WITHDRAWN
University of
Illinois Library
at Urbana-Champaign

THE AMERICAN YEAR BOOK

LITERATURE AND LANGUAGE BIBLIOGRAPHIES FROM THE AMERICAN YEAR BOOK 1910 - 1919

Cumulated Bibliography Series: Number One

Introduction and Indexes by
Arnold N. Rzepecki
Librarian, College Library
Sacred Heart Seminary
Detroit, Michigan

THE PIERIAN PRESS
Ann Arbor, Michigan
1970

International Standard Book Number 87650-013-0

© Copyright 1970, The Pierian Press
All Rights Reserved

An authorized cumulation and reprint
from

THE PIERIAN PRESS
Ann Arbor, Michigan
1970

PREFACE TO THE INDEX

The years covered by these annuals, 1910-1919, were referred to by Van Wyck Brooks in one of his most successful books as "America's coming-of-age." The period of such critics as Randolph Bourne, Brooks, Spingarn, Pound, Mecken, and many others was indeed an era of exceptionally significant critical output. According to Morton Zabell, "The moment was alive with creative energy and rebellion...."[1]

A personal name index to this very important annual bibliographic survey is therefore a very complete list of the names of almost all American critics writing on the literature of the ancient and western world from a stance of new found "internationalism" and critical maturity. A subject approach would show the broad spectrum of interest--the personal names of the authors the critics wrote about does show this.

Personally, the extent and depth of critical work done during this period in such areas as Semitic studies, Scandanavian literature, and especially the Ancient Classics was amazing to me and will probably be one of the strongest features of this work.

One other significant feature emerged from the indexing almost from the beginning. Not only is this index of special value to anyone looking for references to critical works on ancient or Western literature, it also has the special value of reflecting the original, creative literary output of America during this period, 1910-1919. The names of Dreiser, Sandburg, Masters, Frost, Lindsay, Cather, Robinson, and other recognized literary figures appear in the index. The literature of the war years, historical, as well as fictional, is perhaps best represented in these annuals from 1914 on.

It is my hope that this index makes the wealth of material in these annual bibliographic surveys more accessible to the researcher and the literary scholar.

> Arnold Rzepecki
> Librarian
> College Library
> Sacred Heart Seminary
> 1970

---

[1] Zabell, Morton, *Literary Opinion in America*, New York, Harper, 1951, p. 14.

TABLE OF CONTENTS

	Page
Bibliography for 1910	1
1911	23
1912	47
1913	69
1914	90
1915	109
1916	130
1917	154
1918	176
1919	196
Subject Index	219
Personal Name and Main Entry Index	220

1910 LITERATURE AND LANGUAGE

ANCIENT LITERATURE AND PHILOLOGY

ANCIENT LITERATURE

(Additions from Papyri)

CLIFFORD H. MOORE

The recovery of Aristotle's *Constitution of Athens* from an Egyptian papyrus some twenty years ago opened a new period in which the additions made to extant Greek literature by the discoveries of new papyri have been so constant that scholars have come to expect that each year will bring something new and valuable. The past twelve month has not disappointed that expectation, for the seventh volume of the *Oxyrhynchus Papyri* (London, 1910), contains much that is welcome. The papyri published date from the late second to the sixth century of our era. They give us considerable fragments of the *Aetia* and *Iambi* of the Alexandrian poet Callimachus, fairly extensive fragments of a prose treatise on literary composition, portions of the Μισούμενος of the comic poet Menander, a bit from an unknown historical work, and a complete 'Ἐγκώμιον 'Ἑρμοῦ. All this is new, as in a certain sense is a small fragment of the Greek version of the apocalyptic work called the sixth book of Ezra, of which the Latin text only has hitherto been known. The present discovery may give support for the view that the work originated in Egypt. Of works already extant we have some verses from Genesis ii and iii in the Greek version, parts of the first Epistle to the Corinthians, vii–viii, and some verses from the Epistle to the Philippians, iii–iv. Two fragments of Plato's *Phædrus*, one from Xenophon's *Cyropædia*, i, 6, and one from Chariton's romance of *Chæreas and Callirhoë* complete the list.

Of all these the most important are the fragments from the works of Callimachus and the portion of a play of Menander. The former are contained on two leaves which once belonged to a papyrus book. The portion of the *Aetia* recovered from the first leaf amounts to ninety verses, the greater part of which is occupied with the story of Acontius and Cydippe. We also learn that the poet drew this story from Xenomedes, the historian of Ceos in the early fifth century, who has thus been made something more than a name to us; and in fact, Callimachus devotes nineteen verses of this fragment to a summary of Xenomedes's mythical history. The second leaf contains the epilogue to the *Aetia* and some 450 verses of the *Iambi*, of which unhappily a large part are damaged past certain and complete restoration. Enough, however, is preserved to give us the story of Bathycles's cup, adjudged to Thales as the wisest of men, and a tale of the reversal of nature in the reign of Cronos, including a quarrel between the olive tree and the laurel. Although the fragment of Menander's Μισούμενος —*The Hated Man*—are but scanty, yet the large portions of his comedies recovered during the last few years make every additional find doubly welcome.

The considerable fragments of the anonymous prose treatise on literary composition found on papyrus of the third century, but composed between A.D. 50 and 200, present a variety of subjects: the characteristics of Lysias, observations on systems of ethics, omission of names and suppression of facts in various prose writers, criticism of the orators for belittling the achievements of Philip, censure of the diction of Xenophon, and a collection of Atticisms. The historical fragment on papyrus of the third century describes a battle which is as yet unidentified. Finally the encomium on Hermes in twenty-two verses is a rather mediocre effusion, apparently of the second century of our era.

While these are the chief literary finds made known during the past year it should be noted that there has been published a large number of new rescripts, documents, and letters, which add to our knowledge of the nonliterary Greek language in the imperial period and of social and governmental matters in Egypt. Unhappily no papyri containing Latin writings have been recovered.

Among the recent publications of literary works made known in former years must be named Grenfell and Hunt's *Hellenica Oxyrhynchia* (London, 1909), that historical work which was first published by them in *The Oxyrhynchus Papyri*, Vol. V. The authorship of this is confidently claimed for Theopompus by Eduard Meyer in an interesting book *Theopomps Hellenika* (Halle, 1909), but the original editors still hesitate between Theopompus and Cratippus. The fragments of Menander, old and new, have been edited by A. Korte: *Menandrea ex papyris et membranis vetustissimis*, ed. maior (Leipsic, 1910), ed. minor (*ibid.*); and the fragments of the *Hero, Epitrepontes, Periceiromene*, and *Samia* have been provided with introductions, explanatory and critical notes, and a bibliography by Edward Capps in an edition which deserves the warmest praise (Boston, 1910).

Finally may be named the useful collections by George Milligan, *Selections from the Greek Papyris*, University Press, Cambridge, 1910, which offers fifty-five selected texts covering over nine centuries; few can be called literary, but they throw light on the language and history of the period they cover.

SEMITIC PHILOLOGY

MORRIS JASTROW

Within the general field of Semitic philology the completion of Prof. Carl Brockelmann's *Grundriss der vergleichenden Grammatik der Semitischen Sprachen* (Berlin, Reuther and Reichard, 1908–10) merits first mention as a comprehensive work embodying the present state of knowledge by an acknowledged master of the entire field of Semitic philology. After a survey of the character and literature of each one of the Semitic languages and dialects, the phonology is taken up in detail and with equal exhaustiveness, the noun and verb formations and the particles. The division adopted for the Semitic languages is that into east and west, with a further subdivision of the western Semitic languages into northwest Semitic, comprising Canaanitic and Aramaic, and southwest Semitic, covering Arabic and Abyssinian. Babylonian-Assyrian (which is preferable to Brockelmann's Assyrian-Babylonian) is the representative of the eastern Semitic branch, and is significant as the first to branch off definitely from the common trunk. Brockelmann inclines strongly towards including Egyptian in the Semitic group, and also believes in a grade of relationship between the Semitic and Hamitic languages. The attempts to discover a relationship between the Semitic and the Indo-Germanic group have led to no results. Indications point to Arabia as the original home of the Semites, though this, too, is a problem that has not yet been definitely solved.

In Prof. Max L. Margolis' Grammar of the Aramaic idiom of the Babylonian Talmud (German and English editions, Munich, C. H. Beck, 1910) we have the first thoroughly scientific study of the language of the great compilation of Talmudical Judaism. Based on a study of the manuscript material, the grammatical forms are set forth with an application of that exact philological method which is in the main the gift of German scholarship. The work is an important contribution also to the comparative study of Semitic speech.

The *Encyclopœdia of Islam* (German, French, and English) under the general editorship of Prof. Houtsma, of the University of Utrecht, and with the coöperation of a large body of scholars, is progressing very slowly, only six parts having appeared since 1908. When completed it will form a vast storehouse of facts, covering the entire scope of Islamism, historical, geographical, biographical, literary, artistic, legal, and theological.

On the other hand, the publication of the great biographical encyclopædia of Ibn Sa'ad, with sketches of all notable persons in the history of Islamism down to the year 230 of the Hegira—i. e., to the tenth century A.D., is proceeding rapidly under the direction of Prof. Ed. Sachau, of the University of Berlin (Brill, Leiden). Eight volumes of this important mine of valuable historical material have now appeared.

The large archive of clay tablets found in 1906–07, at Boghâz-Köi, by Prof. Hugo Winckler, of the University of Berlin, still awaits publication, but in the meanwhile Winckler has communicated some preliminary results (Die Arier in den Urkunden von Boghâz-Köi in the *Orientalistische Literaturzeitung*, July, 1910) in which he furnishes some specimen translations of the tablets, all bearing, as he believes, on the prominent position occupied in the Hittite Empire by the Aryan population. The thesis rests upon a very doubtful comparison of a term *mariana*, occurring in these tablets with the Vedic *marya*, used in the sense of "heroes." Fortunately the proof for Aryan settlements in central Asia Minor as early as circa 1500 B.C. is independent of such hazardous conjectures. Winckler, himself, furnished a more substantial one by his discovery that the names of Vedic deities, like Varuna and Mitra, occur in the tablets of Boghâz-Köi. Pending the publication of the tablets from which the solution of the Hittite problem may be expected, we have in Prof. John Garstang's *Land of the Hittites* (New York, Dutton, 1910) an admirable survey of explanations and discoveries with a summary of all that we can at present gather from the story of the monuments and inscriptions.

The first volume of L. W. King's *History of Babylonia and Assyria* (London, Chatto & Windus, 1910) covers the earliest period down to the foundation of the Babylonian monarchy circa 2000 B.C. The material for this period is still too scanty to permit of writing a continuous history, but what we have is well utilized by the author, who adds to the value of his work by plans and illustrations and a good map, besides archæological discussions of deep interest. In an important appendix, Mr. King reviews the bearings of the results of the two expeditions of Pumpelly, in 1903–04, to the transcaspian province of Russian Turkestan on the origin of the Sumerians—the non-Semitic settlers of the Euphrates Valley. While not pronouncing a definite opinion, Mr. King inclines to the belief that further explorations will strengthen the view of Pumpelly that the central Asian oasis represents the fountainhead of western Asiatic culture and that the Sumerians may have come from this region.

Besides marking a reaction against the Pan-Babylonistic thesis of German scholars who would interpret the entire culture of antiquity in terms of an astral-mythology that had its origin in the Euphrates Valley, Prof. A. T. Clay's *Amurru, the Home of the Northern Semites* (Phila. S. S. Times, 1910), pleads for an early migration of "Amorites" from northern Syria to Babylonia, and sees pronounced "Amoritish" influences in the early Babylonian pantheon and in myths that have hitherto been supposed to have originated in Babylonia, and from there traveled to the western branches of the Semites, including the Hebrews. The thesis is as novel as it is learnedly and ingeniously worked out, though meager philological evidence is often pushed beyond due bounds.

The *International Critical Commentary* (New York, Scribner's) series has been brought nearer to completion by the addition of *Genesis* by Prof. John Skinner, and *Chronicles* by Prof. Edward L. Curtis, both of which maintain the high standard of thoroughness and completeness from the philological and exegetical point of view that has made the volumes of the series standard authorities recognized as such in Europe as well as this country. About one half of the Old Testament series has now been issued.

INDO-GERMANIC PHILOLOGY
(*Exclusive of the Germanic Languages*)

ROLAND G. KENT

The past few years have been an era of convenient handbooks, containing usually grammar and texts, of comparative grammars of a set of related languages, and of etymological dictionaries; works embodying in concise form the latest results in the field. The most recent are the following:

GEIGER, W.—Elementarbuch des Sanskrit. Heidelberg, Winter, 1910.
GELDNER, K. F.—Der Rigveda in Auswahl, vol. ii (Stuttgart, Kohlhammer, 1909); a commentary to those hymns to which vol. i (1907) forms a glossary.
REICHELT, H.—Awestisches Elementarbuch. Heidelberg, Winter, 1909.
LESKIEN, A.—Grammatik der altbulgarischen Sprache. Heidelberg, Winter, 1909.
BERNEKER, E. — Slavisches etymologisches Wörterbuch. Heidelberg, Winter; part 5 has appeared.
PEDERSEN, H.—Vergleichende Grammatik der keltischen Sprachen, vol. i. Einleitung und Lautlehre. Göttingen, Vanderhoek, 1909.
THURNEYSEN, R.—Handbuch des Altirischen. Heidelberg, Winter, 1909.
BOISACQ, E.—Dictionnaire étymologique de la langue grecque. Heidelberg, Winter, and Paris, Klincksieck. Part v has appeared.
THUMB, A.—Handbuch der griechischen Dialekte. Heidelberg, Winter, 1909.
WALDE, A.—Lateinisches etymologisches Wörterbuch, Ed. 2. Heidelberg, Winter, 1910.

Other convenient handbooks appear below under the names of C. D. Buck and H. C. Tolman.

Karl W. Hiersemann, of Leipsic, acquired in 1909 a collection of 1,294 Sanskrit manuscripts on palm leaves, written mainly in South Indian alphabets, and including a great variety of texts. At latest advices they had not found a purchaser.

American Contributions.—The recent contributions of American scholars include the following:[1]

[1] The author uses the following abbreviations in this text:
AJP., American Journal of Philology; *CP.*, Classical Philology; *CQ.*, Classical Quarterly; *IF.*, Indogermanische For-

INDO-IRANIAN.—C. R. Lanman (Harvard) has completed and edited the late W. D. Whitney's (Yale) translation of and commentary on the *Atharva-veda Sainhitā* (Cambridge, 1905, vols. vii–viii in *Harvard Oriental Series*, edited by C. R. Lanman).

M. Bloomfield (Johns Hopkins) has presented *The Religion of the Veda* (New York, Putnam, 1908) in the *American Lectures on the History of Religions*. His *Vedic Concordance* (Cambridge, 1906, vol. x in *Harvard Oriental Series*) is to be supplemented by a work on the Vedic variants. (See Bloomfield, *JAOS.*, 29, 286–298; and also Michelson, *JAOS.*, 29, 284–285.)

A. V. W. Jackson (Columbia), in his *Persia Past and Present* (New York, Macmillan, 1906), described his travels and researches amid the scenes of Zoroaster's life, and his examination of the cruces in the old Persian inscription of Darius at Behistan. In the *Columbia Indo-Iranian Series*, edited by Jackson, there have recently appeared, vol. v, *Sayings of Buddha, the Iti-vuttaka*, by J. H. Moore, 1908; vol. vi, *Nyaishes or Zoroastrian Litanies*, by M. N. Dhalla, 1908; vol. vii, *Dasarupa, a Treatise on Hindu Dramaturgy*, by G. C. O. Haas, 1910.

H. C. Tolman (Vanderbilt) has issued in the *Vanderbilt Oriental Series* (edited by himself and J. H. Stevenson), an *Ancient Persian Lexicon and Texts* (Nashville, 1908), and a *Cuneiform Supplement* with an *Index Verborum* by E. L. Johnson (Nashville, 1910). These are decidedly the most usable editions of the old Persian inscriptions; the former volume contains the transliterated texts with translation and lexicon, and the latter contains a grammar, a facsimile of the texts, and a concordance. Tolman's note in *AJP.*, 31, 80, if his restoration of the inscription *Darius NRb* be correct, shows conclusively that Darius was a Zoroastrian.

F. Edgerton (Johns Hopkins) has a convincing treatment of the *Origin and Development of Elliptic Dual and Dvandva Compounds* in *KZ.*, 43,

schungen; JAOS., Journal of the American Oriental Society; *KZ.*, Zeitschrift für vergleichenden Sprachforschung, begründet von A. Kuhn.

110-120, and some etymological notes in *IF.*, 24, 291-293.

T. Michelson has written upon the Indian dialects seen in the inscriptions of Asoka's Fourteen Edicts, and seeks to prove that their dialects are not directly descended from classical Sanskrit: *IF.*, 23, 127-131, 219-271, 24. 52-55, 27, 194-195, 296; *KZ.*, 43, 351; *AJP.*, 30, 183-187, 284-297, 416-429, 31, 55-65; *CP.*, 5, 219-220; *JAOS.*, 30, 77-93.

E. W. Burlingame, in *Buddhaghosa's Dhammapada Commentary* (*Proc. Amer. Acad. of Arts and Sciences*, 45, 467-550), gives the titles of the stories, an index to them, and summaries of the first four books.

In *IF.*, 25 and 26, issued as a *Festschrift für Karl Brugmann*, there are four contributions by American scholars: A. V. W. Jackson, *Indo-Iranian Notes*, 25, 177-184; M. Bloomfield, *On Some Disguised Forms of Sanskrit Paçu Cattle*, 25, 185-199; C. D. Buck (Chicago), *Greek Notes*, 25, 257-263; E. W. Fay (Texas), αἴμων and imāgo, 26, 27-42.

Miss W. W. Wilson, *The Soma Offering in a Fragment of Alcman*, *AJP.*, 30, 188-195; E. A. Weldin, *Rigveda, 1. 32, 8*, *AJP.*, 31, 329-330; J. E. Abbott, *Indian Inscriptions on the Fire Temple at Bāku*, *JAOS.*, 29, 299-304.

GREEK AND LATIN.—C. D. Buck's excellent *Grammar of Oscan and Umbrian* (Boston, Ginn, 1904) has been translated with slight omissions into German by E. Prokosch (Wisconsin) under the title *Elementarbuch der oskisch-umbrischen Dialekte* (Heidelberg, Winter, 1905). Buck's *Greek Dialects* (Boston, Ginn, 1910) is also a splendid manual, not identical in method with Thumb's *Handbuch* (see above). Buck is now supervising a series of *Studies in Greek Noun Formation* (*Introduction* by Buck in *CP.*, 5, 323-325), based on collections begun by the late A. W. Stratton, and since extended; the first portion, that on *Labial Terminations* (*CP.*, 5, 326-356), is by E. H. Sturtevant (Barnard), and marks a great advance over previous work.

The late M. Warren (Harvard) offers a brilliant interpretation and restoration of *The Stele Inscription in the Roman Forum*, in *AJP.*, 28, 249-272, 373-400.

E. W. Fay, in *Synthesis Doliolorum Dresseliana* (*AJP.*, 30, 121-138), gives an extremely ingenious interpretation of the Duenos inscription as a humorous archaizing product of a grammarian between the time of Lucilius and that of Quintilian.

Greek and Latin etymologies are discussed by M. Bloomfield in *AJP.*, 29, 78-81 (πρέσβυς); by F. A. Wood (Chicago) in *CP.*, 3, 74-86 (μωέν, maneō, febris, melior, tempus, etc.), 5, 303-308; by E. W. Fay in *KZ.*, 41, 208 (κραιπάλη. crāpula); 42, 86; 42, 382, and 43, 120 (*-ter* of prepositions and adverbs, *cumulus, clēmēns*); 43, 154-160 (*premit, gerit, atrōx*, etc.); *IF.*, 26, 27-42; *CQ.*, 3, 272-278 (*mīles*, etc.); 4, 80-90 (*annus*, etc.); *CP.*, 4, 301-310 (*mēd, tēd*); by C. D. Buck in *IF.*, 25, 257-263 (ἑστία, etc.); by E. H. Sturtevant in *CQ.*, 3, 8-12 (*dīs, mīs*, etc.); *CP.*, 3, 435-440.

A. R. Anderson (Princeton) continues his valuable studies in the language of Plautus by *The Use of the Œ Diphthong in Plautus*, in *CP.*, 4, 291-300.

F. F. Abbott (Princeton) treats *Vulgar Latin in the Ars Consentii de Barbarismis* in *CP.*, 4, 233-47.

LATIN LITERATURE

CHARLES KNAPP

Within the last eighteen months the most important contributions to the study of Latin literature have been made abroad. Foremost is J. W. Duff's *A Literary History of Rome* (London, Unwin Brothers, 1909), an admirable account of Roman literature from the beginnings to the end of the Golden Age, which emphasizes the Roman elements in Latin literature and the originality of the Romans. A review of the book, itself a contribution to the subject, is by K. F. Smith in *American Journal of Philology*, 31.

Less valuable, because less sure in its general grasp, but very suggestive often in details and important since it is the sole book in English devoted to the theme, is H. E. Butler's *Post-Augustan Poetry* (Oxford, Clarendon Press, 1909), dealing with the poets from Seneca the Younger through

Martial and Juvenal. Valuable, too, is F. Plessis's *La Poésie Latine* (Paris, Klincksieck, 1909), a thorough study of Latin poetry from Andronicus to Namatianus, also well reviewed by K. F. Smith, *American Journal of Philology*, 30.

Two of the three volumes of a fine work, *Einleitung in die Altertumswissenschaft*, consisting of papers by various scholars, edited by A. Gercke and E. Norden (Leipsic, Teubner, 1910), have appeared; they contain important articles on Roman meter, literature, religion, and philosophy.

In America most of the work in the field is published in periodicals rather than in book form. Among books the first place is held by C. U. Clark's definitive edition of the text of *Ammianus Marcellinus*, a most elaborate work (Vol. I, Berlin, Weidmann, 1910). We may name also M. H. Morgan's *Addresses and Essays* (New York, American Book Co., 1910), the larger and more important part of which deals with Vitruvius. Much less weighty is F. F. Abbott's *Society and Politics in Ancient Rome*, in which, on the basis of the inscriptions, some light is thrown on matters connected with Latin literature. Finally, a notable article of general interest is P. Shorey's *The Case for the Classics* (Chicago, *The School Review*, 18), especially valuable for bibliographical matter relating to the assault on the classics and the defense.

Volumes of classical studies published by various universities (e. g., California, Columbia, Cornell, Harvard, Michigan, Nevada) contain matters relating to the study of Latin literature, though often on recondite topics of narrow appeal. The *Transactions of the American Philological Association* for 1909 also contains matter of interest to the student of Latin literature.

The *American Journal of Philology*, 31 (Baltimore), and *Classical Philology*, 5 (Chicago), contain various articles within our field. Only a few can be named here. From the former journal we notice E. W. Fay, review of G. Friedrich's *Catulli Veronensis Liber* (Leipsic, Teubner, 1908); A. G. Harkness, *The Final Monosyllable in Latin Prose and Poetry*, which seeks to deduce from the examples cited inferences concerning the influence of accent on verse structure; M. B. Ogle, *Laurel in Ancient Religion and Folk-Lore*, a collection of examples bearing on the theme from both Greek and Latin authors, with comment thereon; E. G. Sihler, *Serviana*, an attempt to set forth something concerning Servius's personality and to discuss him anew as grammarian and rhetorician; R. B. Steele, *Relative Temporal Statements in Latin*, which sets up a new theory of the origin of the subjunctive *cum*-clause (deriving it from Oratio Obliqua), of interest to the student of literature as well as to the grammarian. In *Classical Philology* the articles are even more technical, commonly, and of narrower appeal. J. S. Phillimore, assuming, without proof, that the poem called Culex is by Vergil, proceeds to emend consistently to produce a text which shall show the technical proficiency we expect from Vergil, even in his earliest days, a strangely subjective procedure; E. K. Rand writes on *Early Mediæval Commentaries on Terence* (the concluding pages discuss also the growth of the knowledge of Terence in the Middle Ages); A. L. Wheeler writes on *Propertius as Præceptor Amoris* and *Erotic Teaching in Roman Elegy* (the papers tend to weaken belief in the indebtedness of the Roman elegiac poets to Alexandrian influences). Of a more minute sort are papers on the text of *Livy*, by F. W. Shipley; on that of *Pliny*, by E. T. Merrill and F. E. Robbins; on that of *Catullus*, by B. Ullman.

CLASSICAL PHILOLOGY

PAUL SHOREY

This is not a subject in which we may expect the annual announcement of startling discoveries, nor are American scholars as yet producing epoch-making books. But the development of graduate studies in the past twenty-five years has trained a generation of scholars whose total productivity is creditable to the present and of great promise for the future. Belletristic writers sometimes disparage this work as narrow and technical in its scope, and contrast it invidiously with the comprehensive erudition of Germany or the literary charm of the best French and English essays on classical themes. The work of ambitious professional scholars is naturally in large part technical, but the charge of narrowness is undeserved. In the lack of libraries and other equipment, much of our older scholarship was necessarily limited to special linguistic and syntactical research. But the influence of the new university ideals and of the Archæological Institute with its schools at Athens and Rome, has brought about a change. Specialism with its motto *divide et impera* has taken all knowledge for its province —and to-day nearly every branch and subdivision of philological, archæological, antiquarian, historical, literary inquiry is represented, if not with distinction, at least with credit by some American scholar. This great step in advance is often overlooked in current journalistic censure of American classicism. But a glance at the tables of contents of American philological journals or at the reviews published in *Classical Philology* in the past five years will show that it is a fact.

Periodical Literature. — This increased productivity has been facilitated and fostered by enlarged opportunities for publication. In addition to the *Transactions* of the American Philological Association, and the pioneer *American Journal of Philology*, still brilliantly edited by its founder, Prof. Gildersleeve, we have the *American Journal of Archæology; Classical Philology*, published by the University of Chicago; the *Classical Journal* of the Classical Association of the Middle West and South in co-operation with the Classical Association of New England; the *Classical Weekly*, the organ of the Classical Association of the Middle States; the *Harvard Studies*, now in their twenty-first volume; the *Cornell Studies*, of which the nineteenth volume has just been issued; the *Transactions* of the Connecticut Academy of Arts and Sciences (New Haven), and the *Proceedings* of the American Academy of Arts and Sciences (Boston), which have recently admitted papers on classical themes. Nor is this all. Leading institutions now require the printing of doctoral dissertations and provide an appropriation for the "studies" of the classical departments. Such studies are now published by the universities of Michigan, Wisconsin, Pennsylvania, Illinois, California, Nebraska, Colorado, Nevada, Cincinnati, and many others. Lastly a great deal of unnoticed good work goes into the editing of the various classical series of school and college texts, of which every self-respecting publisher has one.

Much of this productivity is doubtless still amateurish and crude. But it is by no means so futile as the public has been taught to believe. The average doctoral dissertation issued by the larger universities is, to say the least, quite equal to the normal German standard. Good points and genuine if minor contributions to knowledge are frequently made in the "studies" of places whose names a few years ago suggested anything but scholarly associations.

Text-books.—The text-book translated from or based upon a German edition, is being rapidly superseded by works that bear witness to painstaking study and independent scholarship, and when the bigger and better books are ripe the publishers will find place for them in or out of the "series," as they have already found place for such works as the late Prof. Seymour's *Life in the Homeric Age;* for Prof. D'Ooge's *Acropolis*, and for Prof. and Mrs. Allinson's *Greek Life and Letters*.

This general sketch, which seemed necessary as an introduction to the first of these annual reviews, leaves space only for a brief bibliography of the most significant work of the past year in the field of Greek studies. Much of the work, it will be observed, is in the form of journal articles and studies, and doubtless some omitted articles are quite as worthy of inclusion as those here mentioned.

BIBLIOGRAPHY

ALLINSON, F. G. and ANN, C. E.—Greek Lands and Letters. Boston and New York, Houghton Mifflin & Co., 1909.
BONNER, Robert J.—The New Greek Historian. Classical Journal, June, 1910. The Bœotian Federal Constitution. Classical Philology v (1910).

LITERATURE AND LANGUAGE

BOTSFORD, G. W.—The Constitution and Politics of the Bœotian League from its Origin to the Year 387 B.C. Political Science Quarterly, vol. xxv, No. 2. Boston, Ginn & Co.

BUCK, Carl Darling.—Introduction to the Study of the Greek Dialects. Boston, Ginn & Co., 1910.

CAPPS, Edward.—Four Plays of Menander (Hero, Periceiromene, Samia). Epitrepontes. Boston, Ginn & Co., 1910.

DEWING, Henry Bronson.—The Accentual Cursus in Byzantine Greek Prose, with especial reference to Procopius of Cæsarea. Transactions of the Connecticut Academy of Arts and Sciences, vol. xiv. New Haven, 1910. Die Bekehrung im Klassischen Altertum mit besonderer Berücksichtigung des Lukretius. Zeitschrift für Theologie und Medizin, Bd. iii. Heft 11. 1910.

FERGUSON, W. S.—The Athenian Phratries. Classical Philology v (1910).

FLICKINGER, R. C.—Certain Numerals in the Greek Dramatic Hypotheses. Classical Philology v (1910).

GILDERSLEEVE, B. L.—Stahl's Syntax of the Greek Verb (reprint from the American Journal of Philology, vols. xxix and xxx). Baltimore, The Johns Hopkins Press, 1909.

GOODSPEED, E. J.—The Harrison Papyri. Classical Philology, v (1910).

GRAGG, Florence Alden.—A Study of the Greek Epigram before 300 B.C. Proceedings of the American Academy of Arts and Sciences, vol. xlvi, No. 1. Boston, Sept., 1910.

HAWES, C. H. and H.—Crete, the Forerunner of Greece. New York, Harper & Bros., Nov., 1909.

HEIDEL, William Arthur.— Περὶ Φύσεως, a Study of the Conception of Nature among the pre-Socratics. Proceedings of the American Academy of Arts and Sciences, vol. xlv, Part IV. Boston, Jan., 1910.

JONES, H. L.—The Poetical Plural of Greek Tragedy in the Light of Homeric Usage (Cornell Studies in Classical Philology, No. 19). Published for the University by Longmans, Green & Co., 1910.

KERLIN, Robert Thomas.—Theocritus in English Literature. Privately published. Lexington, Va., 1910.

MUSTARD, W. P.—Later Echoes of the Bucolic Poets. A.J.P., xxxv.

PERRIN, B.—The Austere Consistency of Pericles. Transactions of the Connecticut Academy of Arts and Sciences, vol. xv, July, 1909. Recognition scenes in Greek literature. A.J.P., xxx.

PUTNAM, Emily James.—Lucian the Sophist. Class. Phil., iv.

REES, Kelley.—The Three Actor Rule in Menander. Class. Phil., v.

—— The Number of the Dramatic Company in the Period of the Technitæ. A.J.P., xxxi.

SANDERS, Henry A.—The Old Testament Manuscripts in the Freer Collection, Part I. The Washington Manuscript of Deuteronomy and Joshua. New York, The Macmillan Co., 1910.

SCOTT, John A.—Does Homer use the Definite Article? Classical Journal, v (1910).

—— Odyssean Words Found in but One Book of the Iliad. Classical Philology, v (1910).

—— The Influence of Meter on the Homeric Choice of Dissyllables. *Ibid.*, iv (1909).

—— The Effect of Sigmatism as shown in Homer. A.J.P., xxx (1909).

SHOREY, Paul.—A Greek Analogue of the Romance Adverb. Classical Philology, v (1910).

—— Φύσις, μελέτη and ἐπιστήμη. Transactions of the American Philological Association, 1910.

The Seventh Nemean Revisited. American Journal of Philology, xxxi (1910).

WHITE, John Williams.—The Origin and Form of Æolic Verse. Classical Quarterly, iii (1909).

—— The Iambic Trimeter in Menander. Classical Philology, iv (1909).

WRIGHT, Henry B.—Herodotus's Source for the Opening Skirmish at Platæa. Transactions of the Connecticut Academy of Arts and Sciences, vol. xv, July, 1909.

METHODS OF INSTRUCTION IN LATIN AND GREEK

GONZALEZ LODGE

The Curriculum.—The most important advance during the year in the teaching of Latin has been in the matter of curriculum. At the meeting of the American Philological Association, in Dec., 1909, the commission on college-entrance requirements provided for by the association at its former meeting, made a report in which it suggested revolutionary changes in the high-school curriculum. Up to this time there had been a great variety in the specific requirements of the different colleges, though the majority had agreed in requiring four books of Cæsar, six orations of Cicero, and six books of Vergil's Æneid. The commission recommended that the schools should read not less *in amount* than they had done before, but that the emphasis should be laid upon sight translation rather than upon prepared work. In the examination, it recommended that the prepared work should be restricted to two speeches of Cicero and two books of Vergil, and that there should also be examinations in sight reading, which should be of equal value with those in the prepared work, and failure in which should involve failure in the prepared work. The commission also recommended that much greater stress be laid upon oral work, but particularly in the first year. These recommendations have been adopted already by most of the important Eastern colleges, and the State and city of New York have revised their syllabi to harmonize with them. The report has been discussed with considerable detail, especially by the chairman of the commission, Prof. J. C. Kirtland.[1]

The Secondary Schools.—Dr. Ernst Riess[2] has discussed the high-school curriculum from the point of view of the teacher in the public schools, emphasizing the need of more flexible work and less specific demands. Dr. Riess urges that more stress be laid from the beginning upon: translation from English into Latin, mainly at hearing; the acquisition and constant employment of a limited vocabulary. Dr. H. T. Archibald[3] has given detailed suggestions as to the best methods of handling vocabulary from day to day in both Latin and Greek.

Prof. Julius Sachs[4] pleads for an improved standard in the teaching of Latin in the secondary schools with regard first, to training in linguistic power, and second, to the recognition of the vital relation between the content of Roman life and literature and our own literary and practical development. Mr. H. L. Millner[5] makes a comparison between the position of Latin in English and in American schools, to the discredit of the latter, and urges that American schools be given greater flexibility in teaching.

Oral Teaching.—Interest in oral teaching has been much stimulated not only by the report of the commission alluded to above, but by the accounts of the work done in English schools, especially the Perse School, Cambridge, that have been brought back by visiting American teachers. At the last meeting of the National Education Association in July oral teaching was the subject of a Round Table discussion. A report[6] of the work of the Perse School has just been issued by the English board of education. This contains not only a detailed exposition of the method pursued, but also specimens of the work of the individual pupil. It is evident that the conditions in this school are very different from those that prevail in American schools, but much profit can be gained by American teachers from the experiment now being made in this school.

Prose composition has been treated by Profs. J. Elmore,[7] W. S. Gordis,[8] and W. G. Hale.[9] Prof. Elmore urges that, while vocabulary should be limited to the words in common use in the authors read, the material of the exercises should be drawn from within the range of the pupil's experience. Prof. Gordis declares that the *pari-passu* method of treating syntax is the most effective, but there should be coördination of similar, or opposite, constructions by the teacher. Prof. Hale finds that the composition books of the last forty years are all full of faults and unpractical. He urges a shorter book, so arranged that reading and writing go hand in hand in such a way that no construction is used before being taken up, and that it shall be taken up when first reached in reading; further, that constructions should be treated organically.

There has been no serious discussion of the authors read beyond a few papers on Vergil.[10]

Prof. H. F. Allen,[11] in a defense of Greek culture, deprecates strongly the idea that the effect of Greek authors can be gained through translation, or that modern languages have an educational value equal to that of Greek. He meets the criticism that students of Greek cannot read Greek when they leave college, by demanding better methods of teaching, and urges particularly the method pursued in teaching modern languages. There has been little discussion of Greek methods. In addition to Dr. Archibald's article, there is a suggestive paper by Prof. G. A. Williams,[12] setting forth the method he has pursued for twenty years.

Suggestions for stimulating the interest of students are provided in articles by Prof. H. M. Kingery,[13] Miss G. L. Eaton,[14] and Prof. D. P. Lockwood.[15] The production of classical plays[16] is becoming more and more common.

Classics and the New Education.— The symposia of the Michigan Schoolmasters' Club have been continued in a valuable series of studies on the classics and the new education. Prof. E. K. Rand[17] sketches the part played by the classics in the education from the classical period through the dark ages down to the present time, and notes a progressive lowering of the esteem in which they are held, due at the present day to romanticism, materialism, and the breaking down of authority of all kinds. Prof. R. M. Wenley[18] maintains that the classics are classical because in them, as concerns the intellect, we find the secret of eternal life. They enable the average man to realize the winsomeness of literature and art, and also reveal the essentials for which man has ever struggled, will ever struggle. Taught with proper emphasis and recognition of the need of the average student, they will come to their own again. Prof. Paul Shorey[19] summarizes the discussion of the last twenty years, showing that classicists have won a victory at the bar of educated opinion, however slight may be its practical significance. He shows further that classical education is a universal phenomenon of civilization, that higher nonvocational education has always been largely literary and linguistic based on a literature distinctly not ephemeral. For us that literature must continue to be the classics. While it would be too much to expect that all undergraduates should know much classics, it is monstrous that they should not know any.

Latin remains a necessity in anything but an elementary or purely technical education. Greek is not a necessity, but the first of luxuries. In the light of experience no judicious adviser can refuse to "give the horse a chance at the ancient springs" before concluding that he will not drink.

Of great interest to American teachers is a special report[20] of the English board of education on the teaching of classics in the secondary schools of Germany. This gives the results of the investigations of three well-known English scholars into German classical teaching, and forms an excellent supplement to the report of the work in the Perse school.

BIBLIOGRAPHY

1. The Antecedents of the Commission's Report; The Report of the Commission; The New Latin Requirements. Classical Journal, v.
2. Latin in the Secondary Schools. Classical Weekly, iii.
3. Concerning Vocabulary and Parsing in Greek and Latin, Classical Weekly, iii. For an opposing view, see J. Tetlow, The Vocabulary of High School Latin and How to Master It. Classical Journal, v.
4. Improved Standards in Teaching Latin. New York Education Department Bulletin, Dec., 1909.
5. The Function of Latin in School and College. Educational Review, 39.
6. The Teaching of Latin at the Perse School, Cambridge. Educational Pamphlets, No. 20. London, 1910.
7. A Real Basis for Latin Composition. School Review, 18.
8. The Problem of Elementary Latin Composition. Classical Journal, v.
9. Latin Composition in the High School. School Review, 18.
10. SILLS, K. C. W.—The Teaching of Vergil. Classical Journal, v, iii–7. KNAPP, C.—The Scansion of Vergil and the Schools. Classical Weekly, iii. HOSFORD, J.—Vergil and the Transition from Ancient to Modern Literature. Classical Journal, vi.
11. The Case of Greek Again. Educational Review, 39.
12. Problems of Elementary Greek. Classical Weekly, iii, 194–7.
13. Latin Literature in the Secondary Schools. Classical Weekly, iii, 42–4.
14. A Classical Room. Classical Journal, v, 212–3.
15. Widening toward the Past. Classical Journal, 360–4.
16. HAINS, D. D.—Greek Plays in America. Classical Journal, vi, 24–39.
17. The Classics and European Education. School Review, xviii, 441–59.

18. The Classics and the Elective System. School Review, xviii, 513–29. See also Prof. E. G. Sihler on The Elective System in the New York Evening Post, Oct. 1, 1910.
19. The Case for the Classics. School Review, xviii, 585–617.
20. Special Reports on Educational Subjects, vol. xx. London, 1910.

MODERN LANGUAGE AND PHILOLOGY

GERMANIC LANGUAGES

Daniel B. Shumway

Gothic.—The year 1910 has been characterized by great activity in the domain of Germanic languages and literatures. At the close of 1909 a most important addition to our knowledge of Gothic was made, the discovery by P. Glaue and K. Helm, two professors of the University of Giessen, of a new Gothic manuscript, a papyrus fragment of two pages, which came from a village near the ruins of ancient Antinoë in Egypt. It contained a portion of Wulfila's Bible translation of the Gospel of Luke with the corresponding passage in Latin. The discovery is important because it serves to corroborate the belief that there formerly existed bilingual codices of the Bible in Latin and Gothic, such as we find in the small fragment, the *Codex Carolinus* at Wolfenbüttel, and possibly in the original of which the *Brescian Codex* is a copy, and which F. C. Burkitt (*Journal of Theological Studies*, 1899) conjectured to be a copy of a bilingual codex with the Gothic omitted. A facsimile of the fragment with a discussion of the text has been published in E. Preuschen's *Zeitschrift für die neutestamentliche Wissenschaft*, vol. ii, pp. 1–38. This year has also seen the publication of the seventh edition of Braune's well-known *Gotische Grammatik*, of a new and enlarged edition of Streitberg's *Gotisches Elementarbuch*, and a new edition of Wright's handy little *Gothic Grammar*. Finally, Streitberg's admirable edition of the Gothic Bible, with the Greek text on which it is based, has just been completed by the appearance of the second part, containing a Gothic-Greek-German vocabulary.

Middle High German.—In the domain of Middle High German we have a new critical reprint by Fried. Pfaff of the great Heidelberg *Liederbuch*, the most famous of the collections of German *Minnesong*, the first volume of which has thus far appeared. A new translation of the famous epic, the *Nibelungenlied*, into rhythmical prose by Prof. D. B. Shumway, has been published by Houghton Mifflin and quite favorably received; prose having been chosen to make the translation more accurate and literal than is possible with verse. In the period of early New High German the critical Weimar edition of Luther's complete works is being continued, the last volume to appear being the thirty-seventh. A Yale dissertation by Paul Curts discusses Luther's *Variations in Sentence Arrangement from the Modern Literary Usage*, showing that they mostly resemble loose colloquial usages of to-day rather than the strict literary usage.

Modern German.—In modern German literature the unabated interest in Goethe is shown by the appearance of no less than three new critical editions of his works, the one, a selection in six volumes, edited by Erich Schmidt at the request of the Goethe Society. The second is an edition of his complete writings (*Propyläenausgabe*) in forty volumes, of which the first four have appeared. The third is likewise a complete edition in forty parts (*Goldene Klassiker Bibliothek*) and is based on the Hempel edition. There also appeared a jubilee edition of Goethe's *Faust*, containing all the versions of the poem extant (*Urfaust, Fragment,* etc.). At first issued in an expensive subscription edition soon exhausted, it has now been republished in a more moderately priced one. The reception of Goethe's *Faust* in England in the first half of the nineteenth century has been made the subject of an excellent study by W. T. Hanhart (*Columbia University Germanic Studies*). The attitude of the youthful Goethe toward the public forms the subject of an able dissertation by W. R. R. Pinger (*Der

Junge Goethe und das Publikum, University of California Publications) in which he successfully controverts the widespread belief that Goethe was a despiser of the public.

A new popular edition of Schiller, based on the old Hempel edition, has appeared in Berlin (*Goldene Klassiker Bibliothek*). A third edition of Erich Schmidt's monumental biography of Lessing has been issued, and this fall an American edition of Lessing's *Laokoon*, together with Goethe's essay on the statue and Herder's review of Lessing's work, has been published by G. W. G. Howard, of Harvard (Holt & Co.). The introduction contains an admirable essay on Lessing's problems and on the influences under which he wrote. It is almost too long for the purpose, however, and the fact that many parts of the text are omitted, will not cause it to supersede the handy edition of Hamann and Upcott.

A new edition of Arnim and Brentano's *Knaben Wunderhorn* is appearing in Leipsic, and in this country Rob. M. Wernaer has made an excellent and comprehensive study of the *Romantic School in Germany*. Kluge has published the tenth edition of his well-known Etymological Dictionary, R. M. Meyer, the fourth edition of his admirable *History of German Literature in the Nineteenth Century*, and Vogt and Koch have issued an enlarged edition of their *Geschichte der deutschen Literatur* (two volumes, Leipsic). Here in America Geo. M. Priest, of Princeton, has worked over Klee's *Grundzüge der deutschen Literatur* into an excellent and very readable handbook, entitled *A Brief History of German Literature* (Scribner's). Klara Hechtenberg Collitz has prepared a very judiciously selected anthology, entitled *Selections from Early German Literature* (American Book Co.), based on modern German translations. It supplements Calvin Thomas's *Anthology* of the preceding year, as it includes extracts from Gothic and Old Norse, but cannot take its place, as Thomas has brought his selections down to Goethe and Schiller, whereas the former ends with the *Minnesingers*.

German Archives.—An interest in German archives as sources of American history has been growing for some time and has resulted in the Carnegie Institute's sending Prof. M. D. Learned, of the University of Pennsylvania, to Germany for the purpose of investigating the official archives as to the material they contain. This was found to be so abundant that it has led to the establishment of the *Institute of German-American Research* for the publication of the many important documents discovered.. Prof. Learned's report has, however, not yet been made public. The series of the American Germanica has been increased by an excellent treatment of *Schwenkfelder Hymnology* and the sources of the first Schwenkfelder hymn book printed in America by A. A. Seipt, until recently one of the editors of the *Corpus Schwenkfeldianorum*, a monumental edition of Schwenkfeld's writings, and by a detailed study of early German music in Philadelphia by Robt. R. Drummond, in which he shows the important part played by the Germans in the early history of this community.

Scientific Periodicals.—The various American journals devoted to the interests of modern languages and philology, the *Publications of the Modern Language Association*, the *Journal of German and English Philology*, *Modern Philology*, the *German-American Annals*, and the *Modern Language Notes* have been appearing regularly. The *Journal* contained a stimulating article by Prof. Curme on the *Best German Pronunciation*, and one by Emil C. Winter on the *Relation of Schiller to Post-Kantian Idealism*. The Publications of the Modern Language Association contain an article by John C. Ransmeier, showing the close connection between Uhland's *Fortunat und seine Söhne*, and a Parisian version of 1770 to which Uhland had access when studying in Paris, 1810–11. Prof. Calvin Thomas has contributed an interesting article, *The Landsmaal Movement in Norway*, showing the progress that the mother tongue is making there against the domination of the literary idiom, which is essentially Danish in character. Prof. Ernst Voss continues his studies in the literature of the sixteenth century by a reprint of *Der Lutherisch Pfaffennarr*, and Prof. Hoskins has added to his studies in literary criticism with an article entitled *The Place and Function of a Standard in a Genetic Theory*, in which he shows, among other things, that there is no fixed standard of form, but that it varies from age to age, and that, on the whole, changes in art and literature are not the cause, but the result of economic, political, and religious transformations.

Two noteworthy Chicago dissertations are *A Study of Grillparzer's Attitude Toward Romanticism*, by E. J. Williamson, and *A Study of the Technique of K. F. Meyer's Novellen*, by M. L. Taylor, the latter setting forth the inner connection between the external form and Meyer's conception of the characters. The philosophical side of Goethe is discussed in conjunction with Dante and Lucretius by G. Santayana in his *Three Philosophical Poets* (Harvard University Studies in Comparative Literature), and Sudermann's art is briefly treated by Prof. Phelps in his recent book on *Modern Novelists*. Witkowski's brilliant though brief sketch of the *German Drama*, which achieved such instant success in Germany, has been ably translated into English by L. E. Horning (Holt & Co.), and bids fair to become one of the standard handbooks on the subject. Lessing and Schiller are discussed by C. W. Elliott in his work on *The Continental Drama*, and *Ibsen and His Plays* form the subject of a short article by the well-known dramatic critic, Archibald Henderson (*Bookman* for July, 1910). A new translation of Heine's poems by F. K. Ball appeared last year, and a chatty article, *In the Footprints of Heine*, by H. J. Forman, in the Sept. number of the *Bookman*. That Americans are gradually becoming interested in German literature is shown by the fact that a number of translations of German authors have appeared. In addition to Heine's poems, Hauptmann's gloomy tragedy, *Fuhrmann Henschel*, has been translated by M. A. Redlich, and Wildenbruch's charming tale, *Das edle Blut*, by W. O. Lowe, under the title *Story of Cadet Life*. Seidel's little classic, *Leberecht Hühnchen*, has been translated by Jane H. White under the title, *A German Christmas Eve*. Tales by Baumbach and Volkmann have been rendered into English by Ruth G. Schottenfels as *Meadow Sprite and Other Tales of Modern Germany*. The devotional songs of Novalis (Fried. Hardenberg) have also appeared in German and English.

The publication of new school editions of German classics and of German grammars and composition books goes on unabated, but the mere enumeration of their names would take us beyond the limit of this article. The following authors, however, have been edited for the first time: the writings of the German patriot Arndt, by Wm. A. Colwell (Heath & Co.); Annette Droste-Hülshoff's interesting story, *Die Judenbuche*, by Ernst Eckelmann (American Book Co.); further excellent editions of Grillparzer's historical drama, *König Ottaker's Glück und Ende*, by Prof. Eggert, of Michigan; of Otto Ludwig's powerful drama, *Der Erbförster*, by M. C. Stewart, of Harvard; and of Gutzkow's famous play, *Uriel Acosta*, by Profs. Cutting and Noé, of Chicago (all three, Holt & Co.).

German-Americans.—The following books deal with various aspects of German-American life and culture: George von Skal, one time editor of the *New Yorker Staatszeitung* and the author of a well-known book on the American people, treats the history of *German Immigration in the United States*, and sketches the lives of successful German-Americans in an exhaustive study. H. Richards, *The Pennsylvania German in the Revolutionary War*, shows how actively the German elements helped in this great struggle, a part that has never been adequately acknowledged in American histories. H. Winston has sketched the history of the old historical Eagle Schoolhouse Tredyffrin in Chester County and given a chronological list of the German settlers. In this connection mention should be made of A. B. Faust's scholarly work in two large volumes, *The German Element in the United States;* it treats the early German immigration and the influence of German elements in our civilization in such a masterly way that it won the prize above several competitors, and has been called by one of its recent critics "almost monumental."

Selma Lagerlöf.—Passing on to other Germanic languages we find that the interest aroused in Selma Lagerlöf, the Swedish novelist, by her receiving the Nobel prize for literature, is reflected in the appearance of translations of a number of her works. Her quaint and fascinating story *Gösta Berling*, for which she received the prize, and which deals with the curious and romantic adventures of the cavaliers of old Sweden in an inimitable fashion, has been issued in the tenth edition. Further, her *Girl from the Marsh Croft*, a volume of tales, and her charming children's book, *The Wonderful Adventures of Nils*, have been well rendered into English by Velma S. Howard. Her personality is described by Edwin Björkman in the *Review of Reviews*, Jan., 1910.

Swedish Literature.—Tegnér's poetic romance, *Axel*, has again been translated into English by Magnus Bernhard, and the *Education of the Child*, by Ellen Key, the well-known Swedish advocate of woman's rights, has been reprinted from her larger work, *The Century of the Child*. *Swedish Folk Dances* form the subject of a work by Nils W. Berquist. Three volumes of humorous sketches by Alfred Hedenstjerna (*Matmors Friare, Stina i Hornary*, and *Tösabiten pa Grönvik*, and an anthology of Swedish verse (*Poetiskt album ur svenska sangen*) by K. Warburg have been issued in Swedish by the publishing firm Engberg and Holmberg. Two volumes of historical sketches dealing with the sixteenth and seventeenth centuries by the Swedish-Finnish novelist, Zacharias Topelius, *Hertiginnan af Finland* (Duchesses of Finland) and *Ungdomsdrömmar* (Dreams of Youth) have also appeared in the original.

Norwegian Literature.—Taking up the subject of Norwegian literature, we find that the recent death of the great Norwegian poet and novelis, Björnsen, has given rise to a number of articles dealing with him and his works. Thus he has been the subject of sketches by Björkman in *Review of Reviews*, April, 1910, by Max Nordau in the *Bookman*, and by L. C. Wilson in the *North American Review*. Ibsen's tragedy *On the Heights* (Paa vidderne) and his lyric ballads have been translated by W. N. Guthrie. H. Hermannsson, of Cornell, has published a bibliography of the *Sagas of the Kings of Norway and Related Tales*, and G. T. Zoega has prepared a *Concise Dictionary of Old Icelandic* (Oxford Press). On the cultural side Prof. Geo. T. Flom has written a *History of Norwegian Immigration to the United States from the Earliest Beginnings Down to the Year 1848*.

Dutch Literature.—Dutch literature comes in for almost no consideration, the only article on the subject being one by A. S. Van Westrum, *Modern Dutch Literature* in the *Bookman*, Jan., 1910. The author shows how little Dutch literature has been influenced by the movements of other continental literatures. The plays of Heyermann, however, form an exception to this, his *Ship of Good Hope* and *The Ghetto* being modern problem plays and successfully produced both in English and German. In the domain of novels practically the only ones translated into English are three by Louis Couperus, *Eline Vere*, *Footsteps of Fate*, and *Majesty*, and one by Fred. van Eeden entitled *The Quest*. Recently, however, a powerful realistic novel, *Toil of Men*, by Querido, has been published here in an English version.

ROMANCE LANGUAGES

Prof. W. W. Comfort, Cornell University, supplies without accompanying text the following bibliography of the recent important literature of the romance languages:

FRENCH

BAILEY, J. C.—The Claims of French Poetry: Nine Studies in the Greater French Poets. New York, 1909.
BÉDIER, J.—Richard de Normandie dans les Chansons de Geste. Romanic Review, April–June, 1910.
BLONDHEIM, D. S.—Contribution à la Lexicographie française d'après des Sources Rabbiniques. Romania, Avr.–Juillet, 1910.
BROWN, A. C. L.—The Bleeding Lance. Pub. Modern Language Association of America, March, 1910.

1910 LITERATURE AND LANGUAGE

BRUCE, J. D.—Mort Artu, an Old French Prose Romance of the XIIIth Century, being the last division of Lancelot du Lac, now first edited from MS. 342 (Fonds français) of the Bibl. Nat. Halle, 1910.

BRUSH, M. P.—Ysopet III of Paris. Pub. Modern Language Association, Sept., 1909.

CARNAHAN, D. H.—Jean d'Abundance: A Study of his Life and Three of his Works. Univ. of Illinois Bull., vol. vii, No. 1, Sept. 6, 1909.

CERF, B.—Ogier le Danois and the Abbey of St. Faro of Meaux. Romanic Review, Jan.–March, 1910.

CHINARD, G.—Une nouvelle Source d'Atala. Modern Language Notes, May, 1910.

CLAPP, J. M.—An Eighteenth Century Attempt at a Critical View of the Novel: the Bibliothèque universelle des Romans. Pub. Modern Language Association, March, 1910.

CURDY, A. E.—Arthurian Literature. Romanic Review, April–June, 1910; July–Sept., 1910.

FRANK, C. D.—En aller à la Moutarde. Pub. Modern Language Association, March, 1910.

GALPIN, S. L.—On the Sources of Guillaume de Deguileville's Pèlerinage de l'Ame. Pub. Modern Language Association, June, 1910.

GERIG, J. L.—Barthélemy Aneau: A Study in Humanism. Romanic Review, April–June, 1910; July–Sept., 1910.

HAMILTON, G.—Sur la Locution "sa Main a sa Maissele" (Raoul de Cambrai, 1190, 1012). Ztsch. für rom. Phil. xxxiv Band, 5 Heft.

HAMILTON, G. L.—The Sources of the Secret des Secrets of Jofroi de Watreford. Romanic Review, July–Sept., 1910.

JENKINS, T. A.—A new Fragment of the Old French Gui de Warewic. Modern Philology, Oct., 1909.

KASTNER, L. E.—Drummond of Hawthornden and the French Poets of the Sixteenth Century. Modern Language Review, Jan., 1910.

KINNEY, M.—Possible Traces of Huon de Bordeaux in English Ballad Form. Romanic Review, July–Sept., 1910.

KITTRIDGE, G. L.—Chauceriana. Modern Philology, April, 1910.

LANSON, G.—Manuel Bibliographique de la Litt. française moderne, 1500–1900. T. ii; Dix-Septième Siècle. Paris, 1910.

LECOMPTE, I. C.—Le Fablel don Dieu d'Amors. Modern Philology, July, 1910. (Text and translation.)

LOWES, J. L.—The Chaucerian "Merciles Beaute" and three poems of Deschamps. Modern Language Review, Jan., 1910.

LUQUIENS, F. B.—The Reconstruction of the original Chanson de Roland. Translation of the Connecticut Academy of Arts and Sciences, vol. xv.

MATZKE, J. E.—Les Œuvres de Simund de Freine, pub. d'après tous les mss. connus. Paris, 1909. (Société des Anciens Textes français.)

—— On the History of Palatal n in French with special reference to o and open e. Pub. Modern Language Association, Sept., 1909.

MEYER, P.—Les Enfances Gauvain, fragment d'un poème perdu. Romania, Jan., 1910.

NITZE, W. A.—The Fisher King in the Grail Romances. Pub. Modern Language Association, Sept., 1909.

—— The Fountain Defended. Modern Philology, Oct., 1909.

OLIVER, T. E.—Some Analogues of Maistre Pierre Pathelin. Journal of American Folk-Lore, Oct.–Dec., 1909.

RICE, C. C.—The Phonology of Gallic Clerical Latin after the Sixth Century. Harvard University Thesis, 1909.

SCHINZ, A.—"La Profession de Foi du Vicaire Savoyard" et le livre "De l'Esprit." Revue d'histoire littéraire de la France, 17, 2.

SCHOEPPERLE, G.—The Love-Potion in Tristan and Isolt. Romania, Avr.–Juillet, 1910.

SOMMER, H. O.—The Vulgate Version of the Arthurian Romances, edited from MSS. in the British Museum; vol. i, Lestoire del Saint Graal; vol. ii, Lestoire de Merlin. The Carnegie Institution of Washington, D. C.

TOWLES, O.—Imprecation as a Means of Emphasis in Old French Chansons de Geste. Studies in Philology of the University of North Carolina, 1910.

WEEKS, R.—The Boulogne MSS. of the Chevalerie Vivien. Modern Language Review, Jan., 1910.

—— Chevalerie Vivien. Facsimile Phototypes of the Sancti Bertini MS. of the Bibl. Municipale of Boulogne-sur-Mer; with an introduction and notes. University of Missouri Studies, 1909.

WESTON, J. L.—The Legend of Sir Perceval: Studies upon its Origin, Development and Position in the Arthurian Cycle; vol. ii, The Prose Perceval according to the Modena MS. London, 1909.

WILKINS, E. H.—The Belluno Fragment. Modern Language Notes, Feb., 1910.

ITALIAN

BACCI, A. d'Ancona e O.—Manuale della' Letteratura Italiana, vol. vi ed ultimo. Firenze, 1909.

FLETCHER, J. B.—Guido Cavalcanti's Ode of Love. Modern Philology, July, 1909.

HOLME, J. W.—Italian Courtesy—Books of the Sixteenth Century. Modern Language Review, April, 1910.

HUTTON, E.—Giovanni Boccaccio: A Biographical Study. London, 1909.

JACKSON, M.—Antonio Pucci's Poems in the Codice Kirkupiano. Romania, Avr.–Juillet, 1910.

JERROLD, M. T.—Francesco Petrarcha. London, 1909.

JONES, F. N.—Boccaccio and his Imitators, in German, English, French, and Italian Literature. Chicago, 1910.

LEE, A. C.—The Decameron: Its Sources and Analogues. London, 1909.

LIVINGSTON, A. A.—Some Early Italian Parallels to the Locution, "The Sick Man of the East." Pub. Modern Language Association, Sept., 1910.

—— An Important Contemporary Cultivator of the Venetian Dialect: Orlando Orlandini. Modern Language Notes, May, 1910.

—— Gian Francesco Busenello e la Polemica Stigliano-Mariana. Ateneo Veneto, Aug.–Sept., 1910.

McKENZIE, K.—Note sulli antiche Favole Italiane. Misc. di studi critici e ricerche erudite in onore di V. Crescini, 1910.

—— The Problem of the "Lonza," with an unpublished Text. Romanic Review, Jan.–March, 1910.

READE, W. H. V.—The Moral System of Dante's Inferno. Oxford, 1909.

ROBINSON, J. H.—Petrarch's Confessions. Romanic Review, July–Sept., 1910.

SMITH, H. E.—An Early Italian Edition of Æsop's Fables. Modern Language Notes, March, 1910.

SNELL, F. J.—A Handbook to Dante. London, 1909.

VAUGHAN, H. H.—A Brief Study of the Phonology of the Neapolitan Dialect. Romanic Review, April–June, 1910.

WESTON, G. B.—Two lately discovered Letters of Foscolo. Romanic Review, July–Sept., 1910.

SPANISH

BACON, G. W.—The Comedia El Segundo Séneca de España of Dr. Juan Pérez de Montalván. Romanic Review, Jan.–March, 1910. (Anal. of Indebtedness to Cabrera de Córdoba's Felipe Segundo, Rey de España.)

BUCHANAN, M. A.—La Vida es Sueño, vol. i. (Critical text.) Toronto, 1909.

—— Short Stories and Anecdotes in Spanish Plays; No. 2. Modern Language Review, Jan., 1910.

CHURCHMAN, P. H.—Lord Byron's Experiences in the Spanish Peninsula in 1809. Bulletin Hispanique, 1909.

—— Byron and Espronceda. Revue Hispanique, T. xx.

CRAWFORD, J. P. W.—The Devil as a Dramatic Figure in the Spanish Religious Drama before Lope de Vega. Romanic Review, July–Sept., 1910.

—— Trajedia de Narciso of F. de la Cueva y Silva. Edited from the autograph MS., etc. Philadelphia, 1909.

—— Un Hijo que negro á su Padre. Pub. Modern Language Association, June, 1910. (Sixteenth century MS. of an *entremés* here first published.)

FITZGERALD, J. D.—Gonzalo de Berceo in Spanish Literary Criticism before 1780. Romanic Review, July–Sept., 1910.

FITZ-MAURICE-KELLEY. — The Relations between Spanish and English Literature. Liverpool, 1910.

HOUSE, R. E.—The Comedia Radiana of Agustín Ortiz. Modern Philology, April, 1910. (Text and comment.)

LINCOLN, G. L.—Los Alcaldes encontrados; 6a parte. Pub. Modern Language Association, Sept., 1910. (Sixth and final division of the series of *entreméses* entitled Los Alcaldes Encontrados, here first published.)

—— Golondrino y Calandria: An unedited *entremés* of the sixteenth century. Romanic Review, Jan.–March, 1910.

NORTHUP, G. T.—Notes on Don Quijote. Modern Language Notes, June, 1910.

RENNERT, H. A.—The Spanish Stage in the Time of Lope de Vega. New York, 1910.

STUART, D. C.—Honor in the Spanish Drama. Romanic Review, July–Sept., 1910.

GENERAL TOPICS

COPYRIGHT

WILLIAM W. APPLETON

In the United States.—The copyright act now in force went into effect July 1, 1909 and differs materially from previous acts.

The author has the exclusive right to print, publish, translate, dramatize, arrange and adapt, and to deliver or authorize the delivery of the copyrighted work as a lecture, sermon, or address in public for profit. The dramatic author has exclusive right to perform or exhibit in any manner or method, in whole or in part. Works of art are included, models and designs, reproductions of art work, drawings, and plastic works of a scientific or technical character, photographs, prints, and pictorial illustrations. The musical composer has the exclusive right to perform the copyrighted work for profit, to set it in any system of notation or any form of record in which the thought of an author may be recorded and from which it may be read or reproduced. If the composer permits mechanical reproduction, other mechanical reproducers may use the work on payment to author of two cents for each part manufactured. Manufacturers shall furnish, if required by copyright proprietors, on the 20th of each month the number of parts manufactured during previous month, and royalties shall be due on the 20th of the next succeeding month.

Any person entitled to copyright may secure copyright for his work by publication thereof with notice of copyright affixed to each copy, as required by the act. Two copies of work shall be promptly deposited in the copyright office at Washington. If not promptly deposited, the register of copyrights may demand deposit, which must be made within three months from any part of the United States, except an outlying territorial possession of the United States, and within six months from such territory or from any foreign country, in default of which the copyright shall become void.

Copyright shall extend to an author or proprietor, a citizen or subject of a foreign state, only when the alien author or proprietor is domiciled in the United States at the time of first publication, or when the foreign state or nation of which the author or proprietor is a citizen or subject grants by treaty or otherwise to citizens of the United States copyright on substantially the same basis as to its own citizens. The existence of reciprocal conditions are to be determined by the President of the United States by proclamation made from time to time. The President's proclamation of April 9, 1910, included Austria, Belgium, France, Germany, Great Britain and possessions, Italy, Mexico, the Netherlands and possessions, Norway, Portugal, Spain, Switzerland, Chile, Costa Rica, Cuba, Denmark, and Luxemburg was added on June 29, 1910.

Duration.—Duration of copyright is for twenty-eight years from publication, with a renewal term of a further twenty-eight years. The application for renewal of copyright must be made at the copyright office within one year prior to the expiration of the original term of copyright. The copyright of periodical, cyclopedic, and other composite works can be renewed by the proprietor, but all other copyrighted work must be renewed by the author, or by the widow, widower, or children if the author is not living, and in case none of these are living, by the author's executor or next of kin.

Manufacturing Clause.— Books to secure copyright must be manufactured in the United States, except books for the blind, books of foreign language and origin, and English books seeking an *ad interim* protection. In order to give English authors time to arrange for publication in the United States, books in English published abroad may secure an *ad interim* copyright by a deposit of one copy of the foreign edition within thirty days after first foreign publication, and thirty days additional after such deposit are granted, within which the publication of the American edition must take place in order to extend the publication.

Great Britain.—A bill to amend and consolidate the law relating to copyright was introduced in the House of Commons by Mr. Buxton, president of the board of trade, July 26, 1910. The bill, if passed, will replace many existing statutes and amend and extend existing laws.

It extends the period of copyright to the lifetime of author and fifty years thereafter, in line with the recommendation of the Berlin convention. For a cyclopedic or composite work the term for the work as a whole is fifty years. The interests of the public have been safeguarded from the possible perversity of an author's representatives after his death. In case they should withhold a work from publication or place an unreasonable price upon it, or, in case of a drama, ask a prohibitive sum for the right to perform, any one can apply to the comptroller general of patents for a license, and that official will be authorized to adjudicate on the matter, duly respecting the right of royalties.

Copyright means the sole right to produce or reproduce the work or any substantial part thereof in any material form whatsoever, or in any language; to perform, or in the case of a lecture, to deliver, the work or any substantial part thereof in public; and shall include the sole right (*a*) in the case of a dramatic work to convert it into a novel or nondramatic work; (*b*) in the case of a novel or other nondramatic work to convert it into a dramatic work; (*c*) in the case of a literary, dramatic, or musical work, to make any record, perforated roll, or other contrivance by means of which the work may be mechanically performed.

Dramatic work includes any piece for recitation, choreographic work or entertainment in dumb show the scenic arrangement or acting form of which is fixed in writing or otherwise, and any cinematograph production where the arrangement or action form or the combination of incidents represented give the work an original character.

Artistic work includes works of painting, drawing, sculpture and artistic craftsmanship, and architectural works of art and engravings and photographs.

The act permits, at the request and risk of the copyright owner, seizure of pirated editions, the arrest of hawkers or the search of premises without notice or formality. Registration is not compulsory.

Any work to secure copyright must be first published in His Majesty's dominions, but may be published simultaneously in some other place, and shall be deemed to be published simultaneously if the time between the publication in one country and the publication in the other country does not exceed fourteen days.

Turkey.—A complete copyright bill was passed on May 8, 1910, in which copyright is given for a term of the life of the author and thirty years after his death.

South America.—At a meeting of the Pan-American Union, held at Buenos Ayres, the text of the convention on the rights of literary and artistic property was approved Aug. 11, 1910, to be submitted to the various countries represented.

The Argentine.—In Sept. a copyright law was approved by both Argentine chambers, and promulgated by a presidential decree Sept. 23 1910. Under this law scientific, literary, and artistic property is recognized for all works published or edited in the Argentine Republic. The term of copyright is for the lifetime of the author and ten years after his death. In posthumous works the term is twenty years after publication. In Article X it is provided that works published in foreign countries, whatever may be the nationality of the author, are protected if the country of origin has an international convention, or has made special agreement with the Argentine Republic.

The International Copyright Union. —The Conference for the formation of this Union was held first at Berne, Switzerland, in 1886, and met again at Paris in 1896 and at Berlin in 1908. The members of the union are, Germany with protectorates, Belgium, Denmark, Spain and colonies, France with Algeria and colonies, Great Britain, colonies and possessions, Haiti, Italy, Japan, Liberia, Luxemburg, Monaco, Norway, Sweden, Switzerland, Tunis.

At Berlin a new convention of thirty articles was agreed upon, to be ratified not later than July 1, 1910. In case the states did not notify the Berlin convention, they are bound by the text of the former conventions. Belgium, Germany, Haiti, Liberia, Luxemburg, Monaco, Spain, and Switzerland have adopted the Berlin text without reservation; France with a reservation as to works of applied art; Japan with a reservation as to the exclusive right of translation and the public performance of music, and with a reservation as to works of architecture and newspaper articles, and the retroactivity of the provisions of the Berne convention.

The Berlin convention proposed a new basis of international union by guaranteeing to the author of any one of the countries of the union publishing for the first time in any one country copyright in all other countries of the union. This protection is not subject to any formalities whatever, and is declared independent of the existence of copyright in the author's work in his own country. Furthermore, the Berlin convention provides that authors outside of the jurisdiction of any of the countries of the union, publishing for the first time in one of these countries, may enjoy the same rights as national authors. The Berlin convention extended the subject matter of copyright to include works of architecture, pantomimes, when these are fixed in writing, cinematograph productions of an original character, and the reproduction of music by means of mechanical instruments. The Berlin convention proposed a general term of copyright during the life of the author, and fifty years after his death.

It is unfortunate that the United States cannot become a member of the International Union. As long as the United States requires domestic manufacture, or makes copyright depend upon compliance with other formalities, its legislation is not in accordance with the principles of the convention.

SIMPLIFIED SPELLING

Charles P. G. Scott

At the request of the author, the following contribution on the progress of the movement for the simplified spelling of the English language is printed in accordance with the official recommendations thus far made by the Simplified Spelling Board.

The Simplified Spelling Board.—The Simplified Spelling Board was establisht in Jan., 1906, by a number of philologists and literary men and men of affairs, who thought the time had come to make a concerted attempt to regulate and simplify the spelling of the English language. The movement was the outcome of the previous attempts of these men and their predecessors, in the American Philological Association, in the Philological Society of London, and in other societies concernd with literature and education, to bring about a greater regularity in English spelling. In May, 1905, eleven of these men organized themselvs into a committee, and secured from a number of men prominent in literature a promis to use a given number of simplified forms. The list of words was that adopted in 1908 by the National Education Association, namely—*program, catalog, decalog, prolog, demagog, pedagog, tho, altho, thoro, thorofare, thru, thruout.* Over 100 literary men and educators signd this agreement, and the list of signers was soon greatly extended, including teachers and professional persons thruout the United States. Upon this encouragement the committee of eleven receivd a promis from Mr. Andrew Carnegie, who was known as a pronounced advocate of simplified spelling, that he would furnish funds sufficient for the printing of proposals and for the circulation of information and appeals. In Jan., 1906, the committee organized itself into the Simplified Spelling Board, and chose additional members. Offisers were elected, an executiv committee was appointed, and arrangements were made for a campain extending over a period of years. The organization of the board was announced in the public press March 12, 1906, and the first formal proposals for simplification were issued March 21, 1906. These proposals consisted of a pamflet cald *The First Step* (Circular No. 1) and *A List of Common Words Spelled in Two or More Ways,* of which the Board recommended the simpler form for adoption (Circular No. 2; also, enlarged, with references, No. 5, June 18, 1906). These were followd at intervals by other circulars of information and argument, dealing with the educational and literary phases of the subject, with simplified spelling in schools, in universities, in periodicals, in poetry, in publishing, etc.; and many thousand persons in the United States, Canada, and Great Britain, signd a card agreeing to use, as far as may be practicable, the simpler spellings that were recommended by the Simplified Spelling Board.

In the face of much opposition the movement stedily increast in strength, attracting to its support not only a great number of educators and scholars, but many leaders in social, religious, and political reform. The President of the United States, Mr. Roosevelt, announced his approval of the movement Aug. 24, 1906. On Aug. 27 he sent a letter to the Public Printer, directing him to use "in all government publications of the executive departments" the simpler spellings included in "the 300 words enumerated in Circular No. 5" of the Simplified Spelling Board. This action excited much interest thruout the world, and was met by much opposition, and enormous misrepresentation, in the public press. In Dec., 1906, the House of Representativs attacht to an appropriation bill a clause providing in effect that no part of the appropriation should be used for printing in simplified spelling any documents printed by act of Congress. This reduced the Public Printer's use of simplified spellings to documents from the executiv department, not printed by order of Congress. But this action of Congress has not been regarded by educated men as being intellectually conclusiv, and the use of simplified spellings has been kept up by many public officials, in accordance with their personal convictions, and the recommendation of competent advisers. This use is widely prevalent among men in the scientific bureaus, and among officers of the army and navy.

The support given to the movement at the start was greatly increast as a result of the discussion in the newspapers, and every month has shown definit gains in numbers and in influence. The Board has up to date issued twenty-four circulars of the regular series, a number of special circulars, ten special leaflets, and seven numbers of the *Simplified Spelling Bulletin,* a quarterly periodical. All has been done deliberately, temperately, patiently. All the simplified forms thus far recommended by the Board are containd in Circular No. 23. These circulars and the *Bulletin* have been widely circulated thruout the world. Many thousands of persons have signd the card agreeing to use the simplified spellings. Thousands of teachers are using them personally, and many have introduced them into their schools. Some normal schools, as the Iowa State Teachers' College, the Illinois State Normal University, the Colorado State Normal School, and the Normal School at Truro, Nova Scotia, have adopted simplified spellings to the full extent recommended by the Board, and are not only teaching them, but are using them in their publications.

The simpler spellings have been used in a large number of periodicals, of which the Board printed, in Dec., 1908, a list of more than 250. Simplified spellings have also appeard in a number of professional and technical magazines, and are freely used in a number of college journals. Among these simplified spellings, *program* and *catalog* are now establisht as the prevailing forms, and *tho* and *thru* are everywhere common. The influence of the Board is seen also in an extensiv use, in advertizements, of spellings which, if not always "simplified," are at least "insurgent," and mark a revolt against orthografic stagnation. Among men of learning there is now little public opposition, and it would be difficult to find any recognized philologist who would be willing to declare himself against the principle of simplifying English orthografy. Indeed, few educated men can now be found who will maintain that English spelling, of all human inventions, should be kept forever exempt from improvement.

The Simplified Spelling Board in 1909 consisted of forty-six members. The American members were then as follows: E. Benjamin Andrews, O. C. Blackmer, David J. Brewer, James W. Bright, Andrew Carnegie, Clarence G. Child, Samuel L. Clemens ("Mark Twain"), Melvil Dewey, Oliver F. Emerson, David Felmley, Isaac K. Funk, Lyman J. Gage, Richard Watson Gilder, Charles

H. Grandgent, William T. Harris, George Hempl, Thomas Wentworth Higginson, Henry Holt, William James, David Starr Jordan, Thomas R. Lounsbury, Francis A. March, Brander Matthews, William H. Maxwell, William W. Morrow, Theodore Roosevelt, Charles P. G. Scott, Homer H. Seerley, Benjamin E. Smith, Charles E. Sprague, Calvin Thomas, E. O. Vaile, William Hayes Ward, Andrew D. White, and Robert S. Woodward.

The Board also included seven members in England, two in Canada, and two in the Australian Commonwealth, as follows: In England, William Archer, Henry Bradley, Frederick J. Furnivall, H. Stanley Jevons, Sir James A. H. Murray, Walter W. Skeat, and Joseph Wright; in Canada, Alexander H. MacKay and William F. MacLean; in Australia, Thomas G. Tucker; in New Zealand, Sir Robert Stout.

In 1909 the board sufferd the loss of two eminent members, namely, Mr. Richard Watson Gilder and Dr. William T. Harris, and in 1910 of four other distinguisht members—Justice David J. Brewer, Mr. Samuel L. Clemens, Dr. Frederick J. Furnivall, and Prof. William James. The number of members in Dec., 1910, was forty.

Advisory Council.—In 1907 was organized the Advisory Council of the Simplified Spelling Board. The names of the first members were publisht in Jan., 1908. This council consists in great part of scholars, educators, men of science and men of affairs, representing nearly every state in the Union. The number of members in Dec., 1910, was 224. All proposals for simplification are referd to the Advisory Council as well as to the Board before they are recommended to the public for adoption. The members constitute, each in his own locality, centers of information and advice on the subject. The joint body is the largest body of men ever organized for the consideration of the orthografy of any language. It includes a great proportion of the scholars who are recognized as authorities in English philology or in educational science, and it is strengthend by the election of new members from time to time.

In England.—A Simplified Spelling Society has been establisht in Great Britain, with hedquarters at 44 Great Russell Street, London. This society was organized in Sept., 1908, with Prof. Walter W. Skeat, the eminent etymologist, as president, and Mr. William Archer, the well-known dramatic critic, as secretary. Among the officers and members are such eminent men as Sir James A. H. Murray and Dr. Henry Bradley, editors of the Oxford English Dictionary; Sir Frederick Pollock, Sir William Ramsay, the Right Hon. James Bryce, Prof. Gilbert Murray, Prof. Arthur S. Napier, and officials of the Education Department. Many scholars, professors, teachers, and missionaries in the Australian Commonwealth, in Africa, India, China, Japan, the Philippine Islands, and South America, are in correspondence with the Board, and are promoting the movement as an advantage, if not a necessity, to the English language in its contact with other languages. Plans for direct coöperation between the Simplified Spelling Board and the Simplified Spelling Society have been formed, and a conference, leading, it is hoped, to an international commission will be held in London early in 1911.

The movement for simplified spelling is opposed by an immense popular prejudis, and deals with a subject about which the intelligent public knows less than it does about any other subject. The movement has, therefore, been the object of much misrepresentation. The Board is endevoring in its publications to dissipate this prejudis and to diffuse correct information; and it desires that persons who feel any dout about the propriety of the movement, or about its principles, shall ask for the circulars of information publisht by the Board itself, and make up their minds after, and not before, acquiring the information. A request sent to the Simplified Spelling Board, No. 1 Madison Avenue, New York, will bring the necessary information free. Those who are inclined to take an interest in the movement will find it difficult to gather correct information about it from the unprecise utterances of the public press. Circular No. 23, dated March, 1909, contains a full "Alfabetic List of Simplifications in Spelling recommended by the Simplified Spelling Board up to Jan. 25, 1909." These recommendations are all applied in this article. It will be seen that they are far from "radical." They are, in fact, only the "first steps" to a reasonable revision of English spelling. Other simplifications are under consideration, but none have been publisht since the date mentioned.

Esperanto.—The sixth international congress of Esperanto was held in Washington, Aug. 14–20, 1910, the previous congresses having been held annually at Boulogne, Geneva, Cambridge (Eng.), Dresden, and Barcelona. There were present official delegates from twenty-three nations speaking eleven languages, and representatives from other countries speaking as many more. The peculiarity of the congress, distinguishing it from all other international gatherings, was the presentation of all papers and the transaction of all business in the single language of Esperanto, the only exception being in the case of the Chinese delegate, who used his native tongue. A feature of the congress was the address of Dr. Ludwig L. Zamenhof, of Warsaw, Poland, the author or inventor of Esperanto. John Barrett, director of the bureau of republics, and president of the Esperanto Association of North America, presided. Prizes were awarded for the best literary productions in Esperanto, several being awarded to American competitors. The experiences of the Washington congress, and the facility with which the artificial international language was utilized in the proceedings by its members, is claimed as a demonstration that Esperanto is making good its claim to be a feasible and effective medium of international communication, especially for commercial purposes. This claim is not admitted by the adherents of rival artificial languages, of which there are a number, including Volapuk, Bolak, and Ido, the last having also an international organization. It is agreed, even among Esperantists, that Dr. Zamenhof's language possesses certain obvious and unnecessary defects, which impair its simplicity, consistency, and effectiveness. In all probability the more important changes suggested for the improvement of Esperanto will ultimately be adopted.

1911 LITERATURE AND LANGUAGE

ANCIENT LITERATURE AND PHILOLOGY

ANCIENT LITERATURE
(Additions from Papyri)

CLIFFORD H. MOORE

The first three-quarters of the year 1911 have brought greater additions to classical literature than the year 1910. It is true that no single piece is of the interest which the poems of Callimachus possessed; but the total amount of this year's gain is larger and of more varied interest. As often before, we owe a debt of gratitude to the scholarship and energy of Arthur S. Hunt, from whose skilled hand come the two most important volumes of the year: *Catalogue of the Greek Papyri in the John Rylands Library, Manchester* (P. Rylands), and *The Oxyrhynchus Papyri*, vol. viii (P. Oxyr.).

Theological Fragments. — Each volume opens with fragments of theological content, of which the most important are the following: P. Rylands 6, a sixth-century papyrus containing what is apparently quite the oldest extant copy of the Nicene Creed. Although the text does not exactly coincide with any of the other versions known, it offers no very important variants; it closes with a personal confession of faith: "This is my creed, with this language [I shall approach without fear(?)] the terrible judgment seat of the Lord Christ in that dread day when He shall come again in His own glory to judge the quick and the dead and to reign with the saints forever and ever. Amen." Next in interest are 7, a new acrostic Christian hymn; 8 and 9, two liturgical fragments; and 12, a certificate of pagan sacrifice, dating from the Decian persecution. P. Oxyr. 1073 gives us on a vellum leaf of the fourth century parts of Genesis v and vi in the "Old Latin" version preceding Jerome's translation, which are textually important; 1074 and 1075 are two fragments of the Greek version of Exodus xxxi and xl, dating from the third century and therefore older than any known manuscript; 1076 offers a fragment of a new recension of Tobit ii; and 1081 contains an interesting bit of an unknown gnostic gospel.

Classical Texts.—Each volume brings new classical texts. Of these the most important is P. Oxyr. 1082, fragments of *meliambi* by the poet Cercidas. The first fragment preserves portions of two poems. One contains a discussion of the nature of the gods and of divine providence, in which the poet declares that the current beliefs do not square with the facts of life; he will rather leave the fictitious gods to the astrologers, and worship the tried Paean, Giving, and Retribution, that is, beneficence for those afflicted in body or spirit and punishment for wrongdoers. The second poem is erotic, teaching the cheap and easy way of love. Another fragment is apparently biographical, expressing the poet's satisfaction that he has devoted himself to the service of the Muses all his life. The fourth of the larger fragments, which contains a few verses on an uncertain subject, held the final column of the papyrus roll and has the subscription, "The Meliambi of Cercidas the Cynic." Thus we know definitely that Cercidas was a follower of Antisthenes, and from clear references to Zeno the Stoic and his pupil Sphaerus, we must place the poet in the third century B. C. His verses show him to be a graceful writer of no depth and with little poetic gift.

P. Rylands 13 is a fragment of an epic dealing with the story of Linus and the Argive festival of the Arneïdes. With this should be named P. Oxyr. 1085, a second-century fragment of a poem by the Alexandrine versifier Pancrates, hitherto known to us from Athenaeus, who quotes four "not inelegant" verses, to which this discovery adds some 40 more. Pancrates suggested to the emperor Hadrian that a certain kind of lotus, which he declared had sprung from the blood of a man-eating lion slain by the emperor, should be named from the imperial favorite Antinous. The verses so pleased Hadrian that he gave Pancrates free maintenance in the Museum, a generous reward to judge the whole poem by the swollen and diffuse style of the part we have recovered.

Dramatic Texts.—The only significant gain in dramatic literature consists of 28 fairly complete verses from a satyric play, P. Oxyr. 1083. This probably dates from the fifth century B. C. since the choral element seems large, but in spite of the names of two characters, Oineus and Phoenix, it is impossible to determine the author. P. Rylands 15 is the lament of a girl whose lover has been carried away to become a gladiator; and 17 gives us six lines of an epithalamium which suggests the "Epithalamium of Helen" by Theocritus. No. 23 of the same volume contains a fragmentary epitome of the Odyssey, and 26 is one of the happy surprises, for it is nothing less than a part of Apion's "Homeric Glosses," dating from the first century, and therefore but slightly later than the date of composition. New Homeric *scholia* are given in 1086 and 1087 of the P. Oxyr., both of the first century of our era. The former is important for the history of the Aristarchean tradition, while the latter is non-Aristarchean, and gains additional interest by giving us new quotations from no less than 15 different authors.

According to the London *Times* of Nov. 11, Dr. Hunt has announced the recovery of about 400 verses of the "Ichneutae," "The Trackers," a satyric play by Sophocles. The publication of this fragment will be eagerly awaited by scholars.

History.—In the field of history P. Oxyr. 1084 presents a second-century fragment of the first book of Hellanicus's "Atlantis," and 1089 a third-century fragment of an Alexandrian chronicle, in which is mentioned the prefect L. Avillius Flaccus attacked by Philo.

Homer.—Of the fragments of extant literature Homer naturally claims the lion's share in the Rylands volume; no Homeric passages are given from Oxyrhynchus this year. The most interesting is 53, which represents the extensive remains of a vellum book dating from the third or fourth century. The text contains parts of books xii-xv and xviii-xxiv; the largest portions belong to xiii-xiv and xx-xxiv, in fact the lines for the last three books and a half are continuous, although a hole in the center of each leaf causes considerable gaps. The character of the text is "mixed," showing close agreement with no single manuscript or group, so that after all the chief value of this discovery is that it adds a new example to the oldest vellum books known.

The other Greek authors represented are Hesiod, Bacchylides, Herodotus, Hippocrates, Demosthenes, Isocrates, and Polybius.

Latin papyri are so rare that every scrap is welcome. P. Oxyr. 1097, a leaf from a papyrus book of the fifth century, contains Cicero, *De Imperio Cn. Pompei* §§ 60-65, and *In Verrem* II, 1§§1-4 in a text of some critical value; 1098 offers a few fragments of Vergil, *Aeneid* ii, 16-23, 39-46. 1099 and P. Rylands 61 are of especial interest, the former because it contains a fragmentary Latin-Greek vocabulary of words drawn from the *Aeneid* iv, 659-705, and v, 1-6; the latter is a portion of Cicero, *In Catilinam* II, with a parallel translation in Greek. Both date from the fifth century and were intended for Greeks learning Latin. A few marks of quantity and accents are found on the Latin.

SEMITIC PHILOLOGY AND LITERATURE

MORRIS JASTROW

The Elephantine Papyri.—A long expected publication which has appeared just in time to be noticed in this survey is Prof. Eduard Sachau's edition of the "Aramaische Papyrus and Ostraka" (Leipzig, Hinrichs, 1911), the collection of the important finds made some years ago at Elephantine—the little island opposite Assuan. The documents found in the ruins of houses, all in Aramaic and belonging to the 5th century B. C., throw a remarkable and unexpected light on a Jewish military colony established at Elephantine during the period of Persian supremacy in Egypt which maintained relations with the mother-church in Jerusalem. Among the documents are also fragments of the Aramaic original of the famous Aehikar story and parts of the Aramaic translation of the rock inscription of Darius I at Behistun. In all 87 documents are included in this publication, to which an extra volume of facsimiles of the text is attached.

Inscriptions of the Persian Kings.—Belonging to the same period of the Achaemenian dynasty of Persia (c. 545 to 331 B. C.), is Weissbach's edition and translation of the inscriptions of the Persian Kings (*Die Keilinschriften der Achaemeniden*, Leipzig, Hinrichs, 1911). With the exceptions of the two inscriptions of Cyrus, which are in Babylonian, all the other documents are couched in the three official languages of the Persian Kingdom—old Persian, Babylonian and Neo-Elamitic. Prof. Weissbach furnishes a transliteration of all three languages with translations and explanatory notes.

Aramaic.—A useful compilation of the entire material bearing on the position of the Aramæan groups in the history of the ancient Orient and of the prominent position acquired by Aramaic from the 8th Century B. C. throughout Palestine, and Syria up to the district of the Euphrates and Tigris and extending well into Arabia, is represented by Sina Schiffer's "Die Aramäer" (Leipzig, Hinrichs, 1911). That an Aramaic dialect became the common speech even in Babylonia during the two centuries preceding the coming of the Persians is one of the surprising results of recent researches that is being confirmed by steadily increasing material.

Assyriology.—Within the field of Assyriology, the most significant publication of the past year is in the subdivision of archæology. Following up Andrae's valuable treatment of the Anu-Adad Temple excavated by the German expedition at Ashur, the ancient capital of Assyria, Dr. Robert Koldewey, the director of the German excavations at Babylon, has summed up in a splendidly illustrated volume with detailed charts and drawings, the results of the investigations of the temples of Babylon and Borsippa, so far as recovered. (*Die Tempel von Babylon und Borsippa*, Leipzig, Hinrich, 1911). Thanks to this work, we now have a definite view of the interior arrangement of Babylonian sanctuaries.

Sumerian.—The publication of a Sumerian grammar by Stephen Langdon (Paris, Geuthner, 1911), may be taken as an indication of the advance made in our knowledge of the language spoken by the old Sumerian settlers in the Euphrates valley. At the same time Langdon's work shows how much is still doubtful and how defective our knowledge is at many points. Francois Thureau-Dangin, of Paris, now the leading authority on Sumerian has acquired fresh laurels by his *Lettres et Contrats de l'Epoque de la Première Dynastie Babylonienne* (Paris, Geuthner, 1910) —an important collection of documents, containing also two cuneiform tablets from a district Khana of which hitherto little was known.

Another new center from which numerous tablets have recently turned up is Drehem, 3 miles to the south of Nippur. It is to the same indefatigable Thureau-Dangin that we owe the first publication of Sumerian documents from this place. Two larger publications of Drehem tablets are just off the press, one by H. de Genouillac of the collection in Constantinople and in the Louvre, another of Stephen Langdon of those that have been acquired by the Bodleian Library and the Ashmolean Museum of Oxford.

Babylonian.—The activity of the British Museum is represented by three parts of the "Cuneiform Texts" series (Parts 27 to 29), two of which are taken up chiefly with "Birth-Omens" which for the first time enable us to obtain a detailed view of the system perfected by the Babylonian priests in interpreting unusual phenomena—chiefly malformations—observed in new-born infants and in the young of animals. L. W. King has published the first of three volumes of his *History of Babylonia and Assyria* (London, Chatto and Windus, 1910), which comprising a complete treatment of the entire material by a master of the subject will undoubtedly take rank as the standard work on the subject in English. Of works by American scholars, mention should be made of the appearance of two more volumes of the *Assyrian and Babylonian Letters* of the British Museum by Prof. R. F. Harper of the University of Chicago (London, Luzac & Co., 1911). This series of eleven volumes forms a *corpus* of the epistolary literature of Assyria and Babylonia, of equal importance for the light thrown by these letters on historical events, on social conditions and on religious practices. Prof. Jastrow's *Aspects of Religious Belief and Practice in Babylonia and Assyria* (New York, Putnams, 1911) aims to give in a popular form a summary of the main facts of the Babylonian-Assyrian religion, as disclosed by recent researches.

Arabic.—In Arabic literature, the most notable publication is Ignaz Goldziber's *Vorlesungen über den Islam* (Heidelberg, Winter, 1911), which as a treatment of the subject by the greatest living authority ought to appear in an English garb also. The great *Encyclopaedia of Islam* appearing in parts in three languages (English, French and German) is making slow progress, the work extending at present only to BAD. The projectors appear to be in lack of funds to carry on this expensive but highly important undertaking; and it would be a serious loss to science if the *Encyclopaedia* should have to be abandoned for this reason.

Hebrew.—The excavations conducted for a number of years under the auspices of Harvard University through the generosity of Jacob H. Schiff have at last yielded important results. A palace was uncovered which is in all probability the one erected or enlarged by Ahab the King of Israel (9th century B. C.) and numerous ostraka containing important lists of Hebrew proper names have been found. A preliminary account has been furnished by Prof. D. G. Lyon "Hebrew Ostraka from Samaria" (*Harvard Theological Review*, vol. III, pp. 136-146), and an elaborate publication on the excavations is announced as in preparation.

Preliminary reports of important excavations in "underground Jerusalem" conducted by English explorers are being published by Prof. H. Vincent in the *Revue Biblique* (Vol. 8, Nos. 4 and 5). In the "International Series" of commentaries on the Old and New Testament, the volume on Genesis by Prof. H. S. Skinner has appeared (New York, Scribners, 1911), which is by far the best work on the subject that has as yet appeared in English. The treatment is full and explicit and embodies the latest results of critical study of the various documents comprised in Genesis.

INDO-GERMANIC PHILOLOGY

(Exclusive of the Germanic Languages.)

ROLAND G. KENT

The activity of American scholars in this field is such that our entire space is this year devoted to their work.[1]

[1] The following abbreviations are used: *AJA.*, American Journal of Archaeology; *AJP.*, American Journal of Philology; *CP.*, Classical Philology; *CQ.*, Classical Quarterly; *IF.*, Indogermanische Forschungen; *JAOS.*, Journal of the American Oriental Society; *KZ.*, Zeitschrift für vergleichende Sprachforschung, begründet von A. Kuhn; *PAPA.*, Proceedings of the American Philological Association; *PAPS.*, Proceedings of the American Philosophical Society; *TAPA.*, Transactions of the American Philological Association.

Indo-Iranian (see also under "Suffixes and Etymologies").—L. C. Barrett (Trinity) has issued the first edition of Book II of *The Kashmirian Atharva Veda* (*JAOS.*, 30, 187-258), continuing Book I (in *JAOS.*, 26), from a single badly written manuscript, continuing many hymns not known in other versions of the Atharva Veda. G. M. Bolling (Catholic Univ.) and J. von Negelein (Königsberg, Germany) have completed vol. 1 of *The Pariśiṣṭas of the Atharvaveda* (Leipzig, Harrassowitz; part 1, 1909; parts 2 and 3, 1910), giving a text, critical apparatus and indices to this hitherto unpublished work. G. P. Quackenbos (Col. City of N. Y.) gives the text of *The Mayūrāṣṭaka*, an unedited Sanskrit poem by Mayūra, with translation and notes, in *JAOS.*, 31, 343-354. M. Bloomfield (Johns Hopkins), "Some Rig-Veda Repetitions" (*JAOS.*, 31, 49-69; cf. last year); E. W. Hopkins (Yale); "Mythological Aspects of Trees and Mountains in the Great Epic" (*JAOS.*, 30, 347-374), "Magic Observances in the Hindu Epic" (*PAPS.*, 49, 29-40), "Buddha as Tathāgata" (*AJP.*, 32, 205-209); A. V. W. Jackson (Columbia), "The possible Contribution of Oriental Thought to present-day Christianity" (*The 27th Church Congress in the U. S.*, 96-105), "Brahmanism" (Randall and Smith's *Unity of Religion*, 29-37); S. G. Oliphant (Olivet), "Fragments of a lost Myth-Indra and the Ants" (*PAPA.*, 41, lv-lix); E. A. Welden, "The Sāṅkhya term Liṅga" (*AJP*, 31, 445-459). L. Bloomfield (Illinois), in "The Indo-European Palatals in Sanskrit" (*AJP.*, 32, 36-57) presents the theory that Indic spirantized the palatals less soon that did Iranian. F. Edgerton (Johns Hopkins) presents "A Modern Development of the Elliptic Dual" (*KZ.*, 44, 23-25) in Romance dialects, continuing his previous studies (see last year). Oliphant on "The Vedic Dual" (*JAOS.*, 30, 155-185) shows that the dual of words denoting bodily parts is quite rigidly limited in use.

T. Michelson (Smithsonian) continues his researches in the inscriptions of Asoka (*TAPA.*, 40, 23-29; *IF.*, 28, 203-4, 29, 221-6; *JAOS.*, 31, 223-250).

A. V. W. Jackson has just issued another volume of his travels and studies, entitled *From Constantinople to the Home of Omar Khayyam* (New York, Macmillan, 1911).

L. H. Gray (Columbia) gives the text of *The Parsī-Persian Burj-Nāmah, or Book of Omens from the Moon* (*JAOS.*, 30, 336-342), with introduction and translation.

Lydian.—(See XXXIV, *Epigraphy*.)

Suffixes and Etymologies.—H. H. Bender (Princeton) has treated from the phonetic standpoint *The Suffixes -mant and -vant in Sanskrit and Avestan* (Baltimore, 1910), and W. Petersen (Bethany Col., Lindsborg, Kas.), has given a semantic treatment of *The Greek Diminutives in -ιον* (Weimar, 1910); both are exhaustive and scholarly (see review by Edgerton, *AJP.*, 32, 91-97). Edgerton has issued a splendid treatment, both phonetic and semantic, of *The K-Suffixes in the Veda and Avesta* (Leipzig, 1911, reprinted from *JAOS.*, 31, 93-150, 296-342; cf. also *PAPA.*, 40, xxviii f.), and promises to continue his study of this suffix through the later Sanskrit literature. C. W. Peppler (Emory Col., Oxford, Ga.), in "The Termination -κός, as used by Aristophanes for Comic Effect" (*AJP.*, 31, 428-444) shows that this suffix was used by him mainly to ridicule the philosophers and his phonetic for excessive use of words with this suffix.

E. H. Sturtevant (Barnard) continues his "Studies in Greek Noun Formation: Labial Terminations" (*CP.*, 6, 197-215, 450-476; see last year).

E. W. Fay (Texas) has recently been seeking (*CP.*, 6, 315-324; *AJP.*, 31, 404-427) to find the meaning of suffixes as separate words—a line of investigation that seems fruitful, though it will always remain highly conjectural.

Etymologies are treated by Fay in *CQ.*, 5, 119-122 (βασιλεύς), *TAPA.*, 41, 25-53, *JAOS.*, 31, 403-413; and in the articles just mentioned; by H. C. Tolman in *PAPA.*, 41, lxx f.; and by R. G. Kent (Pennsylvania) in *TAPA.*, 41, 5-9 (*mīles*), *JAOS.*, 31, 359-364.

1911 LITERATURE AND LANGUAGE

Greek and Latin (see also under "Suffixes and Etymologies" and "Etruscan," etc.)—H. Collitz (Johns Hopkins) as general editor of the *Sammlung der griechischen Diatektinschriften* has issued vol. IV, part 3 (Göttingen, Vandenhoeck, 1910), by O. Hoffmann (Breslau, Germany), containing grammar and index to the first half of vol. III.

A. R. Anderson (Northwestern), in "Some Questions of Plautine Pronunciation" (*TAPA.*, 40, 99-107), shows that ŏ in older Latin after *u* and *v* was merely graphic for *u*, to avoid writing *VV*, which was ambiguous.

Miss F. M. Bennett (Columbia), "The Duenos Inscription" (*PAPA.*, 41, xxi-xxiv); R. W. Husband (Dartmouth), "The Diphthong -*ui* in Latin" (*TAPA.*, 41, 19-23); W. A. Merrill (California), "On the contracted Genitive in *i* in Latin" (*Univ. of Cal. Publ. in Class. Phil.*, 2, 57-79).

Etruscan, etc.—(See also XXXIV, *Epigraphy*.)

H. C. Tolman (Vanderbilt) proposes an Indo-Germanic etymology for "The Etruscan *aisar, ais, αισοι*" (*PAPA.*, 40, lxxxviii f.).

Husband, in "Race Mixture in Early Rome" (*TAPA.*, 40, 63-81) shows that the language of the so-called Ligurian inscriptions is partly Keltic and partly non-Indo-Germanic, thus proving the Ligurians not Indo-Germanic in language. In *CP.*, 6, 385-401, he discusses the Gallic migrations into Italy.

T. S. Denison, in *The Morphology of the Mexican Verb* (Chicago, 1910), seeks, as in previous publications, to prove the Mexican Indian language Indo-Germanic; but no value can be attached to his theories (cf. Fay's review, *AJP.*, 31, 241 f., of an earlier pamphlet).

GREEK LITERATURE

PAUL SHOREY

There is as yet no occasion for adding anything to the general introduction prefixed to the first of these reports, that for the year 1910. A brief selected bibliography will sufficiently indicate the character of the work done by American Greek scholars during the past year.

BIBLIOGRAPHY

ADAMS, Charles Darwin.—"Notes on the Peace of Philocrates." (*Transactions of the American Philological Association*, XLI (1910), pp. 55-64.)

AUSTIN, Herbert D.—"The Origin and Greek Version of the Strange Feathers Fable." (*Studies in Honor of A. M. Elliott*, vol. I. Baltimore, 1911.)

BAIN, Charles W.—"On ὅπως and ὅπως ἄν." (*Studies in Philology*, vol. VII. Chapel Hill, N. C., The University Press, 1911.)

BOLLING, G. M.—"Homeric Armor and Mr. Lang." (*Catholic Bulletin*, 1910, pp. 669-708.)

BONNER, Campbell.—"Dionysiac Magic and the Greek Land of Cockaigne." (*Tr. A. P. A.*, XLI (1910), pp. 175-185.)
———"The Prenuptial Rite in the *Aetia* of Callimachus." (*Classical Philology*, VI (1911), pp. 402-409.)

BONNER, Robert J.—"The Administration of Justice in the Age of Homer." (*Classical Philology*, VI (1911), p. 12 ff.)

BOTSFORD, G. W.—*A History of the Ancient World*. (New York, The Macmillan Company, 1911.)

BREITENBACH, H. P.—"The *De Compositione* of Dionysius of Halicarnassus considered with reference to the *Rhetoric* of Aristotle." (*Classical Philology*, VI (1911), p. 163 ff.)

DEWING, Henry B.—"The Origin of the Accentual Prose Rhythm in Greek." (*American Journal of Philology*, XXXI (1910), pp. 312-328.)
———"Hiatus in the Accentual Clausulae of Byzantine Greek Prose." (*A. J. P.*, XXXII (1911), p. 188 ff.)

FAIRBANKS, Arthur.—*A Handbook of Greek Religion*. (New York, The American Book Company, 1910.)

FAY, Edwin W.—"Greek βασι-λεύς." (*Classical Quarterly*, London, V, p. 119.)

FLICKINGER, Roy C.—"The Influence of Local Theatrical Conditions upon the Drama of the Greeks." (*Classical Journal*, VII (1911), pp. 3-22.)

GILDERSLEEVE, B. L., and MILLER, C. W. E.—*Syntax of Classical Greek, Pt. II.* (New York, The American Book Company, 1911.)

GOLDMAN, Hetty.—"The *Oresteia* of Aeschylus as Illustrated by Greek Vase Painting." (*Harv. Studies*, XXI (1910), p. 111 ff.)

GOODELL, Thomas D.—"Structural Variety in Attic Tragedy." (*Tr. A. P. A.*, XLI (1910), p. 71 ff.)

1911 LITERATURE AND LANGUAGE

Hains, D. D.—"Greek Plays in America." (*Classical Journal*, vi (1910), p. 24 ff.)

Harry, Joseph Edward.—*The Antigone of Sophocles.* Translated into English verse. (Cincinnati, The Robert Clarke Co., 1911.)

Haskins, Charles H., and Lockwood, Dean Putnam.—"The Sicilian Translators of the Twelfth Century and the First Latin Version of Ptolemy's *Almagest.*" (*Harv. Studies*, xxi (1910), p. 75 ff.)

Heidel, William Arthur.—"The ἄναρμοι ὄγκο of Heraclides and Asclepiades." (*Tr. A. P. A.*, xl (1909), pp. 5-21.)

——"Antecedents of Greek Corpuscular Theories." (*Harv. Studies*, xxii (1911), pp. 111-172.)

Hempl, G.—"The Solving of an Ancient Riddle: Ionic Greek Before Homer." (*Harper's Magazine*, cxxii (1911), pp. 187-198.)

Hewitt, Joseph William.—"The Necessity of Ritual Purification after Justifiable Homicide." (*Tr. A. P. A.*, xli (1910), pp. 99-114.)

——"Major Restrictions on Access to Greek Temples." (*Tr. A. P. A.*, xl (1909), pp. 83-91.)

——see Mather, M. W.

Hoskier, H. C.—*Concerning the Versions of the New Testament.* (London, B. Quaritch, 1910-1911, 2 vols.)

Hutton, Maurice.—"Notes on Herodotus and Thucydides." (*Tr. A. P. A.*, xli (1910), pp. 11-18.)

Johnson, A. C.—*A Comparative Study in Selected Chapters in the Syntax of Isaeus and the Attic Psephismata preceding 300 B. C.* (Athens, Printing Office "Hestia," 1911.) Johns Hopkins University Dissertation.

Keller, William J.—"Xenophon's Acquaintance with the History of Herodotus." (*Classical Journal*, vi (1910), p. 252 ff.)

Macurdy, Grace Harriet.—"Traces of the Influence of Plato's Eschatological Myths in Parts of the Book of Revelation and the Book of Enoch." (*Tr. A. P. A.*, xli (1910), pp. 65-70.)

Mather, M. W., and Hewitt, Joseph William.—*Xenophon, Anabasis, Books I-IV, with introduction, notes and vocabulary.* (New York, The American Book Company, 1910.)

McWhorter, Ashton Waugh.—"A Study of the So-called Deliberative Type of Question (τί ποιήσω;)." (*Tr. A. P. A.*, xli (1910), pp. 157-168.)

Miller, C. W. E.,—See Gildersleeve, B. L.

Murray, A. T.—"On a use of ΔΟΚΩ." (*Classical Philology*, v (1909), p. 488 ff.)

Norlin, George.—"The Conventions of the Pastoral Elegy." (*AJP.*, xxxii (1911), pp. 294-312.)

Ogle, M. B.—"Laurel in Ancient Religion and Folk Lore." (*AJP.*, xxxi (1910), pp. 287-311.)

——"The House Door in Greek and Roman Religion and Folk Lore." (*AJP.*, xxxii (1911), pp. 251-271.)

Pease, Arthur Stanley.—"The Omen of Sneezing." (*Classical Philology*, vi (1911), pp. 429-443.)

Peck, Harry Thurston.—*A History of Classical Philology from the Seventh Century B. C. to the Twentieth Century A. D.* (New York, The Macmillan Company, 1911.)

Peppler, Charles W.—"The Termination -κος as used by Aristophanes for Comic Effect." (*AJP.*, xxxi (1910), pp. 428-444.)

Perrin, B.—*Plutarch's Cimon and Pericles, with the Funeral Oration of Pericles, newly translated, with introduction and notes.* (New York, Scribner's, 1910.)

Petersen, Walter.—*Greek Diminutives in -ιον: a Study in Semantics.* (Weimar. R. Wagner Sohn, 1910.)

Prescott, Henry W.—"The *Versus Inconditi* of Pap. *Oxyrhynch.* 219." (*Classical Philology*, v (1909), p. 158 ff.)

Rand, E. K.—"Horatian Urbanity in Hesiod's 'Works and Days.'" (*AJP.*, xxxii (1911), p. 131 ff.)

Randolph, Charles Brewster.—"The Sign of Interrogation in Greek Minuscle Manuscripts." (*Classical Philology*, v (1909), p. 309 ff.)

Robinson, David M.—"New Greek Inscriptions from Attica, Achaia, Lydia." (*AJP.*, xxxi (1910, pp. 377-403.)

Schauroth, Edward G.—"The ὑποξώματα of Greek Ships." (*Harv. Studies*, xxii, 1911, pp. 173-180.)

Scott, John A.—"Two Linguistic Tests of the Relative Antiquity of the Iliad and the Odyssey." (*Classical Philology*, vi (1911), p. 156 ff.)

——"Words found in the Iliad and in but One Book of the Odyssey." (*Classical Philology*, vi (1911), p. 48 ff.)

——"Repeated Verses in Homer." (*AJP.*, xxxii (1911), pp. 313-321.)

——"Athenian Interpolations in Homer." (*Classical Philology*, vi (1911), pp. 419-428.)

Stuart, Duane Reed.—"The Prenuptial Rite in the New Callimachus." (*Classical Philology*, vi (1911), p. 302 ff.)

Sturtevant, E. H.—"Studies in Greek Noun Formation." (*Classical Philology*, v (1910), pp. 323 ff; vi (1911), p. 197 ff., 450 ff.)

Super, C. W.—*Plutarch on Education.* (Syracuse, N. Y. C. W. Bardeen, 1910.)

TUKEY, Ralph Hermon.—"The Stoic Use of λέξις and φράσις." (*Classical Philology*, VI (1911), pp. 444-449.)
WHITMORE, Charles E.—"On a Passage in Pindar's Fourth Nemean Ode." (*Harv. Studies*, XXI (1910), p. 103 ff.)
WRIGHT, Frederick Warren.—*Studies in Menander*. (Baltimore, The Waverley Press, 1911.) Princeton University dissertation.

LATIN LITERATURE

CHARLES KNAPP

American work in Latin literature still consists mainly of articles in *The American Journal of Philology* (*A. J. P.*), *Classical Philology* (*C. P.*), the *Transactions of the American Philological Association* (*T. A. P. A.*), and in the volumes of studies published under the auspices of various universities. One book, E. G. Sihler's *Annals of Caesar*, a critical biography, comes within our field. In *T. A. P. A.* for 1909, published in 1910, under the title "On Certain Euphonic Embellishments of Propertius," B. O. Foster treats rhyme, vowel repeated, alliteration, syllable repeated, word repeated or echoed, onomatopœia. On Propertius, again, see B. L. Ullman, "The Manuscripts of Propertius" (*C. P.*), and A. L. Wheeler's work on "Roman Elegy" (see below). In *T. A. P. A.*, in "Lucilius and Persius," G. C. Fiske make Lucilius a source for Persius second in importance only to Horace. For a certain tendency of American scholarship see W. P. Mustard, in *T. A. P. A.*, "On the [Latin] Eclogues of Baptista Mantuanus," a writer of the 15th century who knew Vergil well; the same writer's edition of Mantuanus's *Eclogues*; two papers in abstract in the *Proceedings*, bound with *T. A. P. A.*, one by K. P. Harrington, "The Classical Element in 16th Century Latin Lyrics," the other by C. C. Bushnell, "Some New Material dealing with the Classical Influence on Tennyson." In the *Proceedings*, again, C. Knapp, in "The Dramatic Satura among the Romans," defends the Roman tradition concerning the dramatic satura, and promises to give to the subject the exhaustive treatment demanded by its great importance to the student of Latin literature. The abstract in the *Proceedings* of the presidential address of Prof. B. L. Gildersleeve on the "Range and Character of the Philological Activity of America" deserves mention; it is well reinforced by the article of P. Shorey, on "American Scholarship," in *The Nation* for May 11, 1911.

In *C. P.*, G. L. Hendrickson, in a paper entitled "Satura—the Genesis of a Literary Form," urges that, down to 40-30 B. C., the Latin word *satura* was either not in existence at all or at least not in common use as a designation of a form of literature, for the reason that, though Roman satire began with Lucilius, a long time elapsed before it claimed a place as a recognized and independent form of literature needing a specific name.

Other papers making contributions in detail to the study and understanding of Latin literature are: "A Bibliography of Persius," by M. H. Morgan; "The Rhythmical Clausulae in Ammianus Marcellinus," by A. M. Harmon, in *Transactions of the Connecticut Academy of Arts and Sciences*, XVI; "Vahlen's Ennius," by C. Knapp (*A. J. P.*), an elaborate examination of parts of the second edition of Vahlen's great book on Ennius; "The Origin of the Realistic Romance among the Romans," by F. F. Abbott (*C. P.*), an argument that the realistic romance was the invention of Petronius; "Concerning the Oratory of Brutus," by E. J. Philbey (*C. P.*), an argument that in his *Brutus* Cicero does not correctly represent either Brutus's views on oratory or his oratorical style; "The House-Door in Greek and Roman Religion," by M. B. Ogle (*A. J. P.*), an effort to show that the cult connected with the door (*e.g.*, binding the doorposts with wool, fastening on or near the door laurel, cypress, etc.), was concerned originally with the spirits of the dead; "Roman Prayer in its Relation to Ethics," by G. J. Laing (*C. P.*); "The Introduction of Masks on the Roman Stage," by Miss C. Saunders (*A. J. P.*), a good summary and examination of the available evidence and the views based upon it, reinforcing the view that the introduction was between 130 and 91 B. C.; "Erotic Teaching in Roman Elegy" (Part II), by A. L. Wheeler (*C. P.*), which urges that the erotic system of teaching was already highly developed in the New Comedy of Athens and that the Roman elegists drew directly on that comedy; "The Identity of the Child in Virgil's *Pollio* (Eclogue IV), by J. E. Church, Jr., (*C. P.*); "The Convention of the Pastoral Elegy," by G. Norlin (*A. J. P.*), which illustrates the influence of the classics on modern pastoral poetry by pointing out conventions which recur in pastoral poetry from classical times to our own day. This tendency, rather common in America, to trace the influence of the classics on modern literature, especially English, is seen in the second edition of an excellent book, *The Classic Myths in English Literature and Art*, by C. M. Gayley. (See also Prof. Bushnell's paper, referred to above.)

One book not directly concerned with literature proper but sure to prove indispensable to the earnest interpreter of early Latin literature is *Syntax of Early Latin;* Vol. I: *The Verb*, by C. E. Bennett (see reviews of it in *C. P.* by W. G. Hale, in *A. J. P.* by C. Knapp, in *The Classical Weekly*, by A. L. Wheeler).

Most important aid to the study of literature is supplied by adequate lexicons and *indices verborum*. The two important Latin lexicons on which American scholars are engaged, the *Thesaurus Linguae Latinae Epigraphicae*, by G. N. Olcott, and *Lexicon Plautinum*, by G. Lodge (both professors in Columbia University) made progress; of the former 408 pages (into *ara*), of the latter 576 (into *fabula*) have now appeared. Most important for every student of Vergil is M. N. Wetmore's *Index Verborum Vergilianus*, of 554 pages (Yale University Press). An excellent idea of its value may be gained from the review of it by E. K. Rand (*C. P.*). The mention of this paper reminds one of Prof. Rand's "Horatian Urbanity in Hesiod" (*A. J. P.*), and, finally, of the fact that much excellent work in classical literature and philology is done by American scholars in reviews, especially in *A. J. P.* and *C. P.*

METHODS OF INSTRUCTION IN LATIN AND GREEK

GONZALEZ LODGE

College Entrance Requirements.—The Chairman of the Commission on College Entrance Requirements, Prof. J. C. Kirtland,[1] reports 56 colleges and universities as having adopted the recommendations laid down in the report of Dec., 1909, and it is confidently expected that after the examinations of 1912, the old requirements will disappear from most college announcements. The modifications in the curriculum involved in this change have been thoroughly discussed by Prof. Kirtland,[2] while Prof. G. Lodge[3] has set forth the value of the oral method in this connection, and Prof. F. P. Moulton[4] has discussed the methods of training in sight translation. Pres. E. D. M. Gray[5] goes so far as to urge that Latin be taught as a modern language.

Oral Teaching.—The rapid spread of the oral method in Great Britain and the interest which it is arousing among classical teachers is evidenced by the fact that a summer school of Latin, devoted primarily to the exemplification of this method, was held at the University of North Wales during the early part of September. At this school more than a hundred teachers were in attendance and the greatest enthusiasm was manifested. Several new English text-books setting forth this method have been published recently and the two most recent American elementary books likewise provide extensively for this kind of exercise.

Value of Classical Training.—The various *Symposia* of the Michigan Classical Conference have been issued in a single volume[6] which constitutes the strongest, and at the same time the most representative, discussion of the claims of classical study to the earnest consideration of every cultivated man. Particularly important in this book are the discussions in regard to the value of classical training from the point of view of formal discipline and in preparation for the different learned professions. The same points are emphasized in different ways in articles by Prof. F. J. Donnelly,[7] Miss G. H. Goodale,[8] Prof. J. K. Lord,[9] and Prof. Paul Shorey.[10] Statistics of honor men among Dartmouth College students have been prepared by Prof. C. D. Adams,[11] which show that the proportion of classical students who have obtained honors in science is very much greater than that of the distinctly science students, 54 per cent. to 20 per cent. Similar statements showing the same facts have been prepared by Prof. J. W. Hewitt[12] with regard to students in Wesleyan University.

Training of Teachers.—The differences in the training of classical teachers in Germany and in the United States is the subject of an able article by Prof. Julius Sachs.[13] He shows that the fine quality and results of classical teaching in Germany are due to the large amount of knowledge and skill required of German students who expect to be teachers of the classics as well as to the fact that in Germany teaching in the schools is regarded as a life work by those who adopt it.

Prose composition is discussed by A. L. Hodges,[14] who maintains that undue emphasis should not be laid upon this branch of instruction and that the cultural element should not be lost sight of.

Suggestions for stimulating the interest of students are provided in articles by Miss C. J. Allinson,[15] Prof. F. S. Dunn[16] and Prof. F. B. Meyer,[17] while the enthusiasm of students themselves is shown in the prevalence of Greek plays,[18] which continue to be given in a number of universities each year, and other representations of ancient life.

BIBLIOGRAPHY

1. "The Consequents of the Commission's Report." (*Classical Journal*, VI. 330-342.)
2. "The Reconstruction of the Latin Course." (*Educational Review*, XL. 440-454.)
3. "The Oral Method of Teaching Latin." (Report of the National Educational Association, republished *Classical Weekly*, IV. 66-9.)
4. "Sight Tests: Their Aims and How to Prepare Them." (*Classical Journal*, VI. 355-367.)
5. *Latin in the Secondary School*. (Albuquerque, Dec., 1910.)
6. *Latin and Greek in American Education*. (New York, Macmillan, 1911.)
7. "The Profit and Loss of Greek." (*America*, April 22, 1911: reprinted in *Classical Weekly*, IV, 220-221.)
8. "The Classics and the Country Boy or Girl." (*Classical Weekly*, IV, 122-127.)
9. "The Objects and the Results of the Study of Latin." (*Classical Journal*, VI. 233-243.)
10. "American Scholarship." (*Nation*, May 11, 1911.)
11. "Greek and Science." (*Nation*, Feb. 16, 1911.)
12. "The Efficiency of the Student of Greek." (*Nation*, Sept. 7, 1911.)
13. "The Training of the Teacher of the Classics in Germany." (*Educational Review*, XLI. 449-466.)
14. "What and Why in Greek and Latin Composition." (*Classical Weekly*, IV. 90-93.)
15. "Three Factors in Vitalizing the Study of the Classics." (*Classical Journal*, VI. 167-174.)
16. "The Historical Novel in the Classroom." (*Classical Journal*, VI. 296-304.)
17. "Religion and Morality in High School Latin." (*Classical Weekly*, IV. 138-141.)
18. KIRBY, Harriet R.—"A Roman Triclinium." (*Classical Journal*, VI, 260-261.)

MODERN LANGUAGES AND LITERATURE

GERMANIC LANGUAGES

DANIEL B. SHUMWAY

Interest in German and Scandinavian Literature.—Without doubt the most characteristic and significant feature of the year in the department of Germanic languages is the growing interest of the American public in German and Scandinavian literature. This is evidenced not only by the many translations that have appeared, but still more so by the fact that a systematic effort is now being made to translate all the more important modern German authors into English. This monumental undertaking will consist of a series of 20 large volumes of over 500 pages each, under the title: *The German Classics* of the XIX and XX Centuries. In the Scandinavian field, the growing interest has resulted in the forming of an Association for Scandinavian Studies in Chicago. A Committee on Translations was appointed to encourage the translation of Scandinavian works. A brief sketch of the history of Scandinavian study in American universities, from the pen of George T. Flom, appears in the *Transactions* of the meeting, and articles on the Association appeared in the *Dial* of July 1 and in the *Nation* of June 8.

German Translations. — Turning now to modern German literature we find that the following novels and dramas have appeared in translation this year. Gerhart Hauptmann is represented by translations of *The Weavers*, his powerful social drama of the 40's, by Mary Morrison; by his first social drama *Before Dawn*, by Leonard Bloomfield; further by a new translation of his fairy drama *The Sunken Bell*, by one of the *Assumption of Hannele*, of *And Pippa Dances* and of *The Reconciliation*. Hauptmann's latest novel, *Emanuel Quint, der Narr in Christo*, a weird but masterful tale of a weak-minded peasant who is led to believe himself to be a reincarnation of Christ, is well described in *Current Literature*, L. 172-3, under the title of "Hauptmann's Silesian Messiah." Hauptmann's treatment of blank verse is also the subject of a N. Y. Univ. dissertation by C. A. Kraus. Hermann Sudermann is represented by translations of his Biblical drama *Johannes*, of *St. John's Eve*, and of his allegorical play *The Three Heron Feathers*. Friedrich Hebbel, who in recent years has received the recognition long denied him, is represented by the translation of his well known plays *Agnes Bernauer* and *Judith*. Adolf Wilbrandt's masterpiece *The Master of Palmyra* has also appeared in English. Arthur Schnitzler, the Austrian playwright, has been honored by translations of *The Duke and the Actress*, *The Lady with the Dagger*, *The Legacy*, *Living Houses* and *Anatol*, a sequence of dialogues paraphrased for the English stage. All but the last of the above named plays are reprints of the translations which appeared from time to time in *Poet Lore*. A poetic translation of Wagner's *Dusk of the Gods* (*Götterdämmerung*) has appeared from the skilful pen of Oliver Huckel. Wagner's *Autobiography*, which created such a stir in Germany because of its more than candid tone, has likewise been issued in English by Dodd, Mead & Co. A. Julien has also published a study of Wagner's life and works. Frank Wedekind's powerful but repulsive tragedy of childhood, *The Awakening of Spring*, has been done into English by Francis J. Ziegler, who has also rendered several stories by the same author, *The Grisly Suitor*, *Rabbi Ezra* and *The Victim*. An historical drama by Friedrich Eberweiler entitled *Three Holy Kings* has been translated by a member of the Society of Jesus. A few excerpts of Schönherr's masterly tragedy *Faith and Fireside* (*Glaube und Heimat*), which has been the sensation of the year in Germany, have appeared in *Current Literature* for Sept. It is also reviewed by Kuno Francke in the *Nation* of June 15. Modern German drama is treated by P. Pollard in his book *Masks and Minstrels of New Germany*, and W. R. Meyer has discussed the "Technique of Bridging Gaps in the Action of the German Drama Since Gottsched" in *Modern Philology*, VIII, 217-268 and 363-398.

But two German novels have been translated this year. One, the latest work of Gustav Frenssen, bears the title *Klaus Hinrich Baas*. It is the story of the rise of a self-made man in Hamburg, told with all the gripping interest and fidelity to nature so characteristic of Frenssen. Frenssen's literary work is the subject of an appreciative article in the April number of the *Bookman*. The other novel is *Elizabeth Kött* by R. H. Bartsch, which has been translated by Ludwig Lewisohn. One fails to discover the reason for the translation of this rather weak production. No translation, but an estimate of the work of the novelist Spielhagen, who passed away in February, appeared in the *Nation* of March 9 and in the *Review of Reviews* for May. *Tannhäuser*, one of the light but popular verse romances by Julius Wolff, has been rendered into English by C. G. Kendall, and the poet Heine's *Memoirs*, edited by Gustav Karpeles, have been translated by Gilbert Cannan. The interest in Goethe's *Faust* is shown by the issuing of an inexpensive edition of Bayard Taylor's translation in the "Riverside Literature Series," while an expensive edition with 30 full-page colored plates has been prepared by Willy Pogany. The interest in Goethe is further shown by a volume on *Margaret Fuller and Goethe*, containing a sketch of the poet's influence on the transcendentalists; further by a sketch of *Frau Aja, Goethe's Mother*, from the pen of M. Reeks. The great cultural influence of the German immigrants on American civilization is discussed by Rudolf Cronau in an article entitled "The German Element in the United States" in the *Forum* of Sept., and an article "Some German Pioneers" in the *Review of Reviews* of Sept. reviews a similar essay by the same author in the *Gartenlaube*.

German Texts.—The editing of German texts for school use shows apparently no diminution, and only the most important can be mentioned here. Otto Manthey-Zorn has prepared a new edition of Fulda's *Talisman* for Ginn & Co., making the third edition of this play. Camillo von Klenze has made an edition of Hebbel's *Agnes Bernauer* for the Oxford University Press, and issued a new edition of his excellent little volume *Deutsche Gedichte*. An abridged edition of Sudermann's novel *Frau Sorge* has been prepared by Eugene Leser and Carl Osthaus for Heath & Co., and B. J. Vos has edited a new edition of *Wilhelm Tell* for Ginn & Co. The rustic love episode of Scheffel's historical novel *Ekkehard* has been edited, under the title of *Audifax und Hadumoth*, by C. H. Handschin and W. F. Luebke for the American Book Co. An admirable book for students desiring to acquire the vocabulary of economic German is John A. Bole's *Deutsche Wirtschaft*, comprising selections from Loening's *Grundzüge der Verfassung des Deutschen Reiches*, and from Arndt's essay *Deutschlands Stellung in der Weltwirtschaft*. A new departure is also represented by L. Lewisohn's text book on *German Style*, edited for Holt & Co. It consists of selections from the masters of German prose, with excellent analyses and critical notes, and will be found to be of great help in the study of German style.

German Teaching.—The department of the study and teaching of German is represented by the following excellent articles: M. M. Skinner, "Aspects of German Teaching in America" (*Educational Review*, Jan.); S. W. Cutting, "Teaching of German in High Schools and Academies" (*School Review*, April); J. A. Bole, "Writing in German" (*Trans. of Educ. Assn.*, 1910, pp. 529-533); F. Monteser, "Direct Method of Teaching Modern Languages and the Present Conditions in our Schools" (*ibid*, pp. 523-9).

German Philology.—Taking up now the older periods of German, mention should be made of a series of excellent articles on Luther and his work, by A. C. McGiffert, which have been appearing in the *Century Magazine* since Dec., 1910. W. M. Hart, in the July number of *Modern Philology*, discusses the striking similarity of Hans Sachs's *Fastnachtspiel: der Dot im Stock* and Chaucer's *Pardoner's Tale*. The Middle High German period is represented by short articles on Abraham a Santa Clara, by F. S. Law, in the *Musician* for Aug., and on Walther von der Vogelweide, under the title of "The Poet and the Birds," in the *Outlook* for June 24. A cheaper edition of Shumway's prose translation of the *Nibelungenlied* has appeared in the "Riverside Literature Series." Old High German is represented only by L. Armitage's work *Introduction to the Study of Old High German* (Oxford University Press). In the field of Germanic philology, F. A. Wood has compiled an admirable set of tables entitled *Uebersichtstabellen zu Lautentsprechungen und zur Kasusbildung des Nomens und Adjektivs im Germanischen* (Univ. of Chicago Press), and S. Kroesch has discussed the "Semasilogical Development of Words for Perceive, etc., in the Older Germanic Dialects" in *Modern Philology*, VIII, 461-510.

Norwegian.—Turning now to other

Germanic languages we find Norwegian well represented through the continued interest in Ibsen. The following articles concern themselves with him and his works: A. Henderson, "The Evolution of Ibsen's Mind" in his volume *Interpreters of Life;* Edwin Björkman, "The Ibsen Myth" (*Forum,* May); L. W. Smith, "Ibsen, Emerson and Nietzsche—the Individualists" (*Pop. Sc.,* Feb.); "Real Meaning of Ibsen" (*Cur. Lit.,* June); E. F. Curran, "Review of Ibsen's Work" (*Cath. World,* Sept.). E. Dowden in his *Essays Modern and Elizabethan* has also devoted a chapter to Ibsen. Björnson's little two-act play *A Lesson in Marriage* has been translated by Grace I. Colbron. A new reprint of an older translation of Björnson's *Sigurd Slembe,* a powerful story of a tragic episode of Norse history, has been published by W. W. Payne. Arne Norrevang's three-act play *Women and the Fiddlers* has been translated by Herman Sandby; Sir G. W. Dasent has adapted the Norse fairy tales of Asbjörnsen; and Grundtwig's *Fairy Tales from Afar* have been published in a translation by Wessels.

Swedish.—Swedish literature is represented by a translation of Strindberg's greatest play *The Creditor.* Another volume contains three other plays of the same dramatist, *Simoon, Debit and Credit* and *The Outcast;* a third the translation of *The Stronger.* A new translation of Selma Lagerlöf's charming novel *Gösta Berling* has appeared from the pen of Pauline B. Flach. A translation of Ellen Key's work on *Love and Marriage* by Arthur C. Chater serves to acquaint the American public further with her advanced views on this subject. Ernst Rosner's novels *John Herkner* and *Twilight* have been issued by R. G. Badger. "The Scandinavian Element in American Population" is the subject of an article in the *Amer. Hist. Review* for Jan.

Danish.—Neither Danish nor Dutch literature is represented by translations or articles, but under the caption *Denmark and the American Idea,* H. G. Leach writes entertainingly of the kind of American fiction which appeals most to the Danish taste.

ROMANCE LANGUAGES

W. W. COMFORT

Necrology.—The last year has been marked by political and social unrest in the Latin countries of Europe. Little of the first importance in literature has appeared in the immediate past. The deaths in Paris during 1911 of Auguste Longnon and of Gaston Raynaud will be regretted by students of French history and literature. In Italy the veteran Prof. Pio Rajna has been honored by an important volume of studies dedicated to him by his European colleagues.

The past months have witnessed a severe loss to Romance scholarship in this country in the death of Prof. John E. Matzke of the Leland Stanford University in 1910, and of Prof. A. Marshall Elliott of the Johns Hopkins University in 1911. The former had long been a productive scholar in Romance philology, whose work was recognized abroad; the latter had inspired a large number of younger men and had helped to put the study of the modern tongues upon a solid basis in this country by founding *Modern Language Notes* and by aiding in the establishment of the Modern Language Association. At the time of Prof. Elliott's death his friends and former pupils had prepared in his honor a collection of studies, which has since appeared in two volumes. A similar collection of studies in memory of Prof. Matzke is contemplated.

American Publications.—Romance scholars in this country are beset by two evils: the temptation to consume their energies in editing texts for class use at the instigation of publishers; and the temptation to throw their researches into print at the earliest opportunity. As a result of the latter temptation, many of our productive scholars publish their work piecemeal, without the form or comeliness necessary to commend it to the general reader. It is to be deplored that our academic writers in the Romance field seem to be thus unconcerned with literary form *per se.* Unlike those of Europe, our Romance scholars seem not to possess the long breath and the literary sense required to present the results of their study in scrupulous form. Notes, comments, discussions, reviews, abound in our journals; but a stout volume with some literary pretension is a rarity from academic scholars.

Italian Literature.—Another feature of Romance scholarship in this country is its neglect of Italian literature. While Spanish literature is everywhere studied, few advanced students occupy themselves with Italian, and the supply of competent scholars in this field is actually not equal to the demand. America is far behind England in her interest in Italian literature, and it is to be regretted that we have failed to realize that the Italian and Latin literature of the Renaissance, with the divers influences emanating therefrom, offers perhaps the most fruitful field for research in our entire domain.

Present Tendencies.—Speaking more affirmatively of the present trend of Romance studies in this country, we may say that our scholars are concerned rather with literary matters than with pure linguistics or text criticism. Moreover, the literature of the last three centuries receives but scant attention. There are reasons for these two observations: the former is explained by the fact that much of our philological instruction is neither so thorough nor so highly specialized as is the case in Europe, and by the fact that we are ill provided for the study of unpublished texts; the lack of attention paid to more modern literature is due to tendencies at work in our graduate schools.

French Mediæval Literature.—Much is being done both in France and abroad to render the public more familiar with the best literary productions of mediæval France. American scholars are bearing a hand in this important task, while mediævalists everywhere will be gratified by the enterprise of the publishing house of H. Champion et Cie., which has begun to issue a series of popular but scholarly editions of mediæval French texts, formerly inaccessible for class use, under the general direction of M. Mario Roques. It is curious to observe that, in spite of years of discussion, the doctors still disagree upon the two primary problems of mediæval literature, concerning the literary origins of the national epic and of the so-called Breton material. In the discussion of the latter problem, some American scholars have taken an active part.

BIBLIOGRAPHY

ARMSTRONG, E. C.—"The French Shifts in Adjective Position and their English Equivalents." (Baltimore, *Studies in Honor of A. Marshall Elliott,* 1911.)
BOURLAND, C. B.—"*La Dotrina que dieron a Sarra,* Poema de Fernan Perez de Guzman." (*Rev. Hispanique,* t. xxii, pp. 648-686.)
BROWN, A. C. L.—"Chrétien's *Yvain.*" (*Modern Philology,* July 1911.)
BUFFUM, D. L.—"The Songs of the *Roman de la Violette.*" (Baltimore, *Studies in Honor of A. Marshall Elliott,* 1911.)
CRANE, T. F.—"Mediæval Story-books." (*Modern Philology,* Oct. 1911.)
CRAWFORD, J. P. W.—"The Braggart Soldier and the Rufián in the Spanish Drama of the Sixteenth Century." (*Romanic Review,* April-June, 1911.)
——"The Catalan Mascarón and an Episode in Jacob van Maerlant's Merlijn." (Pub. of Modern Language Association, March, 1911.)
"El Decameron in Castellano, manuscrito de El Escorial," edited by F. De Haan. (Baltimore, *Studies in Honor of A. Marshall Elliott,* 1911.)
"Esopo Zuccarino," edited by M. P. Brush. (Baltimore, *Studies in Honor of A. Marshall Elliott,* 1911.)
FLETCHER, J. B.—*The Religion of Beauty in Woman, and Other Essays in Platonic Love in Poetry and Society.* (New York, 1911.)
GALPIN, S. L.—"Influence of the Mediæval Christian Visions on Jean de Meun's Notions of Hell." (*Romanic Review,* Jan.-Mar., 1911.)
GERIG, J. L.—"Barthelemy Aneau: A Study in Humanism," Continued. (*Romanic Review,* Apr.-June, 1911.)
GRANDGENT, C. H.—Dante's *Divina Commedia,* Vol. ii. *Purgatorio.* (Boston, 1911.)
HILL, R. T.—*La Mule sanz Frain,* an Arthurian romance by Paiens de Maisieres, ed., with introduction, notes and glossary. (Baltimore, 1911.)
HOLBROOK, R. T.—*Portraits of Dante from Giotto to Raffael.* (Boston, 1911.)—A critical study, with a con-

cise iconography, illustrated after the original portraits.
JOHNSTON, O. M.—"The Italian Historical Infinitive." (Baltimore, *Studies in Honor of A. Marshall Elliott*, 1911.)
KUERSTEINER, A. F.—"A Textual Study of the First Cantica sobre el Fecho dela Yglesia in Ayala's Rimado." (Baltimore, *Studies in Honor of A. Marshall Elliott*, 1911.)
LANCASTER, H. C.—"A Classic French Tragedy based on an Anecdote told of Charles the Bold." (Baltimore, *Studies in Honor of A. Marshall Elliott*, 1911.)
"Le Contenz dou Monde," edited by T. A. Jenkins. (Baltimore, *Studies in Honor of A. Marshall Elliott*, 1911.)
LIVINGSTON, A. A.—"*The Carmen de Prodicione Guenonis*," translated into English, with textual notes. (*Romanic Review*, Jan.-Mar., 1911.)
LIVINGSTON, A. A.—*I Sonetti Amorosi e Morali di Gian Francesco Busenello; Testo Critico.* (Venezia, 1911.)
LUQUIENS, F. B.—*Three Lays of Marie de France, retold in English Verse.* (New York, 1911.)
MARDEN, C. C.—"Notes for a Bibliography of American Spanish." (Baltimore, *Studies in Honor of A. Marshall Elliott*, 1911.)
MATZKE, J. E.—"The Roman du Châtelain de Couci and Fauchet's Chronique." (Baltimore, *Studies in Honor of A. Marshall Elliott*, 1911.)
MUSTARD, W. P.—*The Eclogues of Baptista Mantuanus.* Edited, with introduction and notes. (Baltimore, 1911.)
NITZE, W. A.—"The Castle of the Grail—an Irish Analogue." (Baltimore, *Studies in Honor of A. Marshall Elliott*, 1911.)
OLMSTED, E. W., and GORDON, A.—A Spanish Grammar. (New York, 1911.)
PIETSCH, Karl.—"Zur Spanischen Grammatik." (I. *Zeitschrift für Romanische Philologie*, XXXIV and XXXV Band., 1911. II. *Modern Language Notes*, April, 1911.)
RICE, C. C.—*Romance Etimologies* (*sic.*). (Pub. of Modern Language Association, June, 1911.)
ROSENBERG, S. L. M.—*La Española de Florencia* of Calderón. Edited, with introduction and notes. (Philadelphia, 1911.)
RUNTZ-REES, Caroline.—*Charles de Sainte-Marthe* (1512-55). (Columbia University, Studies in Rom. Phil. and Lit., New York, 1910.)
SHAW, J. E.—"The Sonnet of Guido Cavalcanti, 'Amore e Monna Lagia'." (Baltimore, *Studies in Honor of A. Marshall Elliott*, 1911.)
SNAVELY, G. E.—"The Ysopet of Jehan de Vignay." (Baltimore, *Studies in Honor of A. Marshall Elliott*, 1911.)
Studies in Honor of A. Marshall Elliott. (2 vols., Baltimore, 1911.)
TUTTLE, E. H.—"Notes on the Spanish Palatals." (*Modern Philology*, Apr., 1911.)
WARREN, F. M.—"French Classical Drama and the *Comédie Larmoyante.*" (Baltimore, *Studies in Honor of A. Marshall Elliott*, 1911.)

ENGLISH LITERATURE

C. G. CHILD

American Scholarship.—In the scientific study of the English language and literature, America continues to emulate, and to strive to combine, virtues which characterize, more or less distinctively, German and American scholarship. Taking both quantity and quality of effective work into account, especially as regards the determination of new truth, patient, minute care in matters of detail which often seem trivial, looking forward to a solid and substantial result at some indefinite point in the future—Germany still holds first place. America, however, is now her close rival in quantity of really valuable research, and gives promise of surpassing her in quality because of a wiser direction of energy toward the attainment of results immediately valuable (in the way both of rendering possible further advance and of coördinating results already gained), and also partly because of a general gradual emancipation from too indiscriminating adherence to German methods and ideals. In America as compared with England there is a more widespread activity in scientific research, a zeal to be fully abreast with the latest advances in knowledge, in marked contrast to the insular indifference or prejudice toward work done in other countries characteristic of England, which insures a greater productivity and a higher average quality in the attainment of new truth and its immediate evaluation. But, in literature, in the higher criticism in which sufficiently wide, varied, and accurate knowledge, powers of philosophic insight and analysis, an ideal of humane culture derived from a life-long liberal training so contrived as to be thorough but not to stifle individuality, are combined with trained taste and a command of expression giving criticism itself a right to be considered literature, America has no one to compare with one or two men in England, and one or two in such a case are worth a multitude of men of lesser gift.

Philology.—A brief survey for the general reader cannot take account of papers treating minute points of scholarship, however useful in their relation, or classroom texts, though perhaps including material of value, but only of general tendencies and of more significant contributions. The past year continued to show the decrease in interest in purely linguistic study, the study of the history of the language, which has characterized the past ten years or more. The teaching of English philology in most universities and colleges consists of little more than the reading of a little Anglo-Saxon and Middle English; and certain universities, which formerly made a specialty of philologic study in their graduate work have turned to the study of literature.

Early English Literature.—With this change is naturally associated a lessening of interest in the study of our earlier literature. In the Old English period (to 1150) there has been no single notable contribution like that of Frederick Tupper's edition of the *Riddles* of 1910. Among the more important publications devoted to this period, we may note the same author's destructive onslaught upon the Cynewulf legend (*Publications of the Modern Language Association*), Moore's examination of the sources of the *Exodus* (*Modern Philology*), the articles by Lawrence and Tupper upon the "*Song of Deor*" (*ib.*), and Kennedy's useful translation of Cynewulf. Klaeber (if we may claim him for America) continues in occasional articles to give earnest of the results of his study of *Beowulf*, pending the publication of his eagerly awaited edition of that poem.

Middle English Literature.—Publications in the general field of Middle English literature (1150-1500) are few. We may note R. H. Griffith's monograph upon the sources of the legend of *Sir Percival of Galles* (University of Chicago), and Miss Keiller's article upon the "Influence of Piers Plowman on the Macro Play of *Mankind*" (*Publications of the Modern Language Association*). American scholarship continues to make almost exclusively its own the field of Chaucerian criticism, especially in the discussion of the vexed questions of chronology, through the work of Miss Hammond, Kittredge, Lowes, Tatlock, Root, Sypherd, C. F. Brown, and W. F. Hart. Reference may here be made to the translation of *Early English Poems* by Pancoast and Spaeth as likely to prove of interest to the general reader, affording as it does a representative anthology of Old English and Middle English verse.

Modern English Literature.—Passing to the Modern period (from 1500), interest continues to center upon the literature of the 16th and 17th centuries, especially the drama. Three helpful papers upon Spenser or connected with him appear in the *Publications of the Modern Language Association*, by Cory ("Spenser, Thomson and Romanticism"), by Greenlaw ("*The Shepherds Calender*"), and by J. B. Fletcher ("A Study in Renaissance Mysticism: Spenser's '*Fowre Hymnes*'"), together with a useful study of French influence upon the beginnings of English classicism by Miss Macintire. To the publications upon Spenser may be added Cory's "The Critics of Edmund Spenser" (University of California Publications). Among works upon the drama, mention may be made of Baskervill's "English Elements in Jonson's Early Comedy," the first volume of Parrott's *Plays and Poems of George Chapman: The Tragedies*, Cunliffe's "The Queenes Majesties Entertainment at Woodstocke" (*Publications of the Modern Language Association*), J. T. Murray's valuable monograph "English Dramatic Companies 1558-1642," G. F. Reynolds's exceedingly helpful article "What we know of the Elizabethan Stage" (*Modern Philology*), Tucker-Brooke's welcome volume, *Tu-*

dor Drama, and Stoll's essay upon the often discussed question of the contemporary intention and conception of the character of Shylock (*Journal of English and Germanic Philology*). Dr. Furness, with the collaboration of his son, continues his variorium edition of Shakespeare, one of the few monumental works of American scholarship. A second edition of Schelling's *Elizabethan Drama*, with revisions and additions, has appeared. Neilson's admirable selection of representative plays under the title *Chief Elizabethan Dramatists excluding Shakespeare* is not merely a class-room text; no better collection is available for the class-room and general reader. Dr. Wallace, whose sensational discovery of a personal deposition signed by Shakespeare, and of new information regarding the site of the Globe Theater, will be remembered, has continued his researches in the Record Office in London. It is rumored that he has made a number of discoveries of note, though not of so striking a nature as those announced.

In the current volume of the *Cambridge History of English Literature*, Springarn contributes the chapter on "Jacobean and Caroline Criticism." In his Harris lectures delivered at Northwestern University, published under the title of "Democracy and Poetry," Gummere links his theories of the communal origin of poetry to an enunciation of the vital and necessary dependence of poetry upon the essential spirit of true democracy. A concordance of Wordsworth, the first publication of the Concordance Society, has been issued under the editorship of Lane Cooper.

Necrology.—During the year Francis Andrew March died at the age of 86—a scholar of world-wide eminence in English philology and letters, a pioneer and chief influence in promoting English studies, a great teacher, and a source of inspiration to numberless students of English throughout his long and active life.

AMERICAN LITERATURE

(*Oct. 1, 1910, to Oct. 1, 1911.*)

ARTHUR HOBSON QUINN

In this review it has seemed best to consider only the most notable productions in creative literature, and to mention works of scholarship only when upon American themes.

Fiction.—In *John Sherwood, Ironmaster*, by Dr. S. Weir Mitchell (Century Co.), we have a powerful psychological study of the character of a manufacturer and inventor, whose life has made him blind to the forces of nature and impervious to the usual human interests, and who through a sojourn in the wilder sections of Maine broadens and enriches his character. The minor characters, especially the insane Benedict Norman and the Maine natives, are well drawn, and the final dramatic situation is admirably conceived.

The Iron Woman, by Margaret Deland (Harpers), shows no decline in the powers of character drawing, plot construction and humorous appeal which the wholly satisfying art of the writer has so long represented. The book continues the story of *The Awakening of Helena Richie*, but among the new characters, Elizabeth Ferguson, the heroine, and the "iron woman," Mrs. Maitland, have added two permanent characters to American fiction.

In *Ethan Frome* (Scribners), Edith Wharton has struck into a new field, the delineation of New England character of the middle classes. One of the terrible tragedies that arise in little communities where all effort is paralyzed by lack of means to escape, is here touched with deep sympathy for human suffering, and with Mrs. Wharton's distinguished art.

The Long Roll, by Mary Johnston (Houghton, Mifflin Co.), presents a remarkable picture of the early Civil War in Virginia, and scores a signal success in depicting the character of Stonewall Jackson. The book would be more interesting if the many campaigns had been more completely fused into one picture of war.

The South after the war is the theme of *The Miller of Old Church*, by Ellen Glasgow (Doubleday, Page & Co.). The hero is a type of the class which rose after the war through ability and changing social and economic conditions. The character sketching is admirable, the descriptions of natural scenery rise to a high level, and for a parallel to the humor of the rustic characters, one has to go to Hardy and George Eliot.

In *Kennedy Square* (Scribners), F. Hopkinson Smith has returned to the scene of an earlier novel to treat again the theme of the South before the Civil War, and has given us his usual charming picture of that time, although the plot and character drawing are somewhat disappointing.

In *The Secret Garden*, by Frances Hodgson Burnett (Stokes), we have a study of the effect of nature upon two children. The story is exquisitely told and is not a child's book but a really notable contribution to fiction. The right feeling, the good sense, the undidactic quality of the book make it one of the best things the author has done. The picture of the sunlit garden and the children in it will live long in the memory.

Pandora's Box, by John Ames Mitchell (Stokes), develops the love story of an American architect and the daughter of an English earl. The cleverness of the conversation, the humorous conception of character, the trenchant criticism of both British and American life, and the touch of psychic influence working through heredity combine to make the book a distinct contribution to the international novel.

The Legacy, by Mary S. Watts (Macmillan), is a well told, if somewhat leisurely novel of life in the Middle West during the last three decades. The great interest of the book lies in the character of the heroine, Letty Breen. The way in which her family pride and lack of moral standards, inherited from her father's family, combined with her mother's industry and sense of duty, work out to form a contradictory yet a very human woman, is masterly.

John Winterbourne's Family, by Alice Brown (Houghton, Mifflin Co.), is a study of responsibilities, typified by several interesting characters, painted with the author's usual skill. The humor is at times very effective; at others, too finely drawn.

The Common Law, Robert W. Chambers (Appletons), is a brilliant if highly colored novel of artist's life in New York. If one forgets the improbability of the chief character, the clever, unabashed and at times powerful treatment of the life described is very strong in its appeal.

A rather unusual book is *The Coward of Thermopylae*, by Caroline Dale Snedeker (Doubleday, Page & Co.). It is a romance of Greece at the time of Marathon and Thermopylae. The author has drawn well the distinction between the Athenian character, with its keen intellectual curiosity and its slighter physical development, and the Spartan military sense and more democratic though less spiritual nature.

Of small bulk but containing a charming love story is Harriet Prescott Spofford's novelette, *The Making of a Fortune* (Harpers).

Queed, by Henry Sydnor Harrison (Houghton, Mifflin Co.), is an interesting study of the change in a man's nature through his gradual awakening to the demands of others upon his sympathy. The characters are well done and the picture of life in a Georgia city of the present day is admirable.

Based upon quite a different phase of Georgia life is *Jane Dawson*, by Will N. Harben (Harpers). This is a story of the poorer classes, in the country, of strong loves and hates, told with a stylistic excellence which makes us wish that the novel had been less of a sermon.

Finally, mention must be made of a western story, *Me—Smith*, by Caroline Lockhart (Lippincott), which in its fidelity to the life described is almost photographic.

Several important collections of short stories have appeared. Under the title *Wandering Ghosts*, by F. Marion Crawford (Macmillan), have been collected seven stories of the late novelist, all of which deal with the supernatural. They vary in excellence, from "The Dead Smile," which is too highly keyed, to "The Upper Berth," which is one of the great short stories of the world, but they are all told with the unfailing charm of the great entertainer.

The Guillotine Club, by Dr. S. Weir Mitchell (Century Co.), contains in the title story, one of the very best of the author's shorter fictions, laid in Paris of the Second Empire, and also several interesting stories with a supernatural basis.

In *Tales of Men and Ghosts* (Scribners), Edith Wharton treats a variety of themes with her usual distinction. Several of the stories reflect a literary atmosphere and have a certain unity in that they deal almost exclusively with men. Two powerful stories of the supernatural complete the volume.

The Finer Grain, by Henry James (Scribners), includes five pieces of fiction, among which the last, "The Bench of Desolation," rises above the rest distinctly, through its human sympathy.

The Empty House, by Elizabeth Stuart Phelps Ward (Houghton Mifflin Co.), is made up of nine of the author's latest stories, in which she did her best work since "The Madonna of the Tubs." All those who believe that America still contains cultivated, respectable people fit for fiction, will like this book.

Members of the Family, by Owen Wister (Macmillan), contains eight stories of Western life, in which some of the characters that he had already developed are met again. Of the stories, the best are the tragic ones, such as "Timberline" or "The Gift Horse," though at times there is also a distinctly successful note of comedy.

In *Later Pratt Portraits*, by Anna Fuller (Putnam), we have eleven portraits of the descendants of "old lady Pratt" made very much alive by delicate characterization, aided by comedy and pathos. Human frailties are touched gently yet artistically in these stories by an art which is content to be judged by those who read completely and with understanding.

A book of short stories containing more promise than actual achievement is *The Sick-a-Bed Lady*, by Eleanor Hallowell Abbott (Century Co.). The author of "Woman's Only Business" has, in all probability, a future.

Poetry and Drama.—In poetry it has not been a very notable year. One of the most important publications is the volume entitled *Poems*, by Madison Cawein (Macmillan). Into this one volume have been condensed by judicious selection the various volumes of Mr. Cawein's verse. Lovers of his poetry will doubtless prefer the larger collected edition in five volumes, but owing to the luxuriance of his poetic ability, the average reader will gain a better idea of his real worth by this selection. The lyric gift, the love of nature and of romance, and the real ability at phrasing which have made Mr. Cawein one of our foremost poets are fully represented in this volume.

In *The Overture and Other Poems*, by Jefferson Butler Fletcher (Macmillan), we have a volume of poems imbued with varied culture from wide reading and containing also interesting experiments in forms such as the sestina. The verse is uniformly well finished and in such a sonnet as "When They Had Slain Their Children to the Idols" a really high note is struck.

At the Silver Gate, by John Vance Cheyney (Stokes), is a volume of rather uneven merit. Such poems as "Presidio" or "Sunset in the Redwoods" are of a high quality. Mention must be made of the illustrations, which are especially charming.

The Immortal Lure, by Cale Young Rice (Doubleday, Page & Co.), contains four plays in verse, of which the general theme is the power of love. The best are "Giorgione," laid in Italy and "The Immortal Lure," laid in India. Mr. Rice has shown an ability in the handling of dramatic blank verse and the situations, if conventional at times, are well established.

Of special interest is the play of *Mona*, the book of the grand opera, by Brian Hooker (Dodd, Mead & Co.) which won the Metropolitan Opera Company prize (see also XXXIV, *Music*). The play is a blank verse tragedy of Britain in the first century A. D. At times it is of remarkable power; and the lyrics are excellent.

1911 LITERATURE AND LANGUAGE

Mention should be made also of the collected edition of Henry Van Dyke's *Poems* (Scribners), and of an interesting experiment in the mingling of abstractions and real characters in *The Treason and Death of Benedict Arnold*, John Jay Chapman (Moffat, Yard & Co.).

The most important reprint is *The Complete Poems of Edgar Allan Poe*, by J. H. Whitty (Houghton Mifflin Co.). The several questions raised by the editor as to textual and biographical matters cannot be discussed in this brief mention, but the volume is one of which no student of Poe can afford to be ignorant.

In prose drama, the most significant publication is *Anti-Matrimony*, by Percy Mackaye (Stokes). This is a clever comedy, a satire on free love and other modern devices which are contrasted with the primary instincts of men and women in a normal state of society. The play is a healthy reaction against the overstrained drama produced by the followers of Ibsen, while owing some of its technique to that writer.

A clever farce by W. D. Howells, *Parting Friends* (Harpers), though very slight as to bulk, is full of bright conversation and revelation of human nature.

Essays and Literary Histories.—In *Imaginary Interviews*, by William Dean Howells (Harpers), we find the author in the mellow fruition of his art, looking out in a calm and friendly way on life, American and foreign, criticizing gently and tolerantly, calling to our minds the inconsistencies of our institutions, but leaving us with a respect for that "finer American average which is the best, and rightly seen, the most interesting phase of civilized life yet known." In these essays, reprinted from the "Easy Chair," are also to be found interesting literary criticism, admirable nature description, and, best of all, the attractive attitude of a man who has arrived and who has sympathy for those still struggling.

Among Friends, by Samuel McChord Crothers (Houghton Mifflin Co.), is a delightful series of familiar essays to be read with interest by every lover of human nature and books. Mr. Crothers's calm, sane attitude does not prevent him from indulging in that species of sparkle which is the life of the familiar essay. "The Anglo-American School of Polite Unlearning" will remain a classic and the very titles of some of the other essays, "The Merry Devil of Education," "The Hundred Worst Books" or "In Praise of Politicians" reveal the promise of what is contained in them.

Learning and Other Essays, by John Jay Chapman (Moffat, Yard & Co.), is a notable series of essays, rather philosophic than familiar, though not at all heavy, and imbued with a wit that is at times brilliant. Several of the essays are on educational topics. In these Mr. Chapman says some true and striking things. In general the volume represents well an enlightened conservatism and real literary ability.

Longfellow and Other Essays, by William P. Trent (Crowell), is a collection of essays and addresses, mostly on literary subjects, and usually occasional in their nature. Perhaps the two most significant essays are "The Relations of History and Literature" and "A Talk to Would-be Teachers," though the entire volume is well worth reading.

There have been two important posthumous publications in the field of the essay. *The Journals of Ralph Waldo Emerson*, edited by Edward Waldo Emerson and Waldo Emerson Forbes (Houghton Mifflin Co.), of which two volumes had already appeared, have been augmented by two more volumes which comprehend the years from 1833 to 1838. This revelation of Emerson's inner life and thought is arranged in a sufficiently connected way to interest the general reader, while the professed student of literature will find the volumes a mine of information concerning the development and the limitations of his art.

In *Genius and Other Essays*, by Edmund Clarence Stedman, edited by Laura Stedman and George M. Gould (Moffat, Yard & Co.), have been collected some of the unpublished essays of Stedman, which while seldom rising to the importance of the essays that appeared during his lifetime, have the note of distinction which always was his. The best are "Genius," "A Belt of Asteroids," "Austin Dobson," and "Keats."

A significant contribution to our literary history is *The Literature of the South*, Montrose J. Moses (Crowell). It is an historical discussion of the literature that has contributed to the sectional development of the South, refreshing in its impartial attitude, and while stronger on its historical than on its critical side, is at times brilliant in its critical appraisement.

Biography.—The *Life and Letters of Edmund Clarence Stedman*, by Laura Stedman and G. M. Gould, 2 vols. (Moffat, Yard & Co.), is not only a thoroughly adequate biography, but also a mine of information concerning our literature since the Civil War. The authors have painted a striking picture of the high heart and indomitable energy of Stedman's character.

Edison, His Life and Inventions, by Frank L. Dyer and Thomas C. Martin (Harpers), is a biography with the qualities of romance. The biographers have arranged their material carefully, with an eye to dramatic situations, and have told their story in a style admirably suited to the general reader who knows little of the technical details of such work as Edison's, and the result is more than a mere narrative. It is a notable contribution to the history of American progress.

Grover Cleveland, by Richard Watson Gilder (Century Co.), is a vitally important picture of the life of Cleveland written by one who knew him intimately. We see the ex-President in his unguarded moments, and we learn to know the great honesty, the unflagging industry of the man. A charming picture is also drawn of the home life of Cleveland and his family, all told with Mr. Gilder's unfailing charm of style.

The Life of Harriet Beecher Stowe, by Charles E. Stowe and Lyman B. Stowe (Houghton Mifflin & Co.), is an intimate personal account of Mrs. Stowe. It is told with a sympathetic understanding of her character and reveals many interesting details of her career.

Another valuable biography is *The Life of Bret Harte*, by Henry C. Merwin (Houghton Mifflin Co.). This is an authentic, well written treatment, which supersedes the English life by Pemberton, whose dates are shown to be at times incorrect. Noteworthy are the chapters on pioneer life in California. It bids fair to be the definitive and authoritative life of Bret Harte.

Three new contributions to the excellent series of American Crisis Biographies, edited by Ellis P. Oberholtzer (Jacobs) are *William H. Seward*, by Edward Everett Hale, Jr., a scholarly book in which the author has gone to original sources for his material; *William Lloyd Garrison*, by Lindsay Swift, written in an easy, fluent style and with great sympathy; and *Stephen A. Douglas*, by Henry P. Willis, an interesting if almost too obviously judicial a picture of the "Little Giant."

Travel.—*The Obvious Orient*, by Albert Bushnell Hart (Appleton), is an admirable description of Japan, China, the Philippines, India, Ceylon, and Egypt, together with an introductory description of the western portion of the United States. The last chapter, summing up the results of the author's observations in his Oriental travels, is especially valuable. The style is clear, pictorial, and flexible.

The North Pole, by Robert Peary (Stokes), is a straightforward book, written in appropriately clear style, without any attempt at heroics and convincing to any unprejudiced mind. It will take its place as one of the permanently important records of human progress.

Over the Border, by William Winter (Moffat, Yard & Co.), is a sympathetic study of Scottish life, scenery and historical associations, and shows Mr. Winter on one of his best sides, the description, in prose, by a poet of a land that he loves. The book is a chronicle of moods of inspiration and will appeal to any one who knows Scotland.

Nature Books.—A book that will be of great interest and appeal to all lovers of nature is *The Lure of the Garden*, by Hildegarde Hawthorne (Century Co.).

SIMPLIFIED SPELLING

Charles P. G. Scott [*]

The movement for the regulation and simplification of English spelling made considerable progress in the year 1911. The Simplified Spelling Board continued its activities with increast means and a larger following. Many thousand additional signatures have been obtaind to the card by which the signer agrees "to use, as far as may be practicable, in his personal correspondence, the simpler spellings that have been recommended by the Simplified Spelling Board." The movement has been especially activ in the Normal Schools of the Middle West. The circulars of the Board have been distributed widely among the faculties and students of these schools, as well as of colleges and universities. There has been an increase of interest in simplified spelling in Canada also. Teachers' conventions in Ontario, Alberta, and Saskatchewan have discust the movement, and past resolutions in its favor.

The Imperial Education Conference, held in London, in April and May, 1911, past a resolution in favor of the simplification of English spelling. The conference resolvd "that the simplification of English spelling is a matter of urgent importance in all parts of the Empire, calling for such practical steps in every country as may appear most conducive to the ultimate attainment of the end in view—the creation, in connection with the subject, of an enlightened public opinion and the direction of it to the maintenance, in its purity and simplicity among all English-speaking peoples, of the common English tongue."

Another notable event was the conference held in London at University College, Sept. 4—12, 1911, between delegates of the Simplified Spelling Board and of the Simplified Spelling Society. The delegates on the part of the Simplified Spelling Board were Prof. Calvin Thomas, of Columbia University; Prof. James W. Bright, of Johns Hopkins University; Prof. Charles H. Grandgent, of Harvard University; Prof. George Hempl, of Leland Stanford University, and Prof. Brander Matthews, of Columbia University. The delegates on the part of the Simplified Spelling Society of Great Britain were Dr. E. R. Edwards, Prof. H. Stanley Jevons, of the University of South Wales; Prof. Daniel Jones; Prof. George Gilbert Murray, of Oxford University, and Prof. Walter Rippmann, of Queen's College. William Archer, Secretary of the Simplified Spelling Society, acted as secretary of the conference.

The conference did not, of course, end the long debate as to plans for the simplification of English spelling. The British delegates, agreeing in the main with the recommendations of the Simplified Spelling Board, so far as they have been publisht, desired to go much farther, and proposed an advanced scheme of simplification. The American delegates, believing that it would be inexpedient to adopt now a scheme including many disputable notations, thought it better to postpone the disputable parts of the scheme until the public is better prepared to accept the changes they will require. In the light of the conference, the British Society is revising its scheme. It proposes to put the matter to the test by extensiv experiment, on lines beyond the point thus far reacht by the Board.

During the year seven new members have been added to the Board. But the Board has sufferd the loss of two distinguisht members—Col. Thomas Wentworth Higginson, who died May 9, 1911, and Prof. Francis Andrew March, the eminent filologist, who died Sept. 9, 1911. Prof. March was the leader among the scholars who more than 30 years ago gave their attention to the promotion of

[*] At the request of the author, who is secretary of the Simplified Spelling Board, this article is printed in accordance with Board's official recommendations.

the movement for the regulation and simplification of English spelling. It was at his instigation that the American Philological Association appointed a standing committee which made an investigation of the matter, approved the change, and recommended definit steps for bringing it about. The establishment of the Simplified Spelling Board, provided with money for the work, was the ultimate result of these efforts.

Two members of the Advisory Council have died during the year, and seven new members have been elected. The Council now consists of 220 members. The Board continues to provide literature and information free, on application to its address, No. 1 Madison Avenue, New York.

COPYRIGHT

WILLIAM W. APPLETON

United States.—A proclamation by the President of the United States issued on Dec. 8, 1910, declared the subjects of the German Empire entitled to all the benefits of Section 1 (e) of the Copyright Act of March 4, 1909, including copyright controlling parts of instruments serving to reproduce mechanically a musical work. Similar proclamations were issued on June 14, 1911, in behalf of Belgium, Luxemburg and Norway, and on November 7, 1911, in behalf of Cuba.

As at present advised, the following countries do not fulfil the reciprocal conditions specified in Section I (e) of the Copyright Act of March 4, 1909: Austria, Denmark, Mexico, the Netherlands and Switzerland.

A presidential proclamation issued May 26, 1911, established general reciprocal copyright relations with Sweden, to go into effect June 1, 1911. The copyright relations with Sweden, however, do not include protection against unauthorized reproduction of music by means of mechanical instruments.

On Aug. 11, 1910, the eight representatives of the United States to the Fourth International Conference of American States signed a "Convention concerning Literary and Artistic Copyright." The convention was also signed by the delegates of the Argentine Republic, Brazil, Chile, Colombia, Costa Rica, Cuba, Dominican Republic, Ecuador, Guatemala, Haiti, Honduras, Mexico, Nicaragua, Panama, Paraguay, Peru, Salvador, Uruguay and Venezuela. It was sent by the President to the Senate on Jan. 26, 1911, for advice and consent to ratification, and its ratification was approved by the Senate on Feb. 15, 1911. Up to this time, however, the convention has not been ratified and proclaimed by the President.

Great Britain.—On Dec. 14, 1911, the House of Commons concurred in the New British copyright bill as passed by the House of Lords. This act will go into force on July 1, 1912. The duration of copyright is for the life of the author and a period of 50 years after his death, provided that after 25 years from the death of the author (or, in the case of a work in which copyright subsists at the passing of this act, 30 years) the work may be reproduced provided the person reproducing pays to the owner of the copyright royalties of ten per cent. upon the published price of the work, subject to regulations made by the Board of Trade.

No assignments of copyright made by the author are valid after the expiration of 25 years from his death, unless made by will, except in the case of the copyright in a collective work, viz.: encyclopædia, dictionary, year book or similar work, newspaper, review, magazine or any work written in distinct parts, by different authors, or in which works, or parts of works, by different authors are incorporated. For photographs, and records by means of which sounds may be mechanically reproduced, the term of copyright is 50 years from the making of the negative or original record. Any person may make such mechanical records provided that such work has received the consent of the owner, and provided royalties shall be paid to the copyright owner within two years after the commencement of this act at the rate of 2½ per cent., and after the expiration of two years, 5 per cent. on the ordinary retail price. After the expiration of seven years, if it appears to the Board of Trade that such rate is no longer equitable, the Board of Trade, after holding a public inquiry, may decrease or increase this rate.

The publication of reports of lectures in newspapers is permitted, unless the report is prohibited by conspicuous written or printed notice affixed before and maintained during the lectures at or about the main entrance of the building in which the lecture is given; any fair dealing with any work for the purpose of private study, research, criticism, review and newspaper summary is not deemed an infringement, and two short passages from an author's works may be published in books for the use of schools, provided that not more than two such passages are published by the same publisher within five years, and the source from which such passages are taken is acknowledged.

The legislature of any "self-governing dominion" of the Empire may repeal any and all enactments relating to copyright passed by parliament (including this act) and enact its own copyright legislation. The term "self-governing dominion" means the Dominion of Canada, the Commonwealth of Australia, the Dominion of New Zealand, the South African Union, and Newfoundland.

The importation of copies made out of the United Kingdom is prohibited, if notice in writing is given to the Commissioners of Customs and Excise by the owners of the copyright.

This act does not require registration, but requires first publication within the parts of the British Dominion to which this act extends, notwithstanding that there has been publication simultaneously in some other place. The work shall be deemed to be published simultaneously if published within fourteen days. The copyright is void if publication is "colorable only and is not intended to satisfy the reasonable requirements of the public."

Delivery of the best edition of a book to the British Museum is required, and a copy of the book on the paper on which the largest number of copies is printed for sale, must be delivered to the Oxford, Cambridge, Edinburgh and Dublin College libraries.

Copies must also be delivered to the National Library of Wales, except in the case of books of such classes "as may be specified in regulations to be made by the Board of Trade."

Canada.—A copyright act was introduced into the House of Commons of Canada on April 26, 1911. This act requires that books are to be printed in Canada, and also requires registration and the deposit of three copies. Notice of copyright must appear in all publications, except paintings, drawings and works of sculpture, for which the signature of the author will be sufficient. Under this act it is possible to exclude all editions not manufactured in Canada. Simultaneous publication within 14 days is required. The book may be reprinted, if the market is not supplied, and much authority is given to the Minister of Agriculture, who has charge of copyright matters. This act was not passed at the last session of the Canadian Parliament, but it is possible that a similar bill may be introduced by the new government.

Australia.—A somewhat similar bill was introduced into the Australian Senate on Oct. 4, 1911, which requires that books must be printed from type set in Australia, or plates made therefrom. There must also be simultaneous publications within 14 days. This bill has passed the third reading, and may soon become a law.

1912 LITERATURE AND LANGUAGE

ANCIENT LITERATURE AND PHILOLOGY

ANCIENT LITERATURE
(Additions from Papyri)

CLIFFORD H. MOORE

Sophocles' "The Trackers."—As in previous years, the important additions to ancient literature in 1912 are given us by Dr. A. S. Hunt. The ninth volume of the *Oxyrhynchus Papyri* brings as its greatest prize considerable portions of a satyr play by Sophocles, the *Ichneutae*, "The Trackers" (no. 1174). The portion recovered amounts to something less than four hundred lines, many of which are incomplete. The papyrus fragments are written in an uncial hand of the latter part of the second century of our era. To scholars the arrangement of the lines, the punctuation, and the critical marks are all of interest; but the majority will find their concern with the plot and dramatic treatment.

The play is based on the exploits of the child Hermes in stealing Apollo's cattle, and inventing the lyre. The scene is on Mount Cellene, in Arcadia; the *dramatis personae* are Apollo, Silenus, the nymph Cyllene, and probably Hermes; the chorus naturally consists of satyrs. In the prologue Apollo announces that his cattle are lost, and offers a reward for them; he declares that he has vainly searched in Thrace, Thessaly, and Bœotia. Silenus with attendant satyrs appears and offers to undertake the search. As a reward for success, Apollo promises freedom and gold. Thus the satyrs become the "trackers" and give the name to the play. Led by the confused hoofprints to the entrance of a cave, the chorus are suddenly terrified by strange sounds which issue therefrom —the notes of the lyre, which the marvelous boy has just invented. Silenus, who is unable to quiet his terrified followers for long, presently knocks at the mouth of the cavern. The nymph Cyllene appears, reproves the satyrs for their conduct, and warns them that they must keep her secret: within she is caring for the new born child of Zeus and Maia, who although not yet six days old, has grown to youth's stature and has made a lyre from a tortoise shell and some cowhide. The mention of the last rouses the suspicions of the satyrs, who declare their belief that here is the thief of Apollo's herd. Cyllene's indignant assertion of the child's innocence ends the connected portions of the play. Yet enough besides remains to show that Cyllene was discomfited, that Apollo appeared and gave Silenus and his band the promised rewards. Probably in the last portions Hermes was confronted by Apollo, acknowledged his guilt, and assuaged his brother's wrath by the gift of the lyre.

In the portions recovered there are comic touches and opportunities for even boisterous action, but nothing equal to one or two scenes in the *Cyclops* of Euripides. Probably, as Dr. Hunt remarks, the humor of the piece was chiefly developed in the (missing) scene in which the tricky child faces the indignant Apollo.

In making the theft of the cattle precede the invention of the lyre, Sophocles differs from the *Homeric Hymn*, and shows the antiquity of the form of the story which Apollodorus chose. Original with the poet were probably the device of having the satyrs discover the cattle, and the selection of Mt. Cyllene as the hiding place. The time of composition is as uncertain as before, save that the metrical strictness seems to point to an early date. Although the lines naturally show more resolutions than those of the tragedies, there is not the freedom which we find in the *Cyclops*. The diction remains distinctly tragic, with a slight admixture of every day words and expressions.

Sophocles' "Eurypylus."—A second series of fragmentary papyri (no. 1175) apparently contain portions of a tragedy of Sophocles hitherto unknown, to which the editor gives the name *Eurypylus*, for it obviously dealt with the Trojan War, and related the killing of Eurypylus by Neoptolemus. Although numerous, the fragments are too seriously injured to tell us much. It seems clear, however, that apart from Eurypylus and Neoptolemus, Astyoche, mother of the former, was one of the characters. We have broken lines from the messenger's speech announcing the death of Eurypylus, Astyoche's lament, which in unusual fashion interrupts the messenger's tale, and some brief lyrics. Possibly other lines refer to the place of the hero's burial; but unhappily little can be determined with certainty.

The *Ichneutae* and the *Eurypylus* have also been published separately by Dr. Hunt with the Clarendon Press.

Satyrus' "Life of Euripides."—The third important find is a long *Life of Euripides* by Satyrus, preserved on a fragmentary papyrus, also of the second century after Christ. To our surprise the life is in the form of a dialogue between one principal and two subordinate speakers. It is popular, diffuse, and contains many quotations and anecdotes. In it are discussed Euripides' life, style, place in the development of tragedy, and his views on all kinds of subjects; there is, however, no criticism of the tragedies in the extant fragments. The whole forms a welcome addition to our knowledge of Peripatetic biography.

Besides these three important items we have the usual fragments of extant secular and theological works, of which no detailed mention can here be made.

SEMITIC PHILOLOGY AND LITERATURE

Morris Jastrow

Philology.—Within the field of comparative Semitic philology, the *Grundriss der vergleichenden Grammatik der semitischen Sprachen*, by Prof. Carl Brockelmann, the first volume of which, comprising the chronology and etymology, is now complete and of which during the last year the syntax has begun to appear, merits special mention. It is the most elaborate and most scientific investigation of the kind that has as yet been attempted; and it has already proved to be an invaluable reference work for all students of philology, because of the careful manner in which the enormous mass of material has been put together and discussed. Of the "Syntax," four parts have appeared, covering the various forms of the simple sentence, the noun, pronoun, the object, and the various time-relationships. On the completion of the work full indices will be added, through which alone a publication of this kind can be made fully serviceable.

Encyclopedia of Islam.—Another undertaking of interest to circles outside the range of Semitic studies is the Encyclopedia of Islam, which began to appear as far back as 1908, but of which only a few parts have been issued. This publication, fathered by the International Union of Scientific Academies, aims to cover the geography, ethnology and biography of the Mohammedan peoples. The parts appear simultaneously in German, French and English, and some idea of the scope may be gained if one considers that the 768 pages in small print and in two columns which have thus far appeared, carry the work down to BOG only. The editors, Profs. Houtsma and Hartmann, have secured the coöperation of Arabists in all parts of the world. In the last part special mention should be made of the valuable article on the Berbers by the most eminent authority on the subject, Professor René Basset.

LITERATURE AND LANGUAGE

Assyriology.—An important publication within the field of Assyriology is the work on *Babylonian Boundary Stones and Memorial Tablets in the British Museum*, published in two volumes, by L. W. King. The value of the 36 texts (some of them very elaborate) published here, consists partly in the light these boundary stones throw upon legal conditions during the various periods of Babylonian history and partly in the symbols of the gods which accompany the stones and which are of the greatest possible importance in the study of the religious ideas developed in Babylonia and Assyria.

Cuneiform Texts.—Of a large collection of cuneiform tablets, found at Drehem (near Nippur) and scattered throughout the museums of Europe, several volumes have been published. M. H. de Genouillac has prepared a volume of texts from this place found at Constantinople and Brussels, Stephen Langdon, of Oxford, some of the texts that have found their way to England, and Mr. King, of the British Museum, a selection of those that were acquired by that institution. The texts are of importance chiefly because of the dates attached.

Prof. A. T. Clay, of Yale University, has added two more volumes to the series of cuneiform texts published by the Museum of the University of Pennsylvania (Vol. II, Parts 1 and 2, of the new series), which furnish several hundred additional texts from the Persian and Cassite periods and thus supplement earlier volumes by Prof. Clay in this important series. The same author has also brought out a most important compilation of the "Personal Names found in Cuneiform Texts of the Cassite Period," presenting material of great philological value.

Tello Excavations.—MM. Heuzey and Thureau-Dangin have begun the publication of a work on the *Nouvelles Fouilles de Tello*, furnishing detailed accounts of the more recent excavations at Tello, begun as far back as 1881, and continued since the death of M. Sarzec by Gaston Cros. Of special value in the latest part of this work to appear is an account of an old Babylonian necropolis, carefully dug out, which has added much information as to the manner in which the dead were buried in the days of the early Babylonian rulers.

INDO-EUROPEAN PHILOLOGY
(Exclusive of the Germanic Languages)

ROLAND G. KENT

This department has been enlarged to embrace also the field of Greek and Latin syntax; it may most conveniently present the work of American scholars in the form of a bibliography. Especial attention may be called to the work of Bloomfield, Edgerton, Haas and Oliphant in Sanskrit; of Fay in the origin of Latin suffixes (see also AMERICAN YEAR BOOK, 1911, p. 779), of Sturtevant in Greek noun formation, of Scott in Homeric diction (see also AMERICAN YEAR BOOK, 1911, p. 781), and of Steele in the syntax of Livy.

BIBLIOGRAPHY

Abbreviations: *AJP., American Journal of Philology; CP., Classical Philology; CQ., Classical Quarterly; CW., Classical Weekly; JAOS., Journal of the American Oriental Society; JRAS., Journal of the Royal Asiatic Society; KZ.,· Zeitschrift für vergleichende Sprachforschung, begründet von A. Kuhn; PAPA., TAPA., Proceedings, Transactions of the American Philological Association.*

General and Miscellaneous

PROKOSCH, E.—"Phonetic Tendencies in the Indo-European Consonant System." (*AJP.*, 33, 195-202.)—"A tentative program" for "grouping our present knowledge of apparently isolated phonetic laws."

——"A Slavic Analogy of Verner's Law." (*AJP.*, 32, 431-5.)

Indo-Iranian

BLOOMFIELD, M.—"On Instability in the Use of Moods in Earliest Sanskrit." (*AJP.*, 33, 1-29.)—A demonstration that many verb forms are used interchangeably, without difference of meaning, in the Vedic hymns.

——Review of W. Caland, *Das Vaitānasūtra des Atharvaveda*. (Göttingische gelehrte Anzeiger, 174, 1-19.)

EDGERTON, F.—"A Hindu Book of Tales: the *Vikramacarita*." (*AJP.*, 33, 249-84.)—A "provisional preface" to a forthcoming critical edition.

FRACHTENBERG, L. J.—"Allusions to Witchcraft and Other Primitive Beliefs in the Zoroastrian Literature." (Dastur Hoshang Memorial Volume, Bombay, 1911, pp. 399-453.)

GRAY, L. H.—"The *Dūtāṅgada* of Subhaṭa, now first translated from the Sanskrit and' Prākrit." (*JAOS.*, 32, 58-77.)

HAAS, G. C. O.—"The *Daśarūpa*, a Treatise on Hindu Dramaturgy." (Vol. VII, Columbia Univ., Indo-Iranian Series.)—A valuable critical edition, with translation and commentary.

HOPKINS, E. W.—"The Epic Use of Bhagavat and Bhakti." (*JRAS.*, 1911, 727-38.)

JACKSON, A. V. W.—"The Literature of India and Persia." (Pp. 43-66 in Columbia Univ. Faculty Lectures on Literature, 1911.)

——"The Zoroastrian Idea of Archangels." (*The New Age*, 14, 615-7.)

MICHELSON, T.—"Asokan Miscellany." (*AJP.*, 32, 441-3.)

——"On Some Irregular Uses of *me* and *te* in Epic Sanskrit, and Some Related Problems." (*JRAS.*, 1911, 169-77.)

OLIPHANT, S. G.—"The Vedic Dual: Part VI, The Elliptic Dual; Part VII, The Dual Dvandva." (*JAOS.*, 32, 33-57.)

TOLMAN, H. C.—"Identification of the Ancient Persian Month *Garmapada* in the Light of the Recently Found Aramaic Papyrus Fragments." (*AJP.*, 32, 444-5.)

——"Notes on the Recently Found Aramaic Papyrus Fragments of the Behistan Inscription." (*PAPA.*, 42, 1-liv.)

Greek and Latin: Linguistics and Syntax

ALLEN, B. M.—"The Dative with Compound Verbs in Latin." (*CW.*, 5, 170-3.)

BUCK, C. D.—*Corrections and Additions to Buck's Introduction to the Study of the Greek Dialects*. (Boston, Ginn & Co., 1912.)

FAY, E. W.—"Two Latin Hoaxes." (*Wochenschrift für klassische Philologie*, 28, 986-991.)

——"The Latin Dative: Nomenclature and Classification." (*CQ.*, 5, 185-95.)

——"Lucilius on *ī* and *ei*." (*AJP.*, 33, 311-6.)—Against Kent's article on a similar topic.

HARRINGTON, K. P.—"Protases—Category Versus Fact." (*CW.*, 5, 114-7.)

KEEP, W. L.—"The Separation of the Attributive Adjective from Its Substantive in Plautus." (Univ. Calif. Publications in Classical Philology, 2, 151-64.)

KENT, R. G.—"Lucilius on *ei* and *ī.*" (*AJP.*, 32, 272-293.)

——"Zu den orthographischen Regeln des Lucilius." (*Glotta*, 4, 299-302.)

KIRK, W. H.—"Genereller Plural im Lateinischen." (*Glotta*, 3, 278.)

LEASE, E. B.—"The Dative with Prepositional Compounds." (*AJP.*, 33, 285-300; a similar article in *CJ.*, 8, 7-16.)

MACURDY, Miss G. H.—"A Note on the Vocative in Herodotus and in Homer." (*CP.*, 7, 77-8.)

MENDELL, C. W.—*Sentence Connection in Tacitus*. (New Haven, Yale Univ. Press, 1911.)

MILLER, C. W. E.—" Τὸ δέ in Lucian." (*TAPA.*, 42, 131-45.)

SCOTT, J. A.—"Patronymics as a Test of the Relative Age of Homeric Books." (*CP.*, 7, 293-301.)

STEELE, R. B.—*Case Usage in Livy: III, The Accusative; IV, The Ablative*. (Leipzig, Brockhaus, 1912.)—Following his studies on the genitive and the dative.

——"The Endings *-ēre* and *-ērunt* in Dactylic Hexameter." (*AJP.*, 32, 328-32.)

STURTEVANT, E. H.—"Notes on the Character of the Greek and Latin Accent." (*TAPA.*, 42, 45-52.)

——" Γυμνός and *nudus*." (*AJP.*, 33, 324-9.)

ULLMAN, B. L.—"Horace Serm. I, 6, 115, and the History of the Word *Laganum*." (*CP.*, 7, 442-9.)

Suffixes and Etymologies

BENDER, H. H.—"Notes on Indo-Iranian *-vant*." (*Indogermanische Forschungen*, 30, 137-8.)—Addenda to his book mentioned last year.

FAY, E. W.—"Vedic *mātari-śvan* = *materiae-puer*." (*KZ.*, 45, 134-5.)

——"Derivatives of the root *bhē* (*y*)—'to strike'; bind.'" (*AJP.*, 32, 403-20.)

——"Composition or Suffixation? Latin Words Ending in *-āgo*, *-ūgo*, *-īgo*; the Latin Suffix *-(u)lentus*." (*KZ.*, 45, 111-33.)

GRAY, L. H.—"On the Etymology of Τραγῳδία." (*CQ.*, 6, 60-3.)

HUSBAND, R. W.—"Zeta." (*PAPA.*, 42, xxvi-xxx.)—A study of the origin of ζ in all Greek words.

KENT, R. G.—"Latin *mille*, and Certain Other Numerals." (*TAPA.*, 42, 69-89.)

MYRICK, A. B.—"A Note on the Etymology of *involare*." (*AJP.*, 32, 446-7.)

OLIPHANT, S. G.—"American Surnames of Hellenic Origin." (*PAPA.*, 42, xxxiv-xxxix.)

STURTEVANT, E. H.—"Studies in Greek Noun Formation: Labial Terminations, III." (*CP.*, 7, 420-41.)—A continuation of his previous studies. WOOD, F. A.—"Etymologische Miscellen." (*KZ.*, 45, 61-71.) ——"Notes on Latin Etymologies." (*CP.*, 7, 302-34.) — Supplementing Walde's *Lateinisches etymologisches Wörterbuch,* especially on the semantic side.

GREEK LITERATURE

PAUL SHOREY

The *American Journal of Philology,* the *American Journal of Archæology, Classical Philology,* and the other periodicals mentioned in the first annual review for 1910 (p. 162), continue the publication of excellent if not always epoch-making work on a wide variety of subjects, by a considerable number of scholars, among whom may be named as contributing to the output of the present year, Professors Adams, Buck, Bollinger, Bonner, Capps, Dickerman, Harry, Heidel, Rees, Robinson, Scott, Smith, and Sturtevant.

Especially to be noted perhaps are Prof. Heidel's article on "Anaximander" in *Classical Philology,* Buckler and Robinson's Greek Inscriptions from Sardes in the *American Journal of Archæology* (see XXXII, *Epigraphy*), and Charles R. Post's Dramatic Art of Sophocles in the twenty-third volume of "Harvard Studies." Further than this it is unnecessary to compile a formal bibliography from the tables of contents of these journals. The *Transactions of the American Philological Association* publish annually a fairly complete bibliography of the members of the Association for the preceding year.

Two readable books, the *Harvard Essays on Classical Subjects,* by eight members of the faculty, and the *Columbia Lectures on Greek Literature,* to which representatives of six universities contributed, may serve, and were perhaps designed, to remove the reproach that American scholarship is confined to the dative case. From a more technical point of view the most important single book of the year is Prof. John Williams White's *The Verse of Greek Comedy.* The entire material is exhaustively re-interpreted on the principles of the so-called "New Metric," for which Prof. White has exhibited in the past few years the zeal of a convertite. His lucid and temperate discussion of the controversy is the first treatment of the revolutionary doctrine that makes it intelligible both to supporters and opponents. With this and the translation of Schroeder's article on the "New Metric" by the present reporter in the April number of *Classical Philology,* the chief documents in the case are easily accessible to the limited public that concerns itself with such things. Prof. William Scott Ferguson's *Hellenistic Athens* is an excellent example of broad historical work based on the specialist's minute knowledge. Prof. Perrin's *Plutarch's "Nicias"* and *"Alcibiades," translated with Introduction and Notes,* is the third of a series of three volumes, and completes his presentation to the English reader of Plutarch as a source and Plutarch's sources for the greatest century in the history of Athens. The *Classical Papers of Mortimer Lamson Earle* contain much that scholars will be glad to have collected in this convenient form, and are a fitting memorial to one too early lost to American scholarship. Dr. Frank E. Robbins' *The Hexaemeral Literature* (Chicago dissertation) is a solid study in the hitherto somewhat neglected field of the influence of Greek philosophy on the interpretation of *Genesis.* Dr. Samuel Lee Wolff's elaborate monograph on the *Greek Romances in Elizabethan Prose Fiction* is published under the auspices of the Columbia University department of English and comparative literature. Dr. H. T. Archbald's *The Fable as a Stylistic Test in Classical Greek Literature* is a Johns Hopkins dissertation.

The appearance of the first 15 volumes of the "Loeb Library of Translations from the Classics with accompanying Texts," is an event which would deserve record here even apart from the considerable place which is to be assigned to American scholars in the execution of the great plan.

The death of Prof. Goodwin (see *Classical Philology* for July, the *Classical Journal* for October, and Prof. Gildersleeve in *American Jour-*

nal of Philology, vol. 33, p. 367) is felt as a personal loss by his many pupils and by the still wider circle of those who were taught by his books or took pride in his fame.

LATIN LITERATURE

CHARLES KNAPP

American work in Latin literature still consists mainly of articles in the periodicals and in the volumes of studies published under the auspices of various universities. Several books, however, fall within this field and the kindred field of Roman history (see the bibliography below, under Abbott, Botsford, Earle, and Harvard Essays). One important book, Olcott's *Thesaurus Linguae Latinae Epigraphicae,* was brought to an untimely end, after the publication of three more fascicles in 1912 (17-19), by the death of the author.

More attention, apparently, is being paid by American scholars to text criticism. Here belongs a book of great value, a critical edition of Ammianus Marcellinus (Berlin, Weidman, 1910), by C. U. Clark (see also the bibliography, under Foster, Hatch, and Johnson). A notable event was the publication of *The Classical Papers of Mortimer Lamson Earle.* Prof. Earle, who died in 1905, was an adept in the criticism and emendation of Greek and Latin texts. His collected papers deal mainly with Greek authors, but contain much of interest to the student of Latin literature, especially in connection with Horace. The tendency to trace the influence of Latin authors on later ages was not so much in evidence (see, however, the bibliography, under Gummere).

American scholars are giving much attention to rhythm in Latin prose writers, following here Zielinski. In his edition of Ammianus (see above), Prof. Clark lays much stress on such matters. So, too, did Prof. Harmon in his paper on the "Rhythmical Clausulæ in Ammianus Marcellinus," to which reference was made last year (see also the bibliography below under Shipley). A warning against such studies is uttered by Paul Shorey, in a review of C. Zander's *Eurythmia vel Compositio Rhythmica Prosae Antiquae,* (*Classical Philology,* 6.494-497).

Much good work appears in reviews. Doctors' dissertations, too, not infrequently give results of importance and promise well for the future. Lack of space, however, forbids mention of such work in detail. The space available can best be devoted to a bibliography with a few words of comment accompanying some of the titles listed.

BIBLIOGRAPHY

Abbreviations are employed as follows: *AJP., American Journal of Philology; CJ., Classical Journal; CP., Classical Philology; CW., Classical Weekly; HS., Harvard Studies; PAPA., Proceedings of the American Philological Association; TAPA., Transactions of the American Philological Association.*

ABBOTT, Frank Frost.—*The Common People of Ancient Rome.* (New York, Scribners, 1911.)
BOTSFORD, G. W.—*A History of the Ancient World.* (New York, The Macmillan Co., 1912.) Pages 311-538 deal with Rome.
CHASE, George H.—See *Harvard Essays, infra.*
DE WITT, Norman W.—"A Campaign of Epigram Against Marcus Antonius in the Catalepton." (*AJP.,* 33, 317-333.)
EARLE, Mortimer Lamson.—*The Classical Papers of Mortimer Lamson Earle.* (New York, Columbia University Press, 1912.)
ELMORE, J.—"Some Phases of Martial's Literary Attitude." (See *Matzke Memorial Volume,* in *Stanford University Studies,* No. 7.)
FLICKINGER, Roy C.—"ΧΟΡΟΥ in Terence's *Heauton,* etc." (*CP.,* 7, 24-34.)—An argument that in this play of Terence there was a chorus, which carried two different rôles.
FOSTER, B. O.—An exhaustive review of Hosius's text of Propertius, and of a text of Catullus, Tibullus and Propertius by Ellis, Postgate and Phillimore. (*AJP.,* 33, 330-342.)
FRANK, Tenney.—"The Import of the Fetial Institution." (*CP.,* 7, 335-342.)
GUMMERE, Richard M.—"Seneca the Philosopher in the Middle Ages and the Early Renaissance." (*PAPA.,* 41, xxxviii-xli.)
HARMON, A. M.—"The Protesilaudamia Lævii." (*AJP.,* 33, 186-194.)
HATCH, W. H. P.—"A Manuscript of Jerome's *De Viris Illustribus,* belong-

ing to the General Theological Seminary in New York." (*HS.*, 23, 47-69.)
Harvard Essays on Classical Subjects.
—Contains eight essays, four of which touch Latin literature, thus: CHASE, George H., "The New Criticism of Roman Art" (1-31); MOORE, Clifford H., "Greek and Roman Ascetic Tendencies" (97-140); MORGAN, Morris H., "Some Aspects of an Ancient Roman City" (141-172); RAND, E. K., "Ovid and the Spirit of Metamorphosis" (207-238).
INGERSOLL, J. W. D.—"Roman Satire: Its Early Name." (*CP.*, 7, 59-65.)
JEROME, Thomas S.—"The Tacitean Tiberius: a Study in Historiographic Method." (*CP.*, 7, 265-292.)
JOHNSON, Dora.—"The Manuscripts of Pliny's Letters." (*CP.*, 7, 66-75.)
KELLOGG, George D.—"The Painting of the Crow and Two Vultures in Plautus' *Mostellaria*, 832 ff." (*PAPA.*, 41, xlii-xlv.)
KNAPP, Charles.—"Notes on *etiam* in Plautus." (*TAPA.*, 41, 115-137.)
——"References to Painting and Literature in Plautus and Terence." (*PAPA.*, 41, xlvi-liii.)
——"The Dramatic Satura and Its Assailants." (*AJP.*, 33, 125-148.)
LODGE, Gonzales.—"Greek Influence on Roman Literature." (In *Greek Literature*, pp. 267-296, New York, Columbia University Press, 1912.)
McCREA, Nelson G.—"Latin Literature." (*CW.*, 5, 194-199). Reprinted from *Lectures on Literature at Columbia University.* (New York, Columbia University Press, 1911.)
MOORE, Clifford H.—See *Harvard Essays, supra.*

MORGAN, Morris H.—See *Harvard Essays, supra.*
OLIPHANT, Samuel G.—"The Use of the Omen in Plautus and Terence." (*CJ.*, 7, 165-173.)
PEASE, Arthur S.—"The Omen of Sneezing." (*CP.*, 6, 427-443.)
PRESCOTT, Henry W.—"The Position of 'Deferred' Nouns and Adjectives in Epic and Hexameter Verse." (*CP.*, 7, 35-58.)
RAND, Edward K.—See *Harvard Essays, supra.*
REES, Kelley.—"The Significance of the Parodoi in the Greek Theater." (*AJP.*, 32, 377-402.)—The paper bears also directly and indirectly on the Roman theater.
ROLFE, John C.—"On Lucan, V, 424 ff. (Additional Notes on *Vela Cadunt*)." (*PAPA.*, 41, lix-lxv.)
SCHAUROTH, Edward G.—"The ΥΠΟ ΖΩΜΑΤΑ of Greek Ships." (*HS.*, 22, 173-179.)—Throws light, if sound, on Horace, Odes 1, 14, 6-9. The author thinks of "undergirders of rope, or perhaps chains, transversally stretched across the ship's hold under the deck, and attached at either end to one of the stout rib pieces."
SHIPLEY, F. W.—"The Heroic Clausula in Cicero and Quintilian.' (*CP.*, 6, 410-418.)
——"The Treatment of Dactylic Words in the Rhythmic Prose of Cicero." (*TAPA.*, 41, 139-156.)
ULLMAN, B. L.—"Horace and Tibullus." (*AJP.*, 33, 149-167.)
WEBB, Robert H.—"An Attempt to Reconstruct the γ Archetype of Terence's Manuscripts." (*HS.*, 22, 55-110.)
——"On the Origin of Roman Satire." (*CP.*, 7, 177-189.)

MODERN LANGUAGES AND LITERATURE

GERMANIC LANGUAGES AND LITERATURE

DANIEL B. SHUMWAY

German Fiction.—The ever-growing interest in German literature is evinced by the increasing frequency of the translations from modern German authors. In some cases the work has hardly made its appearance in Germany before arrangements are made for translating it into English. This is the case with Gerhart Hauptmann's latest novel *Atlantis*, dealing with an American theme, a translation of which, by Adele and Thomas Seltzer, has just been issued by B. W. Huebsch. The powerful woman novelist Clara Viebig is the subject of an article in the *Review of Reviews* for May, and a volume of her short stories, entitled *Guilty, and Other Short Stories* has been translated by O. F. Theis. Ludwig Ganghofer's *Gewitter im Mai* and two short stories by Heinz Tovote, *Frau Agna* and *Mutter*, have been issued in German by Brentano. Margarete Böhme's story, *A Department Store*, translated by Ethel C. Mayne, has been published by Appletons, and her art as novelist discussed in the *Bookman* for June. O. E. Lessing discusses Liliencron, Dehmel, Hauptmann and others in his latest critical work *Masters of Modern German Literature*. The classic writers are not entirely forgotten for the moderns, Carlyle's translation of Goethe's master novel *Wilhelm Meister* having been reissued by Dutton in Everyman's Library. Further, J. McCabe has furnished us with a new life of Goethe, *The Man and His Character* (Lippincotts), H. W. Boynton has discussed him in his volume, *The World's Leading Poets* (Holt), and *Gleams from Goethe* have been chosen and translated with an introduction by H. Attwell. In the general field, J. G. Robertson has followed his earlier work on German literature by a new one entitled *Outlines of the History of German Literature*. The influence of Dante Gabriel Rossetti on German literature is discussed by L. A. Willoughby in a work issued by the Oxford University Press. In the nature of scientific monographs are J. F. Haussmann's article "German Estimation of Novalis from 1800 to 1850" in *Modern Philology* for January, and A. E. Gubelmann's *Study on the Sensuous in Hebbel's Lyric Poetry*, issued by the Yale University Press. An admirable anthology of German lyrics in translation is the *Oxford Book of German Verse, from the 12th to 20th Century*, prepared by H. G. Fiedler with a preface by Gerhart Hauptmann.

German Drama.—This field is, as usual, well represented. A. Dukes in a recent work, *Modern Dramatists*, has discussed the more important German ones, among others Hauptmann and von Hofmannsthal. Four plays of Hauptmann have been translated by Ludwig Lewisohn and a second volume is in preparation. Two of Wagner's most important music dramas, the *Mastersingers of Nuremberg*, and *Tristan and Isolde*, have been translated by the well known critic W. J. Henderson and published by Dodd, Mead & Co. The story of Bayreuth, as told in Wagner's *Bayreuth Letters*, has been published in Caroline V. Kerr's translation by Small, Maynard & Co. Scientific in character are the following essays and dissertations: "Heroines in the Dramas of Grillparzer," by Eliz. A. Hermann (*Modern Philology*); *The History of the Chorus in the German Drama*, by Elsie W. Helmrich (Columbia University Studies); and *The Philology of Schiller in Its Historical Relations*, by Emil C. Wilm (Luce & Co.).

German Texts.—The following dramas have been edited for school use: Hebbel's *Agnes Bernauer*, by M. B. Evans (Heath); Lessing's *Nathan der Weise*, by J. G. Robertson (Putnam); Schiller's *Don Carlos*, by F. W. C. Lieder (Oxford). This latter is especially welcome, as this play had not as yet been edited in America. In prose works, Freytag's historical novel, *Das Nest der Zaunkönige*, has been abridged and edited by E. C. Roeder and C. H. Handschin (Heath), and two stories of A. von Keller, *Die drei gerechten Kammacher* and *Frau Regel Arnrean und ihr Jüngster*, issued by the Oxford University Press. A. F. W. Grimm's interesting story, *Aus der alten Kaffeemühle, Geschichten aus dem Studentenleben*, has been published by the Antigo Publishing Co. New editions of frequently edited tales are: Hauff's *Das kalte Herz*, by F. J. Holzwarth and W. J. Gosse (American Book Co.); Storm's *Immensee*, by C. G. Elmer and J. G. Neumarker (Merrill); Wildenbruch's *Das edle Blut*, by Allyn, and the same author's *Der Letzte*, by J. H. Beekman (American Book Co.). J. H. Hülshof has prepared a *Deutsches Lesebuch* (Jenkins), F. Betz a well chosen selection of German humor, *Deutscher Humor aus vier Jahrhunderten* (Heath), and C. W. Collman a volume of *Easy German Poetry for Beginners* (Ginn & Co.). Among the new grammars the conversational method of Dr. Max Walther of Frankfurt, who gave model lessons in New York last winter, prepared in collaboration with Karl A. Krause under the title *Beginners' German* (Putnam), deserves to head the list. Next comes the admirable *Elementary German Grammar*, by E. C. Wesselhoeft, who has had such success with his composition books. Other grammars are *Progressive Lessons in German*, by R. W. Huebsch and R. F. Smith; *German for Daily Use*, by E. P. Prentys (Jenkins); *A First*

German Book, by G. T. Ungold (Putnam); and *A Conversational Grammar*, by J. Bithell (Putnam).
German Teaching.—This department is represented by the following articles: C. H. Handschin, "Problems in the Teaching of Modern Languages" in *Education* for Dec., 1911; "Historical Sketch of the Gouin Series-System of Teaching Modern Languages and of its Use in the United States," by the same author in the *School Review* for March; C. F. Kayser, "May the Modern Languages be Regarded as a Satisfactory Substitute for the Classics" in the *Educational Review* for May; E. D. Wright, "Foreign Language Requirements for the A. B. Degree" in the *Classical Journal* for May.
German Philology.—The most important event in this field is the appearance of a new series of scientific monographs edited by Prof. Collitz of Johns Hopkins and entitled *Hesperia, Schriften zur germanischen Philologie*. The series is opened by a brilliant scholarly investigation, *Das schwache Präteritum und seine Vorgeschichte*, from the pen of the editor, to which he has prefixed a most interesting and impartial résumé of what American scholarship has thus far accomplished in Germanic philology for the enlightenment of those European scholars who are disposed to disregard American publications. As No. 2 of the series there appeared the dissertation of Mary C. Burchinal on *Hans Sachs and Goethe, A Study in Metre*, which sheds but little additional light on this moot question, but gives a detailed account of the views of her predecessors. An able dissertation, introducing new ideas into the field of syntax, has been written by Richard Fey on *Neuhochdeutsche Appositions-Gruppen*. Though printed in Halle it was offered for the degree of Ph.D. at the University of Pennsylvania. Of importance is also the issuing of an English edition of Vietor's *Kleine Phonetik*, by W. Rippmann, under the title *Elements of Phonetics, English, French and German* (Dutton). L. Bloomfield has written an excellent study of the "E-Sounds in the Language of Hans Sachs" in *Modern Philology* for April, and B. Boezinger a dissertation on *Das historische Praesens in der älteren deutschen Sprache* (Leland Stanford, Jr., University). The earlier New High German is represented by a novel based on Luther's life by W. S. Davis, entitled *The Friar of Wittenberg* (Macmillan). Further, the first volume of an English translation of Zwingli's *Latin Works and Correspondence with Selections from His German Works* has been issued by Putnam. The Middle High German period is represented by a new verse translation of the *Nibelungenlied*, by Arthur S. Way, under the title *Lay of the Nibelung Men* (Putnam). Belonging more to the domain of German philosophy, but of great general interest are the several translations of Nietzsche's works and biography. His autobiography, *Ecce Homo*, has been translated by A. M. Ludovici, who has translated also Nietzsche's *Twilight of the Idols*, his *Antichrist* and *Notes on Zarathustra*. M. Mügge has rendered Nietzsche's *Early Greek Philosophers and Other Essays*, and P. N. Cohn his *Human, All Too Human, a Book for Free Spirits*. Elizabeth Foerster Nietzsche's almost too flattering life of her brother has been translated by A. M. Ludovici. The first volume, *The Young Nietzsche*, dealing with his life from 1844 to 1876, has already appeared; the second, *The Solitary Nietzsche*, is now in press.

Swedish.—The interest in the austere Swedish poet Strindberg, due in part to his death during the year, overshadows that in all other Scandinavian writers. His works are being rapidly translated into English and numerous critical estimates of his art have appeared. So many are there, in fact, that space will permit of the enumeration of only the most important. For a full bibliography the reader is referred to the complete list given by Prof. Arch. Henderson in the *Bulletin of Bibliography* for July. The following plays have appeared: *The Father, Countess Julie, the Outlaw, The Stronger*, translated by Edith and Warner Oland (Luce & Co.); *Easter* and *Lucky Peter*, translated by Velma S. Howard;, *The Dream Play, The Link*,

The Dance of Death, translated with an introduction by Edwin Björkman, who has translated also the tragicomedy, *There Are Crimes and Crimes,* and who has just issued a further volume containing *Miss Julie, The Stronger, Creditors* and *Parriah.* A. Dukes gives an estimate of Strindberg in his *Modern Dramatists.* The works of Ellen Key, the Swedish champion of free love, continue to be translated into English, her *Love and Ethics,* by M. B. Brothwick and F. L. Wright, and *Morality of Women and Other Essays,* by M. B. Brothwick alone. A sequel to Karin Michaelis' much talked of novel, *The Dangerous Age,* entitled *Elsie Lindtner,* has been translated by Beatrice Marshall. Hjalmar Söderberg is discussed and called a "lesser Anatole France of the Far North," by Edwin Björkman in *Is There Anything New.* The Augustana Book concern has issued three volumes of Swedish tales in the original, and as a sign of the increasing interest in the study of the Scandinavian tongues, we have a school edition of Gustaf Geijerstam's *Mina Pojkar,* edited by J. Alexis with an introduction and notes, in the college and high school series of Swedish authors issued by the same firm.

Norwegian.—In Norwegian literature Ibsen, as usual, stands in the front rank of interest. His collected works have been revised and edited with an introduction by W. Archer (Scribners). A. Dukes discusses his influence in his *Modern Dramatists,* and Otto Heller has written an excellent book on his *Plays and Our Problems* (Houghton Mifflin). Bjöornson's play, *When the New Wine Blooms,* has been translated by Lee M. Hollander for the series of Poet Lore Plays, and his art is discussed by A. Dukes in his *Modern Dramatists.* *Norse Tales* are retold for little children by F. Freeman and R. Davis. Scientific in character are A. C. Crowell's *Introductory Lessons to Old Icelandic* and J. W. Hartmann's dissertation on *The Gangu Krolfssaga, a Study in Old Norse Philology* (Columbia University Studies). The new society for the advancement of Scandinavian, organized in Chicago in 1911, has issued a second number of its *Proceedings.*

Danish.—The most important translation from this language is George Brandes' well known work, *Main Currents in Nineteenth Century Literature,* published in six volumes by Macmillans. Of great interest also is the translation of three plays of Ludwig Holberg, the father of Danish comedy, by H. W. L. Hime, indicating, as it does, a revival of interest in the earlier literature of this country. J. Grant Cramer has translated Grundtvik's *Fairy Tales.*

Dutch.—The literature of Holland is better represented than in 1911 when no article or translation appeared. During the year *The Hundred Best Dutch Poems* have been published by Geo. W. Jacobs & Co., and A. Dukes has discussed the well known dramatist, Herman Heijermanns, who, like the German playwrights, shows strongly the influence of Ibsen. Petrus Blok's monumental *History of the Netherlands* in five volumes has just been completed by the issue of the fifth volume on the 18th and 19th centuries, translated by A. Bierstadt (Putnam).

ROMANCE LANGUAGES AND LITERATURE

BENJAMIN P. BOURLAND

Necrology.—Rufino José Cuervo died in Paris, July 17, 1911. He was born at Bogotá in 1844, spent nearly all his life in philological study, and was among the most exact and thorough of scholars in Spanish, easily the first of all who have come from South America. His principal works were the repeated editions of Bello's celebrated grammar, and his *Diccionario de construcción y régimen de la lengua castellana,* a splendid work of which but two volumes have been published. It is understood that the manuscript for the continuation has been left complete. Gustav Groeber, professor at Breslau 1874-1880, at Strassburg 1880-1909, died at Strassburg Nov. 6, 1911; a man of very broad learning and interests, one of the first scholars of Germany, known to all students of the Romance languages everywhere as the founder and editor of the *Zeitschrift für romanische Philologie*, and editor of the *Grundriss der romanischen Philologie*. Wilhelm Cloëtta, professor at Jena 1893-1909, and at Strassburg from the latter year, died Sept. 25, 1911. His principal interest was in the history of literature, his chief works studies of the *Moniage Guillaume* and the *Enfances Vivien*. Marcelino Menéndez y Pelayo died at Santander, May 19, 1912. He was the first man of letters and scholar of Spain, and a great figure in the scholarship of the world. From the very long list of his important writings we note the *Historia de los Heterodojos de España*, *Historia de las Ideas Estéticas en España*, the *Antología de Poesías Líricas*, and the long series of *Estudios*. At his death he was professor of the Universidad Central, Director of the Royal Academy of History, and Director of the National Library, all of Madrid.

There is no special change to be observed in the position of Romance studies in the world, and in this country. No great discovery, or epoch-making publication marks the year 1912. In this country, there is to be observed a slight decrease in the output of class-room editions, and an encouraging, though very slight, increase in the publication of purely scientific effort. American scholars continue to find their greater interest in Spanish and Old-French literature.

BIBLIOGRAPHY

ALDEN, Raymond Macdonald.—"The Doctrine of Verisimilitude in French and English Criticism of the Seventeenth Century." (*Matzke Memorial Volume*, Stanford University, 1911.)
ALEXANDER, Luther Herbert.—*Participial Substantives of the -ata Type in the Romance Languages, with Special Reference to French.* (New York, Columbia University Press.)
ALLEN, Clifford Gilmore.—"The Relation of the German 'Gregorovius auf dem Stein' to the Old French Poem 'La Vie de Saint Gregoire.'" (*Matzke Memorial Volume*, Stanford Univ.)
BLONDHEIM, D. S.—"Provençal *aib, ab, aiba,* Portuguese *eiva.*" (*Modern Language Notes*, 27, 1.)
——"Spanish *zaranda,* Portuguese *ciranda.*" (*Ibid.*, 27, 3.)
——"Maimon." (*Romania*, 41, 2.)
——"Judéo-espagnol *abediguar.*" (*Ibid.*)
BRIGGS, William Dinsmore.—"Spenser's 'Faerie Queene,' III, II, and Boccaccio's 'Fiammetta.'" (*Matzke Memorial Volume*, Stanford University.)
BROWN, Arthur C. L.—"On the Independent Character of the Welsh Owain." (*Romanic Review*, 888, 2-3.)
BRUCE, J. D.—"Arthuriana." (*Ibid.*)
BUCHANAN, M. A.—"Spanish Literature, Exclusive of the Drama." (*Romanisches Jahresbericht*, XI, 4.)
BUFFUM, Douglas L.—"The Refrains of the *Cour de Paradis,* and of a *Salut d'Amour.*" (*Modern Language Notes*, 27, 1.)
CARROLL, J. S.—*Dante Expositions.* (New York, G. H. Doran Co.)
CHURCHMAN, P. H.—"The Beginnings of Byronism in Spain." (*Revue Hispanique*, XXIII, 64.)
COESTER, A.—"A Bibliography of Spanish-American Literature." (*Romanic Review*, III, 2-3.)
CRAWFORD, J. P. Wickersham.—"Teofilo Folengo's *Moschaca,* and Jose de Villaviciosa's *La Mosquea.*" (*Publications of the Modern Language Association of America*, 27, 3.)
DAY, Th.—*Beiträge zur Geschichte der Anrede im Französischen zu Beginn der Neuzeit.* (Heidelberg, 1912.)
ESPINOSA, Aurelio M.—"New Mexican Spanish Folktales." (*Journal of American Folklore*, XXIV, 94.)
——"Old French *ne—se—non* in Other Romance Languages." (*Matzke Memorial Volume*, Leland Stanford University.)
GAY, Lucy M.—"Sources of the *Académie de l'Art poëtique* of Pierre de Deimier: Peletier du Mans." (*Publications of the Modern Language Association of America*, 27, 3.)
GRIFFITH, Reginald Harvey.—*Sir Perceval of Galles: a Study of the Sources of the Legend.* (University of Chicago Press.)
HAMILTON, George L.—"*Sur la date et quelques sources du Thezaur de Pierre de Corbian.*" (*Romania*, XLI, 2.)
——"*La source d'un épisode de Baudouin de Sebourc.*" (*Zeitschrift für romanische Philologie*, XXXVI, 2.)
HILL, Raymond Thompson. — "The *Enueg.*" (*Publications of the Modern Language Association of America*, 27, 2.)
HILLS, Elijah Clarence.—"Dante's Versification." (*Romanic Review*, III, 2-3.)
JOHNSTON, Oliver Martin.—"Origin of the Legend of Floire and Blancheflor." (*Matzke Memorial Volume*, Stanford University.)
KUERSTEINER, Albert F.—"The Use of the Relative Pronoun in the Rimado de Palacio." (*Revue Hispanique*, XXIV, 65.)

Lancaster, H. Carrington.—"Two Lost Plays by Alexandre Hardy." (*Modern Language Notes*, XXVII, 5.)
——"Crinesius on French Pronunciation." (*Ibid.*, XXVII, 3.)
Lewis, Charles B.—"*Die Altfranzösischen Versionen der lateinischen Historia Apollonii Regis Tyri.*" (*Romanische Forschungen*, XXXIV, 1.)
Matzke, John Ernst.—"The Oldest Form of the Beves Legend." (*Modern Philology*, IX, 3.)
——"Gaston Paris." (*Matzke Memorial Volume*, Stanford University.)
——"The Development and Present Status of French Dialectology." (*Ibid.*)
Nitze, William A.—"The Sister's Son and the *Conte del Graal.*" (*Modern Philology*, IX, 1.)
Northup, George Tyler.—"The Italian Origin of the Spanish Prose Tristram Versions." (*Romanic Review*, III, 2-3.)
Pietsch, Karl.—"*Zur Spanischen Grammatik.*" (*Modern Language Notes*, XXVII, 6.)
——"*Zur Spanischen Grammatik.*" (*Modern Philology*, IX, 3.)
——"Duecho Once More." (*Modern Philology*, IX, 1.)
Post, C. R.—"The Sources of Juan de Mena." (*Romanic Review*, III, 2-3.)
Price, William Raleigh.—*The Symbolism of Voltaire's Novels, with Special Reference to Zadig.* (New York, Columbia University Press.)
Rennert, Hugo A.—*The Spanish Pastoral Romances.* (Publications of the University of Pennsylvania.)
Robertson, D. Maclaren.—*A History of the French Academy.* (New York, G. W. Dillingham Co.)
Ruutz-Rees, C.—"Charles Fontaine's *Fontaine d'Amour* and *Sannazaro.*" (*Modern Language Notes*, XXVII, 3.)
Smith, Hugh A.—"Studies in the Epic Poem 'Godefroi de Bouillon." (*Publications of the Modern Language Association of America*, XXVII, 2.)
——"A Prose Version of the '*Sept Sages de Rome.*'" (*Romanic Review*, III, 1.)
Stuart, Donald Clive.—"The Source of Gresset's *Méchant.*" (*Modern Language Notes*, XXVII, 2.)
Terracher, A.—"*Note sur le Pour et le Contre de Voltaire.*" (*Ibid.*)
Tuttle, Edwin H.—"Hispanic 'Alteru' and 'Altu.'" (*Modern Language Review*, VII, 3.)
Umphrey, G. W.—"The Aragonese Dialect." (*Revue Hispanique*, XXIV, 65.)
Warren, F. M.—"The Troubadour *canso* and Latin Lyric Poetry." (*Modern Philology*, IX, 2.)
——"Enéas and Thomas' *Tristan.*" (*Modern Language Notes*, XXVII, 4.)
Waxman, Samuel Montefiori.—"The Religion of Rabelais." (*Romanic Review*, III, 2-3.)
Wright, C. H. C.—*A History of French Literature.* (New York, Oxford University Press.)

Texts and Translations

"*Auto de la Quinta Angustia que Nuestra Senora passo al Pie de la Cruz.*" Published by J. P. Wickersham Crawford. (*Romanic Review*, III, 2-3.)
"*La Bataille de Trente Anglois et de Trente Bretons.*" Edited by Henry Raymond Brush. (*Modern Philology*, IX, 2 and 3.)
"'*Las Borlas Veras.*' *Comedia famosa de Lope de Vega Carpio.*" Edited by S. E. Millard Rosenberg. (Publications of the University of Pennsylvania.)
"*Comedia a lo Pastoril, para la noche de Navidad.*" Published by J. P. Wickersham Crawford. (*Revue Hispanique*, XXIV, 66.)
"*Gaspar de Avila. Tercera jornada de las Fullerias de Amor.*" Published by J. P. Wickersham Crawford. (*Revue Hispanique*, XXIV, 66.)
"*La Mule sanz Frain*, an Arthurian Romance." Edited by Raymond Thompson Hill. (Baltimore, J. H. Furst Co.)
"The Rimed Chronicle of the Cid." Edited by Benjamin P. Bourland. (*Revue Hispanique*, XXIV, 66.)
"The Triumph of Death, translated out of Italian by the Countess of Pembrooke." Published by Frances Berkeley Young. (*Publications of the Modern Language Association of America*, XXVII, 2.)

ENGLISH LANGUAGE AND LITERATURE

C. G. Child

Innumerable texts, reviews and minor notes, often of great value and attesting the industry of American scholars, must necessarily be excluded from the narrow limits of this article, the object of which is to indicate the general trend of activity in the field of English.

Philology.—The continued neglect of linguistic study is to be deplored. It is not an arid and barren discipline, but, properly considered, a humanity, and, for the graduate student, through the character of the training it affords, a helpful correction to the futile æstheticism and dilettantism which students so often display. Articles on linguistic matters are more numerous than last year; among them may be mentioned Bright's on an idiom of the comparative in Anglo-Saxon (*Mod. Lang. Notes*), Hale on the harmonizing of grammatical nomenclature (*Publ. Mod. Lang. Association*), Miss Pound on "Intrusive Nasals in Present Day English" (*Eng. Studien*), Curme on the relative (*Journal of Eng. and Germ. Phil.*), F. A. Wood's articles as touching English, and the admirable work of the Dialect Society in studying American English (*Dialect Notes*).

Old English Period (449-1150).—Articles in this field are, as usual, few, but good: Bright on "Exodus" (*Mod. Lang. Notes*), S. Moore on the same poem (*Mod. Phil.*), F. Tupper, Jr., on the Cynewulfian runes (*Mod. Lang. Notes*) and notes on various poems (*Journal Eng. and Germ. Phil.*), Lawrence on the "Haunted Mere" in "Beowulf" (*Publ. Mod. Lang. Association*), J. M. Hart on ll. 168-9 of that poem (*Mod. Lang. Notes*), and Klaeber's valuable reviews of works upon it in a number of periodicals.

Middle English Period (1150-1500).—Sommer has continued the publication of the Arthurian Vulgate (Carnegie Institution). Welcome contributions are Lawrence's "Medieval Story" (Columbia Lectures), Mosher's *Exemplum* (Columbia Press), Miss Dudley's striking demonstration of the Egyptian elements in the "Body and Soul" legend (Bryn Mawr Monographs), and F. Tupper's delightful article on Giraldus Cambrensis (Sewanee). Hemingway's rendering of the *Morte Arthur* will be welcomed (Houghton Mifflin Co.). American activity in the study of Chaucer may continue to be a matter of pride: Kittredge (*Mod. Phil.*); Root (*Eng. Stud.*); Hathaway (*ibid.*); C. Brown, Lowes, MacCracken, S. Moore, Miss Hammond, H. S. V. Jones (*Mod. Lang. Notes*—the last named also in *Publ. Mod. Lang. Association*). Special mention must be accorded to the first complete rendering of Chaucer in modern English by Tatlock and Percy Mackaye, published in a sumptuous format (Macmillan).

In the still too little explored 15th century, MacCracken has published a poem on Ralph, Lord Cromwell (*Mod. Lang. Notes*), of interest in relation to Lydgate (see also Miss Hammond, *ibid.*), and S. Moore a most helpful article on "Patrons of Letters in Norfolk and Suffolk, c. 1450" (*Publ. Mod. Lang. Association*). In relation to the earlier drama, see Mackenzie's "New Source for *Mankind*" (*ibid.*), Spenser's volume on "Corpus Christi Pageants in England" (Baker and Taylor), and Cady on the Towneley cycle (*Journal Eng. Germ. Phil.*). The publication by Flügel and others of early song-miscellanies in *Anglia* is continued by Padelford, "English Songs in Ms. Selden B. 26."

Modern English (1500-date).—To the reviewer it seems as if nine out of ten scholars in America devoted themselves to the drama of the 16th and 17th centuries. Spenser is not wholly neglected: Greenlaw (*Mod. Phil.*); Cory, whose volume also touches on the Fletchers and Milton (University of California); Bruce (*Mod. Lang. Notes*); Padelford ("Allegory of the Faerie Queene," Ginn). Other works, not on the drama, are: Wolff's *Greek Romances in Elizabethan Prose Fiction* (Columbia Studies); Miss Hatcher's admirable article on "Aims and Methods of Elizabethan Translators" (*Eng. Stud.*); Tieje's "Expressed Aim of the Long Prose Fiction from 1579 to 1740" (*Mod. Phil.*), and Westcott's publication of a "find" of some little interest, namely, new poems of James I of England (Columbia Series). But new editions and articles in the field of the drama are innumerable: Wallace's *Evolution of the Drama to the Time of Shakespeare;* Miss Foster, "Dumb Show before 1620" (*Eng. Stud.*); Boland, *Time in Elizabethan Drama* (Yale Studies); Graves, "Religious and Political Plays" (*Mod. Phil.*); W. J. Lawrence, *The Elizabethan Playhouse and Other Studies* (Lippincott) and "Light and Darkness in the Elizabethan Theatre" (*Eng. Stud.*); Graves on the Elizabethan stage (*Mod. Phil.*); Forsythe on *Jeronimo* (*Mod. Lang. Notes*); a sheaf upon Shakespeare—Scholl, *Winter's Tale*

(*Mod. Lang. Notes*); Law, *Richard III* (*Publ. Mod. Lang. Association*); Tynan, "Greene and 'Shakspere'" (*ibid.*); Hanford, "Suicide in Shakespeare" (*ibid.*); Padelford, *As You Like It* (*Sewanee Review*); Northup, "Bibliography" (*Journal Eng. Germ. Phil.*); Arnold on the soliloquies (Columbia Press); William Winter, *Shakespeare on the Stage* (Moffatt, Yard & Co.); Henneman's *Shakespeare and Other Papers* (reprints: University of the South); Stoll, "Criminals in Shakespeare" (*Mod. Phil.*); Adams on Jonson (*Mod. Lang. Notes*), and on Heywood (*Eng. Stud.*); Miss M. L. Hunt on Thomas Dekker (Columbia Press; also *Journal Eng. Germ. Phil.*); Pierce, **Dekker** and Ford (*Anglia*); Adams, Hausted's *Rival Friends* (*Journal Eng. and Germ. Phil.*), and Brathwaite's *Mercurius Britannicus* (*Mod. Lang. Notes*). The Restoration period is represented by Forsythe's article on Shadwell (*Journal Eng. Germ. Phil.*). Here, in leaving the 17th century, may be mentioned Hall's monograph on *Idylls of Fishermen* (Columbia Press), Hasting's article on "Errors and Inconsistencies in *Robinson Crusoe*" (*Mod. Lang. Notes*), Hand Browne's delightful article on "Scottish Ballads" (*Sewanee Review*), and with the latter Belden's discussion of the relation of balladry to folk-lore (*Journal of American Folk Lore*). The 18th century is, as usual, scantily represented: Havens, "The Romantic Aspects of the Age of Pope" (*Publ. Mod. Lang. Association*); Wells, "Henry Fielding and the Crisis" (*Mod. Lang. Notes*). Among literature relating to the 19th century, it is always difficult to draw a line between constructive criticism and popular exposition, and only really helpful contributions can be here noted. Among them may be noted C. E. Morgan's *Rise of the Novel of Manners* (Columbia Press); Cunliffe's "Modern Thought in Meredith's Poems" (*Publ. Mod. Lang. Association*); Lounsbury's *Early Literary Career of Robert Browning* (Scribner); W. S. Johnson's *Thomas Carlyle, 1814-1831* (Yale Press); Barley's "The Morality Motive in Contemporary English Drama" (University of Texas); the volume of *Lectures on Literature* delivered at Columbia by members of its faculty (Columbia Press); Neilson's stimulating *Essentials of Poetry*, and Reed's substantial volume of *English Lyrical Poetry* (Yale Press), a gallant attempt to encompass in more than mere outline the range of our lyrical verse from its beginnings to the present day.

The founding of the *English Journal* (University of Chicago Press) may be noted. In this connection, success may be wished for every influence tending to ameliorate the deplorable evils incidental to the college requirements for admission in English.

Necrology.—Horace Howard Furness, editor of the *Variorum Shakespeare*, died Aug. 13 in his 79th year. His work, one of the greatest monuments of American scholarship, will be continued by his son, Horace Howard Furness, Jr., for some years associated with his father as collaborator.

AMERICAN LITERATURE

(*Oct. 1, 1911, to Nov. 15, 1912*)

ARTHUR HOBSON QUINN

This review includes those works of creative literature that are of notable worth or have attracted such widespread interest that a judgment upon them seems necessary in this place. Works of scholarship are mentioned only when upon distinctly American themes.

Poetry and Drama.—While *The Poems and Dramas of George Cabot Lodge* (2 vols., Houghton Mifflin Co.) include of course no poems written in the limits of our period, they are of such importance in the history of American Literature that they must take precedence in the year's review. The verse dramas "Herakles" and "Cain" and the sonnets placed George Cabot Lodge easily first in these fields, while as the apostle of revolt he was always significant.

In *The Singing Man*, by Josephine Preston Peabody (Houghton Mifflin Co.), we find another example of the poetry of revolt and of criticism of social conditions. Hatred of oppression, a wide love of humanity, combined with a constructive optimism make these new poems of Mrs. Marks perhaps the most notable volume of new poems of the year. The artistic finish of the verse, and the high sincerity of the impulse were to be expected from the author of "The Piper."

The Little Gray Songs from St. Joseph's, by Grace Fallow Norton (Houghton Mifflin Co.), are real poetry. The simplicity, the inevitability that belong to high art are manifested in these lyrical cries of pain born of a great soul bearing with courage a hopeless doom. It is many a day since America has produced poetry like the fifth, the eleventh, the twenty-fourth or the thirtieth of these songs.

Far Quests, by Cale Young Rice (Doubleday, Page & Co.), shows a remarkable, at times a great, ability in phrasing, a keen delight in nature and a deep insight into the human aspects of passion.

Scum of the Earth, by Robert Haven Schauffler (Houghton Mifflin Co.), is a volume with a few poems that are worth while, "Scum of the Earth," "Marsyas," and "Washington," combined with some "fillers in." The title poem has a good basic thought and a good climax.

The Sailor Who Has Sailed, by Benjamin R. C. Low (John Lane), contains a number of poems that reveal careful workmanship, and now and then striking phrases. The author never descends to tricks or devices to gain attention. While there is no new note struck, there is at times decided distinction.

The Candle and the Flame, by George Sylvester Viereck (Moffatt, Yard & Co.), contains some verses that reveal a lyric swing and poetic vocabulary, but nothing vitally new. It is destructive criticism that is found; there is nothing constructive.

Tomorrow, by Percy Mackaye (Stokes), is the most significant drama of the year. The art of Mr. Mackaye, deepening and becoming more convincing, has produced a play which treats bravely and constructively a great problem in modern life. The production of a better race is made the theme of a play that is practically adapted for the stage and is also literature.

The Novel.—The novel of the year is unquestionably *The Reef*, by Edith Wharton (Appletons). The brilliant phrasing, the careful planning of the effect, the establishment of standards of social and moral conduct have rarely been equalled, even in Mrs. Wharton's own work. In the character drawing, she has added to the gallery of her portraits the figure of Anna Leath, a truly wonderful picture of the refined, cloistered woman, and in the character of the hero she has shown again her signal ability in visualizing the attitude of man toward woman. The other characters, especially the adventuress, are deftly sketched.

In *The Heroine in Bronze*, by James Lane Allen (Macmillan), the author, leaving for the time the manner of *The Bride of the Mistletoe* and *The Doctor's Christmas Eve*, has written simply a charming love story, in which are revealed also some of his theories of art. The hero, sure of himself, is a finely drawn character and the heroine is rarely conceived.

The Voice, by Margaret Deland (Harpers), is a novelette, in which the realism of character drawing, the idealism of the point of view and the combination and harmonizing of the natural and the spiritual that have become characteristic of Mrs. Deland's work are shown in their fullness of power.

The Inheritance, by Josephine Daskam Bacon (Appletons), is a vitally interesting story in which the writer has accomplished the unusual task of representing the attitude of a boy and a man with distinct success. The character drawing is fine. The main thesis, the inheritance of the hero's traits from his father and his mother, is really wonderfully done.

Tante, by Anne Douglas Sedgwick (Century Co.), is a brilliant portrayal of the character of an absolutely selfish woman, set off by a carefully studied background of English and continental life, social and artistic. The somewhat leisurely progress of the novel is atoned for by the brilliance of the style.

The Butterfly House, by Mary Wilkins Freeman (Dodd, Mead & Co.), is a story which, though based on a rather improbable situation, is told with Mrs. Freeman's conscientious art. The carefully restrained humor, and the utter abandonment of any cloak to realism are clearly to be recognized in this latest book of the author's.

The Street Called Straight (Harpers) is an interesting novel which derives its main interest from the admirable contrast of the characters of an American business man and an English army officer, rivals for the love of a cultivated American girl. The case for America has rarely been better put, and the style is distinguished.

Alexander's Bridge, by Willa S. Cather (Houghton Mifflin Co.), is a study of the effect of two different women upon a strong man's nature, and the consequent struggle between the claims of love, duty and professional pride on one side, and on the other, the love and the memory of his youth. There is a distinction of style and a fine reticence of passion that are unusual to-day.

In *The Citadel*, by Samuel C. Merwin (Century Co.), we have a novel which depends for its interest on its timeliness. The hero, John Garwood, a congressman, is made the concrete representative of the most advanced progressive ideas, which are put in an interesting manner, though at times the artistic unity is marred by a too definite preachment. The character drawing is good, but the types of the reactionary politicians are very conventional.

A Hoosier Chronicle, by Meredith Nicholson (Houghton Mifflin Co.), is a thoroughly entertaining novel with good character sketching, some humor, and a well arranged plot. The life described is laid in Indiana mainly during the last decade, and a good picture is drawn of political and social conditions there. The relations of Sylvia and her father while he is not known to her and later when she makes her appeal to him on his own account are skillfully drawn.

Jennie Gerhardt, by Theodore Dreisler (Harpers), presents a very realistic story of a girl's life as determined by the pressure of circumstances into a mould where it seemed impossible to shape that life in accordance with the usual moral and social standards. The character drawing is good.

A Man's World, by Albert Edwards (Macmillan), is a very interesting story of a man's growth and development away from narrow and conventional moral standards to a broader knowledge of life. There is an objective quality—the characters are of interest only as they affect the main character, not in themselves.

To M. L. G. (Stokes) is a remarkable book in some ways, revealing frankly and with an eye to the picturesque, phases of theatrical life from which the glitter and tinsel have been removed, leaving the sordid side exposed in a most realistic manner. That the book is a revelation of a personal experience for the purpose of recalling a lover (as the preface states) is somewhat difficult to believe.

The Sentence of Silence, by Reginald Wright Kauffman (Moffat, Yard & Co.), is a very realistic description of a young man's career, with the thesis that children should be enlightened as to sex matters instead of being allowed to find out the great facts of life themselves. The climax is handled rather skillfully. That the book will serve any useful purpose is questionable, since the philosophy of life expressed by Judith Kent. the heroine, places the whole question of purity in women on a low plane, and the book is so framed that this seems to be the author's standpoint.

A great contrast to this type is *Mother*, by Kathleen Norris (Macmillan). This is a story based upon a study of average American middle life, containing a direct criticism of the small family so common at the present day. It is appealing in its natural quality.

1912 LITERATURE AND LANGUAGE

The Rich Mrs. Burgoyne, a later book, also by Mrs. Norris (Macmillan), is similar to *Mother* in its general atmosphere, yet shows versatility in the treatment of character. It satirizes gently the pretence and the nervous strain of American life in well-to-do society of a small town in California. Both stories have a healthful influence.

The Old Nest, by Rupert Hughes (Century Co.), is a simple yet appealing story of the relations of parents and children, touching upon the lack of fidelity to the memories of one's youth.

Belonging to the same general type of novel, *The Love that Lives*, by Mabel Osgood Wright (Macmillan), is a rather placid story of life in a small New England town, with accurate and sympathetic character drawing. The note of self-sacrifice is simply and delicately touched.

The Heart of Us, by T. R. Sullivan (Houghton Mifflin Co.), is a pleasant leisurely novel of Boston life, with a flavor of society, mingled with some pictures of theatrical life. The love story of Staunton Ives and Dorothy Ashley is rather weak.

Another contrast to the realistic stories above mentioned is *Beauty and the Jacobin*, by Booth Tarkington (Harpers). This is a brilliant novelette of the Terror, told almost exclusively in dialogue.

Both Sides of the Shield, by Major Archibald Butt (Lippincott), which is a novelette dealing with a contrast between Northern and Southern ideals, derives its chief interest from the personality of the author. The story, while not highly original, is told in a straightforward interesting manner.

The Ordeal, by Charles Egbert Craddock (Lippincott), is a story of Tennessee, dealing with the search of a mother for her child who has been kidnapped by the mountaineers, in order to hide the crime of murder. There is a sense of dignity in the style and the descriptions are good.

The Recording Angel, by Corra Harris (Doubleday, Page & Co.), is a novel of Georgia life written with a penetrating sense of the moral contrasts of life and revealing a keen wit. Some pages are sparkling with brilliant sentences, which even at times draw one's attention away from the plot.

The Mountain Girl, by Payne Erskine (Little, Brown & Co.), is a story laid in the Carolina mountains, told in a fresh and interesting manner. The characters are vividly portrayed.

The Goodly Fellowship, by Rachel C. Schauffler (Century Co.), has an unusual plot, concerned largely with the adventures of missionaries in Persia. Despite the somewhat ragged style, the book holds one's attention.

The Charioteers, by Mary Tappan Wright (Appletons), is a rather forceful story of moral issues, with a nervous, slightly overstrained style, but presenting some good character drawing.

Stover at Yale, by Owen Johnson (Stokes), is a much discussed story of college life with a sound thesis, the necessity of democracy in that life. There is some vivid writing, but the importance of the particular local institutions attacked is somewhat over emphasized.

Short Stories.—*From the South of France*, by Thos. A. Janvier (Harpers), is a collection of stories, revealing an intimate knowledge of modern Provençal types, and written in a style that is a refreshment to the spirit. The comedy is real, growing out of the characters and their relations and is based on the broadest and keenest knowledge of human nature.

In Sixes and Sevens, by O. Henry (Doubleday, Page & Co.), we have another volume from the story teller who could pack into a very few words characterization of the most definite kind, conveyed in language that is frequently slangy, and at times artificially highly colored, but nevertheless is often vigorous to the point of distinction.

Following O. Henry at some distance perhaps, but with a reality that is sometimes startling, *Buttered Side Down*, by Edna Ferber (Stokes), deals with the shop girl, the waitress and the second-rate actress in a way which, despite slang and a strain for attention, has a grip upon life that counts.

The Raid of the Guerilla, by Charles Egbert Craddock (Lippincott). In this collection of short stories, Miss Murfree continues to depict the life of the Tennessee mountaineers, which she made so long ago her own. While the plots are at times slight, the style is distinguished and the descriptive power is frequently remarkable.

Mothers to Men, by Zona Gale (Macmillan), continues the stories of Friendship Village which have delighted so many readers. If this volume never quite reaches the level of her *Pelleas and Etarre*, it nevertheless stands out among the lesser books of stories for the unfailing distinction of its style.

Vistas of New York, by Brander Matthews (Harpers), is concerned with revelations of phases of metropolitan life, some tragic and some comic. They are told with the writer's usual facility in expression and in some cases, as "In a Hansom," with real power.

In *Behind the Dark Pines*, by Martha Young (Appletons), the author, while an evident imitator of Joel Chandler Harris, has struck at times a fresh note, and there is a crispness and unity about the stories that make them attractive.

Biography.— *Emerson's Journals* (4 vols.), 1838-55, edited by Edward W. Emerson and Waldo Emerson Forbes, is continued this year in the production of four volumes carrying the work from 1838 to 1855. Notwithstanding the omission of significant comment on Emerson's part on such events as the Divinity School address of 1838, or the address on "The Transcendentalist," 1842, it is hard to estimate properly the importance of this publication. It shows Emerson on sides that his works do not reveal, touches of humor that one hardly expects, in short a human side which in his case is especially valuable. The development of his interest in slavery and in communities, his views of Carlyle, Tennyson and of Thoreau, his trip to England in 1847-8, and many other phases of biographical value are to be found in a new setting.

In *Mark Twain, a Biography* (Harpers) Albert Bigelow Paine has written a remarkable biography. Personal association and careful search through Mark Twain's works have enabled the biographer to represent adequately the writer whose work lent itself so thoroughly to biographical treatment.

In *The Life and Times of Winslow Homer* (Houghton Mifflin Co.), William H. Downes has written in all probability the definitive life of that painter. After a sympathetic exposition of Homer's place in American art, he traces the course of his development from his beginning as an illustrator, through his Civil War sketches, his interpretation of negro life, and, most important, his pictures of the sea and the seafaring folk. The book is splendidly illustrated with reproductions of Homer's masterpieces.

Of unusual interest is the volume entitled *The House of Harper*, by J. Henry Harper. It is the biography of a firm rather than of an individual, but it also is to a certain extent a section of the history of our literature. Important details concerning some of the foremost authors of the last century are told in an interesting style, with a wealth of detail, and an eye for the essential that are frequently striking.

Woodrow Wilson, the Story of His Life, by William Bayard Hale (Doubleday, Page & Co.), is a clear, interesting account of Woodrow Wilson, the President-elect, written from an authoritative point of view. While the style is at times careless, the masterly way in which the author makes clear the development of Mr. Wilson's character and the progress of his fight for democracy makes the book a notable one.

The Letters of Sarah Orne Jewett, edited by Annie Fields (Houghton Mifflin Co.), is a collection of letters that are literature. Miss Jewett's interested, joyous attitude toward life is revealed in a series of comments upon books, nature and people, exquisite in expression and dictated by sound judgment and tender sympathy with whatever she came in contact. An admirable introduction is furnished by Mrs. Fields.

Personal Traits of Abraham Lincoln, by Helen Nicolay (Century

Co.), is a book which is pleasant and chatty and would give to one unacquainted with Lincoln's life a fair, if somewhat idealized picture of some phases of his career. It adds little, however, to what has already been published concerning Lincoln.

Lee, the American, by Gamaliel Bradford, Jr. (Houghton Mifflin), is a very sympathetic study of Robert E. Lee, calm and dispassionate, more concerned with painting a general portrait than with establishing a chronology. The biographer has preserved an objective attitude and has arrived at his result by means of sifting evidence from a great number of sources.

Of interest as a contrast is *Robert E. Lee, Man and Soldier*, by Thomas Nelson Page (Scribners). The treatment here is much more subjective, and consequently not so judicial, but Lee's life is treated as part of a social condition, and the biography is animated by sympathy and complete understanding.

The Life of George Cabot Lodge, by Henry Adams (Houghton Mifflin Co.), is a very sympathetic and a quite authoritative life of the poet whose untimely death cut off the promise of great achievement. The chronicle of Lodge's development is admirably treated.

The True Daniel Webster, by Sydney George Fisher (Lippincott), is told in an unpretentious, chatty style, and with an apparently thorough knowledge of Webster's life. Though a bit diffuse in places, it will undoubtedly become one of the standard lives of Webster.

Under the Old Flag, by James Harrison Wilson (Appleton), is an autobiography of an experienced soldier in the Civil War, the Spanish War and the Boxer Uprising in China. All the operations of these armies are viewed through General Wilson's eyes, and the result is a very interesting and valuable personal account.

The Promised Land, by Mary Antin (Houghton Mifflin Co.), is an interesting if somewhat too detailed account of the life of a girl of Russian-Jewish stock, both in Russia and in this country. The book is chiefly of importance as an argument for democracy and for the organization of American society.

Essays and Addresses.—*Humanly Speaking*, by Samuel McChord Crothers (Houghton Mifflin Co.), is another volume of the series which has made its author one of our foremost essayists. For keen wit, clarity of vision, surety of poise, and broad human sympathy, such essays as these are not surpassed in English or American literature to-day.

Democracy and Poetry, by Francis B. Gummere (Houghton Mifflin Co.), in the distinction of the style and the broad, non-technical attitude of the writer falls clearly within the domain of creative literature. It is a sane yet enthusiastic plea for intelligent constructive democracy.

American Addresses, by Joseph H. Choate (Century), forms the most notable collection of its kind in recent years. Here are grouped together a series of addresses delivered from 1864 to 1911, upon momentous political occasions, important educational gatherings, or other celebrations of like character. Those who have heard Mr. Choate speak will be glad to have preserved the best of the production of one of our really great orators.

Travel and Description.—In *From Constantinople to the Home of Omar Khayyam*, by A. V. Williams Jackson (Macmillan), we have combined the methods of the scholarly investigator and the entertaining narrator of travels. The result is a charming book, in which the historical and personal elements are more emphasized than the political.

Italian Castles and Country Seats, by Tryphosa Bates Batcheller (Longmans Green & Co.), is a series of letters, presenting a pleasant chatty account of social Italy, with a background of history, by one who has had large opportunities to become acquainted with her material. The illustrations are not by any means of the usual kind, but represent the more intimate side of Italian life very satisfactorily.

The Flowing Road, by Casper Whitney (Lippincott), is a valuable record of travel in South America, mainly on the Orinoco and the Rio

Negro. There is a constant spice of danger in the account of the winter's journey through a country about which even yet there is a great deal of misrepresentation.

Footprints of Famous Americans in Paris, by John Joseph Conway (John Lane), is an interesting compilation of facts concerning Franklin, Jefferson, Tom Paine, Longfellow and other famous Americans. The best sketches are those dealing with the less well known men.

A rather unusual book is *European Years, the Letters of an Idle Man*, edited by George E. Woodberry (Houghton Mifflin). Here are reprinted letters from a Bostonian, living abroad, from 1876-1905, containing not only descriptions of places, but also comments upon politics and society, which have now an historical as well as an absolute interest.

Nature Books.—*The Lure of the Garden*, by Hildegarde Hawthorne (Century Co.), bids fair to become a classic for garden lovers. The distinctive note of the work is a social one; the chapter on "Our Grandmothers' Gardens" reveals a nice feeling for the distinction between the Northern and Southern attitude toward the garden. The illustrations by Parrish and others add greatly to the charm of the book.

More philosophical is *Time and Change*, by John Burroughs (Houghton Mifflin Co.). Here the nature lover will find topics such as scientific faith, evolution, the great ice sheet of the North, the formation of the Yosemite Valley, and other themes, both abstract and concrete, treated in an attractive way. The preface contains an apology for the "hard science" discussed in the book, but the science is really not very difficult; as a matter of fact, it is a bit obvious.

Moths of the Limberlost, by Gene Stratton Porter (Doubleday, Page & Co.), is a fascinating study of moth life in that district of Indiana which the writer has made her own. In the opening chapter she draws a distinction between a nature lover and a naturalist, and it is as one of the former that she writes.

Anthologies and Literary Histories.
—*Yale Book of American Verse*, by Thomas R. Lounsbury (Yale Univ. Press). The charmingly written Introduction, "A Word about Anthologies," justifies the publication of this volume, but the specifically trained student of American literature must regretfully refuse to recommend it as a guide to what is best in our poetry. An anthology which omits all of Longfellow's sonnets, all of Field's child verse, and leaves out George Cabot Lodge altogether, dismisses itself from serious consideration as an authority.

History of American Literature, by William B. Cairns (Oxford Univ. Press), is another attempt at a history of our literature that proceeds along conventional lines and adds no fresh viewpoint.

JOURNALISM

Gerhard R. Lomer

The Pulitzer Foundation.—The School of Journalism of Columbia University, founded by the benefaction of the late Joseph Pulitzer (d. 29 Oct., 1911), proprietor of the New York *World* and the St. Louis *Post-Dispatch*, was opened in September. In an article in the *North American Review* for May, 1904, Pulitzer stated the aim of the foundation to be "to make better journalists, who will make better newspapers, which will better serve the public." In this will, dated April 16, 1904, he expressed the purpose of this gift more explicitly as "to assist in attracting to the profession [of journalism] young men of character and ability and also those already engaged in the profession to acquire the highest moral and intellectual training." To realize this ideal, Pulitzer gave to the trustees of Columbia one million dollars in 1904, and made provision for the gift of another million if at any time within seven years after his death the School shall have been in successful operation for three years.

He also arranged for three annual traveling scholarships of $1,500 each for graduates of the school. The School of Journalism will occupy eventually a special building on the University grounds, which is now in process of construction and which is expected to be ready in September, 1913. The administration of the School is vested in an advisory board consisting of Samuel Bowles, *Springfield Republican;* Nicholas Murray Butler, Columbia University; John Langdon Heaton, New York *World;* George S. Johns, St. Louis *Post-Dispatch;* Victor Freemont Lawson, *Chicago Daily Tribune;* St. Clair McKelway, *Brooklyn Eagle;* Charles Ransom Miller, New York *Times;* Edward Page Mitchell, the *Sun,* New York; Ralph Pulitzer, the New York *World;* Whitelaw Reid (chairman), New York; Melville Elijah Stone, Associated Press, New York; Charles H. Taylor, Boston *Globe;* Samuel Calvin Wells, Philadelphia *Press.* The director of the School is Talcott Williams, formerly editorial writer of the Philadelphia *Press.* There is a teaching staff of 25 members.

The course of study covers four years and leads to the degree of B. Lit. Candidates for admission must be at least 17 years of age and must present a certificate of good moral character or of honorable dismissal from some other institution. Specially qualified students are admitted to advanced standing. In 1912 the school had a grand total of 104 students, of which 59 were matriculated, 22 non-matriculated, and 23 registered in Columbia College. The distribution by years was: 61 first year; 15 second year; 14 third year; and 14 fourth year. Twenty-one states and one foreign country are represented.

The First National Newspaper Conference.—The first National Newspaper Conference in the United States, suggested by newspaper men, was held in Madison, Wis., July 29-Aug. 1, 1912, under the auspices of the Extension Division of the University of Wisconsin. The general question under consideration was: "Are newspaper and magazine writers free to tell the truth? If not, why not, and what can be done about it?"

The Conference grew out of an impromptu discussion on journalism which took place in October, 1911, at one of the meetings of the "Conference on Social and Civic Center Development" then in session in Madison. The widespread interest that has been shown in this first Newspaper Conference has led those who had charge of it to the belief that it should be permanently established as an annual convention.

The meetings were largely attended by the newspaper men of Wisconsin, but the programme included the names of journalists of national reputation. Newspapers, magazines and press agencies were all represented, and a good deal of difference of opinion was expressed in the answers which the various speakers gave to the question before the Conference, both in the formal papers and in the informal discussion.

Underlying all the discussion was the question, first, whether the Press at the present time is serving its own ends, the public good, or unseen interests; and, second, whether the Press has a definite function to perform and special duty to fulfill with regard to the education and the leadership of public opinion. Particular aspects of the problem involved, such as the following, called for separate discussion: Is the public getting all the truth to which it is entitled? Can the impartiality of the news agencies be fairly challenged? How is news service affected by the cost of the plant, by advertising, and by the non-journalistic interests of the capitalistic owner? Can the newspaper be regarded merely as a business proposition, if it is to be a factor in social amelioration? Can commercial journalism justify itself, or must there eventually be endowed or public newspapers?

The speakers also considered the necessity of some definite study of newspapers with a view to determining the relative amount of space devoted to desirable and to undesirable news. While some accused the papers of unreliability and of unjust discrimination in the publication of news, other speakers, especially those representing the better known and more conservative journals, emphasized the constant and careful effort made by the newspapers to secure and to publish the truth, and to keep continually in mind the public welfare and not any private interest.

Federal Control of Newspapers.— Legislation attached to the Post Office Appropriation bill, signed by the President Aug. 24, attempts, in the opinion of the newspapers, to establish a censorship of journalism under pretense of regulating the carriage of the mails. It is provided:

That it shall be the duty of the editor, publisher, business manager, or owners of every newspaper, magazine, periodical, or other publication to file with the Postmaster-General and the Postmaster at the office at which said publication is entered, not later than the first day of April and the first day of October of each year, on blanks furnished by the Post Office Department, a sworn statement setting forth the names and Post Office addresses of the editor and managing editor, publisher, business manager, and owners, and in addition the stockholders, if the publication be owned by a corporation, and also the names of known bondholders, mortgagees, or other security holders; and also, in the case of daily newspapers, there shall be included in such statements the average number of copies of each issue of such publication sold or distributed to paid subscribers during the preceding six months.

A copy of such sworn statement shall be published in the second issue of such newspaper, magazine, or other publication printed next after the filing of such statement. Any such publication shall be denied the privileges of the mail if it shall fail to comply with the provisions of this paragraph within ten days after notice by registered letter of such failure.

That all editorial or other reading matter published in any such newspaper, magazine or periodical for the publication of which money or other valuable consideration is paid, accepted, or promised, shall be plainly marked "advertisement." Any editor or publisher printing editorial or other reading matter for which compensation is paid, accepted, or promised, without so marking the same, shall upon conviction in any court having jurisdiction be fined not less than fifty dollars ($50) nor more than five hundred dollars ($500).

A suit to test the constitutionality of the law, endorsed by the American Newspaper Publishers' Association, was begun in New York early in October by the Journal of Commerce and Commercial Bulletin Co., publishers of the *Journal of Commerce*. Frank Hitchcock, Postmaster General, George W. Wickersham, Attorney General, Edward M. Morgan, Postmaster at New York, and Henry S. Wise, Federal District Attorney at New York, were named as defendants. It was charged in the complaint that the legislation was void, being in conflict with the First and Fifth Amendments to the Constitution of the United States, and an order was asked restraining the defendants from attempting to enforce it. The trial of the suit was expedited in every possible way. Judge Learned Hand, of the U. S. District Court at New York, on Oct. 15, sustained a demurrer filed on behalf of the Government and dismissed the petition of the complainant, granting the complainant an appeal from his order. Similar action was taken on Oct. 17 in a second suit filed by the Lewis Publishing Co., New York, publishers of the *Morning Telegraph*. The cases thus advanced to the docket of the U. S. Supreme Court, before which they were argued Dec. 2, but no decision had been announced at the end of the year. On Dec. 14, a bill amending the law was introduced in the House, which provides that newspapers shall file a statement showing the names of officers and owners, but not requiring the names of stockholders owning less than 5 per cent. of the stock. The requirements for statements of indebtedness and circulation and for the labeling as "advertisement" of paid reading matter are eliminated.

1913 LITERATURE AND LANGUAGE

AMERICAN LITERATURE
(Nov. 15, 1912, to Nov. 15, 1913)
EDWARD EVERETT HALE

Fiction.—The greatest productivity in creative literature has been as usual of works of fiction. Speaking roundly, we may say that the publication of fiction has been somewhat less than in 1912. Of the books designed to appeal to a cultivated audience, which make only a small proportion of the whole, there are about 350 by American authors. Of English novels republished in America there are about half as many. Of the best fiction the proportion is somewhat different. In almost any list of "best novels" a full half is likely to be by English authors. The following review includes only the work of American writers, with mention of a few English or Canadian authors who are practically domesticated in the United States.

The most popular forms of fiction are still the tales of adventure, mystery, or romance which became respectable from a literary standpoint some twenty-five years ago. The best examples of fiction, however, show the seriousness of interest in reality, in actual life, that was a note of the nineteenth century. It is not that there are so many "transcripts of life" or so many discussions of problems, but that so many writers even of romantic or idealistic tendency seem to be intent on particular phases of actual life or on some secret of life that lies beneath the everyday surface.

First to be named should be William D. Howells' *New Leaf Mills* (Harpers). Mr. Howells has been for years in character and achievement the chief figure in American fiction and this book shows the ripe and mature nature of one who has long known life. In it Mr. Howells goes back to the days of his youth and presents the manners and characters that he sees through the vista of half a century of experience.

Next to be noted is a set of stories dealing with the life-experience of some man or woman. In this group will be found more books that have attracted wide attention than in all other groups put together. Life-stories of women are: Ellen Glasgow's *Virginia* (Doubleday, Page & Co.), the plain but touching story of a woman of the old order who lives on into the new; Albert Edwards' *Comrade Yetta* (Macmillan), the life-experience of a Jewish girl in New York who rises from speeder in a sweat-shop to be a leader in the great social movement; Edith Wharton's *The Custom of the Country* (Scribners), a highly polished account of a sordid struggle for social success; Robert Herrick's *One Woman's Life* (Macmillan), an equally vivid account of a life of the same sort, less sordid and more probable; F. A. Kummer's *A Song of Sixpence* (Watt), still another and more sensational account of the American adventuress; Mary Johnston's *Hagar* (Houghton, Mifflin Co.), the life of a girl born in the quiet conventionality of the old South who becomes a cosmopolitan and a feminist; Daniel C. Goodman's *Hagar Revelly* (Mitchell Kennerley), ostensibly a study of why women go wrong; with others of less note. Stories of men are Mrs. Watts' *Van Cleve* (Macmillans), an almost historical study of an American and of America for the last 30 years; Coningsby Dawson's *A Garden without Walls* (Holt), a theory of life presented in so charmingly idealized and imaginative a form that one almost forgets that there is a theory in it; Henry R. Miller's *The Ambition of Mark Truitt* (Bobbs, Merrill & Co.), a very able statement of what might be the career of a modern captain of industry; Basil King's *The Way Home* (Harpers), a story of a young man which offers also an answer to one of the religious questions of the day; Nelson Lloyd's *David Malcolm* (Scribners), the development of a mountain boy into a cosmopolitan journalist; Grace Lutz's *Lo, Michael* (Lippincotts), a well-founded story, though of slight actuality, of a man who rose from the slums and recognized his responsibilities to those he had left behind. These books are very different in character and degree of excellence, but all claim attention as stories of men and women who distinctly stand for some definite thing.

Akin to these are the books which present some social group or some phase of life, not, as a rule, because anything of importance is enacted therein, but because the phase of life or group of people is significant or interesting. Such are Weir Mitchell's *Westways* (Century Co.), which has for its subject a family and a community as affected by the storm of the Civil War; Meredith Nicholson's *Otherwise Phyllis* (Houghton, Mifflin Co.), a fine picture of a typical American character against an Indiana background; Miss Cather's very beautiful study of life on the prairie farm, *Oh Pioneers!* (Houghton, Mifflin Co.); Mrs. Stratton-Porter's *Laddie* (Doubleday, Page & Co.), which gives us the feeling of the farm and the countryside; Mrs. Wiggins' *Waitstill Baxter* (Houghton, Mifflin Co.), a picture of country life in Maine; A. Mulder's *The Dominie of Harlem* (McClurg), a story full of the local color of Dutch life in Michigan; and several more. A few books deal with some single question: such is Winston Churchill's *The Inside of the Cup* (Macmillan), a most stimulating presentation of one of the most fundamental things in the religious life of to-day; such also is Miss Robins' *My Little Sister* (Dodd, Mead & Co.), a poignant presentation of the awful possibilities of one of the accepted evils of our social system. Such, too, are practically some books which are not ostensibly studies of social questions, like Miss Bryant's *Ruth Anne* (Lippincotts), a book full of life in which a love story is so soaked in social atmosphere as itself to take rather a minor place in the reader's mind, and Miss Münsterberg's *Anna Borden's Career* (Appletons), in which the social interest often conceals the satire on the woman who turns this way and that in her effort to be selfish in the altruistic modes approved by society. Of this kind, strangely enough is Jack London's *The Valley of the Moon* (Macmillan), which begins with a picture of current conditions and people trying to better them by current remedies, and continues with the author's solution of "back to the land." Also to be noted here are Francis Lynde's story of alleged politics, *The Hon. Senator Sagebrush* (Scribners), and J. M. Forman's excellent presentation of the suffrage movement in *The Opening Door* (Harpers). Some of these books are historical, like Stewart Edward White's *Gold*, a book which is meant to present not a story or a character, but the life of the fortyniner; and Mary Johnston's *Cease Firing* (Houghton, Mifflin Co.), and Thomas Dixon's *The Southerner* (Appletons), two books in which the writers seek to discern the real forces beneath the chaos and glamour of the great war, the hardships, the dangers, the romance and the idealism. Even John Fox's *The Heart of the Hills* (Scribners) differs from his earlier stories of romantic incident because he is absorbed in what is really an important phase of national life, namely, the emerging of the mountaineer. So the other mountain stories are apt to be studies of conditions rather than stories of incident, like Francis N. Greene's excellent *The Right of the Strongest* (Scribners), and in lesser measure C. N. Buck's *The Call of the Cumberland* (Watt). F. H. Spearman's *Merrilie Dawes* (Scribners) is a romantic tale enough, but belongs here because under the romance lies the especial interest in a definite phase of life, that of the stock exchange. So also Miss Marjorie Patterson's *The Dust of the*

Road (Holt) has its love story, but its real interest is as a picture, very vivid and curious, of the theatre life. Among the books, realistic or not, which are occupied with actual fact, we must put a number of novels founded on the complications of sex, as Mr. Vance's *Joan Thursday* (Little, Brown & Co.), Miss DeJeans' *The House of Thane* (Lippincotts), Upton Sinclair's *Sylvia* (Winston), and Mrs. Martin's *The Parasite* (Lippincotts). Among the books full of the spirit of social questioning many will think we should place the book which is the most notable of the year, namely, Henry S. Harrison's *V. C.'s Eyes* (Houghton, Mifflin Co.). This is undoubtedly a book of characters, manners, problems, life itself, but differs from all those mentioned above in its structural power. While others are content to detail a career, to present a phase of life, to discuss a question, Mr. Harrison has felt it better to tell a fine story and let phases of life, social questions, careers and characters show for what they will. And herein he stands almost alone, for those who wish to show us life are usually indifferent to the emotional power of story, and those who have a story to tell are generally indifferent to, or perhaps unconscious of, character and life.

The main interest of a great many of the books of the year lies in their stirring portrayal of adventurous incident, their baffling mystery, or their sentiment of romance. First to be named in this group is Rex Beach's *The Iron Trail* (Harpers). The book depicts a passing civilization, it is true, but it is read because there is something to be done of which the novelist tells us the story. There are many other of these stories of adventure in the great world. Among the best stories of the woods are H. Footner's *Jack Chanty* (Doubleday, Page & Co.), J. O. Curwood's *Isobel* (Harpers), and H. H. Knibb's *Stephen March's Way* (Houghton, Mifflin Co.). The great West has its stories of adventure, A. M. Chisolm's *Precious Waters* (Doubleday, Page & Co.), Zane Grey's *Desert Gold* (Harpers), Ridgewell Cullom's *Night Riders* (Jacobs), and many more.

Indeed, there are stories of romance and adventure over the whole world, from T. E. Harre's *The Eternal Maiden* (Kennerley), a story of the Esquimaux, to Rowland Thomas's tropical *Fatima* (Little, Brown & Co.). The East arouses many imaginations, as, for example, in Mr. Isham's *An Aladdin from Broadway* (Bobbs, Merrill & Co.), Mason and Hilliard's *The Bear's Claws* (McClurg), Harold MacGrath's *Parrot & Co.* (Bobbs, Merrill & Co.), and others. There seem to be no real Zenda stories this year, though G. B. McCutcheon's *A Fool and his Money* (Dodd, Mead & Co.) comes somewhere near them. Here belong some of the historical novels. Most of these are Civil War stories; some are serious studies on a large scale and have been already mentioned. John Luther Long's *War* (Bobbs, Merrill & Co.) is in the beginning a most attractive picture of the life of a quiet Maryland farm in war time, but later becomes more a story of intrigue and adventure. Others are more frankly stories of incident and excitement, like Miss Lincoln's *The Lost Despatch* (Appletons), and Chittenden Marriott's *Sally Castleton, Southerner* (Lippincotts). Apart from Civil War stories there are few pieces of historical fiction to be noted, Canon Brady's *The Fetters of Freedom* (Dodd, Mead & Co.) and Miss Kingsley's *Veronica* (Appletons) being most worthy of remark. There have been as usual a large number of detective stories, some of which have given a new turn to familiar motives. Mrs. Rinehart's *The Case of Jennie Brice* (Bobbs, Merrill & Co.) and Miss Bunker's *Diamond Cut Diamond* (Bobbs, Merrill & Co.) are good examples of the author's ingenious craft. Burton Stevenson's *The Gloved Hand* (Dodd, Mead & Co.) has some new elements, but is not so strong as the stories which gave him his reputation. H. K. Webster's *The Ghost Girl* (Appletons) and Maximilian Foster's *The Whistling Man* (Appletons) are ingenious, but do not seem to call for additional remark. *The Bishop's Purse*, however, by Oliver Herford and Cleveland Moffett, is noteworthy. It is confusing in its multiplicity of action, but the presentation of character is on a far higher plane than is common in detective stories. *November Joe*, by Hesketh Pritchard (Houghton, Mifflin Co.), is an ingenious attempt to translate a detective story into terms of the great outdoors. But though ingenious in conceiving the detective of the woods, the author had but slight ability to give an idea of the medium in which he worked. The feeling for nature in the book is slight. Owen Johnson in *The Sixty-first Second* (Stokes) has not been more fortunate in his combination of detective story and society novel. He is so absorbed in portraying his social *milieu* that he does not keep alive any interest in the solution of his mystery. Arthur Stringer's *The Shadow* (Century) is perhaps not to be called a detective story. It is the tale of a world hunt after a criminal and good after its kind. Of the stories of social life not otherwise mentioned the chief would be Robert Chambers' *The Business of Life* (Appletons), in which the author ballasts his fashionable story of club and country-house with a definite idea on one of the aspects of the social life of to-day, and Booth Tarkington's *The Flirt*, a picture of a violent though somewhat conventional flirt against a background of some Middle West metropolis.

Such a division of the fiction of the day indicates only two great impulses and therefore must omit a number of books of value. Such are Mrs. Burnett's *T. Tembarom* (Century Co.), which we might call a good old-fashioned story of a lost heir, told with unfailing spirit, sympathy and invention; H. E. Rives's *The Valiants of Virginia* (Bobbs, Merrill & Co.), a story of a very modern man in ideally characteristic surroundings of the Old South; and Stephen Whitman's *The Isle of Life* (Scribners), a wildly romantic story of lurid cast, but of a good deal of skill in handling. Miss Eleanor Abbott's *The White Linen Nurse* (Century Co.) is a whimsical but most attractive love story, as full of feeling for life as though it were an absolute "transcript." Still unclassified are G. R. Chester's Wallingford stories, of which two have appeared during the year. Critics have striven to find in these extravaganzas a presentation of a specifically American phase of life, but one hardly likes to import such an element of seriousness into such amusing creations. There have been a number of pure extravaganzas: Emerson Hough's *The Lady and the Pirate* (Bobbs, Merrill & Co.) is not without a true feeling for the beauty of romance; L. J. Vance's *The Day of Days* (Little, Brown & Co.) is something that makes one feel as though it must be fact, though we know absolutely that it must be the wildest fiction; Miss N. W. Putnam's *The Impossible Boy* (Bobbs, Merrill & Co.) is a very attractive imagination of the road and the town. There are, finally, a number of books that come very near extravagance, humorous sketches like J. C. Lincoln's *Captain Pratt's Patients* (Appletons), Mrs. Greene's *Everbreeze* (Appletons), Irving Bacheller's *The Taming of Griggsby* (Harpers), all practically continuations of well established favorites.

Short Stories.—The short stories collected into permanent form are an almost infinitely small part of the vast number written. It would be useless, therefore, to try to gather from the few that do so appear anything significant in regard to tendencies or influences. One of the best collections is Mrs. Josephine Daskam Bacon's *The Strange Cases of Dr. Stanchon* (Appletons). Mrs. Bacon has, perhaps, not made the character of the great alienist a perfectly definite and enduring figure, but the stories are extremely good. Miss E. Singmaster's *Gettysburg* (Houghton, Mifflin Co.) contains as fine examples of the short story as will be seen. These stories of Gettysburg in the war and in later years offer in a few pages an extraordinarily wide gamut of passion and emotion. Thomas Nelson Page's *The Land of the Spirit* (Scribners) is more significant in its idea than in its execution; these stories are good specimens of Mr. Page's work, though they do not really do much to reveal the "deepening note of thought and feeling" which the author sees in American life. Miss Alice Brown is well known as a member of the group of New England story-tellers and her

Vanishing Points (Macmillan) is a good example of the fine observation and delicate expression which is common to them. Another collection of much the same sort but with rather more pulse of life is Anna Nicholas' *The Making of Thomas B a r t o n* (Bobbs, Merrill & Co.). These tales of everyday life in Indiana and elsewhere have a great charm. Anne Douglas Sedgewick's work is well known; in *The Nest* (Scribners) she has grouped some of her later work with some of her earliest in a volume as remarkable for its observation as for its cleverness of statement. The "quiet" stories, as we may call them, are chiefly by women. More uproarious are the men's stories. Jack London's *Night Born* (Century Co.) is as vital and bloody as most of his work, and as interesting. C. E. Mulford in *The Coming of Cassidy* (McClurg) gives more typical cowboy stories of the heroes of Bar-20. Ralph D. Paine's *Captain O'Shea* (Scribners) is a collection of original and exciting stories, with a good central figure of the modern adventurer. *Murder in Any Degree* by Owen Johnson (Century Co.) is characteristic of the author's new manner, smart and striking, and yet very different from his transcripts of school and college life. Mr. J o h n s o n seems hardly well enough settled in his new field for his work to have really fine quality. Of detective stories, A. B. Reeves' *The Poisoned Pen* (Dodd, Mead & Co.) contains a record of the work of Craig Kennedy, the inventor of the application of the methods and discoveries of physical science to the detection of crime. Mrs. Green's *Masterpieces of Mystery* (Dodd, Mead & Co.) is more old-fashioned, as one may say; less modern, but with more mystery. These are her first short stories in a field where she has long been a conspicuous figure. In *Blister Jones* (Bobbs, Merrill & Co.) John T. Foote gives much of the feeling of the world of the racing circuit. The book gives an excellent notion of the good and bad in a life that gives both good and bad in a man plenty of chance. Charles G. D. Roberts' *The Feet of the Furtive* (Macmillan) is a collection of his well-known animal tales, full of the tragedy of the forest.

Biography. — Next to fiction the most striking department of literature during the year is undoubtedly biography. This is characteristic of a year in which the chief novels have been more biographies than anything else. The most striking book in this division, both by subject and by treatment, is the *Autobiography* of Theodore Roosevelt (Macmillan). Few men of our day have had more varied and interesting experience, and of these none has had the gift of incisive style that makes this book so effective. There is nothing like it for an idea of the American in action. Next to it should be placed the *Reminiscences of Augustus Saint Gaudens* (Century), not a formal autobiography, but nevertheless a fine record of the life of the greatest American artist of our time, one who did most to give the American spirit a beautiful and enduring form. In *A Small Boy and Others* (Scribners) Henry James gives an account of his boyhood in New York and London. In style it will not disappoint the lovers of James at a much later period; in substance it is a very interesting combination, namely, Henry James and his environment, both American and English. John Muir's *The Story of My Boyhood and Youth* (Houghton, Mifflin Co.) is an interesting account of his early days in Wisconsin. Mrs. Amelia E. Barr's *All the Days of My Life* (Appletons) is a remarkable record of one widely, but not well known, but whose life is worth knowing. The book gives a simple and vivid picture of a rich and varied life. Few that we know give a better example of reverence and faith and of untiring patience and energy. Jack London's *John Barleycorn* (Century) might be called a special autobiography; it is an account of Jack London's life as a drinking man. To men who drink or have drunk it will be as curious a statement of experience as they have ever read. To those who do not drink it will be as forcible a piece of evidence as they have ever had. Its literary value would seem to come from its author's ability to ₩write with extraordinary frankness. T h e *Autobiography of George Dewey, Admiral of the Navy* (Scribners) is an important story told in plain, clear style. It presents not only the very notable public services of Admiral Dewey, but in its record of his life gives us a valuable view of the American navy for half a century. *Retrospections* by Hubert Howe Bancroft (Bancroft Co.) is a most interesting view of a remarkable man. The most undeniable value is in his account of the gathering of the material and the writing of his historical works. As to his view of the history of his own time there will be great difference of opinion. The fourth and fifth volumes of John Bigelow's *Retrospections of an Active Life* (Doubleday, Page & Co.) continue one of the valuable records of the nineteenth century. The latest volumes go no farther than 1879, but they offer an admirable means of gaining some of the tone and color of the years immediately following the Civil War. Few works of the kind give us so much fact and gossip with so little prejudice or ill feeling. *The Life and Letters of Charles Eliot Norton* (Houghton, Mifflin Co.) begins the record of a life which was of the greatest influence in the history of culture in America. These volumes give us an intimate view of Norton's relations with the chief literary men of America. More significant, perhaps, are the letters to literary men of England which give us even a higher idea of Norton's character than we might otherwise have had. The *Letters and Recollections of Alexander Agassiz* (Houghton, Mifflin Co.) presents a good idea of a career that will be more interesting to most readers than that of the author's famous father. Mr. Agassiz was not so great a teacher as Louis Agassiz, but he was remarkable as an investigator. William Winter's *The Wallet of Time* (Moffat, Yard & Co.) is a survey of the American stage for half a century by the man best qualified to write it. Doubtless many will not agree with his ideas, but it is impossible to deny the great value of such a view. The *Life and Letters of Gen. G. G. Meade* (Scribners), edited by his son and grandson, is very timely in this year of Gettysburg. The most valuable feature is the long series of letters to his wife, giving account of daily doings and opinions of the men of his time. Frederic Bancroft has edited the *Letters, Speeches and Correspondence of Carl Schurz* (Putnams) in a collection which gives abundant material and leaves the man to speak for himself. It reveals the amiable private character and gives a good idea of the fine public life of one who was typical of the best American life of his time. Mrs. De Koven's *Life and Letters of John Paul Jones* (Scribners) is a thorough and painstaking study of an important life, able and sympathetic, if not always with the strictly critical spirit of the historian. John Jay Chapman's *William Lloyd Garrison* (Moffat, Yard & Co) is as brilliant a piece of biographic work as any of the year. Written absolutely from the Garrisonian standpoint, it is a very telling presentation of the value of Garrison's life. *A Sunny Life: Samuel June Barrows*, by Isabel C. Barrows (Little, Brown & Co.), records a life useful, influential and fine, besides being sunny. Mary E. Phillips's *James Fenimore Cooper* (Lane) is a book which has long been needed. It gathers contemporary material of great value both in word and picture. As a personal record it will probably never be superseded. Alexander Irvine's *My Lady of the Chimney Corner* (Century Co.) is a charming account of his mother as he remembers her in the early days in Ireland. It is written more as though a bit of fiction than in the conventional form of biography and is all the more interesting therefor. Miss Helen A. Clarke's *Browning and his Century* (Doubleday, Page & Co.) is not exactly a biography, nor a criticism, but a study of the relation of Browning to the great forces of his age, by one who has long studied the poet and his work.

Poetry and Drama. — In poetry much has been written that is charming and beautiful without being great. The award of the Nobel prize to Rabindranath Tagore, the great popular approval of Rudyard Kipling shown by a vote of 22,000 out of 40,000 taken recently in England by a popular weekly, the devoted appreciation of the Countess de Noailles in France, lead us to ask whom Americans can think of in the same way.

1913 LITERATURE AND LANGUAGE

We do not find among the newer voices any that satisfy such a desire. Mr. Moody and Mr. Lodge are not yet eclipsed. Earlier singers like James Whitcomb Riley and Josephine Preston Peabody, though they have published no poems during the year, are not outsung. Of those familiar to us George E. Woodberry (Merrymount Press) publishes three poems full of the vitality of a vision that sees through the chaos of the contending moment. Madison Cawein in *The Republic* (Stewart & Kidd) expresses his old feeling for nature in new forms, some of them of his very best. Clinton Scollard in *Lyrics from a Library* (George William Browning) reminds older readers of a time when *vers de société* was more popular than now. His latest work adds to his earlier reputation for clever brilliancy a ripened tenderness that comes with years. Bliss Carman's *Echoes from Vagabondia* (Small, Maynard & Co.) are really echoes of the earlier voice which made the poet well known. There are some whose work appears for the first time in book form. Mr. Benét's *Merchants from Cathay* (Century Co.) is a volume of poems well indicated by the name, for his imagination wanders in the strange exotic lands of romance, though his verse is willing to bind itself by the ordinary laws of present poetry. Mrs. C. R. Robinson, on the other hand, in *The Call of Brotherhood* (Scribners), keeps close at home, her work being distinguished by evident sincerity and deep feeling. Miss Fanny Stearns Davis is still different. In *Myself and I* (Macmillan) she shows a sentiment of poetic intuition, a feeling for the significant in a world of beautiful phenomena that is most individual. Kenneth Rand in *The Dirge of the Sea* (Sherman, French & Co.) has felt the call to wander over the road and across the wave and has the gift to make us feel it. If we did not confine our view to collected poetry, we should mention much more. In the drama we have relatively, at least, more action of imagination, though very little of it appears in book form. Josephine Preston Peabody's *The Wolf of Gubbio* is a dramatic rendering of one of the legends of St. Francis. The wolf is a real wolf which has stolen a child, but is led by the saint to bring him back. It is a subject well fitted for the delicate and imaginative work of the poet. George Middleton's *Tradition* (Holt), on the other hand, is a collection of one-act plays of contemporary life. The plays are passionate crises in life, generally arising from the power of tradition in convention. They are quite as strong as *Embers*, by which Mr. Middleton first became known to lovers of literature.

Essays and Criticism.—Among the books which might be variously classified as essays or criticism the most important is Paul Elmer More's *The Drift of Idealism* (Houghton, Mifflin Co.). This volume has the qualities of learning and judgment which have become familiar through the earlier volumes of the "Shelburne Essays," but in this case the studies are carefully planned to present a single topic, namely, Romanticism, something in which it need hardly be said Mr. More wholly disbelieves. Neither does Irving Babbitt, whose *Masters of Criticism* (Houghton, Mifflin Co.) is an excellent presentation of the chief French critics of the 19th century. It is chiefly valuable, however, because of the author's own critical view, which is strongly anti-romantic, and presents the author as a judicial critic of superior training and power. Max Eastman's *The Enjoyment of Poetry* (Scribners) is another good piece of criticism, a book full of perceptive appreciation, discrimination, which is meant to give and does give, not an analysis of a psychologic state, but an incentive to artistic pleasure. A contrast with the foregoing books is Gerald Stanley Lee's *Crowds* (Doubleday, Page & Co.), a study of the world in general, or more particularly of democracy, in the now familiar manner of its author. Hamilton Mabie's *American Ideals* (Macmillan) is a series of lectures on America delivered before Japanese audiences. The nature of the occasion called for a certain simplicity, but it allowed many general views and summaries which make the book rather an unusual review and history of American culture. Oscar Straus's *The American Spirit* (Century Co.) is not a connected treatment, but a collection of articles and addresses by a man who has great gifts of ability and character and great opportunity to use them. Mr. Straus is a public man of the highest type; the present volume deals with a variety of topics which his broad experience has given him a chance to study. Helen Keller's *Out of the Dark* (Doubleday, Page & Co.) contains the author's thoughts on the position of woman and her education, the possibility of preventing blindness and of educating those whose blindness has not been prevented. Theodore Roosevelt's *History as Literature and Other Essays* (Scribners) includes four noteworthy utterances, the author's addresses at the Sorbonne and before the University of Berlin, the University of Oxford, and the American Historical Association, as well as a number of articles that have appeared in periodicals. It need not be said that the author by no means shows himself the scholar of the university. Rather is he the scholar who has learned to know the world, who returns with information for his whilom brethren. We may add note of a few works more specifically critical. The current interest in the drama takes form not only in creative work, but in such studies as Charlton Andrews' *The Drama of To-day* (Lippincotts) an excellent general view; Archibald Henderson's *European Dramatists* (Stewart & Kidd), a book showing wide reading and excellent judgment; C. Weygandt's *Irish Plays and Players* (Houghton, Mifflin Co.), a careful study of a timely subject; Elizabeth R. Hunt's *The Play of To-Day* (Lane), a theoretical book very practically illustrated; and Brander Matthews' *Shakespeare as a Playwright* (Scribners), which gives a view of this topic at once scholarly and practical.

Travel and Description.—There have been fewer notable books of travel than usual. Mr. Howells' *Familiar Spanish Travels* (Harpers) has not merely the observation of an interesting phase of life as seen through an interesting temperament, which one always finds in Mr. Howells, but also much of the matured wisdom which comes of living in a large way. Stewart Edward White's *African Camp Fires* (Doubleday, Page & Co.) is more than a mere record of travel. His narration of fact has much of the charm of his fiction, not that his imagination alters conditions, but that he imparts an element of humanity into whatever interests him. Somewhat like it, but really very different is Arley Munson's *Jungle Days* (Appletons), an account of the experiences of an American missionary doctor in India. Most interesting of all in topic is Belmore Browne's *Conquest of Mount McKinley* (Putnams), though the book is really much more than an account of a great achievement, because it gives so much of the human temper which made the achievement at once difficult and possible. Another book of the great Northwest is Stanley Washburne's *Trails, Trappers and Tenderfeet* in western Canada (Holt), a well written and illustrated account, full of the spirit of muskeg and mountain.

MODERN LANGUAGES AND LITERATURE

GERMANIC LANGUAGES

DANIEL B. SHUMWAY

German Fiction and Drama.—The chief interest of the year in this field has centered around the translation of Gerhard Hauptmann's novel, *Atlantis*, which appeared toward the close of 1912. It was the subject of many reviews, and gave rise to investigations concerning the events described. Thus Rudolf Tombo, Jr., in *Modern Language Notes* for January, traces some of the scenes to the author's experiences in America. In the same number Professor Tombo discusses the identity of the *Hassenpflugs* in Hauptmann's earlier novel, *The Fool in Christ*, and tries to prove that they were modeled on the brothers Heinrich and Julius Hart, who played an important rôle in the literary revolution of the early nineties. Hauptmann's grotesque festival play, written in the style of an old puppet play, with strong resemblances to Goethe's *Faust*, has been the subject of an animated discussion because of its being prohibited by the German Crown Prince after a few performances in

Breslau. An account of it will be found in the *Outlook* for July and in *Current Opinion* for August. The January number of the latter magazine also has an article on Hauptmann as the greatest German playwright since Goethe. Hauptmann's dramas have appeared in translation in two volumes by Ludwig Lewissohn. Excerpts from C. Rössler's *Five Frankforters*, an admirable play dealing with the Rothchilds, are given in *Hearst's Magazine* for Sept., 1913. Ernst Hardt's beautiful verse drama, *Tristan and the Jester*, has been translated by John Heard, Jr.; and *Professor Bernhardi*, an amusing comedy of the Austrian dramatist Arthur Schnitzler, has been translated and adapted by Mrs. Emil Pohl. The relation of another Austrian dramatist, Hoffmannsthal, to Greek tragedy in his tragedies *Electra* and *Œdipus*, has been ably discussed by George W. Baker in the *Journal of English and German Philology* (XII, 383-406). The dramatic art of Max Halbe is treated by Charles Norris in *Modern Language Notes* for June. Most interesting are the articles of A. von Ende upon German drama, in the *Nation* of Jan. 2 and July 17. The author discusses Hauptmann's *Gabriel Schilling's Flucht*, Fulda's latest drama, *Der Seeräuber*, a romantic comedy in verse, Carl Hauptmann's play, *Die lange Jule*, and a number of other playwrights and their plays.

In the field of the novel the most noteworthy publications are *Similde Hegewalt*, a character study by Beyerlein, the author of *Jena und Sedan*, and a novel by Clara Viebig, translated under the title *Son of his Mother* by H. Raahauge. Hauff's *Caravan Tales* have been freely adapted and retold by J. G. Hanstein. W. W. Florer has an interesting note on Gustav Frenssen in *Modern Language Notes* for May, reviewing Elster's life of Frenssen and illustrating it with data supplied by Frenssen himself in a letter to Florer. Two valuable bibliographies have been published, one by Rudolf Tombo, Jr., on recent German fiction, in *Modern Language Notes* for April, another on important German dramas since 1871 in the New York *Times*' "Review of Books" of Feb. 16. A well written article by Dorothea Gerard, on *Recent German Fiction* in *The Nineteenth Century* for Sept, 1913, deals with the latest novels of Baroness von Heyking (*Ille Mihi*), of Walter Bloem (*Volk wider Volk*) and of Alfons Paquet (*Kamerad Flemming*).

Among the classical writers Goethe, as usual, holds the center of interest. Günther Jacoby, who made an interesting attempt a few years ago to prove that Herder served as the model for *Faust*, examines in the *Journal of English and German Philology* (XII, 1-19) Burdach's argument to prove that *Faust* was modeled on Moses and concludes that not the living but the dying *Faust* shows traits taken from Moses and to a greater extent than Burdach suspects. G. Schaafs discusses (*ibid.*, 20-31) a few "Faust Paralipomena," and W. Page Andrews has added another to the long list of *Faust* commentaries by a work entitled *Goethe's Key to Faust, a Scientific Basis for Religion and Morality*. Goethe's autobiography has been retranslated by Minnie S. Smith as *Poetry and Truth of my Own Life* for Bohn's Popular Library. P. H. Brown has published a volume on the *Youth of Goethe*. A. Baumgarten has issued a life of Goethe in German (*Goethe, sein Leben und seine Werke*). Hamilton Mabie discusses the attitude of the twentieth century toward Goethe in the *Outlook*, Sept. 27, 1913, under the caption, *The Young Goethe*. The sources of two of Goethe's poems, *Das Blutlied* and *Mignon*, are investigated by G. Schaaf in *Modern Language Notes* for February and March.

W. C. Hilmer has published a book on *Rime in Schiller's Poems*, and C. M. Newport, of the University of Wisconsin, has written on *Woman in the Thought and Work of Hebbel*. Francis W. Kracher has discussed Lessing's theory of pity in *Modern Language Notes* for May, showing that it differed from Aristotle's and still has a value for our times.

German Philology.—In this field, which includes the literature of the older periods, E. Classen has discussed *Vowel Alliteration in the Old Germanic Languages* (Longmans). A *Wörterbuch und Reimverzeichnis zu* dem *Armen Heinrich von Hartmann von Aue*, by Guido C. Riemer, has appeared as Number 3 of the "Hesperia Series." As Number 4, B. Q. Morgan discusses *Nature in the Middle High German Lyrics*. Myrtle M. Mann treats of "*Die Frauen und die Frauenverehrung in der Höfischen Epik nach Gottfried von Strassburg*" in the *Journal of English and German Philology* (XII, 355-387). W. F. Luebke investigates the "Language of Berthold von Chiemsee" in his *Tewtsche Theologcy* of 1528, in *Modern Philology* (X, 207-263). Arthur T. J. Remy treats of the "Origin of the Tannhäuser Legend" in the *Journal of English and German Philology* (XII, 32-77), showing that it is a combination of a Celtic myth and a Christian legend which has been developed in Germany. The *Nibelungenlied* has again been translated, this time by Arthur S. Way under the title *Lay of the Nibelung Men* (Putnam). Jessie L. Weston's admirable translation of *Parzival* has been reprinted from the edition of 1884.

German Texts and Teaching.—There has been as usual considerable activity in the production of school texts, but only two editions of important dramas can be mentioned here. They are both by Grillparzer, the one *Libussa*, edited with an introduction by G. O. Curme (Oxford), the other *Des Meeres und der Liebe Wellen* by Martin Schütze (Heath).

In pedagogy Charles H. Handschin has published an extensive treatise on the "Teaching of Modern Languages in the United States" as Bulletin 3 of the *U. S. Educational Bureau*. The importance of phonetics in teaching German is pointed out by E. Prokosch in the *Transactions* of the National Education Association for 1912 (p. 733). C. A. Krause discusses the "Trend of Modern Language Instruction in the United States" in the *Educational Review* for March, and M. D. Learned advocates the introduction of German into the grade schools in the *German-American Annals* for January-April.

German-American Relations.—This ever-growing field is represented by a number of interesting works and articles. Preston A. Barba continues his study of Friedrich A. Strubberg's life and novels in the *German-American Annals* for May and contributes an article on the "American Indians in German Fiction" to the same number. Charles Brede also continues his studies of "German Drama on the Philadelphia Stage" by treating the period from 1812 to 1815 (*ibid.*). W. Scholl shows the influence of Schiller's "*Lied von der Glocke*" on Longfellow's "Building of the Ship" and other poems, in *Modern Language Notes* for February. Otto Lohr has written on the *German Element of New Netherland* (Stechert), and O. Lohan on *Das Deutschtum in den Vereinigten Staaten von Amerika* (Steiger). Adolf Rambeau has published studies on the culture of this country under the title *Aus und über Amerika* (Stechert). *Deutsch-Amerikanische Gedichte* is the title of a volume of verse by M. Raible.

Swedish.—The interest in Strindberg is still well sustained. Edith and Warner Oland have continued their translations of his plays by issuing *Comrades, Facing Death* and *Easter. The Confessions of a Fool* has been translated by Ellie Schleussner, *Lucky Peter* by Velma S. Howard, *On the Seaboard* by Elizabeth C. Westergren, *Son of a Servant, The Inferno, Zones of the Spirit* by Clarence Field, and *Married*, twenty stories of married life, by Ellie Schleussner. Estimates of Strindberg and his works will be found in the *Nation* for July 17, in the *Living Age* for Feb. 22 and in the *Dial* for Jan. 16. A Swedish life of the Swedish essayist Ellen Key by Nyström-Hamilton has been translated by Anna Fries, with an introduction by Havelock Ellis. It is rather unfavorably reviewed in the *Varien* of Sept. 11, 1913. Ellen Key's essay on Rahel Varnhagen, the most brilliant of the coterie of literary Jewesses of Berlin in the early nineteenth century, has been translated by A. G. Chater, with an introduction by Havelock Ellis. Gustaf Janson's *Lognerna* has been done into English under the title *Pride of Man*. An estimate of the novels of Selma Lagerlöf will be found in *Living Age* for May.

Norwegian.—This language is represented mainly by the plays of Björnsen and Ibsen. Thus Ed. Björkman has translated *The Gauntlet, Beyond Our Power*, and *The New System;* and three comedies have been rendered by R. F. Sharp, all by Björnsen. Ibsen's drama *The Warrior's Mound* and its relation to the author's romantic tales are discussed by A. M. Sturtevant. His lyrics and *Brand* have been translated by F. E. Garrett. Indridi Einarsson's five-act drama *Sword and Crozier* has been added to the list of the "Poet Lore" plays by Lee M. Hollander. *Norse Fairy Tales* have been rendered and edited by Geo. N. Dasent (Lippincotts). Recent Scandinavian books are discussed by A. Kildal in the *Nation* of April 3.

In the field of Old Norse W. A. Craigie has prepared a volume of *Icelandic Sagas* for the "Cambridge Manuals of Science and Literature" (Putnams). A. LeRoy Andrews has continued his studies in the *Old Norse Sagas* in *Modern Philology* for April. K. A. Mortensen's *Handbook of Norse Mythology* has been translated from the Danish by A. C. Crowell. Prof. Geo. T. Flom has contributed "Semiasological Notes on Old Scandinavian Flík" in the *Journal of English and German Philology* (XII, 78-92). J. A. Holvik has published a *Second Book of Norse Literary Selections*.

Danish.—In this field we greet with great satisfaction the revival of the plays of Ludwig Holberg, the famous Danish dramatist of the early eighteenth century, who influenced among others the youthful Lessing. Three of his comedies have been translated by H. W. L. Hime under the titles, *Henry and Pernille, Captain Bombastis Thunderton*, and *Scatterbrain*.

ROMANCE LANGUAGES AND LITERATURE

BENJAMIN P. BOURLAND

The scientific activity of American scholars in the Romance languages has of late years been devoted principally to French and Spanish. Investigation in these fields has continued keen in 1913, while it may be put down as the capital event of the year, that Italian has received in large measure the attention it deserves. Aside from a number of smaller pieces of research, we note the publication in the field of Italian literature of three important books: Professor McKenzie's *Concordance to Petrarch;* Professors Rand and Wilkins' *Concordance to the Latin Works of Dante*, and the volume of the *Paradiso*, which completes Professor Grandgent's edition of the *Divina Commedia*. In French, the study of the mediæval epos has flourished as usual, and Professor Borgerhoff, in another line, has made an important contribution to the history of the relations of English and French literature in the eighteenth century. In Spanish, Miss Bushee's discerning and reprinting of the *Sucesos of Mateo Alemán* is a telling contribution to the history of prose fiction. Dr. Bacon's study of Juan Pérez de Montalván and Professor Lancaster's book on Pierre du Ryer both claim the attention of students of the theatre, as will Miss Smith's work on the *commedia dell' arte*.

In the world field there is no great change to set down. The most important publication is the rapid appearance of Professor Meyer-Lübke's *Romanisches Etymologisches Wörterbuch*, whereof the half already issued proves that when it is done, it will supersede all predecessors.

Necrology.—Gustav Koerting died at Kiel on Feb. 3 at the age of 67. He was one of the most widely known of Romance scholars and had devoted most of his energy to the encyclopædia of his subject. He edited the *Französische Studien*, founded, with the late Professor Koschwitz, the *Zeitschrift für Französische Sprache und Literatur;* published a *Handbuch der romanischen Philologie;* and was best known for his *Lateinisch-Romanisches Wörterbuch*, which though open to severe criticism, and always severely criticized, has been for twenty years an indispensable companion to every Romance philologist. Carl Wahlund, honorary professor in the University of Upsala, died on April 23 at the same age. He was the author of many studies, mostly in French Literature, and the collector of a fine library, which before his death he gave to the University of Upsala. Among his works are editions with Hugo von Feilitzen, of

the *Enfances Vivien;* and of the French prose version of the *Voyage of St. Brendan.*
Arturo Graf, professor in the University of Turin, died in the last week of April. He was born in Athens in 1848, and was one of the most widely known scholars of the world in the folklore of the Middle Ages. His best known works are *Miti, Leggende e Superstizioni del Medio Evo; Attraverso il Cinquecento.* Count Angelo de Gubernatis died in Rome on Feb. 26. He was born at Turin in 1840, was professor, first, in Florence at the Istituto di Studi Superiori, since 1891 in the University of Rome. Among his very numerous works we note the *Storia Universale della Letteratura,* and a series of volumes on mythology.

BIBLIOGRAPHY

ADAMS, Edward L.—"Word Formation in Provençal." (*University of Michigan Studies,* Humanistic Series, II, New York, 1913.)
BABBITT, Irving.—*The Masters of Modern French Criticism.* (London, Boston and New York, 1913.)
BACON, George W.—"The Life and Dramatic Works of Doctor Juan Pérez de Montalván." (*Revue Hispanique,* XXVI, 69-70.)—A full and new treatment of the *Life,* with an exhaustive analysis of each one of the plays.
BOOKER, John M.—"The French Inchoativ Suffix *-iss* and the French *ir* Conjugation in Middle English." (*Studies in Philology of the University of North Carolina,* IX.)
BORGERHOFF, Joseph L. — *Le Théâtre Anglais à Paris sous la Restauration.* (Paris, 1912.)
BORLAND, Lois.—"Montgomerie and the French Poets of the Early Sixteenth Century." (*Modern Philology,* XI, 1.)
BURNAM, J. M.—*An Old Portuguese Version of the Rule of Benedict.* (Cincinnati, 1912.)
CRANE, T. F.—"New Analogues of Old Tales." (*Modern Philology,* XI, 3.)
CRAWFORD, J. P. Wickersham.—"Suárez de Figueroa's *España Defendida* and Tasso's *Gerusalemme Liberata.*" (*Romanic Review,* IV, 2.)
——"The Seven Liberal Arts in the *Vision Delectable* of Alfonso de la Torre." (*Ibid.,* IV, 1.)
——The "Vision Delectable" of Alfonso de la Torre and Maimonides' "Guide of the Perplexed." (*Publications Modern Language Association of America,* XXVIII, 2.)
CRITCHLOW, F. L.—*The Arthurian Kingship in Chrétien de Troyes.* (Princeton University Press, 1912.)
CROSS, Tom Peete.—"Notes on the Chastity-testing Horn and Mantle." (*Modern Philology,* X, 3.)
ESPINOSA, A. M.—"Cuentitos populares nuevo-mejicanos y su transcripción fonética." (*Bulletin de Dialectologie Romane,* IV, 4.)
——"Old Spanish *fueras.*" (*Romanic Review,* IV, 2.)
FAY, Percival B.—*Elliptical Partitive Usage in Affirmative Clauses in French Prose of the Fifteenth and Sixteenth Centuries.* (Paris, 1912.)
FLETCHER, J. B.—"The Allegory of the *Vita Nuova.*" (*Modern Philology,* XI, 1.)
FORTIER, Alcée.—"Casimir Delavigne *Intime.*" (*Publications Modern Language Association of America,* XXVIII, 2.)
GERIG, John L.—"Barthélemy Aneau, a Study in Humanism." (*Romanic Review,* IV, 1.)
HAMILTON, George L.—"Sources of the Symbolical Lay Communion." (*Romanic Review,* IV, 2.)
HENDERSON, E. F.—*Symbol and Satire in the French Revolution.* (New York, 1912.)
HIBBARD, Laura.—"The Sword Bridge of Chrétien de Troyes and its Celtic Original." (*Romanic Review,* IV, 2.)
JENKINS, T. Atkinson.—"French Etymologies." (*Modern Philology,* X, 4.)
KINNEY, Muriel.—"Notes on the Geography of Huon de Bordeaux." (*Romanic Review,* IV, 1.)
LANCASTER, H. C.—*Pierre du Ryer, Dramatist.* (Washington, D. C., Carnegie Institution.)
——"Pierre du Ryer Écrivain dramatique." (*Revue d'histoire littéraire de la France,* XX, 2.)
LANG, H. R.—"A Passage in the *Danza de la Muerte.*" (*Romanic Review,* III, 4.)
——"Old Portuguese *Brou.*" (*Ibid.*)
LANGLEY, Ernest F.—"The Extant Repertory of the Early Sicilian Poets." (*Publication Modern Language Association of America,* XXVIII, 3.)
LIVINGSTON, Arthur.—"Concerning an Aspect of Concettismo." (*Modern Language Review,* Cambridge, England, VIII, 3.)
——*Sebastiano Rossi, imitatore e plagiario di Gian Francesco Busenello.* (Venezia, C. Ferrari, 1912.)
——*La Vita Veneziana nelle opere di Gian Francesco Busenello.* (Venezia, V. Callegari, 1913.)
——"The Jocose Testament of G. Contarini and a Group of Venetian Revellers of the Seicento." (*Romanic Review,* III, 4.)
LUQUIENS, Frederick B.—"The Reconstruction of the original *Chanson de Roland.*" (*Romanic Review,* IV, 1.)
MACKENZIE, Kenneth.—*Concordanza delle Rime di Francesco Petrarca.* (Oxford, Clarendon Press, 1912.)
MASON, J. F.—*The Melodrama in France from the Revolution to the Beginning of the Romantic Drama, 1791-1830.* (Baltimore, 1912.)
MOORE, Olin.—"The Young King, Henry Plantagenet, in Provençal and Italian Literature." (*Romanic Review,* IV, 1.)
NORTHUP, George T.—"The Spanish Prose *Tristram* Source Question." (*Modern Philology,* XI, 2.)
——"Old Spanish *Brunda.*" (*Modern Language Notes,* XXVII, 7.)
PATON, Lucy A.—"Notes on Manuscripts of the Prophécies de Merlin." (*Pub-

1913 LITERATURE AND LANGUAGE

lications Modern Language Association, XXVIII, 2.)
PIETSCH, K.—"Concerning MS. 2-G-5 of the Palace Library at Madrid." (*Modern Philology,* XI, 1.)
RAND, E. K., and WILKINS, E. H.—*Dantis Aligherii operum latinorum concordantiae.* (Oxford, Clarendon Press, 1912.)
SCHINZ, Albert.—*Les accents dans l'écriture française.* (Paris, Champion, 1912.)
———"*Histoire de l'Impression et de la Publication du 'Discours sur l'Inégalité,' de J. J. Rousseau.*" (*Publications Modern Language Association of America,* XXVIII, 2.)
———"*La question du Contrat Social.*" (*Revue d'Histoire Littéraire de la France,* XIX, 4.)
SCHLATTER, Edward B.—*The Development of the Vowel of the Unaccented Initial Syllable in Italian.* (Madison, Wisconsin, 1913.)
SEARLES, Colbert.—*Catalogue de tous les Livres de feu M. Chapelain.* (Stanford University, California, 1912.)
SMITH, Hugh A.—"Studies in the Epic Poem Godefroi de Bouillon." (*Publications Modern Language Association of America,* XXVIII, 1.)
———"The Composition of the *Chanson de Willame.*" (*Romanic Review,* IV, 1 and 2.)
SMITH, Winifred.—*The Commedia dell' Arte.* (New York, Columbia University Press, 1912.)
STOWELL, William H.—"Personal Relations in Mediæval France." (*Publications Modern Language Association of America,* XXVIII, 3.)
STUART, Donald C.—"Stage Decoration and the Unity of Place in France in the Seventeenth Century." (*Modern Philology,* X, 3.)
TREAT, Ida.—*Un cosmopolite du XVIII Siècle: Francesco Algarotti.* (Trévoux, 1913.)
WILKINS, E. H.—"The Enamorment of Boccaccio." (*Modern Philology,* XI, 1.)
YOUNG, Karl.—"*La Procession des Trois Rois at Besançon.*" (*Romanic Review,* IV, 1.)

Texts

Becerro de Benevivere II. Published by John M. Burnam. (*Romanic Review,* III, 4.)
BOSCÁN, Juan.—*Las treinta.* Published by Hayward Keniston. (New York, Hispanic Society of America, 1912.)
———*La Divina Commedia.* Edited and annotated by Charles H. Grandgent; Vol. III, *Paradiso.* (Boston, 1913.)
Farça a manera de tragedia 1537. Reprinted by Hugo Albert Rennert. (*Revue Hispanique,* XXV, 67.)
Historia Meriadoci and *De Ortu Waluuanii.* Edited by J. Douglas Bruce. (Göttingen, 1913.)
"Some Poems of Dr. Juan Pérez de Montalván," published by George W. Bacon (*Revue Hispanique,* XXV, 68.)
SEDAINE, Michel-Jean. — *Le Philosophe sans le Savoir.* Variorum critical edition by Thomas Edward Oliver. (Urbana, Illinois, 1913.)
"The *Sucesos* of Mateo Alemán." Reprinted by Alice H. Bushee. (*Revue Hispanique,* XXV, 68.)

George Ticknor's *Travels in Spain.* Edited by George N. Northup. Toronto, 1913.

ENGLISH LANGUAGE AND LITERATURE

C. G. CHILD

The following summary of American activity in the study of English can in the space available merely indicate the general trend of scholarly activity during the year without attempting to include numerous texts, reviews and minor articles even though often of great technical value.

A volume of papers contributed by colleagues and pupils of George Lyman Kittredge was issued (Ginn) in commemoration of his completion of 25 years of service in Harvard University. A review of its contents, covering a wide range of subjects, is not possible here, but it is pleasant to record this just tribute to a great teacher, a master in many fields as well as his own, an inspiration to all who seek his aid, both in the scientific study, and in the appreciation, of literature.

Other works of general reference are Schelling's *English Lyric* (Houghton, Mifflin Co.), Brander Matthew's *A Study of the Drama* (Houghton, Mifflin Co.), and Bryton's *London in English Literature* (University of Chicago).

Philology.—Curme has continued his fruitful investigations in the field of syntax (*Journal Eng. and Germ. Phil., Mod. Lang. Notes, Publ. Mod. Lang. Assoc., Eng. Stud.*), and is awakening profitable discussion in Germany. The exhaustive monograph of Callaway (Carnegie Institution) on *The Infinitive in Anglo-Saxon* promises to rank as a monument of American scholarship. Other articles, always few, in this field are Kenyon's "An Idiomatic Order of Words" (*Mod. Lang. Notes*) and Krapp's suggestive "Standards of Speech and their Values" (*Mod. Phil.*).

Old English Period (449-1150.—Among more notable contributions may be instanced Bright and Ramsay's *Notes on the "Introduction"* to the *WS. Psalms* (Clarendon Press), Klaeber's welcome edition of texts relating to the "Fall of Man" (Heidelberg), his papers on Beowulf (*Ang-*

lia), Belden's article on the same poem (*Mod. Lang. Notes*), Cook's discussion of the dates of the Ruthwell and Bewcastle crosses (Yale Press), Williams' monograph on *Gnomic Poetry* (Columbia Press), Tupper's striking article on *Deor*, and on the British Museum transcript of the Exeter Book (both in *Anglia*), various notes on old English poems by Tupper and Klaeber (*Jour. Eng. and Germ. Phil.*), and Miss Fisk's paper on "Animals in Early English Ecclesiastical Literature" (*Publ. Mod. Lang. Assoc.*), which links this period with the next.

Middle English Period (1150-1500). —Booker's *Middle English Bibliography* (Heidelberg), though unavoidably incomplete, will be of material assistance. Helpful original investigations are Miss Sandison's *Chansons d'Aventure in Middle English* (Bryn Mawr Monographs), Cross on the "Chastity-Testing Horn and Mantle" (*Mod. Phil.*), Miss Hammond's article on the *Prologue* to Lydgate's *Story of Thebes* (*Anglia*), and Root's discussion of the methods of mediæval publication (*Publ. Mod. Lang. Assoc.*). Miss Rickert's paper on John Bret (*Mod. Phil.*) revives the discussion of the multiple authorship of *Piers Plowman*. Emerson's review (*Mod. Lang. Notes*) of Bateson's edition of *Patience* is of positive constructive value. Sommer continues his publication of the *Vulgate Version of the Arthurian Romances* (Carnegie Institute). Cady writes on the "Wakefield Group in the Towneley Cycle" (*Jour. Eng. and Germ. Phil.*).

Continued devotion to the study of Chaucer, in the success of which for many years America may take pride, is attested by the articles of Karpinksi (*Mod. Lang. Notes*), Hulbert *Mod. Phil.*), Shannon (*Publ. Mod. Phil.*), Emerson (*Romanic Review, Mod. Phil.*), Tatlock (*Anglia, Jour. Eng. and Germ. Phil.*), S. Moore (*Anglia, Mod. Phil.*), Shannon (*Publ. Mod. Lang. Assoc.*), and the monographs of Hulbert (University of Chicago) and Fansler (Columbia Press), while Tupper's article in the *Nation* announces an epoch-making discovery in relation to Chaucer's design in the *Canterbury Tales*.

Modern English (1500-date).—In the early 16th century may be noted Lois Borland's essay on Montgomery (*Mod. Phil.*). Less work seems to have been done in the Elizabethan field than usual. Spenser is the subject of articles by Baskervil (*Pub. Mod. Lang. Assoc.*), Reed Smith (*Mod. Lang. Notes*), Graham (*ibid.*), Padelford (*Mod. Phil.*) and of a monograph by Higginson (Columbia). Cunliffe has published his important edition of *Early English Classical Tragedies* (Clarendon), and Boyer a most interesting volume on *The Villain as Hero in the Elizabethan Drama* (Routledge). Articles upon Shakespeare include H. S. V. Jones (*Mod. Lang. Notes*), Adams (*ibid.*), Northup (*Jour. Eng. and Germ. Phil.*), Stoll (*Mod. Phil.*), Darzan (*Mod. Phil.*), Newcomer (*Mod. Phil.*), Gray (*Jour. Eng. and Germ. Phil.*), Moriarty, (*Mod. Phil.*), and Tupper (*Publ. Mod. Lang. Assoc.*), as well as several on the sonnets. Jonson is the subject of a monograph by Judson (Yale Studies) and an interesting note by McDaniel (*Mod. Lang. Notes*). Other monographs and articles are: on Heywood by Miss Bates (*Jour. Eng. and Germ. Phil.*) and Graves (*Mod. Phil.*); Richard Brome, by Andrews (Yale Studies); Decker and Ford by Pierce (*Anglia*); *The Arraignment of Paris* by Graves (*Mod. Lang. Notes*); "The Broken Heart" by Baskervil (*ibid.*); "The Late Lancashire Witches" by Andrews (*ibid.*). An unusual number of articles have appeared on Milton, by Friedland, Gilbert, Lockwood, Nicholson and Hart (all in *Mod. Lang. Notes*) and by Thompson (*Publ. Mod. Lang. Assoc.*). Other notable contributions on the literature of the 17th and subsequent centuries are those of Miss Hughes on Vaughan (*Mod. Lang. Notes*); Scheurer, "The Town Shifts," 1671 (*Anglia*); Heinzelmann and Griffith on Pope (*Mod. Phil.*); Croissant on Cibber (*Kansas Humanistic Studies*); Tieje on "Realism in Pre-Richardsonian Fiction" (*Publ. Mod. Lang. Assoc.*); Trent on Defoe (*Cambridge History*); two articles by Welles on Fielding (*Publ. Mod Lang. Assoc., M. L. N.*); Morton on the "Spenserian Stanza in the 18th Century" (*Mod. Phil.*); Chew on

1913 LITERATURE AND LANGUAGE

Byron and Croly (*Mod. Lang. Notes*); Fuess's monograph on "Byron as Satirist" (Columbia Press); Phelps on "Browning in Germany" (*Mod. Lang. Notes*). Interesting examples of the oral tradition of old ballads in America are given by Belden (*Jour. of Am. Folk-Lore*), by Woods (*Mod. Lang. Notes*) and by Carrie A. Harper (*ibid.*). An important contribution to the history of contemporary literature is Cornelius Weygandt's *Irish Plays and Playwrights* (Houghton, Mifflin Co.).

Necrology.—William Hande Browne died Dec. 13, 1912, in his 84th year. A devoted student of English literature in general, a specialist in Early Scottish literature, his modesty prevented adequate recognition of his wide and accurate knowledge. He will be gratefully remembered by his students, many of whom, owing to the gentleness and quietness of his method of instruction, often not till long after learned to realize how much they owed to his teaching and example.

ANCIENT LITERATURE AND PHILOLOGY

ANCIENT LITERATURE
(*Additions from Papyri*)
CLIFFORD H. MOORE

The most important collection of literary and theological papyri to be noticed this year is that contained in the first volume of the publications of the Società Italiana per la ricerca dei Papiri greci e latini in Egitto, edited by Professor Girolamo Vitelli under the title *Papiri Greci e Latini* (Firenze, 1912), which appeared too late for review in the YEAR BOOK for 1912. Of the 112 numbers, 31 are theological or literary. The most of these call for no particular notice, and none is of such great interest as a number which have been published in recent years.

Theological Fragments. — Of the biblical fragments, Number 2, a piece of a parchment codex of the fourth century containing Luke xxii, 45-47, 50-53, is of importance to scholars as it omits verse 51, thus possibly lending some support to the suspicions of Weiss that the original text of Luke has been expanded at this point. Number 6, fragments of the *Protevangelium* of James, is not especially valuable so far as the text is concerned, save that the passages here given tend to favor the view that the work is a unit, but the date of the fragments, the fourth century, disproves the claims of certain scholars who have held that the work originated in the fifth or sixth century. Valuable also are the two scanty fragments, Number 7, of the *Apocalypse of Elias*, which has been hitherto known in the Coptic versions. Another fragment, Number 65, of the sixth century, seems to contain scholia to a medley of biblical texts, the relation between which is obscure. A portion of a roll, Numbers 26 and 27, makes welcome additions to the scanty hagiographic papyri. On the *recto* is a part of the legend of Saint Paphnutius and the *verso* gives us a similar part of the story of Saint Christina. The latter belongs to a Greek version older than any hitherto known to us, apparently to that from which the Latin version was made.

Greek Classical Texts.—Most of the literary fragments contain parts of extant works and add little to our knowledge. New are two fragments of comedies, Numbers 99 and 100, but the lines cannot be satisfactorily restored or assigned. A leaf of the third century, Number 17, contains six sepulchral epigrams celebrating the virtues of an unknown Euprepius to whom his daughter erected a monument. The verses have slight literary merit; many phrases can be paralleled from Kaibel's collection. They have many corrections and alternate versions between the lines in the original hand. Two fragments, Numbers 19 and 85, give us glimpses of ancient schools, for they belonged to pupils' note books. The first contains elementary notices relating to the Trojan War, while the second gives a detailed description of a *chreia*.

Latin Classical Texts.—Papyri containing Latin works are rare, but this volume brings us three bits, Numbers 20, 21 and 110, from Cicero, *In Verr.*, act. 1, 1, Vergil, *Aen.*, iv, 66-

83

68, 99-102, and Sallust, *Bell. Cat.*, 10-11. The lines from Cicero tend to confirm the text in two places against the charge of interpolation which the learned have brought, but otherwise have no value. The fragments of Vergil and of Sallust show that they were prepared for Greeks learning Latin, for the latter has marks of quantity and a number of interlinear Greek glosses, one of which is incorrect apparently; the former also has the long quantity marked several times as well as accents indicating the prose, not the verse, accent. These remind one of *Oxyr. Pap.* 1099 and *Pap. Rylands* 61, which were noticed in the YEAR BOOK for 1911 (p. 776).

Mention should be made of th handy volume published by Dr. A. S. Hunt in the "Oxford Classical Texts" under the title *Tragicorum Graecorum Fragmenta Papyracea nuper reperta.* It contains the *Indagatores, Eurypylus* and *Achaeorum Conventus* of Sophocles, the *Hypsipyle, Cretes,* and *Melanippe Vincta* of Euripides, and certain anonymous satyric fragments. Finally it should be noted that Alfred Körte has begun a review in the *Archiv für Papyrusforschung* (V, pp. 531 ff.) of all the literary texts published during the past six years.

GREEK LITERATURE

WILLIAM ARTHUR HEIDEL

The *American Journal of Philology,* the *American Journal of Archæology, Classical Philology,* and the other periodicals mentioned in the YEAR BOOK for 1910 (p. 162), continue the publication of excellent articles on a wide variety of subjects. Especially to be noted of the output of 1913 are: Professor Bolling's "Contributions to the Study of Homeric Metre," part II, in the *American Journal of Philology;* the continuation of Buckler and Robinson's "Inscriptions from Sardes," II and III. Professor Robinson's "Inscriptions from the Cyrenaica," and W. B. Dinsmoor's "Attic Building Accounts," I-III, in the *American Journal of Archæology;* Professor Buck's "Interstate Use of the Greek Dialects," Professor Scott's "Paris and Hector in Tradition and in Homer" and "The Assumed Duration of the War of the *Iliad,*" and Professor Flickinger's "Tragedy and the Satyric Drama," in *Classical Philology;* Professor Adams's "Are the Political Speeches of Demosthenes to be Regarded as Political Pamphlets?" Professor Baker's "Some of the Less Known MSS. of Xenophon's *Memorabilia,*" and Professor Hewitt's "On the Development of the Thankoffering among the Greeks," in the *Transactions of the American Philological Association.*

Of books intended for the literary public the year has not been prolific. Perhaps Professor Harmon's excellent edition of Lucian in the "Loeb Classical Library" deserves especial mention as one of the best fruits of this great undertaking. Prof. Milton W. Humphreys has rendered in his admirable edition of *Demosthenes On the Crown* a labor of love which bears eloquent witness to the vitality of classical studies. In "An Athenian Critic of Life" (*Yale Review,* April, 1913) Professor Goodell presents a sympathetic study of Sophocles. The writer published in the *Proceedings of the American Academy of Arts and Sciences* (May, 1913) a series of studies entitled *On Certain Fragments of the Pre-Socratics: Critical Notes and Elucidations.* American scholars have in recent years published some of their best work in foreign periodicals; thus, Prof. H. W. Prescott's "ΕΒΑΡΟΟΝ" (Theocritus, *id.,* I, 139, 140) appeared in the *Classical Quarterly* (July, 1913). Among archæological publications may be mentioned Dr. G. W. Elderkin's *Problems in Periclean Building* and Edith H. Hall's *Excavations in Eastern Crete; Sphoungaras.*

The year has brought forth few doctoral dissertations on Greek subjects: among them we may note Lilly Ross Taylor's *The Cults of Ostia* and Mary Hamilton Swindler's *Cretan Elements in the Cults and Ritual of Apollo* (both of Bryn Mawr), Dr. Donald B. Durham's *The Vocabulary of Menander Considered in its Relation to the* Κοινή (Princeton), and Dr. George M. Calhoun's *Athenian Clubs in Politics and Litigation* (Chicago). The last-mentioned is an exceptionally full and valuable study of an interesting phase of ancient life.

1913 LITERATURE AND LANGUAGE

As usual, much good work is done in the reviewing of the most notable books. Such reviews appear not only in the classical periodicals, but also in those of a more general character, such as the *Nation*, and in journals devoted to related special subjects, such as the *Philosophical Review*. Among the classical periodicals the *American Journal of Philology* publishes the fullest and most detailed reviews. The *Transactions and Proceedings of the American Philological Association* publish annually a fairly complete bibliography of the members of the Association for the preceding year.

Greek studies in America should receive added impetus from the honor conferred upon one of their most brilliant exponents in the appointment of Prof. Paul Shorey to the Roosevelt Professorship at the University of Berlin for the year 1913-14. While the selection was doubtless directly a personal tribute, indirectly it testifies to the breadth of classical culture in that the appointee is required to lecture on subjects relating to American life and institutions.

LATIN LITERATURE

CHARLES KNAPP

Owing to the conditions of publication in the United States, American work in Latin literature and kindred fields consists largely of articles in periodicals,[1] and in the volumes of studies in classical philology brought out under the ægis of learned societies or various universities. In 1913, however, appeared a notable book, an edition of Tibullus, with elaborate introduction and notes, by K. F. Smith. This, the first thoroughgoing and complete edition of Tibullus published in America, is likely long to remain the definitive edition of that author. *Roads from Rome*, by Anne C. E. Allinson, is an interesting group of essays on Catullus, Propertius, Horace, Ovid and his wife, etc.

Contributions to the study of various authors have been made in the following articles: "Catullus Carmen 2," by E. W. Fay (*CP.*, VIII, 301-309), a defense of the substantial integrity of this poem as it stands; "Cicero the Stylist: An Appreciation," by G. Showerman (*CJ.*, VIII, 180-192); "Was Cicero Successful in the Art Rhetorical?" by J. E. Granrud (*CJ.*, VIII, 234-243); "The Ferentinum of Horace," by W. B. McDaniel (*TAPA.*, XLIII, 67-72), which identifies the Ferentinum of Horace, *Epistles* 1, 17, 6-8, with a hamlet of that name near the Aqua Ferentina and Lucus Ferentinae, in the Alban region, where the cities of the Latin League used to hold their general assemblies; "Lucilius on EI and I," by R. G. Kent (*AJP.*, XXXIV, 315-321), a continuation of a discussion by the same author and E. W. Fay of various passages in Lucilius, and so of value to the student of Latin literature; "The Creation Story in Ovid Metamorphoses," by F. E. Robbins (*CP.*, VIII, 401-414), an argument that Ovid's source is to be found, not in any specific author, Greek or Roman, but in the general teaching of the Stoics, familiar to every educated Roman in Ovid's time; "The *Amphitruo* of Plautus," by H. W. Prescott (*CP.*, VIII, 14-22), an argument that there is in this play a change of scene, from the space before the house of Amphitruo to the harbor; if so, the play has another claim to distinction as a play unique, since changes of scene are very rare in extant Greek and Roman tragedy and comedy both, outside of Aristophanes; "The Composition of the *Rudens* of Plautus," by Cornelia C. Coulter (*CP.*, VIII, 57-64), who sees evidence of *contaminatio*, or the combination of materials got from two (Greek) plays, which, in this case, were laid in different places; "Suetonius and his Biographies," by J. C. Rolfe (*Proceedings of the American Philosophical Society*, LII, 206-225); "A Manuscript of Jerome's *De Viris Illustribus* belonging to the General Theological Seminary," by W. H. P. Hatch (*HS.*, XXIII, 47-70); "The Dialogue of Tacitus," by W. Peterson (*AJP.*, XXXIV, 1-14), dealing with the manuscript history of the work, which called forth a reply from

---
[1] Periodicals are cited in this article under the following abbreviations: *AJP.*, *American Journal of Philology*; *CJ.*, *Classical Journal*; *CP.*, *Classical Philology*; *CW.*, *Classical Weekly*; *HS.*, *Harvard Studies*; *TAPA.*, *Transactions of the American Philological Association*.

A. Gudeman (*ibid.*, 243-246); "The Tragedy of Dido," by H. H. Yeames (*CJ.*, VIII, 139-150, 193-202). Two papers on Horace, "Horace's View of the Relations between Satire and Comedy," by H. R. Fairclough (*AJP.*, XXXIV, 183-193), and "Horace, *Epistles*, II, i, 139 ff. and Livy, VII, 2," by C. Knapp (*TAPA.*, XLIII, 125-142), are part also of the discussion of the Roman tradition that there was in early times a form of the Roman drama called *Satura;* to the same discussion belongs "Satura and Satire," by B. L. Ullman (*CP.*, VIII, 172-194), which proposes an excellent explanation of the puzzling word *satura* and discusses the use of that word in Latin writers.

Two papers dealt with prose rhythm: "Preferred and Avoided Combinations of the Enclitic *Que* in Cicero," by F. W. Shipley (*CP.*, VIII, 23-47) and "*De Clausulis a Flavio Vopisco Adhibitis*," by Susan H. Ballou, published abroad.

The tendency, strong in recent years, to trace the influence of the classics on later literatures, is seen in *The Classical Origin and Tradition of Literary Conceits*, by M. B. Ogle (*AJP.*, 34, 125-152), and *Classical Traditions in Early German and Romance Literature*, by the same author (*Mod. Lang. Notes*, December, 1912). Here, too, mention may be made of *Further Notes on Sicilian Translations of the Twelfth Century* (translations from the Greek into Latin), by C. Haskins (*HS.*, 23, 155-160).

Recently much work has been done in translating classical authors into English. Of foremost interest here is the "Loeb Classical Library" (of translations), to which many American scholars are under pledge to contribute, though none has in fact done so as yet, in Latin. A book entitled *Cato and Varro: The Treatises on Roman Farm Management done into English, with Notes of Modern Instances, by a Virginia Farmer*, is of interest, because Cato had not been done into English, but unfortunately the author's enthusiasm is not matched by sound understanding of the Latin originals.

This article may well close with a notice of papers and books in fields more or less directly ancillary to the study of Latin literature. Webster's *Ancient History*, with a companion volume, *Readings in Ancient History*, has been well received. In "A Roman Astrologer as a Historical Source: Julius Firmicus Maternus" (*CP.*, VIII, 415-435), Lynn Thorndike seeks to show that in Firmicus's work we have a clear and faithful picture of society in his time. We may note also "On the Legality of the Condemnation and Trial of the Catilinarian Conspirators," by G. W. Botsford (*CW.*, VI, 130-132), and "The Prosecution of Cataline's Associates," by R. W. Husband (*CJ.*, ii, 4-26).

In lexicography we may note *Index Verborum Catullianus*, M. N. Wetmore, which well continues the same author's masterly *Index Verborum Vergilianus* (1911); for reviews of these books, by G. Lodge and C. Knapp, see *CW.*, VI, 101-103, 109-111, 124.

In Latin grammar, of papers contributory to an understanding of Latin authors mention should be made of *Case Usage in Livy*, by R. B. Steele, published in Germany; "The Participial Usage in Cicero's Epistles," R. B. Steele (*AJP.*, XXXIV, 172-182); *The Future Periphrastic in Latin* (*id.*, *CP.*, VIII, 457-476); "*Neve* and *Neque* with Imperative and Subjunctive," by E. B. Lease (*AJP.*, XXXIV, 255-275). Important is "The Development of Copulative Verbs in the Indo-European Languages" (*TAPA.*, XLIII, 173-200), which deals with substitutes for the copula *sum* and its equivalents in various languages, including Latin.

INDO-EUROPEAN PHILOLOGY
(*Exclusive of the Germanic Languages*)

ROLAND G. KENT

General.—E. H. Sturtevant gives a valuable review of "Recent Literature in Comparative Philology" (*CW.*,[1] VI, 116-9). Under the title "Ueber grammatische Perseverationserscheinung-

---

[1] Periodicals are cited under the following abbreviations: *AJP.*, American Journal of Philology; *CJ.*, Classical Journal; *CP.*, Classical Philology; *CW.*, Classical Weekly; *IF.*, Indogermanische Forschungen; *JAOS.*, Journal of the American Oriental Society; *TAPA.* and *PAPA.*, Transactions and Proceedings of the American Philological Association.

en," H. Oertel deals with modifications of words in assimilation to preceding words (*IF.*, XXXI, 49-66). C. L. Meader (*TAPA.*, XLIII, 173-200) shows that verbs meaning stand, sit, lie, remain, go, grow, appear, find, etc., have in various Indo-European languages developed into mere copulas, but mostly where there is a middle or reflexive meaning. W. G. Hale proposes changes in "The Classification of Sentences and Clauses" (*PAPA.*, XLIII, xxix-xxxii; and A. W. McWhorter discusses the "Mood of the Question" and the "Mood of the Answer" (*ibid.*, xliii-xlix).

Indo-Iranian. — In the "Columbia University Indo-Iranian Series," edited by A. V. W. Jackson, Vol. VIII has appeared: *Vāsavadattā, a Sanskrit Romance by Subandhu*, translated, with an introduction and notes, by Louis H. Gray. L. C. Barrett has issued "The Kashmirian *Atharva Veda*. Book III" (*JAOS.*, XXXII, 343-90), in style similar to his publication of the first two books in the same periodical. M. Bloomfield (*IF.*, XXXI, 156-77) shows that in the oldest Sanskrit the finite verb may vary in position in the clause without the slightest change of meaning. A theory on the difficult question of the relations of Vedic, Sanskrit and Prakrit is set forth by W. Petersen in *JAOS.* (XXXII, 414-28); a partial reply to his views is given by T. Michelson (*ibid.*, XXXIII, 145-9).

Other articles are M. Bloomfield, "The Sikh Religion," in *Studies in the History of Religions* (169-86), presented to C. H. Toy (New York, 1912); E. W. Hopkins, "Sacred Rivers of India," in the same volume (213-29); F. Edgerton, "*Pañcadivyāhivāsa*, or Choosing a King by Divine Will" (*JAOS.*, XXXIII, 158-66); R. G. Kent, "Classical Parallels to a Sanskrit Proverb" (ibid., 214-6); W. H. Schoff, "Proposed Identification of Two South Indian Place-names in the *Periplus*" (*Jour. Royal Asiatic Soc.*, January, 1913, 130-3), and "Tamil Political Divisions in the First Two Centuries of the Christian Era" (*JAOS.*, XXXIII, 209-13).

H. C. Tolman (*Amer. Jour. of Archæology*, XVII, 85-6 and *PAPA.*, XLIII, liv-lvii), discusses the ethnological types and the dress of the figures on the grave relief of King Darius, and shows that the long flowing robe is Persian, and the tightly fitting coat and trousers are Median, reversing the usual belief on the point.

Greek and Latin: Linguistics and Syntax.—C. D. Buck (*CP.*, VIII, 133-59) shows that in treaties and other documents of interest to more than one community in ancient Greece much mixture of dialects occurred. The usages of οὐ and μή are discussed by T. D. Goodell and by B. L. Gildersleeve (*AJP.*, XXXIII, 436-49), and instances of ὅταν with causal meaning without temporal significance are adduced by A. C. Pearson (*ibid.*, 426-35).

C. L. Durham's "Formal Latin and Informal Latin" (*CW.*, VI, 97-101) and G. D. Kellogg's "Characterization of Gallic Latin" (*ibid.*, 90-4) are useful summaries on those subjects. F. F. Abbott's "Note on the Latin Accent" (*CP.*, VIII, 92-3) argues that the accent of the masses was a stress accent, imitating that of Greek. Some problems of "Hidden Quantities" are dealt with by C. D. Buck (*Class. Review*, XXVII, 122-6); a reply to this is to be found on pp. 160-2 of the same volume. E. H. Sturtevant (*TAPA.*, XLIII, 57-66) shows that the *ui* in *cui* and *huic* was a diphthong of which the *u* was the vowel element. W. G. Hale (*IF.*, XXXI, 272-5) argues that as the perfect tense denotes completion, the perfect subjunctive in prohibitions in Latin came to indicate thoroughness or finality. R. B. Steele (*AJP.*, XXXIV, 172-82) studies the uses of the participles in Cicero's *Epistles* and compares them with similar usages in Livy; he presents also (*CP.*, VIII, 457-76) a study of "The Future Periphrastic in Latin," down to Suetonius. E. B. Lease (*AJP.*, XXXIV, 255-75) gives the first instalment of the history of "*Neve* and *Neque* with the Imperative and Subjunctive," down to Apuleius. R. C. Flickinger (*ibid.*, 276-99) gives a detailed history of "The Accusative of Exclamation in Epistolary Latin," continuing his study of the same construction in Plautus and Terence (*ibid.*, XXIX). C. C. Mierow (*CP.*, VIII, 436-44) discusses "Adverbial

Usage in Eugippius." R. G. Kent (*TAPA.*, XLIII, 35-56) discusses the results upon the vowels of the Roman dislike for writing the same letter twice in succession, and the linguistic inferences to be drawn therefrom; replies (*AJP.*, XXXIV, 315-21) to Fay's article on the orthographic rules of Lucilius (*ibid.*, XXXIII, 311-6); treats certain phenomena of "Purpose Clauses" (*CJ.*, IX, 35-6); and attempts to complete the interpretation of the inscription on "The Oscan Slingshot of Saepinum" (*IF.*, XXXII, 196-202).

Word Formation and Etymology.— E. W. Fay has an elaborate study on "Derivatives of the Root *Sthā* in Composition" (*AJP.*, XXXIII, 377-400, and XXXIV, 15-42); in the *Bulletin* of the University of Texas for Jan. 15, 1913, he has a detailed exposition to prove that "Indo-European Verbal Flexion was Analytical." E. H. Sturtevant concludes his "Studies in Greek Noun Formation: Labial Terminations" (*CP.*, VIII, 65-87, 334-48). S. G. Oliphant (*JAOS.*, XXXII, 393-413) argues that Sanskrit *dhénā* means "voice" or "song." E. W. Hopkins, in "Sanskrit *Kabāiras* or *Kubāiras* and Greek *Kabeiros*" (*ibid.*, XXXIII, 55-70), shows the original identity of the two seemingly different divinities.

E. W. Fay proposes an etymology for Vedic *suśiśvi-s* (*ibid.*, XXXII, 391-2); shows (*CJ.*, VIII, 253-6) that Latin *comes it* is used almost in the meaning "goes with," though this is not recognized even by the great *Thesaurus Linguae Latinae* now appearing; shows (*Class. Quarterly*, VII, 202-7) that the study of the etymology of words will often throw light on the syntactical constructions used with them; and presents a study of English "chews," "chooses" and their etymological cognates (*Jour. of Eng. and Germ. Philology*, XII, 425-33). Latin *pontifex* is etymologized by J. M. Burnam (*Berliner philologische Wochenschrift*, XXXIII, 254-5) as "maker of purity," and by R. G. Kent (*CP.*, VIII, 317-26) as "maker of the paths" between this world and the world of the gods and the dead. B. L. Ullman (*ibid.*, 172-94) discusses the etymology and meaning of *satura*. E. H. Sturtevant (*CW.*, VII, 29-30) reviews interestingly several new etymologies of recent date. L. Van Hook (*PAPA.*, XLIII, lix-lx) shows that the Greek rhetorical term ψυχρότης means "fustian" rather than "frigidity." (B. W. Mitchell (*CW.*, VI, 202-6) gives a popular account of the meaning of the names of the squirrel in many languages, under the title "In the Shadow of his Tail."

SEMITIC PHILOLOGY AND LITERATURE

MORRIS JASTROW

Syriac Book of Medicine.—A work of first-class importance is E. A. Wallis Budge's edition of *The Syriac Book of Medicine* (Oxford Univ. Press) based on a manuscript in the possession of a native of Mosul. While the manuscript itself is not so very old, it represents a compilation made on the basis of older works and thus embodies the traditional medicine of Syria. While the general point of view is that of Greek medicine, which made its way everywhere in the ancient world, the author, or rather authors, of this compilation have added to their work all the traditional lore and folklore of medicine, including astrology and divination as a means of determining the outcome of disease. Added to the work is a long list of what the compiler calls "the medicines of the country," which are the old popular remedies that undoubtedly go back to very early days. The publication thus forms a connecting link joining the later medicine of Syria with the early traditions that may be traced back to the medicine of the Babylonians and Assyrians.

Aramaic Incantation Texts.—The medicine of the ancient Orient (and for that matter, of the modern Orient) was never entirely divorced from incantations and it is therefore a natural step to pass from Budge's important work to Prof. James A. Montgomery's edition of the Aramaic *Incantation Texts from Nippur*, likewise accompanied by translations. These texts are found on clay bowls discovered by the University of Pennsylvania Expedition to Nippur, in the upper strata of the mound. The bowls, which are covered with drawings and inscriptions in ink, date approximately from the sixth century of our era. They were buried with the dead who were supposed to be protected from evil demons by the formulae inscribed on the bowls. The publication is interesting from two points of view: first, as illustrating the persistency of belief in the activity of demons far down into the Christian era among both native Jews and Christians; and, secondly, from the point of view of language. In the latter respect Professor Montgomery's work is of the very greatest importance. It affords an insight into the current dialect of Babylonia in the seventh century and since he has added in a glossary a complete list of all words occurring in similar texts published up to the present time, this volume, which is one of the publications of the Babylonian section of the Museum of the University of Pennsylvania, will take its place as a standard work on the subject.

Cuneiform Texts.—Dr. A. T. Clay has added another volume to the long series of *Cuneiform Texts* that we owe to him. In his new publication, which forms Part II of the Babylonian records in the library of J. Pierpont Morgan, Dr. Clay has given us 56 splendidly preserved commercial and legal texts from the Seleucid era (3d century B. C.). Up to the present only a small number of texts from this very late period have been issued. One of the interesting features of Dr. Clay's new publication is the occurrence of a large number of Greek names in the text, most of which the editor has succeeded in identifying. These names illustrate the active influx of Greeks into the Orient, and we thus see at close hand the interchange of Oriental and Occidental ideas brought about through the conquests of Alexander. Curiously enough the name of Alexander appears in these records without the Greek ending *os*, giving us, therefore, the popular pronunciation of the famous name.

A most valuable work, summing up the results of the expeditions conducted by the German expedition on the site of Babylon during the last 13 years, is Dr. Robert Koldewey's *Das Wiedererstehende Babylon* (Leipzig). The volume gives in a most readable form a complete survey, systematically arranged, of the finds made in the various parts of the mound and of their cultural and historical significance.

Islam.—The appearance of a second edition of T. W. Arnold's well-known book *Preaching of Islam* (New York) should be noticed. The work appears in a revised form which gives evidence of the activity of the author during the 16 years that have elapsed since the appearance of the first edition. The entire range of the spread of Islamism into Western Asia, into Europe, India, Africa and the Malay Archipelago as well as among the Tartars is most carefully covered.

Ancient History of the Near East.—Another work of general interest is H. R. Hall's *Ancient History of the Near East* (New York). Mr. Hall, while not claiming to be a specialist along the whole range of subjects covered by him, has made himself thoroughly familiar with a broad field, while his special knowledge of Egyptian and Babylonian history has enabled him to treat such subjects as the older civilization of Greece, of the Hittites and the earlier history of Assyria and Palestine in a manner which throws a great deal of light on the relationships of ancient civilizations to one another. Mr. Hall brings his history down to the Battle of Salamis, a date which only a few decades ago was very close to the beginnings of ancient history. The work is abundantly illustrated and its usefulness further enhanced by several chronological tables.

Moses.—Lastly, in the field of Old Testament criticism, attention should be directed to the work by Prof. Hugo Gressmann on *Moses und seine Zeit*, an investigation thoroughly critical in character, but which by penetrating beyond textual criticism into a historical insight into the sources for the period of Moses, reaches conclusions that are much more positive than those of his predecessors. Moses, despite the legendary accretions about his name, looms up as a genuine historical personage to whom, among other things, the Decalogue in its original form is ascribed by the author of this latest study of the beginnings of the national life of the Hebrews.

1914 LITERATURE AND LANGUAGE

AMERICAN LITERATURE

(*Nov. 15, 1913, to Nov. 15, 1914*)

EDWARD EVERETT HALE

Fiction.—The greatest productivity in creative literature has been, as usual, in works of fiction, although the publication of novels has been at least somewhat less than in 1913. It is impossible to present exact statistics on this subject; the entire production of fiction in books and periodicals of all kinds is now so very great that no one makes an attempt to comprehend it. Even in the limited statistics of the *Publishers' Weekly*, which include books only and not all of them, the term "fiction" is so vague that comparison with other figures does not indicate very much. But lists formed in about the same way in 1914 and 1913 of books designed to appeal to a cultivated audience would give rather fewer American novels in 1914—about 300 books which come to some sort of notice. Of English books republished in America the proportion is smaller than in 1913.

Since our review closes with Nov. 15, we note little of the influence of the great event of the year. The war broke out in August, by which time arrangements had already been made for fall publication. The influence of the war on literature, and doubtless it is deep, must so far be sought in newspapers and periodicals; the novels of the year show little general difference from those of any other year.

Although there are still, as there have been for a good while, a great many tales of mystery, adventure or romance, yet there appears to be a growing proportion of books which show or affect to show some more serious object on the part of the author than the amusement only or the recreation of the reader. Books are still advertised as a delightful relief from "psychological" or "problem" novels, but such appeals are probably made to a particular class of readers. The appeal of the best fiction is more and more to a serious interest. The year, however, has not produced any such large set of life-experiences as appeared in 1913; in that year, as was noted in the last issue of the YEAR BOOK (p. 788), there was a considerable number of books of this kind, biographical if not autobiographical. Theodore Dreiser continues his chronicle of the American financier in *The Titan* (Lane); like its predecessor, the book is astonishingly vivid in spite of its elaborate detail and its lack of formal construction. Mary S. Watts's *The Rise of Jennie Cushing* (Macmillans) is the story of a waif of the slums, whose life brings her into touch with many of the strongest currents of contemporary life. Gertrude Atherton's *Perch of the Devil* (Stokes) shows quite an original figure against a background of mining life in Montana. Robert Herrick's *Clark's Field* (Houghton, Mifflin Co.) is an account of the life of a young girl who inherited undeserved wealth. Kathleen Norris's *Saturday's Child* (Macmillans) is the story of one who has to "work for a living" and presents a real achievement in life, a vital part of the great world. The anonymous *Altogether Jane* (Kennerley), a book of ability in spite of serious faults, is the autobiography of a woman writer of the day. Such books always deal somewhat with the questions and interests of the time, as seen from the angle of some particular character. There are more books which are discussions of a more general nature. Josephine D. Bacon's *To-day's Daughter* (Appletons) gives the experience in marriage of the daughter of Dr. Stanchon and of several of her friends; problems arise to which the doctor offers solution, less convincing as a rule than the earlier labors of the great alienist. Owen Johnson in *The Salamander* (Bobbs, Merrill Co.) offers the reader a study of a specific type created by our modern city conditions, but the general appeal of the book is emotional rather than sociological. Much the same thing may be said of the anonymous *Home* (Century Co.), a much truer book, which would be interesting (and probably often is) without its constant implication of the saving power of the ingrained habits and affections of home. George R. Chester, whose "Wallingford" stories have been regarded by some as exhibitions of a phase of American life, comes out more strongly (with Lilian Chester) in *The Ball of Fire* (Hearst International Library Co.), which gives a good deal of real criticism of religion and finance as they exist in our large cities. We cannot say whether Mr. Chester would consider his amusing *Tale of Red Roses* (Bobbs, Merrill Co.) a sociological study; it gives a picture (rather conventional and journalistic) of a political boss. Another book dealing with religion more directly and less successfully is George Kibbe Turner's *The Last Christian* (Hearst), which tells of the gradual wasting away of a country congregation. A certain immediate interest attaches to Frederick Palmer's striking *The Last Shot* (Scribners), though perhaps to its disadvantage, for current events have such an intensity that fiction pales before them. Samuel H. Adams's *The Clarion* (Houghton, Mifflin Co.) is an excellent story of a man who bought a newspaper and insisted on running it on a clean and independent basis. Will N. Harben's *The New Clarion* (Harpers) deals with much the same subject in the Alabama setting in which the author is at home. The anonymous *The Goldfish* (Century Co.) presents itself as the actual confessions of a successful man; it is not necessary that it should be a fact to be of interest. Perhaps we may mention here the very popular *Eyes of the World* by Harold B. Wright (Book Supply Co.), in which the author criticises very severely the literary and artistic circles of our day. A few books deal with questions of marriage. M. H. Urner's *The Woman Alone* (Hearst) gives a drab view of an affair with a mistress, and Basil King's *The Letter of the Contract* (Harpers) is the story of a divorced woman. Most of these novels go straight at their subject; Mitchell Keays's *Mrs. Brand* (Small, Maynard & Co.), however, while full of modern ideas, presents them with clever satire, and Jesse L. Williams' *So They Were Married* (Scribners) is also amusingly put.

Next to such books would come the books inspired by the tone or feeling of some place or some particular phase of life. Here one must speak first of George W. Cable's *Gideon's Band* (Scribners), in which are gathered the character and sentiment of a phase of life now passed away, the steamboat life on the Mississippi. And we should place next it the work of another of those who did so much to make "local color" interesting to Americans, namely, Charles Egbert Craddock, whose last book, *The Story of Duciehurst* (Macmillans), is of Mississippi rather than of the mountains by which she first became known. The Southern mountains are not so prominent in fiction as they were in 1913, but we must note Lucy Furman's *Sight to the Blind* (Macmillans), which ought to receive mention as a study of mountain life, though perhaps not accurately under the head of fiction. Joseph C. Lincoln, who is best known for his pictures of Cape Cod life, now gives one by contrast; in *Kent Knowles, Quahaug* (Appletons), a Cape Cod pair go abroad, and in *Cap'n Dan's Daughter* (Appletons) a Cape Cod family inherit money and make an experiment in the society life of a city.

But American fiction has rather diverged from the story of local color of the last century, which aimed chiefly at the portrayal of particular places and phases of life, often close at hand and well known. There are a great many books of distinctive color and atmosphere, but it is rarely very carefully studied, and generally makes its appeal by its out of the way romance, rather than by its familiar realism. There have been in 1914 a great number of stories of the ranch, often very good. H. M. Knibbs's *Overland Red* (Houghton, Mifflin Co.) adds to the general interest of ranch life and incident a curious character combined of the tramp and the cowboy; B. M. Bowers' *The Ranch at the Wolverine* (Little, Brown & Co.) also has more effort at character than some of the author's other books; J. Gregory's *Under Handicap* (Harpers) besides its atmosphere has a good idea at bottom; Zane Gray's *The Light of Western Stars* (Harpers) has that writer's usual appreciation of the great expanses of the Southwest; Dana Coolidge's *Batwing Bowles* (Stokes) makes a good case for the tenderfoot. There are a large number of novels of the woods, chiefly the Canadian, some by well-known writers, as Ralph Connor's *Patrol of the Sun Dance Trail* (Revell), Harold Bindloss' *For the Allinson Honor* (Stokes), H. Footner's *Sealed Valley* (Doubleday, Page & Co.), and Virgie Roe's *The Primal Lure* (Dodd, Mead & Co.). There is an unusual freshness in B. W. Sinclair's *North of Fifty-three* (Little, Brown & Co.), a fine flavor of the woods in Stanley Washburne's *Two in the Wilderness* (Lippincotts), and an especial wintry touch in Alice Jones's *Flame of Frost* (Appletons). J. O. Curwood in *Kazan* (Bobbs, Merrill Co.) has given the story of an escaped sledge-dog who returns to his own kind. Along with these belong two or three books of achievement, as one might say: Ridgewell Cullom's *The Way of the Strong* (Jacobs) is the story of a superman in Alaska and the wheatfields of Canada; Francis Lynde's *The City of Numbered Days* (Scribners) is the tale of a great immigration project; Ednah Aiken's *The River* (Bobbs, Merrill Co.) is the story of the bridling of the Colorado River. Of course our writers range far abroad, but there are not so many exotics in 1914 as is often the case. One of them is among the best books of the year; Samuel Merwin's *Anthony the Absolute* (Century Co.), the story of two Americans in Japan, has a fineness of feeling and a gift of character that are rare. Mary H. Bradley's *The Palace of Darkened Windows* (Appletons) is an Egyptian adventure, and *Felicidad* by R. Thomas (Little, Brown & Co.) is of an island in the Pacific. There are a good many stories of adventure, but none which have attracted much attention. The chief is Jack London's *The Mutiny of the Elsinore* (Macmillans), a book which takes us back to the author's earlier days. L. J. Vance in *The Lone Wolf* (Little, Brown & Co.), the story of a reformed Apache, is good but not quite up to the possibilities. We need only mention G. B. McCutcheon's *The Prince of Graustark* (Dodd, Mead & Co.). Here (as well as elsewhere) may be put that remarkable compound *Diane of the Green Van* by Leona Dalrymple (Reilly & Britton), an extraordinary reminiscence of almost all kinds of fiction previously known, from the novel of the open road to the story of international intrigue. There are many detective stories but no new ideas of importance. H. K. Webster's *The Butterfly* (Appletons) has charm and fancy as well as the usual ingeniousness. Anna Katherine Greene's *Dark Hollow* (Dodd, Mead & Co.) has her usual astonishing and well sustained mystery. R. Gillmore's *The Alster Case* (Appletons) has one very ingenious element which we do not remember ever to have met with before. His *The Opal Pin* (Appletons) is not so good, nor Carolyn Wells's last, *Anybody but Anne* (Lippincotts). N. S. Lincoln's *The Man Inside* (Appletons) is better.

Of historical novels there are none so good as the best of earlier years. Mary Johnston's *The Witch* (Houghton Mifflin Co.), a somber story of free life and the power of superstition in the days of Elizabeth, though finer in its conception than her earliest work, lacks some in its working out. Thomas Dixon's *The Victim* (Appletons) is a picture of Jefferson Davis and will be at once compared with his previous view of Abraham Lincoln; we do not esteem it so highly, either in its historical accuracy or its literary power. In *The Hidden Children* (Appletons) Robert W. Chambers fills out the series of historical novels which he conceived years ago, and which, we feel, shows him at his best. There are a number of other novels of American history. Crittenden Marriott's *The Ward of Tecumseh* (Lippincotts) is a good story of the wilderness after the Revolution. Beulah M. Dix's *Maid Melicent* (Hearst) is a story of Puritan and Cavalier in the Massachusetts colony. Marah E. Ryan's *The House of Dawn* (McClurg) is an interesting story of Mexico in the days of the Spaniards. Several are of the Civil War: Randall Parrish's *The Red Mist* (McClurg), E. Cummings' *Marmaduke of Tennessee* (McClurg) and Kate and Virgil D. Boyles' *The Hoosier Volunteers* (McClurg). In Newell D. Hillis' *The Story of Phaedrus* (Macmillans) and Henry Van Dyke's *The Lost Boy* (Harpers) we have a filling out of conceptions suggested by the Bible.

Such a summary, although based on some very obvious lines of interest both on the part of author (as it would seem) and of the reading public, fails to include many books which are neither markedly realistic nor romantic. Some of the best novels of the year belong to neither group. Julian Hinckley's *E* (Duffield) is one of those books which present a large view of society with all sorts of people; it might be compressed to advantage, but even as it stands it displays admirable appreciation of character and of the real courses of life. Coningsby Dawson's *The Raft* (Holt) has the romantic and poetic feeling which was so attractive in *The Garden without Walls* and the same appreciative feeling for childhood. Marie Van Vorst's *Big Tremaine* (Little, Brown & Co.) is a fine and well told story of Southern life in spite of some veiled inconsistencies and conventionalities. Rex Beach in *The Auction Block* (Harpers) is not so happy in his views of social life as in the rougher element where we learned to know him. We should note among the well-told love stories rather out of the common run, Louise K. Mabie's *The Lights are Bright* (Harpers), Henry Miller's *The House of Toys* (Bobbs, Merrill Co.) and Jennette Lee's *The Woman in the Alcove* (Scribners). Among the noteworthy books of the year are some which depend for their interest upon some original or well drawn character. In *The Poet* (Houghton, Mifflin Co.) Meredith Nicholson gives an appreciation of Eugene Field that will extend to many the affection which was formerly more confined; in *Penrod* (Doubleday, Page & Co.) Booth Tarkington (encouraged perhaps by the reception of the younger brother in *The Flirt*) gives a study of boy character. Finally we shall note the humorous books and the extravaganzas. Chief among the former is W. J. Hopkins' *Burbury Stoke* (Houghton, Mifflin Co.), so genuinely excellent that it is a shame to speak of it merely as humorous. As for the extravaganzas the most successful is E. D. Biggers' *Love Insurance* (Bobbs, Merrill Co.), which, when you once grant its frank impossibility, goes on with great spirit and interest.

Short Stories.—But a small proportion of the short stories written ever appear in book form, and an analysis of those which do appear would signify little. Some of them, however, should be recorded if nothing more. Mary Wilkins Freeman's *The Copy Cat* (Harpers) is a collection of her well known New England portraits. Zona Gale's *Neighborhood Stories* (Macmillans) offer as good a picture of the Middle West and have a real value as social suggestion beside their value as stories. Less attractive but equally good are Mrs. Van de Water's stories of married life in *The Shears of Delilah* (Putnams). Some of these collections are grouped around a character. Lucy Pratt's *Ezekiel* and *Ezekiel Expands* (Houghton, Mifflin Co.) are remarkable pictures of a little negro boy; in this one slight figure Miss Pratt has summed up the history and character of a race. Two collections continue the depiction of character already known to us: Julie Lippman's *Martha and Cupid* (Holt), a record of Martha as wife and mother, and Edna Ferber's *Personality Plus* (Stokes), a view of Emma McChesney as developed by her son Jock. There are a number of detective stories: A. B. Reeves in *The Dream Doctor* (Appletons) is ultra-scientific in his applications of science to the discovery of mysteries and crimes, while Percy Brebner's *Christopher Quarles* (Dutton) returns to the pure intellectuality of the great original. There is an excellent collection of Charles G. D. Roberts' animal stories in *Hoof and Claw* (Macmillans).

Biography. — As usual there are many good biographies and autobiographies, the latter generally the more interesting. These reminiscences, memories and what not have an appeal and value as evidence or revelation of American life. First in most minds will come Brand Whitlock's *Forty Years of It* (Appletons), the story of a fine kind of American democrat, with views of two others of the same sort, "Golden Rule" Jones and Tom Johnson of Cleveland. Another book equally striking is *In My Youth* (Bobbs, Merrill Co.), said to be by Robert Dudley, which gives a personal view of a most interesting phase of the life of our country now for ever passed away; it is a view of the Middle West in the making, a phase of life so near as to be remembered by a few and yet so different from our own time as to seem a different epoch. There are two memorials of successful and well known men, the *Memories of My Youth* (Putnams) by George Haven Putnam, and *My Autobiography* by S. S. McClure (Stokes), two curiously different books, but with much in common as American documents. Here, too, should be placed two other records of Americans. Edward A. Steiner is well known by his work with the immigrants and his story *From Alien to Citizen* (Revell) will be read with sympathy by many. Another book equally worthy of note is A. M. Rihbany's *A Far Journey* (Houghton, Mifflin Co.); the author is an American who twenty years ago landed in America practically penniless, and is now the clergyman of an influential church in one of our large cities. A very different kind of career is that of Al Jennings, told in *Beating Back* (Appletons), who began as a cowboy, became an outlaw and a convict, and has by this time got so far back as to carry the Democratic primaries in Oklahoma for the nomination for governor, although he failed of election. Two other views of life may be interestingly compared: Gen. F. Funston's *Memories of Two Wars* (Scribners) is a most exciting story, though told in a plain and unadorned fashion, of a man who leaped almost at a bound into position and public notice which experience shows to have been amply deserved. W. L. Comfort's *Midstream: A Chronicle at Half Way* (Doran) is a much more vigorous presentation of a life that by its very nature was one of thought rather than action.

Besides these books, of which several would most properly be considered autobiographic, are several other collections of material. Henry James in *Notes of a Son and Brother* (Scribners) would seem to claim no higher title for this second volume of his reminiscences. We are not clear as to whether the chief value of the book is biographic or autobiographic, but value there surely is. Horace Traubel's third volume of *Walt Whitman in Camden* (Kennerley) continues a work so well known as to need no description. Another book of exceptional value is *Little Women Letters from the House of Alcott* (Little, Brown & Co.) by Jessie Bonstelle and Marian de Forest, which gives a better and more comprehensible idea of Bronson Alcott than would be gathered from many more elaborate biographies.

Of true biographies, the finished records of lives esteemed great, there are not very many, though some are noteworthy. *The Letters and Journals of S. F. B. Morse* (Houghton, Mifflin Co.) is a much needed account of a most distinguished American based on much private material. Equally important is *Our Friend John Burroughs* (Houghton, Mifflin Co.) by Clara Barrus. Here also we have much that is autobiographic; indeed the book is rather material for a life than an attempt even at a final estimate and judgment. The same thing may be said of *Thomas Wentworth Higginson* (Houghton, Mifflin Co.) by his wife, a valuable record of the history of our country during the last century. Different in character are the *Confederate Portraits* (Houghton, Mifflin Co.) by Gamaliel Bradford, a series of careful historical studies. Winifred Holt's *A Beacon for the Blind* (Houghton, Mifflin Co.) is the life of Henry Fawcett. The author was led to this subject by her devotion to the cause of the blind, for Henry Fawcett lost his sight at the

1914 LITERATURE AND LANGUAGE

age of twenty-five. She has given her book a good name, for it convincingly shows what remarkable things can be accomplished by courage and character.

Poetry.—The poetry of the year comes, to the chronicler at least, as the product of many conflicting and confusing influences. Groups and categories form and dissolve and reform with an irregularity distressing to the systematizer and delightful to the lover of poetry. Some very obvious tendencies may be noted; one is toward a sort of democracy. Walt Mason still prints the quintessence of the commonplace (no easy matter to get at) in the appearance of prose in the corner of the daily papers. Vachel Lindsey in *The Congo and Other Poems* (Macmillans) is said to be the poetic expression of the Middle West. Arturo Giovanitti (*Arrows in the Gale*, Hillacre Book House) presents his testimony in words to go with the socializing testimony of his act. Patrick MacGill, ex-ditch-digger and navvy, sings of the "underworld, the great oppressed" in *Songs of the Dead End* (Kennerley). Miss Harriet Munroe in *You and I* (Macmillan) writes of the Panama Canal, the turbine, the telephone, State St., Chicago, and other modern matters. Conrad Aiken in *Earth Triumphant* (Macmillans) feels that a story is the thing that all will listen to.

This democratic tendency showing itself in the stuff of poetry, also finds expression in form in the work of several poets who express themselves in free rhythms. Among these we note Amy Lowell (*Sword Blades and Poppy Seed*, Macmillans), who has not only won recognition for her work in practice, but has presented her principles in theory in an essay on *vers libre*. Arthur Stringer does likewise in *Open Water* (Lane). It is not possible in a record to discuss such matters: we had supposed that Heine and Walt Whitman and Henley had made it possible for a poet to express himself as he chose without explaining that rhyme and rhythm were not among poetic necessities. James Oppenheim, however, does not think so, for he has explanations for the "polyrhythms" of his *Songs of the New Age* (Century Co.). Horace Traubel, of course, in *Chants Communal* (A. and C. Boni), offers no explanation for continuing the Whitman tradition.

All these are in a measure innovators, rebels in a world where there are many who are content with the old paths. Of these others we count the most original Robert Frost, whose *North of Boston* (David Nutt), though it may be compared with others in being blank-verse pastoral, has such fine and intense sincerity as differentiates it at once. Paul Laurence Dunbar's complete poems, most of which were known before, have been published. Others already known have published during the year: Coningsby Dawson's *A Night in Florence* continues the stroke of imaginative idealism which we found in his earlier poems; Edward S. Martin (*Poems*, Scribner), the late Madison S. Cawein (*Minions of the Moon*, Stewart & Kidd) and Henry Van Dyke (*The Grand Canyon*, Scribners) are too well known to call for more than record of their new volumes.

Essays and Criticism.—In the field of criticism nothing is so worthy remark as *Notes on Novelists* by Henry James (Scribners). Whatever one may think of James' creative work, there can be no question that the utterance of one who for half a century has been a close observer of the fiction of the world has a distinction rarely equaled. There will be many who will hold that James cannot write with sympathy, hardly even with openmindedness, on one-half of the field of fiction. Yet with this book as with his early criticisms, one is glad to take what there is without quarreling over what there is not. Another book by a veteran, though not exactly in this present field, is *Mont St. Michel and Chartres* (Houghton, Mifflin Co.) by Henry Adams. Mr. Adams is well known as an historian of our own land, but here he devotes himself to a presentation of the medieval spirit in architecture, poetry, and philosophy. Another important book is *The Challenge of Facts and Other Essays* (Yale University Press), a continuation of the series of writings of the late William G. Sumner, a book of wide significance, if it properly represents the influence of the author. Of books by men still in the harness, as one might say, one that has attracted a good deal of attention is Richard C. Cabot's *What Men Live By* (Houghton, Mifflin Co.), an analysis of the main elements in life. The most considerable work of criticism is that by W. C. Brownell entitled *Criticism* (Scribners). In the practice of literary criticism Alden Sampson's *Studies in Milton* (Moffat, Yard & Co.) should be particularly remarked and in later literature Archibald Henderson's *The Changing Drama* (Holt), a work showing wide reading and great skill in perceiving system in the chaotic conditions of the modern theater. Another piece of criticism is Kenyon Cox's *Artist and Public* (Scribners), a book by a master of painting which yet deals with the subject in a simple and unprofessional manner. We note also two books of a kind which seems to arise particularly from the legal profession. John Marshal Gest's *The Lawyer in Literature* (Boston Book Co.) and Theron G. Strong's *Landmarks of a Lawyer's Lifetime* (Dodd, Mead & Co.) are somewhat more interesting to the lawyer than to the lay reader, but they well deserve reproduction in book form.

MODERN LANGUAGES AND LITERATURE

GERMANIC LANGUAGES AND LITERATURE

DANIEL B. SHUMWAY

German Fiction and Drama.—The steadily increasing interest in German literature is shown by the large number of dramas and novels that have been translated during the year. Volumes III and IV of Lewissohn's translation of Hauptmann's works have appeared, volume III containing the domestic dramas, *The Reconciliation (Friedensfest), Lonely Lives (Einsame Menschen), Colleague Crampton* and *Michael Kramer*, and volume IV three symbolic and legendary dramas, *The Assumption of Hannele, The Sunken Bell*, and *Henry of Aue*. K. Holl has published a biography of Hauptmann containing much valuable . d hitherto unknown material relative to the poet and his works. Hauptmann's latest play, *Der Bogen des Odysseus* (Lemcke), has been issued in America. Sudermann is represented by an edition of his recent historical play, *Die Lobgesänge des Claudius* (Lemcke). A number of Schnitzler's plays have been translated by H. B. Samuel (McClurg), and Björkman has also translated three of his plays, *The Lonely Way, Interlude,* and *Countess Mizzi*. Hofmannsthal's one-act play, *Death and the Fool*, has been rendered by Elizabeth Walter (Badger). Three plays of Hebbel have also appeared in Dutton's "Everyman's Library." Garnet Smith has an interesting sketch of the development of German drama from the beginnings of the naturalistic movement down to the present time in the *Quarterly Review* for January. Count de Soissons treats of "Recent Dramatic Movements in Germany" in the *Contemporary Review* for February, the study covering selected works of Sudermann, Schmidtbonn, Elsner, Rapp and Stucken. Amelia von Ende discusses in the *Nation* (xcviii, 370) the latest dramas of Sudermann, Wedekind, Halbe, Eulenburg, Thoma and others. A study of the *Continental Drama of To-day* has been published by B. H. Clark (Holt).

German fiction is equally well represented. At the head of the list stands a translation by G. C. Page of Goethe's famous novel *Wilhelm Meister's Theatrical Mission*, with an introduction by Harry Mayne. Gottfried Keller's charming idyl, *Village Romeo and Juliet,* has been translated by A. C. Bahlmann, with an introduction from the pen of Edith Wharton (Scribner). Bertha Suttner's recent novel, *When Thoughts Will Soar,* dealing with the feminist movement, has been done into English by N. H. Dole (Houghton). Wolzogen's humorous musical story of Weimar and Lizst has been translated under the title of *Florian Mayr* by E. W. Breck and C. H. Genung (Huebsch). Herzog's well-known musical novel, *Das Lebenslied,* has been rendered by Adele Lewisohn under the title *Story of Helga* (Dutton). Paul Schreckenbach's powerful historical romance, *The King of Rothenburg,* translated by A. L. Bookstaver (Badger), will delight all lovers of that quaint town. Very timely is the translation by Stella Bloch of Walter Bloem's *The Iron Year*, presenting as it does a graphic picture of certain phases of the Franco-Prussian War. Fred. Eisemann has published in translation six of Schnitzler's erotic and mystic tales under the title of *Viennese Idylls* (Luce). Two other tales of the same author, "She Never Knew" and "Dead Men Tell No Tales," have been rendered by Beatrice Marshall in the *Fortnightly* for January and June. In an illuminating article on "Recent German Fiction" (*Nineteenth Century*, March) Dorothea Gerard gives detailed accounts with extracts of new novels by Kellermann, Bartsch, Schnitzler, Mann, Ertl and Stratz. Amelia von Ende discusses in the *Nation* of July 9 novels by Hegeler, Lietger, Thoma and Ehrenstein.

German poetry is represented by a translation of Heine's *Poems and Ballads* by Robert Levy (Macmillan) and by a rendering of his masterly satire *Atta Troll* by Herman Scheffauer (Huebsch).

Among the essays on German literature the most pretentious is A. W. Porter's *Outlines of German Romanticism* (Ginn), intended as a manual for students and treating the subject in a novel fashion. Porterfield has also written on "Poets as Heroes of Epic and Dramatic Works in German Literature" in *Modern Philology* for June. Other important essays are: C. E. Vaughn, *Influence of English Poetry on the Romantic Revival on the Continent* (Oxford); R. W. Macan, "Goethe in Rome" (*Fortnightly*, January); Charles Handschin, "Goethe's Abfall von der Gotik" (*Mod. Phil.*, June); F. H. Adler, *Herder and Klopstock, a Comparative Study* (Stechert); Fritz Winther, *Das Gerettete Venedig* (Univ. of Cal.); Ernst Feise, "Zur Entstehung, Problem und Technik von Goethe's Werther" (*Jour. of Eng. and Ger. Phil.*, January); Fred. C. Braun, "Margaret Fuller's Translation and Criticism of Goethe's Tasso" (*ibid.*, April).

Germanic Philology.—In this field the following important articles and monographs have appeared: Harry F. Colling, "The Language of Freytag's *Ahnen*" (*Jour. of Eng. and Ger. Phil.*, April), showing his frequent use of foreign words and archaisms; Philip Seiberth, "A Study in the Principles of Linguistic Change" (*ibid.*, January); F. A. Bernstorff, *Use of the Word "Derselbe" from the Classic Period of German Literature to the Present Day* (Banta); Bruno Boezinger, *Das historische Präsens in der älteren deutschen Sprache* (Leland Stanford Univ.). Leo Wiener made an unsuccessful attempt to prove that the Gothic Bible does not represent the language of Ulfilas in an article entitled "Philological Fallacies" in the *Nation* for May 7 (see also *ibid.*, June 11). In the Old High German period F. A. Wood has well rendered the *Hildebrandslied* into English alliterative verse (Univ. of Chicago Press). In Middle High German T. W. Rolleston has retold *Parsifal, or the Legend of the Holy Grail* (Crowell); Jessie L. Weston, in *The Quest of the Holy Grail*, has given a clear account of the various sources and the theories pertaining to this complicated subject. Gertrud Schoepperle has published a thorough and systematic study of the sources of *Tristan and Isolt* (Ottendorfer Series of German Monographs). H. A. Guerber in his *Book of the Epic* treats of the *Nibelungenlied* and other German epics. Julius Goebel contributes an article on the art of Walther von der Vogelweide to the April issue of the *Journal of English and German Philology*.

German-American Relations.—In this field a new annual has been launched, *Amerikanische Geschichtsblätter*, edited by Julius Goebel. It contains a large number of valuable articles on German settlements and migrations in America. J. T. Ochs' work, *Der Deutsche Amerikanische Farmer*, discusses the part played by the German-Americans in the colonization of the United States. Preston A. Barba has continued his studies of the influence of America on German literature with an article "Cooper in Germany" (*German-American Annals* for January), and A. B. Faust has published the "Graffenried Manuscript C," the most complete of the manuscripts relating to the settlement of Newbern, N. C. (*ibid.*).

German Texts and Teaching.—In this field, for want of space, only a few of the most important texts can be mentioned. A new edition of Schiller's *Braut von Messina* has been prepared by K. H. Breul (Putnam); Frenssen's *Jörn Uhl*, edited by W. W. Florer (Heath); Carl Schurz's *Lebenserinnerungen* by Edward Manly (Allyn & Bacon); Spielhagen's *Das Skelett im Hause* by Marie Goebel (Oxford German Series). Mrs. Collitz has published a second volume of her German anthology under the title *Selections from Classical German Literature*, comprising selections from the reformation period to the beginning of the nineteenth century. G. O. Curme has written a *First German Grammar*, a skillful combination of grammar and reader. In the department of teaching the University of Wisconsin has issued an *Experimental Study of Methods of Teaching High-School German* from the pen of M. M. Clarahan; and C. H. Bell has compared German and American schools and educational methods in "Experiences of an American Exchange Teacher in Germany" (*Educational Review*, January).

Swedish.—In this field the activity in translating Strindberg's works continues unabated. Edith and Warner Oland have published *Swanwhite*, *Advent* and *The Storm* (Luce); Clara Fried has rendered *Advent* (Badger) and *Fair Haven and Foul Strand* and *The Growth of a Soul* (McBride, Nast); Elizabeth G. Westergren and Ellie Schleussner have each translated Strindberg's story of the East Skerry Islands, the one under the title *On Seaboard*, the other *By the Open Sea;* Edwin Björkman has contributed the additional translations *After the Fire, Debt and Credit, The Thunderer, Advent* and *Simoon.* Selma Lagerlöf's romantic picture of old Swedish life has been well translated by Anna Barwell as *Liliecrona's Home* (Dutton); selected tales of the same authoress have been edited in the original for American schools by Jules Mauritzson under the title *Valda Berättelser* (Augustana Book Co.). Tegner's *Fritiof's Saga* has likewise been edited by A. O. Stromberg (*ibid.*). Ellen Key's *Renaissance of Motherhood* has been rendered by Anna E. B. Fries (Putnam) and Hilles Grane's *Song of the Rose* by A. W. Kjellstrand (Augustana).

Norwegian.—In this field William Archer has published an entirely revised edition of his well-known translation of Ibsen's works (Scribner). A number of Ibsen's plays, including *The Pretender, The Pillars of Society,* etc., have been translated by R. F. Sharp for "Everyman's Library" (Dutton), and G. B. Shaw has continued his *Quintessence of Ibsen* down to the latter's death (Brentano). Björkman has finished a second series of Björnsen's plays, comprising *Love and Geography, Beyond Human Might* and *Laboremus* (Scribner), accurate but somewhat marred by vulgarisms and Germanisms. Knut Hamsun, a novelist of some prominence, though little known here, is now represented for the first time in English in the translation by Carl C. Hyllested of his novel, *Shallow Soil,* a study of young Norway. Norse sagas are represented by the *Song of Frithiof,* retold in modern verse by G. C. Allen (Doran), by the Icelandic saga of *Grettir the Strong* of the eleventh century translated by G. A. Hight (Dutton), and by *Svold, a Norse Sea Battle,* a poem by S. F. B. Lane (Scribner). Andersen's *Fairy Tales and Other Stories* have been revised and in part newly translated by W. A. and J. K. Craigie. (Oxford); Asbjörnsen's *Norse Fairy Tales* by G. W. Dasent (Lippincott), and *Norwegian Folk and Fairy Tales* by H. L. Braeksted under the title *Round the Yule Log* (Lippincott). In the *Nation* (xcviii, 206) Arne Kildal discusses recent Scandinavian plays and novels, calling special attention to Heiberg's *Bed of State (Paradesengen)*, dealing with the sickness and death of Björnsen, as the most sensational book of the season in Norway. The attempt that is now being made to reinstate the ancient language of Norway, the *Landsmaal*, as a literary tongue is discussed by Ingebright Lillehei in the *Journal of English and German Philology* for January, and by E. M. Bacon in the *Dial* for March 16, the former believing it will be successful, the latter, whose article is entitled "Anti-Babel," doubting it.

1914 LITERATURE AND LANGUAGE

Danish.—The revived interest in Holberg noted in the last issue (p. 798) is shown by a study of his comedies by O. J. Campbell (Harvard Univ. Press). Two plays of Hjalmar Bergstrom, *Karen Borneman*, a plea for the sex freedom of women, and *Lyngaard and Co.*, dealing with industrial conflicts, have been translated by Edwin Björkman (Kennerley). G. H. Borrow has rendered *Danish Romantic Ballads* into English (Putnam). Franz de Jessen's *Katya*, a romance of Russia, has been translated from the Danish by W. J. A. Worster (Luce), Jens Jörgensen's *Lourdes* by Ingeborg Lund with a preface by Hillaire Belloc (Longmans), and Martin Nex's *Pelle the Conqueror* by Jesse Muir (Holt). H. J. Hanson has published a comparative Norwegian-Danish-English dictionary (J. Anderson).

ROMANCE LANGUAGES AND LITERATURE

Benjamin P. Bourland

The year 1914 has not seen any departure from the usual courses in the pursuit of Romance studies in America, unless Professor Schevill's *Ovid and the Renascence in Spain* be considered an excursus into a field of a new kind. An examination of the year's publications suggests that activity in work about the Old-French epic is less than heretofore; that later French literature is proving increasingly tempting to younger scholars; that the study of classical Spanish is abundantly holding its own; that the renewed activity in Italian matters noted in the last issue (p. 798) can hardly be held to continue; that the preponderance of the literary over the grammatical interest subsists in about the usual ratio; and that the pedagogical aspects of the field are being more keenly considered, as is shown by a decrease in the output of hastily made text-books.

Necrology.—Frédéric Mistral died on March 25 at Maillane, the village in Provençe where he was born on Sept. 8, 1830, and where he spent nearly all of his life. Mistral was the accepted leader of the group of men of letters, the Félibres, whose purpose it is to rehabilitate Provençal as a literary language, and the greatest figure in Provençal letters of his time and of many centuries. He won international recognition, and received many honors in France and elsewhere (Nobel Prize, 1904). He was best known as a poet (*Mireillo*, 1859; *Calendan*, 1867; *Nerto*, 1884, and many other volumes), but he also made a notable contribution to scholarship in his *Trésor dou Félibrige*, a massive lexicon of modern Provençal (1878). Hermann Suchier, until 1913 professor in the University of Halle, died July 4, 1914, at the age of 66. Suchier was one of the pillars of the older German school of Romance philology. His work was in French and Provençal, and was concerned in large measure with Norman. His influence as a teacher was very great and his works numerous and influential. Alcée Fortier, professor of Romance languages in Tulane University, died on Feb. 14 at the age of 57; besides being the author and editor of numerous books in French literature and history, he was deeply concerned with the earlier history of Louisiana, and for many years was president of the State Historical Society.

Bibliography

Altrocchi, Rudolph.—"The Story of Dante's *Gianni Schicchi* and Regnard's *Légataire Universel.*" (Publ. Mod. Lang. Assoc., xxix, No. 2, 1914.)

Austin, Herbert D.—*Accredited Citations in Ristoro d'Arezzo's "Composizione del Mondo."* (Baltimore, Johns Hopkins Univ., 1913.)

Blossom, F. A.—*La Composition de Salammbô d'après la correspondance de Flaubert.* (Ibid.)

Bruce, J. Douglas.—"The Development of the Mort d'Arthur Theme in Mediæval Romance." (*Romanic Rev.*, iv, No. 4, 1913.)

Buchanan, M. A.—"Spanish Literature Exclusive of the Drama. General Histories, Studies and Collected Texts, 1891-1910." (*Krit. Jahresber. Fortsch. Roman. Phil.*, xii.)

Buffum, D. L.—"The Sources of the *Roman de la Violette.*" (*Romanic Rev.*, iv, No. 4, 1913.)

Chatfield-Taylor, H. C.—*Goldoni, a Biography.* (New York, Duffield, 1914.)

Coleman, A.—*Flaubert's Literary Development in the Light of His "Mémoires d'un fou," "Novembre,"* and

99

1914 LITERATURE AND LANGUAGE

"Éducation Sentimentale." (Baltimore, Johns Hopkins Univ., 1914.)
COSENZA, Mario E.—*Francesco Petrarca and the Revolution of Cola di Rienzo.* (Chicago, Univ. of Chicago Press, 1914.)
CRAWFORD, J. P. Wickersham.—"The Influence of Seneca's Tragedies on Ferreira's *Castro* and Bermúdez' *Nise lastimosa* and *Nise laureada.*" (*Mod. Phil.*, xii, No. 3, 1914.)
——. "Inedited Letters of Fulvio Orsini to Antonio Agostin." (Publ. Mod. Lang. Assoc., xxviii, No. 4, 1913.)
CRU, R. Loyalty.—*Diderot as a Disciple of English Thought.* (New York, Lemcke & Büchner, 1914.)
DUNLOP, Geoffrey A.—"The Sources of the Idyls of Jean Vauquelin de la Fresnaye. (*Mod. Phil.*, xii, No. 3, 1914.)
DUTTON, George B.—"The French Aristotelian Formalists and Thomas Rymer." (Publ. Mod. Lang. Assoc., xxix, No. 2, 1914.)
FARNSWORTH, W. O.—*Uncle and Nephew in the Old French "Chansons de geste."* (New York, Lemcke & Büchner, 1913.)
FAY, P. B., and COLEMAN, A.—*Sources and Structure of Flaubert's "Salammbô."* (Baltimore, Johns Hopkins Univ. Press, 1914.)
FISCHER, Walter P.—*The Literary Relations between La Fontaine and the "Astrée" of Honoré d'Urfé.* (Philadelphia, Univ. of Pennsylvania, 1913.)
FOULET, Lucien.—*Le Roman de Renard.* (Paris, Champion, 1914.)
GEDDES, J., Jr.—"Canadian French." (*Krit. Jahresber. Fort. Roman. Phil.*, xii.)
HAMILTON, George L.—*"L'histoire de Troie dans l'art du moyen-âge avant le Roman de Troie."* (*Romania*, xlii, No. 168, 1913.)
HOPKINS, Annette B.—*The Influence of Wace on the Arthurian Romances of Crestien de Troyes.* (Chicago, Univ. of Chicago Press, 1914.)
HOUSE, Ralph E.—"The Sources of Bartolomé Palau's *Farsa Salamantina.*" (*Romanic Rev.*, iv, No. 3, 1913.)
JONES, E. C.—*Saint Gilles.* (Paris, Champion, 1914.)
KEIDEL, George C.—*Old French Fables.* (Baltimore, Johns Hopkins Univ. Press, 1914.)
KINROSS, Martha.—*Tristram and Isoult.* (New York, Macmillan, 1914.)
NITZE, William A.—"The Romance of Erec, Son of Lac." (*Mod. Phil.*, xi, No. 4, 1914.)
ROBINSON, J. H., and ROLFE, H. W.—*Petrarch; the First Modern Scholar and Man of Letters.* 2d ed. (New York, Putnam, 1914.)
SCHEVILL, Rudolph.—*Ovid and the Renascence in Spain.* (Berkeley, Univ. of California Press, 1913.)
SEARLES, Colbert.—*"L'Académie française et Le Cid."* (*Rev. d'Hist. Litt. de la France*, xxi, No. 2, 1914.)
SHELDON, E. S.—*Some Remarks on the Origin of Romance Versification.* (Boston, Ginn, 1913.)
WARSHAW, J.—"The Identity of Somaize." (*Mod. Lang. Notes*, xxix, Nos. 2 and 3, 1914.)
WEEKS, R.—"General Phonetics," 1909. (*Krit. Jahresber. Fort. Roman. Phil.*, xii.)

Texts

RICHEUT, *Old French Poem of the Twelfth Century.* With Introduction, Notes and Glossary by Irville C. Lecompte. (*Romanic Rev.*, iv, No. 3, 1913.)
Spanish Treatise on Chess-Play written by order of King Alfonso the Sage in the Year 1283. Manuscript of the Royal Library of the Escorial. With an introduction by John G. White of Cleveland. (Leipzig and London, Quaritch, 1913.)
Troya Abrasada, de Pedro Calderón de la Barca y Juan de Zarabeta. Published by George Tyler Northup. (*Revue Hispanique*, xxix, No. 75, 1913.)
Correspondance de Voltaire, 1726-1729. Edited by Lucien Foulet. (Paris, Hachette, 1913.)
Vulgate Version of the Arthurian Romances. Edited from manuscripts in the British Museum by H. Oskar Sommer, vol. vii; supplement, *Le Livre d'Artus*, with glossary. (Washington, Carnegie Institute, 1913.)

ENGLISH LANGUAGE AND LITERATURE

C. G. CHILD

In the brief space available for this review it is possible only to indicate the general trend of American scholarship, and reference to many texts, reviews and articles upon points of detail, though technically of importance, must be omitted.

Philology.—Except for minor notes and textual criticism (Emerson's emendations of *Patience* in *Modern Language Notes* here deserve special mention) but little work has been accomplished, though the record is, on the whole, better than in the past two or three years. The most important single contributions have been F. A. Wood's "Some Parallel Formations in English" (*Hesperia*), Miss Babcock's article on inflexional *l* in its metric relations (*Publ. Mod. Lang. Assoc.*), and Curme's articles on "The Analytic Genitive in Germanic" (*Mod. Phil.*) and "The Origin and Force of the Split Infinitive" (*Mod. Lang. Notes*). Other contributions are F. N. Scott's "Order of Words in Certain Rhythmic Groups" (*Mod. Lang. Notes*), Kenyon's " 'Ye' and 'You' in the King James Version" (*Publ. Mod. Lang. Assoc.*), Read's "A Vernerian Sound Change in English" (*Eng. Stud.*), and Tucker Brooke's survey of "Germanic Studies in England 1559-1689" (*ibid.*). The need of proceeding at once with an *American Dialect Dictionary*, at cost otherwise of irreparable loss, has again been urged by Mead at the meeting of the Modern Language Association. The *Report* of the Joint Committee on Grammatical Nomenclature has been the subject of much comment in educational journals.

Old English Period (449-1150).—There has been less productive work in this field than usual. Reference may be made to B. C. Williams's "Gnomic Poetry in Anglo-Saxon" (Columbia), Olsen's "Beowulf and the Feast of Bricriu" (*Mod. Phil.*), Cook's *Some Accounts of the Bewcastle Cross* (Yale Univ. Press), and Miss Dudley's article on "The Grave" (*Mod. Phil.*), which links this period with the next.

Middle English Period (1150-1500).—The publication of McKnight's *Middle English Humorous Tales in Verse* (Heath) and Miss Shackford's useful volume of translations, *Legends and Satires from Medieval Literature* (Ginn), is welcome. Gerould's valuable article on the legend of St. Christina (*Mod. Lang. Notes*), Miss Spalding's *Middle English Charters of Christ* (Bryn Mawr *Monographs*), Miss Hammond's article on Lydgate (*Anglia*), and Sommer's *Structure of Le Livre d'Artus* (Hachette) should be especially noted; and, in the field of the drama, Karl Young on the Easter play (*Publ. Mod. Lang. Assoc.*), Bonnell on the *Prophet's Play* (*Publ. Mod. Lang. Assoc.*), Mackenzie on Henry Medwall's *Nature* (*ibid.*), and the latter's volume on *The English Moralities* (Ginn). America has not failed to distinguish herself, as for years past, in the study of Chaucer. There are important contributions by Lowes (*Mod. Phil.*), Tatlock (*Publ. Mod. Lang. Assoc.* and *Mod. Lang. Notes*), Carleton Brown (*Eng. Stud.*, Sept., 1913), Sypherd (*Publ. Mod. Lang. Assoc.*), Fansler (Columbia), and Jefferson (*Jour. Eng. and Germ. Phil.*), and Kuhl (*Publ. Mod. Lang. Assoc.*). The most notable contribution—one of the highest importance—is the paper (*ibid.*) by Frederick Tupper establishing the fact that Chaucer used the seven deadly sins as a leading motif in the *Canterbury Tales*.

Modern English Period (1500 to Date).—SeBoyer has written upon Skelton (*Mod. Lang. Notes*), and Tieje on "The Critical Heritage of Fiction in 1579" (*Eng. Stud.*). Special interest in the study of Spenser, manifested during several years, continues; here may be noted the articles of Padelford (*Jour. Eng. and Germ. Phil.*), Fletcher (*ibid.*), Long (*Mod. Lang. Notes, Anglia, and Eng. Stud.*), Lowes (*Publ. Mod. Lang. Assoc.*), and Hall (*ibid.*). There are, as usual, many papers and monographs upon the drama of the 16th and 17th centuries. Dutton writes upon "Dramatic Fashions Illustrated in Six Old Plays" (*Jour. Eng. and Germ. Phil.*) and Chislett upon *Ralph Roister Doister* (*Mod. Lang. Notes*). Wallace, who has distinguished himself by recent brilliant discoveries in English archives, treats *The First London Theater* (*Univ. of Nebraska Studies*) and proposes some startling theories in "The Evolution of the English Drama" (*Shakespeare Jahrbuch*). Reynolds (*Mod. Lang. Notes*), Graves (*Jour. Eng. and Germ. Phil.*), and Lawrence in the second series of his admirable studies of *The Elizabethan Playhouse* (Macmillan) treat the structure and conventions of the Elizabethan stage. Elizabethan tragedy is discussed by Alden (*Jour. Eng. and Germ. Phil.*) and by Fansler in *The Evolution of Technic in Elizabethan Tragedy* (Row, Peterson, and Co.). Of volumes upon Shakespeare may be mentioned Neilson and Thorndike's *The Facts About Shakespeare* (*Tudor Shakespeare*) and Stewart's *Some Textual Difficulties in Shakespeare* (Yale Univ. Press). Articles upon Shakespeare include studies by Adams (*Mod. Lang. Notes*), Kelsey (*Jour. Eng. and Germ. Phil.*), Mason (*Mod. Phil.*), Schreiber (*Publ. Mod. Lang. Assoc.*), and Tolman (*ibid.*). Penniman, in his edition of Jonson's *Poetaster* and Dekker's *Satiromastix* ("Belles Lettres Series") summarizes, and advances upon, his own previous work and that of others upon the war of the theaters. Adams discusses the authorship of *A Warning to Fair Women* (*Publ. Mod. Lang. Assoc.*), and contributes notes upon Henry Glapthorne's *Wit in a Constable* (*Jour. Eng. Germ. Phil.*). Nettleton treats of the *English Drama of the Restoration and Eighteenth Century* (Macmillan). Of especial note are Gayley's detailed study of *Beaumont the Dramatist* (Century Co.) and Schelling's survey of *English Drama* (Dent) from its beginnings to Sheridan. Milton is the subject of a volume by E. N. S. Thompson, *Essays on Milton* (Yale Univ. Press), and of articles by H. W. Peck (*Publ. Mod. Lang. Assoc.*) and Gilbert (*Mod. Lang. Notes*). Strauss has edited a volume of Farquhar in the "Belles Lettres Series." Articles of a scientific character dealing with the period from the close of the 17th century to the present are, as usual, few in proportion to the extent of time and its importance. Here may be cited Snyder on "Stuart and Jacobite Lyrics" (*Jour. Eng. and Germ. Phil.*), Bernbaum on Mrs. Behn's biography (*Publ. Mod. Lang. Assoc.*), Dutton on Thomas Rymer (*ibid.*), Elwood Smith on unidentified letters of Pope (*ibid.*), Hughes on *Clarissa Harlowe* (*Jour.*

Eng. and Germ. Phil.), Snyder on Thomas Gray (*Mod. Phil.*), Stork on the influence of the ballad on Wordsworth and Coleridge (*Publ. Mod. Lang. Assoc.*), Routh on the influence of Coleridge, Keats, and Shelley on Poe (*Mod. Lang. Notes*), Olivero on Hood and Keats (*ibid.*), Chew on Byron (*ibid.*), Eaton on De Quincey (*Jour. Eng. and Germ. Phil.*), Schultz on Scott's use of Chaucer (*Mod. Lang. Notes*), and Jaeck on John Oxenford (*Jour. Eng. and Germ. Phil.*).

The ballad is reserved for a word of special mention, not merely because American scholarship must always take a special interest in this field, owing to the monumental work of Child on *English and Scottish Ballads*, and Gummere's work upon the origins of poetry, but for a special reason noted below. In addition to the essay by Stork, above, may be listed Moore's article on "Omission of Central Action in English Ballads" (*Mod. Phil.*), and Forsythe's on "Modern Imitations of the Popular Ballad" (*Jour. Eng. and Germ. Phil.*). It is desirable to call special attention to the movement to gather oral versions of old ballads and native ballads still current in America (in which the Society of American Folk Lore has already done service) under the leadership of Belden and Alphonso C. Smith (see the *South Atlantic Quarterly* and the *Nation*). In this connection may be noted the continuation of the work of Lomax in gathering American folk songs (see abstract of his paper read at the meeting of the Modern Language Association).

ANCIENT LITERATURE AND PHILOLOGY

ANCIENT LITERATURE
(*Additions from Papyri*)

CLIFFORD HERSCHEL MOORE

There are fewer literary papyri to notice this year than in previous years, although the publication of documents still goes on apace. The Società Italiana per la ricerca dei Papiri greci e latini in Egitto brought out its second volume too late in 1913 for the last issue of the YEAR BOOK. Of its 44 numbers 18 are from works previously known, four being texts of the Old and New Testaments and nine Homeric. A fragment of the Gospel according to Luke (No. 124) follows the version represented by a number of the manuscripts of the Itala, omitting xxii, 62 (καὶ ἐξελθὼν ἔξω ἔκλαυσεν πικρῶς); it is therefore important as the first Greek manuscript known which supports the Latin manuscripts at this place. The other sacred fragments offer nothing remarkable.

Of the other texts already known

No. 117 is noteworthy, for it is a fourth-century fragment of the *Gynecology* of Soranus, a medical writer of the time of Trajan and Hadrian. The verso offers some variants from the text given in the unique codex Parisinus Græcus 2153 (c); the recto contains an incomplete passage which seems to belong to the text lost in a lacuna of c (=p. 300.19 Rose) and may therefore with future discoveries become important.

Among the fragments of new texts appears a part of a *florilegium sententiarum* (No. 120) which shows little new in substance, although the collection does not seem to be closely related to any of the known *florilegia*. No. 123 is a fragment of Sappho, apparently identical in content with a small fragment discovered by Hunt among the Oxyrhynchus papyri. No. 128 is a part of a rhetorical exercise (μελέτη) in which Lacedæmonian steersmen under Lysander argue their right to rewards for their victory over the Athenians. The battle in question may well have been Ægospotami, but the papyrus gives no certain indication. Nos. 130 and 131 may be related. Both are in hexameters. The former contains some 48 broken verses of a Hesiodic *Eoeae*, the lines telling of the race between Hippomanes and Atalanta; the latter is a portion of some Theban story. A medical fragment (No. 132), some half-verses of the *Hecale* of Callimachus (No. 133), a prose mythological fragment (No. 135), fragments of an unknown comedy (No. 143), and a part of an unknown life of Demosthenes (No. 144) may become important through later discoveries. Thirteen fragments grouped under No. 147 contain bits of the Pæans of Pindar; six of these certainly belong to the sixth and seventh Pæans published by Grenfell and Hunt (Oxyrh. Pap., v); the others cannot be placed with certainty.

More important than are these, however, are 87 verses from a comedy by Menander (?), No. 126, preserved on three pieces of parchment; the writing dates from the fifth century. The goddess Tyche speaks the prologue, which was apparently of the expository type. The dialogue preserved is insufficient to enable us to reconstruct the plot; but the verses tell us of a marriage, of a miser (φιλάργυρος) who may have given his name to the play, and of the sudden death of Smicrines' brother; a rascally slave Davus announces a great misfortune and quotes Carcinus and Euripides to the mystification and annoyance of Smicrines; and then the verses break off. Still the whole is a welcome addition to our growing *corpus Menandreum*.

Finally we should notice an interesting paraphrase in Latin hexameters of Virgil *Æn.* 1, 477ff.

In ΔΙΚΑΙΟΜΑΤΑ, edited by the Greek Society of Halle (Weidmann, Berlin, 1913), we find five literary fragments of which the most important are some half-hexameters from a Hellenistic epic, some half-lines of Sappho, and three substantial fragments of Æschines against Timarchus.

Lastly we should call attention to six lectures by E. M. Walker of Queen's College, Oxford, published under the title *The Hellenica Oxyrhyncia* (Oxford, 1913), in which the author inclines to favor the attribution to Ephorus.

GREEK LITERATURE

WILLIAM ARTHUR HEIDEL

The *American Journal of Philology*, the *American Journal of Archæology*, *Classical Philology*, and the other periodicals mentioned in the YEAR BOOK for 1910 (p. 162), continue the publication of excellent articles on a wide variety of subjects. A new illustrated magazine, *Art and Archæology*, made its first appearance in July, 1914. Although general and popular in character, it may be expected to present occasionally matters bearing indirectly, if not directly, on Greek literature. Among articles in periodicals for 1914 may be noted the following: G. M. Bolling, "The Archetype of Our Iliad and the Papyri," B. O. Foster, "The Duration of the Trojan War," J. A. Scott, "Two Homeric Personages," A. C. Johnson, "The Date of Menander's Andria," in the *American Journal of Philology*; G. M. Calhoun, "Documentary Frauds in Litigation at Athens," Paul Shorey, "Plato's Laws and the Unity of Plato's

Thought, I," J. A. Scott, "Athenian Interpolations in Homer, Part II," in *Classical Philology;* E. B. Clapp, "On Certain Fragments of Pindar," T. D. Goodell, "χρή and δεῖ," in the *Classical Quarterly;* F. A. Hall, "A Comparison of the Iphigenias of Euripides, Goethe, and Racine," in the *Classical Journal;* C. R. Post, "The Dramatic Art of Menander," in *Harvard Studies in Classical Philology;* A. R. Anderson, "Repudiative Questions in Greek Drama, and in Plautus and Terence," F. G. Allinson, "Some Passages in Menander," R. B. English, "Heraclitus and the Soul," in *Transactions of the American Philological Association.*

The year has brought forth several books which appeal to the student of Greek literature as well as the general reader. *Ancient Greece: a Sketch of Its Art, Literature, and Philosophy Viewed in Connection with Its External History from Earliest Times to the Age of Alexander the Great,* by H. B. Cotterill (Stokes), *Athens and Its Monuments,* by C. H. Weller (Macmillan), Furtwängler and Ulrich's *Greek and Roman Sculpture,* translated by Horace Taylor (Dutton), *Euripides and His Age,* by Gilbert Murray (Holt), are among the best of the number. In the "Loeb Classical Library" have appeared *Quintus Smyrnæus,* by A. S. Way, and *Plato,* vol. I, by H. N. Fowler, and Professor Wright's excellent *Works of the Emperor Julian,* has reached the second volume. Professor C. F. Smith, who had before produced good editions of Thucydides, Books III and VII, has given us a scholarly edition of Thucydides, Book VI (Ginn).

The number of American doctoral dissertations of the year is not large. The best, and also the one which possesses most interest for the student of literature, is a Yale dissertation, "The Influence of Isocrates on Cicero, Dionysius and Aristides," by H. M. Hubbell. "The Kings of Lydia, and a Rearrangement of Some Fragments from Nicolaus of Damascus," a Princeton dissertation, by Leigh Alexander, is of value to the historian. Another Princeton dissertation, "The House-Door on the Ancient Stage," by W. W. Mooney, is a useful study of the drama.

LATIN LITERATURE

CHARLES KNAPP

Though American work in Latin literature and allied fields consisted in 1914, as usual, mainly of articles in periodicals,[1] several books deserve attention. One, by E. G. Sihler, *Cicero of Arpinum,* is a political and literary biography, and a guide to the study of Cicero's writings. A translation of Vitruvius' important work on architecture, written by the late M. H. Morgan, of Harvard University, was published, with illustrations and original designs prepared under the direction of H. L. Warren.

A selected list of articles and dissertations follows, arranged according to the Latin authors with which they deal primarily: "The Helvetian Campaign. Was Cæsar Wise or Willful?" by A. T. Otis (*CJ.,* ix, 241-250, 292-300); "Catullus, LXVIII, A and B," by Tenney Frank (*AJP.,* xxxv, 67-78); "The Impeachments of Verres and Hastings: Cicero and Burke," by H. V. Canter (*CJ.,* ix, 199-211); *The Influence of Isocrates on Cicero, Dionysius, and Aristides,* by H. M. Hubbell, a Yale University dissertation; "The Prosecution of Archias," by R. W. Husband (*CJ.,* ix, 165-171); "Cicero's Judgment of Lucretius," by H. W. Litchfield (*HS.,* xxiv, 147-159); "The Conclusion of Cicero's *De Natura Deorum,"* by A. S. Pease (*TAPA.,* xliv, 25-37); "Lucilius: The *Ars Poetica* of Horace, and Persius," by G. C. Fiske (*HS.,* xxiv, 1-36); a review of H. Magnus' monumental critical text-edition of the *Metamorphoses* of Ovid (*AJP.,* xxxv, 207-211) and a review of R. Schevill's *Ovid and the Renaissance in Spain* (*Univ. of California Publ. in Mod. Phil.,* iv, 1-268; reviewed in *AJP.,* xxxv, 330-335), both by K. F. Smith, and distinct contributions to the study of Ovid; "The Greek Motives of the First Scene of Plautus' *Menæchmi,*" by G. D. Kellogg (*PAPA.,* xliv, xxxii-xxxiv); "The Presentation of Classi-

---

[1] Periodicals are cited thus: *AJP., American Journal of Philology; CJ., Classical Journal; CP., Classical Philology; CW., Classical Weekly; HS., Harvard Studies; TAPA.* (*PAPA.*), *Transactions (Proceedings) of the American Philological Association.*

cal Plays," by D. D. Hains (*CJ.*, ix, 189-198, 251-260, 344-353); "Notes on Plautus and Terence," by C. Knapp (*AJP.*, xxxv, 12-31); "The Plot of the *Querolus* and the Folk-Tales of Disguised Treasure," by D. P. Lockwood (*TAPA.*, xliv, 215-232); "The House-Door on the Ancient Stage," by W. W. Mooney, a Princeton University dissertation; "Roman Comedy," by W. A. Oldfather (*CW.*, vii, 217-222); "The Site of Roman Dramatic Performances," by Catharine Saunders (*TAPA*, xliv, 87-97); "More About the Dialogus of Tacitus," by W. Peterson (*AJP.*, xxxv, 74-78); "Tertullian and the Pagan Cults," by G. J. Laing (*PAPA.*, xliv, xxxv-xxxvii); reviews of Smith's edition of Tibullus, a work noticed a year ago, by A. L. Wheeler (*AJP.*, xxxv, 461-470) and B. L. Ullman (*CW.*, vii., 212-214); "Varroniana," by E. W. Fay (*AJP.*, xxxv, 149-162, 245-267).

Less definitely connected with particular authors are the following: a review of Leo, *Geschichte der Römischen Literatur*, I, by J. W. D. Ingersoll (*CW.*, vii, 188-190); "The Latin Epyllion," a study of the shorter poems in Latin and the reëstablishment and development of romanticism, by C. N. Jackson (*HS.*, xxiv, 37-50); a review of Duff, *A Literary History of Rome*, by E. S. McCartney (*CW.*, vii, 164-168); "The Abuse of Fire," a study of fire "miracles" in ancient times, by W. B. McDaniel (*ibid.*, 121-125, 129-132); "Some Greek, Roman and English Tityretus," a study of the persistent tradition, from classical times, of the semi-respectable street roisterer, with special reference to the etymology of "Tityretu" as a name for such roisterers, by W. B. McDaniel (*AJP.*, xxxv, 52-66: the author derives the name from *Tityrus*, in the sense of a Satyr); *The Birds of the Latin Poets*, by E. W. Martin, a Leland Stanford University publication; "The Story of the Strix: Ancient," a study of the ancient tales of a woman-bat, by S. G. Oliphant (*TAPA.*, xliv, 133-149); "A Study of the Social Position of the Devotees of the Oriental Cults in the Western World, Based on the Inscriptions," by D. N. Robinson (*TAPA.*, xliv, 151-161); "Dramatic 'Satura'," by B. L. Ullman (*CP.*, ix, 1-23).

A concise and simple statement of the matters at issue between various students of ancient metrical systems, Greek and Roman, is to be found in "The Old and New in Metrics," by R. W. Husband (*CJ.*, ix, 212-221); this paper was inspired by the publication, in 1912, of J. W. White's *The Verse of Greek Comedy*, which was reviewed by P. Shorey (*CP.*, viii, 99-104, 217-220; see also *ibid.*, 214-217, for reply by Professor White).

Reference was made in the last issue (p. 805) to the part played by American scholars in the preparation of the "Loeb Classical Library." During 1914 the volumes added include translations of Horace, *Odes*, by C. E. Bennett, of Cicero, *De Officiis*, by W. Miller, and of Suetonius, complete, by J. C. Rolfe.

That the interests of scholars in Latin literature take a wide range is evidenced by W. P. Mustard's edition of *The Piscatory Eclogues* of Jacopo Sannazaro, and by *De Rinucio Aretino Græcarum Litterarum Interprete*, by D. P. Lockwood (*HS.*, xxiv, 51-109). (For works on Latin syntax see *Indo-European Philology*, *infra.*)

SEMITIC LANGUAGES AND LITERATURE

Morris Jastrow, Jr.

The Hittites.—The progress made in unraveling the mystery of the Hittites merits a place here because the work within this field is largely carried on by Semitists. R. Campbell Thompson has hit upon a new method for the decipherment of the puzzling script in a monograph, "A New Decipherment of Hittite Hieroglyphics," published by the Society of Antiquaries of London. Basing his attempt chiefly upon a long inscription found at Carchemish in 1911, Mr. Thompson by a most ingenious and patient process of reasoning and of combination succeeded in reading correctly a number of proper names occurring in this and in other Hittite inscriptions. With this as a basis he has been able to pass on to other words and, while many of his results are still problematical, it looks very much as though the key discovered by him were correct.

A volume of Hittite texts, written in cuneiform characters and found in the course of excavation at Boghazkoi conducted by the late Prof. Hugo Winckler, is in course of preparation. Twenty-six little vocabularies comprised in this volume form the subject of a preliminary study by Prof. Friedrich Delitzsch, who shows that these vocabularies contain hundreds of Hittite words writte: in cuneiform characters, together with their equivalents in Babylonian and Akadian. As a consequence we now know the actual pronunciation and meaning of many Hittite words, as well as case endings and verbal forms.

For those interested in a general survey of the Hittite civilization, we may refer to Eduard Meyer's *Reich und Kultur der Chetiter* (Boston, 1914), an excellent monograph with full illustrations.

Assyriology.—The two most important works in the domain of Assyriology are the *Grundzüge der Sumerischen Grammatik* and the *Sumerisches Glossar* by Prof. Friedrich Delitzsch. Through these two works the study of Sumerian is finally placed on a sound basis, though there are still many problems in the language awaiting explanation. With the help of these two handbooks of Sumerian every Assyriologist is now in a position to pass on to the study of the older non-Semitic language of Babylonia.

Prof. A. T. Clay, of Yale University, has added, as editor of the *Babylonian Records in the Library of J. Pierpont Morgan*, two more volumes to the series, one prepared by the editor and furnishing 56 legal documents of Babylonia dating from the latest period (312 to 65 B. C.). Especial interest attaches to these texts because of the large number of Greek names occurring in them and Professor Clay has been particularly happy in the explanation of these names. The other volume (number 3 of the series) is by Dr. Clarence E. Keiser, of Yale University, who publishes for the first time a large number of tags or labels attached to merchandise or to animals and containing in a summary manner indications of the objects or animals forwarded through a messenger or on a boat. The texts published throw a further interesting light on the commercial methods in vogue in ancient Babylonia.

Two other publications in the domain of Assyriology are Dr. M. Schorr's *Alt-babylonische Rechtsurkunden* and Professors Kohler and Ungnad's *Assyrische Rechtsurkunden*, the former furnishing translations and valuable commentaries on some 300 of the older commercial and legal documents of Babylonia, the latter doing the same for almost 700 documents of the same class belonging to the Assyrian period.

Islam.—Prof. D. S. Margoliouth has brought to a close his great edition of Yaqut's *Dictionary of Learned Men*, published by the trustees of the E. J. W. Gibb Memorial of England. This biographical dictionary, one of the most important in the whole range of Arabic literature, contains notices of several thousand individuals, writers, statesmen, theologians, etc.; it is thus a mine of most valuable information for the student of Mohammedan and Arabic history. The same Professor Margoliouth has just published a series of "Lectures on the Early Development of Mohammedanism," which is an endeavor to trace the growth of Islamic ideas from the inside rather than from the outside point of view.

Old Testament.—Within the Old Testament field the usual large number of publications by German, French, English and American scholars have been forthcoming, among the most important being Prof. R. C. H. Charles' translation and commentary on *Apocrypha and Pseudepigrapha of the Old Testament* (2 vol., Oxford and Clarendon Press), based on the most minute and a•curate studies of the original texts. Mention may be also made of the *Festschrift*, published in celebration of the seventieth birthday of Prof. Julius Wellhausen of Göttingen, the leading Biblical student of the day, whose early researches formed a most important epoch in the critical study of the Old Testament. Professor Wellhausen is equally eminent as an Arabic scholar and in recent years has brought out important investigations on the New Testament. It was therefore particularly appropriate that his pupils and friends in all parts of the world should have united in preparing a *Festschrift* which contains articles by distinguished scholars in the three divisions of Professor Wellhausen's remarkable activity.

INDO-EUROPEAN PHILOLOGY
(Exclusive of the Germanic Languages)
ROLAND G. KENT

General.—L. Bloomfield's *Introduction to the Study of Language* (Holt) is an excellent manual, presenting the results of linguistic and phonetic study up to the present day. It covers part of the field of W. D. Whitney's *Language and the Study of Language*, published in 1867, but it supplements and corrects that work rather than entirely supersedes it, since the older book is larger and fuller and of such saneness of treatment that even the lapse of nearly 50 years has failed to destroy its value, though in details it must now be corrected.

The *Report of the Joint Committee on Grammatical Nomenclature*, appointed by the National Educational Association, the Modern Language Association of America and the American Philological Association, was issued at Chicago in the closing days of 1913, and sets forth a uniform terminology for grammar, applicable to all the languages studied in the schools of this country, in an attempt to reduce the waste of effort entailed by learning different sets of technical terms for different languages; it has met with much commendation, but also with considerable hostile criticism.

E. Prokosch, under the title *Die Stabilität des germanischen Konsonantensystems* (*IF.*,[1] xxxiii., 377-94), discusses the development of the consonants of the original speech in the separate languages.

[1] Periodicals are cited under the following abbreviations: *AJP.*, *American Journal of Philology*; *CJ.*, *Classical Journal*; *CP.*, *Classical Philology*; *CQ.*, *Classical Quarterly*; *CW.*, *Classical Weekly*; *IF.*, *Indogermanische Forschungen*; *JAOS.*, *Journal of the American Oriental Society*; *TAPA.*, *Transactions of the American Philological Association*.

Indo-Iranian.—Three volumes have recently appeared in the "Harvard Oriental Series," edited by C. R. Lanman: XII and XIII, *The Panchatantra-text of Purnabhadra*, by J. Hertel (critical commentaries, etc.; the text in vol. xi, previously published); and XV, *Bharavi's Poem, Kiratarjuniya, or Arjuna's Combat with the Kirata, translated from the original Sanskrit into German and explained*, by C. Cappeller.

M. Bloomfield presents (*Proc. Amer. Philos. Soc.*, lii, 616-50) a very interesting and valuable account of "The Character and Adventures of Muladeva," the arch-rogue and trickster of Hindu literature, gathered from many widely scattered sources. Other articles in the Indian field are C. R. Lanman, "Buddhaghosa's Treatise on Buddhism, Entitled the 'Way of Salvation': Analysis of Part I, 'On Morality'" (*Proc. Amer. Acad. Arts and Sci.*, xlix, 149-69), and "Hindu Law and Custom as to Gifts" (*Anniversary Papers by Colleagues and Pupils of G. L. Kittredge*, 1-14); G. M. Bolling, "The Çantikalpa of the *Atharvaveda*" (*JAOS.*, xxxiii, 265-78); E. A. Welden, "The Samkhya Teachings in the *Maitri Upanisad*" (*AJP.*, xxxv, 32-51); E. W. Hopkins, "Gleanings from the *Harivansa*" (*Festschrift für Ernst Windisch*, 68-77); F. Edgerton, "Vedic *sabhā*." (*Kuhns Zeitschrift*, xlvi, 173-8); A. J. Edmunds, "Identification of Asoka's First Buddhist Selection" (*Jour. Royal As. Soc.*, 1913, 385-7); D. Osborne, "A Græco-Indian Engraved Gem" (*Am. Jour. of Archæology*, xviii, 32-4); R. G. Kent, "The Chronology of Certain Indo-Iranian Sound Changes" (*JAOS.*, xxxiii, 259-62).

In the Iranian field the most notable product of the year is *A Catalogue of the Persian Manuscripts presented to the Metropolitan Museum of Art, New York, by Alexander Smith Cochran*, prepared and edited by A. V. W. Jackson and A. Yohannan, and issued as volume I of the "Columbia University Indo-Iranian Series," of which Professor Jackson is general editor (vols. II-VIII appeared in previous years). Other articles are: Jackson, "Art in Persian Manuscripts" (*Nation*, xcvi, 627-8), "The Ancient Persian Conception of Salvation According to the *Avesta*, or Bible of Zoroaster" (*Am. Jour. Theol.*, xvii, 195-206), "On a Statue of Zoroaster in New York City" (*Sanj Vartman*, Bombay, Sept., 1913), "Notes on Allusions to Ancient India in Pahlavi Literature" (*Festschrift für Ernst Windisch*, 209-212); L. H. Gray, "Iranian Miscellanies" (*JAOS.*, xxxiii, 281-94); H. C. Tolman, "Does *yaunā takabarā* (*Dar. NRa*) signify 'Shield (i. e. *Petasos*)-wearing Ionians'?" (*Proc. Am. Philol. Assoc.*, xliv, p. liii-lv).

Etymology and Phonology, General and Classical.—Very considerable contributions in etymology, running through the whole field of Indo-European languages, are made during the year by E. W. Fay (*CQ.*, viii, 50-60; *IF.*, xxxii, 330-2 and xxxiii, 351-67; *TAPA.*, xliv, 107-26; *Jour. Eng. and Germ. Phil.*, xii, 540-1; *AJP.*, xxxv, 149-62 and 245-67, with the linguistic material indexed 149-50); and by F. A. Wood (*CP.*, ix, 145-159; *Mod. Lang. Notes*, xxix, 69-72). G. Hempl (*TAPA.*, xliv, 185-214) interprets "The Tell el Amarna Texts" as "old Doric" Greek, but his view is highly improbable. F. C. Babbitt (*Berliner Phil. Wochenschr.*, xxxiv, 1055) interprets Athena's epithet Τριτογένεια as 'daughter of the third-born,' since her father Zeus was third in the genealogical line Uranus, Cronus, Zeus. C. D. Buck (*CP.*, ix, 370-3) answers negatively the query "Is the Suffix of βασίλισσα, etc., of Macedonian Origin?" W. H. Schoff, on "The Name of the Erythræan Sea" (*JAOS.*, xxxiii, 349-362), disputes the view of Miss Hoyt (*JAOS.*, xxxii, 115-9).

E. H. Sturtevant adds some important details on "The Genitive and Dative Singular of the Latin Pronominal Declension" (*TAPA.*, xliv, 99-105). C. D. Buck champions the validity of Greek "HΣΣE as Evidence for *esse*" (*CR.*, xxviii, 157-8). E. W. Fay (*AJP.*, xxxiv, 497-9) again as; sails Kent's views on the value of the fragments of Lucilius for Latin orthography (*A. Y. B.*, 1913, p. 807). R. G. Kent has etymological articles on *pomerium* (*TAPA.*, xliv, 19-24) and *puer* (*IF.*, xxxiii, 169-71). Miss E. Fahnestock and Miss M. B. Peaks present data for "A Vulgar Latin Origin for Spanish *padres* meaning 'Father and Mother'" (*TAPA.*, xliv, 77-86). F. H. Lee has an interesting paper on the "Etymological Tendencies of the Romans" (*CW.*, vii, 90-6). E. W. Nichols contributes valuable studies in word-meanings in his "Semantic Variability and Semantic equivalents of *-oso-* and *-lento-*" (Yale doctoral dissertation).

Latin Syntax.—A truly noteworthy product of American scholarship is C. E. Bennett's *Syntax of Early Latin*, Vol. II, *The Noun* (Allyn & Bacon, Boston), following Vol. I, *The Verb*, after an interval of four years. An exhaustive review, in part hostile, is given by C. Knapp in *AJP.*, xxxv, 268-93. Professor Bennett's two volumes supersede all previous treatments of the subject, and will remain the standard work in this field for many years.

The following special investigations may be noted: J. J. Schlicher, "The Historical Infinitive" (*CP.*, ix, 279-94 and 374-94); A. R. Anderson, "Studies in the Exclamatory Infinitive" (*C.P.*, ix, 60-76), "The Unity of the Enclitic *Ne*" (*CP.*, ix, 174-88) and "Repudiative Questions in Greek and Latin" (*TAPA.*, xliv, 43-64); R. B. Steele, "The Participle in Livy" (*AJP.*, xxxv, 168-78), and "The Passive Periphrastic in Latin" (*TAPA.*, xliv, 5-17); E. D. Cressman, "The Genitive and Ablative of Description" (*CJ.*, ix, 122-7); R. G. Kent, "Some Tense Sequences in Cæsar's *De Bello Gallico*" (*CW.*, vii, 77-8 and 88).

1915 LITERATURE AND LANGUAGE

AMERICAN LITERATURE

(Nov. 15, 1914, to Nov. 15, 1915)

EDWARD EVERETT HALE

Novels.—The year 1915 has not been noteworthy so far as fiction is concerned. There has been no great change either in the amount of fiction produced or in the kind. There has been very little that seems to have been inspired or suggested by the great public interest of the year, the European War. There have been no extraordinary best sellers; there have been more books than usual on the best selling lists but none has attained the popularity that has often been recorded. There have been a number of novels a good deal talked of or written about, but none that has made any such impression as can be remembered of novels of recent years. The more prominent novelists have produced as a rule nothing that will change their reputation. Those who come into notice for the first time do so usually with work of an accustomed kind. Within the established lines, however, there has been much excellent work. There are not so many of the biographical novels as in some years and the best of them nowadays are apt to give us a view of surroundings as well as of personal life. Dorothy Canfield's *The Bent Twig* (Holt) is quite as remarkable for its exhibition and criticism of the intellectual life of America as it is for its development of the character of an interesting woman from a childhood in a remarkable home through the troubled seas of a life of leisure and opportunity. Miss W. S. Cather in *The Song of the Lark* (Houghton, Mifflin Co.) gives the life and training of a Swedish girl, born and brought up in a little town in Colorado, who became a great singer; the figure of the great artist is well given and the earlier environment of western life is also good, although its necessity is not so clear. Ernest Poole's *The Harbor* (Macmillans) has been much discussed as a view of the industrial and social conditions of New York City, presented under the symbol of New York Harbor and a life of one who lived by it from boyhood to manhood with constant relation to its moods and phases. Winston Churchill in *A Far Country* (Macmillans) follows his later idea of studying the main currents of the life of to-day and presents the experience of a boy who grew up to be a corporation lawyer in a great middle-western city with an important part in the politics and business affairs of the nation. Mrs. Norris's *The Story of Julia Page* (Doubleday, Page & Co.) is another excellent presentation of a life story, in this case of a girl who makes her way from a dubious half-and-half sort of society to a place among the really best people of the country, and finds there much the same sort of difficulty that her mother had found in a coarser phase of life. Theodore Dreiser pauses in his study of the American financier to give an account of a so-called artist in *The "Genius"* (Lane), a man, however, at bottom not so very unlike the man of business Mr. Dreiser has heretofore presented.

Somewhat different from these are the books which have a reminiscence of what used to be called a "problem novel." There are few books at present which are definitely devoted to any social question, so-called, although as with several which we have just mentioned there are a number which are distinctly moulded by a desire to write about some of the ideas which interest people nowadays. Of these latter one of the best is Judge Grant's *The High Priestess*

(Scribners), written with the desire to present a possible case in the current view of feminism, but not too strongly charged with that idea to lose individuality as a picture of life and character. The same may be said of Booth Tarkington's *The Turmoil* (Harpers) which gives the contrast between our American business aptitude and our interest in other matters. John Corbin's *The Edge* (Duffield) deals with the question of private rather than public economy. Miss N. W. Putnam's *The Little Missioner* (Appletons) deals with no one question but is largely modeled by ideas in politics and religion. Alice Gerstenberg's *The Conscience of Sarah Platt* (McClurg) and James Hay's *The Man Who Forgot* (Doubleday, Page & Co.) are more definite dealings with problems, one a private question and the other public, namely, temperance. Minnie J. Reynold's *The Crayon Clue* (Kennerley) is a bright and spirited story of graft and tyranny in the public schools in Bartown. Mrs. Frances Allen's *Her Wings* (Houghton, Mifflin Co.) is a semi-humorous view of the suffrage question.

Of the many books which are most remarkable for what is often called "the spirit of place," we may mention first those which present or sometimes merely try to present the life of New York City, which, so far as fiction is concerned at least, is naturally the typical big city of the country. In most cases these books give rather a superficial view of a flashy exterior, the extravagant semi-public sensational life in which the restaurant and theatre represent play and the stock exchange represents work. Such for instance is Rupert Hughes' *Empty Pockets* (Harpers), which although it begins as a detective story goes on with the idea of giving a view of New York life. Reginald W. Kauffman's *Jim* (Moffatt, Yard & Co.) gives also this dazzling, glittering side of New York life, as does Gouverneur Morris's *When My Ship Comes In* (Scribners), which also has a considerable theatrical element to it, being a story of the theft of a play. Owen Johnson's *Making Money* (Stokes) also seems to belong here. George Bronson Howard's *God's Man* (Bobbs-Merrill Co.) presents a curious understage of the same sort of thing. Robert W. Chambers' *Athalie* (Appletons) has the contrasting note of the beautiful old country place and the accompanying motive or idea of a correspondence between the spiritual and the physical life. James L. Forbes' *The Great Mirage* (Harpers) is a story of newspaper life in New York but gives strongly the idea that this hectic sensational outer life is but a bubble to be pricked by whoever would know the real life of the great city. G. Corson's *Blue Blood and Red* (Holt), a well written book of great promise, is devoted to something of the same view, although it has so little of theory and so much of life that perhaps its main idea is not sufficiently obvious. James Oppenheim's *The Beloved* (Huebsch) is a love story of Greenwich Village, showing in its manner something of a change from the author's earlier work. Therese Tyler's *The Dusty Road* (Lippincotts) is a story of uncompromising realism of Philadelphia society.

There are also, as there have been for some time, stories of local color. Of these Elsie Singmaster's *Katy Gaumer* (Houghton, Mifflin Co.) is a picture of convincing fidelity of life among the Pennsylvania Germans. Mrs. H. R. Martin's *Martha of the Mennonite Country* (Doubleday, Page & Co.) tells of one of the religious communities of the same state; Arnold Mulder's *Bram of the Five Corners* (McClurg) joins to a view of life among the Dutch communities in Michigan the consideration of a painful possibility which perhaps arises much more often than it comes to public notice. Mr. Lincoln's *Thankful's Inheritance* (Appletons) is, like most of his books, a Cape Cod story. Joseph Hergersheimer's *Mountain Blood* (Kennerley), Mrs. Paine Erskine's *A Girl of the Blue Ridge* (Little, Brown & Co.), C. N. Buck's *The Code of the Mountains* (Watt), deal in widely different ways and phases with the life of the eastern mountaineers. Several of the books otherwise mentioned have a strong element of local color, generally in the beginning, in the account of the early days of their chief figure. C. W.

1915 LITERATURE AND LANGUAGE

Camp's *Sinister Island* (Dodd, Mead & Co.) runs into romance and mystery, and so does C. T. Jackson's *John, the Fool* (Bobbs-Merrill Co.) but of both the prevailing note is atmosphere.

These stories of place run naturally into stories of adventure, but the real story of adventure rarely gets any very true idea of locality; a touch of atmosphere or scenery is generally all that is attempted. The great West is still the scene for most of the "adventure stories," sometimes on a ranch, sometimes in a mine, sometimes on a Mexican border, sometimes as far north as Alaska and the Columbia River. One can do no more than mention the names of Ridgewell Cullom's *The Law Breakers* (Jacobs); Zane Gray's *The Lone Star Ranger* and *The Rainbow Trail* (Harpers); H. H. Knibbs' *Sundown Slim* (Houghton, Mifflin Co.); Caroline Lockhart's *The Man from the Bitter Roots* (Lippincotts); F. Lynde's *The Real Man;* H. Willsie's *Still Jim* (Stokes); these are the best of many. Here too, except that there is more to it than to the others, one would put Rex Beach's *The Heart of the Sunset* (Harpers), although it is by no means the author's best work. There are also a number of stories of adventure in Canada. Harold Bindloss' *Harding of Allenwood* (Stokes) is a story of the Saskatchewan. I. O. Curwood's *God's Country and the Woman* (Doubleday, Page & Co.) is a lively melodrama of the Canadian Northwest. R. Pocock's *The Cheerful Blackguard* (Bobbs-Merrill Co.) is a smart tale of the Canadian mounted police. S. Shaw's *A Siren of the Snows* (Little, Brown & Co.) is a tale of a puzzling case which called a secret-service agent to the far North. W. Elwood's *Guimo* (Reilly & Britton) is not exactly of adventure but of life in the Philippines. We might put here also Sinclair Lewis's *The Trail of the Hawk* (Harpers), a story of the life of Carl Ericson, a Minnesota boy who was seized with a passion for the aeroplane, a book full of good notes of American life. A few stories are directly inspired by the war: Robert W. Chambers' *Who Goes There* (Appletons); W. S. Dyer's *Pierrot; Dog of Belgium* (Doubleday, Page & Co.); A. B. Reeves' *The War Terror* (Hearst); B. E. Stevenson's *Little Comrade* (Holt); all of them interesting though none of them great. W. L. Comfort's *Red Fleece* (Doubleday, Page & Co.) carries on the idea of his earlier book on the Russia-Japanese War. P. J. Brebner's *The Turbulent Dutchess* (Little, Brown & Co.) seems like a belated and rather lonely Zenda story. We shall not even name the score or more detective stories, which show that this fascinating form has by no means lost its charm.

There are as always a considerable number of historical novels, some of considerable merit. Stewart Edward White's *The Gray Dawn* (Doubleday, Page & Co.) is chiefly a chronicle of a phase of our nation's history at a most interesting period. This is the second volume of Mr. White's series on early life in California of which the first appeared in 1914. A book of something the same kind but of narrower scope is Eleanor Atkinson's *Johnny Appleseed* (Harpers), a story of frontier life a hundred years ago when Jonathan Chapman was planting appleseeds around the bare homes of Ohio. James Lane Allen's *The Sword of Youth* (Century) is a story of the Civil War, leisurely and elaborated in style like most of the works of its author. Mary Johnston in *The Fortunes of Garin* (Houghton, Mifflin Co.) has left the American themes which first brought her into notice and presents a very good study of mediæval life in southern France in the time of the Crusades.

There are a number of books which do not fall in such obvious classes. Henry S. Harrison's *Angela's Business* (Houghton, Mifflin Co.) is, like his recent books, not without its reflection of questions and problems, but it is in the main a story of the love affairs of several young people, a lighter story than some of its author's but equally well told. Samuel Merwin's *The Honey Bee* (Bobbs-Merrill Co.) also has a reflection of current questions in its figure of Hilda Wilson, the capable business woman. She is the honey bee, the one whose life is taken up in work, who has nothing to do with other affairs of life, except we might add, in this particular story where she has new interests, curious and diverse enough to satisfy anybody. Mrs. Josephine D. Bacon's *Open Market* (Appletons), like her last book, is a commentary on married life, based upon what is really a bit of extravagance, but proceeding from such premises in a natural and convincing manner. George A. Chamberlain's *Through Stained Glass* (Century) is a book which maintains the reputation made by the author in his anonymously published *Home*. Both books have a vast range of human experience and an ability to probe human nature to considerable depths. Mrs. Gene Stratton-Porter's *Michael O'Halloran* (Doubleday, Page & Co.) is something of a variation of her earlier stories of the Limberlost. It does give us a glimpse or two of nature, but is in the main taken up in questions of city life. David Grayson's *Hempfield* (Doubleday, Page & Co.) shows us the influence of the same spirit in the lives of interesting men and women that is already familiar to readers of the author's other works. Mrs. Mary Hallock Foote's *The Valley Road* (Houghton, Mifflin Co.) is an interesting story of an engineer's family in California. There are a few books which are, as we might say, garments for ideas that the author has deeply had at heart. Will Levington Comfort's *Lot & Co.* (Doran) is a protest against the hard and grasping game of grab so current in our present life. Jack London's *The Star Rover* (Macmillans) is an adaptation of the idea of the passage of the soul through many lives, although it must be confessed that the author gives us no notion of any particular connection between the lives he recalls, so that the book is more like a series of short stories than anything else. There are not as many humorous books as in some years but we ought to mention H. C. Wilson's *Ruggles of Red Gap* (Doubleday, Page & Co.); Ruggles is an ultra English valet who in the guise of his master compares Red Gap with older civilization.

Short Stories. — The number of short stories published in the periodicals is so enormous that it is impossible to form more than a vague idea of fashions and tendencies, and the number published in collections is too small to give any real notion of the matter. Rather the best are Harvey O'Higgins' *The Adventures of Detective Barney* (Century), an amusing set of stories about a boy who studied to be a detective; Dorothy Canfield's *Hillsboro People* (Holt), a collection of excellent stories of Vermont; Mrs. Deland's *Around Old Chester* (Harpers), characteristic stories of Dr. Lavendar's people; Montague Glass's *The Competitive Nephew* (Doubleday, Page & Co.), giving us more of the world to which his earlier books introduced us; Edna Ferber's *Emma McChesney & Co.* (Stokes), some further adventures of this interesting business woman not only in business but in other fields. H. E. Porter's *Pepper* (Century) is a series of Harvard stories published under the name of Holworthy Hall. E. E. Ferris' *The Business Adventures of Billy Thomas* (Macmillans) is a number of stories on business matters, amusing and suggestive. Lucy Pratt's *Felix Tells It* (Appletons) gives the conversations of a boy showing plenty of observation though hardly the charm of *Ezekiel*. A. B. Reeves' *The War Terror* (Hearst) is a further series of the deeds of Craig Kennedy, not all about the war. George Fitch's *Homeburg Memories* (Little, Brown & Co.) are country town sketches, full of attractive memories. C. E. VanLoan's *Buck Parvin and the Movies* (Doran) is a book which would almost serve as a guide to the motion-picture business. Sewall Ford's *Shorty McCabe on the Job* (Clode) is a tale of Shorty's experience with strange bequests. This dozen books is but a drop from the bucket of short-story literature, yet it will give a notion of the general tendencies of the short story, though somewhat superior to the rest in quality.

Poetry.—The poetry of the year goes on in its escape beyond old bounds. In more senses than one it is "an extravagant and erring spirit." Both in what they say and the way they say it our poets put behind them the old poetic substance or the old poetic form or both. The most consistent and successful effort at large expression in free forms that has appeared for some time is Lincoln Colcord's *Vision of War* (Macmillans), a noble view of war and the present war in relation to democracy, humanity, and a more spiritual life. Equally free in form is Edgar L. Master's *Spoon River Anthology* (Macmillans), which with remarkable originality gives a cynical and gloomy presentation of life when once it is past. It is a saturnine development of "The evil that men do lives after them," and presents with unruffled temper characters and phases of life that even fiction has not often touched. More lyric in utterance is J. G. Fletcher in *Irradiations* (Houghton, Mifflin Co.); he uses free rhythms for the expression of feelings which, if they be not universal, might certainly be, for they seem elemental in character, unconditioned by culture or custom. Fanny S. Davis in *Crack-o'Dawn* in more accustomed forms gives utterance to a sentiment which is continually being aroused out of its daily round of pleasure in nature and fancy and the world to glimpses and understandings of the larger life of God and humanity. Two popular poets may be reckoned in this group of such as would broaden the bounds of poetry, though on the surface quite different from the rest; Berton Braley in *Songs of the Workaday World* (Doran), with poems of all sorts of stray and strange men from all over the world, and Walt Mason, whose *Horse Sense* (Macmillans) has long been known to all readers of the newspapers. Edwin Markham's *Shoes of Happiness* (Doubleday, Page & Co.) contains the author's poems of a dozen years, which if it has nothing so striking as the famous "Man with the Hoe" is yet cut out of the same piece. Several other books have something of the same note, as Joyce Kilmer in his *Trees and Other Poems* (Doran) and Margaret Widdemer in *The Factories* (Winston). More of a consistent whole in its idea is Witter Bynner's *New World* (Kennerley), developed from his earlier poem, "The Immigrant." Though we can only mention a few titles, we should note the increasing interest in writing plays, more especially by Edgar Arlington Robinson in *The Porcupine* (Macmillans) and Alice Brown in *Children of Earth* (Macmillans). There are several collections of one-act plays, for example, George Middleton's *Possessions* (Holt) and Percival Wilde's *Dawn* (Holt).

Biographies.—There are a number of good biographies and autobiographies, though nothing quite as good as some of the most striking things of the last few years. In the autobiographies George Haven Putnam in *Memories of a Publisher* (Putnams) carries on the series begun in 1914 in a volume which has even more interest. Rev. Lyman Abbott in his *Reminiscences* (Houghton, Mifflin Co.) is not merely a fit record of a life full of different kinds of important work but it gives also a view of the varied scenes in which Dr. Abbott's life has been passed. Equally important and interesting, or indeed more interesting, for it is told with a never failing sense of humor, is Dr. Anna K. Shaw's *The Story of a Pioneer* (Harpers). Dr. Shaw has always been pushing ahead and this is a most interesting account of her work. William Winter's *Vagrant Memories* (Doran) is a combination of the series of reminiscences which are the fruit of a long life devoted to an interest in the stage with exceptional opportunities for knowledge of it. They are full of anecdote, comment, philosophy, appreciation, and bring back to mind the old-time great ones of the theatre in the days of William Warren and Edwin Booth. Hiram Maxim's *My Life* (McBride, Nast & Co.) is perhaps hardly a contribution to American literature, but it is a most amusing and interesting account of a man of importance. *Letters to a Friend* and *Travels in Alaska* by the late John Muir (Houghton, Mifflin Co.) continue a remarkable series of writings, of which the publishers announce there still remain others unpublished. Poultney Bigelow's *Prussian Memories* (Putnams) is a volume of vigorous criticism of recent German ideals and American practice, put in the form of reminiscences of many years spent in Germany at different times.

Of the more formal biographies the chief is W. R. Thayer's *Life of John Hay* (Houghton, Mifflin Co.) based upon diaries and copious correspondence. It is particularly valuable for the light it throws on what were current politics ten and fifteen years ago in China and elsewhere, and its comment on contemporary statesmen. There is also a very full picture of the earlier years, and especially of John Hay's life in the White House as Secretary to Lincoln. Percy H. Epler's *Life of Clara Barton* is the first adequate account of the life of this well known figure of modern philanthropy. The book gives a full length figure; indeed it is almost an autobiography, for the original material in the hands of the author was very great. The same might be said of Wm. B. Parker's *Edward R. Sill* (Houghton, Mifflin Co.) which gives an account of the poet's own life in the poet's own words, for Sill was a great letter-writer. It was worth while to make such a picture of this fine nature that took so little pains to make himself known. We ought to mention, but can do nothing more, O. W. Firkins' *Ralph Waldo Emerson* (Houghton, Mifflin Co.); Wm. H. Dall's *Spencer F. Baird* (Lippincotts); and F. L. Bullard's attractive little sidelight on Lincoln, called *Tad and his Father* (Dodd, Mead & Co.).

Essays and Criticism.—The year has produced a number of notable collections of essays. First to be mentioned is John Burroughs' *The Breath of Life* (Houghton, Mifflin Co.), in which that great lover of nature and the open air meditates over a lifetime of observation and seeks to draw conclusions as to the secret of life. Paul E. More in the latest volumes of the Shelburne Essays, *Aristocracy and Justice* (Houghton, Mifflin Co.), presents the positive side of the argument which his last volume presented critically, the argument for what may be thought of as classicism in form and thought or at any rate something other than the individualism so current to-day in act and morals. John Jay Chapman's *Greek Genius* (Scribners) is something of an antidote to this last, though probably not so meant. But the writer is so constant in his desire to get beneath the conventionalism of pedants and people in general that his studies must be a pleasure to the individualist, even though they deal with a classic like Euripides and a standard like Shakespeare. Gerald Stanley Lee's *We* (Doubleday, Page & Co.) is an effort to show that the problem of the present day lies not so much in the conduct of nations as in the living of daily lives. There is a considerable number of books of literary or general criticism. Horace J. Bridges in *Criticisms of Life* (Houghton, Mifflin Co.) gives a number of studies of the wandering fires and blind guides of the day in a good solid book with much in it. James Huneker's *Ivory, Apes and Peacocks* is the latest collection of that author's scintilating delineations of novelties in modernity, chiefly in painting and music. Miss Amy Lowell's *Six French Poets* (Macmillans), a study of some of the poets of France of the present generation, is one of the most interesting expressions of current ideas on poetry. John Curtis Underwood's *Literature and Insurgency* (Kennerley) is made up of ten studies of recent American authors from Mark Twain to Robert W. Chambers.

MODERN LANGUAGES AND LITERATURE

ENGLISH LANGUAGE AND LITERATURE

ALBERT C. BAUGH

During 1915, as a result of the war in Europe, America has become almost the sole producer of scholarly work in the field of English philology and literature. So extensive has been the work done that it is impossible to notice here all the year's books, articles and editions of texts relating to the subject. Moreover, almost no mention can be made of the many notes on isolated details and specific points of text criticism, valuable as they are to the special student. It is only possible to indicate the general trend of American scholarship during the year.

English Philology.—Investigation of a purely philological character has been less extensive than research in the literature. Francis A. Wood has written on "So-called Prothetic Y and W in English" (*Jour. Eng. and Ger. Phil.*), G. O. Curme has continued his discussion of "The Development of Modern Groupstress in German and English" (*ibid.*) and W. F. Bryan has published "Studies in the Dialects of the Kentish Charters in the Old English Period." J. F. Royster's "The *Do* Auxiliary—1400 to 1450" (*Mod. Phil.*), A. S. Cook's "Archaic English in the Twelfth Century" (*Scottish Hist. Rev.*), and C. H. Grandgent's "Fashion and the Broad A" (*Nation*) may also be mentioned.

Old English Literature (449-1150).— In the field of Anglo-Saxon or Old English literature very little work has been done. Mention may be made of W. W. Lawrence's "Beowulf and the Tragedy of Finnsburg" (*Pub. Mod. Lang. Assoc.*), S. Moore's "Notes on the Old English *Christ*" (*Herrig's Archiv*), and A. S. Cook's "The Date of the Old English Inscription on the Brussels Cross" (*Mod. Lang Rev.*). In view of the little that has been done in 1915 on this portion of English literature, it may be noted that in some cases American scholars who have done their best work in the period have shown a tendency to permit their interests to stray into other channels.

Middle English Literature (1150-1500).— One of the matters most needing treatment in Middle English literature has been taken up by T. A. Knott in "An Essay toward the Critical Text of the A-Version of Piers the Plowman" (*Mod. Phil.*), and the same writer has contributed a valuable discussion of "The Text of Sir Gawayne and the Green Knight" to *Mod. Lang. Notes*. Another poem by the author of "Sir Gawayne" ("Cleanness") has been discussed in a note by O. F. Emerson (*Mod. Lang. Rev.*). H. L. Creek has treated "The Author of Havelok the Dane" (*Englische Studien*), Miss G. H. Campbell has printed texts of "The Middle English *Evangelie*" (*Pub. Mod. Lang. Assoc.*), and Carleton Brown has a note on "A Homiletical Debate between Heart and Eye" (*Mod. Lang. Notes*). P. E. Kretsmann's "A Few Notes on 'The Harrowing of Hell'" (*Mod. Phil.*) and Miss A. M. Jenney's "A Further Word as to the Origin of the Old Testament Plays" (*ibid.*) treat important subjects in Middle English literature. Lydgate has had the attention of R. Withington in "Queen Margaret's Entry into London, 1445" (*Mod. .Phil.*), and Skelton has been discussed in two articles by J. M. Berden (*Mod. Lang. Notes* and *Pub. Mod. Lang. Assoc.*). Recently there has appeared *A Literary Middle English Reader* edited by A. S. Cook. A work of exceptional value that has been eagerly awaited by students of Middle English literature is the bibliography by Carleton Brown of the Middle English religious and didactic literature in verse, which is about to come from the press.

As in recent years, America has again led the world in both the extent and quality of her contributions to the study of Chaucer. Most important of the year are Prof. Kittredge's volume entitled *Chaucer and His Poetry*, six lectures delivered in 1914 at Johns Hopkins University, and J. L. Lowes' article, "Chaucer and the Seven Deadly Sins" (*Pub. Mod. Lang. Assoc.*), a criticism of the views recently advanced by Tupper (especially in *ibid.*, xxix). Kittredge has also written on Chaucer's relation to Guillaume de Machaut in two articles (*Mod. Lang. Notes* and *Pub. Mod. Lang. Assoc.*), and Lowes has discussed "Chaucer and Dante's Convivio" (*Mod. Phil.*) and "The Prioress's Oath" (*Rom. Rev.*). "The Plan of the Canterbury Tales" has been treated by H. S. V. Jones (*Mod. Phil.*), while the Position of Group C in the Canterbury Tales" has been taken up by Samuel Moore (*Pub. Mod. Lang. Assoc.*). Karl Young contributes a note on "Chaucer and the Liturgy" (*Mod. Lang. Notes*), W. O. Sypherd maintains his position as regards "The Completeness of Chaucer's House of Fame" (*Mod. Lang. Notes*), and O. F. Emerson discusses the question "What is the Parlement of Foules?" (*Jour. Eng. and Ger. Phil.*). Frederick Tupper is the author of an interesting article on "The Quarrels of the Canterbury Pilgrims" (*ibid.*), another on "The Pardoner's Tavern" (*ibid.*), and notes in *Mod. Lang. Notes*. Finally may be noted Robertson's "Elements of Realism in the

Knight's Tale" (*Jour. Eng. and Ger. Phil.*) and A. S. Cook's "Beginning the Board in Prussia" (*ibid.*).

Modern English Literature (since 1500).—The transition from the Middle English to the Modern English period is well represented by an excellent article by Ronald S. Crane on "The Vogue of Guy of Warwick from the Close of the Middle Ages to the Romantic Revival" (*Pub. Mod. Lang. Assoc.*). In sixteenth-century literature apart from the drama there has been a tendency of late in America to focus attention on Spenser. F. M. Padelford writes on "The Political, Economic and Social Views of Spenser" (*Jour. Eng. and Ger. Phil.*), and P. W. Long discusses "Spenser and Sidney" (*Anglia*) and "Spenser's 'Muiopotmos'" (*Mod. Lang. Rev.*). H. D. Gray has added "A Possible Interpretation of Lyly's *Endimion*" (*Anglia*) to the number already existing. The connection between the Elizabethan age and the classics has been touched upon by Miss H. M. Blake in "Golding's Ovid in Elizabethan Times" (*Jour. Eng. and Ger. Phil.*), and Miss C. D'Evelyn has discussed the "Sources of the Arthur Story in Chester' *Love's Martyr*" (*ibid.*). As is to be expected, the drama has received much attention. The third volume of *Representative English Comedies* under the general editorship of C. M. Gayley has appeared, and numerous articles on Shakespeare and his contemporaries have been published in the periodicals. H. D. Gray has treated "The First Quarto Hamlet" (*Mod. Lang. Rev.*) and, as regards Shakespeare's non-dramatic work, "The Arrangement and the Date of Shakespeare's Sonnets" (*Pub. Mod. Lang. Assoc.*). J. Phelps has written on "Father Parsons in Shakespeare" (*Archiv*). F. L. Schoell has discussed the relation of "George Chapman and the Italian Neo-Latinists of the Quattrocento" (*Mod. Phil.*). C. M. Gayley's book on *Francis Beaumont, Dramatist*, is significant. Of somewhat similar title is A. H. Nason's *James Shirley, Dramatist*. "The Relation of Shirley's Plays to the Elizabethan Drama" is the title of a Columbia thesis by R. S. Forsythe. A late Elizabethan play, Glapthorne's *Wit in a Constable*, has been treated specifically by D. L. Thomas (*Jour. Eng. and Ger. Phil.*). An interesting question of source has been discussed by J. S. P. Tatlock, "The Welsh 'Troilus and Cressida' and its Relation to the Elizabethan Drama" (*Mod. Lang. Rev.*), and L. Wann has considered "The Oriental in Elizabethan Drama" (*Mod. Phil.*). Finally, from among other articles may be mentioned Miss E. M. Albright's "To be Staied" (*Pub. Mod. Lang. Assoc.*), R. Withington's "The Lord Mayor's Show for 1623" (*ibid.*), and, as belonging to a later time, E. C. Baldwin's "The 'Character' in Restoration Comedy" (*ibid.*).

The eighteenth century is connected with the preceding period on its critical side by J. Routh's "The Purpose of Art as Conceived in English Literary Criticism of the Sixteenth and Seventeenth Centuries" (*Englische Studien*) and *The Rise of Classical English Criticism* (New Orleans). A collection of *Critical Essays of the Eighteenth Century, 1700–1725* has been edited by W. H. Durham. An important volume on the age of Johnson published during the year is C. B. Tinker's *The Salon and English Letters*. Articles on Swift and on the *Dunciad* of 1728 are to be found in the *Nation* and *Modern Philology* respectively.

Space permits mention of only two works bearing on the nineteenth century: S. C. Chew's *The Dramas of Lord Byron: a Critical Study* and the late Thomas R. Lounsbury's *Life and Times of Tennyson*. The latter book was the last thing Professor Lounsbury wrote before his death at the age of 77, on April 9, 1915. An indefatigable worker, the author of many important works, including three volumes of Chaucer studies, and books on Shakespeare and almost every phase of our language and literature, he was one of America's best known and most respected scholars. One other loss to American scholarship must be noted. On Nov. 14, 1914, Ewald Flügel died at his American home in California. At the time of his death he was engaged upon the monumental *Chaucer Dictionary* which he was preparing under the auspices of the Carnegie Foundation and which he had completed approximately as far as F. His death is a great loss to Chaucerian scholarship, and it is to be sincerely hoped that a way will be found for carrying on the work to which he so tirelessly devoted himself and which has been so unfortunately left unfinished.

GERMANIC LANGUAGES AND LITERATURE

Daniel B. Shumway

German Fiction and Drama.—The anti-German feeling engendered in America by the European War does not seem to have materially diminished the interest in German literature. Hauptmann's modernization of the old *Parsival* legend has been translated by Oakley Williams (Macmillans) and the pathological character of the protagonists of his plays admirably set forth by Philo M. Buck, Jr., in the *Unpopular Review* for April. Sudermann's well known problem play *Honor* (*Die Ehre*) has been rendered into English by H. R. Bauhakhage with a preface from the pen of Barrett H. Clarke. A translation of Beyerlein's military drama *Taps* (*Zapfenstreich*), long familiar to the American public from its stage performances, has been made by A. Swickhard (Luce & Co.). Wedekind's powerful tragedy *Earth Spirit* (*Erdgeist*) has been translated by S. A. Eliot for Boni, and an admirable study of the dramatist's work with scenes from two of his plays given by Frances C. Fay in the *Drama* for August. A racy description of Hermann Bahr, the "Austrian Bernhard Shaw," and his dramas appeared in the *Forum* for March from the pen of H. F. Rubeinstein. E. Sheldon's weak melodramatic dramatization of Sudermann's novel the *Song of Songs* (*Das Hohelied der Liebe*) is severely criticized in the *Nation* of Jan. 21. R. T. Falconer has written on *German Tragedy and Its Meaning for Canada* (Univ. of Toronto Press) and E. W. Roessler on *Soliloquy in Modern German Drama* (Lemcke).

German fiction is not as well represented as the drama. The most important translation is that of Bernhard Kellermann's *Tunnel*, a capital picture of certain phases of American finance and enterprise. Richard Stratz's latest novel, *His English Wife*, has been translated by C. C. Curtius (Longmans) and unfavorably reviewed in an article on "England in Recent German Fiction" (*Living Age*, Jan. 9), as being a childish picture of English life and a glorification of German military circles. Baroness von Heyking is represented by a new edition of her *Letters Which Never Reached Him* and a new work *Lovers in Exile* (Tschun), giving an interesting view of life in China (Dutton). Adolf Schumacher has published an excellent study of *Lassalle as a Novelistic Subject of Spielhagen*.

In the field of lyric poetry some of the many German poems called forth by the war have been rendered into English in two special articles, the one "German Poets and the War" (*Review of Reviews*, Feb. 15) dealing with the work of Dehmel, Lissauer, Vierordt, Hermann Hesse, etc., and the other "German War Poets of Today," by A. Salmon (*Living Age*, Feb. 13), praising the work of Dehmel and translating three lyrics. Lissauer's "Chant of Hate," which has produced more sensation than any other war poem, appears in English translations in the *Outlook* (Oct. 28, 1914) and in the *Nation* (March 11, 1915). A. von Ende gives an interesting review of "Recent German Poetry" (*Nation*, Aug. 5), dealing with Karl Henschel, Max Dauthendey, Adolf Frey, Stephan George and lesser lights. An excellent translation of Dehmel's beautiful lyric "The Working Man" (*Der Arbeitsmann*) by Alice S. Blackwell appeared in the *Survey* for March 13. Anna Bunston has well treated "German Soldier Songs" in the *Living Age* for April 10. After speaking of several popular ballads she gives excellent translations of Hauff's "*Reitersmorgenlied*" and "*Soldatenmut*," of Herwegh's "*Reiterlied*," and especially of Körner's beautiful "Prayer before Battle," and points out the prominence of death in the soldiers' songs. In another admirably written article in the *Living Age* (Aug. 28), the same author treats at length the "German Idea of Death," aptly illustrating it by references to the *Nibelungenlied*, to Goethe and to various writers of the Romantic school.

The second volume of the new periodical, the *Germanistic Society Quarterly*, contains a number of well written essays on German literature. One by A. W. Porterfield discusses "Some Things We Owe to German Romanticism" (pp. 115-134). Bertha R. Coffmann concludes her study of the "Influence of English Literature on Hagedorn" (pp. 75-98). Paul R. Pope writes on "Richard Wagner's Debt to Literature" (June number). Julian S. Haskell contributes two articles on "*Quellenstudien zu Gerhart Hauptmann*," treating first "*Stauffer Bern als Urbild des Gabriel Schillings*" in the March number, and "*Der Einfluss Nietzsches auf Hauptmanns Einsame Menschen*" in the June number. More biographical in character is an interesting account of Karl Schönherr, the author of *Glaube und Heimat*, from the pen of Fr. Schönemann (*ibid*, p. 93). Chas. A. Thurber has privately issued a work on Fritz Reuter, containing some things about his life and a translation of a few of his humorous verses. Paul Carus, a well known writer on philosophical subjects, has published a very readable book on *Goethe: With Special Consideration of His Philosophy* (Open Court), in which he not only discusses Goethe's philosophy and religion, but treats of many lesser lights grouped about the central sun of German literature. E. G. Jaeck has published a study on *Mme. de Staël and the Spread of German Literature* (Oxford) and L. M. Price one on the *Attitude of Gustav Freytag and Julian Schmidt toward English Literature* (Johns Hopkins). "Dryden's Relation to Germany in the Eighteenth Century" is discussed by M. D. Baumgarten (Univ. of Nebraska).

German Philology.—In the field of German philology C. C. Mierow has rendered Jordanes' *History of the Goths* into English (Princeton Univ. Press), R. J. Kellogg has written on "Gothic Rendering of Greek Recurrents" (*Mod. Phil.*, June, 1915), C. M. Lotspeich discusses the "Physiological Aspects of Verner's Law" (*Jour. Eng. and Ger. Phil.*, xiv, 348), O. P. Rein treats of "Mixed Preterites in German" (*Hesperia*, No. 4), and H. O. Schwabe the *Semantic Development of Words for Eating and Drinking in Germanic* (Univ. of Chicago Press). More cultural in character is M. H. Haertel's study of the *Social Conditions in Southern Bavaria in the Thirteenth Century as Shown by Meier Helmbrecht* (*Trans. Wisconsin Acad. of Science, Arts and Letters*, xvii, No. 2); also Geo. M. Priest's *Germany Since 1740* (Ginn), and Ernest B. Bax' *German Culture Past and Present* (McBride, Nast & Co.).

German-American Relations.—In this field the most important publication of the year is undoubtedly E. M. Fogel's exhaustive work on the *Beliefs and Superstitions of the Pennsylvania Germans* (American Germanica Press), in which he has collected and compared over two thousand homely proverbs. Further, Preston A. Barba has published a comprehensive study of *Cooper in Germany* (Univ. of Indiana Studies, No. 2), Chas. F. Brede continues his work on the "German Drama in English on the Philadelphia Stage," bringing it down to 1822 (*German-American Annals*), and Louis C. Baker begins his similar study of the New York stage (*ibid.*). The *Narrative of Johann Carl Buettner in the American Revolution* has been issued by the University of Chicago Press, and J. A. Hoefli's experiences of a young Swiss immigrant in California and New York under the title *Erlebtes und Erstrebtes, vergilbte Tagebuch-Blätter* (Stechert).

German Texts and Teaching.—In this field as usual only the more important publications can be mentioned. The appearance of a school edition of Goethe's first novel *Werthers Leiden* by Ernst Feise (Oxford German Series) fills a long felt need. New editions of Thomas' *Hermann und Dorothea* and of Palmer's *Wilhelm Tell* have been issued by Holt. G. O. Curme has prepared an edition of Grillparzer's symbolical drama *Libussa* with an admirable introduction (Oxford). J. T. Hatfield has compiled a volume of *Shorter German Poems for Secondary Schools* (Heath). Two war stories by Liliencron, *Umzingelt* and *Der Richtungspunkt*, have been edited by W. H. David (Oxford), and three of Wildenbruch's tales under the title *Lachendes Land* by L. M. Price (*ibid.*). Ludwig von Arnim's amusing story *Der*

Tolle Invalide has been edited by A. E. Wilson (Putnams). Worthy of mention among the grammars are a new edition of Vos' *Essentials of German* (Holt) and *Eine Ausführliche Deutsche Grammatik in gedrängter Form* by Mabel L. Bishop and Florence McKinley (Heath). In the field of teaching Charles K. Handschin has published an excellent survey of the "Facilities for Graduate Instruction in Modern Languages in the United States" (Miami Univ.). The same author deprecates the use of texts of second-rate writers for elementary language work (*Education*, May) and also tells how the report of the committee on modern language can be made helpful (*School and Society*, June 5). The school of education of the University of Illinois has published (Bull. 12) "Suggestions and References for Modern Language Teachers" by T. E. Oliver. S. M. Waxman writes on the "Teaching of the Pronunciation of Foreign Languages," in the *Educational Review* for June. C. A. Krause has issued in book form four lectures on the *Reform Method in America* which he delivered in German in the Marburg summer school (Stechert).

Swedish.—In the field of Swedish there has not been as much activity as in the last two years. The interest in Strindberg, however, is continued by the translation of a number of his stories under the title *German Lieutenant and Other Stories* (McClurg). Translations of two of Tegner's famous poems have been issued together, the one the familiar "Children of the Lord's Supper" by Longfellow, the other the "Frithiof's Saga" by W. L. Blackley (Scandinavian Classics, ii). A volume of Agnes Wergeland's posthumous poems (*Efterladte Digte*) has been published by the Free Church Book Concern. By far the most noteworthy book of the year, however, is the translation of Selma Lagerlöf's religious romance *Jerusalem*, which in masterly fashion describes the attempts of Swedish peasants to found a colony in Palestine. It is translated by Velma S. Howard with an introduction by H. G. Leach. In the field of literary criticism, A. B. Benson has traced the *Old Norse Elements in Swedish Romanticism* (Columbia Univ. Germanic Studies). K. C. Babcock has treated the *Scandinavian Element in the United States* (Univ. of Illinois Studies in the Social Sciences, iii, No. 3), and Alfred Fonkalsrud has written a work on *Scandinavians, a Social Force in America*. As usual a number of works in Swedish have been issued by the Augustana Book Co.: *Hemlös* from the German of L. Haarbeck, *Heliga Birgittas Pilgrimsfärd* by Verner von Heidenstam, *I Västerland*, a collection of prose and poetry by Oliver A. Linder, and *Pa Heidelberget* with other tales from the German. Ole E. Rolvaag's *Paa glemte veie* has been published by the Augsburg Publishing Co.

Norwegian.—Apart from a translation of Ibsen's symbolical drama *Brand* by F. E. Garrett (Everyman's Library, Dutton), modern Norwegian literature is practically not represented. In the field of literary criticism A. M. Sturtevant discusses Ibsen's comedy of adventure *Sankthansnatten* (*St. John's Eve*) in the *Journal of English and German Philology* (xv, 357). An unfavorable review of Sigurd Ibsen's social problem play *Robert Frank* as translated by Marcia K. Johnson (Scribners) appeared in the *Nation* (Feb. 11), the writer pointing out that Sigurd Ibsen possesses none of his father's dramatic ability and is much better in his previous rôle of essayist. The older literature is represented by the *Story of Griselda in Iceland* (*Kvaethi um Grisilla*) by Rögnvaldsson Thorvaldur which has been edited by Haldor Hermannsson (*Icelandica*, vii, Cornell Univ.) and by a volume of *Norse Legends* compiled by A. E. Sims and M. L. Harry (World Book Co.). G. T. Flom has treated the *Phonology of the Dialect of Aurland* (Univ. of Illinois). Revised second editions have been published of P. Groth's *Norwegian Grammar* (Stechert) and of Michelet's *First Year of Norse* (Free Church Book Concern). In the line of travel A. E. Olsen has published *The Land of the Norsemen* (Holt).

Danish.—In this field the interest in Holberg is continued by translations of three of his comedies, *Jeppe of the Hill* (*Jeppe paa Bierget*), the *Political Tinker* (*Den politisk Kan-*

destober) and *Erasmus Montanus*, by O. J. Campbell and F. Schank (Scandinavian Classics, i). The only other work of Danish literature to appear is Gjellerup's *Pilgrim Kaminita*, trans. by J. E. Logie (Dutton).

Dutch.—Dutch, which was conspicuous by its absence in 1914, is fairly well represented in 1915. A Middle Dutch legend *Beatrijs* has been edited with critical notes and a glossary by A. J. Barnouw (Philological Society's Publications, iii, Oxford). The death of the Dutch novelist Maarten Maartens, who wrote his works in English, has been the signal for appreciative notices in the *Bookman* (Sept.) and in the *Outlook* (Aug. 18). A new novel of his, *Eve, An Incident of Paradise Regained*, has been published by Dutton. In the field of lyric poetry Geertruide Vogel's poems have been rendered into English under the title of *Spring Flowers* by L. Edna Walter (Macmillans).

ROMANCE LANGUAGES AND LITERATURE

Benjamin P. Bourland

American Contributions.—Whether it be that the present European conditions are affecting the accessibility of sources, and thereby the availability of American scholars for certain forms of scientific work pursued by them of late years, the outstanding fact of the year's review of the work in the Romance territory for 1915 is the absence of any larger study of the real problems of language and literature, especially in the Old French field. In Spanish, the publication of the first volumes of Schevill and Bonilla's edition of the complete works of Cervantes marks the beginning of a very important enterprise, which is being carried out with fine scholarship; in Italian, and in the general phases of the subject, there has been no noteworthy contribution from the scholars of this country. The year's production of translation of important matter from the Romance literatures has been unusual, both in quantity and quality; *per contra*, the volume of published texts is very small.

Necrology.—Alessandro D'Ancona, born at Pisa Feb. 20, 1835, died there Nov. 8, 1914. He was for 50 years professor in the University of Pisa, and won high esteem among scholars throughout the world as one of the foremost interpreters and historians of Italian literature. Among his very numerous writings may be mentioned his *Scritti Danteschi, Studi di Letteratura Popolare, Origini del Teatro in Italia, Poesia Popolare Italiana*. He was at one time editor of the *Nazione*, at Florence, and was the founder and editor of the *Rassegna Bibliografica della Letteratura Italiana*. Rodolfo Renier, born at Treviso in 1857, died at Turin in January, 1915. At the time of his death he was professor of the comparative history of Romance literature in the University of Turin. Besides having contributed largely to the scientific development of his field, he was distinguished as co-founder and editor (with Novati) of the very important *Giornale Storico della Letteratura Italiana* and of the collection *Studi Medievali*. Paul Hervieu, of the French Academy, born at Neuilly sur Seine Sept. 2, 1857, died at Paris Oct. 28, 1915. He was educated at the Lycée Condorcet, admitted to the Paris bar, and later served in the diplomatic corps of his country. His writings include, besides several novels, a long list of plays (as *Les Tenailles*, 1895, *La Loi de l'Homme*, 1897, *La Course au Flambeau*, 1901, *L'Enigme*, 1903, *Le Dedale*, 1905, *Le Réveil*, 1907) which gained for him an undisputed place among the very best dramatic authors of his time. Heinrich Schneegans, professor of Romance philology in the University of Bonn, died Oct. 7, 1914, aged 51 years. His most distinguished work was on the French literature of the earlier Renaissance. (*Geschichte der grotesken Satire*, 1894.)

Bibliography

Buchanan, M. A.—"Cervantes and Books of Chivalry." (*Mod. Lang. Notes*, xxix, No. 8, 1914.)
Cannan, Gilbert.—*Satire*. (New York, Doran, 1915.)
Cerf, Barry.—"Rabelais: an Appreciation." (*Romanic Rev.*, vi, No. 2, 1915.)
Crawford, J. P. W.—"Echarse pullas, a Popular Form of *tenzone*." (*Romanic Rev.*, vi, No. 2, 1915.)
———. "The Influence of Seneca's Tragedies on Ferreira's *Castro* and Bermúdez' *Nise Lastimosa* and *Nise Laureada*." (*Mod. Phil.*, xii, No. 3, 1914.)

1915 LITERATURE AND LANGUAGE

CERF, Barry.—"The Source of Juan del Encina's *Eglogo de Fileno y Zambardo*." (*Rev. Hispanique*, xxx, 1914.)
———. *The Spanish Pastoral Drama*. (Philadelphia, Univ. of Pennsylvania, 1915.)
CROSS, Tom Peete.—"The Celtic Elements in the Lays of Lanval and Graelent." (*Mod. Phil.*, xii, No. 10, 1914.)
DUNLOP, Geoffrey A.—"The Sources of the Idyls of Jean Vauquelin de la Fresnaye." (*Ibid.*, No. 3, 1914.)
FISHER, Lizette A.—"Dante's Idea of the Sensible Appearance of Spirits beyond the Grave." (*Romanic Rev.*, v, No. 3, 1914.)
FLETCHER, Jefferson B.—"Dante's Second Love." (*Mod. Phil.*, xiii, No. 3, 1915.)
FORTIER, Edward J.—*Les lettres françaises en Louisiane*. (Quebec, Imprimerie de l'Action Sociale, 1915.)
GALPIN, Stanley L.—"Elements of Christian Eschatology in French Allegory of the XIII and XIV Centuries." (*Romanic Rev.*, vi, No. 2, 1915.)
GEDDES, James.—*Bibliographical Outline of French-Canadian Literature*. (Papers of the Bibliographical Society of America, viii, Nos. 1 and 2, 1914.)
GUÉRARD, Albert Léon.—"The Academic Study of French Civilization." (*Publ. Mod. Lang. Assoc. of America*, xxx, No. 3, 1915.)
HARVITT, Helen J.—"Eustorg de Beaulieu: a Disciple of Marot." (*Romanic Rev.*, v, No. 3, 1914; vi, Nos. 1, 2, 1915.)
HAXO, Henry E.—"Denis Piramus, *La Vie de Saint Edmunt*." (*Mod. Phil.*, xii, Nos. 6, 9, 1914.)
HIBBARD, Laura A.—"Guy of Warwick and the Second Mystère of Jean Louvet." (*Ibid.*, xiii, No. 3, 1915.)
HILL, Raymond T.—"The Enueg and Plazer in Mediæval Italian and French Literature." (*Publ. Mod. Lang. Assoc. of America*, xxx, No. 1, 1915.)
HILLS, E. C.—*Some Spanish-American Poets*. (Colorado Springs, Colorado College, 1915.)
JAMES, Henry.—*Notes on Novelists*. (New York, Scribners, 1914.)
JONES, E. C.—"Saint Gilles, *Essai d'histoire littéraire*." (Paris, Champion, 1914.)
LANCASTER, H. Carrington.—"The Dates of Corneille's Earlier Plays." (*Mod. Lang. Notes*, xxx, No. 1, 1915.)
———. "Gaillard's Criticism of Corneille, Rotrou, DuRyer, Marie de Gournay and Other Writers." (*Publ. Mod. Lang. Assoc. of America*, xxx, No. 3, 1915.)
LANG, Henry R.—"Notes on the Metre of the Poem of the *Cid*" (second article). (*Romanic Rev.*, v, No. 4, 1914.)
LOOMIS, R. S.—"Richard Coeur de Lion and the Pas Saladin in Mediæval Art." (*Publ. Mod. Lang. Assoc. of America*, xxx, No. 3, 1915.)
MCKENZIE, K.—*Per la Storia dei Bestiarii Italiani*. (Turin, Loescher, 1914.)
MOORE, Olin.—"The Young King in the *Recits d'un Ménestrel de Reims* and Related Chronicles." (*Romanic Rev.*, vi, No. 1, 1915.)
MORGAN, H. T.—*Port-Royal, and Other Studies*. (New York, Longmans, 1915.)

MORLEY, S. G.—"*El Uso de las combinaciones métricas en las comedias de Tirso de Molina*." (*Bull. Hispanique*, 1914.)
NORTHUP, George T.—"The Influence of George Borrow on Prosper Mérimée." (*Mod. Phil.*, xiii, No. 3, 1915.)
PALMER, J.—*Comedy*. (New York, Doran, 1915.)
POST, C. R.—*The History of Allegory in Spain*. (Cambridge, Harvard Univ. Press, 1915.)
RENNERT, H. A.—"Bibliography of the Dramatic Works of Lope de Vega, based on the Catalogue of John Rutter Chorley." (*Rev. Hispanique*, xxxiii, No. 83, 1915.)
SÁNCHEZ, N. V.—*Spanish and Indian Place Names of California*. (San Francisco, A. M. Robinson, 1915.)
SEARLES, Colbert.—"Corneille and the Italian Doctrinaires." (*Mod. Phil.*, xiii, No. 3, 1915.)
———. "Stendhal and French Classicism." (*Publ. Mod. Lang. Assoc. of America*, xxx, No. 3, 1915.)
SERONDE, Joseph.—"A Study of the Relation of Some of the Leading French Poets of the XIV and XV Centuries to the Marqués de Santillana." (*Romanic Rev.*, vi, No. 1, 1915.)
SHAW, J. Eustace.—"Dante's *Gentile Donna*." (*Mod. Lang. Rev.*, x, Nos. 2, 3, 1915.)
SMITH, Horatio E.—"Balzac and the Short-Story." (*Mod. Phil.*, xii, No. 6, 1914.)
SMITH, R.—*The Life of Cervantes*. (New York, Dutton, 1915.)
STEPHENS, Winifred.—*French Novelists of To-day*. (Revised ed.) (New York, Lane, 1914.)
STURGIS, G. F.—*The Psychology of Maeterlinck as Shown in His Dramas*. (Boston, Badger, 1915.)
TEMPLE, Maud Elizabeth.—"Robert Ciboule and His *Vie des Justes*: an Academic Moralist of the Fifteenth Century." (*Romanic Rev.*, vi, No. 1, 1915.)
TRAIL, Florence.—*A History of Italian Literature*. (Boston, Badger, 1914.)
TUTTLE, Edwin H.—"Notes on Romanic Speech History." (*Mod. Lang. Rev.*, ix, No. 4, 1914.)
UPHAM, T. Cogswell.—*The Life of Madame Guyon*. (New York, Revell, 1914.)
WARREN, F. M.—"The Enamoured Moslem Princess in *Orderic Vital* and the French Epic." (*Publ. Mod. Lang. Assoc. of America*, xxx, No. 3, 1914.)
———. "A Possible Forerunner of the National Epic of France." (*Ibid.*)
WHITMORE, Charles E.—"Fazio degli Uberti as a Lyric Poet." (*Romanic Rev.*, v, No. 4, 1914.)
WILKINS, Ernest H.—"The Derivation of the Canzone." (*Mod. Phil.*, xii, No. 9, 1914.)
WILLIAMS, O.—*Giosuè Carducci*. (Boston, Houghton, Mifflin, 1914.)
WOODBRIDGE, Benjamin.—"Biographical Notes on Gatien de Courtilz, Sieur du Verger." (*Mod. Lang. Notes*, xxx, No. 5, 1915.)
———. "Gatien de Courtilz, Sieur du Verger, A Precursor of Lesage." (*Mod. Lang. Rev.*, ix, No. 4, 1914.)

1915 LITERATURE AND LANGUAGE

WOODBRIDGE, Benjamin.—"The Novels and the Ideas of Madame Marcelle Tinayre." (Austin, University of Texas, 1915.)

Texts

Obras Completas de Miguel de Cervantes Saavedra. Published by Rudolph Schevill and Adolfo Bonilla. Vols. I and II, *La Galatea* (Madrid, B. Rodríguez, 1914); Vols. III and IV, *Persiles y Segismundo* (*Ibid.*, 1915).

Piscatory Eclogues of Jacopo Sannazaro. Published by W. P. Mustard. (Baltimore, Johns Hopkins Univ. Press, 1914.)

Romancero nuevomejicano. Published by Aurelio M. Espinosa. (*Rev. Hispanique*, xxxiii, No. 84, 1915.)

Translations

Giovanni della Casa, *A Renaissance Courtesy-Book: Galateo of Manners and Behaviour.* With introduction by J. E. Spingarn. (Boston, Updike, 1915; Humanists' Library, No. 8.)

Chrétien de Troyes. *Eric and Enid.* Translated by W. W. Comfort. (New York, Dutton, 1914; Everyman's Library.)

Dante Alighieri, *The Divine Comedy.* Translated by H. Johnson. (New Haven, Yale Univ. Press, 1915.)

Lope de Vega, *The New Art of Making Plays.* Translated by William Tenney Brewster. With an introduction by Brander Matthews. (New York, Dramatic Museum of Columbia Univ., 1914.)

The Song of Roland. Translated into English Verse by Leonard Bacon. (New Haven, Yale Univ. Press, 1914.)

Santa Teresa de Jesús, *Minor Works.* Translated by the Benedictines of Stanwood, with notes and introduction by the Rev. Benedict Zimmermann. (New York, Benzinger, 1914.)

Spanish Legends and Traditions. Translated from the Originals by H. A. Reed. (Boston, Badger, 1914.)

Vives, J. L., *On Education.* A translation of the *De tradendis disciplinis*, with an introduction by Fisher Walton. (New York, Putnams, 1914.)

ANCIENT LITERATURE AND PHILOLOGY

ANCIENT LITERATURE
(*Additions from Papyri*)

CLIFFORD HERSCHEL MOORE

This year brings the tenth volume of the *Oxyrhynchus Papyri*, which, like its predecessors, gives us a rich harvest of fragments from works extant and unknown. Of the theological numbers the one of most importance is 1224, part of a papyrus book of the fourth century, giving six defective columns from an uncanonical gospel. These contain some new words of Jesus, a passage dealing with the call of Peter (*cf.* Luke V, 1-10), and another passage describing the feeling of the scribes, Pharisees, and priests at seeing Jesus consorting with sinners.

The prizes among the classical fragments are those which contain poems of Sappho (1231 and 1232) and Alcaeus (1233 and 1234). No less than 56 fragments of the second century are included under 1231, most of them so mutilated as to be at present of little value. Happily the first gives us five and a half consecutive and nearly complete stanzas, portions of two poems, one of which mentions Doricha, while the second expresses the writer's longing for Anactoria; then follow half verses which coincide with PSI 123, noticed in the last issue of the YEAR BOOK (p. 765). All the fragments under 1231 are in Sapphic measure; No. 56 stood at the end of the roll and gives us the welcome information that this was the first book of Sappho's collected poems and contained 1,320 verses. No. 1232, from a roll of the third century, gives us parts of two poems. Of the first little can be determined, but the second has 20 verses on the marriage of Hector and Andromache written in the Sapphic pentameter of 14 syllables.

The portions of Alcaeus are more fragmentary. 1233 contains 34 numbers in various metres. We can detect the subjects of certain pieces: one is addressed to Melanippus on death, a second contrasts Helen and Thetis, a third is addressed to the Dioscuri, and a fourth to Aphrodite. The fragments of 1234 have scholia, one of which attests the authorship. Apparently the poems belong to the στασιωτικά. Pittacus is certainly the subject of one.

Interesting also is 1235, containing incomplete arguments to two plays of Menander the 'Ιέρεια and the ῎Ιμβριοι. These apparently come from a work which contained outlines of all the plays. No. 1236 gives 22 known verses of Menander's *Epitrepontes* (459-480 K.) and some new verses besides; 1237 some very fragmentary lines of the same dramatist's *Colax.*

In a chrestomathy of historical and mythological matter (1241) the most interesting part to us is a list of Alexandrian librarians from Apollonius the Rhodian to Apollodorus. A second century fragment of Babrius (1249) is chiefly important for bringing the date of the poet well within the second century. A similar reduction in date is made by an early fourth century fragment of the Clitophon and Leucippe of Achilles Talius (1250). The date of the papyrus shows that the author must have written soon after 300 A. D., or at the latest within a generation of Heliodorus and not in the fifth century as Rohde or in the sixth as Schmidt believed.

The third volume of the *Papiri Greci e Latini* of the Italian Society is given chiefly to documents, but it also contains two astrological fragments edited by Fr. Boll (157,158) which are important and some epic fragments (253) modelled on Nonnius. These begin with a description of a battle between the Romans (Αὐσονιῆες) and some unknown foes, but it is impossible to say that this subject is continued through the remaining pieces.

GREEK LITERATURE

WILLIAM ARTHUR HEIDEL

The Year's Work in Classical Studies, 1914 (John Murray), now in its ninth year, though not of equal excellence in its several chapters, is a valuable year book. The writer of this article hopes hereafter to give a general survey of the year's work in Greek literature; at present the difficulty of obtaining books from Continental countries renders the plan impracticable. The precedent of former years will therefore be followed until the *bellum omnium contra omnes* shall have ceased.

Among the articles in American journals may be mentioned: F. G. Allinson, "Menander's *Epitrepontes*," and B. O. Foster, "The Trojan War Again" (*Am. Jour. of Philol.*); R. J. Bonner, "The Four Senates of the Boeotians"; G. M. Calhoun, "Perjury before Athenian Arbitrators"; F. H. Fobes, "Textual Problems in Aristotle's Meteorology and Mediæval Versions of Aristotle's Meteorology"; A. Shewan, "The Oneness of the Homeric Language" (*Class. Philol.*); I. M. Linforth, "Hippolytus and Humanism"; J. W. Hewitt, "The Thank-offering and Greek Religious Thought"; J. W. Cohoon, "Rhetorical Studies in the Arbitration Scene of Menander's *Epitrepontes*" (*Trans. Am. Philol. Assoc.*); C. H. Haskins, "Mediæval Versions of the Posterior Analytics"; W. A. Heidel, "Hippocratea I"; O. J. Todd, *Quo Modo Aristophanes Rem Temporalem in Fabulis Suis Tractaverit* (Harvard Studies, xxv, xxvi). Among American doctoral dissertations may be mentioned: J. W. Kern, "Ἀνά and κατά in Composition and with Case," and H. P. Houghton, "Moral Significance of Animals as Indicated in Greek Proverbs" (Johns Hopkins); T. A. Buenger, "Crete in Greek Tradition" (Pennsylvania); Eleanor S. Duckett, "Studies in Ennius" (Bryn Mawr).

The following volumes have appeared in the Loeb Classical Library (Macmillans): E. Cary, *Dio's Roman History*, I, II, III; B. Perrin, *Plutarch's Lives*, I, II.; H. B. Dewing, *Procopius*, I.; W. Miller, *Xenophon's Cyropædia*, I, II.

Archæology, which must keenly interest the student of Greek literature, is well represented by H. R. Hall, *Ægean Archæology* (Putnams), and especially by E. H. Minns, *Scythians and Greeks: A Survey of Ancient History and Archæology on the North Coast of the Euxine from the Danube to the Caucasus* (Putnams).

Among the books of the year dealing with history should be mentioned the second edition of J. B. Bury's admirable *History of Greece* (Macmillans), and Ida C. Thallon's *Readings in Greek History from Homer to the Battle of Chaeronea: A Collection of Extracts from the Sources* (Ginn). The latter is a scholarly book presenting in English matters of importance to the historian. W. L. Snyder's *The Military Annals of Greece* (Badger) is a book of slight merit calculated for the general public. W. S. Davis, *A Day in Old Athens* (Allyn & Bacon), presents a view of Athenian private life in the fourth century. Much more interesting and attractive is Mrs. R. C. Bosanquet's *Days in Attica* (Macmillans), which passes in review Greek life from prehistoric times to the present. Homer, as always, claims his share of the scholar's attention. Austin Smyth, *The Composition of the Iliad* (Longmans), seeks to show that the Iliad at one time consisted of 13,500 lines, divided into 45 sections of 300 lines each, with major divisions after the 15th and 30th of these. One had hoped that such essays had passed with a certain generation of German scholars. J. A. K. Thomson, *Studies in the Odyssey* (Clarendon Press), seeks a solution of the problems of the poem in the historical study of the myth of Odysseus, who is for the author a divinity. There is unquestionably much of value in the book; but one may be sure that this view, like others that have gone before, is but a passing phase of Greek studies. A. B. Cook, *Zeus: A Study in Ancient Religion*. Vol. I: *Zeus, God of the Bright Sky* (Putnams), is a monumental work of unquestionable merit. The philosophy of the Greeks is well represented by three works. A. W. Benn's *The Greek Philosophers* (Dutton) appears in a second edition, much improved. J. Burnet's *Greek Philosophy*, Part I. *Thales to Plato* (Macmillans), briefly restates the author's account given in his *Early Greek Philosophy*, and adds a highly suggestive but debatable interpretation of the Sophists, Socrates, and Plato. E. Bevan's *Stoics and Sceptics* (Clarendon Press) gives in four lectures an interesting view of certain phases of later Greek thought. The Oxford Translation of Aristotle (Clarendon Press) continues to give us valuable renderings of that important author. The year has brought forth two issues, the first containing *De Mundo*, by E. S. Foster, and *De Spiritu*, by J. F. Dobson; the second, *Magna Moralia*, by St. George Stock, *Ethica Endemia* and *De Virtutibus et Vitiis*, by J. Solomon. The latter contains also an introduction by Mr. Stock, in which he presents strong arguments for the view that the three books (*E. N.* v., vi., vii.: *E. E.* iv., v., vi.), which are common to the texts of the *Nicomachean* and the *Endemian Ethics*, belonged originally to the latter, not (as is commonly believed) to the former.

The Greek drama also receives some attention. O. R. A. Byrde, *Euripides' "Heracles"* (Clarendon Press) gives an excellent brief commentary on the play. J. E. Harry, *The Greek Tragic Poets: Emendations, Discussions, and Critical Notes* (Univ. of Cincinnati Studies, ix.) presents in collected form essays in part previously published. The book displays acumen and wide reading, but reveals also a want of sober judgment and self-criticism. R. T. Elliott, *Aristophanes' "Acharnians"* (Clarendon Press), is a work of ripe scholarship, as is also L. L. Forman, *Aristophanes' "Clouds"* (American Book Co.). The most notable book of the year in this field is J. W. White, *The Scholia on the "Aves" of Aristophanes with an Introduction on the Origin, Development, Transmission, and Extant Sources of the Old Greek Commentary on His Comedies*. The value of this work extends far beyond the scope of its immediate subject.

To Greek historical prose refer W. R. M. Lamb, *Clio Enthroned: A Study of Prose-form in Thucydides* (Putnams), and E. M. Walker, *The Hellenica Oxyrhynchia* (Clarendon Press), the former concerned with the development of historical style and ideals, the latter with a vexed question of authorship.

Prof. A. T. Robertson, who six years ago issued a valuable *Short Grammar of the Greek New Testament*, now gives us *A Grammar of the Greek New Testament in the Light of Historical Research* (Doran), which has already reached a second edition. It is a monumental work of prodigious learning, which reflects honor on American scholarship. It is easily the best book in its field.

F. W. Hall, *A Companion to Classical Texts* (Clarendon Press), is an invaluable aid to all who would concern themselves with Greek or Latin texts, and contains the best available introduction to textual criticism. Two works in the same field, issued by the Clarendon Press, come from the pen of Prof. A. C. Clark: *Recent Developments in Textual Criticism* and *The Primitive Text of the Gospels and Acts*. The former, an inaugural lecture, deals primarily with Latin, but its method and conclusions apply equally to Greek. The latter, concerned with omissions or interpolations in certain MSS., which it subjects to an arithmetical test based on the inferred number of letters in a MS. line, has started a lively controversy which is still *sub judice*. Prof. B. L. Gildersleeve, for nearly 40 years professor of Greek in Johns Hopkins University and recognized leader of Greek studies in America, has retired in order to husband his strength for the completion of various tasks he has set himself, but will continue to edit the *American Journal of Philology*, which he founded. Prof. Martin L. D'Ooge, for 45 years an honored instructor in Greek in the University of Michigan, and the author of several notable books, died Sept. 12.

LATIN LITERATURE

CHARLES KNAPP

Even more than usual American work in Latin literature and allied fields has consisted, in 1915, of articles in periodicals.[1] Mention should be made, however, of one book, the second edition of the *New International Encyclopedia*, edited by F. M. Colby and Talcott Williams, of which 16 volumes were issued in 1914-15. These volumes contain a very wide array of articles in the whole broad field of classical philology, including, of course, numerous important articles dealing especially with Latin literature. The revision of these articles was entrusted to C. Knapp.

A selected list of articles follows, arranged according to the Latin authors with whom they deal primarily: "A Witticism of Asinius Pollio," by G. L. Hendrickson (*AJP.*, xxxvi, 70), a fresh discussion of the famous saying of Asinius Pollio that Livy's writings were marked by *Patavinitas;* "The Year of Caesar's Birth," by M. E. Deutsch (*TAPA.*, xlv, 17), an attempt to fix, by inference, a date not determinable by direct evidence: the author decides for 100 B. C.; "Caesar, Cicero and Ferrero," by E. G. Sihler (*AJP.*, xxxv, 379; xxxvi, 19), an adverse and well founded criticism of Ferrero's well known books on Roman history; "Catullus as an Elegist," by A. L. Wheeler (*AJP.*, xxxvi, 155), an attempt to define more clearly Catullus's position in the history of Græco-Roman elegy; "An Analysis of Cicero, *Cato Maior*," by C. Knapp (*CW.*, viii, 177, 185); "The Prosecution of Milo: A Case of Homicide, with a Plea of Self-Defence," by R. W. Husband (*CW.*, viii, 146); "The Prosecution of Sextus Roscius: A Case of Parricide, with a Plea of Alibi and Non-motive," also by R. W. Husband (*CW.*, viii, 90, 98); "On the Date of Cic. *Fam.* XI., i," also by E. T. Merrill (*CP.*, x, 241); "Cicero and Bithynicus," by E. T. Merrill (*CP.*, x, 432), an attempt to fix the dates of two letters, *Ad Familiares*, vi, 16-17, addressed to a certain Bithynicus; "Men's Names in the Writings of Cicero," by H. L. Axtell (*CP.*, x, 386), a study of men's names in the body of Cicero's writings (not in the superscriptions of his letters); "Eugippius and the Closing Years of the Province of Noricum Ripense," by C. C. Mierow (*CP.*, x, 166); "*Molle atque Facetum*," by C. N. Jackson (*HS.*, xxv, 117), a new effort to fix the meaning of this famous phrase in Horace, *Sermones* I, x, 44; "Horace, *Sermones*, I, i," by C. Knapp (*TAPA.*, xlv, 91), an attempt, by careful analysis, to trace the movement of thought in the piece as a whole, and to fix finally the meaning of various disputed passages in this *Sermo;* "The Personal References in the Satires of Horace," by Dorothy Printup (*CJ.*, xi, 112), a proof that Horace was not afraid to name the living, and to name them adversely; "Horace, Catullus and Tigellius," by B. L. Ullman (*CP.*, x, 270), an argument that Horace named only one Tigellius, and always satirically, and that Catullus and he were at one in opposition to that Tigellius, because both were, in matters of style, Atticists, Tigellius a lover of Asianism: in a word, Horace and Catullus were completely in agreement concerning the

---
[1] Periodicals are cited thus: *AJP., American Journal of Philology*; *CJ., Classical Journal; CP., Classical Philology; CW., Classical Weekly; HS., Harvard Studies*; *TAPA., Transactions of the American Philological Association.*

literary matters with which Horace, *Sermones*, I, x, deals; "Medical Allusions in the Works of St. Jerome," by A. S. Pease (*HS.*, xxv, 74); "Ovid's Experiences with Languages at Tomi," by H. S. Gehman (*CJ.*, xi, 50); "Some Sources of Comic Effect in Petronius," by K. Preston (*CP.*, x, 260); "The Tradition of Pliny's Letters," by E. T. Merrill (*CP.*, x, 8), an outline of the tradition of Pliny's letters from their first appearance to the days of the early printed editions; "The Modern Note in Seneca's Letters," by R. M. Gummere (*CP.*, x, 139); "Apragopolis, Island-Home of Ancient Lotus-Eaters," by W. B. McDaniel (*TAPA.*, xlv, 29), an argument that the island which Suetonius (*Life of Augustus*, 98, 4) calls *Apragopolis*, and places near Capri, is Monacone: the author holds that 2,000 years ago Monacone was a far larger and more attractive island, reminding us that in the same period Capri itself has sunk many feet; "Notes on Suetonius," by J. C. Rolfe (*TAPA.*, xlv, 35); "The *Tinus* in Virgil's Flora," by H. R. Fairclough (*CP.*, x, 405), a defence of *tinus* versus *pinus* as the correct reading in several passages of Virgil's *Georgics*, and an identification of the *tinus* with *Viburnum Tinus L.;* "Virgil and the Country Pastor," by C. P. Parker (*CW.*, viii, 74), an interesting analysis of the motifs of the *Georgics* of Virgil.

Less definitely connected with a particular author are the following: "Rhetorical Studies in the Arbitration Scene of Menander's *Epitrepontes*," by J. W. Cohoon (*TAPA.*, xlv, 141), of importance to students of Plautus, Terence, and especially Quintilian; "The Pastoral, Ancient and Modern," by W. P. Mustard (*CW.*, viii, 161); "Mediæval Versions of the Posterior Analytics of Aristotle," by C. H. Haskins (*HS.*, xxv, 87); "National *Exempla Virtutis* in Roman Literature," by H. W. Litchfield (*HS.*, xxv, 1), a consideration of the persons cited by various Latin writers as embodiments of national virtues, such as *aequitas, fides, pietas, fortitudo;* "The Story of the Strix: Isidorus and the Glossographers," by S. G. Oliphant (*TAPA.*, xlv, 49), a continuation of the article noted in the YEAR BOOK for 1914 (p. 767); "The Significance of the Wing-Entrance in Roman Comedy," by Eleanor F. Rambo (*CP.*, x, 411), a paper of interest to students of Plautus and Terence both; and "Ancient Appreciation of Mountain Scenery," by W. W. Hyde (*CJ.*, xi, 70), an account of the attitude of many writers, Greek and Latin both, toward mountains.

SEMITIC LANGUAGES AND LITERATURE

MORRIS JASTROW, JR.

The European War has seriously interfered with scientific activity in the field of Semitics as in other fields. This is particularly felt in the case of an international undertaking like the *Encyclopedia of Islam*, of which nothing has appeared since the summer of 1914. Other undertakings that have been announced, particularly in Germany and France, have been delayed.

In England there has been some activity, and special mention should be made of a series of volumes issued by the British Academy under the Schweich Lecture Foundation. C. H. W. Johns has published as his contribution an interesting study on the relations between *The Laws of Babylonia and the Laws of the Hebrew Peoples*, showing traces of direct borrowing by the latter; and one of the Louvain professors, Dr. A. Van Hoonacker, who was the Schweich lecturer in 1914, has given (in French) a valuable study on the Judæan Colony at Elephantine in the sixth and fifth centuries before this era, summarizing the results of the remarkable Aramaic documents found in that region. F. C. Burkitt, the well-known English scholar, has given a general survey of Jewish and Christian apocalyptists which illustrates the narrowess of the dividing line between the two divisions.

In this country the Museum of the University of Pennsylvania has been particularly active during the year. It has brought out, in the Babylonian Section, a substantial volume of Sumerian texts by Dr. Edward Chiera on *Legal and Administrative Documents from Nippur, Chiefly from the Dynasties of Isin and Larsa*, which furnishes new material for a period hitherto poorly represented. Dr. Chiera has well under way a further series of volumes of Sumerian texts, furnishing long lists of proper names and representing school exercises carried on in the temple of Nippur thousands of years ago. In the same period is a volume of Sumerian texts of the oldest period known to us, by Prof. George A. Barton, under the title *Sumerian Business and Administrative Documents from the Earliest Times to the Dynasty of Agade*. Prof. Arthur Ungnad contributes a volume of *Babylonian Letters of the Hammurabi Period* which are as interesting as they are varied in contents. And finally, Dr. Stephen Langdon, of Oxford, has published in the same series a tablet containing, according to his interpretation, the Sumerian epic of Paradise, the Flood and the fall of man. Of the interest of the text there is no doubt, but it is questionable whether scholars will be ready to accept Dr. Langdon's somewhat fanciful interpretation.

Prof. R. W. Rogers has brought out a sixth edition of his well known *History of Babylonia and Assyria*. The new edition, largely rewritten, embodies much new material that has been added to our knowledge of various periods in Babylonian-Assyrian history; and since Professor Rogers is an unusually conscientious student who overlooks nothing, his two volumes are to be recommended as the best general work on the subject. In this connection may be mentioned also the writer's work on the *Civilization of Babylonia and Assyria*, which is an endeavor to cover in a single volume the entire subject for the general reader. Besides two chapters devoted to the excavations and to the method of decipherment, the volume contains a survey of Babylonian-Assyrian history, two chapters on the religion and the cult, a survey of commerce and law, a rather full discussion of Babylonian-Assyrian art, and copious specimens of the literature. The book, it may be added, is elaborately illustrated by reproductions of monuments bearing on all phases of the civilization.

Anton Deimel has published, under the title *Pantheon Babylonicum*, an elaborate lexicon of the names and dates found in the cuneiform inscriptions. To this compilation, which has been carried out with great care, the author has added an introduction discussing the ideas underlying proper names and cognate problems, including a comparison between Babylonian and Hebrew religious ideas.

Of a general character is the study of Johannes Petersen of the oath among the Semites, with particular reference to the Mohammedans (*Der Eid bei den Semiten*) which is to be particularly recommended to students and which will be found valuable in a comparative study of religious customs.

The splendid series of publications containing the results of the Princeton University archæological expedition to Syria has been enriched by three substantial volumes, comprising the Greek and Latin inscriptions in northern and southern Syria, by Messrs. Littman, Magie and Stuart, and also a volume of Nabataean inscriptions, by Prof. Littman of the University of Strassburg, the value of which is increased by an admirable introductory chapter outlining the character and general contents of the inscriptions and a survey of grammatical results. The texts are accompanied by brief but illuminating comments. Parallels from other languages and scripts have been abundantly introduced.

Little has appeared in the field of Arabic studies during the year. The activity of the Gibb Memorial Series has been interrupted on account of the war, but, on the other hand, the first volume has appeared in a series instituted in memory of Prof. M. J. de Goeje, the great Arabic scholar who was for so many years one of the ornaments of Leyden University. It is a publication of a text of Al-Mufaddal Ibn Salama entitled *Fakhir*, and edited by Dr. C. A. Storey. The work is an exceedingly interesting compilation of popular Arabic phrases with an indication of their origin.

Several important Arabic texts that were promised for 1915 have failed to make their appearance owing, no doubt, to the war. It may be proper to state, however, that two important works in the field of Mohammedanism may soon be expected to appear, to wit, *Aspects of Islam*, by Professor Goldziher of the University of Budapest, now being printed by the Yale University Press, and the lectures on Mohammedanism delivered by Prof. C. Snouck Hurgronje, of the University of Leyden, 'in this country, in the spring of 1914. The latter volume will be published by Putnams and was in press at the end of the year.

INDO-EUROPEAN PHILOLOGY
(*Exclusive of the Germanic Languages*)

ROLAND G. KENT

General.—L. Bloomfield's "Sentence and Word" (*TAPA*.,[1] xlv, 65) argues that the sentence is the original unit of speech, and that the progress is from an associational articulation of the utterance toward a structure in which there is an apperception of the separate elements. A. W. McWhorter, in "Notes in Syntax: Verb Function" (*PAPA*., xlv, xxiii), deals with the restrictions which the accessory factors of the form exercise upon the use of the form in the sentence. C. D. Buck has a detailed study of the original meanings of the "Words of Speaking and Saying in the Indo-European Languages" (*AJP*., xxxvi, 1, 125). W. Petersen, in "*Der Ursprung der Exozentrika*" (*Indogermanische Forschungen*, xxxiv, 254), seeks to show that compound adjectives of the type ροδοδάκτυλος start as substantives and later develop the adjectival use. R. G. Kent gives brief summaries of papers dealing with the linguistic side of Indo-European philology, read at meetings of learned societies in the United States from March, 1913, to June, 1914 (*Indogermanisches Jahrbuch*, ii, 217). H. S. Gehman handles a hitherto neglected subject, "The Interpreters of Foreign Languages among the Ancients" (doctoral dissertation, Univ. of Pennsylvania), supplementing it with brief articles on kindred topics (*CW*., viii, 9; *PAPA*., xlv, xvii; *CJ*., xi, 50).

Indo-Iranian.—In the Harvard Oriental Series, edited by C. R. Lanman, Volume xvii has appeared: *The Yoga-system of Patañjali, or, the Ancient Hindu Doctrine of Concentration of Mind;* embracing the mnemonic Rules, called *Yoga-sūtras*, of Patañjali; and the Comment, called *Yoga-bhāshya*, attributed to Veda-vyāsa; and the Explanation, called *Tattva-vāiçāradī*, of *Vāchaspati-miçra;* translated from the original Sanskrit by J. H. Woods. Woods has translated also the *Maniprabhā* in his article "The *Yoga-sūtras* of Patañjali as illustrated by the Comment called 'The Jewel's Lustre' or *Maniprabhā*" (*JAOS*., xxxiv, 1). A few notes on "Pāli Lexicography" are given by C. R. Lanman (*PAPA*., xlv, xxii).

S. G. Oliphant continues his studies in "The Vedic Dual; Part II, The Dual in Similes" (*JAOS*., xxxv, 16), showing that in the Vedic literature the elements compared regularly agree in number, and applying this principle to the interpretation of passages. L. C. Barret has published "The Kashmirian *Atharva Veda*, Book Four" (*JAOS*., xxxv, 42; see A. Y. B., 1913, p. 806, and 1911, p. 779); 15 of the 40 hymns in the book consist of material mainly new. Passages in the *Atharva Veda* are freshly interpreted by F. Edgerton (*AJP*., xxxv, 435) and by R. G. Kent (*JAOS*., xxxiv, 310). F. Edgerton's "Hindu Beast Fable in the Light of Recent Studies" (*AJP*., xxxvi, 44, 253) is a valuable critique of, and corrective to, Hertel's "*Pañcatantra: seine Geschichte und seine Verbreitung*."

The Madrassa Jubilee Volume, in honor of Sir Jamsetjee Jejeebhoy, issued at Bombay, contains three articles by American scholars: "Allusions in Pahlavi Literature to the Abomination of Idol-Worship," by A. V. W. Jackson; "The Story of Cambyses and the Magus, as told in the Fragments of Ctesias," by C. J. Ogden; "The Grave of King Darius at Naksh-i-Rustam," by H. C. Tolman. The last-named has written also on "The Middle Iranian Representation

---

[1] Periodicals are cited under the following abbreviations: *AJP*., *American Journal of Philology; CJ*., *Classical Journal; CP*., *Classical Philology; CQ*., *Classical Quarterly; CW*., *Classical Weekly; JAOS*., *Journal of the American Oriental Society; PAPA*., *TAPA*., *Proceedings* and *Transactions of the American Philological Association*.

of I. E. ṇ and ṛ" (*PAPA.*, xlv, xxviii).

Etymology and Phonology, General and Classical.—E. W. Fay continues his progress in identifying suffixes as independent elements, in "Indo-Iranian Word Studies, II" (*JAOS.*, xxxiv, 329), and has a valuable study in root contamination in his "Indo-European Initial Variants of *DY- (Z-) / Y- / D-*" (*CQ.*, ix, 104). H. H. Bender, in "The Accent of Sanskrit *-mant* and *-vant*" (*IF.*, xxxiv, 383) shows the relation of the accent of the adjectives with these suffixes, to that of the stems from which they are formed. W. Petersen has a monograph upon "The Greek Diminutive Suffix -ισκο-, -ισκη-" (*Trans. Conn. Acad. Arts and Sciences*, xviii, 139). C. D. Buck's "Lesbian αι for ā and η" (*CP.*, x, 215) presents corrected interpretations of forms found in the new papyrus fragments in the Lesbian dialect. G. Hempl interprets the Hittite inscriptions written in cuneiform script, as a dialect of Greek (*Nation*, ci, 324).

A. R. Anderson has made a complete collection of the instances of "EIS in the Accusative Plural of the Latin Third Declension" (*TAPA.*, xlv, 129). E. W. Fay discusses the passages relating to "*Nigidius Grammaticus; Casus Interrogandi*" (*AJP.*, xxxvi, 76). G. H. Cohen suggests that the frequentative verbs in *-tāre* started from *frequentāre* (*CP.*, x, 217). J. C. Rolfe removes from the list of Roman provinces "The So-called Callium Provincia" (*AJP.*, xxxvi, 323). A. L. Frothingham's "Grabovius-Gradivus, Plan and Pomerium of Iguvium" (*AJP.*, xxxvi, 314) is an important contribution to the understanding of the Umbrian bronze tablets. Miss Irene Nye offers an improvement in the interpretation of *rihtúd amnúd* in the Oscan inscription known as the Cippus Abellanus (*CP:*, x, 218). E. W. Fay proposes another interpretation of the difficult portion of the inscription on the Oscan slingshot from Saepinum (*Rivista di Filologia*, xliii, 614).

Syntax, Greek and Latin.—A. T. Robertson's *Grammar of the Greek New Testament in the Light of Historical Research* (Doran) is an exhaustive and scholarly volume, embodying the fruits of the periodical literature up to the time of its publication, both in matters of grammar and in those of exegesis; it utilizes the sidelights thrown by the Greek of the inscriptions of Asia Minor and the neighboring islands, and by the language of the papyrus documents found in Egypt (see also *Greek Literature*, *supra*). F. E. Robbins discusses "Προλαμβάνειν with the Genitive" (*CP.*, x, 77).

The substantial accuracy of the term "Sequence of Tenses" and its pedagogical utility are defended by A. T. Walker (*CJ.*, x, 246, 291) and by R. G. Kent (*CW.*, ix, 2, 9), against the attacks made by W. G. Hale (*AJP.*, vii-ix) and by the *Report of the Joint Committee on Grammatical Nomenclature* (*A. Y. B.*, 1914, p. 769). J. J. Schlicher gives his third and concluding paper on "The Historical Infinitive" (*CP.*, x, 54; see ix, 279, 374), dealing with the imitation and decline of the construction.

1916 LITERATURE AND LANGUAGE

AMERICAN LITERATURE

(Nov. 15, 1915, to Nov. 15, 1916)

EDWARD EVERETT HALE

Fiction.—The greatest productivity in creative literature in the United States during 1916 has been, as usual, in works of fiction. The publication of novels and short stories, however, seems to have been somewhat less than that of 1915, which was somewhat greater than the publication of 1914. It is impossible to present exact statistics on this subject; the entire production of fiction in books and periodicals is now so very great that no one makes an attempt to comprehend it. The statistics published in the *Publishers' Weekly*, however, give some idea of the total production of books which may be called fiction. The total number of books (including pamphlets) published in the United States in 1914 was 8,563; in 1915 it was 6,932; the figures for 1916 are not yet available. Of these the books classified as fiction by American authors in 1914 numbered 689; in 1915, 643; for 1916 the figures are not yet complete but an estimate based on the publication of the first six months would give a total of 626. Of these books about one-fourth are usually new editions of books published in other years. Of this considerable amount of fiction, which includes but a very few of the immense number of stories and novels published in the many periodicals, only about a half attract any general attention. Lists or summaries regularly published by the *Dial* and other literary papers rarely mention more than half of what is included in the statistics as fiction. The *Dial* lists included 216 in 1914, 231 in 1915, and 212 in 1916, a result somewhat different from what one would have inferred from the general statistics.

Of this great number of novels and short stories a few present themselves to notice as "best sellers." Of these the following have been most popular: Booth Tarkington's *Seventeen* (Harpers); Eleanor H. Porter's *Just David* (Houghton, Mifflin Co.); Ellen Glasgow's *Life and Gabriella* (Doubleday, Page & Co.); Frank H. Spearman's *Nan of Music Mountain* (Scribners); Henry K. Webster's *The Real Adventure* (Bobbs-Merrill Co.); Jean Webster's *Dear Enemy* (Century Co.); Harold Bell Wright's *When a Man's a Man* (Book Supply Co.); Kathleen Norris's *The Heart of Rachel* (Doubleday, Page & Co.); Mary K. Rinehart's *Tish* (Houghton, Mifflin Co.); and Rupert Hughes's *Clipped Wings* (Harpers.) These names have appeared more than once on the monthly lists of best sellers, and some will appear oftener still, for the books published in the fall have not yet had time to make due impression on the public mind. The precise relation of these lists to literature is not known. They have now been published by the *Bookman* and the *Publishers' Weekly* for a good many years. A study of the best sellers in the past shows that many books once enormously popular have no claim to lasting remembrance. But this fact expresses merely one of the truisms of literary history. It is also the case that some best sellers are books of real value, and further that many books of real value never become best sellers. Still the lists show certain directions of popular interest and certain ways of meeting it.

There have been during the year a number of severe criticisms of American literature, some by Americans, some by others. The general point of such criticism has generally been either that our fiction is commercial, such as will please our rather conventional and sentimental reading public, or else that it is not especially American, that it is rather a pale copy of foreign work. In the mass of fiction published, much will be found open to either one or the other criticism. But the books that have attracted more general attention are not apt to be at fault in either direction. They are generally very American in subject as well as in general style, and if they suffer from conventionality and sentimentality it is from sharing unconsciously in the common faults of our time as of most other times. Most of our better novels, nowadays, are of the kind that used to be called "realistic"; they are views of the life about us that we all know. A good many of them are strongly colored with the ideas that now interest people,—some of the best with different conceptions of the position and possibilities open to women in modern life. Ellen Glasgow's *Life and Gabriella* (Doubleday, Page & Co.) is the story of a Southern girl who, finding that she must leave her husband, makes a career for herself. Mrs. Deland's *The Rising Tide* (Harpers) presents with the author's usual clear-sighted sympathy the case of the ambitious girl who finds herself in revolt against the life about her. Henry K. Webster's *The Real Adventure* (Bobbs-Merrill Co.) gives the experience of a woman who feels that marriage cannot be true union unless a woman can feel herself a somebody who can be independent if necessary. Sara M. Cleghorn's *The Spinster* (Holt) is a girl who with the easy opportunity of comfortable marriage in pleasant circumstances chooses rather to make an individual career for herself. Others are stories of men, sometimes written with an idea of a "theory of life." G. A. Chamberlain's *John Bogardus* (Century Co.) tells the wanderings in search of experience of a young man who had been carefully trained for academic ease. Charles G. Norris's *Amateur* (Doran) shows the mistakes of a young man in the so-called artistic circles of New York. Willard H. Wright's *The Man of Promise* (Lane) is a rather hectic and conventional account of a youthful genius who felt that he must burst the barriers of current conventionalism and made a failure of it. Elias Tobenkin's *Witte Arrives* (Stokes) is a far more convincing record of a young immigrant who grew into a fine and true American. In some books the author has been interested chiefly in some definite phase of modern life, as in Nathan Kussy's *The Abyss* (Macmillans), which is a careful study, with here and there a touch of literary tradition, of the world of tramp, bum, and hobo; or in Kate L. Bosher's *People Like That* (Harpers), a somewhat less realistic story of "the other half"; or in Florence Olmstead's *Father Bernard's Parish* (Scribners), which presents through the medium of an engaging story the mixed population of upper New York; or in W. W. Wells's *The Whirligig of Time* (Stokes), which deals with student life. Quite by itself is Booth Tarkington's amusing and natural tale of boy life, *Seventeen* (Harpers). There are not so many stories of careful local color as there used to be. Grace King's *The Pleasant Ways of St. Médard* (Holt) is a beautiful and delicate picture of Louisiana at the close of the war, full of the sentiment of place and the spirit of the character that has made the new South. J. S. Dresser's *Gibbie of Clamshell Alley* (Dodd, Mead & Co.) is a fine story of a little boy in a New England fishing village. Joseph C. Lincoln's *Mary 'Gusta* (Appletons) is one of his well known Cape Cod stories, as amusing and true as any of his earlier work. But more books still have little especial idea or local color; they are simply stories of American life, told generally by people who know well the circumstances which they describe; if they have some definite idea concerning life it does little more than give direction to their work. Mrs. Watts's *The Rudder* (Macmillans) is a novel of central Ohio with a number of characters carefully studied and fully presented. Samuel Merwin's *The Trufflers* (Bobbs-Merrill Co.) is full of the present Bohemian atmosphere of Washington Square, but is well marked by the conviction that such life is merely a rooting about for enjoyment. Juliet W. Tompkins' *The Seed of the Righteous* (Bobbs-Merrill

Co.) is an excellent study of a family who have been so long traditionally engaged in works of philanthropy that they can not rid themselves of the idea that they have a great claim on the public. Basil King's *On the Side of the Angels* (Harpers) presents a married life in which a man marries one girl while loving another. Alice Brown's *The Prisoner* (Houghton, Mifflin Co.) is a story of New England life not much colored by the questions that might have arisen from the character who suggests the title to the book. Jack London's *The Little Lady in the Big House* (Macmillans) is a story of a superman and a superwoman who were content to live in California. Meredith Nicholson's *The Proof of the Pudding* (Houghton, Mifflin Co.) is one of his later interesting presentations of life in a city of Indiana. G. L. Richmond's *Under the Country Sky* (Doubleday, Page & Co.) is a very good love story with considerable feeling for the atmosphere suggested by the title. Stephen F. Whitman's *Children of Hope* (Century Co.) tells the adventures of a clever American family who went to Italy to spend a fortune that had fallen to them. Owen Johnson's *The Woman Gives* (Little, Brown & Co.) is rather an extravagant tale of redemption placed in a Bohemian atmosphere in New York. Philip Curtiss's *Between Two Worlds* (Harpers) is a really excellent story of a young man of wealth and position who was led to marry a vaudeville singer. F. O. Bartlett's *The Wall Street Girl* (Houghton, Mifflin Co.) is a somewhat more idyllic treatment of the same theme, except that in this case the girl is a stenographer in a broker's office. *Enoch Crane*, begun by F. Hopkinson Smith and finished by his son, F. Berkeley Smith (Scribners), is one of the author's stories of "old New York." *Those about Trench* by E. H. Lewis (Macmillans), one of the best books of the year, is an account of a set of medical students from all nations who have gathered about a famous doctor in Chicago.

It is probable that there are few enough masterpieces among the above, but they are not to be criticised as lacking in nationality. They are, like most good fiction nowadays, views of the particular life that the author happens to know and understand There is no straining to make them "American," but on the other hand, except in a few places there is little foreign influence. Nor can they all in all be called commercial or sentimental. The authors have as a rule the habits of thought and feeling that are normal among us, and are therefore apt to take much the general view in regard to manners and morals that their readers do. It does not seem from their work that they consciously violate their sense of truth to please their readers or any one else.

There are few historical novels this year. W. D. Howell's *The Leatherwood God* (Century Co.), though colored by many recollections of his youth, is yet a historical picture of a singular and interesting phase in the life of our country. E. L. White's *El Supremo* (Duttons) is a very interesting and very carefully studied story of Dr. Francia, the dictator of Paraguay a hundred years ago. E. T. Harré's *Behold the Woman* (Lippincotts) is based on the story of Mary of Alexandria, but is swelled out by detail instead of being vitalized by historical imagination. F. P. Sullivan's *The Portion of a Champion* (Scribners) is a very successful rendering of the spirit of the old Celtic hero world. There are a few novels of American history, of which Emerson Hough's *The Magnificent Adventure* (Appletons) and Samuel McCoy's *Tippecanoe* (Bobbs-Merrill Co.) are best worth note.

There is slight lessening of the great number of stories of adventure and of mystery, but it must be confessed that they do not excite the notice that they did a while ago. Oswald Kendall's *The Romance of the Martin Connor* (Houghton, Mifflin Co.) has a gaiety of spirit and an eye for character that gives his book real quality. Stewart E. White in *The Leopard Woman* (Doubleday, Page & Co.), a story of the African veldt, is not quite as interesting as in his books on our American wilderness. Frank H. Spearman's *Nan of Music Mountain* (Scribners), despite some conventionalities, is the best of a number of "wild West" stories. For the rest we must be content to name: Rex Beach's *Rainbow's*

End (Harpers); Bertrand W. Sinclair's *Big Timber* (Little, Brown & Co.); B. M. Bowers's *The Phantom Herd* (Little, Brown & Co.); Harold Bindloss's *The Coast of Adventure* (Stokes); C. T. Brady's *Baby of the Frontier* and, with C. T. Brady, Jr., *The Web of Steel* (both Revell); Isabel B. Patterson's *The Shadow Riders* (Lane); Ridgewell Cullom's *The Golden Woman* (Jacobs); J. D. Curwood, *The Hunted Woman* (Doubleday, Page & Co.). From this list it will be seen that most of the well-known favorites are continuing their work. We put together a few books inspired by the European War. F. A. Kummer's *The Second Coming* (Dodd, Mead & Co.) presents the coming of our Lord to different representative people engaged in the present struggle. Cleveland Moffett's *The Conquest of America* (Doran) is what one would imagine from the title. The war has also inspired Robert W. Chambers in *The Girl Philippa* (Appletons), George B. McCutcheon in *From the Housetops* (Dodd, Mead & Co.), and Ridgewell Cullom in *The Men Who Wrought* (Jacobs). Of detective stories, the best worth mentioning is William MacHarg's and Edwin Balmer's *The Blind Man's Eyes* (Little, Brown & Co.), but those who cultivate this form of literature will be interested also in: Gertrude Atherton's *Mrs. Balfame* (Stokes); Geraldine Bonner's *The Black Eagle Mystery* (Appletons); Arthur Stringer's *The Door of Dread* (Bobbs-Merrill Co.); A. B. Reeve's *Constance Dunlap* (Hearst); Nevil M. Hopkins's *The Strange Cases of Mason Brandt* (Lippincotts); Percy J. Brebner's *The Master Detective* (Duttons).

There remain a number of books which do not fall readily into any of the above classifications, among them a number of the amusing extravaganzas that have always been found in our literature. Of these rather the most amusing is Alice Duer Miller's *Come Out of the Kitchen* (Century Co.), not, as might be imagined, a suffrage document, but the tale of a young man who rented a fine old Southern mansion, with service included. Charles Sherman's *Only Relatives Invited* (Bobbs-Merrill Co.) is an elaboration of the possibilities of divorce, and N. W. Putnam's *Adam's Garden* (Lippincotts) is the story of a young man who lived in a vacant lot in the upper part of New York City and was visited by a young lady in an aeroplane.

It will be remarked that a number of well known writers have published no novels in the period covered by this review, for instance, Henry S. Harrison, Winston Churchill, Edith Wharton, Robert Herrick, Mary Johnston, Willa S. Cather, Dorothy Canfield, Gene Stratton Porter, Frances Hodgson Burnett, Theodore Dreiser, among others.

Short Stories.—Americans have always liked to write and read short stories, for a variety of reasons, and some of the best of short stories are American. But so very many are published nowadays, chiefly in the periodicals, that no one can really do more than pick out a few for notice. Of the collections of short stories published during the year, two offer themselves at once as in marked contrast. *Xingu* by Mrs. Edith Wharton (Scribners) is (with the exception of two stories inspired by her life in France during the war, the best in the book) a collection of stories of modern society, fine and subtle relations of the rather sophisticated life that Mrs. Wharton has taken as her general subject. Jack Lait's *Beef, Iron and Wine* (Doubleday, Page & Co.), on the other hand, consists of short rapid daily cuts at life of a very different sort, the life of the police, the bum, the chorus girl, the gangster. Such things stand almost poles apart in story writing. Between them are to be found all sorts of variations. Jack London's *The Turtles of Tasman* (Macmillans), the last publication before his death, is a volume very representative of the varied interests in his spirited life. H. K. Webster's *The Painted Scene* (Bobbs-Merrill & Co.) is a first-rate collection of stories on a phase of life quite familiar to the writer, that which centers about a musical-comedy theatre. Hamlin Garland's *They of the High Trails* (Harpers) is an admirable collection of tales in the author's best vein, stories of the life of cowboy, prospector, farmer, in the upper levels of Montana. Booth Tarkington's *Penrod* *and Sam* (Harpers) is a collection of chips left after hewing out his recent figure of the American boy. One can not do more than mention Irvin Cobb's *Local Color* (Doran), James B. Conolly's *Head Winds* (Scribners), a collection with more breadth and depth than is usual with him, Dorothy Canfield's *The Real Motive* (Holt), Rex Beach's *Crimson Gardenia* (Harpers). Finally, one should note the 81 prize *Short Stories from Life* (Doubleday, Page & Co.), a collection made from the 30,000 sent in response to an offer of a number of prizes.

Poetry.—The new currents of American poetry have grown in strength and fulness during the year. Beside new volumes there have been several collections of newer poetry, and one or two new periodicals have been founded, chiefly devoted to poetry. For many the chief volume of poetry of the year will be Edwin Arlington Robinson's *The Man against the Sky* (Macmillans). The book shows to advantage the author's gift for real character and real language. Others will prefer the very different *Songs and Satires* of Edgar Lee Masters (Macmillans), which is manifestly of the same stuff as his much talked-of volume of last year, *Spoon River Anthology*, although the lack of unity in form and conception detracts a little from its effect. Other volumes will best be grouped under the heads of older and younger poets. Of the former should be noted Edith M. Thomas' *The Flower from the Ashes* (Mosher Co.), Bliss Carman's *April Airs* (Small, Maynard & Co.), Robert U. Johnson's *Poems of War and Peace* (Bobbs-Merrill Co.), Josephine P. Peabody's *The Harvest Moon* (Houghton, Mifflin Co.), and Ella Wheeler Wilcox's *World Voices* (Hearst). It does not seem necessary to add a snatch of criticism to each of these, for their authors are well known and these volumes will not change their general reputation. Of the radicals of the newer school are to be mentioned Amy Lowell's *Men, Women and Ghosts* (Macmillans) and James Oppenheim's *War and Laughter* (Century Co.), as well as L. Untermeyer's —— *and Other Poets* (Holt), which latter will serve both for amusement to the lover of parody and help to the student of contemporary verse. Less representative of current tendencies but full of poetry are Hermann Hagedorn's *The Maze* (Macmillans) and Josephine Burr's *Life and Living* (Bobbs-Merrill Co.).

Biography.—There are a number of interesting autobiographies of interesting people. Charles Francis Adams's *An Autobiography* (Houghton, Mifflin Co.) is a sincere personal account of the life of a man representative of the best in American life at a time of deep importance to America. Charles A. Eastman's *From the Deep Woods to Civilization* (Houghton, Mifflin Co.) is the story of a Sioux Indian who educated himself and became an influential American citizen. Frederick W. Seward's *Reminiscences of a War-Time Statesman and Diplomat* (Putnams) contains the recollections of a man who had great opportunities to see what was occurring in the public life of the nineteenth century. *Notes of a Busy Life* by B. J. Foraker (Stewart & Kidd) is the autobiography of a well known political leader of our day, and being modestly and simply written, is full of things that will do much to improve one's ideas on political history. Edward L. Trudeau's *Autobiography* (Doubleday, Page & Co.) is the record of the famous doctor of Saranac Lake who is so warmly remembered for his work in aid of those afflicted with what used to be one of the great scourges of America. *The Letters of Richard Watson Gilder*, edited by Rosamond Gilder (Houghton, Mifflin Co.), gives a personal view of one who was not only the editor of a great periodical but a poet on the one hand and a man deeply interested in public life on the other. Beside these and other autobiographies there are a number of biographies written largely on the basis of letters, journals, etc., which partake largely of the autobiographic character. Most important among these are the lives of Mrs. Julia Ward Howe and of Booker T. Washington. The former is by two daughters, Laura E. Richards and Maud H. Elliott (Houghton, Mifflin Co.), and presents in an autobiography and letters a singularly interesting account of one of the leading women of the nineteenth century. *The Life of Booker T.*

Washington by Emmet J. Scott and Lyman B. Stowe (Doubleday, Page & Co.) gives a life of the great negro educator from personal sources. Here also is to be mentioned H. B. Rankin's *Personal Recollections of Abraham Lincoln* (Putnams), a book which not only presents some new details on the life of the great President but gives new comment on matter already known. Of definite biography there is not very much. Two volumes of the careful studies of Gamaliel Bradford, *Union Portraits* and *Portraits of Women* (Houghton, Mifflin Co.) will add to his reputation in this direction. Among longer careful studies are Albert J. Beveridge's *The Life of John Marshall* (Houghton, Mifflin Co.), which presents only the beginning of the career of the great jurist, and Charles S. Olcott's *Life of William McKinley* (Houghton, Mifflin Co.)

Essays and Criticism.—The essays of the year may be separated into those which follow the literary form of the essay with the desire of expressing general thoughts and ideas in life, and those which use the essay as a medium for the presenting of definite schemes of thought. Of the former the most noteworthy are *The Pleasures of an Absentee Landlord* by S. McC. Crothers (Houghton, Mifflin Co.), an essayist of well known distinction, and *Counter Currents* by Agnes Repplier (Houghton, Mifflin Co.), who here goes rather deeper than her wont into the questions of contemporary life. Of the latter kind the most noteworthy are *Under the Apple Trees* by John Burroughs (Houghton, Mifflin Co.), a collection of wide range but in the main illustrating the author's later thought on the philosophy of life; *Problems of American Government* by Elihu Root (Harvard University Press), a series of studies by one of the clearest of American political thinkers; and *Estimates in Art* by F. J. Mather (Scribners), a collection of excellent critical studies by one who has not only a wide range of knowledge and interest, but also a firm hold on fundamental ideas. Of importance also is Elizabeth L. Pennell's *Nights* (Lippincotts), personal reminiscences of the art and literature of the end of the nineteenth century by one who had remarkable opportunities to know the leading workers in art and letters and the leading currents of thought. There has been published, of course, a good deal of literary study and criticism, of which may be mentioned favorably, the semi-popular *How to Know Wordsworth* by C. T. Winchester (Bobbs-Merrill Co.), with the books in the same series on *Dante* by A. M. Brooks and *DeFoe* by William P. Trent (see also *English Language and Literature*, *infra*).

Necrology.—Several well-known authors have died during the year. On Feb. 1 Henry James died at Rye, England; although he had become a British subject he was still regarded as one of the great figures of our national literature. The following also are to be noted: John T. Trowbridge, Feb. 12; Richard Harding Davis, April 11; Jean Webster, June 11; James Whitcomb Riley, July 22; Josiah Royce, Sept. 14; Frank Dempster Sherman, Sept. 19; Norman Duncan, Oct. 18; Mollie Elliott Seawell, Nov. 15; Jack London, Nov. 22.

MODERN LANGUAGES AND LITERATURE

ENGLISH LANGUAGE AND LITERATURE

Albert C. Baugh

The most noticeable characteristic of American scholarship during 1916 in the field of English philology and literature is its abundance. As yet the war, though it has increased the difficulties of research, has not appreciably affected the productivity of American scholars. The work of some American students published in periodicals like *Anglia* and *Englische Studien*, however, must be omitted in the following *résumé* because of the inaccessibility of recent numbers of these publications. All other omissions, if they are intentional, are made necessary by lack of space.

English Philology.—The number of philological papers published during the year is rather small. Francis A. Wood treats "Old English Diphthongs in Middle and New English" (*Jour. of Eng. and Germ. Phil.*),

Prof. Bright discusses "Anglo-Saxon 'umbor' and 'seld-guma'" (*Mod. Lang. Notes*), and C. M. Lotspeich illustrates the physical principle which he thinks is involved in Verner's law in a note on the "Pronunciation of -tu- in English" (*Jour. Eng. and Germ. Phil.*). A. G. Kennedy treats *The Pronoun of Address in English Literature of the Thirteenth Century*, and O. F. Emerson writes on "English or French in the Time of Edward III" (*Romanic Rev.*). In the Shakespearean period H. M. Ayres discusses *The Question of Shakespeare's Pronunciation*, and M. P. Tilley collects "Some Evidence in Shakespeare of Contemporary Effort to Refine the Language of the Day" (*Pub. Mod. Lang. Assoc.*).

Old English Literature (449-1150).—Touching the *Beowulf*, Fr. Klaeber has published "Observations on the Finn Episode" (*Jour. Eng. and Germ. Phil.*), and Professor Bright has discussed "Beowulf 489-490" (*Mod. Lang. Notes*). Cynewulf has been the subject of several contributions, including Samuel Moore's "The Old English *Christ*: Is It a Unit?" (*Jour. Eng. and Germ. Phil.*), Miss A. M. Jenney's "A Note on Cynewulf's 'Christ'" (*Mod. Lang. Notes*), G. H. Gerould's "Cynewulf's 'Christ,' 678-679" (*ibid.*), B. S. Monroe's "The Anglo-Saxon *Juliana*" and "Notes on the Anglo-Saxon Andreas" (*ibid.*).

Middle English Literature (1150-1500).—In the general period of Middle-English literature a long-felt need has been supplied by J. E. Wells, *A Manual of the Writings in Middle English, 1050-1400*. A convenient volume of translations has been published by W. A. Neilson and K. G. T. Webster under the title, *Chief British Poets of the Fourteenth and Fifteenth Centuries*. Numerous notes and articles on individual works and topics have appeared. Miss H. E. Allen prints "Two Middle-English Translations from the Anglo-Norman" (*Mod. Phil.*) and contributes "A Note on the Lamentation of Mary" (*ibid.*). F. A. Patterson prints "A Sermon on the Lord's Prayer" (*Jour. Eng. and Germ. Phil.*), and Miss G. H. Campbell publishes texts of "The Middle English *Evangelie*" (*Pub. Mod. Lang. Assoc.*). "Hitherto Unprinted Manuscripts of the Middle English *Ipotis*" have been edited by Miss J. D. Sutton (*ibid.*). R. B. Pace's "The Death of the Red Knight in the Story of Perceval" (*Mod. Lang. Notes*) and W. C. Curry's "The Judgment of Paris" (*ibid.*) treat subjects touching the Middle-English romance. A valuable study of the *Saints' Legends* has been published by G. H. Gerould ("Types of Eng. Lit. Series"), and the author of this volume has also discussed "The Source of the Middle English Prose Saint Elizabeth of Spalbeck" (*Anglia*). Two important contributions to the literature of "Sir Gawain and the Green Knight" have appeared during the year, one a book by Professor Kittredge which he calls *A Study of Gawain and the Green Knight*, the other an article by J. R. Hulbert entitled simply "Syr Gawayn and the Grene Knyght" (*Mod. Phil.*). "More Notes on 'Patience'" have come from O. F. Emerson (*Mod. Lang. Notes*) and Professor Manly notes a query of the late Professor Marsh on "The Authorship of Piers the Plowman (*Mod. Phil.*).

A number of publications relating to Chaucer are evidence of the continued interest of American scholars in a field which they have made so much their own. With a few exceptions, however, the work of the year has not been quite so significant as that of 1915. Frederick Tupper has continued to maintain his sins-theory in "Chaucer's Sinners and Sins" (*Jour. Eng. and Germ. Phil.*). J. L. Kenyon makes "Further Notes on the Marriage Group in the Canterbury Tales" (*ibid.*). Several articles treat of Chaucer's relation to other writers. H. M. Cummings' "The Indebtedness of Chaucer's Works to the Italian Works of Boccaccio" (*Univ. of Cincinnati Studies*), Miss H. Seibert's "Chaucer and Horace" (*Mod. Lang. Notes*), and J. S. P. Tatlock's "Chaucer and Wyclif" (*ibid.*) may be mentioned. The latter also discusses "'Bretherhed' in Chaucer's 'Prolog'" (*ibid.*) and Miss E. P. Hammond writes on "Chaucer and Dante and Their Scribes" (*ibid.*). Professor Tupper has made an interesting contribution on "Chaucer and Trophee" (*ibid.*) which is supplemented by O. F. Emerson's "Seith Trophee" (*ibid.*). Tupper has also rediscovered in "Chaucer and Richmond" some things that were suggested in 1894 in the *Academy*, and a similar rediscovery appears in H. J. Savage's supplementary note, "Chaucer's 'Long Castel'" (both in *Mod. Lang. Notes*). In "Hereos Again" J. L. Lowes adds a note to his earlier discussion of the point (*ibid.*), and Carleton Brown has discussed "Chaucer and the Hours of the Blessed Virgin" (*ibid.*). A number of notes and articles by Prof. A. S. Cook may be mentioned: "Skelton's 'Garland of Laurel' and Chaucer's 'House of Fame'" (*Mod. Lang. Notes*), "Chaucer's *fraknes*" (*ibid.*), "Two Notes on Chaucer" (*ibid.*), and "The Historical Background of Chaucer's Knight" (*Trans. Conn. Acad.*). Finally, this summary of Chaucerian scholarship may be brought to a close with mention of H. B. Hinckley's "Chauceriana" (*Mod. Phil.*).

Of Middle-English literature subsequent to Chaucer, J. M. Berdan discusses "The Poetry of Skelton, a Renaissance Survival of . Medieval Latin Influence" (*Romanic Rev.*), and Miss Hammond contributes a note on "*The Lover's Mass* in England and Spain" (*Mod. Phil.*). Concerning the ballad, S. B. Hustvedt has had published by the American Scandinavian Foundation *Ballad Criticism in Scandinavia and Great Britain during the Eighteenth Century*. "The English Ballad of Judas Iscariot" is discussed by P. F. Baum, who has treated also "The Medieval Legend of Judas Iscariot" (both in *Pub. Mod. Lang. Assoc.*). W. H. Schofield's "The Chief Historical Error in Barbour's *Bruce*" (*ibid.*) may be put here. The early history of the drama has received considerable attention. Mention must be made of F. G. Calderhead's "Morality Fragments from Norfolk" (*Mod. Phil.*), Carleton Brown's "The Towneley 'Play of the Doctors' and the 'Speculum Christiani'" (*Mod. Lang. Notes*), R. G. Coffman's "The Miracle Play in England—Nomenclature" (*Pub. Mod. Lang. Assoc.*), W. K. Smart's "Some Notes on *Mankind*" and A. S. Cook's "Another Parallel to the Mak Story" (both in *Mod. Phil.*).

Modern English Literature (since 1500).—The interest which American scholars have shown in Spenser during the last few years continues to increase. As a result of this interest we now have *A Concordance to the Poems of Edmund Spenser* by C. G. Osgood. "Spenser's Birth-date" and "Spenseriana: The Lay of Corinda" are notes by P. W. Long in *Mod. Lang. Notes*. Miss J. M. Lyons discusses "Spenser's *Muiopotmos* as an Allegory" (*Pub. Mod. Lang. Assoc.*), and J. Erskine treats "The Virtue of Friendship in the *Faerie Queene*" (*ibid.*). F. M. Padelford's "Spenser and the Spirit of Puritanism" (*Mod. Phil.*), R. Bolwell's "Notes on Alliteration in Spenser" (*Jour. Eng. and Germ. Phil.*) and E. Fulton's "Spenser, Sidney, and the Areopagus" (*Mod. Lang. Notes*) may also be mentioned. G. P. Krapp's *The Rise of English Literary Prose* treats the history of English prose up to Bacon. T. K. Whipple connects "Isocrates and Euphuism" (*Mod. Lang. Rev.*). *Elizabethan Translations from the Italian* is the title of a volume by Miss M. A. Scott. Milton has received considerable attention during the year. E. N. S. Thompson has published *John Milton: A Topical Bibliography*, and F. M. Darnall has discussed "Milton's *L'Allegro* and *Il Penseroso*" (*Mod. Lang. Rev.*). The latter is the title of a brief note by A. Thaler, who has published also a note on "Milton and Thompson" (*Mod. Lang. Notes*). W. F. Warren's *The Universe as Pictured in Milton's Paradise Lost*, and Miss M. Barstow's "Milton's Use of the Forms of Epic Address" (*Mod. Lang. Notes*) may receive notice in this connection.

Because of the popular interest in the celebration of the tercentenary of Shakespeare's death, Shakespeare and the Elizabethan drama have received unusual attention during the year. Among more general works, Arthur B. Stonex has published his excellent study of "The Usurer in Elizabethan Drama" (*Pub. Mod. Lang. Assoc.*), V. S. Frieburg has examined *Disguise Plots in Elizabethan Drama*, and J. S. P. Tatlock has studied "The Siege of Troy in English Literature, Especially in Shakespeare and Heywood" (*Pub. Mod. Lang. Assoc.*). The early history of the masque is touched on by R. Withington in "After the Manner of Italy" (*Jour. Eng. and Germ. Phil.*), and C. R. Baskerville presents "Some Evidence for Early Romantic Plays in England" (*Mod. Phil.*). The same writer discusses "John Rastell's Dramatic Activities" (*ibid.*) and H. N. Hillebrand treats "Sebastian Westcote, Dramatist and Master of the Children of Paul's" (*Jour. Eng. and Germ. Phil.*). "The Authorship of *Gorboduc*" is an interesting note by J. E. Gillet (*Mod. Lang. Notes*). *Common Conditions*, an early play, has been edited by C. J. Tucker-Brooke as the first of the Yale Elizabethan Club Reprints. The connection between *Froissart and the English Chronicle Play* has been investigated by R. M. Smith.

A number of notable works on Shakespeare have been published in the anniversary year. A. W. Pollard and Miss H. C. Bartlett have compiled *A Census of Shakespeare's Plays in Quarto*. More immediately connected with the tercentenary celebration are the address by Professor Kittredge and the volumes of miscellaneous contributions published especially to commemorate the event. *Shakespeare's England* is an English publication, as is also the elaborate *Book of Homage to Shakespeare* edited by I. Gollancz. But the latter work contains numerous contributions by American scholars, including an important paper by Professor Schelling on "The Common Folk of Shakespeare" and others by Professors Manly, Brander Matthews, Phelps, Mr. H. H. Furness, Jr., etc. Two somewhat similar volumes have been published in America: *Shakesperian Studies by Members of the Department of English and Comparative Literature in Columbia University;* and *Shakespeare Studies by Members of the Department of English of the University of Wisconsin*. The latter especially contains some significant articles on the Elizabethan drama. Attention may be directed to F. G. Hubbard's "Locrine and Selinus," J. R. Moore's "The Function of the Songs in Shakespeare's Plays," Karl Young's "An Elizabethan Defense of the Stage," T. H. Dickinson's "Some Principles of Shakespeare Staging," and Louis Wann's "The Collaboration of Beaumont, Fletcher and Massinger." Independent studies of separate plays have appeared such as E. E. Stoll's *Othello: an Historical and Comparative Study*, T. S. Graves' paper "On the Date and Significance of *Pericles*" (*Mod. Phil.*), and W. Graham's "The Cardenio-Double Falsehood Problem" (*ibid.*). Briefer notes on *Hamlet, Love's Labours Lost,* and *All's Well That Ends Well* will be found in *Mod. Lang. Notes*. The technique of the stage in Elizabethan times is treated in A. H. Thorndyke's *Shakespearean Theatre*, and in somewhat more popular form in O. L. Hatcher's *A Book for Shakespeare Plays and Pageants*. T. S. Graves in "The 'Act-Time' in Elizabethan Theatres" (*Univ. of N. Carolina Studies in Phil.*) settles an important question, and Miss Charlotte Porter explains "How Shakespeare Set and Struck the Scene for *Julius Cæsar* in 1599" (*Mod. Lang. Notes*). Space does not permit the mention of some recent Baconian literature which continues to appear in spite of such articles as John Munro's "More Shakspere Allusions" (*Mod. Phil.*). Apart from the drama, R. M. Alden has published a variorum edition of *The Sonnets of Shakespeare* and contributed two articles on "The 1640 Text of Shakespeare's Sonnets" (*Mod. Phil.*) and "The 1710 and 1714 Texts of Shakespeare's Poems" (*Mod. Lang. Notes*).

In turning from Shakespeare to his contemporaries in the drama we may note two books, D. H. Madden's *Shakespeare and His Fellows* and J. C. Jordan's *Robert Greene*. Greene has been the subject also of three articles in the magazines: C. W. Lemmi, "The Sources of Greene's *Orlando Furioso*" (*Mod. Lang. Notes*), H. D. Gray, "Greene as a Collaborator" (*ibid.*), and Miss E. M. Albright, "Eating a Citation" (*ibid.*). Ben Jonson is represented by several articles, the chief of which are W. D. Briggs' "Studies in Ben Jonson" (*Anglia*), the same author's "Source-Material for Jonson's Plays" (*Mod. Lang. Notes*), and A. B. Stonex's "The Sources of Jonson's *The Staple of*

News" (*Pub. Mod. Lang. Assoc.*). W. E. Farnham has examined the "Colloquial Contractions in Beaumont, Fletcher, Massinger, and Shakespeare as a Test of Authorship" (*ibid.*). Various anonymous plays have been the subject of study. H. M. Ayres discusses "*Cæsar's Revenge*" (*ibid.*), J. Q. Adams, Jr. treats "Captain Thomas Stukeley" (*Jour. Eng. and Germ. Phil.*), and C. R. Baskerville is to be read "On Two Old Plays," *Old Custom* and *A Fig for a Spaniard* (*Mod. Phil.*). Later seventeenth and eighteenth century verse has recently had greater attention paid to it. J. W. Good has issued a volume of *Studies in the Milton Tradition*, and C. L. Powell has made known some "New Material on Thomas Carew" (*Mod. Lang. Rev.*). Miss C. Rinaker's "Thomas Edward's Sonnets" (*Mod. Lang. Notes*) and E. B. Reed's "Herrick and *Naps upon Parnassus*" (*ibid.*) are notes in the period. M. E. Smith treats "The Fable and Kindred Forms" (*Jour. Eng. and Germ. Phil.*) and adds "Notes on the Rimed Fable in England" (*Mod. Lang. Notes*). The "Non Dramatic Pastoral in Europe in the Eighteenth Century" is the title of an article by H. E. Mantz (*Pub. Mod. Lang. Assoc.*). A. H. Shearer discusses "Theophania: An English Political Romance of the Seventeenth Century" (*Mod. Lang. Notes*), C. A. Moore treats "Shaftsbury and the Ethical Poets in England, 1700-1760" (*Pub. Mod. Lang. Assoc.*), and E. Osborne examines the poetry of the period for "Oriental Diction and Theme in English Poetry, 1740-1840" (*Univ. of Kansas Humanistic Studies*).

The post-Elizabethan drama continues to attract a steadily increasing number of students. F. and J. W. Tupper have edited a collection of *Representative English Dramas from Dryden to Sheridan*. G. P. Dutton takes up "Theory and Practice in English Tragedy, 1650-1700" (*Englische Studien*), E. Bernbaum studies *The Drama of Sensibility, 1696-1780*, and C. S. Duncan writes on "The Scientist as a Comic Type" in the drama (*Mod. Phil.*). "Congreve as a Romanticist" is treated by H. S. Canby (*Pub. Mod. Lang. Assoc.*), and the opinions of *Pepys on the Restoration Stage* have been collected by Miss Helen McAfee. Under the title, "A Bluestocking of the Restoration," P. E. More has contributed an interesting paper to the *Nation* on Mrs. Aphra Behn.

English fiction receives treatment at the hands of W. L. Phelps, *The Advance of the English Novel*, and its beginnings are touched on in two papers: A. H. Upham's "Notes on Early English Prose Fiction" (*Mod. Lang. Notes*), and E. B. Reed's reprint of "Three Characters by Henry Molle" (*ibid.*). *The French Revolution and the English Novel* is the title of a book by Allene Gregory tracing an important influence on English fiction. H. M. Dargan discusses "The Nature of Allegory as Used by Swift" (*Univ. of N. Carolina Studies in Phil.*) and J. M. Thomas writes on "Swift and the Stamp Act of 1712" (*Pub. Mod. Lang. Assoc.*). An excellent book on its subject is W. P. Trent's *Defoe: How to Know Him*. Fielding's *Covent-Garden Journal* has been edited by G. E. Jensen in two volumes. Jensen has also written on "Fashionable Society in Fielding's Time" (*Pub. Mod. Lang. Assoc.*) and has discussed in *Mod. Lang. Notes* "The Crisis: A Sermon" and "An Apology for the Life of Mrs. Shamela Andrews, 1741," both of which have been attributed to Fielding. Other studies in the novel that may be noted are J. B. Barton's "Laurence Sterne and Charles Nodier" (*Mod. Phil.*), G. F. Whicher's volume, *The Life and Romances of Mrs. Eliza Haywood*, and W. T. Hale's *Madame D'Arblay's Place in the Development of the English Novel*.

A few other works concerning later periods will suffice to complete this survey. G. F. Richardson treats *A Neglected Aspect of the English Romantic Revolt* (*Univ. of Cal. Pub.*), and S. C. Chew asks "Did Byron write '*A Farrago Libelli'?*" (*Mod. Lang. Notes*). An elaborate biography of Wordsworth in two volumes has been published by G. M. Harper with the title *William Wordsworth: His Life, Works and Influence*. The latest volume of the *Cambridge History of English Literature* contains one contribution by an American, the chapter on *Hazlitt* by W. D. Howe. Bliss Perry's *Thomas Carlyle: How to*

Know Him and W. L. Phelps' *Robert Browning: How to Know Him* are volumes in the same series with Trent's book on Defoe, mentioned above. Wm. Chislet, Jr. has written on "Stevenson and the Classics, 1850-1894" (*Jour. Eng. and Germ. Phil.*), H. L. Cohen has treated *The Ballade*, and F. N. Scott has discussed "Vowel Alliteration in Modern Poetry" (*Mod. Lang. Notes*). Among books of a more general character, Lane Cooper's *Methods and Aims in the Study of Literature*, C. E. Whitmore's *The Supernatural in Tragedy*, Miss L. J. Wylie's *Social Studies in English Literature*, T. De Vries' *Holland's Influence on the English Language and Literature*, and P. H. Boynton's *London in English Literature* help to increase the bulk of work done by American scholars, in spite of unfavorable conditions, and to mark the year as one unusually productive in American scholarship.

GERMANIC LANGUAGES AND LITERATURE

Daniel B. Shumway

German Fiction and Drama.—The interest aroused in the drama through the work of the Drama League and kindred organisations is shown by the number of translations of German and Scandinavian dramas during the year. Thus, Max Halbe's powerful tragedy *Youth* (*Jugend*) and George Hirschfeld's problem play *Mothers* (*Mütter*) have both been translated by Ludwig Lewisohn for the Drama League Series (Doubleday). Hugo von Hofmannsthal's verse drama *Madonna Dianora* has been rendered into English by Harriet B. Boas for the Contemporary Dramatists Series (Badger). The sixth volume of Hauptmann's dramatic works, edited by Lewisohn, has been published by Huebsch; it is entitled *Later Dramas in Prose* and contains *The Maidens of the Mount, Griselda* and *Gabriel Schilling's Flight*. Wedekind's *Erdgeist* is reviewed in the *New Republic* of April 22, and Hauptmann's *Weavers* is the subject of several brief notices in the *New Republic* (Dec. 25, 1915), *Nation* (Dec. 30, 1915) and *Current Opinion* (March). P. M. Buck discusses Hauptmann and Tragedy (*Nation*, June 16). In an article *Arthur Schnitzlers dramatische Werke* (*Germanistic Quarterly*, iii, 106) M. G. Beach points out that Schnitzler has much of Schopenhauer's philosophy but not his pessimism. Robert A. Falconer has written on *German Tragedy and Its Meaning for Canada* (*Univ. of Toronto Press*). In two interesting articles on "Literary Adaptations in Hauptmann's *Versunkene Glocke*" (*Germanistic Quart.*, March and June) Henry Wood has shown the dramatist's indebtedness to various works of Mörike in the creation of his main characters.

In the field of fiction, very few German novels have been rendered into English. The most important is Wolzogen's satirical novel *Third Sex* (*Das dritte Geschlecht*) translated for Macauley & Co. Friedrich Friedrich's popular novel *Obstinate Maid* has been translated from the twenty-first German edition by May E. Ireland (Jacobs). Heinrich Heine's fascinating *Nordseebilder* have been rendered under the title *North Sea* by H. M. Jones (Open Court Pub. Co.) G. C. L. Riemer has translated Gustav Freytag's famous essay on *Dr. Luther* for the Lutheran Publishing Co. Rolf Weber has a well written article "*Das religiöse Problem bei Gerhart Hauptmann,*" discussing Hauptmann's religious views in his novel *Emanuel Quint* and other works (*Jour. Eng. and Germ. Phil.*, xv, 390). Friedrich Schoenemann, "*Deutsche und Amerikanische Romane,*" I (*Germanistic Quart.*, iii, 96), begins a brief study of the novels of these two nations. O. W. Long, "English and American Imitators of Goethe's Werther" (*Mod. Phil.*, Aug., 193) discusses various poems, novels and satires which owe their inspiration to Goethe's youthful work.

Lyrics are well represented in the year's activities. A selection of Goethe's poems has been edited by Martin Schuetze with a study of the development of Goethe's art and view of life (Ginn & Co.). Margaret Münsterberg has published a number of her admirable translations under the title *A Harvest of German Verse* (Appletons). H. L. Fiedler has prepared a *Book of German Verse from Luther* to *Liliencron* (Oxford Univ. Press). M. E. Weber has collected *Passages in Prose and Verse from German Literature of the Nineteenth Century* (Putnams). L. Lewisohn has published a volume on the *Spirit of Modern German Literature* (Hübsch), and C. H. Towne has written on the "Lyrics of the Fatherland" (*Bookman*, Oct., 125). A poem by Ludwig Fulda, "In the Express Train," appeared in the *Bookman* for October (p. 12) and three songs from Heine have been translated by A. Gray (*Living Age*, Sept. 16, 706). "German Poets and the War" is the subject of a short article in *Living Age* (April 15). P. S. Barto has a volume *Tannhäuser and the Mountain of Venus* (Oxford Univ. Press). Charles W. Stork has treated "Hofmannsthal as a Lyric Poet" (*Nation*, May 18). "Goethe and Eckermann" is the subject of an article in the *Unpopular Review* for July (p. 73).

Of essays on German literature there are a goodly number. H. D. Sedgwick treats the waning influence of Goethe under the caption "A Forsaken God" (*Atlantic Monthly*, March, 346). Frederick A. Braun, "Goethe as Viewed by Emerson" (*Jour. Eng. and Germ. Phil.*, Jan., 23) has sketched the development of Emerson's opinions of Goethe from unstinted condemnation to strong admiration. Julius Goebel discusses the meaning of Goethe's poetical fragment *Geheimnisse* (*ibid.*, July, 335). Edw. Hauch sketches *Gottfried Keller as a Dreamer and Idealist* (Columbia Univ. Press). A. Kenngott treats the Swiss hero *Jürg Jenatsch in Geschichte, Roman und Drama* (Washington Univ. Ser. 4, vol. ii). "Schiller's Influence on Goethe's Novel Wilhelm Meisters Lehrjahre" is the subject of an article by O. E. Plath (*Mod. Lang. Notes*, May, 257). Ernst Feise has investigated the metrical forms of Schiller's *Lied von der Glocke* (*Jour. Eng. and Germ. Phil.*, April, 213). G. P. Jackson has continued his study of the "Rhythmic Form of the German Folksongs" (*Mod. Phil.*, June, 65). A. O. Lovejoy has discussed the "Meaning of 'Romantic' in Early German Romanticism," I (*Mod. Lang. Notes*, Nov., 385). In an article entitled "Drama und Epos in der deutschen Renaissance" (*Jour. Eng. and Germ. Phil.*, Jan., 35), Jos. E. Gillet shows that previous to the advent of the English comedians in Germany the German dramas were written to be read rather than to be performed. Kuno Franke has published an interesting study on *Personality in German Literature before Luther* (Harvard Univ. Press). Finally, Emma G. Jaeck has discussed *Mme. de Stael and the Spread of German Literature* (Oxford Univ. Press).

German Philology.—In the general field T. W. Arnoldson has published a study on the *Parts of the Body in Older Germanic and Scandinavian* (Univ. of Chicago Press). E. H. Sehrt has made an exhaustive investigation *"Zur Geschichte der Westgermanischen Konjunktion 'Und' "* (*Hesperia*, No. 8) and also written an article on "Grimmelshausen as Dialectologer" (*Mod. Lang. Notes*, June, 338) showing the novelist's thorough knowledge of German dialects. H. O. Schwabe continues his study of the "Germanic Coin Names" (*Mod. Phil.*, June, 105). F. A. Wood, "Some Verb Forms in Germanic" (*ibid.*, June, 121), has treated the survival of the injunctive, the dual, the ē aorist in Germanic and of the West-Germanic form *deda*. C. Reining has a study of *Verbs compounded with "aus," "ein,"* etc., as contrasted with those *compounded with "heraus," "hinaus," "herein," "hinein,"* etc. (Leland Stanford Univ.). In the field of Gothic, A. Green and L. Bloomfield in a long review of Wiener's *Commentary to the Germanic Laws and Medieval Documents* (*Jour. Eng. and Germ. Phil.*, April, 293) have convincingly shown the untenable character of Wiener's iconoclastic views concerning Gothic and the unsoundness of his method of procedure. In Old High German P. R. Kolbe treats the "Strophic Form of the *Georgslied*" in his third article on "Variation in the O. H. G. Post-Otfridian Poems" (*Mod. Lang. Notes*, Jan., 19). A. M. Sturtevant discusses the "*Syntax des Verbums 'Meinen' im ahd.*" (*Mod. Lang. Notes*, Feb., 85.) In Middle High German P. S. Barto, "*Der Sitz von König Artus Hof im Wartburgkrieg und Lohengrin*" (*Jour. Eng. and Germ.*

Phil., xv, 377), discusses the Germanic idea that mysterious personages have their seats in mountains. In a similar article entitled "*Elementargeister* as Literary Characters in M. H. G. Epics" (*ibid.*, April, 177), H. W. Puckett interestingly shows that fairies rarely appear in these poems, but that such creatures as dwarfs, giants, mermaids and wild men and women are to be met with in abundance. H. W. Church, "The Compound Tenses in Middle High German" (*Jour. Eng. and Germ. Phil.*, Jan., 1), shows that in general the same distinctions between the perfect and preterite were made then as today.

German Texts and Teaching.—In this field another edition of Grillparzer's *Des Meeres und der Liebe Wellen* has been prepared by J. L. Kind for the Oxford Series. An abbreviated edition of Otto Ernst's charming autobiographical novel *Asmus Sempers Jugendland* has been edited by Carl Osthaus (Heath). Many new editions of short German stories and new German readers have appeared, but lack of space forbids mentioning them by name. The following have issued German grammars: P. S. Allen (Ginn), Paul V. Bacon (Allyn), M. B. Evans and H. C. Keidel (Adams), E. Otto (Stechert), E. Otto and J. Wright (Stechert). In the field of pedagogy O. T. Thwing is represented by a well written article on "Education According to Goethe" (*School and Society*, April 8, 505). James M. Andress has written on *Herder as an Educator* (Stechert) and Carl A. Krause discusses his favorite topic, "Why the Direct Method for a Modern Language?" (*Educational Rev.*, March.) A. W. Porterfield has an article on the "Study of German in the Future" (*School and Society*, Sept. 23,473) and S. Bluhm on "Education in the New Germany" (*ibid.*, Sept. 30, 503).

German-American Relations.—This field is well represented. The war has produced a large number of lyrics in this country which have been collected by Irving T. Sanders under the title *Aus Ruhmreicher Zeit* (Stechert). George Sylvester Viereck, the ablest of German-American poets, has likewise issued poems inspired by the war under the caption *Songs of Armageddon and Other Poems* (Kennerly). Rudolf E. Rehbach has published a volume entitled *Mariae Höllenfahrt und Andere Gedichte* (Stechert). In the drama, Charles F. Brede continues his study of the "German Drama on the Philadelphia Stage to 1830" (*German-American Annals*, xviii, 60), and Louis C. Baker concludes his investigation of the "German Drama on the New York Stage to 1830" (*ibid.*, 3). John T. Geissendoerfer discusses Dickens' influence on Raabe, Ebner-Eschenbach and other German novelists (*Germanica Americana*, No. 19). Iola K. Eastburn has treated "Whittier's Relation to German Life and Thought" (*ibid.*, No. 20). An exceedingly able study on "Benjamin Franklin and Germany" has been made by Beatrice M. Victory (*ibid.*, vol. 21). In three well written articles on "*Die Deutschen im offentlichen Leben der Vereinigten Staaten 1848-1865*" (*Germanistic Quart.*, Dec., 1915-June, 1916), G. A. Betz has sketched the attitude of the German-Americans to the different political parties of the period and their opposition to slavery. Charles F. Dapp gives a biographical sketch of the German printer and publisher Johann Heinrich Miller, who was at one time associated with Benjamin Franklin (*German-American Annals*, xviii, 118). Camillo von Klenze has published a thoughtful discussion of *Die Zukunft der Deutschen Kultur in Amerika* (Stechert). The year book of the German-American Historical Society of Illinois also contains a number of articles on German-American relations.

Swedish.—That the interest in Strindberg is undiminished is evinced by the appearance of the *Plays of the Fourth Series*, comprising *The Bridal Crown, The Spook Sonata, The First Warning* and *Gustav Wasa*, translated by Edwin Björkman (Scribners), and by a volume containing *Swanwhite, Advent* and *The Storm*, translated by Edith and Warner Oland (Luce). Charles Wharton Stork, who so ably translated German lyrics for the *German Classics of the Nineteenth Century*, has added to his reputation by most acceptably rendering *Selected Poems of Gustav Fröding*, a poet all too little known in this country (Macmillans). Amandus Johnson has issued an abridgement of his larger work under the title *Swedes on the Delaware*. The well known essayist Ellen Key is represented by an article on "War and the Sexes" (*Atlantic Monthly*, June, 837). A few notes on Selma Lagerlöf appeared in the *Bookman* (Sept., 37). A number of new poems in Swedish have been published by Julius B. Baumann under the title *Fra Vidderne* (Augsburg Pub. Co.). Swedish grammars have been written by H. Fort (Stechert) and A. May (Stechert), while A. L. Elmquist has written on *Swedish Phonology*.

Norwegian.—Ibsen as usual heads the list in this field. His *Peer Gynt* has been translated in the original metres by R. E. Roberts (Modern Drama Series), his *Brand* rendered by F. E. Garrett (Everyman's Library, Dutton), and his *Kongsemnerne*, edited for school use by J. A. Holvik and P. J. Eikeland (Augsburg Pub. Co.). W. E. Jenkins has prepared an historical sketch entitled *Before and After Ibsen* for the Drama League. C. J. Little has written *Biographical and Literary Studies on Ibsen* (Abingdon Press). A. Leroy Andrews in "Further Influences on Ibsen's Peer Gynt" (*Jour. Eng. and Germ. Phil.*, Jan., 51) points out the influences of Oehlenschläger's *Aladdin* on Ibsen's drama. Turning to Björnson we find that his charming story *En Glad Gut* has been edited by G. R. Vowles. A study on *Ballad Criticism in Scandinavia and Great Britain during the 18th Century* by Sigurd B. Hustvedt forms volume ii of the American Scandinavian Foundation's publications. In the field of Old Norse, A. C. Brodeur has translated Snorri Sturluson's *Prose Edda* (*Scandinavian Classics*, v) and S. Laing has rendered the same author's *Heimskringla*, dealing with the Olaf sagas (Everyman's Library). A. Pitt-Kethley has simplified Sir G. W. Dasent's *Tales from the North* for children (Dutton). Halldor Hermannsson has treated *Icelandic Books of the Sixteenth Century* (Cornell Univ. Press). A brief notice on the "Literature of Iceland" by H. W. Dresser appeared in *Home Progress* (v., 295). Philological in character is A. M. Sturtevant's "Study of the Old Norse Word *Regin*" (*Jour. Eng. and Germ. Phil.*, April, 251) in which he traces its development and change of meaning in the various Germanic languages.

Danish.—Andersen's fairy tales never lose their charm and during the year three volumes of them have appeared, one by V. P. Windmere (Rand), and two by Mrs. E. Lucas (Dutton). In the field of the novel, *Child Andrea* by Karin Michaelis has been translated by J. N. Laurvik. In the drama, E. Björkman has translated two of Hjalmar Bergstrom's plays: *Karen Borneman*, and *Lyngaard and Co.* (Modern Drama Series). Under the title *Modern Icelandic Plays*, Mrs. H. K. Schlanche has translated two problem plays, *Eyvind of the Hills*, and *The Hraun Farm*, written by the Danish dramatist Johann Sigurjonsson but situated in Iceland. A. Kildal has given a review of recent Scandinavian books (*Nation*, April 13). Wm. J. Harvey and Chud Repplen have published a survey of Danish life, institutions and culture under the title *Denmark and the Danes* (Pott). Two Danish grammars have appeared, one by E. J. Thomas, *Danish Conversation Grammar*, the other by H. Forchthammer, *How to Learn Danish* (both issued by Stechert).

Dutch.—A Dutch history of the United States, written by A. Meyer and entitled *Geschiednis van het Amerikaansche Volk van af de ontdekking tot op Heden*, has been published by Eerdmans Sevensma Co. T. G. G. Valette's *Dutch Conversation Grammar* and his *Dutch Reader* have been published by Stechert. A brief account of "Flemish Folksongs" is to be found in the *Nation* (June, 623).

ROMANCE LANGUAGES AND LITERATURE

BENJAMIN P. BOURLAND

American Contributions.—The effects of the war in Europe continue to show themselves in the product of American scholarship in the Romance field during the year, in that there is a dearth of articles the preparation of which presupposes easy and frequent communication with the libraries of the Old World, and a tendency, hitherto negligible in this country, to polemic writing on smaller points of interpretation. This latter may be taken to be at once a symptom of a certain sort of maturity and an indication of the difficulty of getting firsthand access to new matter. Still, there has been a fairly large publication of texts, which, though none is of first-rate importance, all have value, and there has been good work in the field of the mediæval popular tradition. There has been also not a little useful writing of criticism of the more popular kind.

On the pedagogic side, the significant fact has been the continued increase in the study of Spanish, and the willingness, here and there, to make the new interest in Latin-America sufficient cause for the development of work in South-American Spanish, sometimes at the expense of the Castilian. The published work in this special field, whatever its promise, cannot be said as yet to have furnished any great contribution to Romance scholarship. The year, take it all through, has brought neither the completion nor the beginning of any large work.

Necrology.—Francesco Novati, born at Cremona in January, 1859, died at Milan late in December, 1915. Professor in the university of Milan, president of the Academy there, co-editor with R. Renier of the *Giornale Storico della Letteratura Italiana*, and editor of the *Studi Medievali*, he was one of the most distinguished and most useful scholars in the field of Italian literature. Alfred Holder, born at Vienna on April 4, 1840, died in January, 1916, at Carlsruhe, where he was director of the Grand-Ducal Library. Among his many and multifarious writings, his *Altkeltischer Sprachschatz* (1896), and his edition of *Saxo Grammaticus* (1886) are of importance to Romance scholarship. Giuseppe Pitrè, born at Palermo on Dec. 23, 1841, died there on Aug. 10. He was the greatest authority on all branches of Sicilian folklore. Among his many writings may be mentioned the *Biblioteca delle Tradizioni Popolari Siciliane* (28 vols., Palermo, 1871-1914) and his editorship of the *Archivo per lo Studio delle Tradizioni Popolari* (23 vols., 1882-1907), and of the 16 volumes of the *Curiosità Popolari Tradizionali* (1885-1890). He fought in Palermo, with Garibaldi, in 1860. José Echegaray, born at Madrid in March, 1833, died on Sept. 15. He was distinguished as mathematician, engineer, poet, and dramatist, and served his country at different times as Minister of Finance and of Education, and as Postmaster-General. Of his many plays, written 1875-1900, the best is *El Gran Galeoto*. Auguste-Emile Faguet, of the French Academy, professor of the Faculté des Lettres at Paris, died there on June 7. He was born at La Roche-sur-Yon on Feb. 18, 1847. He was a learned and discriminating critic of French literature, and a voluminous writer for many periodicals and newspapers. His principal contributions to scholarship are contained in a series of volumes of Literary Studies on the XVI, XVII, XVIII, and XIX centuries, 1885-1900, a book entitled *Les Politiques et Moralistes du XIXe Siècle* (1899).

BIBLIOGRAPHY

ALTROCCHI, Rudolph.—"An Old Italian Version of the Legend of St. Alexis." (*Romanic Rev.*, vi, No. 4.)
BARTON, Francis B.—"Laurence Sterne and Charles Nodier." (*Mod. Phil.*, xiv, No. 4.)
BAUM, P. F.—"The English Ballad of Judas Iscariot." (*Pub. Mod. Lang. Assoc.*, xxxi, No. 2.)
———. "The Mediæval Legend of Judas Iscariot." (*Ibid.*, xxxi, No. 3.)
———. "Roland 3220, 3220a." (*Romanic Rev.*, vii, No. 2.)
BRONK, Isabelle.—"Notes on Méré." *Mod. Lang. Notes*, xxx, No. 8.)
CARNAHAN, D. H.—"Some Sources of Olivier Maillard's 'Sermon on the Passion.'" (*Romanic Rev.*, vii, No. 2.)
CHINARD, G.—"*Notes sur le Voyage de Chateaubriand en Amérique.*" (Univ. of California Pub. in Mod. Phil., 1915.)
———. "*Notes sur le Prologue d'Atala.*" (*Mod. Phil.*, xiii, No. 11.)
———. "Early Intellectual Intercourse between France and America." (*Univ. of California Chronicle*, xvii, 1915.)
CIPRIANI, C. J.—"Future and Past Future." (*Mod. Phil.*, xiii, No. 7.)
CLARK, Barrett H.—*Contemporary French Dramatists.* (London, Stewart and Kidd, 1915.)
COHEN, Helen Louise.—*The Ballade.* (New York, Columbia Univ. Press, 1915.)
CUSHING, M. L.—*Baron d'Holbach; a Study of Eighteenth Century Radicalism in France.* (New York, Lemcke & Buechner, 1915.)

1916 LITERATURE AND LANGUAGE

CUTHBERT, Father.—*The Romanticism of St. Francis.* (New York, Longmans, 1915.)

DARGAN, E. Preston.—"Trissino, a Possible Source for the *Pléiade*." (*Mod. Phil.*, xiii, No. 11.)

———. "Balzac and Cooper. *Les Chouans*." (*Ibid.*, xiii, No. 4.)

DAVID, Henri.—*Théophile Gautier; Le Pavillon sur l'Eau. Sources et traitement.*" (*Ibid.* xiii, No. 7, and xiii, No. 11.)

DEY, W. M.—"The Latin Prefix *pro*—in French." (*Univ. of North Carolina Studies in Phil.*, xii, No. 4.)

ELLERY, Eloise.—*Brissot de Warville; a Study in the History of the French Revolution.* (Boston, Houghton, Mifflin, 1915.)

EMERSON, O. F.—"English or French in the Time of Edward III." (*Romanic Rev.*, vi, No. 2.)

ESPINOSA, A. M.—"Notes on the Versification of *El misterio de los Reyes Magos.*" (*Ibid.*, vi, No. 4.)

———. "New-Mexican Spanish Folk-Lore." (*Jour. Am. Folklore*, 1915.)

———. "Studies in New-Mexican Spanish," Part III. (*Rev. de Dialectologie Romane*, vi, 1015.)

FOULET, L.—*A Bibliography of Medieval French Literature for College Libraries.* Ed. by A. Schinz and G. A. Underwood. (New Haven, Yale Univ. Press, 1915.)

GEORGE, W. L.—*Anatole France.* (New York, Holt, 1915.)

GOLDSMITH, P. H.—*A Brief Bibliography of Books . . . Relating to the Republics Commonly Called Latin American.* (New York, Macmillans, 1915.)

GUTHRIE, K. S.—*Perronik the "Innocent," a Breton Legend.* (Brooklyn, Comparative Literature Press, 1915.)

HAWKINS, R. L.—*Maistre Charles Fontaine, Parisien.* (Cambridge, Harvard University Press, 1916.)

HENDRIX, W. S.—The *Auto da Barea do Inferno* of Gil Vicente and the Spanish *Tragicomedia Alegorica del Parayso y del Infierno.* (*Mod. Phil.*, xiii, No. 11.)

HULBERT, J. R.—"Syr Gawayn and the Grene Knyt." (*Ibid.*, xiii, Nos. 8 and 12.)

JAECK, Emma G.—*Madame de Staël and the Spread of German Literature.* (New York, Oxford University Press, 1916.)

JOHNSTON, O. M.—"Dante's *Divina Commedia* and the Medieval Conception of the Comedy." (*Mod. Lang. Rev.*, xi, No. 3.)

KENYON, H. A.—"Color Symbolism in Early Spanish Ballads." (*Romanic Rev.*, vii, No. 3.)

LANG, H. R.—"Provençal *Dos, Aposta, Affon.*" (*Ibid.*, vii, No. 2.)

LANCASTER, H. C.—"Relations between French Plays and Ballets, 1581-1650." (*Pub. Mod. Lang. Assoc.*, xxxi, No. 3.)

LOWELL, Amy.—*Six French Poets.* (New York, Macmillans, 1916.)

LOWES, J. L.—"Chaucer and Dante's *Convivio.*" (*Mod. Phil.*, xiii, No. 7.)

MACDONALD, G. R.—*Spanish-English and English-Spanish Commercial Dictionary.* (New York, Putnams, 1915.)

MCKENZIE, Kenneth.—"Francesco Griselini and His Relation to Goldoni and Molière." (*Mod. Phil.*, xiv, No. 3.)

MATTHEWS, Brander.—*The Chief European Dramatists.* (Boston, Houghton, Mifflin, 1916.)

MOORE, Olin H.—"The Naturalism of Alphonse Daudet." (*Mod. Phil.*, xiv, No. 3.)

NEWCOMER, C. B.—"The *Puy* at Rouen." (*Pub. Mod. Lang. Assoc.*, xxxi, No. 2.)

NITZE, W. A.—" '*Sans*' *et* '*matière*' *dans les Œuvres de Chrétien de Troyes.*" (*Romania*, xliv, 1915.)

———. "Concerning the word 'Graal,' 'Greal.' " (*Mod. Phil.*, xiii, No. 11.)

PHELPS, W. L.—"Browning in France." (*Mod. Lang. Notes*, xxxi, No. 1.)

SALVIO, A. de.—"Studies in the Dialect of Basilicata." (*Pub. Mod. Lang. Assoc.*, xxx, No. 4.)

SCHOELL, F. L.—"George Chapman and the Italian Neo-Latinists of the Quattrocento." (*Mod. Phil.*, xiii, No. 4.)

SIRICH, E. H.—*A Study in the Syntax of Alexandre Hardy.* (Baltimore, Furst, 1915.)

STEPHENS, Winifred.—*French Novelists of To-Day.* Second series. (New York, Lane, 1916.)

UNDERWOOD, G. A.—"Rousseauism in Two Early Works of Madame de Staël." (*Mod. Phil.*, xiii, No. 7.)

WARREN, F. M.—"A Byzantine Source for Guillaume de Lorris' *Roman de la Rose.*" (*Pub. Mod. Lang. Assoc.*, xxxi, No. 2.)

———. "On the Early History of the French National Epic." (*Mod. Phil.*, xiv, No. 3.)

WARSHAW, J.—"Recurrent '*Préciosité.*' " (*Mod. Lang. Notes*, xxxi, No. 3.)

WILKINS, E. H.—"The Invention of the Sonnet." (*Mod. Phil.*, xiii, No. 8.)

Translations

D'ANDELI, Henri.—*The Battle of the Seven Arts: a French Poem of the 13th Century.* Ed. and trans. by L. T. Pretino. (Berkeley, Univ. of California, 1916.)

PETRARCH.—*Some Love Songs.* Trans. and annotated with a Biographical Introduction by W. Dudley Foulke. (New York, Oxford Univ. Press, 1915.)

PHELPS, Ruth Shepard.—"A Translation of Cene da la Chitarra's 'Parodies on the Sonnets of the Months.'" (*Romanic Rev.*, vi, No. 3.)

ROLLAND, Romain.—*Michelangelo.* Trans. by F. Hoppin. (New York, Duffield, 1915.)

TAMAYO Y BAUS, M.—*A New Drama (Un Drama Nuevo).* Trans. by J. D. Fitz-Gerald and T. H. Guild. (New York, Hispanic Soc. of America, 1915.)

Texts

CERVANTES.—*Comedias y entremeses.* (*Obras completas tomo V edición publicada con notas por Rodolfo Schevill y Adolfo Bonilla.* Madrid, Rodríguez, 1916.)

The Poetry of Giacomo da Lentino, Sicilian Poet of the Thirteenth Century. Pub. by E. F. Langley. (Cambridge, Harvard Univ. Press, 1915.)

LOPE DE VEGA.—*Novelas a la Señora Marquesa Leonarda.* (*Reproduktion der Ausgaben von 1621 und 1624* ... *von John D. Fitz-Gerald und Leonora A. Fitz-Gerald,* (*Romanische Forsch.,* 1913.)

MEJIA DE LA CERDA, Luis.—*"El Juego del Hombre: auto sacramental."* Published by Louis Imbert. (*Romanic Rev.,* vi, No. 3.)

Li Romans dou Lis. Ed. with introduction by F. C. Ostrander. (New York, Columbia Univ. Press, 1915.)

"Les Sentiments de l'Académie Française sur le Cid." Published by Colbert Searles. (Minneapolis, *Univ. of Minnesota Studies in Lang. and Lit.*, 1916.)

"Traditional Ballads from Andalucía." Pub. by A. M. Espinosa. (*Flügel Memorial Volume*, Stanford Univ., 1916.)

"Venice in 1723; the Student Riots of Padua and the Execution of Gaetano Fanton in the Macaronic Poem *Strages Innocentium*." Published by Arthur Livingston. (*Romanic Rev.*, vii, No. 2.)

"Venice in 1727: Sonnets on the Execution of Domenico Althan." Published by Arthur Livingston. (*Mod. Lang. Notes*, xxxi, No. 6.)

ANCIENT LITERATURE AND PHILOLOGY

ANCIENT LITERATURE

(*Additions from Papyri*)

CLIFFORD HERSCHEL MOORE

Again in 1916 the chief publication of literary papyri comes from the skilled hands of the Oxford editors. The eleventh volume of the *Oxyrhynchus Papyri* is given wholly to literary and religious texts, while the twelfth volume will contain only documents.

Eleven new classical numbers in all are offered us. The list opens with parts of Hesiod's *Catalogue of Women* (1358 and 1359). In the first number one fragment deals with the story of Europa, following the tradition which made the Sarpedon of the *Iliad* the son of Europa and Zeus; the second, more fragmentary than the first, seems to contain the story of the pursuit of the Harpies by the Boreadae. The scanty remains published in 1359 apparently deal with the legends of Auge and Telephus, and of Diomedes and Hyacinthus. Among the most important discoveries are some drinking songs by Bacchylides (1361), but of the 48 fragments only two are complete enough to be intelligible. The first gives us 17 verses in praise of wine, addressed apparently to Alexander, son of King Amyntas of Macedon, to whom Pindar dedicated an ode. The other, of which 10 verses are fairly complete, is dedicated to Hiero. Internal evidence shows that it was composed later than 476 B. C., and that the poet was not in Sicily; it seems also to contain a reference to the fifth ode of the British Museum papyrus.

Considerable remains of the *Aetia* and *Iambi* of Callimachus have been published already from Oxyrhynchus. No. 1362 presents a new fragment of the former work, dealing with the association of Peleus with the island Icus, and with the ceremonies which celebrated the hero's arrival. Some new fragments of the *Iambi* (1363) are too scanty to do more than give hope for the future.

A notable addition to the early sophistic literature is made by a fragment of the treatise *On Truth* by Antiphon the Sophist (1364), a contemporary of Socrates. The theme is the antithesis between natural and human law. The writer seeks to justify furtive breaches of the law, and urges that obedience is wholly a matter of personal expediency; a little later he points out that distinctions of birth are entirely artificial.

A third century papyrus sheet (1365) contains an anonymous account of the origin and rise of Orthagoras, tyrant of Sicyon in the first half of the seventh century B. C., who has hitherto been hardly more than a name. Some pieces from the epitome of Hermippus' works *On Lawgivers*, *On the Seven Wise Men*, and *On Pythagoras*, made by Heracleides Lembus (1367), give the end of the first book and the beginning of the second, with a subscription attesting authorship and subject. This discovery completely disposes of certain conjectures by the learned as to the nature and scope of Heracleides' work. We have also a fragment (1368) from an unknown romance, which dealt in the usual way with the adventures of a certain Glaucetes. Finally we must name a scanty fragment of an unknown Attic orator (1366).

Students of religion will welcome Nos. 1380-82 and 1384. The first of these is a long invocation to Isis on an early second-century papyrus, which we at once compare with parts of the eleventh book of Apuleius' *Metamorphoses* and with other similar passages. The second, also of the same century, is in praise of Imouthes-Asclepius, and the third gives the end and title of a story illustrating the ἀρετή of Zeus-Helios-Sarapis. The fourth contains two fragments, apparently belonging to an uncanonical gospel or gospels, along with some medical recipes. A bit from a sailor's song (1383) completes the list of new literary texts.

Of the theological fragments, 1357 deserves especial notice. It contains a calendar of church services at Oxyrhynchus for five months of the year 535-6, which forms one of the most interesting documents concerning the early Egyptian church that has yet come to light.

Of extant classical authors some large pieces have been found, no one of which is of great textual value. But the lengthy passages from Aristophanes' comedies (1371-74) on fifth-century papyri and a long fragment of Thucydides VII (1376) are welcome. To the scanty finds of Latin works we can add a new fragment of Livy I (1379), and No. 62 of the second volume of the *Rylands Papyri*, which contains a translation into Greek from some unknown Latin work.

GREEK LITERATURE

WILLIAM ARTHUR HEIDEL

The *Year's Work in Classical Studies, 1915* (John Murray), now in its tenth year, gives in the main a satisfactory review of the more important works dealing with Greek literature. The authors of the several chapters, however, like the writer, have been greatly handicapped by conditions resulting from the European War. Scarcely any publications have arrived from Germany since March, and once more the hope of presenting a general survey of the year's work is a hope deferred until better times. Meanwhile we shall continue the practice of former years in giving prominence to publications in American journals.

In the *Transactions of the American Philological Association* (1915) appear, among others, the following studies: "Hephaestion and Irrationality," by M. W. Humphreys; "The Wanderings of Dardanus and the Dardani," by G. H. Macurdy; "The ΟΔΥΣΣΗΣ of Cratinus and the *Cyclops* of Euripides," by R. H. Tanner; "Democritus' Theory of Sense Perception," by R. B. English; "Early Cyprian Greek," by George Hempl. The presidential address of Prof. E. P. Morris, "A Science of Style," deserves particular attention as a thoughtful essay in a difficult field.

In the *American Journal of Philology* (now edited jointly by Profs. B. L. Gildersleeve and C. W. E. Miller) we note the following titles: "The Latest Expansion of the *Iliad*," by G. M. Bolling; "A Point in the Interpretation of the *Antigone* of Sophocles," by Charles Knapp; "The Personality of the Epicurean Gods," by G. D. Hadzsitz; "Mimnermus and Propertius," by D. B. Durham; "ΟΠΩΣ and ΟΠΩΤΑΝ" by B. L. Gildersleeve.

In *Classical Philology* the following articles may be mentioned: ΤΥΧΗ ΠΡΟΛΟΓΙΖΟΥΣΑ and the Identification of the Speaker of the Prologue," by C. H. Moore; "The ΔΡΑΠΕΤΙΔΕΣ of Cratinus and the Eleusinian Tax Decree," by R. H. Tanner; "Assumed Contradictions in the Seasons of the *Odyssey*," by J. A. Scott; "The Lot Oracle at Delphi," by F. E. Robbins; "Narrative and Speech Scansion in Homer," by A. Shewan; "Isocrates and the Epicureans," by H. M. Hubbell; "Plutarch's *Alexander* and Arrian's *Anabasis*," by R. B. Steele.

American doctoral dissertations on Greek subjects for the year which have come to the notice of the writer are few. *Lucian's Atticism*, by R. J. Deferrari, a Princeton dissertation, is a meritorious study of style, which ought to be pursued further and should lead to interesting results. *A Study of Archaism in Euripides*, by C. A. Manning (Columbia Univ. Press), opens up an alluring field and throws new light on the art of the dramatist. *The Platonism of Plutarch*, by Roger Miller Jones, a dissertation of the University of Chicago (Collegiate Press), is the work of an exceptionally able scholar and deserves high praise.

The books of the year are fewer than might have been expected. Here especially the war has caused a lessening of publication. The study of Greek literature ought to profit by the admirable *Greek Grammar* (for schools and colleges), by Prof. Herbert Weir Smyth, unquestionably the best brief grammar in English. The Loeb Classical Library (Putnams) continues to add to the debt we owe to Mr. Loeb and the editors. Nine volumes have appeared during the year in the Greek series. *Marcus Aurelius Antoninus*, by C. R. Haines, fully justifies the editors in bringing out a new translation; it is safe to say that many who have read the imperial sage in English only will henceforth use this charming guide to a knowledge of the Greek original. *Hesiod, the Homeric Hymns and Homerica*, by H. G. Evelyn-White, is valuable for much besides the excellent translation of the text. In the *Pindar*, by Sir. J. E. Sandys, many an admirer of the Theban bard will find his favorite text; even after the rendering of Myers, this new translation is assured of a cordial welcome. Prof. B. Perrin has added two volumes to his version of the *Lives* of Plutarch, which is the best we have, and E. Cary another volume of Dio's *Roman History*. A. J. Brock gives us a competent rendering of Galen's treatise *On the Natural Faculties*, and W. R. Paton presents the first volume of a *Greek Anthology* in a happy translation. Lovers of romance will welcome heartily the volume which contains the *Daphnis and Chloe* of Longus, translated by J. M. Edmonds, and *Parthenius*, translated by S. Gaselee.

Sir J. E. Sandys, who had given us an invaluable *History of Classical Scholarship* in three volumes (1903, 2d ed. 1906), now issues a *Short History of Classical Scholarship* (Putnams), which all friends of the classics will prize for its succinct and readable information in compendious form. *Greek Genius and Other Essays*, by John Jay Chapman (Moffat, Yard), contains an appreciative study of Euripides calculated to appeal to the general reader of good literature. *The Greek Tradition: Studies in the Reconstruction of Ancient Thought*, by J. A. K. Thomson (Macmillans), is a stimulating book, less adapted to instruct than to provoke thought. There is much which the author does not know about the subjects he discusses, but he writes as one who has lived where there is abundant intellectual stimulus and has profited by it. His book is good reading for a scholar.

Homer and History, by Walter Leaf (Macmillans), is much the most important book we have to notice. It is the work of a scholar keenly alive to the best classical study of our time and prepared by years of intelligent research to contribute to a saner thought in regard to Homer. Mr. Leaf is certainly right in dating "Homer" far earlier than many scholars have been accustomed to place him, and, questions of detail apart, he is clearly right in laying the emphasis not on minutiæ of statement but on the relation of the Homeric epics to the early history of the eastern Mediterranean basin.

Greek philosophy has little to boast of. *Socrates, Master of Life*, by W. E. Leonard (Open Court Pub. Co.), is a charming essay and, perhaps, the most satisfactory brief account we have of the great Athenian sage. *The Stoic Philosophy*, by Gilbert Murray (Putnams), a Conway lecture, is charming reading, but possesses not a single solid merit as an account of Stoicism.

Among works on archæology the student of things Greek ought not to overlook a book of prime importance, particularly to Americans, the *Handbook of the Cesnola Collection of Antiquities from Cyprus*, by John L. Myres (New York, Metropolitan Museum of Art). In view of the public neglect of the collection because of its supposed spuriousness, it is well to emphasize the fact that with trifling exceptions the antiquities contained in it are shown to be genuine. How important they may prove to be in view of the probability, even the certainty, of intimate relation of ancient Cyprus to Minoan Crete, no one can now forecast.

Several books should be mentioned which, though not works of distinguished scholarship, will surely interest friends of Greek literature. *The Glory that was Greece,* by J. C. Stobart (Lippincott), now, in its second edition, is at once one of the most readable and one of the most beautifully illustrated books about Greece that have appeared in a generation. Joseph Pennell's drawings *In the Land of Temples* (Lippincotts) catch, as only a true artist's pencil can, the very spirit of Greece, Sicily, and Magne Græcia. *Women of the Classics,* by Mary C. Sturgeon (Crowell), is a beautiful book, charmingly made and written in a style to delight the reader.

LATIN LITERATURE

CHARLES KNAPP

The second edition of *The New International Encyclopedia* (A. Y. B., 1915, p. 762) was completed by the publication of volumes xvii-xxiii. The revision of the classical articles in these, as in the earlier volumes, was made by C. Knapp.

To the Loeb Classical Library (A. Y. B., 1913, p. 805) several translations of Latin authors have been contributed by American scholars: of Cicero, *De Officiis,* by W. Miller; of Horace, *Odes and Epodes,* by C. E. Bennett; of Ovid, *Heroides and Amores,* by G. Showerman; of Ovid, *Metamorphoses* (two vols.), by F. J. Miller; of Suetonius, complete (two vols.), by J. C. Rolfe; of Vergil, *Eclogues, Georgics,* and *Aeneid,* I-VI, by H. R. Fairclough. Other important translations are, Vergil, *Eclogues and Georgics,* by T. C. Williams; and two in the University of Michigan Studies, Humanistic Series, xi, the one, *Robert of Chester's Latin Translation of the "Algebra" of Al-Khowarizmi,* by L. C. Karpinski, the other of *The Prodromus of Nicolaus Steno's Dissertation Concerning a Solid Body Enclosed by Process of Nature within a Solid Body,* by J. G. Winter. The original of the former book was made in the ninth century, the Latin version in the twelfth. On the value of the original see D. E. Smith, in *Science* (xliii, 389).

Interpreting the term literature somewhat broadly, so that it shall include all articles which will be of real service to the student of Latin literature, we proceed to give a selected list of articles, arranged according to the Latin authors with whom they deal primarily[1]: "Verbatim Reports of Augustine's Unwritten Sermons," by R. Deferrari (*TAPA.,* xlvi, 35), an argument that in Augustine's "Sermons" we possess unrevised long-hand transcriptions of short-hand verbatim reports; "By-Paths in Cæsarean Bibliography," by F. S. Dunn (*CW.,* ix, 65); "Cæsar *B. G.,* III., 12, 1—a Review and an Interpretation," by S. G. Oliphant (*AJP.,* xxxvii, 282), a defense of the manuscript text, and an interpretation of Cæsar's words as meant to apply only to the actual facts of his experience with the tides while he was fighting the Veneti, and as, in this sense, absolutely correct; "A Vexed Passage in the *Gallic War* (v, 16)," by F. G. Moore (*AJP.,* xxxvii, 206); "The International Law of the Gallic Campaigns," by M. Radin (*CJ.,* xii, 8); "A Lee Shore," by A. R. Wightman (*CW.,* ix, 130), a discussion of Cæsar, *De Bello Gallico,* IV, 28, 3; "Later Echoes of Calpurnius and Nemesianus," by W. P. Mustard (*AJP.,* xxxvii, 73); "Quintus Curtius Rufus," by R. B. Steele (*AJP.,* xxxvi, 402), an attempt to prove that Curtius wrote in the first years of the reign of Alexander Severus; "Interpretatiunculae," by E. W. Fay (*CW.,* ix, 162), a discussion of Horace, *Carmina,* II, 15, and of Vergil, *Eclogues,* V; "Horace and Valerius Cato," by G. L. Hendrickson (*CP,* xi, 249), an argument that the verses prefixed in many manuscripts to Horace, *Sermones,* I, 10, but usually rejected by scholars, were in fact written by Horace himself; "*Molle atque Facetum,*" by M. B. Ogle (*AJP.,* xxxvii, 327), a refutation of the explanation advanced by C. N. Jackson (*HS.,* xxv) of the famous words of

---

[1] Periodicals are cited thus: *AJP., American Journal of Philology; CJ., Classical Journal; CP., Classical Philology; CQ., Classical Quarterly; CW., Classical Weekly; HS., Harvard Studies; TAPA., Transactions of the American Philological Association.*

Horace, *Sermones*, I, 10, 44; "Horace an Atticist," by M. B. Ogle (*CP*., xi, 156), a denial that Horace was an Atticist, in opposition to the explanation of Horace, *Sermones*, I, 10, given by B. L. Ullman (*CP*., x, 270); "The Lucretian Theory of Providence," by G. D. Hadzsits (*CW*., ix, 146); "Criticism of the Text of Lucretius," by W. A. Merrill (*University of California Publications in Classical Philology*); "Some Features of Ovid's Style: I. Personification of Abstractions," by F. J. Miller (*CJ*., xi, 516); "The New Critical Edition of Ovid's *Metamorphoses*," by E. K. Rand (*CP*., xi, 46), an examination, in the main adverse, of the critical text-edition of the *Metamorphoses* published by Magnus (1914); "Petronius, Poggio, and John of Salisbury," by E. T. Sage (*CP*., xi, 11), an argument that John of Salisbury knew all parts of Petronius, though it is not certain that he had a manuscript of Petronius; "Atticism in Petronius," by E. T. Sage (*TAPA*., xlvi, 47); "Mimnermus and Propertius," by D. B. Durham (*AJP*., xxxvii, 194), in opposition to the view of Wilamowitz that Mimnermus was a model for the "Cynthia" book of Propertius; "Seneca's Epigrams," by K. P. Harrington (*TAPA*., xlvi, 207); "Notes on Tibullus," by K. F. Smith (*AJP*., xxxvii, 131), dealing with the literary tradition of Tibullus in modern times; "An Attempt to Date the Composition of Aeneid VII," by Gertrude M. Hirst (*CQ*., x, 87); "Is Donatus's 'Commentary on Virgil' Lost?" by E. K. Rand (*CQ*., x, 158).

Less definitely connected with a particular author are the following: "The Clausula and the Higher Criticism," by Susan H. Ballou (*TAPA*., xlvi, 157), a discussion of the way in which the doctrine of rhythmical clausulae in prose writings may help to decide questions of authorship; "*Fortunatus Et Ille*," by T. Frank (*CJ*., xi, 482), an attempt to explain why the Romans, who were deeply sensitive to the beauties of nature, so seldom in literature gave expression to that sensitiveness; "The Personality of the Epicurean Gods," by G. D. Hadzsits (*AJP*., xxxvii, 317); "The Crooked Plow," by F. Harrison (*CJ*., xi., 323), a criticism by a man of affairs, skilled also in farming, of scholars' descriptions of the Roman plow, and a declaration that the Romans, with a less perfect instrument than we possess, plowed well and, indeed, probably better than many do today; "Legislation against Political Clubs During the Republic," by R. W. Husband (*CW*., x, 11, 18, 26); "On the Expulsion of Foreigners from Rome," by R. W. Husband (*CP*., xi, 315); "Election Laws in Republican Rome," by R. W. Husband (*CJ*., xi, 535); "Liberal Studies in Ancient Rome," by C. Knapp (*Educational Rev.*, li, 237); "The Defeat of Varus and the German Frontier Policy of Augustus," by W. A. Oldfather and H. Canter (*University of Illinois Studies in the Social Sciences*, iv), in opposition to current views which attach great importance to this defeat of the Romans (for an abstract of the paper, by W. A. Oldfather, see *CJ*., xi, 226; for a review of it, by R. V. D. Magoffin, see *CW*., x, 47); "The Interpretation of Roman Comedy," by H. W. Prescott (*CP*., xi, 125), a presentation of the tendencies dominant at present in the higher criticism of Plautus and Terence, of the weakness of modern method here, and the possibility of a different point of view and safer courses of procedure; "An Analysis of the Pagan Revival of the Late Fourth Century," by D. N. Robinson (*TAPA*., xlvi, 87); "Advertising among the Romans," by E. T. Sage (*CW*., ix, 202); "Elision and Hiatus in Latin Prose and Verse," by E. H. Sturtevant and R. G. Kent (*TAPA*., xlvi, 129; for an abstract of this paper, by E. H. Sturtevant, see *CJ*., xii, 34); "The Roman *Magistri* in the Civil and Military Service of the Empire," by A. E. R. Boak (*HS*., xxvi, 73); "The '*Magistri*' of Campania and Delos," by A. E. R. Boak (*CP*., xi, 24); "The Cost of Living in Roman Egypt," by L. C. West (*CP*., xi, 293).

SEMITIC PHILOLOGY AND LITERATURE

Morris Jastrow, Jr.

The Hittites.—The European War again has interfered very seriously with the productivity of European scholarship in the field of Semitic philology and literature, and the difficulty of obtaining German publications forces the chronicler to omit almost entirely publications of that country. Fortunately, just before the more rigorous measures of the British Government against securing importations from Germany came into force, the preliminary results of researches of Friedrich Hrozny, of the University of Vienna, on Hittite inscriptions, found some years ago at Boghaz-köi by the expedition headed by the late Hugo Winakler and now gathered in Constantinople, were given in the *Mitteilungen* of the German Oriental Society. Through the study of the Hittite words transliterated into the Babylonian Cuneiform on clay tablets found at Boghaz-köi, accompanied by translations in the Sumerian and Akkadian (the non-Semitic and Semitic speech of the Euphrates Valley), Dr. Hrozny appears to have definitely established the character of the Hittite language as Aryan. His results have been endorsed by such eminent authorities as Profs. Eduard Meyer of the University of Berlin and Harri Holma of Helsinfors University, who also has published an interesting study on these lists of Hittite words and forms. In consequence of the war, the publication of the Boghaz-köi texts in Constantinople has been delayed. The volume was practically ready for publication when the war broke out. With the advance now made through the researches of Dr. Hrozny and the former investigations of R. C. Thompson of England, and Prof. Friedrich Delitzsch of Berlin, there is every reason to look forward to a definite solution of the Hittite linguistic problem as soon as the publication shall have been placed at the disposal of scholars.

Babylonia.—L. W. King, the most distinguished and most indefatigable of English Assyriologists, has followed up his *History of Sumer* and *Akkad* by a *History of Babylonia* (Stokes), covering the period from the foundation of the monarchy (c. 2350 B. C.) down to the Persian conquest in 539 B. C. It is by far the most complete presentation of the subject that has yet been issued, and is moreover written in so attractive a style as to appeal to the general public and not merely to the specialist. In a special chapter, Mr. King has given a summary, about 70 pages, of the remarkable work of the excavations carried on on the site of the ancient city of Babylonia by the German Orient Society for the past 16 years. Accompanying the summary are illustrations of some of the finds, and a valuable series of plans of buildings, walls, tombs and gates which enables the reader to form an idea of the great city as it appeared in the days of Nebuchadnezzar. Of especially absorbing interest is the chapter on the age of Hammurapi (2123-2081 B. C.) which marks an earlier climax in the history of the city of Babylon.

Mohammedanism.—Within the field of Arabic studies in Mohammedanism there are three notable publications, two of them in English. The lectures delivered by the distinguished professor of Arabic at the University of Leyden, C. Snouck Hurgronje, in the spring of 1914 in this country, have now been published under the title *Mohammedanism* (Putnams). While in the scope of this volume Professor Hurgronje touches only upon the general features of the religion and its history, the presentation is done in such a masterly manner as to compensate for the lack of details. For those desiring a more detailed exposition, Prof. Ignatz Golziher's work on *Mohammed and Islam* issued in English translation by the Yale University Press is strongly to be recommended as an authoritative work on the subject. Professor Golziher, who has no superior as a profound student of Mohammedan theology, sets forth the results of a lifelong study of Mohammedan law and Mohammedan dogmatism and Mohammedan sects in a series of chapters of fascinating interest and full of details not to be found anywhere else, at least in English form. Professor Golziher has also issued a volume in the De Goeje Foundation, established at the University of Leyden in memory of the late Professor De Goeje. As No. 3 of the publications of this Foundation there has just appeared the Arabic text of Ghazali's polemical writing aimed against the Batiniyya Sect of Mohammedanism (*Streitschrift des Gazali gegen die Batiniyya Sekte*), with a long introduction and a detailed analysis of the contents of the work. This sect, more commonly known as the Ismaelitic, was one which advocated as its main doctrine the infallibility of the Imams as the successors of Mohammed. Ghazali, who more than any other Arabic philosopher was instrumental in establishing Mohammedan orthodoxy, subjects the doctrines of the Batiniyya to a close and rigid criticism and shows how their views are a contradiction of the teachings of Mohammed. The work was written about the year 1094 when the sect seemed to have reached the zenith of their influence.

The Old Testament.—Within the field of the Old Testament, especial mention should be made of Professor George A. Barton's *Archæology and the Bible*, by far the most complete treatment of the subject, covering indeed every phase and abundantly illustrated (114 plates). It is an indispensable handbook for all students of the Bible, by a scholar of perhaps unsurpassed authority. Of a smaller compass is P. S. Hancock's very useful *Archæology of the Holy Land*, which presents the results of excavations and archæological research in Palestine.

INDO-EUROPEAN PHILOLOGY

(*Exclusive of the Germanic Languages*)

ROLAND G. KENT

General. — W. Petersen presents (*AJP.*,[1] xxxvii, 173, 255) important studies in "The Origin of the Indo-European Nominal Stem-Suffixes"; he suggests that endings became associated with ideas suggested by the word in its entirety, and were then transferred to other words as suffixes with this significance. A. F. Bräunlich gives (*Indogermanische Forschungen*, xxxv, 237) "A Theory of the Origin of Hypotaxis." He argues that the coördinating construction became subordinating when coordination was incapable of expressing the meaning, e. g., when the main clause was negative. E. W. Fay, under the title "*Pro Domo Mea*" (*AJP.*, xxxvii, 62, 156), supports with new material his previous etymological interpretations of numerals, superlatives, compounds of *sthā*, and verb flexion. H. C. Tolman discusses the Indo-European base $g^w em\bar{e}$ and shows that there is no reason to posit a root $gw\bar{a}$ (*PAPA.*, xlvi, xviii). C. D. Buck has an illuminating account of "Language and the Sentiment of Nationality" (*Amer. Pol. Sci. Rev.*, x, 44). H. S. Gehman discusses "Plutarch's Observation of the Superiority of Latin over Greek as a Means of Expression" (*CJ.*, xi, 237) and the detection or concealment of nationality when persons speak a foreign language (*CW.*, ix, 74, x, 35, and *PAPA.*, xlvi, xvii). R. G. Kent continues his reports of papers on Indo-European linguistics, read at meetings in the United States (*Indogermanisches Jahrbuch*, iii, 202; see *A. Y. B.*, 1915, p. 765).

Indo-Iranian.—E. W. Hopkins, in "Epic Mythology" (vol. III, Pt. 1, Sec. b of the *Grundriss der indoarischen Philologie und Altertumskunde*, Trübner, Strassburg), gives a systematic account of the mythology of the two great Sanskrit epics. M. Bloomfield has a fundamental treatment of "The Etymology and Meaning of the Sanskrit Root *Varj*" (*JAOS.*, xxxv, 273), and another "On Recurring Psychic Motifs in Hindu Fiction, and the Laugh-and-Cry Motif" (*JAOS.*, xxxvi, 54), designed to pave the way to a lexicon of such motifs. F. Edgerton has "Studies in the *Veda*" (*JAOS.*, xxxv, 240), with new interpretations of three passages in the *Chandogya Upaniṣad*, and "Sources of the Filosofy of the *Upaniṣads*" (*JAOS.*, xxxvi, 197), in which he supports the views that there is no single unified system of philosophy in the *Upaniṣads*, and that all the ideas in at least the older *Upaniṣads* are set forth or clearly foreshadowed in the older Vedic texts. H. S. Gehman demonstrates the development

---

[1] Periodicals are cited under the following abbreviations: *AJP.*, *American Journal of Philology*; *CJ.*, *Classical Journal*; *CP.*, *Classical Philology*; *CW.*, *Classical Weekly*; *JAOS.*, *Journal of the American Oriental Society*; *PAPA.*, *TAPA.*, *Proceedings, Transactions of the American Philological Association*.

of the meaning of "*Adhi-brū* and *adhi-vac* in the *Veda*" (*JAOS.*, xxxvi, 213). C. J. Ogden presents "Lexicographical and Grammatical Notes on the *Svapnavāsavadatta* of Bhāsa" (*JAOS.*, xxxv, 269), his gleanings in a study preliminary to an edition of the play. T. Michelson, in "Asokan Notes" (*JAOS.*, xxxvi, 205), gives a series of critical notes on the interpretation of the "Edicts" of Asoka.

Greek.—F. Eakin, in "The Greek Article in First and Second Century Papyri" (*AJP.*, xxxvii, 333), and C. W. E. Miller, in "Note on the Use of the Article before the Genitive of the Father's Name in Greek Papyri" (*ibid.*, 341), formulate the usages of the article in the papyri, and warn against the supposition of haphazard use and also against some current formulations as to its use. H. N. Sanders gives an historical study of "AN with the Future" (*ibid.*, 42), showing that there was a reluctance to use it about 400 B. C. and then again in Lucian's time. B. L. Gildersleeve has (*ibid.*, 210) a note on "ΟΠΩΣ and ΟΠΩΣ ΑΝ." J. W. Kern deals with "ἀνά and κατά: in Composition and with Case" (Ph. D. dissertation, Johns Hopkins Univ.). L. Van Hook shows (*CJ.*, xi, 495) that "The Degradation in Meaning of Certain Greek Words Meaning 'Work'" does not prove that honest toil was looked upon by the ancient Athenian as dishonoring, though this view has been taken by some. W. Petersen argues that "Greek Pronominal Adjectives of the Type ποῖος" (*TAPA.*, xlvi, 59) start from the Indo-European genitive plural in *-oisōm*, and shows that their use to designate quality was a later development. C. D. Buck interprets (*CP.*, xi, 211) the linguistic material in "The Inscriptions of Halae" published by Miss Goldman in the *American Journal of Archæology* for 1915 (p. 438). G. Hempl (*TAPA.*, xlvi, 229) interprets as Greek two early Cyprian documents, and seeks to prove that they are intermediate in alphabet between the Minoan script of Crete and the Cyprian syllabary.

Latin.—Details in the etymology of certain Latin words are handled by F. A. Wood (*CP.*, xi, 208) and E. W. Fay (*Zeitsch. für vergleichende Sprachforschung*, xlvii, 184). E. Riedel, in "Latin Verb Forms" (*Classical Quart.*, x, 165), gives a careful argument on the development of the shorter forms of the perfect tenses (such as *audiero, nosse, dixti*). E. H. Sturtevant, in "Dissimilative Writing in Republican Latin and *UO* in Plautus" (*CP.*, xi, 202), explains certain non-phonetic writings in classical Latin as due to the persistence of older spellings which represent the pronunciation of an earlier date. Sturtevant and R. G. Kent have a joint article on "Elision and Hiatus in Latin Prose and Verse" (*TAPA.*, xlvi, 129; also in abridged form by Sturtevant, in *CJ.*, xii, 34), in which they show that "elided" final sounds were really dropped and not merely slurred in speaking, and give a history of the prevalance of elision in Latin verse. J. C. Rolfe gives a detailed account of "The Use of *Gens* and *Familia* by Suetonius" (*CP.*, x, 445), in respect to the exact meanings of the words. M. Radin presents "A Latin Vocabulary for Practical Purposes" (*CJ.*, xi, 164), containing 529 reasonably common Latin words with English derivatives.

A. J. Carnoy, in "The Importance of Special Languages in the Study of Vulgar Latin" (*TAPA.*, xlvi, 75), shows how the technical words and meanings of professions and trades passed into the general vocabulary and are reflected in the Romance languages. The discussion on the sequence of tenses (see *A. Y. B.*, 1915, p. 766) is continued by Miss Susan Fowler, Miss E. M. Tyng, and B. M. Allen, and reply made by R. G. Kent (*CW.*, ix, 193). C. Knapp discusses a misunderstood form of double question and double statement (*CW.*, x, 9 and 17). H. C. Nutting gives a psychological explanation of "*Hysteron Proteron*" (*CJ.*, xi, 298); also, under the heading "Where the Latin Grammar Fails" (*CW.*, ix, 153), he discusses the use of the moods and tenses with *cum*. Reply is made by Miss B. R. Burchett and B. L. Ullman (*ibid.*, 192), and rejoinder by Nutting (*ibid.*, x, 16).

1917 LITERATURE AND LANGUAGE

AMERICAN LITERATURE

(*Nov. 15, 1916, to Nov. 15, 1917*)

EDWARD EVERETT HALE

Fiction.—The effect of the war upon imaginative literature so far has not been considerable. The change on the part of the United States from a state of public indecision to a state of actual action occurred too late to influence the spring publications, and the general production of books in 1917 is evidently greater than in the preceding year. The total number of books (including pamphlets) published in the United States in 1914 was 8,563; in 1915 it was 6,932; in 1916 it was 8,430; in 1917 it will probably have been nearly 9,000. The exact figures are not yet available, but an estimate can be made on the basis of the production of the first six months. During this period the books classified as fiction by American authors in 1914 numbered 689; in 1915, 643; in 1916, 703; in 1917, about 750. Of these books about one-fourth are usually new editions of books already published. Of this considerable amount of fiction, which includes but a very few of the great number of stories and novels which appear in the periodicals, only about one-half come to any general notice. Lists and summaries published by the *Dial* and other literary papers rarely mention more than half of what is included in the statistics as fiction. Such lists have varied somewhat in plan of late, but as far as we can judge, they also show an increased amount of fiction over 1916.

Of the novels which have come to such popularity as to find a place in the lists of "best sellers", the following have been in more than one of the monthly lists of 1917: Irving Bacheller's *The Light in the Clearing* (Bobbs-Merrill), Zane Grey's *Wildfire* (Harpers), Ernest Poole's *His Family* (Macmillans), Henry K. Webster's *The Thoroughbred* (Bobbs-Merrill), Basil King's *The Lifted Veil* (Harpers), Eleanor H. Porter's *The Road to Understanding* (Houghton, Mifflin), and Kathleen Norris's *Martie the Unconquered* (Doubleday, Page). In the full list for the year some other names will appear, for the books published in the fall have not at the time of writing had a chance to make their fair impression on the public mind. Still, even with this addition, there will not be so many American "best sellers" as there were in 1916. Lists of this kind often do not include really excellent novels, and often do include books of no lasting value. But they have been kept now for a good many years, and they show certain directions of popular interest. It may be mentioned that no American book published in 1917 has come to any such popularity as *Mr. Britling Sees it Through*.

If we take the general view of fiction offered in the YEAR BOOK for some years past, we shall not see much difference in 1917 in the general interests which have moved the writers, and presumably the readers, of the country. For a good many years now there has existed more or less consciously, in the artistic as well as in the public mind, the idea of a difference between the fiction which finds its interest in the presentation of more or less everyday life of the present day, and that which offers a certain excitement in exotic or out-of-the-way climes and situations. In the last years of the last century the writers of romance were in the ascendant. Year by year, however, though the change has been very gradual, our best writers have turned more and more to the presentation of common life, finding in everyday and ordinary characters and phases of life the interest and emotion which they need. The novel of adventure or mystery, of far lands and exciting situations and strange surroundings, the detective story or the story of the great outdoors, still make up a considerable part of the year's fiction. But the books that attract most attention are of a different sort. The same thing is to be observed in England, where H. G. Wells, who 20 years ago made a reputation by fantastic extravaganzas, now increases his fame by an almost unvarnished account of his own life during the war. We might mention in American fiction Winston Churchill, who 20 years ago delighted multitudes by his vigorous historical romances, but who now for a good many years has given himself mostly to the study of political, religious and social questions, and is able to interest people quite as much as he used to. At the same time it is also to be said that this difference between realism and romance is by no means so important as it once was. Few writers of the novels "of mystery, of romance, of adventure", to use the common phrase of the advertisement, are without a considerable element of current life. They are apt to find their beginning or their setting in some kind of life to which we are all accustomed. Nor are the writers of novels of current life without the elements of romance. The real distinction at the present day would seem to be between a presentation of life which shall embody some more or less definite ideal conception, and the presentation, whether realistic or romantic, of life without any such idealism.

Whether or no such a distinction be well founded, there are a number of novels of 1917 which have at bottom the desire to comprehend or exhibit some general criticism of American life. Ernest Poole's *His Family* (Macmillans) is undoubtedly an interesting story about interesting people, but its people are so chosen as to illustrate typical phases of American life and typical contrasts between the life of the present generation and that of the past. Waldo Frank's *The Unwelcome Man* (Little, Brown) is the story of a man who seeks vainly to find opportunities for the action of his spiritual functions in the life of to-day, and is quite a definite as well as pessimistic criticism of American civilization. Sherwood Anderson's *Marching Men* (Lane), which may seem on the surface almost a naturalistic transcript of life, is in reality the presentation of a great if vague idea as to the character of American life. There are as usual a number of books which are thought of as dealing with social problems of one sort or another, but they are rarely so directly concerned with their problem as was the case 20 years ago. Winston Churchill's *The Dwelling-place of Light* (Macmillans) brings vividly before us the relations of labor and capital, but it is much more informed by a general idea than expressive of any definite solution. Much the same thing may be said of the late D. G. Phillips' *Susan Lenox* (Appletons), though of course this book does not represent the conceptions of the immediate present. Here belongs Upton Sinclair's extremely interesting *King Coal* (Macmillans), as well as Henry K. Webster's *The Thoroughbred* (Bobbs-Merrill), rather a slighter consideration of some of the aspects of modern marriage than his book of two years ago. Mention only can be made of Basil King's *The Lifted Veil* (Harpers), Kathleen Norris's *Martie the Unconquered* (Doubleday, Page), and Eleanor H. Porter's *The Road to Understanding* (Houghton, Mifflin), but Dorothy Canfield Fisher's *Understood Betsy* (Holt) calls for particular note quite as much for its engaging humanism as for its ideas on education. There are also a good many books devoted to some special part of America or phase of American life, but they are rarely so definitely "local" as the stories of local color of a generation ago. Alice Brown's *Bromley Neighborhood*, (Houghton, Mifflin), Mary E. Wilkins Freeman and Florence M. Kingsley's *The Alabaster Box* (Appletons), Edith Miniter's *Our Natupski Neighbors* (Holt), and Robert Cutler's *Louisburg Square* (Macmillans) present New England, city and country. Mrs. H. R. Martin's *Those Fitzenbergers* (Doubleday, Page) and Joseph Hergesheimer's *The Three Black*

Pennys (Knopf) deal respectively with the Pennsylvania Dutch and the Pennsylvania steel mills. Paul Kester's *His Own Country* (Bobbs-Merrill), Mrs. Honoré Wilsie's *Lydia of the Pines* (Stokes), and Mathilde Bilbro's *The Middle Pasture* (Small, Maynard & Co.) are distinctively Southern, while Mary Austin's excellent *The Ford* (Houghton, Mifflin) is Californian. Joseph C. Lincoln's books always have enough local color to them, but of course their chief charm is in their humor and character drawing; *Extricating Obadiah* (Appletons) is based on the mishaps of an old sailor who inherited a fortune. Of the stories devoted to particular phases of the life of our country, some of the best represent Jewish life in America. Of these Sidney Nyburg's *The Chosen People* (Lippincotts) is an excellent first-hand story of a young rabbi in an old conservative congregation, while Abraham Cahan's *The Rise Of David Levinski* (Harpers) gives the career of a Jewish immigrant in New York City. It is perhaps something of an accident that Edna Ferber's *Fanny Herself* (Stokes) should be a Jewish story; the chief interest, as in the author's other books, is in the capable woman of business. Such also is Sinclair Lewis's *The Job* (Harpers), a good unconventional chronicle of a woman who makes a success in the business world. We might put here (they are surely American enough) three studies of youth: Samuel Merwin's *Temperamental Henry* (Bobbs-Merrill), Mary R. Rinehart's *Bab, a Sub-Deb*, (Houghton, Mifflin) and rather more authentic than either, it would seem, K. Keith's *The Girl* (Holt), a singularly interesting and perhaps typical impression of an American girl. There are not a few other novels of American life, which ought not be forced into any classification; the two best are Mrs. Wharton's rather darkly tragic *Summer* (Appletons) and Francis R. Bellamy's good piece of romantic idealism, *The Balance* (Doubleday, Page). Here may be mentioned two characteristic though unfinished posthumous novels by Henry James (Scribners), *The Sense of the Past* and *The Ivory Tower*.

Turning to the other side of the field we have first the historical novels. Of these the chief novel of American history is Irving Bacheller's *The Light in the Clearing* (Bobbs-Merrill), a picture of life in northern New York in the generation before the Civil War, as it centered around the sturdy figure of Silas Wright. Will H. Harben's *The Triumph* (Harpers) is a story of the South of much the same period. Mary Johnstone's *The Wanderers* (Houghton, Mifflin) is a series of connected episodes running through the ages, which shows the author's gradual extension of range and interest. F. J. Stimson's *My Story* (Scribners), a fictional autobiography of Benedict Arnold, should be mentioned, though it can hardly have the influence of its predecessor, *King Noanett*, of 20 years ago. We should mention here also *The Sorry Tale* by Patience Worth (Holt), a story based on Biblical suggestion, concerning which many diverse opinions have been expressed. There are not so many good stories of adventure as there have been in past years. The popular favorite has been Zane Grey's *Wildfire* (Harpers), a story, like all its author's, noteworthy not for its adventure alone but for its deep appreciation of the beauty of our Western country. To be noted here also are Mrs. B. W. Bowers's *Starr of the Desert* (Little, Brown), Ernest Seton Thompson's *The Preacher of Cedar Mountain* (Doubleday, Page), the first novel of a writer otherwise well known, George B. McCutcheon's *Green Fancy* (Dodd, Mead), faithful to the Zenda tradition though in New England, and Robert W. Chambers's *The Barbarians* (Appletons). Several books might be more properly called stories of mystery than of adventure. Frances H. Burnett's *The White People* (Harpers) is a story of second sight; Mrs. Wilson Woodrow's *The Hornet's Nest* (Little, Brown), Allen French's *The Hidingplaces* (Scribners), and W. J. Dawson's *A Daughter of the Morning* (Lane) come here. There are some good detective stories; best (with allowance for difference of taste) is William MacHarg and Edwin Balmer's *The Indian Drum* (Little, Brown). Others have approved

Anna K. Green's *The Mystery of the Hasty Arrow* (Dodd, Mead), Natalie S. Lincoln's *The Nameless Man* (Appletons), or Roman Doubleday's *The Green Tree Mystery* (Appletons). Carolyn Wells's *The Mark of Cain* (Lippincotts) and Nevil M. Hopkins's *The Mystery of Raccoon Lake* (Lippincotts) may also be mentioned, though neither is of the best work of its author. As is usual, some of the best books of the year are the extravaganzas, books often so engaging that one cannot pronounce them preposterous; a type of book pertinaciously American. Of these we name only Meredith Nicholson's *The Madness of May* (Scribners), Holworthy Hall's *What He Least Expected* (Bobbs-Merrill), G. Weston's *Oh Mary Be Careful* (Bobbs-Merrill) and (though it may not come best here) K. F. Gerould's clever, *A Change of Air* (Scribners). There are as ever a number of books of a kind passed over by many as "glad" books, which, however, often have a sterling foundation. Of these the most noteworthy appear to be Alice Hegan Rice's *Calvary Alley* (Century), Belle K. Maniates's *Amarilly in Love* (Little, Brown), Maria T. Daviess's *The Heart's Kingdom* (Reilly & Britton), and Grace S. Richmond's *Red Pepper's Patients* (Doubleday, Page). Finally we mention *The Sturdy Oak* (Holt), a suffrage tract, by 14 well known writers, most of whom have been otherwise mentioned in this review.

Short Stories.—There is of course an enormous number of short stories, of which only a very small proportion are collected in book form. Some idea of this form of American literature is given by E. J. O'Brien's *The Best Short Stories of 1916* (Small, Maynard) and H. T. Baker's *The Contemporary Short Story* (Heath). A curious collection is *The Grim Thirteen* (Dodd, Mead), in which F. S. Greene put together a number of stories which were good but too "grim" to pass the magazine editors. Of the collections by distinctive short-story writers would be M. R. S. Andrews's *The Eternal Feminine* (Scribners), Alden Brooks's *The Fighting Men* (Scribners), A. B. Reeves's *The Treasure Train* (Harpers), and C. E. Van Loan's *Old Man Curry* (Doran).

Poetry.—In 1917 one can more readily than usual take a view of current poetry by the help of two publications on the subject. Harriet Monroe and Alice Corbin Henderson, the editors of *Poetry*, have published *The New Poetry: an Anthology* (Macmillans), containing extracts from the work of about a hundred present-day poets (a good many English), with a preface in which they do something to define the ideas and aims of the present generation of poets. More limited in scope, but more particularly critical, are the four essays in Amy Lowell's *Tendencies in Modern American Poetry* (Macmillans). From these two books one can make a grouping of the writers of poetry of the present day. The half-dozen or more writers who some years ago associated themselves under the name of "imagists" are represented in the year's publishing chiefly by a third volume of selections, *Some Imagist Poets: an Anthology, 1917* (Houghton, Mifflin), and by J. G. Fletcher's *Japanese Prints* (Four Seas Co.) and F. S. Flint's *Goblins and Pagodas*. The general principles of this group have been definitely stated and somewhat understood for two or three years, but they now become more interesting from Miss Lowell's essay on "H. D." and on "Mr. Fletcher." Of several others who at one time or another have been associated with the group, Ezra Pound published in 1917 *Lustra* (Knopf); Robert Frost, who though he does not belong to this, or any other, group, but has some aims in common with them, has published *Mountain Intervals* (Holt), a book with much of the genius which is more and more impressing people. Edgar Lee Masters has published *The Great Valley* (Macmillans), a book in the main, of vigorous Americanism, of poems generally longer than those of the famous book by which he is chiefly known and without their condensed genius. Edwin A. Robinson's *Merlin* (Macmillans) is a rendering from the old legend-cycle of King Arthur. It is an effort at something larger than Mr. Robinson has heretofore done, and does not seem to have the particular powers of phrase and characterization of which he is usually the master. Vachell Lindsay, on the other hand, in his *The Chinese Nightingale* (Macmillans) is just like himself; one may call the poems all sorts of things, but they are indisputably effective, however they are styled.

These poets are obviously modern; it is not that they are devoted to images or free verse or anything else, but they clearly have something of the same sort of thing about them (with perhaps the exception of Mr. Lindsay) and they may easily be thought of together. There are several others who might properly be thought of with them though they do not happen to come within the range of Miss Lowell's treatment. Conrad Aiken's *Turns and Movies* (Houghton, Mifflin), John G. Neihardt's *The Quest* (Macmillans), and James Oppenheim's *The Book of Self* (Knopf) are definitely enough of the newer poetry. It is less easy to see why some of the others in Miss Monroe's collection should be "new" poets, if that term be held to show any general difference from the "old" poets. Sara Teasdale's *Love Songs* (Macmillans) are very charming poems, delightful to read and keep in mind now as they would have been at any time, but it is hard (for the present writer at least) to see any "newness" in them even with the assistance of Miss Monroe and Mrs. Henderson. Much the same thing might be said of Edith Wyatt's *The Wind in the Corn* (Appletons), which contains some poems which finely represent the spirit of America, in a way that, one would say, would have been possible even in the much-condemned Victorian era. W. Bynner's *Grenstone Poems* (Stokes) and Joyce Kilmer's *Main Street and Other Poems* (Doran) have in them poetic qualities which have been attractive before the present decade. There are some poets of our day who do not seem to write "new poetry", if we may judge from our anthology. H. B. Fuller is perhaps absent from being too new. He is best known as a novelist, and it is probable that his *Lines Short and Long* (Houghton, Mifflin) will be read with the same sort of interest that one would have for a short story. New enough but not of the newer school of poets is Grantland Rice, the well known sporting writer, whose *Songs of the Stalwart* (Appletons) express fine, manly ideas in fluent verse. Franklin P. Adams's *Weights and Measures* (Doubleday, Page) is a volume of very amusing and modern verse, though quite unlike what is commonly thought of as the new poetry. Further still from the newer aims is Walt Mason, who continues to interest thousands of readers daily with his homely and sensible ideas and his humorous and ridiculous expression. There have been published during the year Stanley Brathwayte's usual *Anthology of Magazine Verse* (Small, Maynard) and several other collections, of which may be especially mentioned *A Book of Verse of the Great War* (Yale University Press) and *The Poets of the Future: A College Anthology*.

Essays and Criticism.—There are a number of very good volumes of criticism. The best is *On Contemporary Literature* (Holt), a book in which Stuart P. Sherman has included a number of articles written during the last few years which have excited a good deal of attention. As a collection the book has something of an accidental character, but its general tenor is perfectly plain. It is an application of what may be called a classical, a standard, a rational, view of literature to the fiction of the present. Professor Sherman is opposed to Mr. Dreiser and Mr. Wells; he is in sympathy with James and Meredith; he can see the good in a modern novelist like Arnold Bennett, and the badness of an old crusted conservative like Alfred Austin; he finds the real thing in Shakespeare. That school of criticism which has been chiefly represented in this country by the work of P. E. More, Irving Babbitt and W. C. Brownell has now another effective weapon. Quite a different view is to be found in J. E. Spingarn's *Creative Criticism* (Holt). Mr. Spingarn's general position in criticism has been known for a good while; in fact a good deal of this book has been in print before. It is well, however, that we should have it all put together in one volume, for it constitutes a good statement of theory. Amy Lowell's *Tendencies in Modern American Poetry* (Macmillans), which has been already mentioned, is interpretation rather than criticism (if one likes to make a difference); it is clearly the statement of one who knows and sympathizes with the aims and ideas of certain of the present poets in America. Miss Lowell understands the new poetry and wishes to present it to the world. Naturally she approves of it, thinks it good, but these feelings on her part do not exactly constitute criticism in the sense in which most people would use the word. This is not a very important matter, however, and does not take from the value of the book, which, as has been seen, is a most useful clue in the present maze of current poetry. Clayton Hamilton's *Problems of a Playwright* (Holt) is the excellent work of a capable critic already well known. Mr. Hamilton has the advantage of really understanding the theatrical standpoint, so that he can offer more in the way of interpretation than he could otherwise do. A different sort of theatrical criticism, but equally useful, is that of J. K. Towse in *Sixty Years of the Theatre* (Funk & Wagnalls). The author was for a long time critic of the New York *Evening Post*. It is not so much our custom to reprint current dramatic criticism as it is in Paris, for instance, but a certain amount of publishing is good both for journalism and literature. Of the literature that would come more properly under the head of "essays" should be noted David Grayson's *Great Possessions* (Doubleday, Page), a book on the familiar circumstances of country life, and Charles S. Brooks's *There's Pippins and Cheese to Come* (Yale University Press).

Biography.—There are many good biographies, especially of great Americans. The most noteworthy contribution to the history of literature is *Audubon the Naturalist: A History of his Life and Time*, by Francis H. Herrick (Appletons). This is definitive of one of the most distinguished and interesting figures of our art and literature. It is founded on a great mass of original material and developed and illustrated in a very complete and satisfactory way. Based also upon a great range of original material is the *Life and Letters of Edward Everett Hale*, by his son, the present writer (Little, Brown). Dr. Hale was one of the most characteristically American figures of the nineteenth century, and this record of his life seeks to give an idea of the breadth of his personality and the range of his interests and accomplishments. *The Life, Art, and Letters of George Inness*, by his son George Inness, Jr. (Century), gives a long-needed authoritative account of the foremost figure in American landscape painting. John S. Clarke's *Life of John Fiske* (Houghton, Mifflin) gives a personal view of an important thinker and historian of about the same time. James G. Pyle's *Life of James J. Hill* (Doubleday, Page) is of a later figure, one of the characteristic Americans of later years, a great captain of industry. Joseph F. Daly's *Life of Augustin Daly* is an account of a very interesting and significant man. Mr. Daly was the representative figure in the American theatre for the last generation, and this life by his brother has much of the authority and character of an autobiography. *The Life of Joseph H. Choate*, by Theron G. Strong (Dodd, Mead), does not offer itself as a complete and authoritative account, but it is written by a man of literary ability who not only knew Mr. Choate well but is also a leader in his profession. Several autobiographies, or more properly volumes of reminiscence, are especially noteworthy. Most interesting probably is *Mark Twain's Letters*, edited by A. B. Paine (Harpers), a collection of singularly original and unconventional letters of our great humorist and philosopher. Another attractive book is *These Many Years*, by Brander Matthews (Scribners). Mr. Matthews has long been an eminent student and critic of the drama and the theatre, and his book gives something of a record of his long activity as well as the quality of his engaging personality. In *A Son of the Middle Border* (Macmillans) Hamlin Garland has given an account of the first half of his life, from his early days in the Wisconsin farm lands in the years following the Civil War to his beginnings and first successes in literature.

Necrology.—There have died during the year Hamilton Wright Mabie, long known and loved as critic, essayist and editor, Dec. 31, 1916; Franklin B. Sanborn, the last of the great Concord group, Feb. 24; J. J. Piatt, still best known for his early poems, Feb. 16; Ruth McEnery Stuart, whose stories of life in the South were well known, May 6; William J. Lampton, who used to call himself the "father of free verse" by virtue of his experiments in newspaper poetry, May 30; and William Winter, the really great theatrical and dramatic critic, June 30.

MODERN LANGUAGES AND LITERATURE

ENGLISH LANGUAGE AND LITERATURE

ALBERT C. BAUGH

English Philology.—In the *Flügel Memorial Volume*, published by Stanford University, is printed an unpublished paper of Flügel's on "The History of English Philology". In the same volume H. Hilmer considers the origin of speech sounds in "The Main Source of Speech-sounds and the Main Channels of their Spread". *Linguistic Change* is the title of a study by E. H. Sturtevant. C. M. Lotspeich continues his study of ablaut in "A Theory of Ablaut" (*JEGP*.[1]). Studies involving general Germanic conditions are R. M. Ihrig's *The Semantic Development of Words for "walk, run" in the Germanic Languages*, E. H. Sehrt, *Zur Geschichte der westgermanischen Konjunktion "und"*, and F. A. Wood, "Etymological Notes" (*MLN.*). Professor Bright has prepared a new edition of his *Anglo-Saxon Reader*. Prof. O. F. Emerson has treated "The Old French Diphthong *ei* (*ey*) and Middle English Metrics" (*RR.*), and has published notes on "*Afterdiner, Aftermete, Aftersopen*", "*Treson*" and "*Iraland*" (Alfred's *Orosius*, I, 1), all in *Modern Language Review*. A. G. Kennedy's "French Culture and Early Middle English Forms of Address" (*Flügel Mem. Vol.*) and J. L. Barker's "End Consonants and Breath-Control in French and English" (*MP.*) deal with Anglo-French linguistic relations. J. M. Steadman, Jr., has studied "The Origin of the Historical Present in English" (*SP.*).

Old English Literature (449-1150). —"The Beginnings of Poetry" by Louise Pound (*PMLA.*) may best be mentioned here. Oscar L. Olson has worked out *The Relation of the Hrólfs Saga Kraka and the Bjarkarímur to Beowulf*, and other Beowulf items are treated by H. M. Ayres, "The Tragedy of Hengest in *Beowulf*" (*JEGP.*), Alexander Green, "An Episode in Ongentheow's Fall" (*MLR.*), G. W. Mead, "Witherygld of *Beowulf*, 2051" (*MLN.*), and L. M. Hollander, "*Beowulf* 33" (*ibid.*). The Finn episode, too, has had considerable attention. American contributions are Alexander Green, "The Opening of the Episode of Fin in *Beowulf*" (*PMLA.*) and N. S. Aurner, "An Analysis of the Interpretations of the Finnsburg Documents" (*Univ. of Iowa Monogr.*). The *Caedmon Poems* have been translated by C. W. Kenedy, and K. Sisam has a note on "The Caedmonian *Exodus* 492" (*MLN.*). Ruth Perkins writes "On the Sources of the *Fata Apostolorum*" (*MLN.*), and G. H. Gerould takes up "The Old English Poems on St. Guthlac and their Latin Source" (*ibid.*). Cook's review of Browne's *Ancient Cross Shafts at Bewcastle and Ruthwell* (*MLN.*) deserves mention. Incidentally it may be very well noted that the progress of *Old English Scholarship in England from 1566-1800* has been traced by E. N. Adams.

Middle English Literature (1150-1500).—The Middle-English period has been the subject of much recent activ-

---

[1] Periodicals are cited under the following abbreviations: *MLN., Modern Language Notes; MLR., Modern Language Review; MP., Modern Philology; PMLA., Publications of the Modern Language Association of America; JEGP., Journal of English and Germanic Philology; SP., University of North Carolina Studies in Philology; RR., Romanic Review.*

ity. By far the most important contribution of the year is Carleton Brown's epoch making *Register of Middle English Religious and Didactic Verse*, of which Part I ("List of Manuscripts") has been issued by the London Bibliographical Society. Part II, containing indexes and references, is promised for early publication. One of Professor Brown's students, F. A. Foster, has completed her edition of *The Northern Passion* for the Early English Text Society. Frances L. Gillespy has published *Layamon's Brut: A Comparative Study in Narrative Art* (*Univ. of Cal. Publ.*). J. Hinton is the author of two careful articles on Walter Map, "Walter Map's *De Nugis Curialium*: Its Plan and Composition" (*PMLA*.), and "Walter Map and Ser Giovanni" (*MP.*). In the field of the romance reference must be made to the long and painstaking review by Lucy M. Gay of the *Vulgate Version of the Arthurian Romances* (*MP.*). W. C. Curry has sought to recreate *The Middle English Ideal of Personal Beauty*, as found in the metrical romances, etc. R. S. Loomis has made especially his own the study of plastic representations of scenes from the romances. The longest of his studies is *Illustrations of Medieval Romance on Tiles from Chertsey Abbey* (*Univ. of Ill. Stud.*), and this may be supplemented by his "The Tristran and Perceval Caskets" (*RR.*) and an article on Galahad in *Art in America*. He has also published "Verses on the Nine Worthies" (*MP.*), supplementary to the texts presented by Gollancz. Margaret P. Medary has investigated the "Stanza-Linking in Middle-English Verse," especially the romances, and Arthu. C. L. Brown has completed the study by an article "On the Origin of Stanza-Linking in English Alliterative Verse" (both in *RR.*). Professor Brown has also discussed "From Cauldron of Plenty to Grail" (*MP.*). The grail legend is treated by L. A. Fisher in *The Mystic Vision in the Grail Legend and Divine Comedy*. J. C. Hodges, "Two Otherworld Stories" (*MLN.*), and R. S. Loomis, "A Phantom Tale of Female Ingratitude" (*MP.*), touch the romance less closely. On turning to the saints' legends, we may note a suggestive article by G. H. Gerould on "The Legend of St. Wulfhad and St. Ruffin at Stone Priory" (*PMLA.*). Hope Emily Allen has published "The *Speculum Vitae*; Addendum" (*PMLA.*) and "A Note on the Proverbs of Prophets, Poets, and Saints" (*MP.*). A number of miscellaneous topics in Middle-English literature have been treated: L. B. Hessler, *Latin Epigrams of the Middle-English Period*; J. M. McBryde, Jr., "Some Medieval Charms" (*Sewanee Rev.*); E. P. Hammond, "A Manuscript Perhaps Lost" (*MLN.*); and R. Wallerstein, *King John in Fact and Fiction*. An exhaustive paper by A. Taylor, "Dane Hew, Monk of Leicester" (*MP.*) traces the diffusion of a widespread folk tale. Two studies have appeared concerning *Piers Plowman*, T. A. Knott's "Observations on the Authorship of *Piers the Plowman*" (*MP.*) and J. H. Hanford's "Dame Nature and Lady Life" (*MP.*). Two short collections of ballads have been edited by W. M. Hart and G. H. Stempel, respectively, and "The Influence of Transmission on the English Ballads" has been studied by J. R. Moore (*MLR.*). J. M. Berdan has traced "The Influence of the Medieval Latin Rhetorics on the English Writers of the Early Renaissance" (*RR.*). The early drama has received considerable attention. P. E. Kretzmann has published a valuable monograph on *The Liturgical Element in the Earliest Forms of the Medieval Drama*. J. K. Bonnell, "The Easter Sepulchrum in its Relation to the Architecture of the High Altar" (*PMLA.*), C. B. C. Thomas, "The Miracle Play at Dunstable" (*MLN.*), Hardin Craig. "The Pater Noster Play" (*Nation*), G. A. Jones, "A Play of Judith" (*MLN.*) and W. K. Smart, "*Mankind* and the Mummer's Plays" (*MLN.*), all concern intimately the early drama.

Once more it is possible to speak with special satisfaction of the work of American scholars on Chaucer. Professor Kittredge has written at length on "Chaucer's Lollius" (*Harvard Stud. in Class. Phil.*) and in a short article has queried "Lewis Chaucer or Lewis Clifford?" (*MP.*). J. L. Lowes in a communication to the *Nation* announced certain views concerning Chaucer's use of French translations of Latin classics. He has also discussed "Chaucer and Dante" (*MP.*) and "The Second Nun's Prologue, Alanus, and Macrobius" (*ibid.*). Professor Cook has written in detail of *The Last Months of Chaucer's Earliest Patron* (*Trans. Conn. Acad.*) and has contributed "Chauceriana" to the *Romanic Review*. R. K. Root's *The Textual Tradition of Chaucer's Troilus* appeared in 1916. Root has also discussed "Chaucer's Dares" (*MP.*). "The Troilus-Cressida Story from Chaucer to Shakespeare" (*PMLA.*) is the title of a paper by H. E. Rollins. H. B. Hinckley treats "The Debate on Marriage in the Canterbury Tales" (*PMLA.*). S. B. Hemingway makes brief contributions on "Chaucer's Monk and Nun's Priest" and "The Two St. Pauls" of Chaucer's *Pardoner's Prologue* (both in *MLN.*). I. C. Lecompte collates "Chaucer's *Nonne Prestes Tale* and the *Roman de Renard*" (*MP.*) and B. L. Jefferson works out the connection between *Chaucer and the Consolation of Philosophy of Boethius.* E. P. Kuhl has published his conclusions regarding "Chaucer's Burgesses" (*Trans. Wis. Acad.*). M. H. Shackford has made a suggestion in connection with "The Date of Chaucer's *House of Fame*" (*MLN.*) and M. L. Brown has made clearer the resemblances between "The *House of Fame* and the *Corbaccio*" (*MLN.*). "The Sources of Chaucer's *Parlement of Foules*" are studied by W. E. Farnham (*PMLA.*). Finally we may gather together here a few minor notes: J. S. P. Tatlock's note on "The Marriage Service in Chaucer's *Merchant's Tale*" (*MLN.*), his "Puns in Chaucer" (*Flügel Mem. Vol.*), P. F. Baum's "Notes on Chaucer" (*MLN.*), and J. Q. Adams' "William Goddard" (*MLN.*).

Modern English Literature (since 1500).—Spenser has been the subject of several articles in the journals. J. B. Fletcher has called his study "The Painter of the Poets" (*SP.*), and C. G. Osgood has written on "Spenser's Sapience" (*ibid.*). O. F. Emerson has argued the question of "Spenser, Lady Cary and the *Complaints* Volume" (*PMLA.*) and contributed a note on "A New Word in an Old Poet" (*MLN.*). P. W. Long has considered "Spenser and the Bishop of Rochester" (*PMLA.*) and "Spenser's Visit to the North of England" (*MLN.*). F. M. Padelford's "The Women in Spenser's Allegory of Love" (*JEGP.*) also deserves mention. For other Elizabethans, outside the drama, there is less to record. "The Italian Lyrics of Sidney's *Arcadia*" is the title of an article by Clarence Stratton (*Sewanee Rev.*). R. M. Alden has a paper on "The Lyrical Conceit of the Elizabethans" (*SP.*). Lyly's *Euphues* has been critically edited by M. W. Croll and H. Clemons. Finally we may record H. E. Rollin's "Notes on Thomas Deloney" (*MLN.*).

Turning to Shakespeare and the Elizabethan drama, we may first note four studies of the theatre and stage. J. Q. Adams, Jr., has published an admirable volume on the *Shakespearean Play-houses*, in which he reexamines the documents and studies the 22 regular and projected theatres of Shakespeare's time. He has also investigated "The Conventual Buildings of Blackfriar's, London, and the Playhouses Constructed Therein" (*SP.*). T. S. Graves has published "'Playing in the Dark' During the Elizabethan Period" and "Notes on Elizabethan Theatres" (both in *SP.*).

Shakespearean literature presents its usual bewildering profusion. H. H. B. Meyer has compiled *A Brief Guide to the Literature of Shakespeare.* E. Greenlaw writes on "Shakespeare's Pastorals" (*SP.*) and H. D. Gray on "Shakespeare's Last Sonnets" (*MLN.*). M. P. Tilley reconciles "Shakespeare and Italian Geography" (*JEGP.*), F. M. Padelford distinguishes "The Gothic Spirit in Shakespeare" (*So. Atlan. Quart.*), and S. P. Sherman discloses "The Humanism of Shakespeare" (*Nation*). William Winter has published a third series of his *Shakespeare on the Stage*, and J. M. Manly considers "Cuts. and Insertions in Shakespeare's Plays" in the light of Shakespeare's versification (*SP.*). B. L. Schafer offers "A Study of the Three Unities in Shakespeare's Representative Plays" (*Sewanee Rev.*), and R. A. Law writes "On the Structure of Certain Shakespeare Plays" (*Texas Rev.*). The University of Texas has published *A Memorial Volume to Shakespeare and Harvey* containing contributions by Professors Manly, Bright, Barrett Wendell, etc. H. D. Gray in "The Authorship of *Titus Andronicus*" (*Flügel Mem. Vol.*) proposes the Shakespearean authorship of the play with revision by other men. Individual plays are also treated by A. R. Brubacher, *Shakespeare's King Richard III;* H. D. Gray, "The Purport of Shakespeare's Contribution to *1 Henry VI*" (*PMLA.*); Wm. Chislett, Jr., "On Shakespeare's *Julius Cæsar*" (*Flügel Mem. Vol.*); and J. H. Hanford, "A Platonic Passage in Shakespeare's *Troilus and Cressida*" (*SP.*). Tucker Brooke offers an interpretation of "Hamlet's Third Soliloquy" (*SP.*), which is opposed by S. A. Tannenbaum's, "Hamlet Prepares for Action" (*ibid.*). Similarly, M. W. Croll makes "A Suggested Emendation" to *1 Henry IV*, II.iv.133ff. which is answered by J. S. Kenyon's "The 'Sow's Tale'"(both in *Nation*). Other textual notes are M. P. Tilley's "A Good Kissing Carrion" to *Hamlet*, II.ii.182 (*MLR.*) and H. D. Gray's "Antony's Amazing 'I Will to Egypt'" (*MP.*). Finally, attention may be directed very briefly to a few more general titles: H. B. Sprague, *Studies in Shakespeare;* R. A. Law, "Shakespeare in Puritan Disguise" (*Nation*); *Papers on Playmaking*, published by the Dramatic Museum of Columbia University; A. W. Crawford, *Hamlet, an Ideal Prince and other Essays in Shakespearean Interpretation;* and J. W. Postgate, *Homage to Shakespeare.*

Three plays of Ben Jonson have been edited in the Yale Studies: *Every Man in His Humour*, by H. H. Carter; *Catiline, His Conspiracy*, by L. H. Harris; and *The Case Is Altered*, by W. E. Selin. T. S. Graves briefly discusses "Jonson's *Epicoene* and Lady Arabella Stuart" (*MP.*), W. D. Briggs connects "*Cynthia's Revels* and Seneca" (*Flügel Mem. Vol.*). Briggs also continues his search for Jonson's sources in "Source-Material for Jonson's *Epigrams* and *Forest*" (*Classical Phil.*) and "Source-Material for Jonson's *Underwoods* and Miscellaneous Poems*" (*MP.*). The University of Pennsylvania has issued the first series of its *Studies in English Drama*. The volume contains A. Gaw, "Tuke's Adventures of Five Hours, in Relation to the 'Spanish Plot' and to John Dryden"; R. Jewell, "Heywood's Faire Maid of the West"; J. L. Carver, "The Valiant Scot, by J. W."; C. C. Gumm, "Sir Ralph Freeman's Imperiale"; C. Stratton, "The Cenci Story in Literature and in Fact"; and M. G. McCauley, "Function and Content of the Prologue, Chorus, and Other Non-Organic Elements in English Drama". The present writer has edited William Haughton's *Englishmen for My Money, or A Woman Will Have Her Will*. E. D. Adams prints "A Fragment of a Lord Mayor's Pageant" (*MLN.*), E. C. Dunn discusses "John Rastell and *Gentleness and Nobility*" (*MLR.*), and E. B. Daw is the author of two papers concerned with minor items—"*Love Fayned and Unfayned* and the English Anabaptists" (*PMLA.*) and "Two Notes on *The Trial of Treasure*" (*MP.*). Various suggestions of the sources of individual plays have been made or examined. E. R. Macauley prints "Notes on the Sources for Medwall's *Nature*" (*MLN.*), Tucker Brooke writes "On the Source of *Common Conditions*" (*MLN.*), W. D. Briggs, "On the Sources of *The Maid's Tragedy*" (*MLN.*), and W. G. Stanard on a source of *Edward III* in "Edward III and the Countess of Salisbury" (*Nation*). C. W. Lemmi is the author of a brief note on "*Tamburlaine* and Greene's *Orlando Furioso*" (*MLN.*) and J. J. Parry writes of "A New Version of Randolph's *Aristippus*" (*ibid.*). C. R. Baskerville concludes his presentation of "Some Evidence for Early Romantic Plays in England" (*MP.*) and has added a supplementary note on "An Elizabethan Eglamour Play" (*ibid.*). *The Early Romantic Drama at the English Court* is the title of a dissertation by L. M. Ellison. Karl Young has written of "William Gager's Defence of the Academic Stage" (*Trans. Wis. Acad.*) and R. M. Alden in "The Invasion of Tragedy by Comedy" (*Texas Rev.*) has supplemented an earlier article (*JEGP.*, xiii). Two phases of verse structure have received attention in F. G. Hubbard's "A Type of Blank Verse Line Found in the Earlier Elizabethan Drama" (*PMLA.*) and C. W. Cobb's "A Further Study of the Heroic Tetrameter" (*MP.*).

Later seventeenth- and eighteenth-century verse is much neglected. It is strange that Milton has attracted so few scholars. J. H. Hanford has written on "The Dramatic Element in *Paradise Lost*" (*SP.*) and E. C. Baldwin has "A Note on *Paradise Lost* IX" (*MLN.*). "The Temptation in *Paradise Regained*" (*JEGP.*) by A. H. Gilbert and the edition of "Of Reformation Touching Church-Discipline in England" by W. T. Hale are the only other Milton items of any extent. H. M. Ayres writes of "Chapman's *Homer* and Others" (*Nation*), E. B. Reed prints "Two Seventeenth Century Hunting Songs" (*MP.*), and J. J. Parry has edited *The [Selected] Poems and Amyntas of Thomas Randolph*. C. A. Moore asks "Did Leibniz Influence Pope's Essay?" (*JEGP.*). C. S. Northup has issued his *Bibliography of Thomas Gray*, and J. P. Kaufman quotes "Stockdale on Gray's Productivity" (*MLN.*). "The Two Versions of Grongar Hill" are treated by G. Greever (*JEGP.*). More general in its scope is C. A. Moore's "The Return to Nature in English Poetry of the Eighteenth Century" (*SP.*), and rather intensive is H. A. Burd's *Joseph Ritson: A Critical Biography*.

The post-Restoration drama has been treated in R. Wright's *Political Play of the Restoration*. R. S. Forsythe has completed his *Study of the Plays of Thomas D'Urfey, with a reprint of "A Fool's Preferment"* (*Western Reserve Stud.*), J. T. Hillhouse has edited Fielding's most successful play, *The Tragedy of Tragedies*, and S. T. Williams has published a volume on *Richard Cumberland: his life and dramatic works*. H. L. Bruce lists additional "English Adaptations of Voltaire's Plays" (*MLN.*), and Miss L. B. Campbell considers "The Rise of a Theory of Stage Presentation in England during the Eighteenth Century" (*PMLA.*).

English fiction has been studied by A. J. Tieje in *The Theory of Characterization in Prose Fiction prior to 1740*. H. J. Savage has discussed "The Beginnings of Italian Influence in English Prose Fiction" (*PMLA.*). H. S. Hughes devotes considerable space to "An Early Romantic Novel" by one Mary (Mitchell) Collyer (*JEGP.*). Miscellaneous prose of the eighteenth century has been treated by Dorothy Foster, "The Earliest Precursor of Our Present-Day Monthly Miscellanies" (*PMLA.*), and C. N. Greenough, "The Development of the *Tatler* Particularly in Regard to News" (*ibid.*). P. H. Houston writes of "Some Contemporary Criticism of Dr. Johnson" (*Texas Rev.*), E. N. S. Thompson examines "The Discourses of Sir Joshua Reynolds" (*PMLA.*) and discusses "Tom Brown and Eighteenth-Century Satirists" (*MLN.*). S. C. Chew finds "An English Precursor of Rousseau" (*MLN.*) and W. H. Graves, in *Junius Finally Discovered*, argues for Paine's authorship of the *Letters*.

Lack of space prevents more than a brief treatment of the later periods of English literature. Mention may be made of Neilson's *Burns: How to Know Him;* notes on Byron and Keats (*MLN.*), and L. N. Broughton's *Concordance to the Poems of Keats*. C. T. Winchester has published *Wordsworth: How to Know Him*, W. H. Vann records "Two Borrowings of Wordsworth" (*MLN.*), G. M. Harper writes of "Wordsworth at Blois" (*Texas Rev.*), and E. L. Bradsher discusses "The First American Edition of the Lyrical Ballads" (*So. Atlan. Quart.*). "Rossetti's *House of Life*" is the subject of a paper by F. M. Tisdel (*MP.*). A Hazlitt item is recorded by J. Zeitlin, "Philosophy for Schoolboys" (*Nation*), and Matthew Arnold should be studied in S. P. Sherman's *Matthew Arnold: How to Know Him* and Irving Babbitt's review in the *Nation*. R. M. Alden has published in the same series *Alfred Tennyson: How to Know Him*, and E. M. Robinson has written a thesis on *Tennyson's Use of the Bible*. F. E. Pierce follows "The Hellenic Current in English Nineteenth-Century Poetry" (*JEGP.*), and M. R. Thayer traces *The Influence of Horace on the Chief English Poets of the Nineteenth Century*. In *The Naming of Charac-*

ters in the *Works of Charles Dickens* E. H. Gordon treats a rather obvious subject. Stevenson has received several treatments including R. H. Rice's *Stevenson: How to Know Him,* G. S. Hellman's edition of *Poems Hitherto Unpublished,* and E. C. Knowlton's "A Russian Influence on Stevenson" (*MP.*). The modern novel receives attention in A. P. Webb's *Bibliography of the Works of Thomas Hardy, 1865-1915,* R. P. Utter's "The Work of Thomas Hardy" (*Sewanee Rev.*), S. P. Sherman's "The Aesthetic Idealism of Henry James" (*Nation*), and Wilson Follett's "A New View of De Morgan" (*Yale Rev.*). In the later poetry we may note A. E. Trombly's article on "The Poetry of A. E." (*Texas Rev.*), J. E. Meeker's volume on *The Life and Poetry of James Thomson* ("*B. V.*") and H. Fineman's *John Davidson: A Study of the Relations of His Ideas to His Poetry.* In the drama two very good books have appeared, T. H. Dickinson's *The Contemporary Drama of England* and E. A. Boyd's *The Contemporary Drama of Ireland.* L. R. Morris's *The Celtic Dawn, a Survey of the Renaissance in Ireland, 1889-1916* is a slighter work. E. H. Bierstadt has issued a volume on *Dunsany the Dramatist,* and W. L. Sowers treats the same writer in "A New Influence in Our Theatre" (*Texas Rev.*). Mention may be made of R. Burton's *Bernard Shaw, the Man and the Mask.*

A few books of a more general character may complete this survey. In criticism W. C. Brownell has published a volume called *Standards,* J. E. Spingarn one which he calls *Creative Criticism,* and Gertrude Buck has written on *The Social Criticism of Literature. The Rhythm of Prose* has been investigated by W. M. Patterson, and "Cadence in English Prose" by F. M. Foster. Assuredly there is no decrease in the production of American scholars during the past year.

GERMANIC LANGUAGES AND LITERATURE

Daniel B. Shumway

German Literature.—The fact that the United States for the greater part of the year has been engaged in war with Germany has naturally resulted in far less activity in translating from the German than heretofore. In the field of philology and literary criticism, however, there are fully as many excellent articles as before the war.

In the field of drama and fiction the English edition of Gerhard Hauptmann's works has been continued by the publication of the seventh volume, containing *Elga* and *The Bow of Odysseus,* translated by Ludwig Lewisohn, and the *Commemoration Masque* (*Festspiel*) by G. B. Q. Morgan. Excellent translations of four plays of the Austrian dramatist Arthur Schnitzler (*The Hour of Recognition, The Big Scene, The Festival of Bacchus* and *His Helpmate*) have appeared under the title *Comedies of Words,* with an introduction by Pierre Loving (Stewart & Kidd); see W. Haynes, "Arthur Schnitzler, Dramatist of Psycho-analysis" in the *Dial* (July 19, p. 63). Hugo von Hofmannthal's play *Everyman,* based on the old English morality play, has been rendered into English blank verse by G. Sterling and R. Ordynski (Robertson). Frank Wedekind is represented by the fifth edition of his powerful tragedy, the *Awakening of Spring* (N. L. Brown), and by a translation of his *Pandora's Box* (Shay). Steiger has reprinted a number of the amusing comedies of R. Benedix: *Günstige Vorzeichen, Die Hochzeitsreise, Die Lügnerin, Ohne Pass* and *Die Phrenologin,* and also *Paulas Geheimnis* by Oscar Blumenthal and *Die Schulreiterin* by E. Pohl. Joseph Wiehr has discussed Carl Hauptmann's *Verhältnis zur Heimatkunst* (*Jour. Eng. and Ger. Phil.,* April, p. 226. Nor have the classical dramatists been forgotten. Lessing's *Minna von Barnhelm* has been translated by Otto Heller (Holt), *Nathan der Weise* by Patrick Maxwell, with an introduction by George Kohut (Bloch). J. T. Hatfield discusses "Lessing's Feeling for Classic Rhythms" (*Jour. Eng. and Ger. Phil.,* April, p. 187) and Brander Matthews deals with Lessing in an article "Three Theorists of the Theatre" (*Art World,* April, p. 24). Goethe is represented only by an article by Julius Goebel, "Traces of the Wars of Liberation in Goethe's *Faust*"

(*Jour. Eng. and Ger. Phil.*, April, p. 195), and Schiller by an interesting article by F. W. C. Lieder on "Bayard Taylor's Adaption of Schiller's Don Carlos" (*ibid.*, Jan., p. 27). The purpose of the German drama in the sixteenth and seventeenth centuries is the subject of an able article by Jos. E. Gillet in the *Publications of the Modern Language Association* (Sept., p. 430).

For the first time in many years no German novel has been translated, and only a brief notice of Johann Stilgebauer's war novel *Inferno*, which was forbidden in Germany, has been given in the *Review of Reviews* (Feb., p. 207). L. M. Price in an article "Karl Gutzow and Bulwer Lytton" (*Jour. Eng. and Ger. Phil.*, July, p. 397) has shown that Gutzow was not so dependent on Lytton as Julian Schmidt would have us think.

In the field of lyric poetry A. W. G. Randall has interestingly discussed "German War and the German Poets" (*Contemporary Rev.*, June, p. 747) and translated poems of Hauptmann, Sudermann, Dehmel, Lissauer, Fritz von Unruhe and others. F. W. Herzberger has published a timely volume of *Luther Songs and Ballads* with a biographical account of the great reformer. That the interest in Heinrich Heine never seems to wane is shown by the translation of 325 of his poems by Louis Untermyer (Holt). An interesting experiment has been made by A. Gray (*Living Age*, Jan., p. 194), who has rendered three of the best known of Heine's lyrics into Scotch dialect verse, with a result that is quaint, pretty and altogether charming.

The field of literary criticism is well represented. O. H. Werner discusses the question of the *Unmarried Mother in German Literature* (*Columbia Univ. Press*), E. F. Clark treats of the "Grobianus of Hans Sachs and its Predecessors" (*Jour. Eng. and Ger. Phil.*, July, p. 390). N. C. Brooks describes the "Hans Sachs Stage" (*ibid.*, April, p. 208). Goethe's ideas of the human race and its capabilities are discussed by John F. Coar in an article entitled "Goethe's Philanthropy" (*Germanistic Soc. Quart.*, March, p. 1). J. F. Haussmann shows "E. T. A. Hoffmann's Influence on Haupt" (*Jour. of Eng. and Ger. Phil.*, Jan., p. 53), and Cecil A. Moore, in "Did Leibniz Influence Pope's Essay on Man?" (*ibid.*, Jan., p. 84), denies that the influence was in any way direct. G. P. Jackson continues his studies of the "Rhythmic Form of the German Folk Song, *Mod. Phil.*, June, p. 79), treating of the various strophic forms. T. F. Crane gives the "External History of the *Kinder and Hausmärchen* of the Brothers Grimm" (*ibid.*, June, p. 65).

German Philology.—In the general field of philology E. Prokosch, "*Die deutsche Lautverschiebung und die Völkerwanderung*" (*Jour. of Eng. and Ger. Phil.*, Jan., p. 1), tries to show, contrary to the general belief, that the contact of the Teutons with foreign nations put an end to the Germanic sound shift. Most interesting is the ingenious attempt of C. M. Lotspeich ("*A Theory of Ablaut*", *ibid.*, April, p. 173) to prove that the qualitative ablaut is due to difference of stress and is therefore really quantitative. Hermann Collitz discusses the "Ablaut of Gothic *speiwan*" (*Mod. Phil.*, June, p. 103), showing by Sanskrit parallels that it is an old word of the first ablaut class. T. W. J. Heuser, under the title "*Deutsche Sprachreinigung*" (*Germanistic Soc. Quart.*, March, p. 26), gives an interesting review of the attempts to supplant foreign words by native ones in German. In an article on "Culture and Kultur from the Viewpoint of a Philologist" (*Educ. Rev.*, March, p. 227) the same scholar discusses the difference between the German and English words. The older period is represented by an article by C. N. Gould on the "Syntax of *at* and *ana* in Gothic, Old Saxon and Old High German" (printed privately). Joseph Wright has rewritten and enlarged his *Middle High German Primer* for the third edition (*Oxford Univ. Press*).

German Texts and Teachings.—In the field of German texts J. L. Kind has continued his editions of Grillparzer's plays by one of *Sappho* (*Oxford Univ. Press*). Rudolph Herzog's interesting novel *Die Burgkinder* has been abridged and edited by O. G. Boetzkes (Heath). A new edition of

Goethe's *Hermann und Dorothea* has been prepared for the Oxford series by F. W. C. Lieder. O. Burkhard has compiled *German Poems for Memorizing* (Holt). Two new editions of Paul Heyse's ever popular tale *L'Arrabbiata* have been published and a literal translation made by V. E. Lyon. German readers have been prepared by E. W. Roessler, F. E. Bell, P. S. Allen and P. Scherer, and a science reader by F. W. Scholz (*Macmillans*). The following German grammars have been issued: M. P. Whitney and L. L. Stroebe, *Brief Course in German* (Holt), R. W. Huebsch and R. F. Smith, *Progressive Lessons in German* (Heath), M. H. Haertel and G. C. Cast, *Elements of German Grammar for Review* (Heath). Deserving of special mention is *A First German Book* by Frederick Betz and W. R. Price (Am. Book Co.) after the direct method, in which each lesson is based on a carefully chosen anecdote calculated to hold the attention of the pupil. In the field of pedagogy C. H. Handschin has discussed the "Study of German during the War" (*School and Society*, Sept., p. 253).

Scandinavian.—In the general Scandinavian field G. T. Flom has published "Studies in Scandinavian Paleography" (*Jour. Eng. and Ger. Phil.*, July, p. 416). In the Swedish field the most important event is the publication of Selma Lagerlöf's works in a nine-volume translation (Doubleday Page). To accompany the edition the publishers have had H. E. Maule prepare an account of the author under the caption *Selma Lagerlöf, the Woman and Her Message*. August Strindberg's *Married* has appeared in the Modern Library of the World's Best Books (Boni & Liveright). The most talked of Swedish poet of the year has been the Nobel Prize winner, Karl Gustav Werner von Heidenstam, whose work has been the subject of several articles by C. W. Stork (*Nation*, Nov. 30, 1916; *Bookman*, Feb., p. 589; *Independent*, April 2, p. 26), which are illustrated by admirable translations of several of his poems. He has been treated also by Svea Bernhard (*Poetry*, April, p. 35), who points out that he is as popular as Lagerlöf and that the literary renascence in Sweden begins with him. C. W. Stork has given fresh proof of his ability as a translator by issuing a volume of selections from the best Swedish lyricists under the title *Anthology of Swedish Lyrics*. Maret Michelet has written in Swedish a brief survey of Mathilde's Wergeland's life under the title *Glimt fra Agnes Mathilde Wergelands liv* (Free Book Concern). Swedish tales have been published, one *Oberst Heg og hans Gutter* by W. T. Ayrer (Fremad), and others under the title *Vildros, ett nytt Knippe* by Carl A. Lönnquist (Augustana Book Concern).

In the Norwegian field the popularity of Ibsen is evinced by new translations of his plays. His *Doll's House*, *Ghosts* and *Enemy of the People* appear in the Modern Library of the World's Best Books. Dutton has issued a volume containing Ibsen's *Pretenders* and other plays. Signs of the increasing attention paid to the study of Norwegian in American schools are a school edition of Björnsen's *En Glad Gut* which has been prepared by J. A. Holvik (Augsburg Publ. Concern), and an edition of a German translation of Ibsen's *Ein Volksfeind* by J. L. Blyesen (Oxford Univ. Press). Doran has published an authorized translation of Jörgensen's *Klokke Roland* under the title *False Witness*.

Two translations from the Danish have appeared, one by Ingeborg Lund of the stirring experiences in the German army of a Schleswig Dane, Erich Erichsen, under the title *Forced to Fight* (Robert McBride), the other a compilation from war time sermons of German clergymen made by J. P. Bangs and translated by Jessie Bröchner under the caption *Hurrah and Hallelujah* (Doran).

ROMANCE LANGUAGES AND LITERATURE

BENJAMIN P. BOURLAND

American Contributions.—The effect of the war upon the output of Roman scholarship in the United States is more and more apparent with each year. Inaccessibility of sources, lack of the inspiration that is won only by free and constant intercourse with the best minds of Europe, and the diversion of men from scholarly to other fields of exertion have affected as well the quantity as the quality of the work produced.

French.—Miss LeDuc's study of Gontier Col is a real contribution to the history of humanism in France. Thieme has published a major treatise on the history of French verse. Fisher's edition of Pierre de Beauvais' *Vie de St. Eustache* is the principal publication in the field of Old French. Stacpoole's *François Villon* has qualities that make it welcome in a subject excellently treated heretofore.

Note should perhaps be made of the fact that numerous manuals have been issued during the year for the help of Americans in the various services in France. A few of these are good of their kind, and some are the work of scholars. None is in any sense a contribution to learning. They are mentioned here as an example of the influence of the war.

Spanish.—The tendency toward Latin America is even stronger in 1917 than in the year preceding, or it may be that 1917 has seen the publication of much matter the preparation of which dates from 1915-16. As yet we have principally text books, but in his *Literary History of Spanish America* Coester has made a beginning on the side of scholarship. In pure Castilian we note Mr. How's translation of the Lazarillo, from Foulché-Delbosc's text, with Wagner's introduction.

Italian.—The outstanding contribution in Italian is Grandgent's volume of McBride lectures, *The Ladies of Dante's Lyrics*. To be noted also is the same author's popular book on *Dante* in the Duffield series.

Necrology.—Robert Edouard Pellissier was killed in the Battle of the Somme, Aug. 29, 1916. He was born on May 12, 1882, at La Ferrière in the French Jura, came to the United States in 1896, studied at Harvard, and from 1911 was of the faculty of Leland Stanford Jr. University, where he was still assistant professor at the time of his death. When the war broke out he was one of the first to sail to France and join the army to serve his native land. He first served as a private, then as sergeant, lastly as lieutenant in the French army. His death, mourned greatly by his friends and colleagues, has taken from the United States a scholar of as high a promise, and a man of as distinguished a character as can be found in any part of the world. Albert Frederick Kuersteiner, since 1898 professor in the University of Indiana, died at Indianapolis on June 9, 1917, after long suffering, admirably borne. He was 51 years old. He was a ripe and sound scholar in French and Spanish, and bore a very high reputation as a teacher. William Henry Fraser, professor of Italian and Spanish in the University of Toronto, died on Dec. 28, 1916.

BIBLIOGRAPHY

BEAUMARCHAIS, P. A. C. de.—*Le Mariage de Figaro.* Ed. by E. F. Langley. (New York, Oxford Univ. Press, 1917.)
COESTER, Alfred.—*The Literary History of Spanish America.* (New York, Macmillans, 1917.)
DARÍO, Rubén.—*Eleven Poems.* Tr. by T. Walsh and Salomón de la Selva. Introduction by Pedro Henríquez Ureña. (New York, Putnams, 1916.)
GRANDGENT, Charles Hall.—*Dante.* (New York, Duffield, 1916.)
———— *The Ladies of Dante's Lyrics.* (Cambridge, Mass., Harvard Univ. Press, 1917.)
LE DUC, Alma deL.—"Gontier Col and the French Pre-Renaissance." (*Romanic Rev.*, vii, 4, and viii, 2; continuation announced.)
The Life of Lazarillo de Tormes and His Fortunes and Adventures. Done out of the Castilian ... by Louis How; introduction by Charles P. Wagner. (New York, Mitchell Kennerly, 1917.)
LUKER, B. F.—*The Use of the Infinitive instead of a Finite Verb in French.* (New York, Lemcke & Buechner, 1916.)
MITCHELL, Julia Post.—*St. Jean de Crèvecoeur.* (New York, Columbia Univ. Press, 1916.)
PIERRE DE BEAUVAIS.—*La Vie de Saint Eustache.* Ed. by John R. Fisher. (*Romanic Rev.*, viii, 1.)
SCHINZ, A.—*J.-J. Rousseau et le libraire-imprimeur Marc-Michel Rey.* (Genève, Jullien, 1916.)
SCOTT, Mary Augusta.—*Elizabethan Translations from the Italian.* (London, Constable, 1917.)
STACPOOLE, H. deVere.—*François Villon. His Life and Times, 1431-1465.* (New York, Putnams, 1917.)
THIEME, Hugo P.—*Essai sur l'histoire du vers français.* Préface de Gustave Lanson. (Ann Arbor, Mich., Wahr, 1917.)

1917 LITERATURE AND LANGUAGE

ANCIENT LITERATURE AND PHILOLOGY

ANCIENT LITERATURE
(*Additions from Papyri*)
CLIFFORD H. MOORE

The year 1917, because of the war, has seen no important publications of literary papyri, strictly speaking, but there appeared in 1916, too late for notice in the last issue of the YEAR BOOK, Part XII, of the *Oxyrhynchus Papyri*, containing documents and letters. The two most important sections are those containing edicts and circular letters and documents emanating from the Senate of Oxyrhynchus, which illustrate the period from Septimius Severus to Constantine; but the whole volume sheds important light upon almost every side of life in Hellenized Egypt.

The collection opens with a rescript of Severus which throws some new light on the methods of appointing collectors of money taxes in villages. It is followed by an edict of Caracalla which shows that the local senators in the capitals of Egypt did not always conduct themselves with senatorial dignity. No. 1408 is an interesting report of a trial, closing with an edict of the prefect, relating to the suppression of brigandage. No. 1412 is the report of a special meeting of the Senate at Oxyrhynchus, called to deal with the transport of grain required by troops. Other documents illustrate the method of procedure and the subjects considered in the local Senate.

Among the rich material contained in the other sections we may mention No. 1424, the letter of a *centurio princeps* of about 318 A. D., which shows how burdensome public office had become by the fourth century. Another declaration of pagan sacrifice (1464), belonging to the Decian persecution of 250 A. D., is here presented, which differs slightly from the normal type of such declarations in that it mentions the imperial decree, θεία κρίσις, and indicates that the writer's family was associated with him in the declaration.

We have previously noticed the lack of Latin documents among Egyptian papyri, but we now have (1466) a request for the appointment of a guardian addressed by a woman to the prefect, Valerius Firmus, written in both Greek and Latin and dating from the year 245. The following number is a petition of the year 263 A. D. of unusual interest, for a woman here presents her claim to be confirmed in her *jus trium liberorum:* inasmuch as she possessed three children and was able to write, she claimed the right to act without a guardian and to enjoy the privileges which a man in similar position would enjoy. Her request was apparently granted. Among the personal letters, Nos. 1492-4 and 1592 have a special interest, as they are among the earliest Christian documents from Egypt, dating from the late third or early fourth century. The formulae of greeting and the pious reflections and good wishes which they all contain, show that such natural expressions had already become fixed in Christian correspondence.

There are given a number of horoscopes which will interest those concerned with ancient astrology. No. 1477 is a portion of a numbered list of questions applied to an oracle, which illustrate the large variety of trivial inquiries directed to ancient shrines. A Gnostic charm for victory (1478) and a Gnostic invocation (1566) likewise observe special mention.

We may call attention also to an article by Bignone in the *Rivista di Filologia* for April, 1917, in which he discusses in an interesting fashion an Epicurean polemic against the Stoic doctrines of providence, fate, and fortune, which has been discovered in the Herculanean Papyrus No. 1670.

GREEK LITERATURE
WILLIAM ARTHUR HEIDEL

The searching of hearts brought about by the European War has led to a thoroughgoing criticism of the aims and methods of education, and the case of the classics has found not only assailants but also admirable champions. *A Defence of Classical Education* by R. W. Livingston (Macmillans), though it is in part a plea of confession and avoidance, is in fact far more than a defence, for it contains an admirable exposition of the salient characteristics especially of Greek literature. *The Assault on Humanism* by Paul Shoey (Atlantic Monthly Co.) is a skillful counterattack by an adroit lawyer and eminent Hellenist. Here and there it gives the impression of "sniping", but on the whole the castigation which it visits on Dr. C. W. Eliot and Abraham Flexner is both fair and deserved. *Value of the Classics* (Princeton Univ. Press) is a monumental memorial of the Classical Conference held at Princeton University on June 2, 1917, containing much of interest to the student of Greek literature.

One of the most delightful books provoked by the war is *Patriotic Poetry, Greek and English*, by W. Rhys Roberts (John Murray), as showing with intent the eternal consolation of the ideal literatures of the world, to which the individual and the race have recourse in all great crises. The Germans, too, have produced books of similar character, but none of like merit. If there are those who would draw from the war the lesson of the need of greater material efficiency, others with the insight and faith of the saving remnant have seen that now more than ever arises the necessity of conserving the higher values, threatened as they have rarely been by vandalism. *The Greek Spirit* by Kate Stephens (Sturgis & Walton), written before the war, *Greek Ideals: A Study of Social Life*, by C. D. Burns (Macmillans), and numerous essays in the periodicals seek to enforce the ideals of ancient Greece as a leaven capable of working in the mass and of saving and quickening what is best in man. In this connection we may mention *Ingram Bywater; the Memoir of an Oxford Scholar*, by W. W. Jackson (Oxford Univ. Press), a living portrait of a deceased Hellenist of large vision and penetrating scholarship, recording the quiet life of a student who passed away while thousands who should have been his successors were risking and giving their lives to preserve the values which he, and others such as he, had created and preserved in the security of the study.

The year has brought forth a number of texts of Greek authors. *Homeri Opera III*, edited by T. W. Allen (Oxford Univ. Press) gives a revised and altogether admirable text of the *Odyssey*, Books I-XII, in a second edition, for the completion of which every lover of Homer will look forward. Eight volumes of the *Loeb Classical Library* (Putnams) devoted to Greek writers have come to hand since the last review. Diôs' *Roman History*, in the excellent translation of E. Cary, has completed the fifth volume. W. R. Paton adds a second of *The Greek Anthology* with an admirable translation and a valuable introduction. H. B. Dewing's *Procopius* also progresses to a second volume, giving us a most desirable addition to our resources. S. Gaselee, who lately translated Parthenius, now puts us under further obligations to him by his text and translation of the romance of *Achilles Tatius;* both are of excellent quality. H. L. Jones has a more difficult task in editing and rendering Strabo, of which work the first volume has appeared; while serviceable, it falls below the standard generally maintained in the Loeb Library. Sir Arthur Hort's *Theophrastus' Enquiry into Plants* (2 vols.), on the contrary, is a masterful rendering of a work of the greatest interest and difficulty, requiring great knowledge and accuracy.

Theophrastus and the Greek Physiological Psychology before Aristotle by G. M. Stratton (Macmillans) gives a general account of Theophrastus as a psychologist of sense perception, a text of the treatise *De Sensibus* accompanied by a translation, and copious notes on the text and translation. *Epictetus, the Discourses and Manual*, translated by P. E. Matheson (Oxford Univ. Press), is altogether admirable as a rendering of the kindly Stoic. *The Prometheus Bound of Aeschylus*, translated by M. C. Wier (Century Co.), is a faithful rendering without outstanding literary merit. *The Rhesus of Euripides*, edited by W. H. Porter (Cambridge Univ. Press), adds an excellent brief edition of a play little read. The most important book of the year is *The Fragments of Sophocles* (3 vols.), edited by A. C. Pearson (Cambridge Univ. Press), who took up the work where it was left on the death successively of Jebb and of Headlam. Containing all the known fragments of Sophocles, with a scholarly commentary and an index to the whole series of volumes, it is a fitting conclusion of the best edition of the great tragic poet, that of Jebb.

The great work, *The Mythology of All Nations* (Marshall Jones), begins auspiciously with the first volume ("Greek and Roman") by W. S. Fox, who gives a useful and interesting survey of the field. *The Days of Alcibiades* by C. E. Robinson (Longmans) draws a picture of life in the Athens of the fifth century, making Alcibiades the central figure. The book admirably serves its purpose of vivifying history. *A Greek Reader for Schools* by C. E. Freeman and W. D. Lowe (Oxford Univ. Press) offers varied readings from the best authors in selections of moderate difficulty. Several studies in detail also should be mentioned. *The Socratic Doctrine of the Soul* by John Burnet (British Academy) presents a valuable study of an important theme. *A History of Greek Economic Thought* by A. A. Trever (Univ. of Chicago Press) is a penetrating and illuminating historical study which admirably covers a neglected subject. *The Ethics of Euripides* by Rhys Carpenter (Columbia Univ. Press) has a vaguer theme and arrives at less satisfactory results. *The Hellenic Origins of Christian Asceticism* by J. W. Swain (Columbia Univ. Press) makes a valuable contribution to the history of religious asceticism. S. Gaselee is to be thanked for his descriptive list of *The Greek Manuscripts in the Old Seraglio at Constantinople* (Cambridge Univ. Press).

Dr. Marion Mills Miller in *The Return of Odysseus* (Stratford Co.) treats in the form of a Greek drama the beautiful tale of Homer. Though not in the truest sense dramatic, the play has caught much of the spirit of the Greek dramatists. *Un Mensonge de la Science Allemande: Les Prolégomènes à Homère de Frédéric-Auguste Wolf*, by Victor Bernard (Hachette), is a war book, intended to cast discredit on German methods. It admirably serves its purpose, but it does far more, for it shows in detail the debt of Wolf, not only to d'Aubignac, but also to other predecessors. One wishes that the learned and entertaining author had more fully demonstrated the utterly untenable position not only of Wolf but of all those, including d'Aubignac, to whom he was indebted.

LATIN LITERATURE

CHARLES KNAPP

To the Loeb Classical Library these translations of Latin works have been added by American scholars: of Seneca, *Tragoediae*, by F. J. Miller (2 vols.); of Seneca, *Epistulae Morales*, Vol. i, by R. M. Gummere.

Following the plan of preceding years, we give a selected list of articles, arranged according to the Latin authors with whom they deal primarily.[1] It is a pleasure to note that some excellent work within the field of Latin literature is being done by writers primarily concerned with modern literature, especially English literature. "Concerning Caesar's Appearance," by M. E. Deutsch (*CJ*., xii, 247); "Caesar as Seen in his Works", by G. Lodge (*CW*., x, 106); "Caesar, De Bello Gallico, iv, 28. 2-3", by T. R. Holmes, A. R. Wightman, and C. Knapp (*CW*., x, 156: see *A. Y. B.*, 1916, p. 768); "Gaius Verres: An Historical Study", by F. H. Cowles (*Cornell Studies in Classical Philology*, xx), of interest especially to students of Cicero's orations against Verres; "*Municipia Fundana*", by J. Elmore (*TAPA*., xlvii, 35), a discussion of the nature of certain *municipia*, a question suggested by Cicero's *Oratio pro Balbo;* "The Prosecution of Murena", by R. W. Husband (*CJ*., xii, 102), a study of matters connected with Cicero's *Oratio pro Murena;* "The Consular Speeches of Cicero", by Catharine Saunders (*CW*., x, 153); "A Concordance to Horace", by Lane Cooper, a very valuable work; "Horace and Valerius Cato", parts II and III, by G. L. Hendrickson (*CP*., xii, 77, 329: see *A. Y. B.*, 1916, p. 768), an effort to identify the adver-

---
[1] Periodicals are cited thus: *AJP*., *American Journal of Philology; CJ*., *Classical Journal; CP*., *Classical Philology; CW*., *Classical Weekly; HS*., *Harvard Studies; TAPA., Transactions of the American Philological Association.*

sary with whom Horace, in *Sermones* I, 10, carries on a discussion about Lucilius, and a general treatment of certain phases of the literary period of transition from Catullus to the early Augustans; "*Molle atque Facetum*", by C. Knapp (*AJP.*, xxxviii, 194), a discussion of the famous phrase used by Horace, *Sermones* I, 10, 44, of Vergil; "Rhetorical Elements in Livy's Direct Speeches", by H. V. Canter (*AJP.*, xxxviii, 125); "Petronius and the Greek Romance", by C. W. Mendel (*CP.*, xii, 158); "The Stratulax Scene in Plautus' *Truculentus*", by E. W. Fay (*Univ. of Texas Bull.*, *Memorial Volume to Shakespeare and Harvey*, 155); "References to Painting in Plautus and Terence", by C. Knapp (*CP.*, xii, 143); "The Plot of the *Epidicus*" of Plautus, by A. L. Wheeler (*AJP.*, xxxviii, 237); "Propertius: A Modern Lover in the Augustan Age", by K. F. Smith (*Sewanee Review*, Jan., 1917); "On a Venetian Codex of Pliny's Letters," by E. T. Merrill (*CP.*, xii, 259); "Pompeius Trogus and Justinus", by R. B. Steele (*AJP.*, xxxviii, 19), an argument that Trogus wrote after Books 90-96 of Livy's great history were published, and that Justinus prepared his epitome of Trogus's work at Rome in 144 or 145 A. D.; "Suetonius and Caesar's German Campaigns", by M. E. Deutsch (*TAPA.*, xlvii, 23); "A Study of Vergil's Descriptions of Nature", by Mabel Louise Anderson; "On the Virgilian *Catalepton* II", by H. R. Fairclough (*TAPA.*, xlvii, 43), an argument that this much-discussed piece is an elaborate *double entendre*, ridiculing T. Annius Cimber for his love of archaic words and ancient spells; "Vergil and Nature", by Mabel V. Root (*CW.*, x, 194); "The Boy Ascanius," by H. O. Ryder (*CW.*, x, 210), a study of the *rôle* played by Ascanius in the Æneid; "Virgil: An Interpretation", by M. S. Slaughter (*CJ.*, xii, 359).

Less definitely connected with a particular author are the following: "Titus Labienus", by F. F. Abbott (*CJ.*, xiii, 4), an account of the career of Caesar's famous *legatus;* "The Birthday as a Commonplace of Roman Elegy", by Helen C. Bowerman (*CJ.*, xii, 310); "Comparative Philology and the Classics", by C. D. Buck (*TAPA.*, xlvii, 65); "The Classics and the Protestant Reformation", by T. A. Buenger (*CW.*, xi, 34); "Compound Adjectives in Early Latin Poetry", by Cornelia C. Coulter (*TAPA.*, xlvii, 153); an elaborate review of C. C. Conrad, *The Technique of Continuous Action in Roman Comedy*, by R. C. Flickinger (*CW.*, x, 147); "The Decline of Roman Tragedy", by T. Frank (*CJ.*, xii, 176); "Chaucer's Lollius", by G. L. Kittredge (*HS.*, xxviii, 47), an argument that Chaucer believed that a Roman named Lollius was author of a work, now lost, on the Trojan War, and that he pretended to be translating this work in his *Troilus*, expecting his readers, however, to see through this transparent literary device and to realize his indebtedness to Boccacio; "On Certain Ancient Errors in Geographical Orientation", by E. T. Merrill (*CJ.*, xii, 88), a paper of interest to students of Caesar, Polybius, Tacitus, etc.; "St. Severinus and the Closing Years of the Province of Noricum", by C. C. Mierow (*Colorado Coll. Pub.*, *Language Series*, ii, 299; "The Antecedents of Hellenistic Comedy", by H. W. Prescott (*CP.*, xii, 405), an article of importance to students of Plautus and Terence; "The Profits of Literature in Ancient Rome", by E. T. Sage (*CW.*, x, 170), a fresh examination of a much-discussed question, which bears on a familiar passage of Horace, *Epistles* II, 2, 51-52, with the conclusion that Roman writers derived profit, not from the sale of copies of their works, but from the sale of their manuscripts and from patrons; "The *Plebs Urbana* in Rome", by E. A. Schnabel (*CW.*, x, 161); "Illogical Idiom", by Paul Shorey (*TAPA.*, xlvii, 205), a discussion involving a consideration of a wide array of passages in Greek and Latin authors; "Roman Literary Characterization", by R. B. Steele (*CW.*, x, 43), a study of the terms used by Latin writers, especially Cicero and Quintilian, to describe the work and style of other authors; "The Sources and the Extent of Petrarch's Knowledge of the Life of Vergil", by D. R. Stuart (*CP.*, xii, 365); "Three as a Magic Number in Latin Literature", by E. Tavenner (*TAPA.*, xlvii, 117); "Epithets of the

Tiber in the Roman Poets", by V. J. Warner (*CW.*, xi, 52); "The Position of Women in the Late Roman Republic", by Helen E. Wiegand (*CJ.*, xii, 378, 423); "Roman Factories", by F. W. Wright (*CW.*, xi, 17).

Several dissertations deserve notice: "The Significance of Certain Colors in Roman Ritual", by Mary Emma Armstrong; "Roman Craftsmen and Tradesmen of the Early Empire", by Ethel H. Brewster; "Goethe's Estimate of the Greek and Latin Writers", by W. J. Keller; "Studies in the Diction of the *Sermo Amatorius* in Roman Comedy", by K. Preston; "Studies in Magic from Latin Literature", by E. Tavenner; "The Influence of Horace on the Chief English Poets of the Nineteenth Century", by Mary Rebecca Thayer; "'Know Thyself' in Greek and Latin Literature", by Elizabeth Gregory Wilkins.

SEMITIC PHILOLOGY AND LITERATURE

MORRIS JASTROW, JR.

The most active medium of publication in the field of Semitics during the year has been the Museum of Archeology of the University of Pennsylvania, which has brought out in the Babylonian Section no less than five volumes. Of these the most important are two volumes by Edward Chiera, giving long lists of Sumerian, Akkadian and "Amoritic" personal names occurring in long cuneiform lists that formed part of the Temple School equipment in ancient Nippur. These lists were used in the Temple School both as copy exercises for the pupils and as a means of explaining the character and composition of the names. As a result of his careful investigation of the hundreds of fragments of these lists now in the University of Pennsylvania Museum, Dr. Chiera has thrown a great deal of new light on the pedagogical methods used in ancient Babylonia. He shows, for example, how the teacher wrote the exercise on the left portion of the tablet which the pupil was expected to copy as closely as he could on the right-hand column, very much, therefore, like modern copybooks.

Stephen Langdon has published three volumes during the year—one of Sumerian liturgical texts, one of Sumerian grammatical texts, and the third a new fragment of the famous epic of Gilgamesh which the University of Pennsylvania Museum was fortunate enough to purchase some years ago. These publications by Dr. Langdon are of considerable importance, but unfortunately, as in the case of his previous publications, the copies are most inaccurately made and there is literally scarcely a page that does not contain errors. This is particularly the case with the important new Gilgamesh fragment, which can hardly be studied properly without a renewed reference to the original tablet. The fragment fills out an important gap in the story, dealing chiefly with the episode between Gilgamesh and his companion Enkidu. The fragment belongs to the Old Babylonian period (not the late Persian period, as Dr. Langdon originally stated in the *Museum Journal*), and by comparison with the late Assyrian version found by Layard among the fragments of the great Royal Library of Nineveh, it is seen that the earlier version, dating from about 2000 B. C., is also much briefer.

Despite the war the De Goeje Foundation of Leyden has continued its activities. Following closely upon the publication of an important collection of Arabic phrases and sayings edited by Prof. C. A. Storey, Prof. Ignaz Goldziher, the well-known authority on Mohammedan theology, has brought out the text of a work by the great orthodox theologian Gazali, directed against the sect commonly known as Isma'ili, but more properly "Batiniyya", a name that emphasizes the tendency of this sect to look for the "inner" meaning in the Koran. Instead of a translation Professor Goldziher gives in running form an epitome of each chapter of this treatise, which, although entirely polemical in character, is nevertheless of value also in making clearer to us the standpoint of Moslem orthodoxy in regard to the exercise of individual judgment. While Mohammedan orthodoxy, which secured a permanent triumph through the great influence of Gazali, is rigidly opposed to deviation from what has once received general consensus, nevertheless free investigation is encouraged and the mere acceptance of a view because traditional is discouraged.

Of more present interest is a little volume by Prof. Snouck Hurgronje on the *Revolt of Arabia*. Professor Gottheil of Columbia University has rendered a real service in making this account of the background of the political movement in Arabia since the war began accessible to English readers (Putnams). Professor Snouck Hurgronje, who knows the Mohammedan East better than any other living scholar, looks upon the movement in Arabia, which has the support of England, as the protest of the national Arabic spirit against the "foreign yoke" imposed in the name of Islam by a power which has little appreciation of the real spirit of Islam. It is too early to judge of the outcome of the revolt, though it is possible that it will lead to a revival of Arabic nationalism and unite the Arabs into a state that will bring about more satisfactory conditions in the Near East than those which existed before the war. As bearing likewise on the situation in the East, I may be permitted to mention my own book on "The War and the Bagdad Railway" (Ohio, 1917, Lippincott), which contains as its main chapter a survey of the history of Asia Minor and proposes a reconstitution of the near East into a series of independent states under international guarantees.

INDO-EUROPEAN PHILOLOGY
(*Exclusive of the Germanic Languages*)
ROLAND G. KENT

General and Miscellaneous.—E. H. Sturtevant in "Linguistic Change" (Univ. of Chicago Press), gives an excellent introduction to the historical study of language, scientific and up-to-date. C. D. Buck's "Comparative Philology and the Classics" (*TAPA*.,[1] xlvii, 65), his presidential address before the American Philological Association, is an admirable survey of the relations between the subjects. Paul Shorey discusses, with many examples, the varieties and psychological basis of "Illogical Idiom" (*ibid.*, 205), common in all languages. Other articles are "Subject and Predicate" (*ibid.*, 13), by Leonard Bloomfield; "On the Need of Establishing Laboratories for Experimental Linguistics and Phonetics" (*PAPA.*, xlvii, xix), by R. J. Kellogg; "The Present Status of the Problem of Races in the Prehistoric Aegean Basin" (*Classical Journal*, xiii, 25), by A. E. R. Boak; "Celtic Studies in the United States" (*Columbia Univ. Quart.*, xix, 30), by J. L. Gerig.

Indo-Iranian.—In the Harvard Oriental Series, edited by C. R. Lanman, three more volumes are to be noted: xx and xxiv, "*Rig-Veda Repetitions*, the repeated verses and distichs and stanzas of the Rig-Veda in systematic presentation and with critical discussion", by Maurice Bloomfield; and xxi, "*Rama's Later History*, or Uttara-Rama-Charita, an ancient Hindu drama by Bhavabhuti, Part I, introduction and translation," by S. K. Belvalkar. A number of difficult Vedic passages are interpreted anew by M. Bloomfield in two articles, "Some Cruces in Vedic Text, Grammar and Interpretation" (*AJP.*, xxxviii, 1), and "On Two Cases of Metrical Shortening of a Fused Long Syllable, Rig-Veda VIII, 13, 18, and VI, 2, 7" (*Aufsätze zur Kultur- und Sprachgeschichte*, Ernst Kuhn Gewidmet, 211). E. W. Hopkins writes on "Indra as God of Fertility" (*JAOS.*, xxxvi, 242), and on "Indic and Indian (= American) Religious Parallels" (*JAOS.*, xxxvii, 72 and 85). R. G. Kent's "Folk-Tales of India" and Franklin Edgerton's "The Hindu Beast Fable and the Story of its Travels" (*Univ. of Pennsylvania Faculty Lectures*, iii, 237 and 359; reprinted from *Old Penn*, xiv, 677 and 773) are mutually supplementary treatments of the theme in semi-popular form.

The sixth volume of *The Mythology of All Races*, edited by L. H. Gray and G. F. Moore, has appeared, containing as its first part "Indian Mythology", by A. B. Keith of Edin-

---
[1] Periodicals are cited under the following abbreviations: *AJP.*, *American Journal of Philology; CP.*, *Classical Philology; CQ.*, *Classical Quarterly; CW.*, *Classical Weekly; JAOS.*, *Journal of the American Oriental Society; PAPA.*, *TAPA.*, *Proceedings, Transactions of the American Philological Association.*

burgh University, and as its second part "Iranian Mythology", by A. J. Carnoy, a valuable handbook of the subject. Other articles by Carnoy are "*La Magie dans l'Iran*" (*Muséon*, i, 171); "Iranian Views of Origins in Connection with Similar Babylonian Beliefs" (*JAOS.*, xxxvi, 300); "The Moral Deities of Iran and India and their Origins" (*Amer. Jour. Theol.*, xxi, 58). On the ancient Persian cuneiform inscriptions we now have E. L. Johnson's *Historical Grammar of the Ancient Persian Language*, forming Vol. viii of the Vanderbilt Oriental Series, a convenient handbook, the only systematic treatment of the topic in English. In the same field, there is an article by H. C. Tolman, "The Graphic Representation of Final Indo-Iranian *a* in Ancient Persian" (*PAPA.*, xlvii, xxix). In the more recent Persian literature, there is "The Allegory of the Moths and the Flame, translated from the Mantiq at-Tair of Farīd ad-Dīn 'Attār," (*JAOS.*, xxxvi, 345), by A. V. W. Jackson; and "A Manuscript of the Manafi' al-Haiawān in the Library of Mr. J. P. Morgan" (*ibid.*, 381), by Abraham Johannan. There are also articles on Iranian and other linguistic topics in Hastings' *Encyclopædia of Religion and Ethics* and in the second edition of the *New International Encyclopædia*, by Jackson, Carnoy, and Raymond Weeks.

Greek and Latin.—The "Studies in Greek Noun Formations", begun by E. H. Sturtevant with "Labial Terminations", has been continued by C. D. Buck, on "Dental Terminations" (*CP.*, xii, 21, 173, 295). E. W. Fay in "Syntax and Etymology: The Impersonals of Emotion" (*CQ.*, xi, 88) explains the impersonal verbs of the type *piget* as having originally had sharp physical meanings; in "Sobriquet and Stem" (*AJP.*, xxxviii, 82) he seeks to show that the final *e* of the *vocative* is by origin a particle used to attract attention. In both of these papers, as also in others (*ibid.*, 228; *CQ.*, x, 229), he defends his thesis that suffixes are really only disguised second elements of compounds; he has an addendum to his interpretation of the Oscan Slingshot of Sae-pinum in the *Rivista di Filologia* (xliv, 512) and an etymology of ὠκεανός in *The Classical Weekly* (x, 200). Problems of composition and of semantics are handled, mainly not in agreement with Fay, by Cornelia C. Coulter, "Compound Adjectives in Early Latin Poetry" (*TAPA.*, xlvii, 153); E. W. Nichols, "The Semantics of Latin Adjective Terminations" (*AJP.*, xxxvii, 417); C. W. Peppler, "The Suffix *-ua* in Aristophanes" (*ibid.*, 459); Walter Petersen, "Latin Diminution of Adjectives" (*CP.*, xi, 426; xii, 49).

In the phonetics and other phenomena of popular and later Latin, E. H. Sturtevant has written on "The Monophthongization of Latin *ae*" (*TAPA.*, xlvii, 107); F. F. Abbott on "The Pronunciation of a Final Consonant when Followed by an Initial Consonant in a Latin Word-Group" (*AJP.*, xxxviii, 73); A. J. Carnoy on "Some Obscurities in the Assibilation of *ti* and *di* before a Vowel in Vulgar Latin" (*TAPA.*, xlvii, 145), "Apophony and Rhyme Words in Vulgar Latin Onomatopœias" (*AJP.*, xxxviii, 265), "Adjectival Nouns in Vulgar Latin and Early Romance" (*Romanic Review*, viii, 166), and "The Reduplication of Consonants in Vulgar Latin" (*Modern Philology*, xv, 31). The absurdities of the etymologies of late Latin grammarians are shown by T. A. Buenger in "The Phonetic Presuppositions of the Fulgentian Etymologies" (*PAPA.*, xlvii, xv), and by W. A. Merrill in "Some Etymologies by Cassiodorus" (*ibid.*, xl).

H. W. Smyth's *Greek Grammar for Schools and Colleges* (Am. Book Co.) has now appeared. Articles on syntactical subjects are as follows: F. H. Fowler, "Determined Futurity in Greek" (*CW.*, x, 178 and 185); Emily H. Dutton, "Studies in Greek Prepositional Phrases: (διά, ἀπό, ἐκ, εἰς, ἐν)" (Univ. of Chicago doctoral dissertation); C. E. Bennett, "Kroll on the Independent Latin Subjunctive" (*CP.*, xii, 121); Jefferson Elmore, "The Subjunctive in Restrictive *Qui* and *Quod* Clauses" (*ibid.*, 253); Miss E. M. Tyng, "An Attempt to Explain Tense Usage in Cicero's Orations" (*PAPA.*, xlvii, xxx).

1918 LITERATURE AND LANGUAGE

AMERICAN LITERATURE
(*Nov.* 15, 1917, *to Nov.* 15, 1918)
EDWARD EVERETT HALE

Book Production.—The war has passed away almost as suddenly as it came, but we cannot yet state, except in the most superficial way, what has been its effect on literature in general and in our country. So far as quantity is concerned, its effect is not yet noticeable in the returns for book production. The total number of books (including pamphlets) published in the United States in recent years has been as follows:

1914	8,563
1915	6,932
1916	8,430
1917	8,820
1918	9,550

The figures for 1918 are estimated on the returns of the first 10 months, but they are probably not far from correct.

War Books.—Of this great number of books produced very many are directly inspired by the war. Not many of them, it may be surmised, will make a figure in future histories of American literature, and many of them belong obviously to history or economics. One could not possibly give here a list of the books, or even kinds of books, belonging to literature that should be noted. But it can be said that few fields of interest are unrepresented. All sorts of people have written—from President Wilson to Private Peat, and from Dorothy Canfield Fisher to the author of *Dere Mable*—and they have written every sort of thing about the war that one can imagine. Our great public men and our historians and diplomatists have written and our soldiers and sailors and nurses have written as well. Our best novelists have turned their experience into fiction, and the most average purveyors of popular reading have seized on the war as a drawing motive.

Some notion of the range of the war-literature may be given by the following summary or selection. President Wilson's messages and addresses have been collected in *In the First Year of the War* (Harpers). Theodore Roosevelt published his manifestos in *The Great Adventure* (Scribners). Secretary Baker at the Front by Ralph A. Hayes (Century) and *Frontiers of Freedom* (Doran), a collection of speeches made by Secretary Baker, give some first-hand ideas from high sources. Henry Morgenthau in *Ambassador Morgenthau's Story* (Doubleday, Page) gives his experiences in Constantinople in a book which has not only historical material of the first value, but also a continuously interesting series of impressions and observations. Ambassador Gerard continues his record in *Face to Face with Kaiserism* (Doran). The history of our relation to the war is presented by John B. McMaster in *The United States in the World War* (Appleton), a book devoted almost entirely to the impressions of the war rendered by the newspapers and other organs of public opinion. More particular books are Gen. Francis V. Greene's *Our First Year of the Great War* (Putnams), Frederick Palmer's *America in France* (Dodd, Mead) and Frank H. Simonds' *History of the World War* (Doubleday, Page). Meredith Nicholson in *The Valley of Democracy* (Scribner) gives a picture of the people and activities of the Middle West permeated with war conditions. On the other hand, there are all sorts of books written about more particular matters. Heywood Broun in *The A.*

E. F., with General Pershing and the American Forces (Appleton), gives a general view of our affairs abroad. W. S. McNutt's *The Yanks are Coming* (Page) reports for the trenches: E. M. Roberts in *A Flying Fighter* (Harper), among others reports for the air; H. D. Trounce in *Fighting the Boche Underground* (Scribner) gives an account of mines, galleries, underground fights, and other such things; Francis A. Collins writes of *The Fighting Engineers* (Century); Malcolm C. Grow in *Surgeon Grow* (Stokes) writes of two years of doctor's work in Russia; Maud Mortimer in *A Green Tent in Flanders* (Doubleday, Page) writes of nursing in Belgium; Isabel Anderson in *Zigzaggings* writes of life in a canteen on the Marne; Burton E. Stevenson in *The A. L. A. in Europe* gives an account of library work with the army; F. A. McMullen and Jack Evans in *Out of the Jaws of Hunland* (Putnams) tell of the adventure of the prisoner. There are many accounts of naval life. Reginald W. Kauffman in *Our Navy at Work* (Bobbs, Merrill), Albert N. Depew in *Gunner Depew* (Reilly & Britton), and J. B. Connolly in *The U-boat Hunters* (Scribners) give various aspects. Besides these books on the more usual manifestations of war and battle are others less obvious. Coningsby Dawson in *The Glory of the Trenches* (Lane) gives a view of the spiritual side of war, while William J. Dawson in *The Father of a Soldier* (Lane) gives the complementary picture. There are not a few books of poems, to be noted elsewhere, and humorous books like *Dere Mable* by Edward Streeter (Stokes).

There are hundreds of other books that may have as much reason to be mentioned as those above noted (who can read them all?), but such a list is enough to give an idea of the general effect of the war on literature. It aroused and stimulated an immense amount of writing upon a deeply moving subject. People were able to write, or at least gained an audience for their writing, who would otherwise have remained unheard, and experiences of body and soul were recorded that might otherwise never have come to expression. Yet all this is in the main more journalism than literature, more the material of literature than literature itself. Sometimes one reads a book like Dorothy Canfield Fisher's *Home Fires in France* (Holt) of which one feels, "This must certainly be something that will last," but even here the critic must confine his emotional sympathy if he wish to render a true account. Probably those are right who say that this war, like other wars, will not have much direct effect on literature, but will affect literature later through the greater fullness and richness of emotion and sympathy that have come into the lives of men and women. Thus Robert Herrick, writing in the *Dial* for Jan. 3, 1918, thinks that the true effect of the war will be when it has "passed into our hearts and souls, having got to be a part of our national consciousness". Something of the sort would seem to be more in accord with the history of literature. Art in the past has generally done more with a rich and general tradition than with immediate and violent stimulants.

Fiction.—When we turn from the very exciting fact to the field of fiction, we find not unnaturally that not only is the fiction more or less colored with war fact, but that there is not so much of it. That is natural; in the presence of such immense happenings as those of the past year one's own little imaginings seem trivial. We are tempted to say, "What are *our* woes and sufferance?" in comparison with all that we daily read and see. As a result, not a few of those who have written fiction recently have either been busy with war work and thus have not written at all, or have been content to report actual fact instead of imagining things less moving. In the lists of "war books", such as those just given, one notices the names of not a few who have been known previously as writers of fiction. Out of a small list like the above there are Mrs. Fisher, Coningsby Dawson, James B. Connolly, Burton E. Stevenson and Reginald Kauffman whose books at other times would be found among the novels of the year. Some of our novelists have taken subjects immediately suggested by the war. Mrs. Wharton has written a beautiful story called *The Marne* (Appleton) to express the feelings that have grown with her work abroad. Other well known novelists have seen in the events and figures of the war something that has stirred them to creation. Such are Mrs. Atherton's *The White Morning* (Stokes), Tilden Freeman's *Khaki* (Macmillan), Mary E. Waller's *Out of the Silences* (Little, Brown), Samuel H. Adams's *Common Cause* (Houghton, Mifflin), Ralph D. Paine's *The Call of the Offshore Wind* (Houghton, Mifflin), R. W. Chambers' *The Laughing Girl* (Appleton), Olive Galbreath's *Miss Amerikanka* (Harper), Rupert Hughes' *The Unpardonable Sin* (Harper), and W. J. Dawson's *The War Eagle* (Lane). Few of these books, however, are direct pictures of the war, such as some that have been written in England or France. We may remember that the greatest war-novels—like Tolstoi's *War and Peace* and Sienkiewicz's *With Fire and Sword*—have been written long after the times they have celebrated.

It would seem, however, that the absolute amount of fiction was less than usual. If we look at the figures again, we find that the number of books classified in the publisher's reports as fiction by American authors was as follows:

1914	689
1915	643
1916	703
1917	707
1918 (estimated)	581

The forms of fiction are much what we have seen for several years, although there is a greater proportion than usual of stories of wild life and adventure, caused perhaps by a restless feeling that fiction ought to be as exciting as the current excitements of fact. Whether this be the reason or not, there is an unusual number of open-air stories of the West or North. One can give something of a guess at them from the authors and titles: Rex Beach, *The Winds of Chance* (Harpers); Zane Grey, *The U. P. Trail* (Harpers); H. H. Knibbs, *The Tang of Life* (Houghton, Mifflin); Peter B. Kyne, *The Valley of the Giants* (Doubleday, Page); Ridgewell Cullom, *The Triumph of John Kars* (Jacobs); B. M. Bowers, *Sky-rider* (Little, Brown); C. A. Seltzer, *"Firebrand" Trevison* (McClurg); Harold Bindloss, *The Lure of the North* (Stokes); Marah E. Ryan, *The Treasure Trail* (McClurg); Robert C. Stead, *The Cow-Puncher* (Harpers); G. G. Van Schaick, *The Peace of Roaring River* (Small). There are fewer stories of the sea: C. T. Brady, *Waif o' the Sea* (McClurg); Randall Parrish, *Wolves of the Sea* (McClurg); and R. E. Smith, *Sea King of Barnegat* (Duffield). Stewart Edward White in *Simba* (Doubleday, Page) returns to Africa, while E. R. Burroughs in *The God of Mars* (McClurg) has got quite off the earth. There are a few good detective stories, N. S. Lincoln's *The Three Strings* (Appleton), F. N. Greene's *The Devil to Pay* (Scribners), and John T. McIntyre's *Ashton Kirke, Criminologist* (Penn) being the most interesting. There are a few good historical novels, of which E. L. White's *The Unwilling Vestal* (Dutton), an excellent and original book, is the best.

The other kind of novel, however, the novel of everyday life and character, is still in the majority as usual in spite of war books and books of adventure. We can give here but a bare suggestion; the directions of interest are not very different from former years. We mention then: Zoe Beckley, *A Chance to Live* (Macmillan); Josephine Daskam Bacon, *On Our Hill* (Scribners); G. W. Cable, *Flower of the Chapdelaines* (Scribners); W. S. Cather, *My Antonia* (Houghton, Mifflin); Croy Homer, *Boone Stop* (Harper); Maria T. Daviess, *The Golden Bird* (Century); Henry B. F. Fuller, *On the Stairs* (Houghton, Mifflin); Zona Gale, *Birth* (Macmillan); H. Hagerdorn, *Barbara Picks a Husband* (Macmillan); Joseph Hergesheimer, *Java Head* (Knopf); Emerson Hough, *The Way Out* (Appleton); J. C. Lincoln, *Shavings* (Appleton); Helen R. Martin, *Maggie of Virginsburg* (Century); Samuel Merwin, *Henry is Twenty* (Bobbs, Merrill); Alice Duer Miller, *The Happiest Time in Their Lives* (Century); Charles G. Norris, *Salt* (Dutton); Kate Norris, *Josse-*

lin's Wife (Doubleday, Page); Ernest Poole, *His Second Wife* (Macmillan); Gene Stratton Porter, *A Daughter of the Land* (Doubleday, Page); S. Strunsky, *Professor Latimer's Progress* (Holt); Booth Tarkington, *The Magnificent Ambersons* (Doubleday, Page); Elias Tobenkin, *The House of Conrad* (Stokes); Mrs. Mary A. Watts, *The Boardman Family* (Macmillan); Henry K. Webster, *An American Family* (Bobbs, Merrill); W. A. White, *In the Heart of a Fool* (Macmillan). Here are two dozen books of which we should like to say a word, but we must be content with the mere record.

Short Stories.—It is perhaps foolish to try to say anything about short stories in a short review like this; there are so many and of so many kinds. E. J. H. O'Brien gives the account of a special student, though too late for us to use. His *Best Stories of 1917 and Yearbook of the American Short Story* (Small) is a necessary authority. He gives not only the best stories that have been published, but also a great deal of biographical and bibliographical material. It is of interest to note that his selection of the best stories includes none of those mentioned in last year's YEAR BOOK. Without Mr. O'Brien's wider range and deeper view, we will mention as worth while a few collections that have got themselves together out of the whole enormous number that are produced. We note Joseph Hergesheimer's *Gold and Iron* (Knopf), three novelettes rather than short stories, which give one a much firmer and more serious impression than most such collections. Daniel Wilber Steele's *Land's End* (Harpers) is introduced by Mr. O'Brien, who gives the writer a position far beyond the reach of most story writers. Among the well known writers Alice Brown publishes her recent work in *The Flying Teuton and Other Stories* (Macmillan); Alice Hegan Rice, *Miss Mink's Soldier* (Century); Fanny Hurst, *Gaslight Sonatas* (Harpers); Edna Ferber, *Cheerful, by Request* (Doubleday, Page). Leo Robbins is a new writer (to us at least); his *Mary the Merry and Other Stories* (Stratford) shows much clever talent. Ellis Parker Butler in *Philo Gubb* (Houghton, Mifflin) has achieved a wonder, a really new kind of detective story, not only humorous, as would be expected, but humorous in a wholly unexpected way. There are a good many war stories, of which A. G. Empey's *Tales from a Dug-Out* (Century) is at least characteristic.

Poetry.—Of course poetry is immensely interesting nowadays. Prof. W. L. Phelps in his *Advance of English Poetry in the Twentieth Century* (Dodd, Mead) says that there never was "a time when there were so many poets in activity, when so many books of poetry were not only read but bought and sold, when poets were held in such high esteem, when so much was written and published about poetry, when the mere forms of verse were the theme of such hot debate". An oldster of an earlier generation may easily agree with him, in thinking of his own youth; in the '80s there was a general notion that deep feeling in poetry had had its day, a great day in truth, but one which had come to an end and had left the clever young men of the end of the century to the charming amusement of French forms and Eighteenth Century octosyllabics, and not too many of them. Nowadays there are certainly more poets and there is certainly more interest in poetry. In the last few years we have seen a very great range from the *Horse Sense* of Walt Mason to the *Irradiations* of J. S. Fletcher. By this time free verse is so general that one need say nothing to explain. Amy Lowell has written *Can Grande's Castle* (Macmillan) in polyphonic prose. The word "prose" refers merely to the way her poetry is printed, namely, in a block like this page; the word "polyphonic" (many-voiced) indicates her rhythmic movement, which is her poetic form. However one may feel about her conceptions of poetic form (some of which she explains in her preface), one will probably feel that in substance, in poetic feeling and fire, she has done something in these lyric narratives that she never did before. Edgar Lee Masters in his *Toward the Gulf* (Macmillan) continues, as he says, the attempts of *The Spoon River Anthology* and *The*

Great Valley to mirror the age and the country in which we live. As in his first volume, his interest here is chiefly in life as it is indicated in those that are gone, but his form is more varied than in the *Anthology* and his field broader. Carl Sandburg's *Cornhuskers* (Holt) and Sherwood Anderson's *Mid-American Chants* (Lane) give more than a hint of their kind by their very names. Mr. Sandburg is more of a poet; Mr. Anderson's great talent shows to better advantage in some of his prose. It is not easy to pick out the best of a great number of books of interest though of lesser value. There is not a little "war verse" that should be recorded; we mention K. G. Duffield's *Bill of the U. S. A.* (Duffield), Berton Braley's *In Camp and Trench* (Doran), E. A. Guest's *Over Here* (Reilly & Britton), C. Divine's *City Ways and Company Streets* (Moffatt), and Mary C. Davies' *The Drums in Our Street* (Macmillan). There are a number of collections, for example, H. A. Gibbons's *Songs from the Trenches* (Harper), C. E. Andrews' *From the Front*, and Frank Foxcroft's *War Verse* (Crowell). One will not inquire too curiously as to the purely poetic character of these verses; they were deeply felt, and they should be deeply felt. For the moment one will not think it wise to try to form estimates. There are one or two books on poetry which are valuable. C. E. Andrews' *The Writing and Reading of Verse* (Appleton) is a very successful attempt at a popular and also sound treatise on meter. W. L. Phelps's *The Advance of English Poetry*, from which we quoted above, is an account marked by much appreciation joined to a great deal of useful information.

Essays and Criticism.—Among the books of essays and criticism may be noted first Joseph W. Beach's *The Method of Henry James* (Yale University), a thorough and careful study of the work of a great American man of letters Those who have been rather dissatisfied with the many vague appreciations and smart generalizations concerning James will be glad to see this study of a different character. Mr. Beach has the method of a scholar, and instead of being content with reading and enjoying and talking, he wants really to know something about his subject. His book is, therefore, the one and only book beside James' own that the student of James cannot afford to miss. One cannot say quite as much of R. C. Holliday's study of *Booth Tarkington* (Doubleday, Page). Neither subject nor study is so noteworthy as the preceding, but it is an excellent thing to make a study of the striking figures of our literature. Another definite piece of work of American criticism is Bernard Berenson's *Essays in the Study of Sienese Painting* (F. F. Sherman). More "modern" than either of the above are Francis Hackett's *Horizons: a Book of Criticism* (Heubsch) and Van Wyck Brooks' *Letters and Leadership* (Huebsch). These collections are by men who are generally thought of in connection with the *New Republic*, a periodical which has lately come to stand for a modern comment on current events in the light of much cleverness and information. It may be remarked here that the *Dial* has removed to New York, and definitely extended its field to include social and political problems as well as the view of literature which formerly satisfied it. The *Dial* is not quite so modern as the *New Republic* and not quite so smart; its editors are older and rather more academic. Beside these books of criticism there are a number of collections of essays of, as we may say, the old sort. C. D. Morley's *Shandygaff* (Doubleday, Page) is a good example, a book made up of essays, stories and sketches, on all sorts of literary and non-literary subjects. The title conveys a sense of the traditional past; it would seem not to be currently understood in the bars and clubs of today. R. C. Holliday's *Walking-stick Papers* (Doran) is another delightful collection of a very cheerful and clever kind. Elizabeth Woodbridge in *Days Out and Other Papers* (Houghton, Mifflin) has a fresh and unhackneyed collection. Three such are more than one usually gets in one year.

Biography.—There is not so much biography this year as heretofore. The most noteworthy thing among the memoirs is *The Education of Henry*

Adams, an autobiography with an Introduction by Henry Cabot Lodge (Houghton, Mifflin). Any account of this distinguished member of this distinguished family would, on the face of it, be of interest. But Henry Adams was not only an Adams but a man of especial gifts and abilities, and his memoirs are therefore full of character. A more definite study is F. E. Leupp's *George Westinghouse* (Little, Brown). This study of the life of a representative American who came to note in a particularly American way is a useful and necessary addition to our means of estimating the powers and duties of our country, Mrs. J. C. Harris's *Life of Joel Chandler Harris* (Houghton, Mifflin) is a delightful account of a very delightful figure in American literature. The *Letters of Anne Gilchrist and Walt Whitman* (Doubleday, Page) are an interesting contribution to our means of knowing more accurately one who is more and more emerging into the position of the great representative poet of America. Arthur N. Davis's *The Kaiser as I Knew Him* (Harpers) will probably not belong to literature, but may be at least remarked. A book of more formal biography is Edward W. Miller's life of Wessel Gansfort in the edition of Gansfort's *Works* published by Putnam. Gansfort was one of the "reformers before the Reformation", and although there is not enough historical material to give a very full idea of his personality and its development, Professor Miller is able to group around him the elements of a great historical period in a very interesting way.

Necrology.—There have died during the year Hubert Howe Bancroft (March 3), the historian of the Pacific Slope; Henry Adams (March 27), the historian mentioned above; John A. Mitchell (June 29), most widely known as one of the founders and editors of *Life;* and Joyce Kilmer, one of the younger poets and critics, killed in battle on Aug. 1.

MODERN LANGUAGES AND LITERATURE

ENGLISH LANGUAGE AND LITERATURE

Albert C. Baugh

English Philology.—In H. Hilmer's "The Origin and Growth of Language" (*JEGP*[1]) an attempt is made to explain language on the basis of concepts, though the results differ from Wundt's. John T. Clark, in *Lexicographical Evolution and Conceptual Progress* (California), considers the testimony which vocabulary affords concerning certain aspects of a people's mentality. C. M. Lotspeich, in "Accent-Mixture and Sound Changes" (*JEGP*), explains consonant shifts and umlaut on the basis of two different types of accent, the Nordic and the Alpine. S. S. Ripins presents "Notes on Old English Lexicography" (*MLN*), and K. Malone attempts an explanation of "The A of Father, Rather" (*MP*). M. Callaway, Jr., has published *Studies in the Syntax of the Lindisfarne Gospels* (Hopkins). R. Taylor offers "Some Notes on the Use of *can* and *couth* as Preterite Auxiliaries in Early and Middle Scottish Poetry" (*JEGP*) before being replaced by *did* about 1500. S. Moore notes "Robert Mannyng's Use of *do* as Auxiliary" (*MLN*) a century earlier than Lydgate, who is the first to use it extensively. R. O. Stidston examines *The Use of "Ye" in the Function of "Thou" in Middle English Literature from MS. Auchinleck to MS. Vernon* (Leland Stanford), J. F. Royster considers "The Causative Use of Hatan" in Old English (*JEGP*), and J. Zeitlin treats "The English Verbal as Adverb" (*Neophilologus*). Rhythmical and metrical studies include Miss A. L. F. Snell's *Pause: A Study of its Nature and its Rhythmical Function in Verse* (Michigan), her "Syllabic Quantity in English Verse" (*PMLA*), and F.

---

[1] Periodicals are cited under the following abbreviations: *MLN, Modern Language Notes; MLR, Modern Language Review; MP, Modern Philology; PMLA, Publications of the Modern Language Association of America; JEGP, Journal of English and Germanic Philology; SP, University of North Carolina Studies in Philology; RR, Romanic Review.* Titles appearing as theses or in the publications of universities are followed where possible by the name of the university.

N. Scott's "The 'Accentual Structure of Isolable English Phrases" (ibid).
Old English Literature (449-1150).—Except for F. G. Hubbard's textual note on "Beowulf 1598, 1996, 2026; Uses of the Impersonal Verb *geweorthan*" (*JEGP*), the only article on Old-English literature is Fr. Klaeber's "Concerning the Relation between *Exodus* and *Beowulf*" (*MLN*), in which the evidence for the priority of the *Exodus* is presented.

Middle English Literature (1150-1250).—In Middle-English literature J. E. Wells has issued a *Supplement* to his *Manual* mentioned two years ago (*A. Y. B.*, 1916, p. 755). Miss C. D'Evelyn has written of "The Middle-English Version of the *Revelation* of Methodius; with . . . the Influence of Methodius in Middle-English Writings" (*PMLA*); Miss Hope Emily Allen presents a lengthy preliminary statement of "The Origin of the *Ancren Riwle*" (*PMLA*), connecting it with Kilburn Priory. Miss Allen has also traced the source of "The Mystical Lyrics of the *Manuel des Pechiez*" (*RR*) and discussed "The *Manuel des Pechiez* and the Scholastic Prologue" (*RR*), casting doubt on William of Waddington's authorship of the Anglo-Norman version. W. H. Hulme has edited *Richard Rolle of Hampole's Mending of Life* from the fifteenth century Worcester Cathedral MS. F. 172 (Western Reserve Univ. Bull.). R. M. Garrett has published *The Pearl: An Interpretation* (University of Washington), and A. J. Perry has printed "Notes on John Trevisa" (*MLN*), showing among other things that Trevisa was dead in 1402.

The fine interest of American scholarship in Chaucer continues unabated. Samuel Moore, in "New Life-Records of Chaucer" (*MP*), prints abstracts of two documents (of 1374 and 1377) touching upon some difficult questions of Chaucer's connection with the controllership of petty customs. Miss M. H. Shackford has reëdited a useful brief Chaucer bibliography (Wellesley). J. L. Lowes, in carrying out his recently proposed intention of demonstrating that Chaucer made use of French translations and adaptations of classical material, shows in "Chaucer and the *Ovide moralisé*" (*PMLA*) that Chaucer knew and used at least part of that work. In line with the same attempt is his "Chaucer's *Boethius* and Jean de Meun" (*RR*). In "The *Franklin's Tale*, the *Teseide*, and the *Filocolo*" (*MP*), Lowes points out a noteworthy borrowing in the *Franklin's Tale* from the *Teseide* and discusses exhaustively the counter claims of Schofield and Rajna regarding the *Filocolo* as Chaucer's source in this tale. W. E. Farnham's "Chaucer's *Clerkes Tale*" (*MLN*) gathers together a number of passages in which Chaucer is closer to Boccaccio's Italian than to Petrarch's Latin, the usually accepted source. F. Tupper discusses "The Envy Theme in Prologues and Epilogues" (*JEGP*) in English literature generally, but with special reference to Middle English and Chaucer. T. A. Jenkins exhaustively comments upon "Deschamps' Ballade to Chaucer" (*MLN*), and is commented upon by G. H. Gerould in "Deschamps as Eustace" (*MLN*). A. S. Cook discusses at length Giovanni da Lignano in "Chaucer's Linian" (*RR*), one of the three Italian contemporaries of Chaucer whom he mentions by name, and adds what he thinks are a fourth allusion to Homer in "Chaucer's Griselda and Homer's Arete" (*Am. Jour. Philol.*). H. B. Hinckley completes our list with "Chauceriana" (*MP*).

The romance has not been wholly neglected. Miss V. D. Scudder has written a good sized volume on *The Morte D'Arthur of Sir Thomas Malory and Its Sources*. Professor Bruce has published elaborate studies of "Pelles, Pellinor, and Pellean in the Old French Arthurian Romances" (*MP*) and "Galahad, Nascien, and Some Other Names in the Grail Romances" (*MLN*). Wm. A. Nitze, in "The Glastonbury Passages in the *Perlesvaus*" (*SP*), tries once more to establish the connection of the *Perlesvaus* with Glastonbury material. R. B. Pace in "*Sir Perceval* and *The Boyish Exploits of Finn*" (*PMLA*) cites an Irish parallel to the romance. Two Middle-English texts have been printed, "Death and Life: An Alliterative Poem" (*SP*) of the fifteenth century, edited by J. H. Hanford and J. M. Steadman, Jr., and a "Dialogue between a Clerk and a Husbandman" (*MLN*) of the same century, printed by Carleton Brown. H. M. Belden's "Boccaccio, Hans Sachs, and *The Bramble Briar*" (*PMLA*) studies intensively this "traditional vulgar ballad". J. McGil's *Folksongs of the Kentucky Mountains* and, though not American, Miss Campbell and Cecil J. Sharp's *English Folk-songs from the Southern Appalachians* deserve mention as attempts to collect English material still traditional in this country. G. L. Kittredge has edited some "Ballads and Songs" (*Jour. Am. Folk-Lore*), and H. E. Rollins prints "Notes on the Shirburn Ballads" (*ibid.*). In folk tales and motives T. F. Crane's "Medieval Sermon Books and Stories and Their Study since 1883" (*Jour. Am. Philos. Soc.*) and his "The Mountain of Nida: An Episode of the Alexander Legend" (*RR*) are especially valuable. A. Taylor traces "The Motive of the Vacant Stake in Folklore and Romance" (*RR*) to a Celtic source, P. F. Baum treats "The Three Dreams or Dream-Bread Story" (*Jour. Am. Folk-Lore*), and M. E. Barnicle connects "The Exemplum of the Penitent Usurer" (*PMLA*) with the morality play. The early drama is always of interest. Hardin Craig, "The Lincoln Cordwainers' Pageant" (*PMLA*), publishes entries in the Lincoln Cordwainers' Company which are incidentally of value as indicating that the Lincoln plays were probably not processional. F. H. Miller points out "Metrical Affinities of the Shrewsbury *Officium Pastorum* and its York Correspondent" (*MLN*); Grace Frank presents evidence that "Revisions in the English Mystery Plays" (*MP*) were often made separately and independently, not in the cycle as a whole; and the present writer has instanced parallels to prove the folk origin of "The Mak Story" (*MP*). Robert Withington, who for some time has been publishing material on the pageant, has issued the first volume of *English Pageantry: An Historical Outline*, and has supplemented it with "The Early 'Royal Entry'" (*PMLA*), showing that the royal entry did not take the form of pageants until 1295, "The Lord Mayor's Show for 1590" (*MLN*), and "A Civic 'Triumph' circa 1700" (*JEGP*).

Modern English Period (since 1500). —The recent favor which Spenser has enjoyed in this country continues as great as ever. Chief among the contributions of the year is H. E. Cory's *Edmund Spenser: A Critical Study* (California). C. H. Whitman has compiled *A Subject Index to the Poems of Edmund Spenser*. A. H. Tolman, in "The Relations of Spenser and Harvey to Puritanism" (*MP*), advocates the view that both men were always Low-Churchmen. Edwin Greenlaw writes of "Spenser's Fairy Mythology" (*SP*), W. F. DeMoss in "Spenser's Twelve Moral Virtues 'According to Aristotle'" (*MP*) replies to Jusserand, showing that Spenser did base his twelve moral virtues on Aristotle, and F. M. Padelford, in "Talus: The Law" (*SP*), tries to show that Talus in the *Faerie Queene* is to be interpreted as the law and the agents who enforce it, not as the abstract principle of justice. O. F. Emerson, in "Spenser's Virgil's Gnat" (*JEGP*), makes a comparative examination of Spenser's translation and the pseudo-Virgilian *Culex;* and A. S. Cook notes "Five Spenserian Trifles" (*JEGP*). Notes on other Elizabethans include J. Q. Adams' proof that "Michael Drayton's *To The Virginia Voyage*" (*MLN*) is a metrical version of certain prose passages in Hakluyt, H. E. Rollins' "New Facts about George Turberville" (*MP*), W. P. Mustard's "Notes on Lyly's *Euphues*" (*MLN*), and R. M. Smith's "The Date and Authorship of Hall's Chronicle" (*JEGP*).

Shakespeare and the Founders of Liberty in America is a timely volume by C. M. Gayley, showing that Shakespeare must have known a number of the members of the Virginia Company. Lawrence Mason has added "Some Further Shakespeare Allusions or Parallels" (*MLN*) to the already extensive list, and A. Thaler has tried to demonstrate that "Shakespeare's Income" (*SP*) probably did not exceed half the total of over £700 a year with which he has been credited. H. D. Gray, in *The Original Version of "Love's Labour's Lost"* with a conjecture as to "*Love's Labour's Won*" (Leland Stanford), attempts to distinguish passage by passage between the play as Shakespeare originally wrote it and the revision that he afterwards made. *Love's Labors Won* is to be found, he thinks, in the main plot of mistaken identity in *Twelfth Night*. F. G. Hubbard, "The *Marcellus* Theory of the First Quarto *Hamlet*" (*MLN*), points to obstacles in the way of Gray's theory that the actor who played the part of Marcellus is responsible for the text of the First Quarto *Hamlet*. Alexander Green in "The Apocryphal *Sir Thomas More* and the Shakespeare Holograph" (*Am. Jour. Philol.*) decides against the theory of Shakespearean collaboration. Finally, M. B. Ruud has done a desirable piece of work in *An Essay toward a History of Shakespeare in Norway*.

Students of the Elizabethan drama are this year under a further debt to J. Q. Adams for gathering together in excellent form *The Dramatic Records of Sir Henry Herbert, Master of the Revels, 1623-1673* (Cornell). W. J. Lawrence treats "The Elizabethan Stage Throne" (*Texas Rev.*). D. Klein, "According to the Decorum of These Daies" (*PMLA*), discusses *Gismund of Salerne* and its revision, *Tancred and Gismund*. Miss G. W. Jones seeks "The Political Significance of the Play of *Albion Knight*" (*JEGP*), and F. G. Hubbard presents "Possible Evidence for the Date of Tamburlaine" (*PMLA*) pointing to 1588. W. D. Briggs attempts to establish June 11, 1572, as "The Birth-date of Ben Jonson" (*MLN*). Miss C. Moore has published the first part of a thesis on *The Dramatic Works of Thomas Nabbes* (Pennsylvania). Massinger and Field's *The Fatal Dowry* has been edited by C. L. Lockert, Jr. (Princeton), and Heywood's *Woman Killed with Kindness* and *Fair Maid of the West* by Katherine Lee Bates with a valuable introduction on Heywood. Heywood is also the subject of R. G. Martin's "A New Specimen of the Revenge Play" (*MP*) and "Notes on Thomas Heywood's *Ages*" (*MLN*).

Milton has provoked some discussion. R. L. Ramsey, "Morality Themes in Milton's Poetry" (*SP*), discusses the medieval elements in Milton and his relation to the plots and characters of the morality play. Jas. H. Hanford asserts that "The Temptation Motive in Milton" (*SP*) is a dominant motive in all his imaginative work. John Erskine in "The Theme of Death in *Paradise Lost*" (*PMLA*) finds an inconsistency between the earlier and later accounts of death in the poem, and E. E. Stoll denies the contention in "Was Paradise Well Lost?" (*ibid.*). Wm. A. Webb writes of "Milton's Views on Education" (*Educ. Rev.*), and E. N. S. Thompson in "Milton's *Of Education*" (*SP*) examines this pamphlet in the light of contemporary educational tendencies. The same author in "A Forerunner of Milton" (*MLN*) cites Henry More's *Psychathanasia* (1642) as championing the Copernican theory, which Milton seems to have accepted.

The seventeenth and eighteenth centuries have always had their devotees. H. T. Perry writes of *The First Duchess of Newcastle and Her Husband as Figures in Literary History* (Harvard). L. D. Wallace, on the evidence of a contemporary letter, sets Dec. 20, 1670-Jan. 9, 1671, as "A New Date for the *Conquest of Granada*" (*MP*), Miss A. E. Gipson has studied *John Home* and his tragedies (Yale), and S. S. Swartley has published a thesis on *The Life and Poetry of John Cutts* (Pennsylvania). The outstanding work of the year in the eighteenth century is Wilbur L. Cross' *The History of Henry Fielding*, the authoritative life of the novelist in three volumes, which scholars have known for years Cross was preparing. Miss H. S. Hughes continues her work in the minor novel in "A Precursor of *Tristram Shandy*" (*JEGP*) and "Translations of the *Vie de Marianne* and Their Relation to Contemporary Fiction" (*MP*). Miss A. I. Hazeltine has written a thesis on *William Shenstone and . . . His Critics* (Wellesley). M. E. Smith considers "The Fable as Poetry in English Criticism" (*MLN*) and offers "A Classification for Fables, Based on the Collection of Marie de France" (*MP*). E. C. Knowlton's "Pastoral in the Eighteenth Century" (*MLN*), R. S. Crane's "Imitation of Spenser and Milton in the Early Eighteenth Century: A New Document" (*SP*), W. H. Durham's "Some

Forerunners of the *Tatler* and the *Spectator*" (*MLN*), showing that Steele's work was a natural development of previous beginnings, and Miss C. Goad's *Horace in the English Literature of the Eighteenth Century* treat various topics in eighteenth-century literature. Towards the end of the century, when we reach the romantic revival, we have to record F. E. Pierce's *Currents and Eddies in the English Romantic Generation*. Mention may also be made of Wm. Haller's *The Early Life of Robert Southey, 1774-1803* (Columbia), F. B. Snyder's "Notes on Burns and the Popular Ballad" (*JEGP*), and Marjorie L. Barstow's *Wordsworth's Theory of Poetic Diction* (Yale). E. C. Baldwin's "Wordsworth and Hermes Trismegistus" (*PMLA*) and S. F. Gingerich's "Shelley's Doctrine of Necessity versus Christianity" (*PMLA*) belong to the same group. B. S. Allen has contributed two papers on Goodwin: "William Goodwin as a Sentimentalist" (*PMLA*) and "The Reaction against William Goodwin" (*MP*).

The nineteenth century has not been so fully discussed. W. Chislett, Jr., has issued a small volume of notes and essays called *The Classical Influence in English Literature in the Nineteenth Century*. W. L. MacDonald, in "Charles Lamb, the Greatest of the Essayists" (*PMLA*), has written an enthusiastic appreciation of Lamb and attempted to define his place in the development of the English essay. Miss Shackford writes of "Swinburne and Delavigne" (*PMLA*). In the novel L. W. Berle contrasts *George Eliot and Thomas Hardy*; J. H. E. Crees devotes attention to *George Meredith: A Study of His Works and Personality*; and J. W. Beach examines *The Method of Henry James*.

We may close this account with a reference to some books on contemporary literature and a few works of a general character. Professor Phelps in *The Advance of English Poetry in the Twentieth Century* republishes essays from the *Bookman* on the poets and poetry of today. In his *The Twentieth Century Theatre* he discusses the contemporary English and American stage. He has also published a little booklet on *Archibald Marshall: A Realistic Novelist*. H. T. and Wilson Follett have gathered together in book form essays on *Some Modern Novelists* from Meredith to Conrad. Wilson Follett has also published *The Modern Novel*, a study of the novel during the last two centuries. S. P. Sherman's *On Contemporary Literature* measures recent writers by the standards of permanent literature. E. A. Boyd issues some Irish literary studies under the title *Appreciations and Depreciations*. W. M. Hart has carefully considered *Kipling the Story Writer* (California), and F. M. K. Foster has compiled a bibliographical survey of *English Translations from the Greek* (Columbia). Finally, George Herbert Palmer has published his Earl lectures of 1917 in a volume called *Formative Types in English Poets*. It includes studies of poets from Chaucer and Spenser to Browning, and forms a notable contribution to American criticism.

GERMANIC LANGUAGES AND LITERATURES

Daniel B. Shumway

German Literature.—Owing to the war with Germany popular articles on German writers have practically disappeared from the magazines and very few translations have been made. Numerous scientific articles, however, testify to the interest still taken by scholars in German literature and philology. Two attempts have been made to show the difference between the older German writers and the militaristic character of modern Germany, one by W. W. Florer in a volume *German Liberty Authors* (Badger), the other in a well written article by F. Tupper, "Battle of the German Books" (*Nation*, Dec., 1917).

In the field of drama and fiction W. A. Hervey has prepared an admirable *Syllabus and Bibliography of the Works of Lessing, Goethe and Schiller* (Lemcke). The seventh volume of Hauptmann's dramas edited by Lewisohn has appeared. Karl Scholz has published an excellent study of *The Art of Translation, with Special Reference to the Dramas of Hauptmann and Sudermann* as Volume xxxvii of the series *Americana Germanica*. A. Henderson has treated of Schnitzler's dramas in his work on *European Dramatists* (p. 397), and one of Schnitzler's novels, *Bertha Garlan*, has appeared in the Modern Library (Boni & Liveright). H. Stevens has made a study of "Description in the Dramas of Grillparzer" (*Pub. Mod. Lang. Assoc.*, xxxiii).

In the field of lyric poetry Chas. W. Stork has continued his admirable translations, this time of the *Lyrical Poems of Hugo von Hofmannsthal* (Yale University Press). J. F. Lambert has published *Luther's Hymns*, and C. A. Williams an hitherto unknown student song of the 16th century (*Jour. of Eng. and Ger. Philol.*, April, 1918).

In the field of literary criticism articles on Goethe are quite numerous. Of chief importance is Calvin Thomas' excellent *Life of Goethe* (Holt), giving the main facts of his life and a detailed criticism of his works. W. J. Keller has interestingly shown how certain passages of the first part of Faust have served as a source for the second part (*Mod. Lang. Notes*, June, 1918). In an article "*Zu Goethes Faust in England*", H. W. Nordmeyer has treated of the Scotchman J. G. Lockhart who was the first to attempt the translation of Faust into English and who did much to break down the prejudice against Goethe in England in the early nineteenth century. Ernst Feise has pointed out the "Influence of Lessing's *Emilia Galotti* on Goethe's *Werther*" (*Mod. Philol.*, Oct., 1917); Geo. M. Baker has discussed the "Healing of Orestes in Goethe's *Iphigenia*" (*ibid.*); and W. A. Chamberlain, "Longfellow's Attitude towards Goethe" (*ibid.*, June, 1918). Two works in German treat of Schiller, the one by A. H. Appelmann the difference between Schiller's and Kant's conceptions of ethics (Stechert), and the other by O. E. Burkhard the treatment of the events leading up to the drama in Schiller's expositions (*Behandlung der Vorgeschichte in der Exposition bei Schiller*, University of Chicago Press). Heinrich Keidel discusses the influence of Plato and Hegel on Hebbel (*Jour. of Eng. and Ger. Philol.*, July, 1918) and A. W. Porterfield traces the influence of Auerbach on Nietzsche (*ibid.*, Feb., 1918).

In older literature Julius Goebel attempts anew the mooted question of the "Evolution of the Nibelungensaga", (*ibid.*, Jan., 1918). John L. Campion reprints an unknown *Tristan* fragment (*Mod. Philol.*, June, 1918). E. F. Clark has shown the "Use of Charms and Exorcisms in the Writings of Hans Sachs" (*ibid.*, Oct., 1918). Joseph Gillet has continued his studies of the older drama with an article "*Ueber den Zweck des Schuldramas in Deutschland im 16. und 17. Jh.*" (*Jour. of Eng. and Ger. Philol.*, Jan., 1918).

German Philology.—In this field several noteworthy articles have appeared. C. M. Lotspeich has continued his accent studies and has tried to show that the Germanic sound shift and mutation are the result of the mixing of two different types of accent, the Nordic and the Alpine (*ibid.*, April, 1918). E. Prokosch in "*Die Indogermanische Media Aspirata*" (*Mod. Philol.*, Feb. and June, 1918), has tried to show that bh, dh, gh were voiceless spirants. H. Collitz has written a further article in support of his views of "Early German Vocalism" (*Mod. Lang. Notes*, June, 1918).

German-American Relations. — In this field George W. Spindler has written an admirable life of the German patriot Karl Follen, who, fleeing from the tyranny of his native land, was instrumental in introducing the study of German into New England (University of Chicago Press). A splendid study of the *German Drama in English on the Philadelphia Stage from 1794-1830* by C. F. Bredé forms Volume xxxiv of the *Americana Germanica* series.

German Texts and Teaching.—In this field a new edition of Goethe's *Tasso* has been prepared by L. G. Robertson (Longmans). Karl F. Münzinger has compiled a *Phonetic Reader* for the Walter-Krause series (Scribner). A critical review of other texts and grammars is given by L. M. Schmidt in *Recent Textbooks in Secondary-School German* (*School Review*, Feb., 1918). The question of the teaching of German in the schools has been the subject of much discussion. Articles on the question will be found in *Education* (March 30), *School and Society* (March and June), and *School Review* (June).

Scandinavian. — In the Norwegian field the interest centres as usual around Ibsen, whose powerful drama *Ghosts* has been novelized by A. Drayatt (Jacobs). A volume of his dramas containing the *Master Builder*, *Pillars of Society* and *Hedda Gabler* has appeared in the Modern Library (Boni & Liveright). A. Henderson has treated Ibsen in his work on *European Dramatists* (p. 73), and B. S. Allen has discussed his fondness for repeatedly using the same *motifs* in "Recurrent Elements of Ibsen's Art" (*Jour. of Eng. and Ger. Philol.*, April, 1918). Nazimova's revival of Ibsen has been made the subject of an article, "Ibsen Once Again", by G. C. Hamilton (*Bookman*, June, 1918). Björnsen's verse romance *Arnljot Gelline* has been well translated by Wm. M. Payne as Volume viii of the *Scandinavian Classics*. Martin B. Ruud has an "Essay toward the History of Shakespeare in Norway" in *Scandinavian Studies and Notes* (iv, 2).

In the Swedish field Strindberg's drama *Miss Julie* has appeared in the Modern Library (Boni & Liveright). His eccentric character has been discussed by Otto Heller in his *Prophets of Dissent* (Knopf). The second part of Selma Lagerlöf's novel *Jerusalem* has been well translated by Velma S. Howard under the title *The Holy City* (Doubleday). Chas. W. Stork has an able article on "Swedish Poetry" in the *American Scandinavian Review* (Nov., 1917, and Oliver A. Lindner one on "Writers of Swedish Life in America" (*ibid.*, May, 1918). Godmundur Kamban's four-act drama *Hadda Padda* has been translated by Sadie L. Peller with a foreword from the pen of the Danish critic George Brandes (Knopf).

In the Danish field Martin Nexö's novel *Pelle the Conqueror* has been translated in two volumes by Jessie Muir and Bernard Miall (Holt).

Dutch is represented by translations of two of Louis Couperus' novels by A. Teixeira de Mattos, *Old People and the Things that Pass* and *Dr. Adriaan* (Dodd, Mead).

ROMANCE LANGUAGES AND LITERATURE

GEORGE L. HAMILTON

French.—During the last year one interest has been paramount, and to no others more than to those whose studies are in those branches of literature that have furnished the bases of modern civilization to the world. Our debt to France, for instance, is due not only to a few adventurers, ships and millions which came to our aid at the beginning of our national history, but because to France we are indebted for maintaining for centuries models of clearness in thinking and perfection in style. American scholarship is paying back part of the debt in its endeavor to elucidate and interpret isolated fragments of her great literature.

In Old French the principal contributions deal with Arthurian literature. M. E. Ogle has confirmed the only rational thesis of "The Sloth of Erec" (*Rom. Rev.*, ix, 1) by illustrations from classical literature. J. Douglas Bruce has continued his valuable studies on the sources of prose romances in his articles "Pelles, Pellinor, and Pellean in the Old French Arthurian Romances" (*Mod. Philol.*, xvi, 113, 337), "Galahad, Nascien and Some Other Names in the Grail Romances" (*Mod. Lang. Notes*, xxxiii, 129), and "The Composition of the Old French Prose *Lancelot* (*Rom. Rev.*, ix, 241), while W. E. Nitze, writing on the "The Glastonbury Passages in the Perlesvaus" (*Univ. of N. C. Studies in Philol.*, xv, 7), continues to give undue authority to one of the latest romances. W. P. Shepard has written an article, which is anything but conclusive, on "Tedbalt of the *Chançun de Guillelmea* and Hugh III, Count of the Maine" (*Rom. Rev.*, ix. 285). Hope Allen in her "Manuel des Pechiez and the Scholastic Prologue" (*ibid.*, viii, 434) and "The Mystical Lyrics of the Manuel des Pechiez" (*ibid.*, ix, 154), in the course of proving her special theses, has developed striking and sane views on vernacular religious literature in mediæval France and England. The publication of "The Middle English Metrical Version of the Revelations of Methodius" and of an abridged version of the Latin text (*Publ. Mod. Lang. Assoc.*, xxxiii, 135) by Charlotte D'Evelyn will be an aid to students of the French version of the same work. The studies of J. L. Lowes on "Chaucer's Boethius and Jean de Meun" (*Rom. Rev.*, viii, 383) and "Chaucer and the *Ovide moralisé*" (*Publ. Mod. Lang. Assoc.*, xxxiii, 312) and T. A. Jenkins' well commented, critical text of "Deschamps' Ballad to Chaucer" (*Mod. Lang. Notes*, xxxiii, 268) are valuable contributions to the intellectual affinities of the two countries concerned. E. S. Sheldon has approached the same subject from a linguistic point of view in his "Some English and Old French Phrases" (*Univ. of N. C. Studies in Philol.*, xv, 1), R. T. Holbrook has added to our knowledge of his subject in his *Étude sur Pathelin Essai de Bibliographie et d'Interpretation* (Elliott Monographs), and Hélène J. Harvitt continues her studies on "Eustorg de Beaulieu, a Disciple of Marot" (*Rom. Rev.* ix, 319). Incidents found in French versions of widely circulated traditions are studied in T. F. Crane's "The Mountain of Nida: An Episode of the Alexander Legend" (*ibid.*, 129), Archer Taylor's "Motif of the Vacant Stake in Folklore and Romance" (*ibid.*, 21) and "Notes on the Wandering Jew" (*Mod. Lang. Notes*, xxxiii, 394), and H. R. Patch on "Mediaeval Descriptions of the Otherworld" (*Publ. Mod. Lang. Ass.*, xxxiii, 601).

Turning to modern French literature, L. C. Lancaster discusses the source and authenticity of "Four Letters of Racine" (*ibid.*, 30) and "Molière's Borrowings from the *Comedie des Proverbes*" (*ibid.*, 208). B. M. Woodbridge has shown how a historical incident passed into one of the first of modern novels in his note, "Mme. de Montespan and la Princesse de Cleves" (*ibid.*, 79). H. L. Bruce in an article on the "Period of greatest Popularity of Voltaire's Plays on the English Stage" (*ibid.*, 20) throws a side light on a portion of his book *Voltaire on the English Stage* (*Univ. of Cal. Publ. in Mod. Philol.*). R. Havens writes on "The Date of Composition of *Manon Lescaut*" (*Mod. Lang. Notes*, xxxiii, 150), while R. C. Whitford throws together a few notes under the title of "Madame de Staël's Literary Reputation in England" (*Univ. of Ill. Studies in Lang. and Lit.*), and "Madame de Staël's Literary Reputation in America" (*Mod. Lang. Notes*, xxxiii, 476). G. C. Chinard has completed his series of studies on an interesting subject in his *L'Exotisme américain dans l'oeuvre de Chateaubriand*. E. P. Dargan continues his "Studies on Balzac" (*Mod. Phil.*, xvi, 351), a bit of literary critical work which has the merit of its own distinctive style. *The Influence of Italy on the Literary Career of Lamartine* by A. Pirazzini forms a volume of the *Columbia University Studies in Romance Philology and Literature*, while the seamy side of the poet's life, based upon his correspondence, is presented to us by D. H. Carnahan in his article, "The Financial Difficulties of Lamartine" (*Mod. Phil.*, xvi, 143), and a most ambitious *Life of Lamartine* in two volumes has been written by H. R. Whitehouse. In his *Sources of the Religious Element in Flaubert's "Salambô"* (Elliott Monographs), A. Hamilton adds one more to the illuminating stylistic studies on the great realist which have been published as the first three volumes of the same series, the fruitful results of the French method of scholarly work in modern literature introduced at Johns Hopkins University a few years ago. H. David has written an informing article on the literary methods of the friend of Flaubert in his "*Les Poésies chinoises de Bouilhet*" (*Mod. Phil.*, xv, 663). In reading O. H. Moore on "Literary Relationships of Guy de Maupassant" (*ibid.*, 645) and "The Romanticism of Guy de Maupassant" (*Publ. Mod. Lang. Assoc.*, xxxiii, 96) one is quite convinced, that if literature is the criticism of life, the criticism of literature demands some experience in life, especially in treating of the work of artists which is the most intense reflection of a living organism. One of our most honored war-time guests, A. Carnoy, at once instructs and delights in his essay, "*L'imagination flamande dans l'Ecole symbolique française*" (*ibid.*, 204). W. W. Comfort has put in a compact form the results of his studies on "The Priest in Modern French Fiction" (*South Atlantic Quart.*, xvii, 113), and R. F. Bowen has told us of "The Peasant Language in Ferdinand Fabre's *Le Chevier*" (*Mod. Phil.*, xv, 675) a technical subject not suitable for treatment in his informing essay on *The Novels of Ferdinand Fabre*. The continual reciprocal borrowing of one literature from another is illustrated in articles by Martha H. Shackford, "Swinburne and Delavigne" (*Publ. Mod. Lang. Assoc.*, xxxiii, 65), L. F. Mott, "Renan and Matthew Arnold" (*Mod. Lang. Notes*, xxxiii, 65), and F. B. Barton, "Laurence Sterne and Théophile Gautier" (*Mod. Phil.*, xvi, 205).

Italian. — C. E. Whitmore offers some new suggestions in his "Studies in the Text of the Sicilian Poets" (*Rom. Rev.*, ix, 269). C. H. Grandgent maintains his position as the first Dante scholar of America in his course of lectures, published under the title of the *Power of Dante*, while Dorothy L. Simons presents some interesting tables in her "Individual Human *Dramatis Personae* of the *Divina Commedia*" (*Mod. Phil.*, xv, 371). A. S. Cook makes some interesting suggestions in "The First Two Readers of Petrarch's Tale of Griselda" (*ibid.*, xv, 633), and gathers together a good deal of inaccessible material upon Petrarch's great legal contemporary Lignano, in the way of a comment on a phrase of Chaucer (*Rom. Rev.*, viii, 553). W. E. Farnham wishes to show in a note, "Chaucer's Clerke's Tale" (*Mod. Lang. Notes*, xxxiii, 193), that the English poet was verbally indebted to Boccaccio's *Decameron* (X, 10), while H. M. Belden, writing on "Boccaccio, Hans Sachs and The Bramble Briar" (*Publ. Mod. Lang. Assoc.*, xxxiii, 327), in the study of an English popular vulgar ballad, extant in both English and American versions, points out the source of an element of that one of Boccaccio tales (IV, 5) best known to us through Keats' dramatic poem *Isabella or the Pot of Basil* (see also *English Language and Literature*, supra). J. L. Lowes makes his usual surprising and substantial additions to our knowledge of Chaucer's sources and art in his "The Franklin's Tale, The Teseide, and the Filocolo" (*Mod. Phil.*, xv, 689), and there are some interesting items in I. de Perott's "Notes on M. A. Scott's Elizabethan Translations from the Italian" (*Rom. Rev.*, ix, 304) and M. P. Tilley's "Della Casa's Galatei in Seventeenth Century England" (*ibid.*, 309). J. Van Horne has a note entitled "Comment on some Posthumous Poems and Fragments of Leopardi" (*Mod. Lang. Notes*, xxxiii, 154), while A. Livingston tells in a way at once informing and amusing what Italian immigrants have made of a combination of their own and our language, of which we have a sample in the article's title, "*La Merica Sanemagogna*" (*Rom. Rev.*, ix, 206).

Spanish.—H. B. Lang completes his "Notes on the Metre of the Poem of the Cid" (*ibid.*, viii, 401; ix, 48), a title which gives no suggestion of the well documented study on the different factors of a widely distributed genre. C. C. Marden's critical text and introduction to the *Libre de Apolonio* (Elliott Monographs) is a fair promise of the excellence of an important work, when completed. R. Scheville's study on *The Dramatic Art of Lope de Vega together with the Dama Boba* (*Univ. of Cal. Publ. in Mod. Philol.*) presents many original views on a much discussed subject and offers a readable text of an unpublished play of the prolific Spanish writer. H. Seris has proved once more the truth of the dictum that there is no such thing as a duplicate of an early printed book in what he writes on "*Una Nueva Variedad de la Edicion principe de Quijoté*" (*Rom. Rev.*, ix, 194). *The Neo-Classic Movement in Spain during the XVIIIth Century* (Leland Stanford Jr. Univ. Publ.) is a well informed book by R. E. Pellissier, a notice of whose death in fighting in a righteous cause, not then officially our own, appeared in the 1917 issue of the YEAR BOOK (p. 731). K. W. Parmelee has an interesting note on the Spanish-American word "Gringo" (*Rom. Rev.*, ix, 108), M. Krepinsky one on "anchova" (*ibid.*, 96), while E. H. Tuttle comments on a number of less common words in his "Spanish Notes" (*ibid.*, 227, 317).

1918 LITERATURE AND LANGUAGE

ANCIENT LITERATURE AND PHILOLOGY

GREEK LITERATURE
William Arthur Heidel

In spite of the severe conditions of the war the publication of books dealing even with subjects apparently so alien as Greek literature and civilization has not ceased; indeed, the reaction noted last year (*A. Y. B.*, 1917, p. 733), tending to emphasize the value of Greek and to make it a more potent factor in the life of today, has not spent itself. In the *Proceedings of the British Academy* (vii) W. Rhys Roberts treats of "Greek Civilization as a Study for the People"; Professor Henry Browne, S. J., of the University of Dublin, gives us *Our Renaissance: Essays on the Reform and Revival of Classical Studies* (Longmans); and Lane Cooper presents *The Greek Genius and Its Influence: Select Essays and Extracts* (Yale University Press, 1917). J. T. Allen's *The First Year of Greek* (Macmillan) by its freshness of treatment seems well calculated to stimulate the study of the language at the only point where under a competent teacher special stimulus is needed. In this connection mention may be made of E. H. Sturtevant's *Linguistic Change: An Introduction to the Historical Study of Language* (University of Chicago Press, 1917) because, though dealing with language study in general, it is by its sound pedagogical sense well suited to aid the student and teacher of Greek.

R. C. Flickinger's *The Greek Theater and Its Drama* (University of Chicago Press, 1918) is an ambitious work on a large subject, touching on many problems and making many minor contributions to the study of the drama, but it leaves much to be desired both in form and content. James Loeb, who has made the cause of classical studies his own and has, by the publication of the Loeb Classical Library and by the previous translation of Croiset's *Aristophanes and the Political Parties at Athens* and *Decharme's Euripides and the Spirit of his Dramas*, enriched the English literature of the Greek drama, now adds to his former benefits by translating, with considerable omissions and adaptations, Professor Legrand's *Daos* under the new and appropriate title, *The New Greek Comedy* (Putnam, 1917), to which the late John Williams White contributed a brief but valuable introduction. Uncertain transport has delayed notice in this place of two books of outstanding merit, the new editions of *The Wasps of Aristophanes* and *The Clouds of Aristophanes* by Benjamin B. Rogers (Bell, 1915, 1916). Long the incomparable standard, Rogers' translations of the plays have been improved in the new edition.

In the Loeb Classical Library two volumes call for notice: E. Cary's *Dio's Roman History* reaches the sixth volume, Professor Perrin's *Plutarch's Lives* the fifth. The excellence of these translations has been commended in former years, and the standard then set is fully maintained.

Paul Elmer More in his *Platonism* (Princeton University Press, 1917) publishes enlarged and extended lectures delivered on the Vanuxem Foundation. While the book will undoubtedly be welcomed as an exposition of the ethical thought of Plato in charming English, its correctness and adequacy as an interpretation are sure to be challenged (see also XXVI, Philosophy). The Medici Society issues, in its Library of Philosophical Translations, the first volume of *Plotinus: The Ethical Treatises*, translated from the Greek by Stephen Mackenna (1917). The work of the translator and the publisher is as nearly perfect as possible. The edition, if peace permits its completion, will be for long the favorite text of the English reader.

Three doctoral dissertations relating to aspects of Greek literature deserve honorable mention. Angela C. Darkow's *The Spurious Speeches of the Lysianic Corpus* (Bryn Mawr) defends a thesis which, if true, renders questions regarding the genuineness or spuriousness of orations attributed to Greek speech-wrights well-nigh nugatory. Though cleverly done, its results will hardly be accepted. J. W. Beardslee, Jr., writes an interesting and valuable study of *The Use of Φύσις in Fifth-Century Greek*

Literature (Chicago). Emily Helen Dutton's *Studies in Greek Prepositional Phrases—διά, ἀπό, ἐκ, εἰς, ἐκ* (Chicago) will be found to be of great use to all careful readers of Greek in determining the meaning of idioms. There remain to be noticed a number of books concerned only indirectly with Greek literature, but of value to the student of Greek in its larger aspects. John B. Edwards gives us an excellent dissertation on *The Demesman in Attic Life* (Johns Hopkins), and Bertha Carr Rider's *The Greek House: Its History and Development from the Neolithic Period to the Hellenistic Age* (Cambridge University Press, 1916), a doctoral thesis presented to the University of London, gives a useful account of a subject which must interest every reader of Greek.

There are likewise a number of books dealing with aspects of Greek religion. Emily L. Shields, in a Johns Hopkins dissertation on *The Cults of Lesbos*, presents in eminently satisfactory form the literary and inscriptional evidence, but does not greatly advance the interpretation of the facts collected. A study of more significance is Pierre Roussel's *Les Cultes Égyptiens à Délos du iiie au i^{er} Siècle av. J.—C.* (Paris, Berger-Levrault, 1916), which enables us to gauge the influence of the Alexandrian cults in one of the leading centers of Greek religion. Alfred Boissier's *Le Culte de Diane en Suisse et l'Origine du Fraumünster à Zürich* (Geneva, Librairie Kundig, 1916) is an historical study of unusual interest. Rendel Harris' *The Ascent of Olympus* (Manchester University Press, 1917) collects studies of the origins of the cults of Dionysos, Apollo, Artemis, and Aphrodite.

Percy Gardner's *A History of Ancient Coinage, 700-300 B. C.* (Clarendon Press, 1918) is a book of capital importance, being the first attempt to trace the history of Greek coinage. Even if specialists should be able to pick flaws in it, its value to the general student of ancient Greece would still be very great. It is pleasant to welcome another book of even greater interest and importance to the student of the classics. The basis of all our study is the ancient texts, and they depend on manuscripts. A. C. Clark, who in 1914 applied the arithmetical test to the omissions in the text of the Gospels and Acts, now gives us a most illuminating study of the subject in *The Descent of Manuscripts* (Clarendon Press, 1918), dealing with omissions of lines and larger units in the manuscripts of Cicero, Asconius, Plato, and Demosthenes. It is not too much to say that his book will mark an epoch in the critical evaluation of manuscripts and the constitution of classical texts.

LATIN LITERATURE

CHARLES KNAPP

During the year considerable attention has been paid to the three great Latin Poets—Lucretius, Vergil, and Horace. W. A. Merrill, long known for his studies in Lucretius, published in *University of California Publications in Classical Philology* (iv) a text of the *De Rerum Natura*. In this he incorporates many of his own emendations, previously published, and attempts (to my mind, rather unsuccessfully), by typographical devices, to indicate the logical divisions of the text. The typographical devices are awkward, and the headings, set frequently within paragraphs, and sometimes even within a sentence, irritate rather than help. But, since critical editions of classical texts have rarely been produced by American scholars, the book well deserves special mention. In the same *Publications* (iii) Merrill presented a paper, "Parallels and Coincidences in Lucretius and Virgil." The exact measure of Vergil's indebtedness, in language and ideas, to his great predecessor is a matter of prime importance, and so Merrill's record is of service and of much value. But his registration of even the simplest verbal coincidences will, after all, delay the final making of such exact measurement. C. J. Keyser, professor of mathematics in Columbia University, published in the *Bulletin of the American Mathematical Society* an interesting paper, "The Rôle of the Concept of Infinity in the Work of Lucretius" (*Classical Weekly*, xii).

We note next a book by that fine scholar, W. Warde Fowler, *Aeneas at* the *Site of Rome: Observations on the Eighth Book of the Aeneid* (Longmans). Fowler draws an interesting parallel between the mission of Aeneas, founder of Rome, and that of Augustus, whose rule is the culmination of the great career of Rome. Aeneas, by the will of the gods, came to Italy to rescue it from chaos and barbarism; Augustus, after the chaos of the civil wars, sought to restore order and to revivify the worship of the gods. T. F. Boyds, whose *Beasts, Birds and Bees of Virgil*, reached a second edition during the year, published also *Virgil and Isiah: A Study of the Pollio, with Translation, Notes, and Appendixes* (Blackwell). Much as Vergil's famous Fourth Eclogue has been studied, each new treatment of the poem is eagerly welcomed.

Horace and His Age: A Study in Historical Background, by J. F. D'Alton (Longmans), covers well the field with which it undertakes to deal—Horace in his relation to Roman politics, the Augustan revival, religion and philosophy, social problems, popular beliefs, the period of the Epistles, and literary criticism. Though one would have welcomed a discussion of Horace's literary art, seeing that Horace's fame and influence have rested not so much on what he said as on matters of form (the way he treated his themes), lovers of Horace will set the book beside Sellar's *Horace and the Elegiac Poets*, as an indispensable part of their Horatian apparatus.

K. F. Smith presented two more of his instructive and delightful essays, under the title "Martial the Epigrammatist", in the *Sewanee Review*, and "The Poet Ovid," in the *University of South Carolina Studies in Philology*.

Parts of certain Latin authors not heretofore readily accessible in English annotated editions have been made available during the year. J. H. Westcott and E. M. Rankin produced a very useful edition, with good introduction and helpful notes, of the *Julius* and the *Augustus* of Suetonius. Though the *Augustus* has long been available in the scholarly edition by E. S. Schuckburgh, this is the first good annotated edition in English of the *Julius*. Of the *Metamorphoses* of Apuleius only the Cupid and Pysche story has been provided with English notes, in the edition by L. C. Purser, but the notes are cumbersome and wordy, and the book expensive. J. P. Pike published in 1918 *The Short Stories of Apuleius* (Allyn & Bacon). The selection of 13 stories, including the Cupid and Psyche, is good, and the introduction helpful, but the notes are likely to prove too brief to be of service to the ordinary reader. J. P. Postgate has published a good edition of Book VIII of Lucan's *Pharsalia* (Cambridge University Press).

A most interesting and inspiring happening of the last year or two is the fact that in war-worn Italy classical scholars have had the courage to begin a new series of critical text editions of Latin authors, to take its place beside the well known Teubner Series and the Oxford Classical Text Series. The new series, which is under the general editorship of Carlo Pascal, is known as the *Corpus Scriptorum Latinorum Paravianum* (it gets the name *Paravianum* from the publishers, I. B. Paravia & Co., Rome, Turin, etc.). The small, convenient, and attractive volumes thus far published, at extremely low prices, include Catullus; Caesar, *De Bello Civili;* Cicero, *De Re Publica;* Minucius Felix, *Octavius;* Plautus, *Stichus;* Plautus, *Captivi;* Tacitus, *Agricola;* Tacitus, *Germania;* Vergil, *Eclogues, Moretum, Copa*, in one volume, the *Catalepton, Maecenas*, and the *Priapeum, Quid Hoc Novi Est*, in another; Ovid, *Tristia;* Ovid, *Ars Amatoria;* Tacitus, *Dialogus;* Cicero, *Pro Milone, Pro Archia*.

W. P. Mustard, well known for his work on late Latin authors, has put classical scholars still further in his debt by his edition of the *Eclogues* of Faustus Androlinus and Iohannes Arnolletus, with good introduction and notes that point out reminiscences of classical authors.

Translations of classical writings seem to come in a steady stream from the presses. Here two must be named, Volume II of a translation of Plautus, by P. Nixon, and a rendering of Juvenal and Persius, by G. G. Ramsay. These works form part of the *Loeb Classical Library*. Nixon's translation is full of life, though at times there is too much straining after effect, particularly in the translation of the various expletives.

For some years past much labor has been expended in the effort to trace the influence of classical writings on English literature. Thus, in 1913, W. T. Myers issued *The Relations of Latin and English During the Age of Milton* (Ruebush-Elkins Co., Dayton, Va.). In 1916 appeared *The Influence of Horace on the Chief English Poets of the Nineteenth Century*, by Mary Rebecca Thayer (Yale University Press), and "Goethe's Estimate of the Greek and Latin Writers", by W. J. Keller (Univ. of Wis. Bull. No. 786). In 1918 Elizabeth Nitchie presented, in an interesting paper, *The Classical Journal* (xiii, 393), "Horace and Thackeray"; Caroline Goad published a very elaborate study (641 pages), *Horace in the English Literature of the Eighteenth Century* (Yale University Press); and W. Chislett, Jr., published *The Classical Influence in English Literature in the 19th Century* (Stratford & Co., Boston).

A very important work, on its surface, indeed, devoted exclusively to Greek things, must be mentioned: *The Greek Theater and Its Drama*, by R. C. Flickinger (University of Chicago Press). By adding much to our understanding of the Greek theatre, this book will minister to a fuller and surer understanding of the two great Roman writers of comedy, Plautus and Terence, whose works are in every case based on Greek originals. (See also *Greek Literature*, supra.)

Lastly, we mention *The Unwilling Vestal*, by Edward Lucas White (Dutton). The author is a teacher of Latin, but also a novelist of distinction (witness his *El Supremo*). For *The Unwilling Vestal* he made a careful study of all the ancient passages bearing on the Vestal Virgins. Granting the correctness of his picture of the Vestals on the archaeological side (there are, I think, few, if any, errors here), I question the psychology of the book; the author makes his heroine, before she is 12, capable of a grand passion for the hero (a strange person, surely), to which she adheres during all the 30 years of her unwilling service as Vestal.

SEMITIC PHILOLOGY AND LITERATURE

MORRIS JASTROW, JR.

The Oriental Club of Philadelphia has published, in commemoration of its thirtieth anniversary, a survey of *Thirty Years of Oriental Studies*. The volume contains an article on "Thirty Years' Progress in Semitics," by Dr. John P. Peters, New York, with a supplementary account by Professor Jastrow of the University of Pennsylvania, followed by a survey of "Thirty Years of Indo-European Studies", by Prof. E. W. Hopkins of Yale University (see also *Indo-European Philology, infra*). The record is particularly gratifying as showing the large part taken in scientific activity both in Semitic and Sanskrit fields by American scholars during the past three decades.

The war has made a serious interruption of scientific work in this country as well as abroad in the field of Oriental studies as in all other branches of scientific work. The record for the year 1918 is therefore somewhat meagre. One notable undertaking of general interest which was completed during the year is the series of *Sacred Books and Early Literature of the East*, edited by Charles F. Horne and comprising no less than 17 volumes. It includes selections from the entire domain of ancient and mediæval Eastern literature, beginning with Babylonia and Assyria and ending with selections from the Apocryphal books of the Old and New Testaments. The translations have been prepared or revised by reliable scholars, and the work, covering a very wide field, in Egypt, Persia, Arabia, Palestine, India, China, Japan, is invaluable as a general reference work, containing a mass of material not found elsewhere.

Another series, *The Mythology of Races*, edited by Dr. L. H. Gray, is making steady progress, signalized by the appearance during the year of a notable volume on *Egyptian Mythology* by W. Max Müller of the University of Pennsylvania. While many of Dr. Müller's views will encounter opposition from his fellow Egyptologists, yet all will recognize the great value of this attempt to penetrate into the inner meaning of the strange beliefs and still stranger speculations found among the ancient Egyptians as revealed by the monuments and by Egyptian texts.

George A. Barton of Bryn Mawr College has added to his previous volumes on Sumerian and Babylonian texts another under the title of *Miscellaneous Babylonian Inscriptions* (Yale University Press). The texts are from the collections in the University of Pennsylvania Museum and should have found a place in the Series published by that institution. The texts are of the very first importance and contain, among other things, a number that throw further light on the early Sumerian view of the creation of the world and of man.

S. A. B. Mercer has compiled a *Sumero-Babylonian Sign List* (Columbia University Press, 1918) which, while it adds nothing new to what was already known, yet may be of use in studying the development of the signs from their archaic to their late forms.

An elaborate series of studies in "Biblical Parallelism" has been issued conjointly by Prof. William Popper of the University of California and Dr. Louis I. Newman. Dr. Popper confines himself to Chapters 1 and 10 of Isaiah, while Dr. Newman takes up the parallelisms in the Book of Amos. The main purpose of the investigation is to establish, through detailed investigation of the literary form in the Prophets, a basis for textual criticism, and more particularly to separate later additions from the original portions of the utterances of the Prophets. A large part of Dr. Newman's work is taken up with parallel methods of composition among the Chinese, Sumerians, and the Finns, as well as in the Syriac and the later Rabbinical literature. The theory remains to be tested.

Perhaps the most important publication of the year in the field of Semitic philology is a volume on *Lydian Inscriptions* by Enno Littmann of Strassburg University, setting forth the results of the excavations at Sardis carried on under the auspices of the American Society for Excavations at Sardis and published by the Society. Hitherto about 13 more or less fragmentary Lydian inscriptions had been published. This number is now considerably enlarged by the discoveries at Sardis, and of special interest and value is a bilingual—Lydian and Aramaic—of considerable length. With the help of the Aramaic as a key Professor Littmann has succeeded in identifying the majority of the characters of the Lydian alphabet, though even with this scarcely more than the beginning of a decipherment of Lydian inscriptions has been rendered possible. The Aramaic translation accompanying the Lydian inscription has been successfully read by Professor Littmann and turns out to be of a mortuary character, dated in the tenth year of King Artaxerxes. The king meant is probably the first of that name, with the surname Longimanus, which would date the inscription date about the middle of the fifth century B.C. It is interesting to thus find the evidence for a considerable Aramaic-speaking population in western Asia Minor at this early period.

INDO-EUROPEAN PHILOLOGY
(Exclusive of the Germanic languages)
ROLAND G. KENT

For several years studies in the origins of the separate cases of nouns in the original Indo-European speech have been appearing, and several of these have been noted in the YEAR BOOK. A careful study of the dative case by Walter Petersen, "Syncretism in the Indo-European Dative" (*Am. Jour. Philol.*, xxxix, 1 and 117), reaches the following conclusions:

The Indo-European dative was in origin an uninflected case of the secondary object, which had certain points of contact with a local case somewhat like the locative in the singular and with the ablative in the plural; from this partially common sphere of usage complete syncretism resulted, so that the uninflected case gave way everywhere to the clearer inflected originally local forms.... This theory of the syncretistic origin of the dative avoids the objections to both local and grammatical theories, combines the advantages of both, and explains other features which both of the other theories cannot explain.

With this interpretation one may compare the somewhat divergent theories of two other American scholars, E. W. Hopkins, who deals especially with the dative in the Hindu Vedas (*Trans. Am. Philol. Assoc.* xxxvii, 87, and *Jour. Am. Oriental Soc.*, xxviii, 360), and E. W. Fay, speaking on the syntax of the case in Latin (*Class. Quart.*, v, 190). Hopkins takes up also the "Origin of the Ablative Case" (*Jour. Am. Oriental Soc.*, xxxviii, 47), and noting that it comprises forms ending in -*os*, identical with the genitive singular or with the dative plural, forms in -d. starting in pronouns as a pseudo-accusative stem form, and forms ending in an adverbial -*tos* of no distinctly specialized meaning, he concludes that the ablative case was a grammatical luxury which developed into a "from" case by a process of specialization.

The tendency of such studies seems to be bringing us near the view that the case system of Indo-European rests upon the use of five elements, *s, m, d, i, bh,* of vague significance, gradually specialized in meaning and combined with one another to form additional endings.

Hopkins has also a valuable account of "Thirty Years of Indo-European Studies" in a volume entitled *Thirty Years of Oriental Studies,* issued in commemoration of 30 years of activity by the Oriental Club of Philadelphia (see also *Semitic Philology, supra*). The writer sketches the progress in the field from 1888 to 1918, with a valuable bibliography of the most important books, and a consideration of the promise of the future. It might be noted also that the American Oriental Society, at its meeting in New Haven in April, 1918, celebrated the seventy-fifth anniversary of its incorporation.

A. H. M. Stonecipher, in his *Graeco-Persian Names* (Vol. IX of the *Vanderbilt Oriental Series*), presents the ancient Persian names that appear in Greek texts, gives their presumable Persian forms and etymologies, and tabulates the phonetic and etymological results in a well systematized way which will be of great value to classicists and to Iranists alike.

The dependence of the study of ancient Indic and Persian religions upon philological studies is such that treatises in these fields belong as much to philology as to religion. In the volume entitled *Religions of the Past and Present,* a series of lectures delivered by members of the faculty of the University of Pennsylvania and edited by J. A. Montgomery, there are chapters on "The Religion of the Veda," "Buddhism," and "Brahmanism and Hinduism," by Franklin Edgerton, and on "Zoroastrianism," by R. G. Kent, which present these themes in a brief and semi-popular yet scholarly form.

L. C. Barret continues his publication, with critical notes, of the Kashmirian Atharva Veda; this instalment is Book V, containing 40 hymns, of which 25 are substantially new, not occurring in other versions of the Vedas (*Jour. Am. Oriental Soc.,* xxxvii, 257).

The valuable studies of W. H. Schoff in the commerce of the ancient Orient are further exemplified in his "Navigation to the Far East under the Roman Empire" (*ibid.*, 240), which, like his previous articles, is a contribution not only to the history of ancient trade, but to the interpretation of the *Peripli* or coasting voyages of merchants which have come down to us in Greek.

The study of the formation of noun stems in Greek continues to receive careful treatment. C. D. Buck, in "Studies in Greek Noun-Formation: Dental Terminations I. 4" (*Class. Phil.*, xiii, 75), handles in detail notably χάρις, θέμις, ἄναξ, and their compounds, with careful citations of the sources of many words not readily ascertainable from previous monographs or lexica. C. W. Peppler has presented (*Am. Jour. Philol.,* xxxix, 173) the fourth part of his "Comic Terminations in Aristophanes" (Part 1, printed separately at Baltimore in 1902; parts 2 and 3, in *Am. Jour. Philol.,* xxxi, 428, and xxxvii, 459), which is important in revealing how derivative words—some familiar, some unusual, and some entirely new—were employed to convey humorous touches in ancient Greek. From his studies it is easily seen that modern humorists in coining strange words to provoke a laugh are but following a very ancient procedure.

1919 LITERATURE AND LANGUAGE
AMERICAN LITERATURE
(Nov. 15, 1918, to Nov. 15, 1919)
EDWARD EVERETT HALE

Book Production.—It is probable that the production of books in the United States would have been larger in 1919 than ever before had it not been for labor troubles, particularly the New York printers' strike, which began at the end of September and for seven weeks hindered production and distribution to a very great degree (see also XV, *Labor*). The total number of books (including pamphlets) published in the United States in recent years has been:

1914	8,563
1915	6,932
1916	8,430
1917	8,820
1918	9,237

The total for 1919 cannot be accurately estimated at the time of writing, chiefly because the printers' strike has interfered with the compilation of the figures. It may be estimated, however, at about 8,000.

Fiction.—Although very vigorous, American fiction in 1919 has not been as interesting as often, partly because of the intrusion of attractions from the outside and partly because of its own failings. Joseph Conrad's *The Arrow of Gold* was enough to discourage many readers and writers of domestic drama, and the extraordinary popularity of the novels of Blasco Ibañez must have had a more distinct and more general effect. Even lesser matters, like the publication of the works of Leonard Merrick, issued with prefaces by other distinguished men of letters, or the choice by Mr. Galsworthy of the *Cosmopolitan* as a vehicle for reaching the American public, may have reduced the demand and thus affected the supply of the native product. The figures of production of books classified in the publishers' reports as fiction by American authors is as follows:

1914	689
1915	643
1916	703
1917	707
1918	594

For 1919 we estimate the figure at about 600.

Aside from these rather mechanical details, the chief matter of annual interest in American fiction has been for many years the production or recognition of some novel which was a thoroughly satisfying expression of the real vitality and vigor of America. Unfortunately one of the best accredited authorities on the subject will not give its judgment for 1919 until long after the YEAR BOOK has gone to press. We mention, therefore, the award of the Pulitzer Prize for the year 1918, although the novel selected is not included in our survey. The award of $1,000 for "the American novel which shall best present the wholesome atmosphere of American life and the highest standard of American manners and manhood" was made to Booth Tarkington for *The Magnificent Ambersons* (A. Y. B., 1918, p. 796), which was certainly a readable and "worth while" book. There were probably some who thought Mrs. Watts's *The Boardman Family* quite as good a picture of sane and wholesome American life, and some who felt that Miss Cather's *My Antonia* was a more beautiful piece of work than either, whatever was to be said of the life which it presented. But most novel readers will have been well pleased with the award. When it comes to 1919, it is hard to predict what the award will be. Mr. Tarkington's *Ramsey Milholland* (Doubleday, Page) may win the prize for him again, for it is a very popular book, and we will not suggest anything else. It may be said, however, that the year's fiction does not include any novels of American life by those who have been thought heretofore most competent to write them. A lot of American novels that has nothing by Mrs. Wharton, Miss Canfield (as she is still called on her title pages), or Miss Cather cannot have the best that we can do, except by the happy chance of some one's emerging who would not previously have been thought of. Sherwood Anderson and Theodore Dreiser come to mind in this connection, though neither has published what could technically be called a novel. Sherwood Anderson's *Winesburg, Ohio* (Huebsch) has so much real feeling for American life and character that one wishes it were a real masterpiece. It lacks constructive power, however, being made up of sketches and stories some of which appeared a good while ago in *The Seven Arts*. It is also too much marred by boyish and sensual fancies to be thought of as a masterpiece. But it does give something which it is better to catch in the tavern than to lose outright even in the temple. It would not be long thought of by one in search of the most wholesome manners and manhood of America, but it does at least suggest that possibly the best pictures of American life and manners can not be entirely sane and wholesome. Mr. Dreiser in the past has not shown much constructive power and he too has suffered from the imputation of sensuality, but his *Twelve Men* (Boni & Liveright) has neither of these faults. These stories have the characteristics of his best work, being founded on wide knowledge and presented with unfailing realism.

Besides these books that have something out of the ordinary about them, there are many others that are good in the well known way that most of us like. We offer a list of what may fairly be called "studies of American life," though a number of them are too highly charged with excitement of divers kinds to allow us to rely on the view presented: Henry G. Aikman, *The Groper* (Boni & Liveright); Josephine D. Bacon, *On Our Hill* (Scribner); Mary H. Bradley, *The Wine of Astonishment* (Appleton); Alice Brown, *The Black Drop* (Macmillan); Zona Gale, *Peace in Friendship Village* (Macmillan); Ellen Glasgow, *The Builders* (Doubleday, Page); Daniel C. Goodman, *The Taker* (Boni & Liveright); Will N. Harben, *The Cottage of Delight* (Harper); Joseph Hergesheimer, *Linda Condon* (Knopf); Arthur Hodges, *The Bounder* (Houghton, Mifflin); Julie M. Lippman, *Flexible Ferdinand* (Doran); George Barr McCutcheon, *Sherry* (Dodd, Mead); Grace S. Mason, *His Wife's Job* (Appleton); Christopher Morley, *The Haunted Bookshop* (Doubleday, Page); Arnold Mulder, *The Outward Road* (Houghton, Mifflin); Kathleen Norris, *Sisters* (Doubleday, Page); William D. Pelley, *The Greater Glory* (Little, Brown); Fleta C. Springer, *Gregg* (Harper); Julian Street, *After Thirty* (Century); Booth Tarkington, *Ramsey Milholland* (Doubleday, Page); Mary H. Vorst, *I've Come to Stay* (Century); Mary H. Watts, *From Father to Son* (Macmillan).

Such a list (even by its omissions) shows considerable material to choose from, but there are many more novels of a different character. The sane and healthful picture of American life, however desirable, is not the most popular thing just now among either the writers or the readers. The novel of "mystery, adventure, romance" is much more obvious, as always, and also more numerous. Our remark last year (A. Y. B., 1918, p. 786) that this passion for excitement was the result of the war was so severely discouraged by an able literary periodical that we will not repeat it but merely wish that we could suggest something better. The fact seems to be that not only are there more stories of adventure (in all sorts of places from the now commonplace wilds of the Canadian Northwest to the romantic walks of Greenwich Village), but also more detective or mystery stories, more stories of domestic emotion, more excitement, in a word, than for several years past. The critics have noted one or two streaks, as one may say, in the general tendency that seem not quite as they should be. It has been pointed out (C. M. Greene, *Bookman*) that those who have heard so much about the high imaginative and spiritual plane to which the world would be uplifted by the war have been disappointed by the material, even commercial, tone of the majority of the novels of the day. Many people beside the book reviewers have wondered at similar results in other expressions of human interest. This does not prove that high imagination and true spirituality were not among the results of the war; it is more likely that such results as these have actually occurred (who can doubt it?), but that it will take some time before they can really manifest themselves in works of art, if not elsewhere. We give a list of the more obvious of the romantic novels, noting that there is much more than usual of the "lure of the untamed West," a pretty sure sign of conventionality; every story here might be described (one of them has been) as a "story of gripping intensity and unusual happenings interwoven with a splendid romance," or if not, it comes pretty near it: David Anderson, *The Blue Moon* (Bobbs, Merrill); Marion Bower and Leon M. Lion, *The Chinese Puzzle* (Holt); B. M. Bowers, *Rim o' the World* (Little, Brown); George A. Chamberlain, *Not All the King's Horses* (Bobbs, Merrill); Robert W. Chambers, *In Secret* (Doran); Dane Coolidge, *Silver and Gold* (Dutton); Ridgewell Cullom, *The Law of the Gun* (Jacobs); James Oliver Curwood, *The River's End* (Houghton, Mifflin); Zane Gray, *The Desert of Wheat* (Harper); Emerson Hough, *The Sagebrusher* (Appleton); Elizabeth Jordan, *The Girl in the Mirror* (Century); H. H. Knibbs, *The Ridin' Kid from Powder River* (Houghton, Mifflin); Jeremy Lane, *Yellow Men Sleep* (Century); Sinclair Lewis, *Free Air* (Harcourt, Brace & Howe); Caroline Lockhart, *The Fighting Sheperdess* (Scribner); F. C. Macdonald, *Sorcery* (Century); A. Merritt, *The Moon Pool* (Putnam); Roy Norton, *Drowned Gold*, (Houghton, Mifflin); A. B. Reeve, *The Soul Scar* (Harper); Vingie Roe, *Tharon of Lost Valley* (Dodd, Mead); Bertrand Sinclair, *Burned Bridges* (Little, Brown); Charles Alden Seltzer, *The Ranchman* (McClurg); Robert Watson *The Girl of the O. K. Valley* (Doran); Honoré Willsie, *The Forbidden Trail* (Stokes); George F. Worts, *Peter the Brazen* (Century).

As always there are a good many books which cannot be pigeonholed as realistic or romantic. Nice, more or less idyllic stories are: C. B. Kelland, *The Little Moment of Happiness* (Harper); Sidney McCall, *Christopher Laird* (Dodd, Mead); Marie C. Oehmler, *A Woman Named Smith* (Century); Henry van Dyke, *The Broken Soldier and the Maid of France* (Scribner). Among the best tales of humor or extravagance so popular and so characteristic a feature of our literature are: Montague Glass, *Potash and Perlmutter Settle Things* (Harper); Wallace Irwin, *The Blooming Angel* (Doran); Peter C. MacFarlane, *The Exploits of Bilge and Ma* (Doubleday, Page); Alice Duer Miller, *The Charm School* (Harper); Harry Leon Wilson, *Ma Pettingill* (Doubleday, Page).

Mary Johnston, our chief writer of historical novels, may come at the end of our list with her *Michael Forth* (Harper), a story of Civil War Reconstruction which recalls some of her best work.

The obvious interest of the war is still important, though more in the periodical press than in books. The magazines continue to show great interest in war topics. A curious little controversy arose in the spring on "the *Atlantic* in war time." A reviewer of DeWolfe Howe's history of the *Atlantic* mentioned elsewhere had spoken of that magazine's "comparative indifference to the Civil War." The statement was challenged, and the reviewer, although conceding verbal indiscretion, pointed out that although there were in every number of the *Atlantic* of the Civil War several articles on war-topics there were always many more entirely untouched by it, whereas in the *Atlantic* even of the present day there are hardly any articles absolutely unconnected with the great struggle. This deep and continued interest, however, does not show itself so much in the more permanent form of books.

Not only is there less of the superficial interest in war topics, but there is less of the deeper emotion that may be supposed to have been stirred by the war. The two problems of a noneconomic nature, or perhaps we should say most capable of literary treatment, that have been most deeply stirred by the war are our feelings about sex and about religion. Yet neither of these motives makes much of an appearance in the literature of the day except in a superficial or perfunctory way.

There have been published two treatises on fiction, Wilson Follet's *The Modern Novel* (Knopf) and Clayton Hamilton's *Manual of the Art of Fiction* (Doubleday, Page). These works have been described by a professional novelist (Henry B. Fuller) in two characteristic sentences. One "whirs and sweeps, aviator-like, through the thin, keen air of theory," and the other "burrows thoroughly and faithfully . . . accomplishes a good amount of serviceable earthwork and helps ventilate and rearrange the general soil." The characterization is not absolutely true to fact but points toward it.

Short Stories.—Of the short story we can, as usual, give but slight account. The mass of short stories published in the popular periodicals is so great that it is a life work to deal with it. Unfortunately E. J. H. O'Brien's *Best Stories of 1919* (Small), like a great deal else that would be useful to the maker of summaries, does not come out in time for us to use. But as we have not mentioned his studies of the work of 1918, it will not be amiss to quote an opinion which we imagine he will repeat in his book on 1919. "There has been a marked ebb this year," he remarks, "in the quality of the American short story. Life these days is far more imaginative than any fiction can be and our writers are dazed by its forceful impact." Something of the same sort, we have thought, might be said of fiction in general. Still, there have been rather more good collections of short stories (relatively) than good novels. We have already mentioned in another connection Mr. Anderson's and Mr. Dreiser's books, which are more like collections of short stories than novels, and though they have no constructive unity, as we may say, they are conceived practically as wholes and are meant to be read as wholes. But quite as good are several others of which the following must serve as a general note. Dorothy Canfield's *The Day of Glory* (Holt) is a volume of stories suggested by her experiences in France; like its immediate predecessor, it shows her fine devotion to a cause as well as her recognized literary ability. Much the same thing might be said of Mrs. Deland's *Small Things* (Appleton); one almost regrets that these writers have been prevented by broader opportunities and the necessities of events from looking around upon their own country. E. L. White has written no novel in 1919, but his *Song of the Sirens* (Dutton) is excellent and has a substance and flavor of its own, like the rest of the work of this author. Joseph Hergesheimer's *The Happy End* (Knopf) is characteristic of the author's usual fine method. Henry van Dyke's *The Valley of Visions* (Scribner) is a collection of stories suggested by his experiences during the war.

Poetry.—Poetry continues to be a challenge to the general reader, or perhaps better an invitation to come and play, even if it be only on the cellar door in the backyard. It is perhaps too scornful and imperious to be an invitation and too gay and childlike to be a challenge, but it has the elements of both. In spite of being occasionally squalid and blasphemous (O. W. Firkins, *Nation*) and more often noisy, it has enough in the way of stronger qualities to make us rather indifferent to its weaknesses. This year Louis Untermeyer has voiced the spirit of the time in his *The New American Poetry* (Holt), and the *New Republic* during the summer made possible a good focussing of different lines of thought by publishing at one time a review of the book by Conrad Aiken with a rejoinder by Mr. Untermyer. The two utterances presented persuasively the two tendencies which may now be observed in American poetry, as well, it may be added, as in American literature as a whole, namely, the feeling for a national and therefore a broadly sympathetic and democratic poetry of ideas and a more definitely æsthetic poetry devoted simply to the love of beauty. It seems as if the poetry of the year was more of the latter kind than of the former. Another book on American poetry is *New Voices* (Macmillan) by Mrs. Marguerite Wilkinson, a book which has had much of the popularity it deserves and shows the popular interest in criticism and poetry, for the book is not only an anthology, but a piece of criticism as well. When it comes to mention particular books of poetry, the task seems so difficult that one wishes to shut his eyes and pick out blindly. We have not followed this course, but another, namely, the selection of something representative in as many different lines as possible, and our order of mention is surely good, being alphabetical: Conrad Aiken, *The Channel Rose* (Four Seas); Stephen V. Benet, *Young Adventure* (Yale Univ. Press); Berton Braley, *Buddy Ballads; Songs of the A. E. F.* (Doran); John Jay Chapman, *Songs and Poems* (Scribner); John G. Fletcher has published not only *The Tree of Life* (Macmillan), but has given those who like theory as well as practice "A Rational Explanation of *Vers Libre*" in the *Dial* of Jan. 11; there has been published a memorial edition of the *Poems, Essays, and Letters* of Joyce Kilmer (Doran) who fell in the war in 1918; Amy Lowell, *Pictures of the Floating World* (Macmillan); John G. Neihardt, *The Song of Three Friends* (Macmillan); Leonard Van Noppen, U. S. N. R. *The Challenge.* The best poems read before the Poetry Club of America during the season of 1918–19 were "Wooden Ships" by David Morton and "Bluestone" by Marguerite Wilkinson; the authors divided the National Arts Prize of $250.

Biography.—No one now living had so many biographies written during his lifetime as Theodore Roosevelt. His death is so recent that no "final" biography has yet appeared, but a sort of pendant to his own account of his life has been published in a series of *Letters to His Children* (Scribner), full of the childlike spirit of real happiness and the love of the realities of life that made him such a sympathetic companion with grown people as well as younger ones. A true and unusual light is thrown on Roosevelt's character in *Bill Sewall's Story of T. R.* (Harper). W. W. Sewall was a Maine guide who had often lived with Roosevelt in the woods and knew him in ways that others were not so likely to see. William R. Thayer's *Life of Theodore Roosevelt* (Houghton, Mifflin) is the most worthy of mention among several other lives published. Among the most characteristic of the many lives of Americans that appear every year is *An American Idyll: The Career of Carleton Parker* (Atlantic Monthly Press) by his wife. Professor Parker was a very unusual man, and this story of his life is not only absorbing and stimulating by its own vitality, but by its suggestion of ideas concerning American education and social problems. Dr. W. T. Grenfell is enough of an American for us to include his autobiography (fortunately still unfinished) *A Labrador Doctor* (Houghton, Mifflin). The most important biography of the year, however, is the *Life of Henry Fielding* by Prof. W. L. Cross (Yale Univ. Press), a remarkable work of laborious inquiry and sympathetic scholarship such as has not appeared for a long while.

Whether it come more properly under the present head or the next we are not sure, but waiving the question, we find great interest in *The Early Years of the Saturday Club, 1850–1870*, by E. W. Emerson (Houghton, Mifflin). Such records are very likely to degenerate into literary gossip, but even literary gossip about our own fathers is of value. Mr. Emerson rises above anything of the sort and gives us a valuable chronicle of one of the literary periods of our history. Of somewhat similar interest, although a slighter work, is M. A. DeWolfe Howe's *The Atlantic Monthly and Its Makers* (Atlantic Monthly Press), an account of one of the most important of the many factors which produced the literature of our country during the last half-century. It does not belong just here, but somewhere must be mentioned Brand Whitlock's great book on *Belgium* (Appleton). To tell the truth the author was so much a part of what he saw that the book is almost as much biography as history. However it be classed, it is an addition to the really memorable books of the year.

Essays.—There appear to be rather more volumes of what in literature are called simply "essays" than there used to be. Here would come Don Marquis's *Prefaces* (Appleton) and F. L. Dunne's *Mr. Dooley on Making a Will and Other Necessary Evils* (Scribner), characteristic productions of humorists of very different types, as well as many more. But of more real importance is John Burrough's *Field and Study* (Houghton, Mifflin), not the last, it will be hoped, of the long row of volumes of the author's essays which have charmed and instructed so many freinds. This volume contains something of the observation of wood and field that we always desire to have of Mr. Burroughs, but it gives mostly his meditations and observations of the spiritual life. Mr. Burroughs says: "When I write about Nature and make much of her beauties, I am writing about God." It tells quite as much as one could otherwise about this kind of literature (in which America has been preëminent) to quote this one sentence from her most popular master of it. It is not an essay, but we also note here William Beebe's *Jungle Peace* (Holt), a truly literary work of a man who, although (or perhaps because) he is a scientist, has a finely imaginative mind as well as an easy gift of expression.

Necrology.—There have died during the year Mrs. Harriet Miller, better known as Olive Thorne Miller, the writer on nature, on Christmas Day, 1918; Theodore Roosevelt, Jan. 6th; Charles E. Van Loan, the best of our writers of sporting stories, March 2; Amelia E. Barr, so long read and loved, March 10; William Morton Payne, long connected with the *Dial*, July 10; John Fox, Jr., the novelist of the Southern mountains, July 8; William N. Harben, one of whose novels is mentioned above, Aug 7; Henry Mills Alden, for more than half a century editor of *Harper's Magazine*, Oct. 7; and Ella Wheeler Wilcox, long and widely known for her verse, Oct. 30.

MODERN LANGUAGES AND LITERATURE

ENGLISH LANGUAGE AND LITERATURE

ALBERT C. BAUGH

Progress in Research.—The period of readjustment has not had as yet a very stimulating effect on English scholarship in America. Although research has continued during 1919 much as it went on during the war, it has resulted chiefly in a goodly number of limited investigations, but has hardly produced any work on a large scale that can be considered of preëminent importance. This, however, was to be expected. Now that the difficulties of research have been materially decreased, we may expect extensive work in English scholarship to be resumed in the United States with gratifying results.

English Philology.—Samuel Moore and T. A. Knott have prepared a short book on the *Elements of Old English*. Frederick Klaeber writes "Concerning the Functions of O. E. *geweorthan* and the Origin of German *gewähren lassen*" (*JEGP* [1]). G. I. Flom discusses "The Origin of the Place-name *Keswick*" (ibid.), and Miss J. M. Lyons in "Frisian Place-names in England" (*PMLA*) supports a view as old as Procopius that the Frisians played a prominent part in the Teutonic settlement of Britain. C. D. Buck has a very interesting article on a fragment of an early Italian bronze urn containing "An ABC Inscribed in Old English Runes" (*MP*). Mention may be made of O. B. Schlutter's "Old English Lexi-

---

[1] Periodicals are cited under the following abbreviations: *MLN, Modern Language Notes; MLR, Modern Language Review; MP, Modern Philology; PMLA, Publications of the Modern Language Association of America; JEGP, Journal of English and Germanic Philology; SP, University of North Carolina Studies in Philology; RR, Romantic Review.* Titles appearing as theses or in the publications of universities are followed where possible by the name of the university.

cal Notes" (*MLN*) and H. G. Shearin's lengthy review (*ibid.*) of Callaway's studies in Old English syntax (*cf. A. Y. B.*, 1918, p. 771). In Middle English Samuel Moore has published *Historical Outlines of English Phonology and Middle-English Grammar*, J. F. Royster has given us "A Note on French-English Word Pairs in Middle English" (*MP*), and John C. Mendenhall has printed a thesis on *Aureate Terms* (Pennsylvania), in which he shows that the fashion by which fifteenth-century English writers adorned their style with rare and unusual words was the product of a continuous clerkly tradition of literary study and criticism. Two books are concerned with the English language in this country: H. L. Mencken's *The American Language: A Preliminary Inquiry into the Development of English in the United States* and G. P. Krapp's *The Pronunciation of Standard English in America*.

Old-English Literature (449–1150). —In Old-English literature *Beowulf* has attracted its usual attention. W. W. Lawrence has published a study of "The Dragon and His Lair in *Beowulf*" (*PMLA*), Frederick Klaeber, Carleton Brown, and Samuel Moore consider textual difficulties (*MLN* and *JEGP*), and W. E. Leonard examines "*Beowulf* and the Niebelungen Couplet" (Wisconsin). A. S. Cook has edited *The Old-English Elene, Phoenix, and Physiologus* and discussed "The Authorship of the Old English *Andreas*" (*MLN*), making a point which he thinks indicates that Cynewulf was the author. O. F. Emerson offers textual "Notes on Old English" (*MLR*), J. W. Bright and R. L. Ramsey present "Notes on the West-Saxon Psalms" (*MLN*), and H. R. Patch studies the slight "Liturgical Influence in The Dream of the Rood" (*PMLA*) as it came from those parts of the church service devoted to the celebration of the cross.

Middle-English Literature (1150–1500).—One of the important poems of early Middle-English literature has had new light thrown upon it by H. B. Hinckley on "The Date of *The Owl and the Nightingale*" (*MP*). Allusions in the poem are used to place its composition between 1176 and 1178. Miss H. E. Allen has printed brief notes "On Richard Rolle's Lyrics" and "A New Latin MS. of the *Ancren Riwle*" (MLR). H. R. Patch treats "Some Elements in Medieval Descriptions of the Otherworld" (*PMLA*). In "The Castle of the Body" (*SP*) C. L. Powell gathers together passages illustrating the allegorical conception of the body as a world, city, or castle. Miss G. G. King discusses "The Vision of Thurkill [in Matthew Paris and Roger of Wendover] and Saint James of Compostella" (*RR*), and Miss G. Schoepperle traces in Celtic literature the superstition of "The Washer of the Ford" (*JEGP*). O. F. Emerson in "Middle-English *Cleanness*" (*PMLA*) has added to a rapidly growing body of textual commentary. Miss C. D'Evelyn, "Piers Plowman in Art" (*MLN*), criticizes an article by E. W. Tristram on "*Piers Plowman* in English Wall Painting." In the romance J. Douglas Bruce has completed his series of long and valuable articles on "The Composition of the Old French Prose *Lancelot*" (*RR*), and in "Mordrain, Corbenec, and the Vulgate Grail Romances" (*MLN*) argues convincingly for the authorship of both romances at Corbie. W. A. Nitze has published the first part of an article "On the Chronology of the Grail Romances" (*MP*), this part being concerned primarily with the determination of the date of the *Perlesvaus* as shortly after 1191. A. C. L. Brown has also begun a study of "The Grail and the English *Sir Perceval*" (*ibid.*), the first part of which is devoted to showing that *Sir Perceval of Gales* is independent of Chrétien's *Conte du Graal*. "The Sources of *St. Erkenwald* and *The Trental of Gregory*" (*ibid.*) by J. R. Hulbert, "Notes on the *Tristan* of Thomas" (*MLR*) by R. S. Loomis, and "Jacques de Vitry and *Boeve de Haumtone*" (*MLN*) by Miss L. A. Hibbard are concerned with other romances. M. B. Ogle, "Some Theories of Irish Literary Influence and the *Lay of Yonec*" (*RR*), shows that there were classical and oriental sources from which the materials of the *Lay* could have been derived. T. P. Cross discusses the chastity-testing mantle in "The Gaelic 'Ballad of the

Mantle'" (*MP*). In the field of popular poetry H. M. Belden has considered the "Folk-Song in America—Some Recent Publications" (*MLN*), and H. G. Shearin records versions of "*Lord Randal* in America" (*MLR*). In "King Cnut's Song and Ballad Origins" (*MLN*) Miss Louise Pound raises a question as to its position in the development of the ballad, and in "The Ballad and the Dance" (*PMLA*) she attacks the belief that the ballad and the song had their origin in the dance. Mention may finally be made of two more general items in Middle English: Miss M. B. Carr's "Notes on a Middle-English Scribe's Methods" (Wisconsin) and the *Census of Incunabula* in America, edited by G. P. Winship (*Bull. New York Public Library*).

Chaucerian scholarship has produced rather slighter results in 1919 than usual, although there are papers of genuine worth to record. Karl Young in "Aspects of the Story of Troilus and Criseyde" (Wisconsin) examines the bearing of the principles of courtly love upon the *rôle* of Pandarus and upon Criseyde's attitude toward marriage. H. R. Patch considers "Troilus upon Predestination" (*JEGP*). H. M. Ayres, "Chaucer and Seneca" (*RR*), makes the most out of the rather slight debt Chaucer owes to Seneca, and E. F. Shannon, "Chaucer and Lucan's *Pharsalia*" (*MP*), reviews the recorded borrowings from Lucan and adds one or two. H. R. Patch writes of "Chaucer's Desert" (*MLN*) in the *House of Fame*, and W. E. Farnham suggests further folk-lore connection for "The Fowls in Chaucer's Parlement" (Wisconsin). E. F. Amy has published a study of *The Text of Chaucer's Legend of Good Women* (Princeton). Miss M. Fabin, "On Chaucer's *Anelida and Arcite*" (*MLN*), compares Chaucer's poem with Machaut's *Lai de la Souscie*. Miss F. M. Grimm investigates the *Astronomical Lore in Chaucer* (Nebraska), and T. O. Wedel studies *The Medieval Attitude Toward Astrology, Particularly in England* (Yale). Brief notes include O. F. Emerson's "Chaucer's Opie of Thebes Fyn" (*MP*), containing two instances of Chaucer's familiarity with mediæval medicine, and J. D. Bruce's note on a proverbial expression in the "Prologue to the Canterbury Tales" (*MLN*).

The early drama has received some attention. G. R. Coffman has published "The Miracle Play in England: Some Records of Presentation, and Notes on Preserved Plays" (*SP*). Karl Young in "A New Version of the *Peregrinus*" (*PMLA*) prints a text from a manuscript in Madrid. L. Wann considers "The Influence of the French Farce on the Towneley Cycle of Miracle Plays" (*Trans. Wis. Acad.*). Miss M. C. Lyle discusses *The Original Identity of the York and Towneley Cycles* (Minnesota), and Miss F. H. Miller, "The *Northern Passion* and the Mysteries" (*MLN*), adduces further parallels showing that the author of the York passion plays used the *Northern Passion* extensively.

Modern English Literature (since 1500).—One of the most useful aids to the study of a poet, if it is properly used, is a concordance to his works. In *A Subject-Index to the Poems of Edward Spenser* C. H. Whitman has filled a long felt want. A. H. Gilbert in "Spenser's Imitations of Ariosto: Supplementary" (*PMLA*) makes additions to those listed by Dodge, and W. P. Mustard traces "E. K.'s Classical Allusions" (*MLN*). The same writer offers a few "Notes on Lyly's *Euphues*" (*ibid.*). S. Harkness analyzes "The Prose Style of Sir Philip Sidney" (Wisconsin). H. E. Rollins discusses "The Date, Authors and Contents of *A Handful of Pleasant Delights*" (*JEGP*), and J. H. H. Lyon has published *The New Metamorphosis, Written by J. M., Gent., in 1600* (Columbia). H. E. Rollins has given us an elaborate and comprehensive study of "The Black-Letter Broadside Ballad" (*PMLA*), and has shown, "Concerning Bodleian Ms. Ashmole 48" (*MLN*), that it is a compilation of much less importance than is generally attached to it. He has also written at some length of "Martin Parker, Ballad-Monger" (*MP*). Miss E. M. Albright in "*Ad Imprimendum Solum*" (*MLN*) maintains against Pollard that the expression did mean "sole rights to printing" and not "to printing only"

(*MLN*). Pollard has replied in the *Library*.

Shakespeare and the Elizabethan drama are subjects of perennial interest. A. H. Tolman has published a series of "Shakespeare Studies" (*MLN*), discussing Shakespeare's supposed references to his marriage, the choosing of the caskets, the epic character of Henry V, and drunkenness in Shakespeare. He has also considered the question, "Why Did Shakespeare Create Falstaff?" (*PMLA*), in a suggestive article, which, however, illustrates a tendency in modern Shakespearean criticism to see in each accidental circumstance a deep or subtle artistic purpose. M. P. Tilley writes on "Shakespeare and the Puritan's 'Pensive Regard for the Well-Bestowal of Time'" (*JEGP*). *King John* has been issued in the Variorum Edition, edited by Horace Howard Furness, Jr. E. E. Stoll has published *Hamlet: An Historical and Comparative Study* (Minnesota). W. W. Lawrence's "The Play Scene in *Hamlet*" (*JEPG*) treats an important and strangely neglected matter, discussion of which has been stimulated by an article of W. W. Greg (*MLR*). H. D. Gray examines the purpose of "The Dumb Show in Hamlet" (*MP*), and H. A. Doak discusses "Ghosts in Shakespeare" (North Dakota). J. D. Rea points to the *Naufragium*, one of the colloquies of Erasmus, as "A Source for the Storm in *The Tempest*" (*MP*), and L. Mason records some "Stray Notes on *Othello*" (*MLN*). Tucker Brooke in "*Titus Andronicus* and Shakespeare" (*MLN*) attacks a paper by H. D. Gray (*cf. A. Y. B.*, 1917, p. 726), thereby provoking a protest from R. M. Alden in "*Titus Andronicus* and Shakespeare Dogmatics" (*ibid.*) and a reply by Gray (*ibid.*). T. M. Parrott in "Shakespeare's Revision of *Titus Andronicus*" (*MLR*) has also considered the problem involved in this play, deciding upon superficial revision by Shakespeare in scenes that he thinks can be approximately determined by metrical tests. J. Q. Adams, "Shakespeare, Heywood, and the Classics" (*MLN*), believes that the company that joined with the Queen's men in the production of Heywood's *Ages* was none other than Shakespeare's, the King's men. Other Shakespearean literature includes E. P. Kuhl's "Shakespeare and *The Passionate Pilgrim*" (*MLN*), A. Morgan's "What Meres Knew About Shakespeare's Sonnets: A Reply to Dr. Carpenter" (*Cath. World*), G. R. Havens' "The Abbé Prévost and Shakespeare" (*MP*), and E. G. Lawrence's *Sidelights on Shakespeare*.

Next to Shakespeare Ben Jonson has been most popular with the critics. J. D. Rea has edited *Volpone* (Yale); D. L. Clark discusses the renaissance theory of poetry and rhetoric in "The Requirements of a Poet: A Note on the Sources of Ben Jonson's *Timber*, Paragraph 130" (*MP*); L. H. Harris considers "Lucan's *Pharsalia* and Jonson's *Catiline*" (*MLN*) and "Local Color in Ben Jonson's *Catiline* and Historical Accuracy of the Play" (*Class. Philol.*); and J. Q. Adams has recorded the vicissitudes of "The Bones of Ben Jonson" (*SP*). J. M. Steadman, Jr., in "The Dramatization of the Robin Hood Ballads" (*MP*), considers the extant plays but not those known only by title. Various sources and parallels are recorded in B. M. Woodbridge's "Marlowe and Jean de Meung" (*MLR*), F. L. Schoell's "G. Chapman's 'Commonplace Book'" (*MP*), E. K. B.'s "*Locrine* and the *Faerie Queene*" (*Nation*), and H. F. Schwarz's "John Fletcher and the *Gesta Romanorum*" (*MLN*). Heywood's *The Captives, or The Lost Recovered* has been edited by A. C. Judson (Yale), and Massinger's *Duke of Milan* by T. W. Baldwin. Lacy Lockert has written of "Marston, Webster, and the Decline of the Elizabethan Drama" (*Sewanee Rev.*). Theatrical matters have received some consideration. In "The Housekeepers of the Globe" (*MP*) J. Q. Adams traces the ownership of the various shares from the organization of the theater until the building was pulled down in 1644. He has also cast doubt upon the identity of "An 'Hitherto Unknown' Actor of Shakespeare's Troupe?" (*MLN*). A. Thaler, "Playwrights' Benefits, and Interior Gathering in the Elizabethan Theater" (*SP*), supplements Lawrence's work on these two topics, and G. F. Reynolds discusses in an interesting paper "Two Conventions of the Elizabethan Stage." (*MP*).

Of seventeenth-century writers Milton has received most attention. A. H. Gilbert has compiled *A Geographical Dictionary of Milton* (Cornell), and E. N. S. Thompson has written on "Milton's Knowledge of Geography" (*SP*). Gilbert has studied "The Cambridge MS. and Milton's Plan for an Epic" (*ibid.*) and pointed out "A Parallel between Milton and Seneca" (*MLN*). R. E. N. Dodge discusses "Theology in *Paradise Lost*" (Wisconsin); G. Sherburn in "The Early Popularity of Milton's Minor Poems" (*MP*) lists chronologically the references to the poem down to 1740; D. H. Stevens considers "The Order of Milton's Sonnets" (*MP*); and J. H. Hanford follows "Milton and the Return to Humanism" (*SP*) through the ages. Notable books have also been written about the English Bible. J. H. Penniman's *A Book About the English Bible* is the most complete discussion. Others include W. L. Phelps' *Reading the Bible*, C. A. Smith's *Keynote Studies in Keynote Books of the Bible*, and D. H. Kyes' *The Literary Style of the Prophetic Books of the English Bible*. S. R. Shafer has traced the course of *The English Ode to 1660* (Princeton). S. E. Leavitt writes on "Paul Scarron and English Travesty" (*SP*). H. M. Belden rallies to Dryden's defense in "The Authorship of 'Macflecknoe'" (*MLN*). D. N. Smith has edited a collection of *Characters from the Histories and Memoirs of the Seventeenth Century*, and J. B. Wharey compares "Bunyan's *Holy War* and the Conflict Type of Morality Play" (*MLN*). In the later drama we may mention L. Wann's "The Oriental in Restoration Drama" (Wisconsin), J. F. Bradley's record of borrowing that amounts to plagiarism in "Robert Baron's Tragedy of *Mirza*" (*MLN*), D. Miles' "A Forgotten Hit: *The Nonjuror*" (*SP*), and Miss L. B. Campbell's "A History of Costuming on the English Stage between 1660 and 1823" (Wisconsin).

In the eighteenth century J. M. Beatty, Jr., points to "Charles Churchill's Treatment of the Couplet" (*PMLA*) as a revolt against the correctness of Pope, and also examines "The Political Satires of Charles Churchill" (*Trans. Wis. Acad.*). C. A. Moore discovers "A Predecessor of Thomson's *Seasons*" (*MLN*), Miss C. Rinaker discusses "Thomas Edwards and the Sonnet Revival" (*ibid.*), and H. W. O'Connor "The Narcissa Episode in Young's *Night Thoughts*" (*PMLA*). G. B. Denton rejects "A Stanza Ascribed to Thomas Gray" (*MP*); A. H. R. Fairchild gives us an interesting little study of "Robert Bloomfield" (*SP*), a minor eighteenth-century poet; and R. C. Whitford goes at length into "Satire's View of Sentimentalism in the Days of George the Third" (*JEGP*). In the eighteenth-century novel R. S. Crane, in "A Note on Richardson's Relation to French Fiction" (*MP*), has proved Warburton's authorship of the preface pointed out by G. C. Macaulay, and the unsoundness of Macaulay's conclusions based on it. Miss H. S. Hughes also discusses "Richardson and Warburton" (*ibid.*). W. Cross in "The Legend of Henry Fielding" (*Yale Rev.*) shows us the real Fielding in contrast with the "bibulous spendthrift and libertine of tradition." Other Fielding items include "Fielding Notes" (*MLN*) by C. W. Nichols, "Fielding's Miscellanies" (*MLR*) by J. E. Wells, and "The Covent-Garden Journal Extraordinary" (*MLN*) by G. E. Jensen. W. Kurrelmeyer records "A German Version of *Joseph Andrews*" (ibid.), and Miss H. S. Hughes publishes "Notes on Eighteenth-Century Fictional Translations" (*MP*). Mention may also be made here of W. Taylor's "The Prose Style of Johnson" (Wisconsin), R. F. Jones' *Lewis Theobald: His Contribution to English Scholarship* (Columbia), H. A. Burd's "Eight Unpublished Letters of Joseph Ritson" (*Trans. Wis. Acad.*), and Miss J. Patton's *The English Village: A Literary Study, 1750–1850*.

The romantic revival in English literature has received considerable attention. F. B. Snyder offers "Notes on Burns's First Volume" (*MP*). Lane Cooper writes on "Wordsworth's Knowledge of Plato" (*MLN*), Miss M. Mead on "Wordsworth's Eye" (*PMLA*), and A. Beatty on "Joseph Fawcett: The Art of War. Its Relation to the Early Development of

William Wordsworth" (Wisconsin). A. W. Crawford, "On Coleridge's *Ancient Mariner*" (*MLN*), suggests that the poem was a criticism of the spiritual feebleness of the church of his day. Miss A. D. Snyder discusses *The Critical Principles of the Reconciliation of Opposites as Employed by Coleridge* (Michigan), and J. H. Hanford considers "Coleridge as a Philologian" (*MP*). Miss M. R. Thayer writes on "Keats: The Eve of St. Mark" (*MLN*), and A. Harvey has published a volume on *Shelley's Elopement*. S. C. Chew in "The Centenary of *Don Juan*" (*Am. Jour. Philol.*) gives a bibliographical survey of the poem and its many sequels. He has also reviewed "The Pamphlets of the Byron Separation" (*MLN*). J. W. Draper's "The Social Satires of Thomas Love Peacock" (*MLN*) and notes by E. Bureta and M. A. Buchanan on "Spanish Ballads Translated by Southey" (*MLN*) should also be recorded.

"Rossetti Studies" have been published by A. E. Trombly (*South Atlantic Quart.*), and "*Festus and The Blessed Damozel*" (*MLN*), by A. D. McKillop, records Rossetti's indebtedness to the former poem. W. B. D. Henderson has written on *Swinburne and Landor: A Study of Their Spiritual Relationship and Its Effect on Swinburne's Moral and Poetical Development*. Miss A. T. Harding combines "Shelley's *Adonais* and Swinburne's *Ave Atque Vale*" (*Sewanee Rev.*). Miss M. E. Mead has published *A Catalogue of The Dr. Samuel A. Jones Carlyle Collection* (Michigan). F. W. Roe considers "Ruskin and the Sense of Beauty" (Wisconsin), and W. F. De Moss traces "An American Influence on John Ruskin" (*ibid*). G. B. Denton, "Herbert Spencer and the Rhetoricians" (*PMLA*), finds wholesale borrowings in *The Philosophy of Style*. In the novel O. F. Emerson prints "Two Notes on Jane Austin" (*JEGP*), R. B. Johnson has gathered together a collection of essays on *The Women Novelists* and Miss M. Tomlinson has written on "The Beginnings of George Eliot's Art" (*Sewanee Rev.*). R. E. Burton has prepared *Dickens: How to Know Him*, and W. C. Phillips has published *Dickens, Reade and Collins,*

Sensation Novelists. A Study in the Conditions and Theories of Novel Writing in Victorian England (Columbia). Lane Cooper has done a very difficult piece of annotating in his edition of Meredith's *Essay on Comedy*, and O. J. Campbell considers "Some Influences of Meredith's Philosophy upon His Fiction" (Wisconsin). Miss R. D. Cornelius discusses "The Clearness of Henry James" (*Sewanee Rev.*), and W. B. Cairns, "Character Portrayal in the Work of Henry James" (Wisconsin). H. Maynadier throws "A Brick at a New Literary Idol" (*Sewanee Rev.*), namely, Samuel Butler's *Way of All Flesh*. A volume on recent literature is J. W. Cunliffe's *English Literature during the Last Half Century*. R. N. Whiteford discusses *Motives in English Fiction*, A. Mordell, *The Erotic Motive in Literature*, and J. F. L. Raschen, "Earlier and Later Versions of the Friendship Theme" (*MP*), part one being concerned with the Damon and Pythias story. Stylistic matters are treated in W. Strunk's *The Elements of Style*, H. L. Creek's "Philosophies of Style" (*JEGP*), P. Seiberth's "The Rhythmical Line" (*ibid.*), M. W. Croll's "The Cadence of English Oratorical Prose" (*SP*), and Miss A. L. F. Snell's "Notes on the Form of *The Dynasts*" (*PMLA*), a continuation of studies listed in the YEAR BOOK for 1918 (p. 771). Miss A. R. Burr's *The Autobiography*, Lane Cooper's "The Making and the Use of a Verbal Concordance" (*Sewanee Rev.*), L. M. Price's *English-German Literary Influences* (California), and W. B. Cairns' *British Criticism of American Writings, 1783–1815* (Wisconsin), are miscellaneous titles requiring mention. G. P. Baker has published an authoritative book on *Dramatic Technique*, L. B. Roland has specialized on *The Technique of the One-Act Play*, and B. H. Clark has collected an anthology of *European Theories of the Drama*. C. E. Whitmore examines "The Nature of Tragedy" (*PMLA*) and formulates "A Definition of Lyric" (*ibid*). In comparative literature Miss R. I. Goldmark's *Studies in the Influence of the Classics on English Literature* (Columbia), Miss E. Nitchie's *Virgil and the English*

Poets (ibid.), and Miss M. L. Lilly's The Georgic: A Contribution to the Study of the Vergilian Type of Didactic Poetry (Hesperia) are all dissertations on the relation of English literature to the classics. One of the most important of recent books is J. L. Lowes' Convention and Revolt in Poetry, a collection of lectures delivered originally at the Lowell Institute.

GERMANIC LANGUAGES AND LITERATURES

Daniel B. Shumway

German Literature.—Although the armistice with Germany has existed for over a year there has been no sign of renewed interest in German literature in the popular magazines. The scientific periodicals contain, as usual, many interesting articles. In the field of the drama the *Poet Lore* translations still continue to acquaint the people of this country with the best in modern German literature; thus, Hofmannsthal's *Madonna Dianora*, Hartleben's *Hanna Jagert*, Kleist's *Feud of the Schroffensteins*, and Hebbel's *Maria Magdelena* have been translated for this series and published (Badger). In addition, translations of Schnitzler's *Gallant Cassian* (Phillips, LeRoy) and Sudermann's *Silent Mill* (Brentano) have been issued. The *Life and Works of Friedrich Hebbel* by T. M. Campbell is also announced (Badger). In the field of literary criticism J. H. Randall discusses the "Problem of Wilbrandt's Meister von Palmyra" (*Mod. Philol.*, June, 1919). A number of interesting articles have appeared on Goethe. Julius Goebel presents "Reminiscences of Plato in Goethe's Faust" (*Jour. Engl. and Ger. Philol.*, April, 1919). John A. Walz gives a new interpretation of the figures hovering over the place of execution in the brief scene, *Nacht, Offen Feld*, of *Faust* (*Mod. Lang. Notes*, May, 1919). M. J. Rudwin in an article *"Des Teufels Schöpferrolle bei Goethe"* (*Neophilologus*, iv, 319) traces the idea of the devil doing creative work back to the Gnostics and shows that Goethe obtained it from Arnold and Jacob Böhme. Wm. C. Cooper treats the "Revision and Completion of Tasso" (*Publ. Mod. Lang. Assoc.*) W. Kurrelmeyer in an article entitled "A Contemporary Criticism of Schiller's Räuber (*Jour. Engl. and Ger. Philol.*, Jan., 1919) reviews a criticism of this play, which appeared in 1783 and which had hitherto escaped the notice of biographers and literary critics. He suggests that the unknown author was J. J. Gerstenberg, the well known translator of Shakespeare.

In the field of fiction the most important publication is that of the life of the mediæval rogue, *Tyl Ulenspiegel in the Land of Flanders and Elsewhere*, a novel written originally by C. T. DeCoster in Dutch but dealing with a German subject. In this case the translation was made from the French version by Geoffrey Whitwith (McBride). An excellent German translation has existed for a number of years. An article dealing with the same subject will be found in the *Nineteenth Century* for January under the title, "*Legende de Thyl Uylenspiegel*, Legend of Old Flanders." A well written essay by H. J. Weigand attempts an interpretation of Heine's odd work, *Das Buch LeGrand* (*Jour. Eng. and Ger. Philol.*, Jan., 1919), calling it a satirical Aristophanic comedy. Martin Schütze continues his "Studies in the Mind of Romanticism by discussing the determining factors in the action and structure of Kleist's dramas (*Mod. Philol.*, June, 1919). O. Walzel, "*Die künstlerische Form der deutschen Romantik*" (*Neophilologus*, iv), treats the artistic theories of the romanticists. D. F. Passmore discusses *Gutzkow's Short Stories* (Banta).

In the field of the lyric a short article in the *Literary Digest* of March 29 gives a survey of German poems appearing during the war and emphasizes the growing importance of Stefan Georg. Jessie Lemont has made a faithful and quite successful translation of the modern German lyricist Rainer Maria Rilke (T. C. Wright), and Martin Schütze apropos of this translation speaks of the same poet as one of the lyrical gem makers of Germany at present (*Dial*, May, 1919). The beautiful lyrics of Walther von der Vogelweide, which never grow old have been englished by Frank Betts (Longmans). An admirable study of *Paul Gerhardt as a Hymn Writer and His Influence on English Hymnody* from the pen of T. S. Hewett has been issued (Yale Univ. Press). The "Humor of Wilhelm Busch" is the subject of an article by T. C. von Stockum (*Neophilologus*, iv).

In older literature there deserve mention the publication of the Middle High German poem *Von dem Jüngsten Tage* by L. C. Willoughby (Oxford Univ. Press) and the "Metrical Study of Georg Rudolf Weckerlin" (*Hesperia*, No. 10.) Although philosophy is not usually treated in this article, one is tempted to mention the excellent work of Wm. Salter on *Nietzsche, the Thinker* (Holt), which is by far the best book in English on this much discussed philosopher.

German Philology.—The articles in the field of German philology all concern themselves this year with word studies. F. A. Wood, "Germanic Etymologies" (*Mod. Lang. Notes*, April, 1919), traces the etymology of 18 different words. W. Kurrelmeyer, "German Lexicography" (*ibid.*, May, 1919), gives early occurrences of 12 different military loan words in German, the same scholar also discusses "Contributions to German Lexicography from the Translation of Heinrich von Eppendorff," of the sixteenth century (*Publ. Mod. Lang. Assoc.*). Aaron Schaffer treats the "Hebrew Words in Gryphius' Horribilicribifax (*Jour. Eng. and Ger. Philol.*). In the field of syntax J. Alexis published a *Study of the German Relative in the Eighteenth Century* (Banta), M. Diez treats *Analogical Tendencies in the German Substantive* (*Univ. of Texas*), and F. W. Pierce, in "The German Adjective and the Use of the Umlaut in its Comparison" (*Mod. Lang. Jour.*, Feb., 1919), presents a useful tabulation of the different classes of adjectives.

German Texts and Teaching.—In the field of German texts and teaching nothing of special importance has appeared. M. L. Perrin and Joel Hathaway have prepared an edition of Baumbach's popular tale *Der Schwiegersohn* (C. E. Merrill). Two tales of Johanna Spyri, *Beim Weidenjoseph* and *Moni der Geissbub*, have been issued (Scott), and the same author's famous child's tale *Heidi* has been published (Saalfield). T. B. Hewett and H. A. Farr prepared a little volume of *German for the American Soldier* (New Haven, Whitlock). Philip S. Allen published a practical German course, *German Without a Teacher* (Drake).

German-American Relations.—Clement Vollmer has written an excellent study of the *American Novel in Germany from 1871-1913* (*Americana Germanica Press*), and L. M. Price has published a full and valuable bibliography of all works dealing with the *Influence of English on German Literature* (*Univ. of Cal.*).

Scandinavian.—In the general Scandinavian field the *American Scandinavian Review* contains, as usual, many translations of stories and poems from Scandinavian languages, as well as articles on the various Scandinavian countries. In the Swedish field the most important publication is the translation of Selma Lagerlöf's powerful novel *Gösta Berling's Saga*, by Lillie Tudeer, for the American Scandinavian Foundation. In this connection it is worthy of note that the gripping story by the same authoress, *The Girl of the Marshcroft*, is being exhibited as a motion-picture film by the International Press Association. Anna Olsson's stories for children have been published under the title *Angelus Gåva* (Augustana Book Co.).

In the Norwegian field the most important publication is the translation of Johan Bojer's strong novel, *The Great Hunger*, by W. J. C. Worster and C. Archer. It is a story of the struggles of a boy of the lower classes much like Frenssen's Jörn Uhl. Björnsen's play *En Fallit* has been edited with an introduction and notes by J. A. Holvik (Augsburg Publ. Co.). In the field of research Wm. H. Eller has written an able study, *Ibsen in Germany, 1870-1900*, for the series "Studies in Literature" (Badger). A. LeRoy Andrews in a short article, "Further Influences upon Ibsen's Peer Gynt" (*Jour. Engl. and Ger. Philol.*, Jan., 1919) speaks of the indirect influence of Goethe's *Faust* through Heiberg's *En Sael efter Döden*.

Dutch.—In the Dutch field much more activity is to be noted than usual. B. K. Kuiper has translated into Dutch Blasco Ibanez' famous novel, *The Four Horsemen of the Apocalypse*, under the title, *De Vier Paarden uit Openbaring* (Eerdmann & Sevensma). The same firm has also published two stories from the life of the Frisian people, *De jonker van Sterrenburg* and *Mooie Marie* by G. I. van der Ploeg. Wouter Nijhoff and M. E. van Kronenberg have prepared a *Nederlandsche Bibliographie* from 1500–1540 (Stechert). M. Goodman has treated of the *Dutch and English on the Hudson* (Yale Univ. Press) and B. K. Kuiper of the Dutch in the United States under the title *Ons Opmaken en Bouwen* (Eerdmann & Sevensma). Another volume in the Dutch language containing a wealth of material for use at festivals and lectures, etc., has been issued by the same firm under the title *Voor Onze Feesten, Voordrachten en Samenspraken*. It was compiled by A. Meyer.

ROMANCE LANGUAGES AND LITERATURES

George L. Hamilton

French.—The aftermath of the war is as unfavorable to scientific research as the war itself. Since we have not suffered the loss of some of the most promising of our younger scholars, as is the case of the European nations, if we have the men, we shall have the occasion in the future to make more serious contributions to erudition, in Romance scholarship as in other fields, than in the past.

In the year 1919 the most extensive and original work of American Romance scholars has been done in the field of Old-French literature. T. A. Jenkins in writing "On alleged Anglo-Normanisms in the Oxford *Roland* (*Mod. Philol.*, xvi, 369) has made an important contribution to the language and date of the best of the French epics. In his "The Descendants of Ganelon—and of Others" (*Rom. Rev.*, x, 149) G. L. Hamilton has shown how a general trait becomes individualized in certain prominent characters. Elizabeth S. Tyler in her Notes on the *Chançun de Wil-lame* (*ibid.*, ix, 396) makes some useful suggestions on the poem of which she has brought out a very convenient edition (Oxford Univ. Press). Laura A. Hibbard in a note on "Jacques de Vitry and *Boeve de Haumstone*," (*Mod. Lang. Notes*, xxxiv) shows how an episode in the adventures of a Crusader has been utilized in more than one French epic. E. S. Sheldon makes some cautious suggestions in his "Notes on Foerster's Edition of *Ivain*" (*Rom. Rev.*, x, 233), while in writing on the date of "*Ile and Galeron*" (*Mod. Philol.*, xvii, 383) he shows reason to discredit the early date of 1167–8, assigned to this work of Gautier d'Arras. J. D. Bruce continues and completes his learned researches on "The Composition of the Old French *Lancelot*," (*Rom. Rev.*, ix, 353; x, 48, 97), and in a note on "Mordrain, Corbenic, and the Vulgar Grail Romances" (*Mod. Lang. Notes*, xxxiv, 385) he discusses the sources and names of certain episodes in the connected group of Arthurian romances. In the first of his articles "On the Chronology of the Grail Romances, I. The Date of the *Perlesvaus*" (*Mod. Philol.*, xvii, 151) W. A. Nitze undertakes to establish definitely his thesis of the early date of one of these works, while in his "Eric's Treatment of Enide" (*Rom. Rev.*, x, 26) he clings vigorously to his own opinion on the motive of Chrétien de Troies' work. A. L. C. Brown in "The Grail and the English *Sir Perceval*" (*Mod. Philol.*, xvi, 553, xvii, 261) throws new light on the independent origin of the English poem on the same theme. R. Loomis throws light upon mediæval literary themes through his iconographical studies, for which he is so well prepared, in his "Notes on the *Tristan* of Thomas" (*Mod. Lang. Rev.*, xiv, 38) and his "Allegorical Siege in the Art of the Middle Ages" (*Am. Jour. Archæol.*, xxiii, 255), while R. T. Hill undertakes to present a critical text of "*La Vie de Sainte Euphrosine*" (*Rom. Rev.*, x, 159, 191), and Alma de L. Le Duc writes on "The Pastoral Theme in French Literature in the Fourteenth and Fifteenth Centuries" (*Mod. Lang. Rev.*, xiv, 398). While T. P. Cross in his article on "The Gaelic Ballad of the Mantle" (*ibid.*, xvi,

649) emphasizes the fact that the most primitive motive appears in modern Celtic versions as showing a Celtic source of a widely diffused tradition found in French works of an early date, M. G. Ogle in his "Some Theories of Irish Literary Influence and the Lay of *Yonec*" (*Rom. Rev.*, x, 123) shows how world-wide is another tale which some scholars find purely Celtic. M. Fabin, writing "On Chaucer's *Anelida and Arcite*" (*Mod. Lang. Notes*, xxxiv, 266), wishes to show the indebtedness of the English poet to Machant's *Lai de la Souscie*. Hélène J. Harvitt shows the high regard in which "Hugues Salel, Poet and Translator" (*Mod. Philol.*, xvi, 595) was held by his contemporaries, if he is only remembered by students of the Renaissance as a translator of the *Iliad*. R. G. Usher in writing on "Francis Bacon's Knowledge of Law French" (*Mod. Lang. Notes*, xxxxiv, 28) throws light on our information about the schooling of a great man and the continued survival of the bastard form of Norman French among English lawyers as late as the seventeenth century. H. C. Lancaster adds to our knowledge of Jodille and Colet in a note in the *Romanic Review* (x, 173), and A. G. H. Spiers has a suggestive article on "Corneille's *Polyeucti* Technically Considered" (*Mod. Lang. Rev.*, xiv, 44). H. Ashton in "The Confession of the *Princess of Clèves*" elucidates further an episode of *Le Princesse de Clèves* of Mme. de la Fayette, based on an episode in the life of Mme. de Montespan. S. E. Lett in writing on "Paul Scarron and English Travesty" (*Univ. of N. C. Studies in Philol.*, xvi, 108) points out how inferior is the type of literature produced in England at the close of the seventeenth century in imitation of French works of the same character. W. Kurrelmeyer in a study on "the Source of Wieland's *Don Sylvio* (*Mod. Philol.*, xvi, 637) shows how largely the German writer is indebted to a French fairy romance of the eighteenth century in one of his works, and the same author has also shown his indebtedness to the most famous of French picaresque novels for names, episodes, and even verbal phrases in a note on "*Gil Blas*, and *Don Sylvio*" (*Mod. Lang. Notes*, xxxiv, 78). R. S. Crane in "A Note on Richardson's Relation to French Fiction" (*Mod. Philol.*, xvi, 495) shows that the English novelist was not indebted to any French models, however much such an influence may be instanced, as is shown by Helen S. Hughes in her "Notes on Eighteenth-Century Fictional Translation" (*ibid.*, xvii, 225). Irving S. Babbitt's historical and critical study on *Rousseau and Romanticism* (Houghton, Mifflin), is as well informed, as suggestive, and as irritating as his earlier valuable works on modern French literature. G. Chinard makes a further contribution to his studies on the sources of Chateaubriand in the introduction and notes to his edition of *Les Natchez, Livres* I and II (*Univ. of Cal. Publ. in Mod. Philol.*, vii, 201), and W. Girard in the completion of his work, of special interests to Americans, "*Du transcendantalisme considéré sous son aspect social*" (*ibid.*, 1) devotes most of his space to discuss the French origins of the movement. A. R. Nykl in a note on "The Talisman in Balsoc's *Peau de Chagrin*" (*Mod. Lang. Notes*, xxxiv, 479) shows how the great novelist thought his readers would be even more ignorant than himself in his treatment of the object around which one of his most widely read stories centers, and P. F. Baum, writing on "The Young Man Betrothed to a Statue" (*Publ. Mod. Lang. Assoc.*, xxxiv, 523) sets forth the long pedigree of the theme of one of Merimée's stories, *Venus d' Ille*. S. P. Shanks in his book on Anatole France gives a well written sketch and appreciation of the life and work of the greatest of contemporary French authors. M. M. Dondo under the title of "*Vers libre*" (*Publ. Mod. Lang. Assoc.*, xxxiv) discusses the rhymical values of the work of the apostles of this advanced school of poetry. A. G. J. Spiers in his paper on "An Ill-Advised Criticism of Cyrano de Bergerac" (*Univ. of N. C. Studies in Philol.*, xvi, 102) takes up the cause of Rostand against the most severe of his critics, Magne, who has impugned the accuracy of the historical details of this celebrated drama.

Spanish.—G. T. Northrup in an article on "The Imprisonment of King

Garcia" (*Mod. Philol.*, xvii, 393) traces the evolution in literature of the fate of the hapless King of Galicia, who died in 1090. R. Schevill in his volumes on Cervantes in the Series of "Master Spirits of Literature" (Duffield), has given us a well considered and readable account of the life and work of the greatest of Spanish authors. J. L. Perrin in his article on "Don Garcia de Mendoza in Ercilla's *Araucana*" (*Rom. Rev.*, ix, 430) shows the part played by the hero in this, the first work of literary merit written on the Western Hemisphere. S. G. Morley continues his studies on the versification of the Spanish poets in his "Studies in Spanish Dramatic Versification of the *Siglo de Oro*, *Alarcón* and *Moreto*" (*Univ. of Cal. Publ. in Mod. Philol.*, vii, 130), and in the same publications we find two interesting articles on nineteenth-century writers, one (*ibid.*, 87) by Elizabeth McGuire, "A Study of the Writing of D. Mariano José de Larra, 1809-1837," in which particular attention is given to the indebtedness of this justly popular writer to French models, and the other, in which more than justice is done to the minor novelist and reactionary, Francisco Navarro Villoslado, by Beatrice Q. Cornish (*ibid.*, 1).

Italian.—A. H. Krappe in a note on "The Legend of the Glove" (*Mod. Lang. Notes*, xxxiv, 16) adds something to our knowledge of the story, of Italian literary origin which was the basis of Schiller's "*Der Handschuh*" but is better known to English readers in the forms of Leigh Hunt and Browning. E. Goygio has gathered some notes on the study of Italian in this country in his "Dawn of Italian Culture in America" (*Rom. Rev.*, x, 250). E. H. Tuttle continues to make suggestions which throw light upon various individual phonetic phenomena in his "Hispanic Notes: *Azarilaziago;* B for U" (*Rom. Rev.*, x, 170), while in his studies on "Vowel-Breaking in Southern France" (*Mod. Philol.*, xvi, 585) and "Notes on Romanic Speech-History (*Mod. Lang. Rev.*, xiv, 105), he shows a capacity for dealing with more general linguistic principles in a way that attracts attention. O. M. Johnston follows the historical development of a French syntactical phrase in his note on "*Que for Jusqu'à ce que* with *Atendre*" (*Mod. Lang. Notes*, xxxiv, 282).

ANCIENT LITERATURE AND PHILOLOGY

GREEK LITERATURE

WILLIAM ARTHUR HEIDEL

Owing to conditions arising from the war certain books that should have received attention earlier can only now be noticed; others already published have not yet come to hand and report of them must be postponed. The publication of a second edition, revised and enlarged, of Van Leenwen's *Euchiridium Dictiones Epicae* (Leyden, Sigthoff, 1918) is to be heartily welcomed.

The Greek dramatists have, as usual, claimed a large share of the attention of writers. A welcome little volume gives *The Acharnians of Aristophanes* as played by the Oxford University Dramatic Society in February, 1914, in a Greek text based on that of the Oxford Classical Texts and in the excellent translation into English verse, reprinted by permission, by R. Y. Tyrrele (Oxford Univ. Press, 1914). *Studies in Greek Tragedy* by Louise E. Matthaei (Cambridge Univ. Press, 1918), founded on lectures given at Newnham College, devotes separate chapters to the *Prometheus Bound* of Æschylus, to the *Ion, Hippolytus*, and *Hecuba* of Euripides, and to the use of accident in plots. These studies are brightly phrased and well considered, being in fact a valuable contribution to the understanding of dramatic literature. Two volumes of the "Columbia University Studies in Classical Philology" should not be overlooked in this connection, namely, Miss Pearl C. Wilson's treatment of *Wagner's Dramas and Greek Tragedy*, and Wm. S. Messer's *The Dream in Homer and Greek Tragedy*. The latter particularly adds not a little to our knowledge of poetic technique in a matter hitherto hardly considered. *The Crimes of the Oedipodean Cycle*, by Henry Newpher Bowman (Badger, 1918), is of some slight value, which is, however, in no way related to the chief interest of the author, for his purpose was to apply the principles of Freud to the interpretation of these myths. One may recognize a certain degree of truth in the Freudian analysis of dreams without sharing Mr. Bowman's enthusiasm for Dr. Abraham's *Dreams and Myths* or believing that this kind of study is likely to shed much light on the Greek dramatists. A consideration of "The Heracles Myth and Its Treatment by Euripides," by G. L. Hendrickson, deserves to be ranked with Miss Matthaei's studies. It is one of the *Classical Studies in Honor of Charles Forster Smith* (see also *Latin Literature, infra*), written by his colleagues (Univ. of Wisconsin, 1919). The same volume contains papers on "The Source of Herodotus' Knowledge of Artabazus," by A. G. Laird, and "A Study of Pindar," by Annie M. Pitman, besides an interesting discussion of certain Fayum papyri, under the title of "An Egyptian Farmer," by W. L. Westermann.

Translations of various Greek works have appeared, chiefly in the Loeb Classical Library (Putnam). Here it is a pleasure to record that Professor Perrin has so promptly completed the sixth and seventh volumes of his admirable translation of Plutarch's *Lives*. Dewing offers the third volume of *Procopius;* C. D. Adams gives a worthy rendering of *The Speeches of Æschines;* and G. W. Butterworth translates three essays of Clement of Alexandria. The first volume of Xenophon's *Hellenica*, containing Books I-V, by C. L. Brownson, is measurably faithful but hardly to be commended as a model; and the version of Pausanias by W. H. S. Jones, of which the first volume has appeared. cannot be regarded as superior to Frazer's, though this instalment gives promise of an excellent and handy edition of that important author. *Selected Essays of Plutarch*, Vol. II, by A. O. Prickard (Clarendon Press, 1918), contains in a charming English translation a number of important treatises, such as that "On the Genius of Socrates," the three "Pythian Dialogues." and that "On Delay in Divine Punishment." F. M. K. Foster's *English Translations from the Greek* (Columbia Univ. Press, 1918) gives a bibliographical survey of real interest and value to the student of classical influences in English literature. A book on this subject, *The Classical Influence in English Literature in the Nineteenth Century and Other Essays and Notes*, by William Chislett, Jr. (Stratford Co., 1918), is too sketchy and inadequate to be of great service. Rarely does one find so delightfully sane an exposition of the claims and possibilities of classical studies as in the charmingly written essay. entitled *Religio Grammatici: The Religion of a Man of Letters*, delivered by Gilbert Murray as the presidential address to the (British) Classical Association (Houghton, Mifflin, 1918). *The History of Religions*, by E. W. Hopkins, (Macmillan, 1918), contains an interesting chapter (xxii) on "Greek Religion." W. R. Halliday's *Greek Divination* (Macmillan, 1913) is a valuable study, though incomplete, and should have been noticed earlier in this series of reviews of Greek literature.

Pagan Ideas of Immortality during the Early Roman Empire, the Ingersoll Lecture (1918) by C. H. Moore (Harvard Univ. Press, 1918), presents a clear sketch of an interesting subject without giving a satisfactory explanation of the origin or associations of these ideas. A work of capital importance is Ernest Barker's *Greek Political Theory—Plato and his Predecessors* (Methuen, 1918). The emphasis on Plato's *Laws* is especially to be commended. L. W. Hopkinson's *Greek Leaders* (Houghton, Mifflin, 1918) contains 11 biographical sketches which may be recommended to teachers of Greek history for collateral reading. T. R. Glover's *From Pericles to Philip* (Macmillan, 1917) treats in an exceptionally vivid way the main events of the greatest period of Greek history. The book will prove to be of equal interest to the general reader and to the historian. *The Platonism of Philo Judæus*, by J. H. Billings (Univ. Chicago Press, 1919), a dissertation of distinct value, discusses exhaustively a subject debated for centuries. *The Biblical Antiquities of Philo*, now first translated from the old Latin version by M. R. James (Macmillan, 1917), is in fact a pseudonym, for it has no relation to Philo. Nevertheless it is a most valuable addition to our resources for the study of the Jewish background of early Christianity. The Society for Promoting Christian Knowledge, to whose support we owe this publication, gives us two other works of equal interest in good English versions: *St. Dionysius of Alexandria; Letters and Treatises*, by E. L. Feltoe, and the *Lausiac History of Palladius*, by W. K. Lowther Clarke. The former will interest students of Epicurus, the latter those who study early monasticism.

We have yet to mention three volumes which more than any of those listed above reflect honor on classical scholarship in America. Two of these should have received earlier notice, *The Old Testament Manuscripts in the Freer Collection* and *The New Testament Manuscripts in the Freer Collection*, both edited by Henry A. Sanders of the University of Michigan (Macmillan, 1917, 1918). Not only are these Greek manuscripts of great interest in connection with the tradition of the texts, but the work of the editor is so entirely adequate to his subject that it will occur to no one to begrudge him the exceptional privilege he has enjoyed of giving to the world publications of such importance. Another work of somewhat similar character is *Aristotelis Meteorologicorum Libri Quattuor. Recensuit indicem verborum addidit F. H. Fobes* (1919). The editor after elaborate preparation and detailed preliminary publication of the results of studies in the manuscript tradition of the *Meteorologica* of Aristotle now gives us a model critical edition of the text, which is sure to be the standard for many years to come. The Aristotelian treatise is in fact one of the most important documents for the historian of Greek science in its earlier stages, and he is bound to use this edition with a confidence he could not have in those of Bekker and Ideler, which are based on a far more limited knowledge of the manuscript tradition. One cannot refrain from thanking the syndics of the Harvard University Press for the worthy publication of so excellent a work.

LATIN LITERATURE

CHARLES KNAPP

It is again possible to record studies in Lucretius and Vergil. C. H. Herford is author of an interesting lecture on *The Poetry of Lucretius* (Longmans). M. S. Slaughter well discusses "Lucretius, the Poet of Science," in *Classical Studies in Honor of Charles Forster Smith* (see below). C. Knapp in "An Analysis of Lucretius, De Rerum Natura I–III," (*Class. Weekly*, xiii) aims to help students to follow Lucretius' thought and the workings of his mind; a by-product of the paper is its proof that transpositions of Lucretius' verses from the places they occupy in the manuscripts is unsound procedure. G. D. Hadzsits discusses carefully "Lucretius as a Student of Roman Religion" (*Trans. Am. Philol. Assoc.*, xlix). H. R. Fairclough has completed his translation of Vergil (Loeb Classical Library) with a rendering of *Aeneid*, vii–xii and of all the poems in the *"Appendix Vergiliana."* W. Warde Fowler continues his masterly studies in Vergil with a volume entitled *The Death of Turnus: Observations on the Twelfth Book of the "Aeneid"* (Longmans). A very useful book is *Vergil and the English Poets* by Elizabeth Nitchie (Columbia Univ. Press).

Every study that deals at all carefully with the earliest remains of Latin writing is welcome. Such a study is T. Frank, "The *Columna Rostrata* of C. Duilius" (*Class. Philol.*, xiv). Admitting the charge that the epitaph as we have it is too fulsome and rhetorical to be attributed to the Romans themselves in 260 B. C., a score of years before Latin literature can fairly be said to begin, Frank accounts for these characteristics by supposing that, in the absence of Roman models, Duilius naturally adopted the style of the Greek honorific inscriptions to be seen in every city of Sicily. He thinks the inscription goes back to 260 B. C., but that, about 150 B. C., some one filled out certain illegible places in the orthography of that day. Our extant version is due to a second restoration made in the early Empire. (See also *Indo-European Philology, infra.*)

In *Classical Philology* (xiv) H. W. Prescott published the sixth of a series of papers on "The Antecedents of Hellenistic Comedy," criticizing the methods of modern students of Roman comedy (Plautus and Terence) and questioning the processes by which they seek to prove the dependence of that comedy on Euripides. C. Knapp (*Class. Philol.*, xiv) discusses "References to Plays, Players, and Playwrights in Plautus and Terence," and also (*Am. Jour. Philol.*, xv). "References to Literature in Plautus and Terence," grouping allusions to the stories (*e. g.*, that of Io, Jason, Hercules, the stories of the Trojan cycle) that figure so largely in Greek literature, especially Greek dramatic literature. E. H. Sturtevant in a paper entitled "The Coincidence of Accent and Ictus in Plautus and Terence" (*Class. Philol.*, xiv) proves once more that in early Latin verse accent and quantity both were factors. He stresses the *rôle* played by accent; he holds, further, that the Latin accent was at once expiratory and musical and dismisses the view of C. E. Bennett that ictus was not stress, but merely the quantitative prominence of the long part of a foot.

In connection with Cicero we note that E. P. Winstedt's translation of the *Letters* (Loeb Classical Library) is now complete (three volumes). Catharine Saunders, in a paper entitled "The ΠΑΛΙΝΩΔΙΑ of Cicero" (*Class. Philol.*, xiv) maintains that the palinode referred to by Cicero, *Ad Atticum*, iv, 5, was a communication sent by Cicero to Pompey, or perhaps directly to Cæsar himself, containing assurances that Cicero would withdraw opposition to Cæsar, in particular on the question of the Campanian land law. This novel view rests on a careful study of various speeches of Cicero, etc. L. H. Harris, "Local Color in Ben Jonson's *Catiline* and Historical Accuracy of the Play" (*ibid.*), notes that Jonson followed his sources (Cicero, Sallust, Plutarch) closely, as a result doing grave injustice to Catiline, who was not as black as these writers paint him. Of interest also to students of Cicero are the articles by C. N. Smiley and G. C. Fiske in *Classical Studies in Honor of Charles Forster Smith* (see below).

Livy's capacity for painting pictures instinct with dramatic imagination and colored with lively human sympathy has often been remarked. R. S. Conway, in a lecture entitled *The Venetian Point of View in Roman History* (Longmans), thinks that in all this Livy was in thorough accord with the tendencies of the Venetian district in which Padua, Livy's birthplace, was situate; the Venetian race, he says, has from the earliest times been remarkable for artistic ability, which culminated in the great painters of the Renaissance.

In connection with Catullus we may note an important article by A. L. Wheeler, "Remarks on Roman Poetic Diction" (*Class. Weekly*, xii), and of interest to students of Cæsar is an article by F. S. Dunn, "Julius Cæsar in the English Chronicles" (*Class. Jour.*, xiv).

A welcome addition to the limited body of material available for the study of Seneca's philosophical writings is an edition, with notes and a translation in French, of *Ad Helviam Matrem De Consolatione*, by Charles Favez. Of interest too is the paper by C. N. Smiley in *Classical Studies in Honor of Charles Forster Smith* (see below). Of great importance is the fine *"Index Verborum Quae in Senecae Fabulis Necnon in Octavia Reperiuntur"* by W. A. Oldfather, A. S. Pease, and H. V. Canter (*Univ. of Ill. Studies in Lang. and Lit.*, iv, Nos. 2-4).

R. B. Steele (*Am. Jour. Philol.*, xl) has a paper entitled "Curtius and Arrian," a demonstration of the extent to which the Latin author Q. Curtius Rufus employed the Greek writer Arrian as a source.

A welcome addition to our apparatus for the study of medieval Latin (the term "medieval" is used here in a very broad sense) is formed by a translation, in the Loeb Classical Library, by H. F. Stewart and E. K. Rand, of Boethius, the *Opuscula Sacra* and the *Philosophiae Consolatio;* and by F. M. Nichols' *Epistles of Erasmus*, Vol. III. In the latter work the epistles of Erasmus, from the earliest to those of his fifty-third year, are arranged in chronological sequence and translated; with the translation is a commentary that justifies the chronological arrangement and adds biographical data.

Worthy of special mention is the volume entitled *Classical Studies in Honor of Charles Forster Smith* (*Univ. of Wisconsin Studies in Lang. and Lit.*, No. 3), consisting of 10 papers by men and women at various times colleagues of Professor Smith at the University of Wisconsin. Of these papers the following are of importance to students of Latin literature (see also *Greek Literature, supra*): C. N. Smiley, "Seneca and the Stoic Theory of Literary Style," a paper of interest to students of Cicero also; G. C. Fiske, "The Plain Style in the Scipionic Circle," a discussion of certain phases of the style of the *Satires* of Lucilius and Horace and of the theories of humor held by these writers (of importance also to students of Cicero); Katharine Allen, "Britain in Roman Literature"; and M. S. Slaughter, "Lucretius, the Poet of Science."

Some reactions of scholars to the book by A. C. Clark, *The Descent of Manuscripts* (*A. Y. B.*, 1918, p. 781), may be noted. One is a review of the book, by C. F. Walters (*Class. Rev.*, xxxiv), a complimentary notice, reënforced by evidence purporting to show that the author had applied Clark's principles successfully to the restoration in various places of the text of Livy. The other is a review (*Class. Jour.*, xiv) by E. T. Merrill, who has worked much on the manuscripts of Pliny the Younger, which is decidedly critical, not to say skeptical, of Clark's methods and results in restoration.

Works less directly connected with Latin literature, but still of importance to workers in' that field, are the following: M. Platnauer, *The Life and Reign of the Emperor Septimius Severus* (Oxford Univ. Press); W. D. Gray, *A Study of the Life of Hadrian Prior to His Accession* (*Smith Coll. Studies in Hist.* iv, No. 2); A. E. R. Boak, "The Master of the Offices in the Later Roman and Byzantine Empires" (*Univ. of Michigan Studies, Humanistic Series*, xiv, Pt. i); G. Ferrero and C. Barbagallo, *A Short History of Rome* (three volumes), of which Vol. I treats the history down through the death of Julius Cæsar and Vol. II, the Empire from 44 B. C. to 476 A. D.; E. Pais, *Dalle Guerre Puniche a Cesare Augusto,* two volumes (Rome, Nardechia); E. Cocchia, *Il Tribunato della Plebe, la sua Autorita Giudiziaria Studiata in Rapporto colla Procedura Civile* (Naples, Pierro, 1917); Elizabeth O'Neill, *Rome: A History of the City from the Earliest Times;* W. Ridgeway, "The Value of the Traditions with Respect to the Early Kings of Rome" (*Class. Jour.*, xiv), an interesting attempt to show that it is futile to reject the traditional Roman account of the regal period of Rome, as Mommsen did on the grounds, first, that the state archives were burned in 390 B. C., and, second, that the traditional stories of the regal period contain supernatural elements. Ridgeway lays stress on the power of memory and oral tradition, and argues, by citing very modern instances, that the supernatural elements may well have attached themselves to what were at first plain and reasonably accurate accounts of actual happenings; C. D. Buck, "Words for 'Battle,' 'War,' 'Army,' and 'Soldier'" (*Class. Philol.*, xiv), an instructive paper, showing, for instance, how widely some ancient classical words for "army" and "soldier" have been appropriated by different nations; E. Meyer, *Cæsars Monarchie und das Principat des Pompejus: Innere Geschichte Roms von 66 bis 44 v. Chr.;* G. de Sanctis, *Storia dei Romani*, Vol. III; J. E. Sandys, *Latin Epigraphy: An Introduction to the Study of Latin Inscriptions* (Cambridge Univ. Press), a very useful book, giving a good collection of materials well arranged; E. B. Lease, "The Number Three, Mysterious, Mystic, Magic" (*Class. Philol.*, xiv) and "The Use and Range of the Future Participle" (*Am. Jour. Philol.*, xl). The latter paper shows that Ovid first realized the stylistic possibilities of the future participle; through Ovid and Livy this particple was brought to its highest development, and to the Latin world "many new and varied nuances of expression were given."

SEMITIC LANGUAGES AND LITERATURES

MORRIS JASTROW, JR.

With the termination of the war communication with Germany has been reopened, and German publishers and booksellers are sending broadcast bibliographies of important books that were issued between 1914 and 1919. The opportunity afforded by a catalogue issued by Harrassowitz of Leipzic to see what has been published in Germany during these years in the Oriental field justifies devoting the space here afforded to a brief survey of the recent activity of German and Austrian scholarship in Semitics. The record is a surprising one in respect to both quantity and quality. The war apparently did not hinder pupils and colleagues of eminent scholars from bringing out the inevitable *Festschrift* on the occasion of a scholar's sixtieth or seventieth birthday. Publications of this character containing larger or smaller collections of papers covering the semitic field have been issued in honor of Eduard Sachau, director of the Oriental Seminary in Berlin; Julius Wellhausen, the great Biblical critic (who died in April, 1917); Count Wolf von Baudissin; Ernst Kuhn, the eminent Indologist and comparative philologist of Munich; Fritz Hommel, also of Munich University; Friederich Karl Andreas; and Ernst Windisch. The list published by Harrassowitz covers almost 500 items of which about two-thirds represent contributions to Semitic philology and archæology and publications of texts; the remaining one-third deals with Egyptology and Indology. Despite the war even new scientific societies have been organized and serials such as *Der Islamische Orient* inaugurated. Periodicals and publications of the various learned academies have proceeded without serious interruption. Perhaps of most general interest is the activity that has been carried on during the war in Hittite researches. Before relations with the Central Powers were broken off, some preliminary reports had reached this country of a successful attempt on the part of an Austrian scholar, Friedrich Hrozny, to solve the mystery of the Hittite script. It now appears that Hrozny has published in three parts a series of Hittite studies, including a detailed analysis of his method of decipherment, together with specimen texts. That the attempt has been regarded as successful may be concluded from various monographs on the subject published by such scholars as Weidner of the University of Berlin and Holma of the University of Helsingfors. In addition, a large number of cuneiform texts from the Hittite center Boghazköi have been published by the German Orient Society. Although presumably many problems still remain to be solved before the decipherment can be said to be complete, it seems definite that the Hittite language has been shown to be Aryan in character, in itself a most important and somewhat astonishing result.

Another feature of the German publications in the Oriental field during the period of the war is the large number of monographs and larger works dealing with the historical and archæological problems in the realm of what until recently was the Turkish Empire. By the side of publication of Turkish documents, grammars, and philological publications, there are numerous large works dealing with art and monuments in the Turkish Empire, studies of geographical problems in Turkish lands, as well as many studies in the field of Arabic philology, all more or less connected with the relations between Turks and the various peoples of the Orient. No doubt this predominance of Turkish studies, leading to increased activity in the Arabic, Syriac, and Aramaic fields, reflects the high hopes entertained by Germany during the war of succeeding in her ambition to control the East. It will be interesting to see what influence the dashing of these hopes by Germany's defeat in the war will have on the direction to be taken by Oriental science in Germany during the next few years.

INDO-EUROPEAN PHILOLOGY
(Exclusive of the Germanic languages)

ROLAND G. KENT

The output of American scholars in Indo-European philology has been much diminished of late by the Great War, since many devoted themselves to the service of their country rather than to research; notably A. V. W. Jackson of Columbia spent several months in Mesopotamia and Persia with the Red Cross, where his acquaintance with the country, the languages, and the people, gained in three previous journeys, rendered him invaluable. Yet perhaps Oriental studies may prove to be a gainer rather than a loser from the war, since Americans have come to feel greater interest in foreign affairs, especially in those of Asia. In recognition of this changed attitude the American Oriental Society, at its meeting in Philadelphia in April, passed resolutions calling for a School of Modern Oriental Languages to be established in this country under Government auspices, at Washington or elsewhere, for the training of young men who may be going to the Orient in consular service or for purposes of commerce (*Jour. Am. Orient. Soc.*, xxxix, 144, 151, 185). The same Society also appointed a committee to prepare a statement setting forth the scope, character, aims, and purposes of Oriental studies, to be presented with the backing of the Society to the higher institutions of learning at which such studies are not represented, in the hope that the desirability of their inclusion in the college curriculum may become evident (*ibid.*, 153).

Two volumes by Maurice Bloomfield, on *Rig-Veda Repetitions* (xx and xxiv in the "Harvard Oriental Series," edited by C. R. Lanman) appeared early in 1919, illustrating the present delays in publication, since they bear the date 1916 on the title page. These list the repeated verses and distichs and stanzas of the Rig-Veda systematically, with critical commentary, facilitating comparative studies in this field. The same scholar's *Life and Stories of the Jaina Savior Pārçvanātha* (John Hopkins Univ. Press) contains the story of the life of the earlier of the two Jaina Saviors who are historical; he is said to have been born in 817 B. C. It includes, in the usual Hindu form of stories, the fundamental doctrines of the Jaina religion, which are here for the first time published to the Occidental world.

Bloomfield's "Fable of the Crow and the Palm Tree" (*Am. Jour. Philol.*, xl, 1) is a further article in his proposed encyclopædia of Hindu fiction, on the motif of a chance occurrence misunderstood as a cause; the crow alights on the tree just before it falls, and the bird's trifling weight appears to be the cause of the tree's fall (*cf.* previous studies by Bloomfield, *Jour. Am. Orient. Soc.*, xxxvi, 54; *Proc. Am. Philos. Soc.*, lii, 616, and lvi, 1; and by E. W. Burlingame, *Jour. Royal As. Soc.*, July, 1917, 429). In much the same field is W. N. Brown's "Pancatantra in Modern Indian Folklore" (*Jour. Am. Orient. Soc.*, xxxix, 1), a comparison of the stories found in that work with the forms in which they appear in the recorded current collections.

Franklin Edgerton has a further study in the Rig-Veda (*Am. Jour. Philol.*, xl, 175; *cf.* xxxv, 435, and *Jour. Am. Orient. Soc.*, xxxv, 240) on "The Metaphor of the Car in the Rigveda Ritual," in which he shows that the whole ritual performance is spoken of as a car, after the likeness of the car of the god Indra; on this basis he gives a new translation of the difficult Rigvedic hymns, x. 51–53, with brief explanatory comments.

In general phonetics, A. J. Carnoy, who has now returned to the University of Louvain after a brief stay at the University of California and a longer sojourn at the University of Pennsylvania, has an illuminating article on "The Real Nature of Dissimilation" (*Trans. Am. Philol. Assoc.* xlix, 101), wherein he advances the theory that dissimilation of sounds takes place by the failure to perform one movement of the articulation which the sound has in common with a preceding or following sound, thereby transforming the sound or making it so nearly identical with another sound familiar to the language, that the hearer repeats the word with the changed sound.

In Lithuanian, H. H. Bender makes some valuable observations in his review of *Lalis's Lithuanian-English and English-Lithuanian Dictionary* (published at Chicago), and of Juskevic's *Lithuanian-Russian Dic-*

tionary (incomplete) (*Am. Jour. Philol.*, xl, 321).

In the phonology of Latin, F. A. Wood advances new views on the development of Indo-European *w* after *t d p b m s* in his "Greek and Latin Etymologies" (*Class. Philol.*, xiv, 245), and E. W. Fay does the same on "The Phonetics of *MR*— in Latin" (*Class. Quart.*, xiii, 37). In semantics, I. D. Hyskell, on "Some Rare Meanings of *Excludo*" (*Class. Philol.*, xiii, 401), traces the development of the meaning "to fashion by hollowing out, carving," argues that it is not due to confusion with *excudo*, *excutio*, and *excido*, and restricts the range of meaning of *excudo*. In syntax, R. C. Flickinger presents a further chapter on "The Accusative of Exclamation" (*Trans. Am. Philol. Assoc.*, xlix, 27; cf. *Am. Jour. Philol.*, xxix, 303, and xxxiv, 276), in which he treats this construction from Lucretius to Ovid; and E. B. Lease writes on "The Use and Range of the Future Participle" (*Am. Jour. Philol.*, xl, 262), showing a very varied and extensive employment. Finally, Tenney Frank has notable observations on two Latin inscriptions of primary linguistic importance: he argues that the *Columna Rostrata* of C. Duellius underwent a restoration about 150 B. C., before its final restoration under the early Empire (*Class. Philol.*, xiv, 74); and he identifies the material of the Forum Stele as coming from north of Cremera, and hence set up either when the Etruscans were masters of Rome or when Rome possessed that part of Etruria. As the latter period is obviously too late, this Stele must, he says, date from the time of the Etruscan dynasty in Rome, which traditionally ended in 509 B. C. (*ibid.*, 87). (See also *Latin Literature, supra.*)

SUBJECT INDEX

American literature,
 39ff, 60ff, 69ff, 90ff,
 109ff, 130ff, 154ff,
 176ff, 196ff
Ancient literature, 1ff,
 23ff, 47ff, 83ff,
 102ff, 122ff, 146ff,
 169ff; see also
 Semitic literature
Classical philology, 6ff;
 see also Latin, Greek
Copyright, 16ff, 45ff
Danish literature, 35,
 56, 79, 99, 119, 143;
 see also Scandinavian
 literature
Dutch literature, 14, 56,
 120, 143, 209
English literature, 37ff,
 58ff, 81ff, 100ff,
 114ff, 135ff, 160ff,
 181ff, 201ff
Germanic languages, 11ff,
 32ff, 53ff, 76ff, 96ff,
 117ff, 140ff, 165ff,
 185ff, 207ff
Greek literature, 28ff,
 51ff, 84ff, 103ff,
 123ff, 147ff, 169ff,
 190ff, 211ff
Indo-European philology,
 86, 107, 128, 152, 174,
 194, 216; see also
 Indo-Germanic philology

Indo-Germanic philology,
 4, 26, 49f; see also
 Indo-European philology
Italian literature, 15ff,
 36ff; see also Romance
 languages and literature
Latin literature, 5ff,
 30ff, 52ff, 85ff, 104ff,
 125ff, 149ff, 171ff,
 191ff, 213ff
Norwegian literature, 14,
 34ff, 56ff, 78ff, 98,
 119, 143; see also
 Scandinavian literature
Romance languages, 14ff,
 35ff, 56ff, 79ff, 99ff,
 120ff, 143ff, 167ff,
 187ff, 209ff
Scandinavian literature,
 167, 187, 208; see also
 Germanic, Swedish,
 Danish, and Norwegian
 literatures
Semitic philology, 2, 25,
 48, 88, 105, 126, 150,
 173, 193, 216
Simplified spelling,
 19ff, 44ff
Spanish literature, 16;
 see also Romance languages and literatures
Swedish literature, 14,
 35, 55, 78, 98, 119,
 142

219

PERSONAL NAME AND MAIN ENTRY INDEX

Abbott, Eleanor Hallowell, 41, 72
Abbott, Frank F., 5, 6, 30, 52, 87, 172, 175
Abbott, Justin E., 5
Abbott, Lyman, 113
Achilles Tatius, 123
Adams, Charles D., 28, 32, 51, 84, 212
Adams, Charles Francis, 134
Adams, E.D., 163
Adams, Edward L., 80
Adams, Eleanor N., 160
Adams, Franklin P., 158
Adams, Henry, 65, 95, 180
Adams, Joseph Quincy, 60, 82, 102, 139, 162, 183, 184, 204
Adams, Samuel H., 91, 178
Adler, Frederick H., 97
Aeneas, 192
Aeschines, 103, 212
Aeschylus, 28, 170, 211
Agassiz, Alexander, 74
Agassiz, Louis, 74
Agostin, Antonio, 100
Ahab, King of Israel, 26
Aiken, Conrad, 95, 158, 199, 200
Aiken, Ednah R., 92
Aikman, Henry G., pseud., see Armstrong, H.H.
Albright, Evelyn M., 116, 138, 203
Alcaeus, 122
Alcibiades, 51, 171
Alcott, Amos Bronson, 94
Alden, Henry Mills, 201
Alden, Raymond Macdonald, 47, 101, 138, 162, 163, 164, 204
Aleman, Mateo, 81
Alexander the Great, 89, 146
Alexander, Leigh, 104
Alexander, Luther Herbert, 57
Alexis, J., 56, 208
Algarotti, Francesco, 81
Allen, B. S., 185, 187
Allen, Bernard M., 50, 153
Allen, Clifford G., 57
Allen, Frances, 110
Allen, G.C., 98
Allen, Hamilton F., 9
Allen, Hope E., 136, 161, 182, 187, 202
Allen, James Lane, 61, 111
Allen, James T., 190
Allen, Katharine, 215
Allen, Philip S., 142, 167, 208
Allen, Thomas W., 170
Allinson, Ann C.E., 7, 85
Allinson, C.J., 32
Allinson, Francis G., 7, 104, 123
Althan, Domenico, 146
Altrocchi, Rudolph, 99, 144
Ammianus Marcellinus, 6, 30, 52
Amy, Ernest F., 203
Amyntas, King of Macdeon, 146
Anaximander, 51
Andersen, Hans Christian, 98, 143
Anderson, A.R., 5, 28, 104, 108, 129
Anderson, David, 198

Anderson, Isabel, 177
Anderson, Mabel L., 172
Anderson, Sherwood, 155, 180, 197, 199
Andreas, Friederich K., 216
Andress, James M., 142
Andrews, A. Leroy, 79, 143, 208
Andrews, Charlton, 76
Andrews, Clarence E., 82, 180
Andrews, Elisha Benjamin, 20
Andrews, Mary R.S., 157
Andrews, William Page, 77
Aneau, Barthelemy, 15, 36, 80
Antisthenes, 23
Antin, Mary, 65
Antonius, M., 52
Antinaus, 24
Antiphon, 146
Apion, 24
Apollo, 47
Apollodorus of Athens, 47, 123
Apollonius at Rhodes, 123
Appelmann, Anton H., 186
Appleton, William A., 16, 45
Apuleius, Lucius, 87, 147, 192
Archer, William, 21, 44, 56, 98
Archias, 104
Archibald, H.T., 9, 10, 51
Ariosto, Lodovico, 203
Aristides, 104
Aristophanes, 27, 29, 123, 124, 147, 190, 195, 211
Aristotle, 1, 28, 77, 123, 126, 170, 183, 213
Armitage, Lionel, 34
Armstrong, Edward C., 36
Armstrong, Harold H., 197
Armstrong, Mary E., 173
Arndt, Ernst Moritz, 13, 34
Armin, Ludwig von, 118

Armin, Mary Annette, 12
Arnold, Benedict, 42, 156
Arnold, Le Ray, 60
Arnold, Matthew, 169, 189
Arnold, Thomas W., 89
Arnoldson, T.A., 141
Arnolletus, Iohannes, 142
Arrian, Flavius, 147, 214
Artaxerxes, King of Lydia, 194
Asbjörnsen, Peter C., 35, 98
Ascanius, 172
Asclepiades, 29
Asclepius, 147
Asconius, Pedianus, Quintus, 191
Ashley, Dorothy, 63
Ashton, Harry, 210
Asinius Pollio, 125
Asoka, King of Magadha, 5, 107, 152
Astyoche, 48
Atalanta, 103
Athenaeus, 24
Atherton, Gertrude, 90, 133, 178
Atkinson, Eleanor, 111
Attwell, Henry, 54
Aubignac, Francois H., abbe d', 171
Audubon, John James, 159
Auerbach, Berthold, 186
Augustine, St., Bp. of Hippo, 149
Augustus, Emperor of Rome, 150, 192
Aurelius, M. Antoninus, 148
Aurner, Nellie S., 160
Austin, Alfred, 158
Austin, Herbert D., 28, 99
Austin, Jane, 206
Austin, Mary, 156
Avila, Gaspar de, 58
Axtell, H. L., 126
Ayrer, W. T., 167
Ayres, Harry M., 136, 139, 160, 164, 203

Baas, Klaus Hinrich, 33
Babbitt, Frank C., 108
Babbitt, Irving, 75, 80, 158, 164, 210

Babcock, Kendric C., 119
Babrius, 123
Bacchylides, 24, 146
Bacci, A. d'Ancona, 15
Bacheller, Irving, 72, 154, 156
Bacon, E. M., 98
Bacon, Sir Francis, 137, 210
Bacon, George W., 16, 79, 81
Bacon, Josephine Daskam, 61, 72, 91, 112, 178, 197
Bacon, Leonard, 122
Bacon, Paul V., 142
Badger, R. G., 35
Bahlmann, A. C., 96
Bahr, Hermann, 117
Bailey, John C., 14
Bain, Charles W., 28
Baird, Spencer F., 114
Baker, George M., 77, 186
Baker, George P., 206
Baker, Harry T., 157
Baker, Louis C., 118, 142
Baldwin, E. C., 116, 164, 185
Baldwin, Thomas W., 204
Ball, Francis K., 13
Ballow, Susan H., 86, 150
Balmer, Edwin, 133, 156
Balzac, Honore, 121, 145, 188, 210
Bancroft, Frederic, 74
Bancroft, Hubert Howe, 74, 181
Bangs, J. P., 167
Barba, Preston A., 78, 97, 118
Barbagallo, Corrado, 215
Barbour, Harriet, 137
Barker, Ernest, 212
Barley, Joseph W., 60
Barnicle, M. E., 183
Barnouw, Adriaan J., 120
Baron, Robert, 205
Barr, Amelia E., 73, 201
Barrett, John, 22
Barrett, L. C., 27, 87, 128, 195
Barrows, Isabel C., 74
Barrows, Samuel June, 74

Barrus, Clara, 94
Barstow, Marjorie L., 137, 185
Bartlett, Frederick O., 132
Bartlett, Henrietta C., 138
Bartlett, John, 163
Barto, Philip S., 141
Barton, Clara, 114
Barton, Francis B., 144, 189
Barton, George A., 127, 152, 194
Barton, J. B., 139
Bartsch, Karl, 97
Bartsch, R. H., 33
Barwell, Anna, 98
Baskervill, Charles R., 38, 82, 138, 139, 163
Bassett, Rene, 48
Batcheller, Tryphosa Bates, 65
Bates, Katherine L., 82, 184
Bateson, Frederick W., 82
Baudissin, Wolf von, 216
Baugh, Albert C., 114, 135, 160, 181, 201
Bauhakhage, H. S., 117
Baum, Paull F., 137, 144, 162, 183, 210
Baumann, Julius, 143
Baumbach, Rudolf, 13, 208
Baumgarten, Alfred, 77
Baumgarten, M. D., 118
Bax, Ernest A., 118
Beach, M. G., 140
Beach, Joseph W., 180, 185
Beach, Rex, 71, 93, 111, 132, 134, 178
Beardslee, John W., 190
Beatty, Arthur, 205
Beatty, James M., 205
Beaulieu, Eustang de, 121, 188
Beaumarchais, Pierre A. C. de, 168
Beaumont, Francis, 102, 116, 138, 139
Beauvais, Pierre de, 167
Becerro de Benevivere, 81
Beckley, Zoe, 178

Bedier, Joseph, 14
Beebe, William, 201
Beekman, L. H., 54
Behn, Aphra, 102, 139
Bekker, Immanuel, 213
Belden, Henry M., 60,
 82, 83, 102, 183, 189,
 202, 205
Bell, Clair H., 98
Bell, Florence E., 167
Bellamy, Francis R., 156
Belloc, Hillaire, 99
Belvalkar, S. K., 174
Benauer, Agnes, 33
Bender, Harold H., 27,
 50, 129, 217
Benedix, R., 165
Benet, Stephen V., 75,
 200
Benn, Alfred W., 124
Bennett, Arnold, 158
Bennett, Charles E., 31,.
 105, 108, 149, 175,
 214
Bennett, Frank M., 28
Benson, Adolph B., 119
Beowulf, 38, 101, 115,
 136, 160, 182, 202
Berdan, John M., 115,
 137, 161
Berenson, Bernard, 180
Bergstrom, Hjalmar, 99,
 143
Berle, Lina W., 185
Bernard, Victor, 171
Bernbaum, Ernest, 102, 139
Berneker, Erich, 4
Bernhard, Magnus, 14
Bernhard, Svea, 167
Bernstorff, Frank A., 97
Berquist, Nils W., 14
Betts, Frank, 208
Betz, Frederich, 59, 167
Betz, G. A., 142
Bevan, Edwyn, 124
Beveridge, Albert J., 135
Beyerlein, Franz A., 77,
 117
Beyle, Marie-Henri, 121
Bharavi, 107
Bhavabhuti, 174
Bierstadt, A., 56
Bierstadt, Edward H., 165
Biggers, Earl D., 93
Bigelow, John, 74

Bigelow, Poultney, 113
Bilbro, Mathilde, 156
Billings, J. H., 212
Bindloss, Harold, 92,
 111, 133, 178
Bishop, Mabel, 119
Bithell, Jethro, 55
Bithynicus, 125
Björkman, Edwin, 14, 35,
 56, 78, 96, 98, 99,
 142, 143
Björnson, Björnstjerne,
 14, 35, 56, 78, 79,
 98, 143, 167, 187, 208
Blackley, William L., 119
Blackmer, O. C., 20
Blackwell, Alice S., 117
Blake, H. M., 116
Blasco Ibanez, Vicente,
 196, 209
Block, Stella, 97
Bloem, Walter, 77, 97
Blok, Petrus, 56
Blondheim, D. S., 14, 57
Bloomfield, Leonard, 27,
 33, 55, 107, 128, 141,
 174
Bloomfield, Maurice, 4,
 5, 27, 49, 87, 107,
 152, 174, 217
Bloomfield, Robert, 205
Blossom, Frederick A.,
 99
Bluhm, S., 142
Blumenthal, Oscar, 165
Boak, Arthur E. R., 150,
 174, 215
Boas, Harriet, 140
Boccaccio, Giovanni, 16,
 57, 81, 136, 172, 182,
 183, 189
Boethius, 162, 188, 214
Boetzkes, Ottilie G.,
 166
Boezinger, Bruno, 55, 97
Böhme, Arnold, 207
Böhme, Jacob, 207
Böhme, Margarete, 53
Boisacq, Emile, 4
Boissier, Alfred, 191
Bojer, Johan, 208
Bole, John A., 34
Boll, Frederick, 123
Bolling, George M., 27,
 28, 84, 103, 107, 147

Bolwell, Robert G., 137
Bonilla, Adolfo, 120, 122, 145
Bonnell, John K., 101, 161
Bonner, Campbell, 28
Bonner, Geraldine, 133
Bonner, Robert J., 7, 28, 51, 123
Bonstelle, Jessie, 94
Booker, John M., 80, 82
Bookstaver, A. L., 96
Booth, Edwin, 113
Bordeaux, Huon de, 15, 80
Borgerhoff, Joseph L., 79
Borland, Lois, 80, 82
Borroughs, John, 66
Borrow, George H., 99, 121
Bosanquet, R. C., 123
Boscan, Juan, 81
Bosher, Kate L., 131
Botsford, George W., 8, 28, 52, 85
Bouilhet, Louis, 188
Bouillon, Godefroi, 81
Bourland, Benjamin P., 58, 79, 99, 120, 143, 167
Bourland, Caroline B., 36
Bowen, R. F., 189
Bower, Marion, 198
Bower, B. M., pseud; see Sinclair-Cowan, Bertha
Bowerman, Helen C., 172
Bowles, Samuel, 67
Bowman, Henry Newpher, 211
Boyd, Ernest A., 165, 185
Boyds, T. F., 192
Boyles, Kate, 93
Boyles, Virgil D., 93
Boynton, Henry W., 54
Boynton, Percy H., 140
Bradford, Gamaliel, 65, 94, 135
Bradley, Henry, 21
Bradley, Jesse F., 205
Bradley, Mary H., 92, 197
Bradsher, Earl L., 164

Brady, Cyrus T., 133, 178
Braeksted, Hans L., 98
Braley, Berton, 113, 180, 200
Brandes, George, 56, 187
Brathwaite, Richard, 60
Brathwayte, Stanley, 158
Braun, Frederick, 97, 141
Braune, Theodor W., 11
Braunlich, A. F., 152
Brebner, Percy, 93, 111, 133
Breck, E. W., 96
Brede, Charles, 78, 118, 142, 186
Breitenbach, H. P., 28
Brentano, Clemens M., 12
Bret, John, 82
Breul, Karl H., 98
Brewer, David J., 20, 21
Brewster, Ethel H., 173
Brewster, William T., 122
Bridges, Horace J., 114
Briggs, William Dinsmore, 57, 138, 163, 184
Bright, James W., 20, 44, 59, 81, 136, 160, 163, 202
Brochner, Jessie, 167
Brock, Arthur J., 148
Brockelmann, Carl, 2, 48
Brodeur, Arthur C, 143
Brody, Canon, 71
Brome, Richard, 82
Bronk, Isabelle, 144
Brooks, A. M., 135
Brooks, Alden, 157
Brooks, Charles S., 159
Brooks, Nathan C., 166
Brooks, Van Wyck, 180
Brothwick, M. B., 56
Broughton, Leslie N., 164
Broun, Heywood, 176
Brown, Alice, 40, 72, 113, 132, 155, 179, 197
Brown, Arthur Charles Lewis, 14, 36, 57, 161, 202, 209
Brown, Carleton, 38, 59, 101, 115, 137, 161, 183, 202
Brown, M. L., 162

Brown, Peter H., 77
Brown, W. N., 217
Browne, Belmont, 76
Browne, George F., 160
Browne, Henry, 190
Browne, William Hand, 60, 83, 190
Brownell, William C., 96, 158, 165
Browning, Robert, 60, 74, 140, 145, 185, 211
Brownson, Carleton L., 212
Brubacher, Abram R., 163
Bruce, Harold L., 164, 188
Bruce, James Douglas, 15, 57, 81, 99, 182, 187, 202, 203, 209
Brugman, Karl, 5
Brush, Henry R., 58
Brush, Murray P., 15, 36
Brutus, Decimus Junius, 30
Bryan, William T., 115
Bryant, Marguerite, 70
Bryce, James, 21
Buchanan, Milton A., 16, 57, 99, 120, 206
Buck, Carl Darling, 4, 5, 8, 50, 51, 84, 87, 108, 128, 129, 153, 172, 174, 175, 195, 201, 215
Buck, Charles N., 70, 110
Buck, Gertrude, 165
Buck, Philo M., 117, 140
Buddhaghosa, 107
Budge, Ernest A., 88
Buenger, T. A., 123, 172, 175
Buettner, Johann C., 118
Buffum, Douglas L., 36, 57, 99
Bullard, F. L., 112
Bulwer Lytton, Lytton E., 166
Bunker, John, 71
Bunston, Anna, 117
Bunyon, John, 205
Burchett, B. P., 153
Burchinal, Mary C., 55
Burd, Henry A., 164, 205
Bureta, E., 206
Burke, Edmund, 104
Burkhard, Oscar, 167, 186
Burkitt, Francis C., 11, 126

Burlingame, Eugene W., 5, 217
Burnam, John M., 80, 81, 88
Burnet, John, 124, 171
Burnett, Frances Hodgsen, 40, 72, 133, 156
Burney, Fanny, 139
Burns, Cecil D., 170
Burns, Robert, 164, 185, 205
Burr, Anna R., 206
Burr, Josephine, 134
Burroughs, Edgar R., 178
Burroughs, John, 94, 114, 135, 201
Burton, Robert, 165, 206
Bury, John B., 123
Busch, Wilhelm, 208
Busenello, Gian Francesco, 16, 37, 80
Bushee, Alice H., 79, 81
Bushnell, Curtis C., 30
Butler, Ellis Parker, 179
Butler, Harold E., 5
Butler, Nicolas Murray, 67
Butler, Samuel, 206
Butt, Archibald, 63
Butterworth, G. W., 212
Bylesen, J. L., 167
Bynner, Witter, 113, 158
Byrde, O. R. A., 124
Byron, George Gordon Noel Byron, 6th., Baron, 16, 83, 102, 116, 139, 164, 206
Bywater, Ingram, 170

Cable, George W., 91, 178
Cabot, Richard C., 96
Cady, Frank, 59, 82
Caesar, Caius Julius, 8, 30, 104, 108, 125, 149, 171, 172, 192, 214
Cahan, Abraham, 156
Cairns, William B., 66, 206
Caland, W., 49
Calderhead F. G., 137
Calderon de la Barca, Pedro, 37, 100
Calhoun, George M., 84, 103, 123

Callaway, Morgan, 81, 181, 201
Callimachus, 1, 28, 29, 103, 146
Calpurnius, 149
Cambrai, Raoul de, 15
Camp, Charles W., 111
Campbell, G. H., 115, 136
Campbell, Lily B., 164, 183, 205
Campbell, Oscar J., 99, 120, 206
Campbell, T. M., 207
Campion, John L., 186
Canby, Henry S., 139
Canfield, Dorothy, 109, 112, 133, 134, 155, 176, 177, 197, 199
Cannan, Gilbert, 34, 120
Canter, Howard V., 104, 150, 172, 214
Capps, Edward, 2, 8, 51
Carcinus, 103
Carducci, Giosue, 121
Carew, Thomas, 139
Carlyle, Thomas, 54, 60, 64, 139, 206
Carman, Bliss, 75, 134
Carnahan, David H., 15, 144, 188
Carnegie, Andrew, 19, 20
Carnoy, A. J., 153, 175, 188, 217
Carpenter, George R., 204
Carpenter, Rhys, 171
Carr, M. B., 203
Carroll, J. S., 57
Carter, Henry H., 163
Carus, Paul, 118
Carver, J. L., 163
Cary, Ernest, 123, 148, 170, 190
Casa, Giovanni della, 122, 189
Cassiodorus, Flavius Magnus Aurelius, 175
Cast, Gottlob C., 167
Catiline, Lucius Sergius, 86, 214
Cather, Willa, 62, 70, 109, 133, 178, 196, 197

Cato Maior, 86, 149, 171
Catullus, Gaius Valerius, 52, 85, 104, 125, 172, 192, 214
Cavalcanti, Guido, 16, 37
Cawein, Madison, 41, 75, 95
Cercidas, 23
Cerf, Barry, 15, 120, 121
Cervantes Saavedra Miquel de, 120, 121, 122, 145, 211
Chamberlain, George A., 112, 131, 198
Chamberlain, W. A., 186
Chambers, Robert W., 40, 72, 92, 110, 111, 114, 133, 156, 178, 198
Chapelain, M., 81
Chapman, George, 38, 116, 145, 164, 204
Chapman, John Jay, 42, 74, 114, 148, 200
Chariton, 1
Charles the Bold, 37
Charles, Robert Henry, 106
Chase, George H., 52, 53
Chateaubriand, Francois, 144, 188, 210
Chater, Arthur C., 35, 78
Chatfield-Taylor, Hobart, 99
Chaucer, Geoffrey, 34, 38, 59, 82, 101, 102, 115, 116, 136, 137, 145, 161, 162, 172, 182, 185, 188, 189, 203, 210
Chester, George R., 72, 91
Chester, Sir Robert, 116
Chew, Samuel C., 82, 102, 116, 139, 164, 206
Cheyney, John Vance, 41
Chiemsee, Berthold von, 78
Chiera, Edward, 126, 127, 173
Child, Clarence G., 20, 37, 58, 81, 100, 102
Chinard, Gilbert, 15, 144, 188, 210
Chisholm, Arthur M., 71
Chislett, William, 101, 140, 163, 185, 193, 212
Chitarra, Cene de la, 145
Choate, Joseph H., 65, 159

Chorley, John Rutter, 121
Chretien de Tr yes, 36,
  80, 100, 122, 145, 202,
  209
Church, Henry W., 142
Church, J. E., Jr., 31
Churchill, Charles, 205
Churchill, Winston, 70,
  109, 133, 155
Churchman, Philip H., 16,
  57
Cibber, Colley, 82
Ciboule, Robert, 121
Cicero, Marcus Tullius,
  8, 9, 24, 30, 53, 83,
  84, 85, 86, 87, 104,
  105, 125, 149, 171,
  172, 175, 191, 192,
  214, 215
Cimber, T. Annius, 172
Cipriani, Charlotte J.,
  144
Clapp, Edward B., 104
Clapp, John M., 15
Clarahan, M. M., 98
Clark, Albert C., 124
  191, 215
Clark, Barrett H., 96,
  144, 206
Clark, Charles U., 6, 52
Clark, Donald L., 204
Clark, E. F., 166, 186
Clark, John T., 181
Clarke, Barrett H., 117
Clarke, Helen A., 74
Clarke, John S., 159
Clarke, William K. L.,
  213
Classén, Ernest, 77
Clay, Albert Tobias, 3,
  49, 89, 106
Cleghorn, Sara M., 131
Clemens, Samuel, 20, 21,
  64, 114, 159
Clement of Alexandria,
  212
Clemons, Harry, 162
Cleveland, Grover, 43
Clifford, Lewis, 161
Cloetta, Wilhelm, 57
Coar, John T. 166
Cobb, C. W., 164
Cobb, Irvin, 134
Cocchia, E., 215
Cochran, Alexander S.,
  107

Coester, Alfred, 57, 168
Coffmann, Bertha R., 118
Coffman, George R., 137
Cohen, G. H., 129
Cohen, Helen L., 140, 144
Cohn, P. N., 55
Cohoon, J. W., 123, 126
Col, Gontier, 168
Colbron, Grace T., 35
Colby, Frank M., 125
Colcord, Lincoln, 113
Coleman, Algernon, 99,
  100
Coleridge, Thomas, 102,
  206
Colling, Harry F., 97
Collins, Francis A., 177
Collins, Wilkie, 206
Collitz, Klara Hechtenberg,
  12, 55, 98
Collitz, Hermann, 28, 166,
  186
Collmann, Chester W., 54
Collyer, Mary, 164
Colwell, William A., 13
Comfort, Will Levington,
  94, 111, 112
Comfort, William W., 14,
  35, 122, 188
Congreve, William, 139
Conolly, James B., 134,
  177
Connor, Ralph, 92
Conrad, Clinton C., 172
Conrad, Joseph, 185, 196
Contarini, G., 80
Conway, John Joseph, 66
Conway, Robert S., 214
Cook, Albert S., 81, 101,
  115, 116, 124, 137,
  160, 162, 182, 183,
  189, 202
Coolidge, Dane, 92, 198
Cooper, James Fenimore,
  74, 97, 145
Cooper, Lane, 39, 140, 171,
  189, 205, 206
Cooper, William C., 207
Corbian, Pierre de, 57
Corbin, John, 110
Cordoba, Cabrera de, 16
Corneille, Pierre, 121, 210
Cornelius, R. D., 206
Cornish, Beatrice, 211
Corson, G., pseud; see
  Sholl, A. M.

227

Cory, Herbert E., 38, 59, 183
Cosenza, Mario, 100
Cotterill, Henry B., 104
Coulter, Cornelia C., 85, 172, 175
Couperus, Louis, 14, 187
Courtilz, Gatien de, 121
Cowles, Frank H., 171
Cox, Kenyon, 96
Craddock, Charles Egbert, 63, 64, 91
Craig, Hardin, 161, 183
Craigie, Jessie K., 98
Craigie, William A., 79, 98
Cramer, Jesse Grant, 56
Crane, Ronald S., 116, 184, 205, 210
Crane, Thomas F., 36, 80, 166, 183, 188
Cratinus, 147
Cratippus, 2
Crawford, Alexander W., 1 163, 206
Crawford, Francis Marion, 40
Crawford, James P. Wichersham, 16, 36, 57, 58, 80, 100, 120
Creek, Herbert L., 115, 206
Crees, James H. E., 185
Cressman, Edmund D., 108
Crevecoeur, Michel G. S. de, 168
Critchlow, F. L., 80
Croiset, Maurice, 190
Croissant, DeWitt, 82
Croll, Morris W., 162, 163, 206
Croly, George, 83
Cromwell, Ralph Lord, 59
Cronau, Rudolf, 34
Cros, Gaston, 49
Cross, Tom Peete, 80, 121, 202, 209
Cross, Wilbur L., 82, 184, 200, 205
Crothers, Samuel McChord, 42, 65, 135
Crowell, A. C., 56, 79
Cru, Robert Loyalty, 100
Cuervo, Rufino Jose, 56

Cueva y Silva, F. de la, 16
Cullom, Ridgewell, 71, 92, 111, 133, 178, 198
Cumberland, Richard, 164
Cummings, E., 93
Cummings, Hubertis M., 136
Cunliffe, John W., 38, 60, 82, 206
Curdy, A. E., 15
Curme, George O., 12, 59, 78, 81, 98, 101, 115, 118
Curran, Edwin F., 35
Curry, Walter C., 136, 160
Curtis, Edward L., 3
Curtiss, Philip, 132
Curtius, C. C., 117
Curtius, Rufus Quintus, 149, 214
Curts, Paul, 11
Curwood, James O., 71, 92, 111, 133, 198
Cushing, M. L., 144
Cuthbert, Fr., 145
Cutler, Robert, 155
Cutting, Starr W., 13, 34
Cutts, John, 184
Cyllene, 47
Cynewulf, 38
Cyrus the Great, 25

d'Abundance, Jean, 15
Dall, William H., 114
Dalrymple, Leona, 92
D'Alton, John F., 192
Daly, Augustin, 159
Daly, Joseph F., 159
D'Ancona, Alessandro, 120
D'Andeli, Henri, 145
Dante Alighieri, 13, 16, 36, 57, 81, 99, 115, 121, 122, 135, 136, 145, 162, 168, 189
Dapp, Charles F., 142
D'Arblay, Frances, Mme., see Burney, Fanny
Dargan, Edwin P., 145, 188
Dargan, H. M., 139
Dario, Ruben, 168
Darius, I. King of Persia, 4, 25, 87, 128

Darkaw, Angela C., 190
Darnall, F. M,, 137
Dasent, George W., 35, 79, 98, 143
Daudet, Alphonse, 145
Dauthendey, Max, 117
David, Henri, 145, 188
David, W. H., 118
Davidson, John, 165
Davies, Mary C., 180
Daviess, Maria T., 157, 178
Davis, Arthur N., 181
Davis, Fanny Stearns, 75, 113
Davis, Jefferson, 92
Davis, Richard Harding, 135
Davis, Roy, 56
Davis, William S., 55, 123
Daw, E. B., 163
Dawson, Coningsby, 69, 93, 95, 177
Dawson, William J., 156, 177, 178
Day, Thomas, 57
DeCoster, C. T., 207
Deferrari, Roy T., 147, 149
Defoe, Daniel, 82, 135, 140
deForest, Marian, 94
Deguilleville, Guillaume de, 15
Dehmel, Richard, 53, 117, 166
Deimel, Anton, 127
Deimier, Pierre de, 57
Dejean, Louis L., 71
Dekker, Thomas, 60, 82, 102
DeKoven, Anna, 74
Deland, Margaret, 39, 61, 112, 131, 199
Delavigne, Casimir, 80, 185, 189
Delitzsch, Friedrich, 10 106, 151
Deloney, Thomas, 162
Democritus, 147
DeMorgan, William F., 165
DeMoss, W. T., 183, 206
Demosthenes, 24, 84, 103, 191

Denison, Thomas S., 28
Denton, George B., 205, 206
Depew, Albert N., 177
DeQuincy, Thomas, 102
Deschamps, Emile, 15, 182, 188
Deutsch, Monroe E., 125, 171, 172
D'Evelyn, Charlotte, 116, 182, 188, 202
DeVries, T., 140
Dewey, George, 73
Dewey, Melvil, 20
Dewing, Henry Bronson, 8, 28, 123, 170, 212
DeWitt, Norman, 52
Dey, W. M., 145
Dhalla, Maneckji N., 4
Dickens, Charles, 142, 165, 206
Dickinson, Thomas H., 138, 165
Diderot, Denis, 100
Diez, M., 208
Dinsmoor, Wayne B., 84
Dio, Cacceianus, Cassius, 123, 148, 170, 190
Dionysius of Alexandria, 213
Dionysus of Halicarnassis, 28, 104
Divine, Charles, 180
Dix, Beulah, 93
Dixon, Thomas, 70, 92
Doak, H. A., 204
Dobson, Austin, 43
Dobson, J. F., 124
Dodge, Robert E. N., 203, 205
Dole, Nathan H., 96
Donatus, Aelius, 150
Dondo, Mathurin M., 210
Donnelly, Francis J., 32
D'Ooge, Benjamin L,, 7
D'Ooge, Martin, 125
Douglas, Stephen A., 43
Dowden, Edward, 35
Downes, William H., 64
Draper, John W., 206
Drayatt, A., 187
Drayton, Michael, 183
Dreiser, Theodore, 62, 90, 109, 133, 158, 197, 199
Dresser, Horatio W., 143

Dresser, J. S., 131
Droste-Hulshaff, Annette, 13
Drummond, Robert R., 12
Dryden, John, 118, 139, 163, 205
Duckett, Eleanor S., 123
Dudley, Louise, 59, 101
Dudley, Robert, 94
Duff, John W., 5, 105
Duffield, Kenneth G., 180
Dukes, Ashley, 54, 56
Dunbar, Paul Laurence, 95
Duncan, Carson S., 139
Duncan, Norman, 135
Dunlop, Geoffrey A., 100, 121
Dunn, Esther C., 163
Dunn, F. S., 32, 149, 214
Dunne, F. L., 201
Dunsany, Edward J., 165
D'Urfey, Thomas, 164
Durham, Charles L., 87
Durham, Donald B., 84, 147, 150
Durham, Willard H., 116, 184
Dutton, George B., 100, 101, 102, 139
Dutton, Emily, 175, 191
Dutton, J. D., 136
Dyer, Frank L., 43
Dyer, William S., 111

Eakin, Frank, 153
Earle, Mortimer Lamson, 51, 52
Eastburn, Iola, 142
Eastman, Charles A., 134
Eastman, Max, 75
Eaton, Arthur W. H., 102
Eaton, G. L., 10
Eberweiler, Friedrich, 33
Ebner von Eschenbach, Marie, 142
Echegaray, Jose, 144
Eckelmann, Ernst, 13, 141
Edgerton, Franklin, 4, 27, 49, 87, 107, 128, 152, 174, 195, 217
Edison, Thomas Alva, 43

Edmonds, John M., 148
Edmunds, Albert J., 107
Edwards, Albert, 62, 69
Edwards, E. R., 44
Edwards, John B., 191
Edwards, Thomas, 139, 205
Eeden, Fredrick von, 14
Eggert, Charles A., 13
Eikeland, Peter J., 143
Einarsson, Indridi, 79
Eisemann, Fred, 97
Elderkin, George W., 84
Eliot, Charles W., 13, 170
Eliot, George, 40, 185, 206
Eliot, Samuel A., 117
Eller, William H., 208
Ellery, Eloise, 145
Elliott, Aaron Marshall, 28, 35, 36, 37
Elliott, Maud H., 134
Elliott, Richard T., 124
Ellis, Havelock, 78
Ellis, Robinson, 52
Ellison, L. M., 163
Elmer, Clement G., 54
Elmore, Jefferson, 9, 52, 171, 175
Elmquist, Axel L., 143
Elster, Otto, 77
Elwood, W., 111
Emerson, Edward Waldo, 42, 64, 200
Emerson, Oliver F., 20, 82, 100, 115, 136, 137, 145, 160, 162, 183, 202, 203, 206
Emerson, Ralph Waldo, 35, 42, 64, 114, 141
Empey, A. G., 179
Encina, Juan del, 121
Ende, Amelia von, 77, 96, 97, 117
English, R. B., 104, 147
Ennius, Quintus, 30
Epictetus, 170
Epicurus, 213
Epler, Percy H., 114
Eppendorff, Heinrich von, 208
Erasmus, Desiderius, 204, 214
Ercilla y Zuniga, Alfonso De, 210

Erichsen, Erich, 167
Ernst, Otto, 142
Erskine, John, 137, 184
Erskine, Payne, 63, 110
Espinosa, Aurelio M., 57, 80, 122, 145, 146
Eugippius, 88, 125
Euripides, 47, 48, 84, 103, 104, 114, 124, 147, 148, 170, 171, 190, 211, 212, 214
Eurypylus, 48, 84
Evans, Jack, 177
Evans, Marshall B., 54, 142
Evelyn-White, Hugh G., 148

Fabin, Madeleine, 203, 210
Fabre, Ferdinand, 189
Faguet, Auguste-Emile, 144
Fahnestock, E., 108
Fairbanks, Arthur, 28
Fairchild, Arthur H. R., 205
Fairclough, Henry R., 86, 126, 149, 172, 213
Falconer, Robert T., 117, 140
Fansler, Dean S., 82, 101
Fanton, G etano, 146
Farmer, Virginia, 86
Farnham, W. E., 139, 162, 182, 189, 203
Farnsworth, William O., 100
Farquhar, George, 102
Farr, Hollon A., 208
Fauchet, Claude, 37
Faust, Albert B., 13, 97
Faustus Androlinus, 192
Favez, Charles, 214
Fawcett, Henry, 94
Fawcett, Joseph, 205
Fay, Edwin Whitfield, 5, 6, 27, 28, 49, 50, 85, 88, 105, 108, 129, 149, 152, 153, 172, 175, 195, 218
Fay, Frances C., 117

Fay, Percival B., 80, 100
Feilitzen, Hugo von, 79
Feise, Ernst, 97, 118, 141, 186
Felmley, David, 20
Feltoe, Charles L., 213
Ferber, Edna, 63, 93, 112, 156, 179
Ferguson, William S., 8, 51
Ferreira, P. Julio, 100, 120
Ferrero, Guglielmo, 125, 215
Ferris, Elmer E., 112
Fey, Richard, 55
Fiedler, Hermann G., 54, 140
Field, Clarence, 78
Field, Eugene, 66, 93
Field, Rachel L., 184
Fielding, Henry, 60, 82, 139, 164, 184, 200, 205
Fields, Annie, 64
Fineman, H., 165
Firkins, Oscar W., 114, 199
Firmicus Maternus, Julius, 86
Fischer, Walter P., 100
Fisher, Dorothy Canfield, see Canfield, Dorothy
Fisher, John R., 168
Fisher, Lizette A., 121, 161
Fisher, Sidney George, 65
Fisk, Earl E., 82
Fiske, George C., 30, 104, 214, 215
Fiske, John, 159
Fitch, George, 112
Fitzgerald, John Driscoll, 16, 145, 146
Fitzgerald, Leonora, 146
Fitzmaurice-Kelly, James, 16
Flaccus, L. Avillius, 24
Flach, Pauline B., 35
Flaubert, Gustav, 99, 100, 188
Fletcher, Jeffersen B., 16, 36, 38, 41, 80, 101, 121, 162

Fletcher, John, 59, 138, 139, 204
Fletcher, John G., 113, 157, 200
Fletcher, Joseph S., 179
Flexner, Abraham, 170
Flickinger, Roy C., 8, 28, 52, 84, 87, 172, 190, 193, 218
Flint, F. S,, 157
Flom, George T., 14, 33, 79, 119, 167, 201
Florer, Warren W., 77, 98, 185
Flügel, Ewald, 59, 116, 160, 163
Fobes, Francis H., 123, 213
Foerster, Elizabeth, 55
Fogel, Edwin M., 118
Folengo, Teofilo, 57
Foller, Karl, 186
Follett, Helen T., 165, 185
Follett, Wilson, 165, 185, 199
Fonkalsrud, Alfred, 119
Fontaine, Charles, 100, 143
Foote, John T., 73
Foote, Mary Hallock, 112
Footner, Hulbert, 71, 92
Foraker, B. J., 134
Forbes, James L., 110
Forbes, Waldo Emerson, 42, 64
Forchhammer, Henri, 143
Ford, John, 60, 82
Ford, Sewall, 112
Forman, Henry J., 13
Forman, J. M., 70
Forman, Lewis L., 124
Forsythe, Robert S., 59, 60, 102, 116, 164
Fort, Henri, 143
Fortier, Alcee, 80, 99
Fortier, Edward L., 121
Foscola, Ugo, 16
Foster, Benjamin O., 30, 52, 103, 123
Foster, Dorothy, 164
Foster, E. S., 124
Foster, Frances A., 59, 160
Foster, Frederick M., 165, 185, 212

Foster, Maximilian, 71
Foulet, Lucien, 100, 145
Foulke, William Dudley, 145
Fowler, Frank H., 175
Fowler, Harold N., 104
Fowler, Susan, 153
Fowler, William W., 191, 213
Fox, John, 70, 201
Fox, William S., 171
Foxcroft, Frank, 180
Frachtenberg, Leo J., 50
France, Anatole, 56, 145, 210
Francis of Assisi, St., 145
Francke, Kuno, 33, 141
Frank, Colman D., 15
Frank, Grace, 183
Frank, Tenney, 52, 104, 150, 172, 213, 218
Frank, Waldo, 155
Franklin, Benjamin, 142
Fraser, William H., 168
Frazer, James G., 212
Freeman, Charles E., 171
Freeman, Frank, 56
Freeman, Mary Wilkins, 62, 93, 155
Freeman, Tilden, 178
Freine, Simund de, 15
French, Allen, 156
Frenssen, Gustav, 33, 77, 98, 208
Fresnaye, Jean Vauquelin de la, 100, 121
Freud, Sigmund, 212
Frey, Adolf, 117
Freytag, Gustav, 54, 97, 118, 140
Frieburg, V. S., 137
Fried, Clara, 98
Friedlander, Gerald, 82
Friedrich, Friedrich, 140
Friedrich, G., 6
Fries, Anna, 78, 98
Froding, Gustav, 142
Froissart, Jean, 138
Frost, Robert, 95, 157
Frothingham, Arthur L., 129
Fuess, Charles M., 83
Fulda, Ludwig, 34, 77, 141

Fuller, Anna, 41
Fuller, Henry B., 158, 178, 199
Fuller, Sarah Margaret, 34, 97
Fulton, Edward, 137
Funk, Isaac K., 20
Funston, F., 94
Furman, Lucy, 91
Furness, Horace Howard, 39, 60, 138
Furness, Horace Howard, Jr., 60, 204
Furnivall, Frederick J., 21

Gage, Lyman J., 20
Gager, William, 163
Gaillard, Auger, 121
Galbreath, Olive, 178
Gale, Zona, 64, 93, 178, 197
Galen, Claudius, 148
Galpin, Stanly L., 15, 36, 121
Galsworthy, John, 196
Ganghofer, Ludwig, 53
Gansfort, Wessel, 181
Gardner, Percy, 191
Garland, Hamlin, 133, 159
Garrett, Fydell E., 79, 119, 143
Garrett, Robert M., 182
Garrison, William Lloyd, 43, 74
Garstang, John, 3
Gaselee, Stephen, 148, 170, 171
Gaston de Paris, 58
Gautier d'Arras, 209
Gautier, Theophile, 145, 189
Gaw, Allison, 163
Gay, Lucy, 57, 160
Gayley, Charles M., 31, 102, 116, 183
Geddes, James, 100, 121
Gehman, H. S., 126, 128, 152
Geiger, Wilhelm, 4
Geijerstam, Gustav, 56
Geissendoerfer, John T., 142
Geldner, K. F., 4
Genouillac, H. di, 25, 49
Genung, Charles H., 96

George III, King of Great Britain, 205
George, Stefan, 117, 207
George, Walter L., 145
Gerard, Dorothea, 77, 97
Gercke, A., 6
Gerhardt, Paul, 208
Gerig, John L., 15, 36, 80, 174
Gerould, Gordon H., 101, 136, 160, 182
Gerould, Katherine F., 157
Gerstenberg, Alice, 110
Gerstenberg, J. J., 207
Gest, John Marshall, 96
Gewidmet, Ernst K., 174
Ghazzali, 151, 152, 173
Gibbons, Herbert A., 180
Gilbert, Allen H., 82, 102, 164, 203, 205
Gilchrist, Anne, 181
Gilder, Richard Watson, 20, 21, 43, 134
Gilder, Rosamund, 134
Gildersleeve, Basil L., 7, 8, 28, 30, 51, 87, 125, 147, 153
Gillespy, Frances L., 161
Gillet, Joseph E., 138, 141, 166, 186
Gillmore, Rufus, 92
Gingerich, Solomon F., 185
Giotto di Bondone, 36
Giovanitti, Arturo, 95
Gipson, A. E., 184
Giraldus Cambrensis, 59
Girard, William, 210
Gjellerup, Karl A., 120
Glaphthorne, Henry, 102, 116
Glasgow, Ellen, 40, 69, 130, 131, 197
Glass, Montague, 112, 198
Glaue, P., 11
Glover, Terrot R., 212
Goad, Caroline, 185, 193
Goddard, William, 162
Goebel, Julius, 97, 141, 165, 186, 207
Goeje, M. J., de, 127, 151

Goethe, Johann Wolfgang von, 11, 12, 13, 34, 54, 76, 77, 96, 97, 104, 117, 118, 140, 141, 142, 165, 166, 167, 173, 185, 186, 193, 207, 208
Golding, Arthur, 116
Goldman, Hetty, 28, 153
Goldmark, Ruth T., 206
Goldoni, Carlo, 99, 145
Goldsmith, Peter H., 145
Goldziher, Ignaz, 26, 128, 151, 173
Gollancz, Israel, 138, 160
Gonzalo de Berceo, 16
Good, John W., 139
Goodale, George H., 32
Goodell, Thomas D., 28, 84, 87, 104
Goodman, Daniel C., 69, 197
Goodman, Milton, 209
Goodspeed, Edgar J., 8
Goodwin, Alfred, 51
Goodwin, William 185
Gordis, Warren S., 9
Gordon, Arthur, 37
Gordon, Elizabeth H., 165
Gosse, W. J., 54
Gottheil, Richard, 174
Gottsched, Johann C., 33
Gould, Charles N., 166
Gould, George M., 42, 43
Gournay, Marie de, 121
Goygio, E., 211
Graf, Artura, 80
Gragg, Florence Alden, 8
Graham, Walter J., 138
Grandgent, Charles H., 21, 36, 44, 79, 81, 115, 168, 189
Grane, Hiller, 98
Granrud, John E., 85
Grant, Judge, 109
Graves, T. S., 59, 82, 101, 138, 162, 163
Graves, W. H., 164
Gray, Alexander, 141, 166
Gray, Edward D. M., 31
Gray, Henry D., 82, 116, 138, 162, 163, 183, 204
Gray, Louis H., 27, 50, 87, 108, 174, 193
Gray, Thomas, 102, 164, 205
Gray, W. D., 215
Grayson, David, 112, 159
Green, Alexander, 141, 160, 183
Green, Anna K., 72, 73, 92, 157
Greene, Clay M., 198
Greene, Francis N., 70, 178
Greene, Francis V., 176
Greene, Frederick S., 157
Greene, Robert, 60, 138, 163
Greenlaw, Edwin, 38, 59, 162, 183
Greenough, Chester N., 164
Greever, Garland, 164
Greg, Walter W., 204
Gregory, Allene, 139
Gregory, Jackson, 92
Grenfell, Bernard P., 2, 103
Grenfell, Wilfred T., 200
Gresset, Jean-Baptiste L., 58
Gressmann, Hugo, 89
Grey, Zane, 71, 92, 111, 154, 156, 178, 198
Griffith, Reginald H., 38, 57, 82
Grillparzer, Franz, 13, 54, 78, 118, 142, 166, 186
Grimm, A. F. W., 54
Grimm, Friedrich M., 203
Grimm, Jakob Ludwig K., 166
Griselini, Francesco, 145
Groeber, Gustav, 56
Grimmelshausen, Hans, 141
Groth, P., 119
Grow, Malcolm C., 177
Grundtvig, Svend H., 35, 56
Gryphius, Andreas, 208
Gubelmann, Albert E., 54
Gubernatis, Angelo de, 80

Gudeman, Alfred, 86
Guerard, Albert Leon, 121
Guerber, Helene A., 97
Guest, Edgar A., 180
Guillaume de Lorris, 145
Gumm, C. C., 163
Gummere, Francis B., 65, 171
Gummere, Richard M., 39, 52, 102, 126
Guthrie, Kenneth S., 145
Guthrie, William N., 14
Gutzkow, Karl F., 13, 166, 207
Guy of Warwich, 15, 116, 121

Haan, F. de, 36
Haarbeck, L., 119
Haas, George Christian Otto, 4, 49, 50
Hackett, Francis, 180
Hadrian, Emperor of Rome, 24, 103, 215
Hadzsits, George D., 147, 150, 213
Haertel, Martin H., 118, 167
Hagedorn, Friedrich von, 118
Hagedorn, Hermann, 134, 178
Haines, Charles R., 148
Hains, D. D., 10, 28, 105
Halbe, Max, 77, 96, 140
Hale, Edward Everett, Jr., 43, 69, 90, 109, 130, 154, 159, 176, 196
Hale, William Bayard, 64
Hale, William G., 9, 31, 87, 129
Hale, William T., 139, 164
Hall, Edith H., 84
Hall, Edward, 183
Hall, Frederic A., 104, 124
Hall, Halworthy, pseud. see Porter, H. E.
Hall, Harry R., 89, 123
Hall, Henry Marion, 60
Haller, William, 185
Halliday, William R., 212

Hamann, A., 12
Hamilton, Arthur, 188
Hamilton, Clayton, 159, 199
Hamilton, G. C., 187
Hamilton, George L., 15, 57, 80, 100, 187, 209
Hammond, Eleanor, 38, 59, 82, 101, 136, 137, 161
Hammurabi, King of Babylonia, 150
Hamsun, Knut, 98
Hancock, P. S., 152
Hand, Learned, 68
Handschin, Charles H., 34, 54, 55, 78, 97, 119, 167
Hanford, James H., 60, 161, 163, 164, 182, 184, 204, 206
Hanhart, W. T., 11
Hanson, Haldor J., 99
Hanstein, J. G., 77
Harben, William N., 40, 91, 156, 197, 201
Hardenberg, Friedrich, 13, 59
Harding, A. T., 206
Hardt, Ernst, 77
Hardy, Alexandre, 58, 145
Hardy, Thomas, 40, 165, 185
Harkness, G., 6
Harkness, S., 203
Harmon, Austin M., 30, 52
Harper, Carrie A., 83
Harper, George M., 139, 164
Harper, Joseph Henry, 64
Harper, Robert F., 26
Harre, E. T., 132
Harre, T. Everett, 71
Harrington, Karl P., 30, 50, 150
Harris, Corra, 63
Harris, Joel Chandler, 181
Harris, Lynn H., 163, 204, 214
Harris, Rendel, 191
Harris, William T., 21
Harrison, Frederic, 150

Harrison, Henry Sydnor, 40, 71, 111, 133
Harry, Joseph Edward, 29, 51, 124
Harry, M. L., 119
Hart, Albert Bushnell, 43
Hart, Heinrich, 76
Hart, James M., 59
Hart, Julius, 76
Hart, W. F., 38
Hart, Walter M., 34, 82, 161, 185
Harte, Bret, 43
Hartleben, Otto, 207
Hartmann, Armen Heinrich, 78
Hartmann, Jacob W., 56
Hartmann, Martin, 48
Harvey, Alexander, 206
Harvey, William J., 143
Harvitt, Helen J., 121, 188
Haskell, Julian S., 118
Haskins, Charles H., 29, 85, 123, 126
Hastings, Agnes, 60
Hastings, James, 175
Hatch, William H. P., 52, 85
Hatcher, O. L., 59, 138
Hatfield, James T., 118, 165
Hatheway, Joel, 208
Hauch, Edward, 141
Hauff, Wilhelm, 54, 77, 117
Haughton, William, 163
Haupt, Paul, 166
Hauptmann, Carl, 77, 165
Hauptmann, Gerhardt, 13, 33, 53, 54, 76, 77, 96, 117, 118, 140, 165, 166, 185
Haussmann, Carl T., 54,,166
Havens, George R., 204
Havens, Raymond, 60, 188
Hawes, C. H., 8
Hawes, Harriet A., 8
Hawkins, Richmond L., 145
Hawthornden, Drummond of, 15
Hawthorne, Hildegarde, 43, 66
Haxo, Henry C., 121

Hay, James, 110
Hay, John, 113, 114
Hayes, Ralph A., 176
Haynes, William, 165
Hazeltine, Alice I., 184
Hazlitt, William, 139, 164
Heard, John, 77
Heaton, John Langdon, 67
Hebbel, Friedrich, 33, 34, 54, 77, 96
Hedenstjerna, Alfred, 14
Hegel, George W. F., 186
Heiberg, Johan, 98, 208
Heidel, William Arthur, 8, 29, 51, 84, 103, 123, 146, 169, 189, 211
Heidenstam, Karl Gustav Verner von, 119, 167
Heijermanns, Herman, 56
Heine, Heinrich, 13, 34, 95
Heliodorus, Bp. of Tricca, 123
Hellanicus, 24
Heller, Otto, 56, 165, 187
Hellman, George S., 165
Helm, K., 11
Helmbrecht, Meier, 118
Helmich, Elsie W., 54
Hemingway, Samuel B., 59, 162
Hempl, George, 21, 29, 44, 108, 129, 147, 153
Henderson, Alice Corbin, 157, 158
Henderson, Archibald, 13, 35, 55, 76
Henderson, Ernest Jr., 80
Henderson, Walter,B.D., 206
Henderson, William J., 54
Hendrickson, George L., 30, 125, 149, 171, 212
Hendrix, William S., 145
Henley, William E., 95
Henneman, John Bell, 60
Henriquez Urena, Pedro, 168
Henry Plantagenet, 80
Henschel, Karl, 117
Heraclides, 29, 146
Heraclitus, 104
Herbert, Henry, 184

Herder, Johann G. von, 12, 77, 97, 142
Herford, Charles H., 213
Herford, Oliver, 71
Hergesheimer, Joseph, 110, 155, 178, 179, 197, 199
Herkner, John, 35
Hermann, Eliz. A.,54
Hermannson, Halldor, 14, 119, 143
Hermes, Trismegistus, 47
Hermippus, 146
Herodotus, 8, 24, 29, 50, 212
Herrick, Francis H., 159
Herrick, Robert, (1591-1674), 139
Herrick, Robert, 69, 90, 133, 177
Hertel, John, 107, 128
Hervey, William A., 185
Hervieu, Paul, 120
Herwegh, Georg, 117
Herzberger, Frederick W., 166
Herzog, Rudolph, 96, 166
Hesiod, 24, 29, 31, 146, 148
Hesse, Hermann, 117
Hessler, L. B., 161
Heuser, Frederick W. J., 166
Heuzey, M. M., 49
Hewett, T. S., 208
Hewitt, Joseph W., 29, 32
Hewitt, Thomas B., 84
Heyking, Baroness von, 77, 117
Heyse, Paul, 167
Heywood, Thomas, 60, 82, 137, 163, 184, 204
Hibbard, Laura, 80, 121, 202, 209
Hiersemann, Karl W., 4
Higginson, James J., 82
Higginson, Thomas Wentworth, 21, 44
Hight, George A., 98
Hill, James J., 159
Hill, Raymond T., 36, 57, 58, 121, 209
Hillebrand, Harold N., 138
Hillhause, James T., 164
Hilliard, Robert, 71
Hillis, Newell D., 93
Hills, Elijah, 57, 121
Hilmer, H., 160, 181
Hilmer, W. C., 77
Hime, H. W. L., 56, 79
Hinckley, H. B., 137, 162, 182, 202
Hinckley, Julian, 93
Hinton, James, 161
Hippocrates, 24
Hippolytus, 123
Hippomanes, 103
Hirst, Gertrude, 150
Hirschfeld, George, 140
Hitchcock, Frank, 68
Hodges, Archibald L., 32
Hodges, Arthur, 197
Hodges, J. C., 161
Hoefli, J. A., 118
Hoffmann, Ernst T. A., 166
Hoffmann, O., 28
Hofmannsthal, Hugo von, 54, 77, 96, 140, 141, 165, 186, 207
Holbach, Baron d', 144
Holberg, Ludwig, 56, 79, 99, 119
Holbrook, Richard T., 36, 188
Holder, Alfred, 144
Holl, K., 96
Hollander, Lee M., 56, 79, 160
Holliday, Robert C., 180
Holma, Harri, 151, 216
Holme, J. W., 16
Holmes, Thomas R.,,171
Holt, Henry, 21
Holt, Winifred, 94
Holvik, Johan A., 79, 143, 167, 208
Holzwarth, Franklin J., 54
Home, John, 184
Homer, 8, 24, 28, 29, 50, 84, 104, 123, 124, 147, 148, 164, 170, 171, 182, 211
Homer, Cray, 178
Homer, Winslow, 64
Hommel, Fritz, 216
Hood, Thomas, 102
Hooker, Brian, 41

Hopkins, Annette, 100
Hopkins, Edward W., 27, 50, 87, 88, 107, 152, 174, 193, 195
Hopkins, Nevil M., 133, 157
Hopkins, William J., 93
Hopkinson, Leslie W., 212
Hoppin, F., 145
Horace, 30, 50, 53, 85, 86, 104, 105, 125, 126, 136, 149, 150, 164, 171, 172, 173, 185, 191, 192, 193, 215
Horne, Charles F., 193
Horning, Lewis E., 13
Hort, Arthur, 170
Hosford, J., 10
Hosius, 52
Hoskier, H. C., 29
Hoskins, Joseph A., 13
Hough, Emerson, 72, 132, 178, 198
Houghton, Herbert P., 123
House, Ralph Emerson, 16
Houston, Percy H., 164
How, Louis, 168
Howard, G. W. S., 12
Howard, George B., 110
Howard, Velma S., 14, 55, 78, 119, 187
Howe, Mark A. De Wolfe, 198, 200
Howe, Julia Ward, 134
Howe, Will D., 139
Howells, William Dean, 42, 68, 76, 132
Hoyt, Mary W., 108
Hrozny, Friedrich, 151, 216
Hubbard, Frank G., 158, 164, 182, 183, 184
Hubbell, Harry M., 104, 147
Huckel, Oliver, 33
Huebsch, Rudolph W., 54, 141, 167
Hughes, Helen S., 82, 102, 164, 184, 205, 210
Hughes, Rupert, 63, 110, 130, 178
Hulbert, J. R., 82, 136, 145, 202

Hulme, W. H., 182
Hulshof, John H., 54
Humphreys, Milton W., 84, 147
Huneker, James, 114
Hunt, Arthur Sturridge, 2, 23, 24, 47, 48, 84, 103
Hunt, Elizabeth R., 76
Hunt, H. L., 60
Hunt, Leigh, 211
Hurgranje, C. Snouck, 128, 151, 174
Hurst, Fanny, 179
Husband, Richard W., 28, 50, 86, 104, 105, 125, 150, 171
Hustvelt, Sigurd B., 137, 143
Hutton, Edward, 16
Hutton, Maurice, 29
Hyllested, Carl C., 98
Hyde, Walter W., 126
Hyskell, Ira D., 218

Ibanez, V. Blasco, see Blasco Ibanez, Vicente
Ibn Sa'ad, 3
Ibsen, Henrik, 13, 14, 35, 56, 78, 79, 98, 119, 143, 167, 187, 208
Ibsen, Sigurd, 119
Ihrig, Roscoe M., 160
Imbert, Louis, 146
Ingersoll, J. W. D., 53, 105
Inness, George, 159
Ireland, Mary E., 140
Irvine, Alexander, 74
Irwin, Wallace, 198
Isham, 71
Isocrates, 24, 104, 137, 147
Ives, Staunton, 63

Jackson, Abraham Valentine William, 4, 5, 27, 50, 65, 87, 107, 128, 175, 217
Jackson, Andrew, 39
Jackson, Carl N., 105, 125, 149
Jackson, Charles T., 111
Jackson, George P., 141, 166

Jackson, Margaret, 16
Jackson, William W., 170
Jacoby, Gunther, 77
Jaeck, Emma G., 102, 118, 141, 145
James, Apostle, 83
James I, King of England, 59
James of Campostello, St., 202
James, Henry, 41, 73, 94, 95, 121, 135, 156, 158, 165, 180, 185, 206
James, Montague R., 213
James, William 21
Janson, Gustaf, 78
Janvier, Thomas A., 63
Jastrow, Morris, 2, 26, 48, 88, 105, 126, 150, 173, 193, 216
Jefferson, Bernard L., 101, 162
Jejeebhay, Jamsetjee, 128
Jenkins, Thomas A., 15, 37, 80, 182, 188, 209
Jenkins, William E., 143
Jenney, A. M., 115, 136
Jennings, Al, 94
Jensen, Gerard E., 139, 205
Jerome, St., 52, 85, 126
Jerome, Thomas, 53
Jerrold, M. T., 16
Jessen, Franz de, 99
Jevons, Herbert Stanley, 21, 44
Jewell, R., 163
Jewett, Sarah Orne, 64
Jodelle, Etienne, 210
Johannan, Abraham, 174
John of Salisbury, 150
Johns, Claude H., 126
Johns, George S., 67
Johnson, Allan C., 29, 103
Johnson, Amandus, 143
Johnson, Dora, 53
Johnson, Edwin Lee, 4, 175
Johnson, Henry, 122
Johnson, Marcia K., 119
Johnson, Owen, 63, 72, 73, 91, 110, 132
Johnson, Reginald B., 206
Johnson, Robert U., 134
Johnson, Samuel, 116, 164, 205
Johnson, Tom, 94
Johnson, William S., 60
Johnston, Mary, 39, 69, 70, 92, 111, 133, 156, 198
Johnston, Oliver M., 37, 57, 145, 211
Jones, Alice, 92
Jones, Daniel, 44
Jones, Ethel C., 100, 121
Jones, Florence N., 16
Jones, G. A., 161
Jones, George W., 184
Jones, Henry S. V., 59, 82, 115
Jones, Horace L., 8, 170
Jones, Howard M., 140
Jones, John Paul, 74
Jones, Reginald F., 205
Jones, Roger M., 148
Jones, Samuel A., 206
Jones, William H. S., 212
Jonson, Ben, 38, 60, 82, 102, 138, 163, 184, 204, 214
Jordan, David Starr, 21
Jordan, Elizabeth, 198
Jordan, John C., 138
Jordanes, 118
Jorgensen, Jens, 99, 167
Judson, Alexander C., 82, 204
Julian the Apostote, Emperor of Rome, 104
Julien, A., 33
Jusserard, Jean A., 183
Justinus, 172
Juvenal, Decimus Junius, 192

Kamban, Godmunder, 187
Kant, Immanuel, 186
Karpeles, Gustav, 34
Karpinski, L. C., 82, 149
Kastner, Leon E., 15
Kauffman, Reginald Wright, 62, 110, 177
Kaufman, J. C., 164
Kayser, Carl F., 55
Keats, John, 42, 102, 164, 189, 206
Keay, Mitchell, 91

Keep, Winthrop L., 50
Keidel, George C., 100
Keidel, H. C., 142
Keiser, Clarence E., 106
Keith, Arthur B., 174
Keith, K., 156.
Kelland, Clarence B., 198
Keller, Adalbert von, 54
Keller, Gottfried, 96, 141
Keller, Helen, 76
Keller, William J., 29, 173, 186, 193
Kellermann, Bernhard, 97, 117
Kellogg, George D., 53, 87, 104
Kellogg, R. J., 118, 174
Kelsey, Charles, 102
Kendall, Calvin, 34
Kendall, Oswald, 132
Keniston, Hayward, 81
Kennedy, Arthur G., 38, 136, 160
Kennedy, Charles W., 160
Kennedy, Craig, 73
Kenngott, Alfred, 141
Kent, Ronald G., 4, 26, 27, 49, 50, 85, 86, 87, 88, 107, 108, 128, 129, 150, 152, 153, 174, 194, 195, 216
Kenyon, Herbert A., 145
Kenyon, John S., 81, 101, 136, 163
Kerlin, Robert Thomas, 8
Kern, J. W., 123, 153
Kerr, Caroline V., 54
Kester, Paul, 156
Key, Ellen, 14, 35, 56, 78, 98, 143
Keyser, Cassius J., 191
Al-Khowarizmi, 149
Kildal, Arne, 79, 98, 143
Kilmer, Joyce, 113, 158, 181, 200
Kind, John L., 142, 166
King, Basil, 70, 91, 132, 154, 155
King, Grace, 131, 202
King, Leonard William, 3, 26, 49, 151
Kingery, Hugh Macmaster, 10

Kingsley, Florence M., 71, 155
Kinney, Muriel, 15, 80
Kinross, Martha, 100
Kipling, Rudyard, 74, 185
Kirby, Harriet, 32
Kirk, William H., 50
Kirtland, John C., 9, 31
Kittridge, George L., 15, 38, 59, 81, 107, 115, 136, 138, 161, 172, 183
Kjellstrand, August W., 98
Klaeber, Frederick, 38, 59, 81, 82, 136, 182, 201, 202
Klein, David, 184
Kleist, Heinrich von, 207
Klenze, Camillo von, 34, 142
Klopstock, Friedrich, 97
Kluge, Friedrich, 12
Knapp, Charles, 5, 10, 30, 31, 52, 53, 85, 86, 104, 105, 108, 125, 147, 149, 150, 153, 171, 172, 191, 213, 214
Knibbs, Henry H., 71, 92, 111, 178, 198
Knott, Thomas A., 115, 161, 201
Knowlton, E. C., 165, 184
Koch, Theodore W., 12
Koerting, Gustav, 79
Kohler, Kaufmann, 106
Kohut, George, 165
Kolbe, Parke R., 141
Koldewey, Robert, 25, 89
Körner, E., 117
Korte, Alfred, 2, 84
Koschwitz, Eduard, 79
Kott, Elizabeth, 33
Kracher, Francis W., 77
Krapp, George P., 81, 137, 202
Krappe, Alexander H., 211
Krause, Carl A., 33, 54, 78, 119, 142
Krepinsky, M., 189
Kretzmann, Paul E., 115, 161
Kroesch, Samuel, 34
Kronenberg, M. E. von, 209

Kuersteiner, Albert F., 37, 57, 168
Kuhl, E. P., 101, 162, 204
Kuhn, Ernst, 216
Kuiper, B. K., 209
Kummer, Frederic A., 69, 133
Kurrelmeyer, W., 205, 207, 208, 210
Kussy, Nathan, 131
Kyes, D. H., 205
Kyne, Peter B., 178

LaFayette, Marie M. Mme, de, 210
Lagerlof, Selma, 14, 35, 78, 98, 119, 143, 167, 187, 208
Laing, Gordon J., 30, 105
Laing, Samuel, 143
Laird, A. G., 212
Lait, Jack, 133
Lamartine, Alphonse de, 188
Lamb, Charles, 185
Lamb, Walter, R.M., 124
Lambert, James F., 186
Lampton, William J., 160
Lancaster, Henry C., 37, 58, 79, 121, 145, 210
Lancaster, L. C., 188
Landor, Walter S., 206
Lane, Jeremy, 198
Lane, S. F. B., 98
Lang, Henry R., 80, 121, 145, 189
Langdon, Stephan, 25, 49, 127, 173
Langley, Ernest F., 80, 168
Lanman, Charles R., 4, 107, 128, 174, 217
Lanson, Gustave, 15, 168
Larra, Mariano Jose de, 211
Laurvik, J. N., 143
Law, Frederick H., 34
Law, Robert A., 60, 162, 163
Lawrence, Edwin G., 101, 204
Lawrence, William J., 59, 184
Lawrence, William W., 38, 115, 202, 204

Lawson, Victor Freemont, 67
Layard, Sir Austen, 173
Leach, Henry G., 35, 119
Leaf, Walter, 148
Learned, Marion D., 12, 78
Lease, Emory B., 50, 86, 87, 215, 218
Leavitt, Sturgis E., 205
Lecompte, Irville C., 15, 100, 162
LeDuc, Alma, 168, 209
Lee, Arthur C., 16
Lee, Francis H., 108
Lee, Gerald Stanley, 75, 114
Lee, Jennette, 93
Lee, Robert E., 65
Leenwen, Van, 211
Legrand, Phillipe E., 190
Leibniz, Gottfried W., 164, 166
Lemmi, C. W., 138, 163
Lemont, Jessie, 207
Lentino, Giacoma da, 145
Leonard, William E., 148, 202
Leopardi, Giacomo, 189
Lesage, Alain Rene, 121
Leser, Eugene, 34
Leskien, August, 4
Lessing, Gotthold, 12, 13
Lessing, Otto E., 53
Lett, Stephen E., 210
Leupp, Francis E., 181
Levy, Robert, 97
Lewis, Charles B., 58
Lewis, Edwin H., 132
Lewis, Sinclair, 111, 156, 198
Lewisohn, Adele, 96
Lewisohn, Ludwig, 33, 34, 54, 77, 96, 140, 141, 165, 185
Lieder, Frederick W. C., 54, 166, 167
Lignano, Giovanni da, 182, 189
Liliencron, Detlev von, 53, 118, 141
Lillehei, Ingebright, 98
Lilly, Marie L., 207
Lincoln, Abraham, 64, 92, 114, 135
Lincoln, George L., 16

Lincoln, Joseph C., 71, 72, 91, 110, 131, 156, 178
Lincoln, Natalie S., 92, 157, 178
Lindner, Oliver A., 119, 187
Lindsay, Vachel, 95, 158
Linforth, Ivan M., 123
Lion, Leon M., 198
Lippman, Julie, 93, 197
Litchfield, H. W., 104, 126
Little, Charles J., 143
Littman, Enno, 127, 194
Livingston, Arthur A., 16, 37, 80, 146, 189
Livingston, R. W., 169
Livy, 50, 85, 87, 108, 125, 147, 175, 214, 215
Lizst, Franz, 96
Lloyd, Nelson, 70
Lockert, C. L., 184, 204
Lockhart, Caroline, 40, 111, 198
Lockhart, John G., 186
Lockwood, Dean P., 10, 29, 105
Lockwood, Laura E., 82
Lodge, George Cabot, 60, 65, 66, 75
Lodge, Gonzalez, 8, 31, 53, 86, 171
Lodge, Henry Cabot, 181
Loeb, James, 190
Logie, I. E., 120
Lohan, Oswald, 78
Lohr, Otto, 78
Lomax, John Avery, 102
Lomer, Gerhard R., 66
London, Jack, 70, 73, 92, 112, 132, 133, 135
Long, John Luther, 71
Long, O. W., 140
Long, P. W., 101, 116, 137, 162
Longfellow, Henry W., 66, 78, 119, 186
Longnon, Auguste, 35
Longus, 148
Lonnquist, Carl A., 167
Loomis, Roger S., 121, 161, 202, 209
Lord, John K., 32

Lotspeich, Claude Meek, 118, 136, 160, 166, 181, 186
Lounsberry, Thomas R., 21, 60, 66, 116
Louvet, Jean, 121
Lovejoy, Arthur O., 141
Loving, Pierre, 165
Low, Benjamin R. C., 61
Lowe, William D., 13, 171
Lowell, Amy, 95, 114, 134, 145, 157, 158, 159, 179, 200
Lowes, John Livingston, 15, 38, 59, 101, 115, 137, 145, 161, 182, 188, 189, 207
Lucan, 53, 192, 203, 204
Lucas, Elizabeth, 143
Lucian, 8, 50, 84, 147, 153
Lucilius C., 30, 50, 85, 88, 104, 108, 172, 215
Lucretius, 13, 104, 150, 191, 213, 215, 218
Ludovici, Anthony M., 55
Ludwig, Otto, 13
Luebke, William F., 34, 78
Luke, Saint, 83, 102, 122
Luker, Benjamin F., 168
Lund, Ingeborg, 99, 167
Luquiens, Frederick B., 15, 37, 80
Luther, Martin, 11, 34, 55, 140, 166, 186
Lutz, Grace, 70
Lydgate, John, 59, 82, 101, 115, 181
Lyle, Marie C., 203
Lyly, John, 116, 162, 183, 203
Lynde, Francis, 70, 92, 111
Lyon, David G., 26
Lyon, John H. H., 203
Lyon, Vivian E., 167
Lyons, J. M., 137, 201
Lysander, 103
Lysias, 1

Maartens, Maarten, 120
Mabie, Hamilton, 75, 77, 160
Mabie, Louise K., 93

McAfee, Helen, 139
Macan, Reginald W., 97
Macaulay, George C., 205
Macauley, E. R., 163
McBryde, J. M., 161
McCabe, James, 54
McCall, Sidney, 198
McCartney, Eugene S., 105
McCaulley, M. G., 163
McClure, S. S., 94
McCoy, Samuel, 132
MacCracken, Henry, 59
McCrea, Nelson, 53
McCutcheon, George B., 71, 92, 133, 156, 197
McDaniel, Walton B., 82, 85, 105, 126
Macdonald, Francis C., 198
McDonald, George R., 145
MacDonald, Wilbert L., 185
MacFarlane, Peter C., 198
McGiffert, Arthur C., 34
McGil, J., 183
MacGill, Patrick, 95
MacGrath, Harold, 71
McGuire, Elizabeth, 211
MacHarg, William, 133, 156
Machaut, Guillaume de, 115, 203, 210
McIntyre, John T., 178
MacKay, Alexander H., 21
Mackaye, Percy, 42, 59, 61
McKelway, St. Clair, 67
Mackenna, Stephen, 190
McKenzie, Kenneth, 16, 79, 121, 145
Mackenzie, William R., 59, 101
McKillop, A. D., 206
McKinley, Florence, 119
McKinley, William, 135
McKnight, George, 101
MacLean, William F., 21
McMaster, John B., 176
McMullen, Fred A., 177
McNutt, William S., 177
Macurdy, Grace H., 29, 50, 147
McWhorter, Ashton W., 29, 87, 128
Madden, Dodgson H., 138

Maerlant, Jacob von, 36
Maeterlinck, Maurice, 121
Magie, David, 127
Magnus, Hugo, 104, 150
Magaffin, Ralph V. D., 150
Maillard, Olivier, 144
Maimonides, Moses Ben, 80
Maiseres, Paiens de, 36
Mallory, Sir Thomas, 182
Malone, K., 181
Maniates, Belle K., 157
Manly, Edward, 98, 136, 138
Manly, John M., 162, 163
Mann, Myrtle, 78
Mann, Thomas, 97
Manning, Clarence A., 147
Mannyng, Robert, 181
Manthey-Zorn, Otto, 34
Mantuanus, Baptista, 30, 37
Mantz, Harold E., 139
Map, Walter, 161
March, Francis A., 21, 39, 44
Marden, Charles C., 37, 189
Margoliouth, David S., 106
Margolis, Max L., 2
Marie de France, 37, 184
Markham, Edwin, 113
Marks, Jeanette, 61
Marlowe, Christopher, 204
Marot, Clement, 121, 188
Marquis, Don, 201
Marriott, Crittenden, 71, 93
Marsh, Edward, 136
Marshall, Archibald, 185
Marshall, Beatrice, 56, 97
Marshall, John, 135
Marston, John, 204
Martial, 52, 192
Martin, Edward S., 95
Martin, Ernest W., 105
Martin, Helen R., 71, 110, 155, 178
Martin, Robert G., 184
Martin, Thomas C., 43
Mason, Grace S., 197
Mason, James F., 80
Mason, Lawrence, 102, 183, 204
Mason, Walt, 113, 158, 179
Massinger, Phillip, 138, 139, 184, 204

Masters, Edgar Lee, 113, 134, 157, 179
Mather, Frank J., 135
Mather, Maurice W., 29
Matheson, Percy E., 170
Matthaei, Louise, 211, 212
Matthews, Brander, 21, 44, 64, 76, 81, 122, 138, 145, 159, 165
Matzke, John E., 15, 35, 37, 58
Maule, Harry E., 167
Maupassant, Guy de, 188
Mauritzson, Jules,
Maxim, Hiram, 113
Maxwell, Patrick, 165
Maxwell, William H., 21
Maynadier, Gustavus H., 206
Mayne, Ethel C., 53
Mayne, Harry, 96
Mayūra, 27
Mc, see Mac
Mead, G. W., 101, 160
Mead, M. E., 205, 206
Meade, George G., 74
Meader, Clarence L., 87
Medary, Margaret P., 161
Medwall, Henry, 101, 163
Meeker, James E., 165
Mejia de la Cerda, Luis, 145
Mena, Juan de, 58
Menander, 1, 2, 8, 30, 103, 104, 122, 123, 126
Mencken, Henry L., 202
Mendell, Clarence W., 50, 172
Mendenhall, John C., 202
Mercer, Samuel A. B., 194
Meredith, George, 60, 158, 185, 206
Merimee, Prosper, 121, 210
Merrick, Leonard, 196
Merrill, Elmer Truesdell, 6, 125, 126, 172, 215
Merrill, William A., 28, 150, 175, 191
Merritt, Abraham, 198
Merton, David, 200
Merwin, Henry C., 43

Merwin, Samuel C., 62, 92, 111, 131, 156, 178
Messer, William S., 211
Methodius, 187
Meun, Jean de, 36, 182, 188, 204
Meyer, Adolph, 143, 209
Meyer, Conrad F., 13
Meyer, Eduard, 2, 106, 151, 215
Meyer, Frederick B., 32
Meyer, Herman H. B., 162
Meyer, Paul, 15
Meyer, R. M., 12
Meyer, W. R., 33
Meyer-Lubke, Wilhelm, 79
Miall, Bernard, 187
Michaelis, Karin, 56, 143
Michelangelo Buonarroti, 145
Michelet, Maret, 119, 167
Michelson, Truman, 4, 5, 27, 50, 87, 153
Middleton, George, 75, 113
Mierow, Charles C., 87, 118, 125, 172
Miles, Dudley H., 205
Miller, Alice Duer, 133, 178, 198
Miller, Charles Ransom, 67
Miller, Charles W., 28, 50, 147, 153
Miller, Edward W., 181
Miller, F. H., 183
Miller, Frank J., 149, 150, 171
Miller, Henry R., 70, 93
Miller, Johann Heinrich, 142
Miller, Marion M., 171
Miller, Olive Thorne, 201
Miller, Walter, 105, 123, 149
Milligan, George, 2
Millner, H. L., 9
Milton, John, 59, 82, 96, 102, 137, 139, 164, 184, 193, 205
Mimnermus, 147, 150
Miniter, Edith, 155
Minns, Ellis H., 123

Minucius Felix, Marcus, 192
Mistral, Frederic, 99
Mitchell, Benjamin W., 88
Mitchell, Edward Page, 67
Mitchell, John Ames, 40, 181
Mitchell, Julia Post, 168
Mitchell, Silas Weir, 39, 70, 71
Moffett, Cleveland, 71, 133
Moliere, Jean Baptiste, 145, 188
Molina, Tirso de, pseud. see Tellez, G.
Molle, Henry, 139
Mommsen, Theodor, 215
Monroe, B. S., 136
Monroe, Harriet, 95, 157, 158
Monteser, Frederick, 34
Montespan, Francoise, Mme de, 210
Montgomerie, Alexander, 80
Montgomery, Albert, 82
Montgomery, James A., 88, 89, 195
Moody, William V., 75
Mooney, W. W., 104, 105
Moore, Cecil A., 139, 164, 166, 184, 205
Moore, Clifford H., 23, 47, 53, 83, 102, 122, 146, 147, 169, 212
Moore, Frank G., 149
Moore, George Foot, 174
Moore, J. R., 138, 161
Moore, Justin Hartley, 4
Moore, Olin, 80, 121, 145, 188
Moore, Samuel, 38, 59, 82, 102, 115, 136, 181, 182, 201, 202
Mordell, Albert, 206
More, Henry, 184
More, Paul Elmer, 75, 114, 139, 158, 190
More, Sir Thomas, 184
Morgan, Arthur E., 204
Morgan, Bayard Q., 78
Morgan, Charlotte E., 60
Morgan, Edward M., 68

Morgan, G. B. Q., 165
Morgan, H. T., 121
Morgan, Morris H., 6, 30, 53, 104
Morganthau, Henry, 176
Moriarty, A., 82
Moricke, Eduard, 140
Morley, Christopher D., 180, 197
Morley, Sylvanus G., 121, 211
Morris, Edward P., 147
Morris, Gouverneur, 110
Morris, Lloyd R., 165
Morrison, Mary, 33
Morrow, William W., 21
Morse, Samuel F. B., 94
Mortensen, K. A., 79
Mortimer, Maud, 177
Morton, Thomas, 82
Moses, 77, 89
Moses, Montrose, J., 42
Mosher, Joseph, 59
Mott, Lewis F., 189
Moulton, Frank P., 31
Al-Mufaddal Ibn Salama, 127
Mügge, Maximillan, 55
Muir, Jessie, 99, 187
Muir, John, 73, 113
Mulder, Arnold, 70, 110, 197
Mulford, Clarence E., 73
Muller, Wilhelm Max, 193
Munro, John, 138
Munson, Arley, 76
Munsterberg, Margaret, 70, 140
Munzinger, Karl T., 186
Murray, Augustus T., 29
Murray, Gilbert, 21, 44, 104, 148, 212
Murray, James A. H., 21
Murray, J. T., 38
Mustard, Wilfred P., 8, 30, 37, 105, 122, 126, 149, 183, 192, 203
Myers, W. T., 193
Myres, John L., 148
Myrick, Arthur B., 50

Nabbes, Thomas, 184
Napier, Arthur S., 21
Nason, Arthur H., 116
Nazimova, Alla, 187

Negelein, J. von, 27
Neihardt, John G., 158, 200
Neilson, William A., 39, 60, 101, 136, 164
Nemesianus, 149
Neoptolemus, 48
Nettleton, George H., 102
Neumarker, J. S., 54
Newcomer, C. B., 82, 145
Newman, Louis I., 194
Nexo, Martin, 99, 187
Nicholas, Anna, 73
Nichols, C. W., 205
Nichols, Edwin W., 108 174
Nichols, Francis M., 214
Nicholson, Meredith, 62, 70, 93, 132, 157, 176
Nicolaus of Damascus, 104
Nicolay, Helen, 64
Nietzsche, Friedrich, 35, 55, 186, 208
Nijhoff, Wouter, 209
Nitchie, Elizabeth, 193, 206, 213
Nitzke, William A., 15, 37, 58, 100, 145, 182, 187, 202, 209
Nixon, Paul, 192
Nodier, Charles, 139, 144
Noe, Sydney P., 13
Nordau, Max, 14
Norden, E., 6
Nordmeyer, H. W., 186
Norlin, George, 29, 31
Norrevang, Arne, 35
Norris, Charles, 77, 131, 178
Norris, Kathleen, 62, 63, 90, 109, 130, 154, 155, 178, 197
Northrup, Clark S., 164
Northrup, George T., 16, 58, 60, 80, 81, 82, 100, 121, 210
Norton, Charles Eliot, 74
Norton, Grace Fallow, 61
Norton, Ray, 198
Novalis, pseud, see Hardenberg, Friedrich
Novati, Francesco, 144
Nutting, Herbert C., 153
Nyberg, Sidney, 156
Nye, Irene, 129

Nykl, A. R., 210
Nystrom, Anton Kristen, 78

O.Henry, 63
Oberholtzer, Ellis P., 43
O'Brien, Edward J., 157, 179, 199
Ochs, J. T., 97
O'Connor, H. W., 205
Oehlenschlager, Adam G., 143
Oemler, Marie, 198
Oertel, Horst, 87
Ogden, Charles J., 128, 152
Ogier le Danois, 15
Ogle, Marbury B., 6, 29, 30, 85, 149, 150, 187, 203, 210
O'Higgins, Harvey, 112
Oland, Edith, 55, 78, 98, 142
Oland, Warner, 55, 78, 98, 142
Olcott, Charles S., 135
Olcott, G. N., 31
Oldfather, William A., 105, 150, 214
Oliphant, Samuel G., 27, 49, 50, 53, 88, 105, 126, 128, 149
Oliver, Thomas E., 15, 81, 119
Olivero, Federico, 102
Olmstead, Florence, 131
Olmsted, Everett W., 37
Olsen, A. E., 119
Olson, Oscar, 101, 160
Olsson, Anna, 208
Omar Khayyam, 27, 65
O'Neill, Elizabeth, 215
Oppenheim, James, 95, 110, 134, 158
Ordynski, R., 165
Orlandini, Orlando, 16
Orsini, Fulvio, 100
Orthagoras, 146
Ortiz, Agustin, 16
Osborne, Duffield, 107
Osborne, Elizabeth, 139
Osgood, Charles G., 137, 162
Ossoli, M.F., Marchesa, see Fuller, Sarah Margaret

Osthaus, Carl, 34, 142
Ostrander, Frederick C., 146
Otis, Alvah T., 104
Otto, Emil, 142
Ovid, 53, 85, 99, 100, 104, 116, 126, 149, 150, 192, 215, 218
Oxenford, John, 102

Pace, Roy B., 136, 182
Padelford, Frederick M., 59, 60, 82, 101, 116, 136, 162, 183
Page, G. C., 96
Page, Thomas Nelson, 65, 72
Paine, Albert Bigelow, 64, 159
Paine, Ralph D., 73, 178
Paine, Thomas, 164
Pais, E., 215
Palau, Bartolome, 100
Palladius, 213
Palmer, Frederick, 91, 118, 176
Palmer, George Herbert, 185
Palmer, John L., 121
Pancoast, Henry S., 38
Pancrates, 24
Paquet, Alfons, 77
Paris, Matthew, 202
Parker, Carleton P., 126, 200
Parker, Martin, 203
Parker, William B., 114
Parmelee, K. W., 189
Parrish, Randall, 93, 178
Parrott, Thomas M., 38, 204
Parry, J. J., 163, 164
Parthenius, 170
Pascal, Carlo, 192
Passmore, D. J., 207
Patch, Howard Rollin, 188, 202, 203
Pathelin, Pierre, 15, 188
Paton, Lucy, 80
Paton, William R., 148, 170
Patterson, Frank A., 136
Patterson, Isabel B., 133
Patterson, Marjorie, 70
Patterson, W. M., 165
Patton, Julia, 205

Pausanias, 212
Payne, William M., 35, 187, 201
Peabody, Josephine Preston, 61, 75, 134
Peacock, Thomas L., 206
Peaks, M. B., 108
Peary, Robert, 43
Pearson, A. C., 87, 170
Pease, Arthur S., 29, 53, 104, 126, 214
Peck, H. W., 102
Peck, Harry T., 29
Pedersen, Holger, 4
Pelayo, Marcelino Menendez y, 57
Peller, Sadie, 187
Pelley, William D., 197
Pellisier, Robert E., 168, 189
Pennell, Elizabeth L., 135
Pennell, Joseph, 149
Penniman, James H., 102, 205
Peppler, Charles W., 27, 29, 175, 195
Pepys, Samuel, 139
Percival of Galles, Sir, 38
Perez de Ayala, Ramon, 37
Perez de Guzman, Fernan, 36
Perez de Montalvan, Juan, 16, 79, 80, 81
Pericles, 8, 29
Perkins, Ruth, 160
Perott, I. de, 189
Perrin, Bernadotte, 8, 29, 51, 123, 148, 190, 212
Perrin, J. L., 211
Perrin, Marshall L., 208
Perry, Aaron J., 182
Perry, Bliss, 139
Perry, Henry T., 184
Pershing, John Joseph, 176
Persius, 30, 104, 192
Peters, John, 193
Petersen, Johannes, 127
Petersen, Walter, 27, 29, 87, 128, 129, 153, 175, 194
Peterson, William, 85, 105
Petrarch, Francesco, 16, 80, 100, 145, 172, 182, 189

Petronius Arbiter, 30, 126, 150, 172
Pfaff, Friedrich, 11
Phelps, Henry P., 138
Phelps, J., 116
Phelps, Ruth Shepard, 145
Phelps, William L., 13, 83, 139, 140, 145, 179, 180, 185,,205
Philbey, E. J., 30
Phillimore, John S., 6, 52
Phillips, David G., 155
Phillips, Mary E., 74
Phillips, Walter C., 206
Philo, Judaeus, 24, 212, 213
Philocrates, 28
Piatt, J. J., 160
Pierce, Frederick E., 82, 164, 185
Pierce F. W., 208
Pietsch, Karl, 37, 58, 81
Pike, Joseph B., 192
Pindar, 30, 104, 146, 148, 212
Pinger, Wilhelm, R. R., 11
Piramus, Denis, 121
Pirazzini, A., 188
Pitman, Annie, 212
Pitre, Giuseppe, 144
Pitt-Kethley, A., 143
Plath, Otto E., 141
Platnauer, Maurice, 215
Plato, 1, 29, 103, 104, 124, 186, 190, 191, 205, 207, 212
Plautus, Titus Maccius, 50, 53, 85, 87, 104, 105, 126, 150, 153, 172, 192, 193, 214
Plessis, F., 6
Pliny the Younger, 6, 53, 126, 172, 215
Ploeg, G. I. van der, 209
Plotinus, 190
Plutarch, 29, 51, 123, 147, 148, 152, 190, 212, 214
Pocock, Roger, 111
Poe, Edgar Allen
Pogany, Willy, 34
Pohl, Emil, 77, 165
Pollard, Alfred W., 138, 203, 204
Pollard, Percival, 33
Pollock, Frederick, 21
Polybius, 24, 172
Pompeius Trogus, 172, 214
Poole, Ernest, 109, 154, 155, 179
Pope, Alexander, 60, 82, 102, 164, 166, 205
Pope, Paul R., 118
Popper, William, 194
Porter, Alfred W., 97
Porter, Charlotte, 138
Porter, Eleanor H., 130, 154, 155
Porter, Gene (Stratton), 66, 70, 112, 133, 179
Porter, Harold E., 112, 157
Porter, W. H., 170
Porter, William Sydney, see O.Henry, pseud.
Porterfield, Allen W., 97, 118, 142, 186
Post, Charles R., 51, 58, 104, 121
Postgate, John P., 52, 192
Postgate, John W., 163
Pound, Ezra, 157
Pound, Louise, 59, 160, 202
Powell, Chilton L., 139, 202
Pratt, Lucy, 93, 112
Prentys, Elsie P., 54
Prescott, Henry W., 29, 53, 84, 85, 150, 172, 214
Preston, Keith, 126, 172
Pretino, L. T., 145
Preuschen, E., 11
Prevost, Antoine Francois, 204
Price, Lawrence M., 118, 166, 206, 208
Price, William Raleigh, 58, 167
Prickard, Arthur O., 212
Priest, George M., 12, 118
Printup, Dorothy, 125
Pritchard, Hesketh, 72
Procopius of Caesarea, 8, 123, 170, 212
Prokosch, Eduard, 5, 49, 78, 107, 166, 186

Propertius, Sextus, 6, 30, 52, 85, 147, 150, 172
Ptolemaeus Claudius, 29
Pucci, Antonio, 16
Puckett, H. W., 142
Pullitzer, Joseph, 66
Pullitzer, Ralph, 67
Pumpelly, Raphael, 3
Purser, Louis C., 192
Putnam, Emily James, 8
Putnam, George Haven, 94, 113
Putnam, Nina W., 72, 110, 133
Pyle, James G., 159
Pythagoras, 146

Quackenbos, George P., 27
Quinn, Arthur Hobson, 39, 60
Quintillian, 53, 126, 172
Quintus of Smyrna, 104

Raabe, Wilhelm, 142
Raahauge, H. M., 77
Rabelais, Francois, 58, 120
Racine, Jean Baptiste, 104, 188
Radin, Max, 149, 153
Rajna, Pio, 35, 182
Rambeau, Adolf, 78
Rambo, Eleanor F., 126
Ramsay, George G., 192
Ramsay, Robert L., 184, 202
Ramsay, William, 21, 81
Rand, Edward K., 6, 10, 29, 31, 53, 79, 81, 150, 212
Rand, Kenneth, 75
Randall A. W. G., 166
Randall, John Herman, 27, 207
Randolph, Charles B., 29
Randolph, Thomas, 163, 164
Rankin, E. M., 192
Rankin, H. B., 135
Ransmeier, John C., 12
Raphael Sanzio, 36
Rapp, William J., 96
Raschen, John F. L., 206
Rastell, John, 163
Raynaud, Gaston, 35

Rea, John D., 204
Reade, Charles, 206
Reade, William H. V., 16
Redlich, A., 13
Reed, Edward B., 60, 139, 164
Reed, Henry A., 122
Reeks, Margaret, 34
Rees, Kelley, 8, 51, 53
Reeve, Arthur B., 73, 93, 111, 112, 133, 158, 198
Regnard, Jean Francois, 99
Rehbach, Rudolf E., 142
Reichelt, H., 4
Reid, Whitelaw, 67
Rein, Orestes P., 118
Reining, Charles, 141
Remy, Arthur T. J., 78
Renan, Ernest, 189
Renier, Rodolfo, 120, 143
Rennert, Hugo A., 16, 58, 81, 121
Repplen, Chud, 143
Repplier, Agnes, 135
Reuter, Fritz, 118
Reynolds, George F., 38, 101, 204
Reynolds, Sir Joshua, 164
Reynolds, Minnie J., 110
Rice, Alice Hegan, 157, 179
Rice, Cale Young, 41, 61
Rice, Clara C., 15, 37
Rice, Grantland, 158
Rice, Richard A., 165
Richard II, King of England, 121
Richards, Laura E., 134
Richardson, George F., 139
Richardson, Samuel, 205, 210
Richmond, Grace L., 157
Rickert, Edith, 82
Rider, Bertha Carr, 191
Ridgeway, William, 215
Riedel, E., 153
Riemer, Guido, 78, 140
Rienzo, Cola di, 100
Riess, Ernest, 9
Rihbany, Abraham M., 94
Riley, James Whitcomb, 75, 135
Rilke, Rainer Maria, 207
Rinaker, Clarissa, 138, 205

Rinehart, Mary Roberts, 71, 130, 158
Rippins, S. S., 181
Rippmann, Walter, 44, 55
Ritson, Joseph, 164, 205
Rives, Hallie E., 72
Robbins, A. A., 6
Robbins, Frank E., 51, 85, 129, 147
Robbins, Leo, 179
Robert of Chester, 149
Roberts, Charles G. D., 73, 94
Roberts, Elizabeth M., 177
Roberts, Richard E., 143
Roberts, William Rhys, 170, 190
Robertson, Archibald T., 124, 129
Robertson, D. M., 58
Robertson, John G., 54
Robertson, L. C., 186
Robins, Elizabeth, 70
Robinson, Corinne R., 75
Robinson, Cyril E., 51, 84, 171
Robinson, David, 29
Robinson, Dwight N., 105, 150
Robinson, Edna M., 164
Robinson, Edwin Arlington, 113, 134, 157
Robinson, James Howard, 16, 100
Roe, Frederick W., 206
Roe, Vingie, 92, 198
Roeder, E. C., 54
Roessler, E. W., 117, 167
Roger of Wendover, 202
Rogers, Benjamin B., 190
Rogers, Robert W., 127
Rohde, Erwin, 123
Roland, L. B., 206
Rolfe, H. W., 100
Rolfe, John C., 53, 85, 105, 126, 129, 149, 153
Rolland, Romain, 145
Rolle, Richard, 182, 202
Rolleston, Thomas W., 97
Rollins, Hyder E., 162, 183, 203
Rolvaag, Ole E., 119

Roosevelt, Theodore, 20, 21, 73, 76, 176, 200, 201
Root, Elihu, 135
Root, Mabel V., 172
Root, Robert K., 38, 82, 162
Roques, M. Mario, 36
Roscius, Sextus, 125
Rosenberg, Solomon L., 37, 58
Rosner, Ernst, 35
Rossetti, Dante Gabriel, 54, 164, 206
Rossi, Sebastian, 80
Rossler, C., 77
Rostand, Edmond, 210
Rotrou, Jean de, 121
Rousseau, Jean Jacques, 81, 145, 164, 168, 210
Roussel, Pierre, 191
Routh, J., 102, 116
Royce, Josiah, 135
Royster, James F., 115, 181, 201
Rubinstein, Harold F., 117
Rudwin, Maximilian J., 207
Runtz-Rees, Caroline, 37, 58
Ruskin, John, 206
Ruud, Martin B., 184, 187
Ryan, Marah E., 93, 178
Ryder, H. O., 172
Ryer, Pierre du, 79, 80, 121
Rymer, Thomas, 100, 102

Sachau, Eduard, 3, 25, 216
Sachs, Hans, 34, 55, 166, 183, 186, 189
Sachs, Julius, 9, 32
Sage, Eva T., 150, 172
Saint Gaudens, Augustus, 73
Sainte-Marthe, Charles de, 37
Salel, Hugues, 210
Sallust, Gaius, 84, 214
Salmon, Arthur L., 117
Salter, William, 208
Salvio, Alfonso de, 145
Sampson, Alden, 96
Samuel, Horace B., 96
Sanborn, Franklin B., 160
Sanchez, Nellie V., 121
Sandburg, Carl, 180

Sandby, Herman, 35
Sanders, H. N., 153
Sanders, Henry A., 8, 213
Sanders, Irving T., 142
Sandison, Helen E., 82
Sandys, John E., 148, 215
Sannazaro, Jacopo, 105, 122
Santa Clara, Abraham, 34
Santayana, George, 13
Santillana, Inigo L., Marquis de, 121
Sappho, 103, 122
Sarzec, M., 49
Satyrus, 48
Saunders, Catherine, 30, 105, 171, 214
Savage, Howard J., 137, 164
Scarron, Paul, 205, 210
Schaafs, G., 77
Schafer, Barbara Louise, 162
Schaffer, Aaron, 208
Schank, F., 120S
Schauffler, Rachel C., 63
Schauffler, Robert Haven, 61
Schauroth, Edward G., 29, 53
Scheffauer, Herman, 97
Scheffel, Joseph, 34
Schelling, Felix E., 39, 81, 102, 138
Scherer, Peter, 167
Schevill, Rudolph, 99, 100, 104, 120, 122, 145, 189, 211
Schiff, Jacob H., 26
Schiffer, Sina, 25
Schiller, Johann Chriptoph Friedrich, von, 12, 13, 54, 77, 78, 98, 141, 166, 185, 186, 207, 211
Schinz, Albert, 15, 81, 145, 168
Schlanche, H. K., 143
Schlatter, Edward, 81
Schleussner, Ellie, 78, 98
Schlicher, John J., 108, 129
Schlutter, O. B., 201
Schmidt, Erich, 11, 12, 123
Schmidt, Julian, 118, 166
Schmidt, Lydia M., 186
Schnabel, E. A., 172
Schneegans, Heinrich, 120
Schnitzler, Arthur, 33, 77, 96, 97, 140, 165, 186, 207
Schoell, Franck L., 116, 145, 204
Schoepperle, Gertrude, 15, 97, 202
Schoff, Wilfred H., 87, 108, 195
Schofield, William H., 137, 182
Scholz, Frederick W., 167
Scholz, Karl, 185
Schonemann, Friedrich, 118, 140
Schonherr, Karl, 33, 118
Schopenhauer, Arthur, 140
Schorr, M., 106
Schottenfels, Gertrude R., 13
Schreckenbach, Paul, 96
Schuckburgh, E. S., 192
Schultz, James W., 102
Schumacher, Adolf, 117
Schurz, Carl, 74, 98
Schutze, Martin, 78, 140, 207
Schwabe, Henry O., 118, 141
Schwarz, Henry S., 204
Scollard, Clinton, 75
Scott, Charles P. G., 19, 21, 44
Scott, Emmett J., 135
Scott, Fred N., 101, 140, 182
Scott, John A., 8, 29, 50, 51, 103, 104, 145
Scott, Mary A., 137, 168, 189
Scott, Walter, 102
Scudder, Vida, D., 182
SeBoyar, Gerald, 101
Searles, Colbert, 81, 100, 121, 146
Seawell, Mollie Elliott, 135
Sedaine, Michel-Jean, 81
Sedgwick, Anne Douglas, 61, 73
Sedgwick, Henry D., 141

Seerley, Homer, 21
Sehrt, Edward H., 141, 160
Seibert, H., 136
Seiberth, Philip, 97, 206
Seidel, Heinrich, 13
Seipt, Allen A., 2
Selin, William E., 163
Sellar, William Y., 192
Seltzer, Adele, 53
Seltzer, Charles A., 178, 198
Seltzer, Thomas, 53
Selva, Salomon de la, 168
Seneca, Lucius Annaeus, 5, 100, 120, 126, 150, 163, 171, 203, 205, 214, 215
Seris, H., 189
Seronde, Joseph, 121
Servius, 6
Severus, Septimius, 168, 215
Sewall, William, 200
Seward, Frederick W., 134
Seward, William H., 43
Seymour, Thomas Day, 7
Shackford, Martha H., 101, 162, 182, 185, 189
Shadwell, Thomas, 60
Shafer, S. R., 205
Shaftesbury, Anthony A., 139
Shakespeare, William., 39, 59, 60, 82, 101, 102, 114, 116, 136, 137, 138, 139, 158, 162, 163, 172, 183, 184, 187, 204, 207
Shanks, S. P., 210
Shannon, Edgar F., 82, 203
Sharp, Cecil, 183
Sharp, Robert F., 79, 98
Shaw, Anna K., 113
Shaw, George Bernard, 98, 117, 165
Shaw, J. E., 37, 121
Shaw, Stanley, 111
Shearer, A. H., 139
Shearin, Hubert G., 202, 203

Sheldon, Edward S., 100, 117, 188, 209
Shelley, Percy B., 102, 185, 206
Shenstone, William, 184
Shepard, W. P., 187
Sherburn, George, 205
Sheridan, Richard B., 102, 139
Sherman, Charles, 133
Sherman, Frank D., 135
Sherman, Stuart P., 158, 162, 164, 165, 185
Shewan, A., 123, 147
Shields, Emily L., 191
Shipley, Frederick W., 6, 53, 86
Shirley, James, 116
Sholl, Anna M., 110
Shorey, Paul, 6, 8, 10, 28, 30, 32, 51, 52, 85, 103, 105, 170, 172, 174
Showerman, Grant, 85, 149
Shumway, Daniel B., 11, 32, 34, 53, 76, 96, 117, 140, 165, 185, 207
Sidney, Sir Philip, 116, 137, 162, 203
Sienkiewicz, Henryk, 178
Sigurdjonsson, Johann, 143
Sihler, Ernest G., 6, 11, 30, 104, 125
Sill, Edward R., 114
Sills, Kenneth C., 10
Simonds, Frank H., 176
Simons, Dorothy, 189
Sims, Albert E., 119
Sinclair, Bertrand W., 92, 133, 198
Sinclair, Upton, 71, 155
Sinclair-Cowan, Bertha, 92, 133, 156, 178, 198
Singmaster, Elsie, 72, 110
Sirich, Edward H., 145
Sisam, Kenneth, 160
Skal, George von, 13
Skeat, Walter W., 21
Skelton, John, 101, 115, 137
Skinner, H. S., 26
Skinner, John, 3
Skinner, Macy M., 34

Slaughter, Moses S., 172, 213, 215
Slemke, Sigurd, 35
Smart, Walter K., 137, 161
Smiley, Charles N., 214, 215
Smith, Alphonso C., 102
Smith, Benjamin E., 21
Smith, Charles A., 205
Smith, Charles F., 104, 211
Smith, Daniel E., 149
Smith, David N., 205
Smith, Elwood, 102, 184
Smith, Frank Berkeley, 132
Smith, Francis Hopkinson, 40, 132
Smith, Garnet, 96
Smith, Horatio E., 16, 121
Smith, Hugh A., 58, 81
Smith, Kirby F., 5, 6, 85, 104, 150, 172, 192
Smith, Lewis W., 35
Smith, M. E., 139
Smith, Minnie S., 77
Smith, Rachel M., 138, 183
Smith, Raymond F., 54, 167
Smith, Reed, 82
Smith, Robert E., 178
Smith, Winifred, 79, 81
Smyth, Austin, 124
Smyth, Herbert Weir, 148, 175
Snavely, Guy E., 37
Snedeker, Caroline Dale, 40
Snell, Ada L. F., 181, 206
Snell, Frederick J., 16
Snyder, A. D., 206
Snyder, Fairmont B., 185, 205
Snyder, Henry N., 102
Snyder, William L., 123
Socrates, 124, 146, 148, 212
Soderberg, Hjalmar, 56
Soissons, Guy J. R., Ct. de, 96
Solomon, Joseph, 124

Sommer, Heinrich O., 15, 59, 82, 100, 101
Sophocles, 24, 29, 47, 48, 51, 84, 147, 170, 171
Soranus, 103
Southey, Robert, 185, 206
Sowers, W. L., 165
Spaeth, John D. E., 38
Spalding, Mary C., 101
Spearman, Frank H., 70, 130, 132
Spencer, Herbert, 206
Spenser, Edmund, 38, 57, 59, 82, 101, 115, 137, 162, 183, 184, 185, 203
Sphaerus, 24
Spielhagen, Friedrich, 33, 98
Spiers, Alexander G. H., 210
Spindler, George W., 186
Spingarn, Joel E., 39, 122, 158, 165
Spofford, Harriet Prescott, 40
Sprague, Charles E., 21
Sprague, Homer B., 163
Springer, Fleta C., 197
Spyri, Johanna, 208
Stacpoole, H. de Vere, 168
Stael-Holstein, Anne Louise, Mme de, 118, 141, 145, 188
Stanard, William G., 163
Stead, Robert C., 178
Steadman, John M., 160, 182, 204
Stedman, Edmund Clarence, 42, 43
Stedman, Laura, 43, 43
Steele, Daniel W., 179
Steele, R. B., 49, 86, 87, 147, 149, 172, 214
Steele, Richard, 185
Steele, Robert R., 6, 50, 108
Steiner, Edward, 94
Stempel, Guido H., 161
Stendahl, pseud, see Beyle, Marie-Henri
Steno, Nicholaus, 149
Stephens, Kate, 170

Stephens, Winifred, 121, 145
Sterling, George, 165
Sterne, Laurence, 139, 144, 189
Stevens, David H., 205
Stevens, Harold, 186
Stevenson, Burton E., 71, 111, 177
Stevenson, James Henry, 4
Stevenson, Robert Louis, 140, 165
Stewart, Hugh F., 214
Steward, Morton C., 13
Stidston, Russell O., 181
Stilgebauer, Johann, 166
Stimson, Frederic J., 156
Stobart, John C., 149
Stock, St. George, 124
Stockdale, Fairbank, 164
Stockum, T. C., von, 208
Stoll, Elmer E., 38, 60, 82, 138, 184, 204
Stone, Melville Elijah, 67
Stonecipher, A. H. M., 195
Stonex, Arthur B., 137, 138
Storey, C. A., 127, 173
Stork, Charles Wharton, 102, 141, 142, 167, 186, 187
Stout, Robert, 21
Stowe, Charles E., 43
Stowe, Harriet Beecher, 43
Stowe, Lyman B., 43, 135
Stowell, William H., 81
Strabo, 170
Strassburg, Gottfried von, 78
Stratton, A. W., 5
Stratton, Clarence, 162, 163
Stratton, George M., 170
Stratz, Richard, 97, 117
Straus, Oscar, 75
Strauss, Louis A., 102
Street, Julian, 197
Streeter, Edward, 177
Streitberg, Wilhelm, 11

Strindberg, August, 35, 55, 78, 98, 119, 142, 167, 187
Stringer, Arthur, 72, 95, 133
Stroebe, Lilian L., 167
Stromberg, A. O., 98
Strong, Theron G., 96, 159
Strubberg, Friedrich A., 78
Strunk, William, 206
Strunsky, Simeon, 179
Stuart, Lady Arabella, 163
Stuart, Donald Clive, 16, 58, 81
Stuart, Duane R., 29, 172
Stuart, Ruth McEnery, 160
Stuart, William, 127
Sturgeon, Mary C., 149
Sturgis, G. F., 121
Sturluson, Snorri, 143
Sturtevant, A. M., 79, 119, 141, 143
Sturtevant, Edgar H., 5, 27, 29, 49, 50, 51, 86, 88, 108, 150, 153, 160, 174, 175, 190, 214
Suarez de Figueroa, Cristobal, 80,
Suchier, Herman, 99
Sudermann, Hermann, 13, 33, 34, 96, 117, 166, 185, 207
Suetonius, Tranquillus, 85, 87, 105, 126, 149, 153, 172, 192
Sullivan, Francis P., 132
Sullivan, Thomas R., 63
Sumner, William G., 95
Super, Charles W., 29
Suttner, Bertha, 96
Swain, Joseph W., 171
Swartley, S. S., 184
Swickhard, A., 117
Swift, Jonathan, 116, 139
Swift, Lindsay, 43
Swinburne, Algernon, 185, 189, 206
Swindler, Mary Hamilton, 84
Sypherd, Wilbur O., 38, 101, 115

Tacitus, Cornelius, 50, 85, 105, 172, 192
Tagore, Rabindranath, 74
Tamayo y Baus, Manuel, 145
Tannenbaum, Samuel A., 163
Tanner, R. H., 147
Tarkington, Booth, 63, 72, 93, 110, 130, 131, 133, 179, 180, 196, 197
Tasso, Torquato, 80, 97, 207
Tatlock, John S. P., 38, 59, 82, 101, 116, 136, 137, 162
Tavenner, Eugue, 172, 173
Taylor, Archer, 161, 183, 188
Taylor, Bayard, 34, 166
Taylor, Charles H., 67
Taylor, Horace, 104
Taylor, Lilly Ross, 84
Taylor, Moron Lee, 13
Taylor, Robert, 181
Taylor, Warner, 205
Teasdale, Sara, 158
Tegner, Esaias, 14, 98, 119
Teixeira de Maltos, Alexander, 187
Tellez, Gabriel, 121
Temple, Maud Elizabeth, 121
Tennyson, Alfred, 30, 64, 116, 164
Terence, 6, 52, 53, 87, 104, 105, 126, 150, 172, 193, 214
Teresa of Jesus, St., 122
Terracher, A., 58
Tertullian, 105
Tetlow, J., 10
Thackeray, William M., 193
Thaler, Alwin, 137, 183, 204
Thalles, 124
Thallon, Ida C., 123
Thayer, Mary R., 164, 173, 193

Thayer, William R., 113, 200
Theis, O. F., 53
Theobold, Lewis, 205
Theocritus, 8, 24, 84
Theophrastus, 170
Theopompus, 2
Thieme, Hugo P., 168
Thoma, Ludwig, 96, 97
Thomas, Calvin, 12, 21, 44, 161, 186
Thomas, Daniel L., 116
Thomas, E. J., 143
Thomas, Edith M., 134
Thomas, Joseph M., 139
Thomas, Rowland, 71, 92
Thompson, Elbert N. S., 82, 102, 137, 164, 184, 205
Thompson, Ernest S., 156
Thompson, Francis, 137
Thompson, Reginald Campbell, 105, 151
Thomson, James, 165, 205
Thomson, James A. K., 124, 148
Thoreau, Henry David, 64
Thorndike, Ashley H., 101, 138
Thorndike, Lynn, 86
Thorvaldus, Rognvaldsson, 119
Thucydides, 29, 104, 124, 147
Thumb, Albert, 4
Thurber, Charles A., 118
Thoreau-Dangin, Francois, 25, 49
Thurneysen, R., 4
Thwing, O. T., 142
Tiberius, Emperor of Rome, 53
Tibullus, Albius, 52, 53, 85, 105, 150
Ticknor, George, 81
Tieje, Arthur J., 59, 82, 101, 164
Tigellius, 125
Tilley, Morris P., 136, 162, 163, 189, 204
Timarchus, 103
Tinayre, Mme Marcelle, 121
Tinker, Chauncey B., 116
Tisdel, Frederick M., 164

Tobenkin, Elias, 131, 179
Todd, O. J., 123
Tolman, Albert H., 204
Tolman, Herbert C., 4, 27, 28, 50, 87, 102, 108, 128, 152, 175, 183
Tolstoy, Leo, 178
Tombo, Rudolf, 76, 77
Tomlinson, M., 206
Tompkins, Juliet W., 131
Topelius, Zacharias, 14
Torre, Alfonso de la, 80
Tovote, Heinz, 53
Towles, O., 15
Towne, Charles H., 141
Towse, John R., 159
Toy, Crawford H., 87
Trail, Florence, 121
Trajan, Emperor of Rome, 103
Traubel, Horace, 94, 95
Treat, Ida, 81
Trent, William P., 42, 82, 135, 139, 140
Trever, A. A., 171
Trevisa, John, 182
Trissino, Giangiorgio, 145
Tristram, E. W., 202
Trombly, Albert E., 165, 206
Trounce, Harry D., 177
Trowbridge, John T., 135
Trudeau, Edward L., 134
Tucker, Thomas G., 21
Tucker-Brooke, C. J., 38, 101, 138, 163, 204
Tudeer, Lillie, 208
Tukey, Ralph H., 30
Tupper, Frederick, 38, 59, 82, 101, 115, 136, 137, 139, 182, 185
Turner, George Kibbe, 91
Turberville, George, 183
Tuttle, Edwin H., 37, 58, 121, 189, 211
Twain, Mark, pseud, see Clemens, Samuel
Tyler, Elizabeth S., 209
Tyler, Therese, 110
Tynan, Brandon, 60
Tyng, E. M., 153, 175
Tyrrell, Robert Y., 211

Uberti, Fazio degli, 121
Uhland, Ludwig, 12
Ullman, Berthold L., 6, 30, 50, 53, 86, 88, 105, 125, 150, 153
Umphrey, George W., 58
Underwood, George A., 145
Underwood, John Curtis, 114
Ungnad, Arthur, 106, 127
Ungold, G. T., 55
Unruhe, Fritz von, 166
Untermeyer, Louis, 134, 166, 199
Upcott, E. A., 12
Upham, Alfred H., 139
Upham, Thomas C., 121
Urena, Pedro Henriquez, see Henriquez Urena, Pedro
Urfe, Honore d', 100
Urner, Mabel H., 91
Usher, Roland G., 210
Utter, Robert P., 165

Vaile, E. O., 21
Valerius Firmus, 168
Valette, T. G. G., 143
Vance, Louis Joseph, 72, 79, 92
Van Dyke, Henry, 42, 93, 95, 198, 199
Van Hook, Larue, 88, 153
Van Hoonacker, A., 126
Van Horne, John, 189
Van Loan, Charles E., 112, 157, 201
Vann, William H., 164
Van Noppen, Leonard, 200
Van Schaick, George G., 178
Van Vorst, Marie, 93
Varnhagen, Rahel, 78
Varro, 86
Vaughan, Henry, 82
Vaughan, Herbert H., 16
Vaughn, C. E., 97
Vega Carpio, Lope Felix de, 16, 58, 121, 122, 146, 189
Vergil, see Virgil
Verner, Karl A., 118, 136
Verres, Gaius, 171
Vicente, Gil, 145
Victory, Beatrice M., 142
Viebig, Clara, 53, 77

Viereck, George Sylvester, 61, 142
Vignay, Jehan de, 37
Villaviciosa, Jose de, 57
Villon, Francois, 168
Villoslado, Francisco Navarro, 211
Vincent, Harry, 26
Virgil, 6, 8, 9, 10, 24, 30, 31, 84, 103, 126, 149, 150, 172, 183, 191, 192, 206, 213
Vitelli, Girolama, 83
Vitruvius Pollio, 6, 104
Vitry, Jacques de, 202, 209
Vives, Juan L., 122
Vogel, Geertrude, 120
Vogelweide, Walther, von der, 34, 97, 207
Vogt, Johan, 12
Volkmann, Richard von, 13
Vollmer, Clement, 208
Voltaire, Francois Marie Arouet de, 58, 100, 164, 188
Vorst, Mary H., 197
Vos, Bert J., 34, 118
Voss, Ernst, 12
Vowles, Guy R., 143

Wagner, Charles P., 168
Wagner, Richard, 33, 54, 118
Wahlund, Carl, 79
Walde, Alois, 4
Walker, Arthur T., 129
Walker, Edward M., 103, 124
Wallace, L. D., 184
Wallace, Malcolm W., 39, 59, 101
Waller, Mary, 178
Wallerstein, Ruth, 161
Walsh, Thomas, 168
Walter, Elizabeth, 96
Walter, Lavinia Edna, 120
Walters, C. F., 215
Walther, Max, 54
Walton, Fisher, 122
Walz, John A., 207
Walzel, O., 207
Wann, Louis, 116, 138, 203, 205

Warburg, K., 14
Warburton, William, 205
Ward, Elizabeth Stuart Phelps, 41
Ward, William Hayes, 21
Warewic, Gui de, see Guy of Warwick
Warner, V. J., 173
Warren, Frederick M., 37, 58, 121, 145
Warren, Herbert L., 104
Warren, M., 5
Warren, William F., 113, 137
Warshaw, Jacob, 100, 145
Warville, Brissot de, 145
Washburne, Stanley, 76, 92
Washington, Booker T., 134
Watreford, Jofroi, 15
Watson, Robert, 198
Watts, Mary H., 179, 196, 197
Watts, Mary S., 40, 69, 90, 131
Waxman, Samuel Montefiori, 58, 119
Way, Arthur S., 55, 78, 104
Webb, A. P., 165
Webb, Robert H., 53
Webb, William A., 184
Weber, E., 141
Weber, Rolf, 140
Webster, Daniel, 65
Webster, Henry K., 71, 92, 130, 131, 133, 154, 155
Webster, Hutton, 86
Webster, Jean, 130, 135
Webster, John, 204
Webster, Kenneth G. T., 136
Weckerlin, George R., 208
Wedekind, Frank, 33, 96, 117, 140, 165
Wedel, Theodore O., 203
Weeks, Raymond, 15, 100, 175
Weigand, Herman J., 207
Weiss, Bernhard, 83
Welden, E. A., 5, 27, 107
Weller, Charles H., 104
Welles, W. W., 131
Wellhausen, Julius, 106, 216

Wells, Carolyn, 92, 157
Wells, Herbert G., 155, 158
Wells, John E., 60, 136, 182, 205
Wells, Samuel Calvin, 67
Wendell, Barrett, 163
Wenley, Robert M., 10
Wergeland, Agnes, 119, 167
Wernaer, Robert M., 12
Werner, Oscar H., 166
Wesselhoeft, Elizabeth C., 54
West, L. C., 150
Westcote, Sebastian, 138
Westcott, Allan F., 59
Westcott, John H., 192
Westergren, Elizabeth C., 78, 98
Westermann, William L., 212
Westinghouse, George, 181
Weston, George, 157
Weston, George Bensen, 16
Weston, Jessie L., 15, 78, 97
Westrum, A. S. Van, 14
Wetmore, Monroe N., 31, 86
Weygandt, Cornelius, 76, 83
Wharey, James B., 205
Wharton, Edith, 39, 41, 61, 69, 96, 133, 156, 178, 197
Wheeler, Arthur L., 6, 30, 31, 105, 125, 172, 214
Whicher, George F., 139
Whipple, Thomas K., 137
White, Andrew D., 21
White, Edward L., 132, 178, 193, 199
White, Jane H., 13
White, John G., 100
White, John Williams, 8, 51, 105, 124, 190
White, Stewart Edward, 70, 76, 111, 132, 178
White, William A., 179
Whiteford, Robert N., 206
Whitehouse, Henry R., 188
Whitford, Robert C., 188, 205

Whitlock, Brand, 94, 200
Whitman, Charles H., 183, 203
Whitman, Stephen, 72, 132
Whitman, Walt, 94, 95, 181
Whitmore, Charles E., 30, 121, 140, 189, 206
Whitney, Casper, 65
Whitney, Marian P., 167
Whitney, William D., 4, 107
Whittier, John Greenleaf, 142
Whitty, James H., 42
Whitwith, Geoffrey, 207
Wickersham, George W., 68
Widdermer, Margaret, 113
Wiegand, Helen E., 173
Wiehr, Joseph, 165
Wieland, Christoph, 210
Wiener, Leo, 97, 141
Wier, Marion C., 170
Wiggin, Kate Douglas, 70
Wightman, A. R., 149, 171
Wilamowitz-Moellendorff, Ulrich von, 150
Wilbrandt, Adolf, 33, 207
Wilcox, Ella Wheeler, 134, 201
Wilde, Percival, 113
Wildenbruch, Ernest von, 13, 54, 118
Wilkins, Elizabeth G., 173
Wilkins, Ernest H., 15, 79, 81, 121, 145
Wilkinson, Marguerite, 200
William of Waddington, 182
Williams, Blanche C., 82, 101
Williams, Charles A., 186
Williams, Jessie L., 91
Williams, Oakley, 117, 121
Williams, Sherman A., 10
Williams, Stanley T., 164
Williams, Talcott, 67, 125, 149
Williamson, Edward J., 13
Willis, Henry P., 43
Willoughby, L. A., 54, 208

Willsie, Honore, 111, 156, 198
Wilm, Emil C.,
Wilson, Anne E., 119
Wilson, H. C., 112
Wilson, Harry Lean, 198
Wilson, James Harrison, 65
Wilson, Louis C., 14
Wilson, Pearl C., 211
Wilson, W. W., 5
Wilson, Woodrow, 64, 156, 176
Winchester, Caleb T., 135, 164
Winckler, Hugo, 3, 106, 151
Windisch, Ernst, 216
Windmere, V. P., 143
Winship, George P., 203
Winstedt, Eric O., 214
Winston, H., 13
Winter, Emil C., 12
Winter, John G., 149
Winter, William, 43, 60, 74, 113, 160, 162
Winther, Fritz, 97
Wise, Henry S., 68
Wister, Owen, 41
Withington, Robert, 115, 116, 138, 183
Witkowski, Georg, 13
Wolf, Frederic-Auguste, 171
Wolff, Julius, 33, 59
Wolff, Samuel Lee, 51
Wolzogen, Hans P., 96, 140
Wood, Francis A., 5, 34, 51, 59, 97, 100, 108, 114, 135, 141, 153, 160, 208, 218
Wood, Henry, 140
Woodberry, George E., 66, 75
Woodbridge, Benjamin, 121, 122, 188, 204
Woodbridge, Elizabeth, 180
Woods, James H., 128
Woodward, Robert S., 21
Wordsworth, William, 39, 102, 139, 164, 185, 205, 206
Worster, W. J., 99, 208

Worth, Patience, 156
Worts, George F., 198
Wright, Charles H. C., 58
Wright, E. D., 55
Wright, F. L., 56
Wright, Frederick W., 30, 173
Wright, Harold B., 91, 130
Wright, Henry B., 8
Wright, Joseph, 11, 21, 142, 166
Wright, Mabel Osgood, 63
Wright, Mary Tappan, 63
Wright, Robert S., 164
Wright, Willard, 131
Wright, Wilmer C., 104
Wulfila, 11
Wyatt, Edith, 158
Wycliffe, John, 136
Wylie, Laura J., 140

Xenamedes, 192
Xenophon, 1, 29, 84, 123, 212

Yeames, H. H., 85
Yohanan, Abraham, 107
Young, Charles E., 205
Young, Frances B., 58
Young, Karl, 81, 101, 115, 138, 163, 203
Young, Martha, 64

Zamenhof, Ludwig L., 22
Zander, Charles, 52
Zarabeta, Juan de, 100
Zeitlin, Jacob, 164, 181
Zeno, the stoic, 24
Ziegler, Frances J., 33
Zielinski, F., 52
Zimmermann, Benedict, 122
Zoega, Geir T., 14
Zoroaster, 108
Zuccarino, Esapo, 36
Zwingli, Ulrich, 55